Communications in Computer and Information Science 2911

Series Editors

Gang Li, *School of Information Technology, Deakin University, Burwood, VIC, Australia*
Joaquim Filipe, *Polytechnic Institute of Setúbal, Setúbal, Portugal*
Zhiwei Xu, *Chinese Academy of Sciences, Beijing, China*

AF737118

Rationale

The CCIS series is devoted to the publication of proceedings of computer science conferences. Its aim is to efficiently disseminate original research results in informatics in printed and electronic form. While the focus is on publication of peer-reviewed full papers presenting mature work, inclusion of reviewed short papers reporting on work in progress is welcome, too. Besides globally relevant meetings with internationally representative program committees guaranteeing a strict peer-reviewing and paper selection process, conferences run by societies or of high regional or national relevance are also considered for publication.

Topics

The topical scope of CCIS spans the entire spectrum of informatics ranging from foundational topics in the theory of computing to information and communications science and technology and a broad variety of interdisciplinary application fields.

Information for Volume Editors and Authors

Publication in CCIS is free of charge. No royalties are paid, however, we offer registered conference participants temporary free access to the online version of the conference proceedings on SpringerLink (http://link.springer.com) by means of an http referrer from the conference website and/or a number of complimentary printed copies, as specified in the official acceptance email of the event.

CCIS proceedings can be published in time for distribution at conferences or as post-proceedings, and delivered in the form of printed books and/or electronically as USBs and/or e-content licenses for accessing proceedings at SpringerLink. Furthermore, CCIS proceedings are included in the CCIS electronic book series hosted in the SpringerLink digital library at http://link.springer.com/bookseries/7899. Conferences publishing in CCIS are allowed to use our online conference service (Meteor) for managing the whole proceedings lifecycle (from submission and reviewing to preparing for publication) free of charge.

Publication process

The language of publication is exclusively English. Authors publishing in CCIS have to sign the Springer CCIS copyright transfer form, however, they are free to use their material published in CCIS for substantially changed, more elaborate subsequent publications elsewhere. For the preparation of the camera-ready papers/files, authors have to strictly adhere to the Springer CCIS Authors' Instructions and are strongly encouraged to use the CCIS LaTeX style files or templates.

Abstracting/Indexing

CCIS is abstracted/indexed in DBLP, Google Scholar, EI-Compendex, Mathematical Reviews, SCImago, Scopus. CCIS volumes are also submitted for the inclusion in ISI Proceedings.

How to start

To start the evaluation of your proposal for inclusion in the CCIS series, please send an e-mail to ccis@springer.com

Hailong Sun · Hongfei Fan · Xiaoping Li ·
Xiaokang Wang · Dongning Liu · Bowen Du ·
Tun Lu
Editors

Computer Supported Cooperative Work and Social Computing

20th CCF Conference, ChineseCSCW 2025
Guangzhou, China, November 7–9, 2025
Revised Selected Papers, Part II

Springer

Editors
Hailong Sun
Beihang University
Beijing, China

Hongfei Fan
Tongji University
Shanghai, China

Xiaoping Li
Guangdong University of Technology
Guangzhou, China

Xiaokang Wang
Zhengzhou University
Zhengzhou, China

Dongning Liu
Guangdong University of Technology
Guangzhou, China

Bowen Du
Tongji University
Shanghai, China

Tun Lu
Fudan University
Shanghai, China

ISSN 1865-0929 ISSN 1865-0937 (electronic)
Communications in Computer and Information Science
ISBN 978-981-92-0287-4 ISBN 978-981-92-0288-1 (eBook)
https://doi.org/10.1007/978-981-92-0288-1

© The Editor(s) (if applicable) and The Author(s), under exclusive license
to Springer Nature Singapore Pte Ltd. 2027

This work is subject to copyright. All rights are solely and exclusively licensed by the Publisher, whether the whole or part of the material is concerned, specifically the rights of translation, reprinting, reuse of illustrations, recitation, broadcasting, reproduction on microfilms or in any other physical way, and transmission or information storage and retrieval, electronic adaptation, computer software, or by similar or dissimilar methodology now known or hereafter developed.
The use of general descriptive names, registered names, trademarks, service marks, etc. in this publication does not imply, even in the absence of a specific statement, that such names are exempt from the relevant protective laws and regulations and therefore free for general use.
The publisher, the authors and the editors are safe to assume that the advice and information in this book are believed to be true and accurate at the date of publication. Neither the publisher nor the authors or the editors give a warranty, expressed or implied, with respect to the material contained herein or for any errors or omissions that may have been made. The publisher remains neutral with regard to jurisdictional claims in published maps and institutional affiliations.

This Springer imprint is published by the registered company Springer Nature Singapore Pte Ltd.
The registered company address is: 152 Beach Road, #21-01/04 Gateway East, Singapore 189721, Singapore

If disposing of this product, please recycle the paper.

Preface

Welcome to ChineseCSCW 2025, the 20th CCF Conference on Computer-Supported Cooperative Work and Social Computing.

ChineseCSCW 2025 was organized by the China Computer Federation (CCF), and co-hosted by the CCF Technical Committee on Cooperative Computing (CCF TCCC) and Guangdong University of Technology, in Guangzhou, China, during 7–9 November 2025. The conference was also supported by Guangdong University of Education, SCHOLAT, Guangdong Hengdian Information Technology Co., Ltd. and Guangzhou Togogo Technology Co., Ltd. The theme of the conference was *Human-Centered Collaborative Intelligence*, which reflects the emerging trend of the combination of artificial intelligence, human-system collaboration, and AI-empowered applications.

ChineseCSCW (known by the initials CCSCW) is a highly reputable conference series on computer-supported cooperative work (CSCW) and social computing in China with a long history. It aims to connect Chinese and overseas CSCW researchers, practitioners and educators, with a particular focus on innovative models, theories, techniques, algorithms and methods, as well as domain-specific applications and systems, from both technical and social aspects in CSCW and social computing. The conference was initially held biennially since 1998, and has been held annually since 2014.

This year, the conference received 196 submissions, and after a rigorous double-blind peer review process in which each submission received at least three reviews, only 50 of them were eventually accepted as full papers, resulting in an acceptance rate of 25.5%. The program also included 13 short papers. Both full papers and short papers were orally presented. In addition, the conference featured 6 keynote speeches, 6 high-level technical forums, the 6th ChineseCSCW Cup Big Data Competition (Final Round), and an awards ceremony. We are grateful to the distinguished keynote speakers, *Weiming Shen* from *Huazhong University of Science and Technology*, *Bin Hu* from *Beijing Institute of Technology*, *Weineng Chen* from *South China University of Technology*, *Zhi Jin* from *Peking University* and *Wuhan University*, *Nong Xiao* from *Sun Yat-sen University*, and *Yucheng Liang* from *Sun Yat-sen University*.

We hope that you enjoyed ChineseCSCW 2025.

November 2025

Tianruo Yang
Zhenyou Wang

Organization

Steering Committee

Ning Gu	Fudan University, China
Bin Hu	Beijing Institute of Technology, China
Xiaoping Liu	Hefei University of Technology, China
Yuqing Sun	Shandong University, China
Yong Tang	South China Normal University, China
Weiqing Tang	China Computer Federation, China
Zhiwen Yu	Harbin Engineering University, China
Shaozi Li	Xiamen University, China
Xiangwei Zheng	Shandong Normal University, China
Tun Lu	Fudan University, China

General Chairs

Tianruo Yang	Zhengzhou University, China
Zhenyou Wang	Guangdong University of Technology, China

Vice Chairs

Xiaoping Li	Guangdong University of Technology, China
Lizhen Cui	Shandong University, China

Program Committee Chairs

Hailong Sun	Beihang University, China
Tun Lu	Fudan University, China
Hongfei Fan	Tongji University, China
Dongning Liu	Guangdong University of Technology, China

Organization Committee Chairs

Xiaokang Wang	Zhengzhou University, China
An Zeng	Guangdong University of Technology, China

Publication Chairs

Hongfei Fan	Tongji University, China
Jian Zhu	Guangdong University of Technology, China

Paper Award Chairs

Bin Guo	Northwestern Polytechnical University, China
Yichuan Jiang	Southeast University, China
Weineng Chen	South China University of Technology, China
Xiaochun Yang	Northeastern University, China

Paper Recommendation Chairs

Yiming Tang	Hefei University of Technology, China
Honghao Gao	Shanghai University, China
Lianyong Qi	China University of Petroleum (East China), China
Yang Chen	Fudan University, China

ChineseCSCW Cup Competition Chairs

Jian Cao	Shanghai Jiao Tong University, China
Ying Gao	South China University of Technology, China
Chaobo He	South China Normal University, China
Zhuowei Wang	Guangdong University of Technology, China

Major Projects Forum Chairs

Yong Tang	South China Normal University, China
Yuqing Sun	Shandong University, China

Outstanding Young Scholars Forum Chairs

Tong Wang	Harbin Engineering University, China
Weineng Chen	South China University of Technology, China

Top-Venue Papers Forum Chairs

Peng Zhang	Fudan University, China
Tengfei Liu	Hangzhou Institute of Technology, Xidian University, China

Publicity Chairs

Xiangwei Zheng	Shandong Normal University, China
Shaohua Teng	Guangdong University of Technology, China
Yinzhang Guo	Taiyuan University of Science and Technology, China
Bo Jiang	Zhejiang Gongshang University, China

Sponsorship Chairs

Xiaoping Li	Guangdong University of Technology, China
Min Jiang	Xiamen University, China
Weihui Dai	Fudan University, China
Jing Gao	Guangdong Hengdian Information Technology Co., Ltd., China

Finance Chairs

Jiacheng Diao	Guangdong University of Technology, China
Lunke Fei	Guangdong University of Technology, China

Website Chairs

Jianguo Li	South China Normal University, China
Ronghua Lin	South China Normal University, China

Program Committee

Tie Bao	Jilin University, China
Ying Bi	Zhengzhou University, China
Zhan Bu	Nanjing Audit University, China
Hongming Cai	Shanghai Jiao Tong University, China
Yongming Cai	Guangdong Pharmaceutical University, China
Yuanzheng Cai	Minjiang University, China
Zhicheng Cai	Nanjing University of Science and Technology, China
Buqing Cao	Hunan University of Science and Technology, China
Donglin Cao	Xiamen University, China
Jian Cao	Shanghai Jiao Tong University, China
Jingjing Cao	Wuhan University of Technology, China
Chao Chen	Chongqing University, China
Chaochao Chen	Zhejiang University, China
Jianhui Chen	Beijing University of Technology, China
Junyang Chen	Shenzhen University, China
Liangyin Chen	Sichuan University, China
Long Chen	Southeast University, China
Longbiao Chen	Xiamen University, China
Ningjiang Chen	Guangxi University, China
Qingkui Chen	University of Shanghai for Science and Technology, China
Wang Chen	China North Vehicle Research Institute, China
Weineng Chen	South China University of Technology, China
Xin Chen	Taiyuan University of Science and Technology, China
Yang Chen	Fudan University, China
Yanru Chen	Sichuan University, China
Yaxi Chen	Southwest Minzu University, China
Yiqiang Chen	Institute of Computing Technology, Chinese Academy of Sciences, China
Zhen Chen	Yanshan University, China
Zonggan Chen	South China Normal University, China
Shiwei Cheng	Zhejiang University of Technology, China
Xiaohui Cheng	Guilin University of Technology, China
Yuan Cheng	Wuhan University, China
Jinhua Cui	Huazhong University of Science and Technology, China
Lizhen Cui	Shandong University, China

Zongmin Cui	Jiujiang University, China
Weihui Dai	Fudan University, China
Wei Dao	Tisson Regaltec Communications Tech. Co., Ltd., China
Xianghua Ding	University of Glasgow, UK
Xinyi Ding	Zhejiang Gongshang University, China
Wanchun Dou	Nanjing University, China
Bowen Du	Tongji University, China
Guodong Du	Yanshan University, China
Changjie Fan	NetEase (Hangzhou) Network Co., Ltd., China
Hongfei Fan	Tongji University, China
Yili Fang	Zhejiang Gongshang University, China
Lunke Fei	Guangdong University of Technology, China
Liang Feng	Chongqing University, China
Shanshan Feng	Shandong Normal University, China
Jiaojiao Fu	East China University of Science and Technology, China
Honghao Gao	Shanghai University, China
Jing Gao	Guangdong Hengdian Technology, China
Liping Gao	University of Shanghai for Science and Technology, China
Shan Gao	Harbin Engineering University, China
Ying Gao	South China University of Technology, China
Yuan Gao	Hunan University, China
Yunjun Gao	Zhejiang University, China
Qingyuan Gong	Fudan University, China
Ning Gu	Fudan University, China
Bin Guo	Northwestern Polytechnical University, China
Kun Guo	Fuzhou University, China
Saidi Guo	Zhengzhou University, China
Wei Guo	Shandong University, China
Yinzhang Guo	Taiyuan University of Science and Technology, China
Tao Han	Zhejiang Gongshang University, China
Fei Hao	Shaanxi Normal University, China
Chaobo He	South China Normal University, China
Fazhi He	Wuhan University, China
Ziyang He	Zhengzhou University, China
Bin Hu	Lanzhou University, China
Daning Hu	Southern University of Science and Technology, China
Liang Hu	Tongji University, China

Wenting Hu	Jiangsu Open University, China
Yanmei Hu	Chengdu University of Technology, China
Changqin Huang	South China Normal University, China
Lu Jia	China Agricultural University, China
Tao Jia	Southwest University, China
Bin Jiang	Hunan University, China
Bo Jiang	Zhejiang Gongshang University, China
Jiuchuan Jiang	Nanjing University of Finance and Economics, China
Min Jiang	Xiamen University, China
Weijin Jiang	Hunan University of Technology and Business, China
Wenchao Jiang	Guangdong University of Technology, China
Yali Jiang	Shandong University, China
Yichuan Jiang	Southeast University, China
Lanju Kong	Shandong University, China
Liqian Lai	Jiaying University, China
Chunying Li	Guangdong Polytechnic Normal University, China
Diankui Li	Jiamusi University, China
Dongsheng Li	IBM Research China, China
Genghui Li	Shenzhen University, China
Guoliang Li	Tsinghua University, China
Hengjie Li	Lanzhou University of Arts and Science, China
Jianguo Li	South China Normal University, China
Jingjing Li	South China Normal University, China
Junli Li	Jinzhong University, China
Li Li	Southwest University, China
Nuo Li	Fudan University, China
Pu Li	Zhengzhou University of Light Industry, China
Renfa Li	Hunan University, China
Shaozi Li	Xiamen University, China
Taoshen Li	Guangxi University, China
Weimin Li	Shanghai University, China
Xiaoping Li	Southeast University, China
Yong Li	Tsinghua University, China
Lu Liang	Guangdong University of Technology, China
Yunji Liang	Northwestern Polytechnical University, China
Hao Liao	Shenzhen University, China
Bing Lin	Fujian Normal University, China
Dazhen Lin	Xiamen University, China
Jinjiao Lin	Shandong University of Finance and Economics, China

Ronghua Lin	South China Normal University, China
Yongguo Ling	Guangxi University, China
Chanjuan Liu	Dalian University of Technology, China
Cong Liu	Shandong University of Science and Technology, China
Debin Liu	Zhengzhou University, China
Dongning Liu	Guangdong University of Technology, China
Hong Liu	Shandong Normal University, China
Huazhong Liu	Hainan University, China
Jing Liu	Xidian University, China
Li Liu	Chongqing University, China
Ning Liu	Shandong University, China
Shijun Liu	Shandong University, China
Shufen Liu	Jilin University, China
Tengfei Liu	Hangzhou Institute of Technology, Xidian University, China
Xiaoping Liu	Hefei University of Technology, China
Ying Liu	University of Chinese Academy of Sciences, China
Yuechang Liu	Jiaying University, China
Yupeng Liu	Harbin University of Science and Technology, China
Zhaowei Liu	Yantai University, China
Zhihan Liu	Central South University, China
Zitao Liu	Jinan University, China
Dianjie Lu	Shandong Normal University, China
Hong Lu	Shanghai Polytechnic University, China
Huijuan Lu	China Jiliang University, China
Qiang Lu	Hefei University of Technology, China
Tun Lu	Fudan University, China
Haoyu Luo	South China Normal University, China
Zhiming Luo	Xiamen University, China
Chen Lv	Shandong Normal University, China
Hongtao Lv	Shandong University, China
Jun Lv	Yantai University, China
Mingjie Lv	Zhejiang Lab, China
Peng Lv	Central South University, China
Pin Lv	Guangxi University, China
Qiujie Lv	Zhengzhou University, China
Xiao Lv	Naval University of Engineering, China
Hui Ma	Zhongshan Institute, University of Electronic Science and Technology of China, China

Keji Mao	Zhejiang University of Technology, China
Chao Min	Nanjing University, China
Li Ni	Anhui University, China
Haiwei Pan	Harbin Engineering University, China
Li Pan	Shandong University, China
Yinghui Pan	Shenzhen University, China
Yijie Peng	Peking University, China
Lianyong Qi	Qufu Normal University, China
Sihang Qiu	National University of Defense Technology, China
Jiaxing Shang	Chongqing University, China
Yanjun Shi	Dalian University of Technology, China
Yuliang Shi	Shanda Dareway Company Limited, China
Na Song	Putian University, China
Xiaoxia Song	Shanxi Datong University, China
Songzhi Su	Xiamen University, China
Hailong Sun	Beihang University, China
Ruizhi Sun	China Agricultural University, China
Yuling Sun	East China Normal University, China
Yuqing Sun	Shandong University, China
Wenan Tan	Nanjing University of Aeronautics and Astronautics, China
Shan Tang	Shanghai Polytechnic University, China
Weiqing Tang	China Computer Federation, China
Xiaoyong Tang	Changsha University of Technology, China
Yan Tang	Hohai University, China
Yiming Tang	Hefei University of Technology, China
Yong Tang	South China Normal University, China
Yizheng Tao	China Academy of Engineering Physics, China
Shaohua Teng	Guangdong University of Technology, China
Fengshi Tian	China People's Police University, China
Zhuo Tian	Institute of Software, Chinese Academy of Sciences, China
Binhui Wang	Nankai University, China
Chengji Wang	Central China Normal University, China
Dakuo Wang	IBM Research, USA
Hongbin Wang	Kunming University of Science and Technology, China
Hongjun Wang	Southwest Jiaotong University, China
Hongpo Wang	Beijing University of Science and Technology, China
Jia Wang	Xinjiang University, China

Jingbin Wang	Fuzhou University, China
Lei Wang	Dalian University of Technology, China
Li Wang	Taiyuan University of Technology, China
Lin Wang	Jinan University, China
Lu Wang	Harbin Engineering University, China
Shuang Wang	Southeast University, China
Tao Wang	Minjiang University, China
Tianbo Wang	Beihang University, China
Tong Wang	Harbin Engineering University, China
Wanyuan Wang	Southeast University, China
Wei Wang	Huazhong University of Science and Technology, China
Xiaogang Wang	Shanghai Dianji University, China
Xiaokang Wang	Zhengzhou University, China
Yijie Wang	National University of Defense Technology, China
Yingjie Wang	Yantai University, China
Zhenxing Wang	Shanghai Polytechnic University, China
Zhiwen Wang	Guangxi University of Science and Technology, China
Zijia Wang	Guangzhou University, China
Zongyue Wang	Jimei University, China
Fengfeng Wei	South China University of Technology, China
Yiping Wen	Hunan University of Science and Technology, China
Ling Wu	Fuzhou University, China
Quanwang Wu	Chongqing University, China
Xiaokun Wu	South China University of Technology, China
Zhengyang Wu	South China Normal University, China
Chunhe Xia	Beihang University, China
Daoxun Xia	Guizhou Normal University, China
Fangxiong Xiao	Jinling University of Science and Technology, China
Jing Xiao	South China Normal University, China
Xiaolan Xie	Guilin University of Technology, China
Yi Xie	National University of Defense Technology, China
Zhiqiang Xie	Harbin University of Science and Technology, China
Yu Xin	Harbin University of Science and Technology, China
Huanliang Xiong	Jiangxi Agricultural University, China
Guandong Xu	Education University of Hong Kong, China

Heyang Xu	Henan University of Technology, China
Hongfeng Xu	Guizhou Normal University, China
Jiuyun Xu	China University of Petroleum, China
Yonghui Xu	Shandong University, China
Yuanbo Xu	Jilin University, China
Xiao Xue	Tianjin University, China
Yaling Xun	Taiyuan University of Science and Technology, China
Jiaqi Yan	Nanjing University, China
Xiaohu Yan	Shenzhen Polytechnic University, China
Bo Yang	University of Electronic Science and Technology of China, China
Chao Yang	Hunan University, China
Dingyu Yang	Alibaba Group, China
Gang Yang	Northwestern Polytechnical University, China
Jing Yang	Hainan University, China
Jing Yang	Harbin Engineering University, China
Lin Yang	Shanghai Computer Software Technology Development Center, China
Qiang Yang	Nanjing University of Information Science and Technology, China
Tianruo Yang	Zhengzhou University, China
Xiangli Yang	Zhengzhou University, China
Xiaochun Yang	Northeastern University, China
Ziyi Yang	Beijing Institute of Technology, China
Yan Yao	Qufu Normal University, China
Xiaoyan Yin	Northwestern University, China
Jianyong Yu	Hunan University of Science and Technology, China
Shanping Yu	Beijing Institute of Technology, China
Xianchuan Yu	Beijing Normal University, China
Xu Yu	Qingdao University of Science and Technology, China
Yang Yu	Sun Yat-sen University, China
Zhengtao Yu	Kunming University of Science and Technology, China
Zhiwen Yu	Harbin Engineering University, China
Zhiyong Yu	Fuzhou University, China
Chengzhe Yuan	Guangdong Polytechnic Normal University, China
Junying Yuan	Guangzhou Southern College, China
An Zeng	Guangdong University of Technology, China
Dajun Zeng	Institute of Automation, Chinese Academy of Sciences, China

Liang Zeng	Beijing Institute of Technology, China
Zhihui Zhan	South China University of Technology, China
Changyou Zhang	Institute of Software, Chinese Academy of Sciences, China
Chaowei Zhang	Yangzhou University, China
Hongbo Zhang	Huaqiao University, China
Jia Zhang	Jinan University, China
Jifu Zhang	Taiyuan University of Science and Technology, China
Jing Zhang	Southeast University, China
Liang Zhang	Fudan University, China
Libo Zhang	Southwest University, China
Miaohui Zhang	Jiangxi Academy of Sciences, China
Peng Zhang	Fudan University, China
Senyue Zhang	Shenyang Aerospace University, China
Shaohua Zhang	Shanghai Business School, China
Wei Zhang	Guangdong University of Technology, China
Xiaowei Zhang	Lanzhou University, China
Xin Zhang	Jiangnan University, China
Ying Zhang	Northwestern Polytechnical University, China
Yong Zhang	Shenzhen Institute of Advanced Technology, Chinese Academy of Sciences, China
Zhiqiang Zhang	Zhejiang University of Finance and Economics, China
Zili Zhang	Southwest University, China
Hong Zhao	Guangzhou Institute of Technology, Xidian University, China
Ruonan Zhao	Zhengzhou University, China
Tianfang Zhao	Jinan University, China
Jiaoling Zheng	Chengdu University of Information Technology, China
Xiangwei Zheng	Shandong Normal University, China
Jinghui Zhong	South China University of Technology, China
Ning Zhong	Beijing University of Technology, China
Jiantao Zhou	Inner Mongolia University, China
Yifeng Zhou	Southeast University, China
Yu Zhou	Shenzhen University, China
Huiling Zhu	Jinan University, China
Jia Zhu	South China Normal University, China
Jianhua Zhu	City University of Hong Kong, China
Jie Zhu	Nanjing University of Posts and Telecommunications, China
Nengjun Zhu	Shanghai University, China

Tingshao Zhu	Institute of Psychology, Chinese Academy of Sciences, China
Xia Zhu	Southeast University, China
Xianjun Zhu	Jinling University of Science and Technology, China
Yanhua Zhu	First Affiliated Hospital of Guangdong Pharmaceutical University, China
Qiaohong Zu	Wuhan University of Technology, China

Contents

Topic C: Crowd Cooperative Computing and Evolutionary Computation

Intelligent Collaborative Vessel Scheduling for Inland Waterway Intersections Based on Improved Multi-agent Deep Reinforcement Learning

Tianfang Lv, Songming Liu, Zihao Cai, Shan Gao(✉), Min Ouyang, and Tong Wang

Harbin Engineering University, Harbin 150001, China
gaoshan08@hrbeu.edu.cn

Abstract. To mitigate frequent navigational conflicts and improve traffic efficiency at inland waterway intersections, we propose a collaborative scheduling framework that integrates a vessel motion model, a dynamic safety domain model, and a multi-agent deep reinforcement learning algorithm. The dynamic safety domain model captures vessel maneuvering behaviors with high precision, accounting for constraints from waterway topology and collision avoidance regulations. Furthermore, we introduce a cooperative control algorithm, termed Multi-Agent Deep Deterministic Policy Gradient enhanced by Long Short-Term Memory and Hybrid Sampling (MALHP-DDPG). This approach leverages LSTM networks and a hybrid sampling strategy to enhance policy exploration diversity and training stability, while preserving experience heterogeneity. Simulation results demonstrate that the proposed approach achieves high robustness and dynamic adaptability, enabling real-time, coordinated, and efficient vessel scheduling in complex intersection scenarios.

Keywords: Inland waterway intersections · Vessel behavior modeling · Collaborative scheduling · LSTM · MADDPG

1 Introduction

In recent years, due to their large transportation capacity, low costs, and environmental benefits, shipping has gradually become a significant mode of transport, playing an increasingly crucial role in economic development [1]. Inland waterway intersections are critical nodes in the maritime transportation system, where high-density traffic flow, complex vessel interactions, and limited maneuverability converge, leading to persistent navigation conflicts and reduced traffic efficiency [2]. As inland waterway transport scales up and its frequency increases, ensuring safe passage for vessels through complex intersections and, on this basis, improving traffic efficiency, has become an important topic within inland vessel traffic management systems.

So far, both domestic and international scholars have explored various methods for coordinating vessel traffic in congested inland waterways or intersections. Traditional

© The Author(s), under exclusive license to Springer Nature Singapore Pte Ltd. 2027
H. Sun et al. (Eds.): ChineseCSCW 2025, CCIS 2911, pp. 3–16, 2027.
https://doi.org/10.1007/978-981-92-0288-1_1

approaches primarily include rule-based and optimization methods. For example, Zhang et al. [3] proposed a collision avoidance decision system for inland vessels based on the International Regulations for Preventing Collisions at Sea (COLREGs), which integrates velocity obstacle (VO) algorithms for dynamic collision avoidance and path optimization. Hua et al. [4] introduced a cloud-shore-ship collaborative architecture for the inland autonomous waterway transport system (i-AWTS), incorporating navigation rules, task rules, and system cooperation rules within the cognitive and application layers. Bellsolà Olba et al. [5] modeled port waterway intersections as queuing systems, constructing an optimization model aimed at maximizing throughput by analyzing vessel conflicts and traffic flow characteristics. Xin et al. [6] proposed a vessel traffic clustering framework for complex waters, utilizing hierarchical bi-objective optimization to balance conflict connectivity and spatial compactness. In recent years, data-driven methods based on intent prediction and behavior modeling have gradually become a research focus. Yuan et al. [7] proposed a trajectory prediction model called GATransformer, which integrates a Graph Attention Network (GAT) and the Transformer architecture, enabling high-precision prediction of multiple vessels' future trajectories in complex intersection waters using AIS data. Chen et al. [8] introduced a Bayesian intent recognition framework for intersection scenarios that combines radar and image information, enabling real-time inference of vessel turning/going straight intentions. Ma et al. [9] developed a vessel encounter intent reasoning model based on a Hidden Markov Model (HMM), significantly enhancing the real-time performance and accuracy of intent inference. Chen et al. [10] proposed a method combining Mixed-Integer Programming (MIP) and Distributed Model Predictive Control (DMPC), focusing on collaborative vessel passage at waterway intersections.

As traffic density increases and scheduling complexity rises, traditional scheduling strategies are increasingly inadequate in addressing the complex demands of safe, coordinated, and real-time vessel operations under changing traffic conditions. In recent years, deep reinforcement learning (DRL) has developed rapidly, gaining attention for its ability to learn optimal strategies through interaction with dynamic environments. For example, Xie et al. [11] developed a COLREGs-compliant multi-vessel collision avoidance DRL method, improving decision-making and training efficiency. Wang et al. [12] proposed a scalable multi-agent deep deterministic policy gradient (Scalable-MADDPG) algorithm for multi-unmanned surface vehicle (USV) coordinated target intrusion scenarios, achieving robust collision avoidance and cooperative maneuvering in complex marine environments (with wind and wave disturbances). Guo et al. [13] introduced a multi-pointer graph network (MPGN) with dual-policy PPO (bi-PPO) framework for port vessel scheduling and tug allocation (VT-COP), modeling the problem as a hierarchical multi-action Markov decision process (MMDP). Wang et al. [14] designed a two-stage DRL algorithm to address the congestion bottleneck at container terminals with four stages (QC-LS-IS-YC). The advantages of DRL methods in terms of learning efficiency, robustness, and optimization capabilities have made them highly effective in complex tasks such as multi-vessel coordination and port scheduling.

Dispatching vessels in confluence zones of inland rivers poses several intrinsic challenges. First, many existing frameworks are designed for isolated or small-scale scenarios and fail to generalize to continuous, high-volume traffic streams. Second, vessel maneuvering involves pronounced inertia and delayed response characteristics, complicating the modeling of real-time interactions and control feedback. Third, the geometric and dynamic characteristics of vessels—including their physical dimensions and spatiotemporally evolving safety domains—are often oversimplified, limiting the reliability of collision avoidance and passage planning in dense environments.

To address the aforementioned challenges, we introduce an integrated innovation that combines the vessel maneuvering model, dynamic safety domain, and reinforcement learning-based intelligent decision-making. The vessel maneuvering model enables precise characterization of individual vessel dynamics, while the dynamic safety domain provides an effective guarantee for safe passage between vessels. Reinforcement learning (RL), in turn, empowers agents to learn optimal dispatch strategies through interaction with the environment. By leveraging the real-time regulatory capability of the dynamic safety domain and the adaptive optimization capability of reinforcement learning, we aim to achieve efficient and dynamic scheduling optimization in confluence zones.

The primary contributions of this work are summarized as follows:

1. We develop a spatiotemporal coupling modeling technique that facilitates cross-scale coordination between individual vessel dynamics and global traffic flow characteristics.
2. We design a multi-objective hybrid reward mechanism that jointly considers dynamic safety domain evaluation, collision risk mitigation, and traffic throughput optimization, thereby enabling fine-grained scheduling control.
3. We integrate a long short-term memory (LSTM) module and a hybrid sampling strategy into the DRL framework to enhance the agent's capacity for long-term temporal reasoning and improve training stability in non-stationary environments.

2 System Model

2.1 Environment Description

The study considers a bidirectional cross intersection within a Traffic Separation Scheme (TSS), where vessels are limited to three maneuvers: straight, left turn, and right turn. They may face three ty pes of conflicts: following, merging, and crossing. Navigation behavior is determined solely by vessel interactions, excluding external factors such as wind, waves, and communication delays. The scheme diagram of study area is shown in Fig. 1.

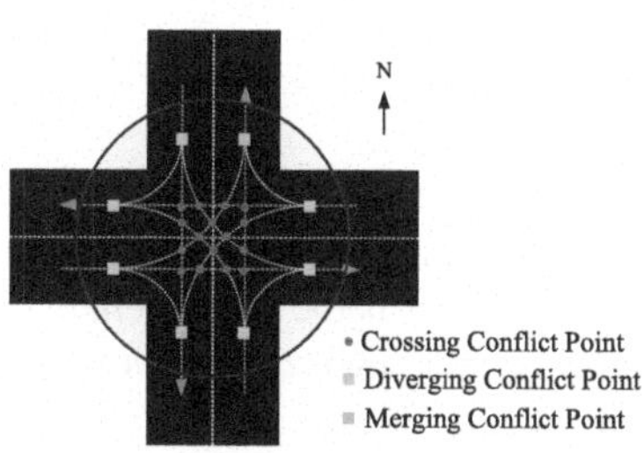

Fig. 1. The scheme diagram of study area.

2.2 Vessel Motion Model

Given the vessel's small turning radius and limited maneuverability, it is essential to account for lateral motions, including yaw and sway. To strike a balance between accuracy and efficiency, a simplified three-degree-of-freedom (3-DOF) model is adopted, as illustrated in Fig. 2. This model effectively captures the key dynamic characteristics of the vessel while reducing computational complexity, thereby enhancing its practicality. The simplified vessel motion equations are presented in Eq. (1).

$$\begin{bmatrix} \dot{x} \\ \dot{y} \\ \dot{z} \end{bmatrix} = \begin{bmatrix} \cos\psi & \sin\psi & 0 \\ \sin\psi & \cos\psi & 0 \\ 0 & 0 & 1 \end{bmatrix} \begin{bmatrix} \mu \\ \nu \\ \omega \end{bmatrix} \tag{1}$$

where x and y denote the vessel's position; ψ is the heading angle; μ is the surge velocity component; ν is the sway velocity component; and ω is the yaw rate.

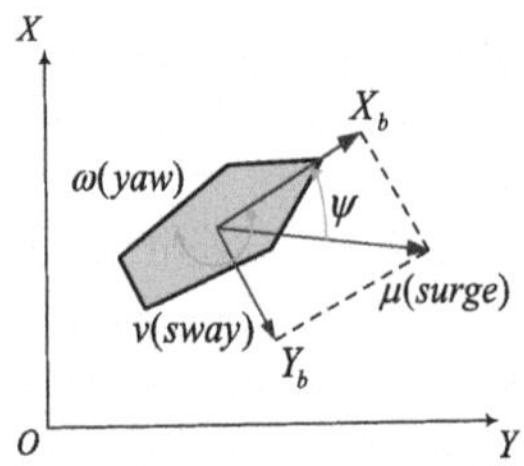

Fig. 2. The scheme diagram of 3-DOF vessel motion model.

2.3 Vessel Dynamic Safety-Domain Model

Intersection navigation can be framed as a resource allocation problem: vessels ensure orderly passage by reserving time windows along their routes or adjusting speed to reduce trajectory overlap and minimize intersection clearance time, thereby improving traffic efficiency. Building on the "virtual lane mapping" method first introduced in [15], this study introduces an extended approach "virtual waterway mapping" to support early decision-making before vessels enter the intersection and to reduce collision risk. The safety distance $D_i(t)$ for vessel i is defined as the sum of its length and braking distance. The schematic diagram is shown in Fig. 3, and the corresponding equations are given in Eq. (2).

$$D_i(t) = D_{0i}(t) + D_{1i}(t) + D_{2i}(t) + l_i = (\sigma + 1)l_i + v_{i(i+1)}t_0 + \frac{v_i(t)^2}{2a_i} \tag{2}$$

where $D_{0i}(t)$, $D_{1i}(t)$ and $D_{2i}(t)$ denote the contributions of vessel length, minimum speed, and braking distance to the safety distance, respectively. r_i and r_{i+1} denote the domain radii of the vessel i and $i+1$. σ is the vessel length coefficient, set to 0.25, l_i is the length of vessel i; v_i and v_{i+1} denote their respective velocities, $v_{i(i+1)}$ is the relative velocity. If there is no vessel ahead of vessel i or $v_i < v_{i+1}$, $v_{i(i+1)} = v_i$. If $v_i > v_{i+1}$,

$v_{i(i+1)} = v_i - v_{i+1}$, t_0 is the braking response time, set to 5 s, a_i is the acceleration of vessel i.

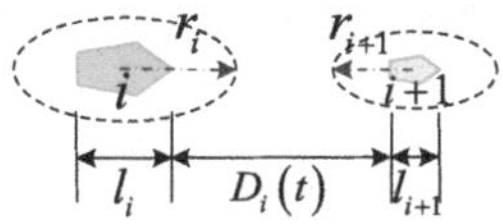

Fig. 3. The schematic diagram of safety distance calculation.

2.4 Multi-agent Scheduling System Modeling

State Space and Action Space. To address scheduling challenges under continuous traffic flow, this study identifies, at the start of each training episode, a set of cooperative vessels likely to interact with each target vessel, forming dynamic coordination relationships. Each vessel agent engages in multi-agent cooperation with its selected partners.

The state space $s_t = [I_i, I_{1i}, I_{2i}, ..., I_{ni}]$, where I_i is the target vessel's information: $I_i = [p_i, v_i, l_i, a_i, w_i]$, where p_i denotes the position; w_i is the intended route. I_{1i}, $I_{2i}, \ldots, I_{ni}$ represent the state information of the n nearest cooperative vessels relative to the target vessel on the same route segment.

The action space consists of the acceleration of the vessel. The action of the target vessel is an acceleration value a_i, where $a_i \in [a_m, a_M]$, a_m and a_M are the minimum and maximum acceleration bounds, respectively. The joint action of the cooperative vessels is defined as $a_{\bar{i}} \in [a_{1i}, a_{2i}, ..., a_{ni}]$.

Multi-objective Reward Function. Vessel scheduling at intersections is a multi-objective optimization problem that seeks to maximize traffic efficiency while ensuring navigational safety. This study designs a multi-objective reward function $r(t)$ that integrates safety, efficiency, and rule compliance. The formulation is defined as follows:

$$r(t) = \begin{cases} \omega_1(r_d(t) + r_t(t)) + \omega_2 r_e(t) + \omega_3 r_s(t) + \omega_4 r_c(t), & \text{normal navigation} \\ 4, & \text{pass through the intersection} \\ -8, & \text{collision intersection} \end{cases} \quad (3)$$

where ω_1, ω_2, ω_3, ω_4 represent the weights assigned to each reward component, set to 1.0, 1.0, 3.0 and 2.0, respectively. $r_d(t)$,$r_t(t)$,$r_e(t)$,$r_s(t)$,$r_c(t)$ respectively represent the reward functions based on spatial and temporal security, efficiency, stability and regularity. Further details are provided below:

Safety Reward. The distance-based safety reward function $r_d(t)$ and the time-based safety reward function $r_t(t)$ are defined as follows:

$$r_d(t) = \begin{cases} \log\left(\left(\frac{S_d(t)}{D_i(t)}\right)^{\beta_d} + 10^{-4}\right) & 0 < S_d(t) < D_i(t) \\ 2 & S_d(t) \geq D_i(t) \end{cases} \quad (4)$$

$$r_t(t) = \begin{cases} -\left(\frac{4}{\tanh(-T_d(t))}\right)^{\beta_t} & 0 < T_d(t) < T_i(t) \\ 2 & T_d(t) \geq T_i(t) \end{cases} \quad (5)$$

where β_d and β_t are exponential modulation factors used to improve the model's sensitivity to potential collision risks. The actual position difference $S_d(t)$ between the target vessel i and its nearest neighboring vessel $i+1$, the actual time gap $T_d(t)$ between them, and the dynamic safe distance threshold $D_i(t)$ and safe time threshold $T_i(t)$, are calculated as shown in Eqs. (6)–(9):

$$S_d(t) = |p_i(t) - p_{i+1}(t)| \tag{6}$$

$$D_i(t) = (\sigma + 1)l_i + v_{i(i+1)}t_0 + \frac{v_i(t)^2}{2a_i} \tag{7}$$

$$T_d(t) = \frac{S_d(t)}{v_i(t) - v_{i+1}(t)} \tag{8}$$

$$T_i(t) = \frac{D_i(t)}{v_i(t) - v_{i+1}(t)} \tag{9}$$

Efficiency Reward. This reward encourages vessels to maintain high speeds and is defined as follows:

$$r_e(t) = \frac{v_i(t) - v_{im}}{v_{iM} - v_{im}} \tag{10}$$

where v_{iM} and v_{im} denote the maximum and minimum speed limits of the vessel, respectively. The reward function is normalized to improve comparability.

Stability Reward. Since vessel heading and speed typically change gradually, stability is essential for effective scheduling. Therefore, reward functions are designed to penalize changes in heading angle and acceleration, is defined as follows:

$$r_s(t) = 1 - \gamma_1 \tanh\left((\Delta\theta)^2\right) - \gamma_2 \tanh\left((\Delta a)^2\right) \tag{11}$$

where $\Delta\theta$ and Δa denote the rate of change in heading angle and acceleration, respectively, while γ_1 and γ_2 represent their corresponding weights, both set to 0.5.

Rule Reward. The International Regulations for Preventing Collisions at Sea (COLREGs) offer structured guidance on the timing and scale of avoidance maneuvers. To promote compliance and encourage reasonable avoidance behavior, a rule-based reward function is defined as follows:

$$r_c(t) = \begin{cases} r_d(t), & \text{c = True} \\ -2, & \text{c = False} \end{cases} \tag{12}$$

where c = True denotes compliance with the rules, while c = False denotes a violation.

3 DRL Algorithm

3.1 Problem Statement

Vessel scheduling is a complex continuous combinatorial optimization problem, making exhaustive enumeration impractical. Although intersection traffic exhibits Markovian characteristics, slow vessel maneuvers, partial observability, and high uncertainty require agents to infer others' intentions. However, MADDPG lacks an explicit memory mechanism, limiting its ability to capture long-term dependencies in dynamic environments. To address this, LSTM is integrated into the MADDPG framework to enhance temporal modeling and improve decision-making in intersection scheduling.

3.2 Multi-agent LSTM Hybrid Prioritized DDPG

MADDPG Overview: The system architecture of the MADDPG framework used in this study is illustrated in Fig. 4. Each vessel agent consists of the following components: Actor Network π, Target Actor Network π', Critic Network Q and Target Critic Network Q', where s_t and a_t denote the state and action spaces, respectively. $\tilde{a}$ denotes the action selected by the Actor Network, while a' denotes the action selected by the Actor Target Network

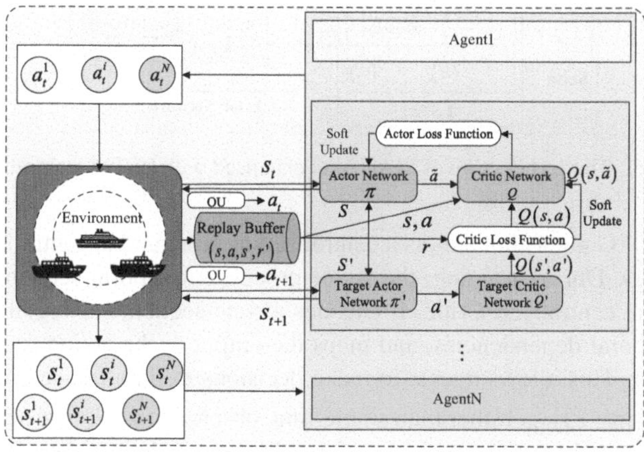

Fig. 4. The system architecture of MADDPG framework.

The Actor Network acts as a trainable controller that maps vessel states to actions. The Critic Network evaluates state–action pairs from a global perspective and guides Actor updates. Target Actor and Target Critic Networks help stabilize training by providing target values for the Critic. A soft update mechanism is used for parameter updates. Interaction data are stored in the experience replay buffer in batches (s, a, s', r'), and OU noise is added to enhance exploration and policy diversity.

In Critic value estimation, considering only the target vessel and its cooperative vessels is sufficient to evaluate coordination effects. The objective function is defined as follows:

$$\begin{cases} J_1(\theta) = \max_{\theta} E_\beta\left[Q^{\omega}_{s_t,a_t}\right] \\ J_2(\omega) = \min_{\omega} E_\beta\left[\frac{1}{2}\left(r_t + \gamma Q^{\omega'}_{s_{t+1},a_{t+1}} - Q^{\omega}_{s_t,a_t}\right)^2\right] \end{cases} \tag{13}$$

In addition to the four networks mentioned above, the algorithm involves the parameters ω of the value network Q, ω' of the target value network Q', and θ of the policy network π, along with the discount factor γ and the immediate reward r_t from the environment at time t.

LSTM-Enhanced MADDPG Architecture. The traditional MADDPG algorithm uses fully connected networks and processes only instantaneous states. With LSTM integration, both the Critic and Actor Networks incorporate LSTM layers to capture historical state sequences. The architecture of MADDPG enhanced with LSTM integration is partially illustrated in Fig. 5. In the figure, h_t denotes the hidden state at time step t, and c_t represents the corresponding cell (memory) state.

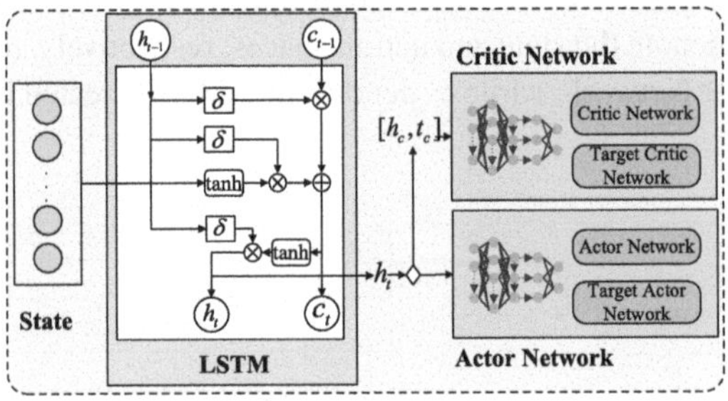

Fig. 5. The architecture of MADDPG enhanced with LSTM integration.

The MADDPG algorithm adopts a centralized training and decentralized execution (CTDE) strategy. During training, the Actor processes temporal sequences more frequently than the centralized Critic, It encodes a state sequence using an LSTM layer to capture temporal dependencies, and maps the output to the action space via a fully connected layer. This allows agents to make decisions at time t based on observation sequences $\tau = \{\tau^{i-1}\}_{i=0}^{l}$, rather than single-time observations τ^t. The sequence length l is configurable, and the action selection formula agent is defined as follows:

$$a_t = \pi_a\left(\left\{\tau^{t-i}\right\}_{i=0}^{l}; \theta\right) \tag{14}$$

The Critic Network receives a state sequence and the current action as inputs. The sequence is first encoded by an LSTM layer, and the resulting hidden representation is concatenated with the action vector. This joint representation is then processed by fully connected layers to estimate the Q-value.

Hybrid Sampling Strategy: To process time-series data, this study employs a sequence buffer to store and manage interaction sequences. Each entire sequence is treated as a single input, and after interacting with the environment, a corresponding single-step experience tuple is extracted and stored in the buffer.

To balance early-stage exploration and later-stage learning efficiency, a hybrid sampling strategy is introduced that adapts dynamically during training. Uniform sampling is used in the initial phase to ensure broad experience coverage, and the strategy gradually transitions to prioritized experience replay (PER), the model can focus on more informative samples.

The final sampling probability, denoted as P_i, for the experience indexed by i, is defined as follows:

$$P_i = \xi(t) \cdot P_i^{PER} + (1 - \xi(t)) \cdot P_i^{UNIFORM} \tag{15}$$

where $p_i^{UNIFORM}$ denotes the uniform sampling probability, and $\xi(t)$ is a linearly increasing scaling function with respect to training steps, used to control the weight of PER:

$$\xi(t) = \min\left(1.0, \xi_0 + \frac{t}{T'}(1.0 - \xi_0)\right) \tag{16}$$

where ξ_0 denotes the initial weight, set to 0.2, and T' denotes the total number of transition steps, set to 10,000.

p_i^{PER} represents the sampling probability in PER, based on a rank-based strategy, and is defined as follows:

$$p_i^{PER} = \frac{1}{rank(i)^{\alpha}} \Bigg/ \sum_{j=1}^{M} \frac{1}{j^{\alpha}} \tag{17}$$

where $rank(i)$ denotes the rank of sample i in the priority queue, M is the total number of samples currently stored in the experience buffer, α is the priority sampling exponent.

To mitigate the policy bias introduced by non-uniform sampling, importance sampling weights are employed:

$$\omega_i = \left(\frac{P_{new}(i)}{P_{old}(i)}\right)^{\beta} \tag{18}$$

where $P_{new}(i)$ and $P_{old}(i)$ denote the sampling probabilities of i under the current and the original policies, respectively, β is the exponent for importance sampling correction.

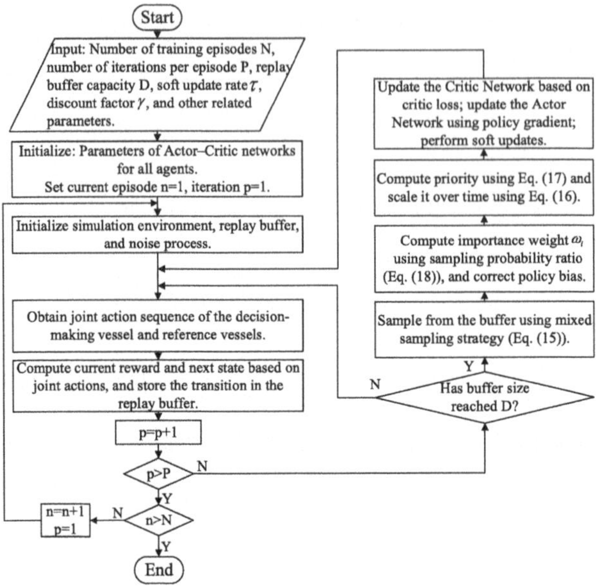

Fig. 6. Flowchart of the proposed algorithm.

Reinforcement Learning Training: The algorithm flowchart is shown in Fig. 6. Agents can share scheduling information to collaboratively search for an optimal strategy, each agent can make near-optimal decisions based solely on the local operating status within its assigned region.

4 Simulation and Analysis

4.1 AIS Data Analysis

The experimental scenario of this study is shown in Fig. 1 and is based on real AIS data for simulation experiments. The data were collected from an inland waterway in the southeastern United States over a two-week period using the Automatic Identification System (AIS). The study area spans approximately 4.93 km north–south and 4.86 km east–west. A total of 322 vessel trajectories were extracted. The AIS data were preprocessed by removing outliers and missing entries, and by filling null values. In the course analysis, a directional tolerance of $\pm$ 40° was applied to each heading to account for the irregular geographic layout of intersections. The relevant results are shown as Fig. 7.

Statistical analysis shows that vessel speeds are primarily distributed between 0.5 and 9 m/s, with accelerations falling within $\pm$ 0.5 m/s^2. The average transit time is approximately 23.83 min. Prior studies have shown that vessel arrivals follow a Poisson distribution, where traffic generation involves determining both vessel attributes and temporal arrival patterns. This study constructs an intersection traffic flow: vessel arrivals are modeled as a Poisson process, and directional arrival ratios are derived from the statistical distribution of AIS data.

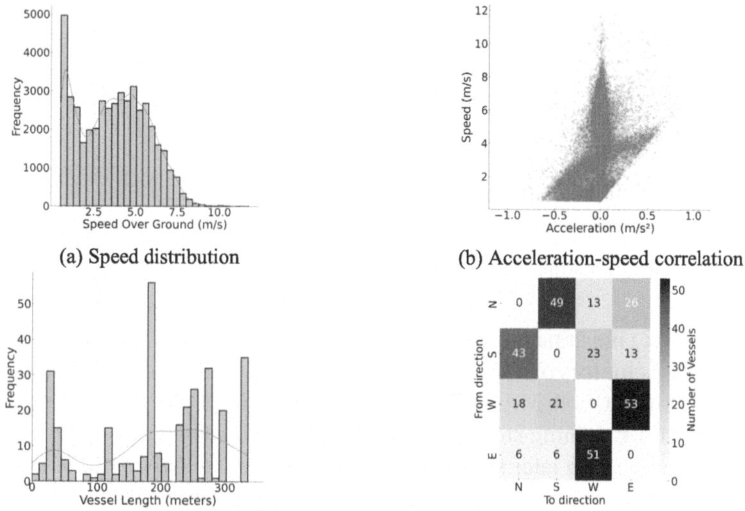

(a) Speed distribution (b) Acceleration-speed correlation

(c) Length distribution (d) Heading distribution

Fig. 7. AIS-based statistical distributions of vessel parameters.

4.2 Hyperparameter Settings

Hyperparameters used in the experiments were listed in Table 1.

Table 1. Hyperparameter Settings.

Hyperparameter	Value	Hyperparameter	Value
Experience buffer capacity	500000	Soft update coefficient	0.998
Training steps T	50000	Batch size	64
Discount factor γ	$0.5 \rightarrow 0.9$	Hidden units	64
Priority exponent α	0.7	LSTM hidden units	64
Importance sampling coefficient β	0.5	Sequence buffer length	12
Actor learning rate	$0.0001 \rightarrow 0$	LSTM time steps	4
Critic learning rate	$0.001 \rightarrow 0$	Exploration noise	0.2

4.3 Results and Analysis

A comparative evaluation of MALHP-DDPG, MALUP-DDPG, and MADDPG was conducted under identical experimental settings. MALUP-DDPG (Multi-Agent LSTM-Augmented DDPG with Uniform Sampling) adopts uniform sampling as its experience replay strategy. The corresponding results are presented below.

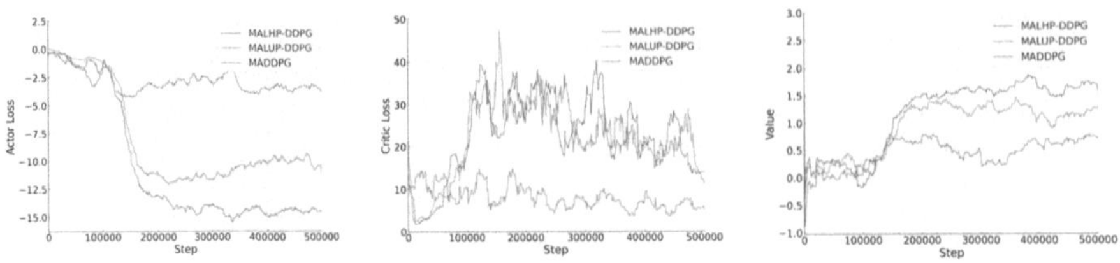

(a) Actor loss curve (b) Critic loss curve (c) Reward curve

Fig. 8. Comparison of training performance between MALHP-DDPG and baseline algorithms.

Figure 8(a)–(c) illustrate the training performance of the three algorithms. As shown in Fig. 8(a), the Actor loss of MADDPG stagnates prematurely, indicating limited learning ability. In contrast, both MALHP-DDPG and MALUP-DDPG converge rapidly after approximately 170k training steps, with MALHP-DDPG showing greater stability and smoother convergence in later stages. Figure 8(b) shows that MALHP-DDPG exhibits higher loss variance, suggesting more active policy exploration. The hybrid sampling mechanism improves the use of high-error samples, enhancing the model's ability to capture complex state–action relationships and improving generalization. As shown in Fig. 8(c), MALHP-DDPG maintains the highest reward level during the mid-to-late training stages, demonstrating its capacity to learn superior policies in complex multi-agent environments. Although slight fluctuations appear toward the end of training, overall performance remains stable and outstanding.

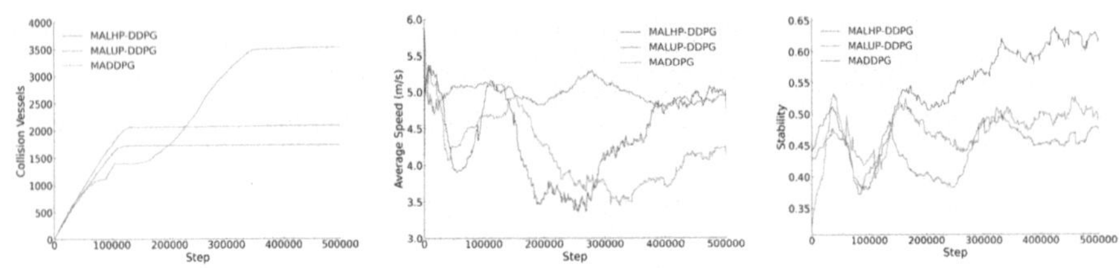

(a) Collision rate (safety) (b) Average speed (efficiency) (c) Action stability (stability)

Fig. 9. Comparison of safety, efficiency, and stability between MALHP-DDPG and baseline algorithms during training.

Figure 9(a)–(c) compare the three algorithms in terms of collision rate (safety), average speed (efficiency), and action stability (stability). Figure 9(a) shows that MALHP-DDPG consistently achieves the lowest collision rate and stabilizes early, demonstrating superior safety control. MADDPG's collision rate increases rapidly and remains high, revealing ineffective avoidance in complex environments. MALUP-DDPG performs comparably to MALHP-DDPG early on but shows slightly higher collision rates later, indicating potential for safety improvement. Figure 9(b) shows the average speed trends. MALHP-DDPG initially sacrifices speed for safety, but after about 250k steps, its speed rises steadily, eventually surpassing MALUP-DDPG and approaching MADDPG, achieving a good balance between safety and efficiency. MALUP-DDPG reaches high speed early but fluctuates later, showing instability. MADDPG maintains high speed at the cost of safety. Figure 9(c) illustrates action stability. MALHP-DDPG steadily improves throughout training, achieving the highest stability and demonstrating strong convergence and robustness. MALUP-DDPG performs slightly better than MADDPG but with limited improvement, while MADDPG remains flat or declines, indicating higher action variability and less reliable behavior.

Overall, MALHP-DDPG exhibits the best balance of safety, stability, and efficiency, making it highly suitable for multi-agent navigation tasks requiring reliability.

Table 2. Performance Comparison Between MALHP-DDPG and Baseline Algorithms.

Evaluation Metrics	Algorithms	Vessel Traffic Flow / Hour				
		15	20	25	30	35
Collision rate / (%)↓	MALHP-DDPG	**0.00**	**0.00**	**0.00**	**0.00**	**0.01**
	MALUP-DDPG	0.00	0.00	0.10	1.11	2.16
	MADDPG	0.00	0.00	1.60	3.17	4.24
Average speed / (m/s)↓	MALHP-DDPG	**5.68**	**5.42**	**5.37**	**5.31**	**5.23**
	MALUP-DDPG	5.19	5.03	4.91	4.64	4.47
	MADDPG	5.47	5.29	5.12	4.91	4.78
Action stability ↑	MALHP-DDPG	**53.06**	**86.82**	**128.37**	**172.29**	**220.89**
	MALUP-DDPG	46.98	59.58	74.25	89.15	105.60
	MADDPG	43.48	51.55	58.48	65.16	72.31

To further evaluate the superiority and coordination precision of the proposed algorithm, a comprehensive comparison was conducted between MALHP-DDPG and the baseline algorithms (MALUP-DDPG and MADDPG) under varying levels of vessel traffic flow, with a consistent vessel-type distribution. As shown in Table 2, MALHP-DDPG consistently achieves the best overall performance across all metrics. It maintains an almost zero collision rate in all traffic scenarios, reflecting excellent collision-avoidance capability, and achieves a balanced trade-off between safety and efficiency by maintaining high average speeds. Moreover, MALHP-DDPG exhibits strong action stability, with its advantages becoming more evident as traffic density increases, resulting in widening performance gaps compared with the other algorithms.

5 Conclusion and Future Work

This paper addresses the challenge of vessel coordination in inland river confluence waters. A novel deep reinforcement learning–based scheduling method, MALHP-DDPG, is proposed to improve scheduling efficiency and reduce conflicts in highly dynamic and multi-objective traffic environments. The method integrates a cross-scale collaborative scheduling model with a Long Short-Term Memory (LSTM) network and a hybrid sampling strategy, enhancing temporal modeling and complex state understanding. Consequently, it improves multi-agent decision quality and behavioral stability in dynamic interactive environments. Simulation results demonstrate that MALHP-DDPG significantly outperforms baseline methods across multiple metrics, achieving faster policy convergence, higher cumulative rewards, and better environmental adaptability. In high-density crossing scenarios, it effectively coordinates multi-vessel navigation, reduces potential conflicts, and achieves a balanced performance in safety, stability, and efficiency, offering an efficient and reliable strategy for complex waterway traffic management.

Acknowledgments. This work was supported in part by the National Natural Science Foundation of China under Grant 62372131, the Key Research and Development Program of Heilongjiang Province under Grant 2023ZX01A20.

References

1. Wenzhang, Y., et al.: Analysis of vessel traffic flow characteristics in inland restricted waterways using multi-source data. Ocean Eng. **317,** 120065 (2025)
2. Şirin, Ö., Or, İ., Altan, Y.C.: Scheduling and simulation of maritime traffic in congested waterways: an application to the Strait of Istanbul. J. Navig. **74**(3), 656–672 (2021)
3. Zhang, G., Wang, Y., Liu, J., et al.: Collision-avoidance decision system for inland ships based on velocity obstacle algorithms. J. Mar. Sci. Eng. **10**(6), 814 (2022)
4. Hualong, C., Man, Z., Yuanqiao, W., et al.: An implementable architecture of inland autonomous waterway transportation system. IFAC-PapersOnLine **54**(16), 37–42 (2021)
5. Bellsolà Olba, X., Daamen, W., Vellinga, T., et al.: A method to estimate the capacity of an intersection of waterways in ports. Transp. A Transp. Sci. **15**(2), 1848–1866 (2019)
6. Xin, X., Liu, K., Loughney, S., et al.: Maritime traffic clustering to capture high-risk multi-ship encounters in complex waters. Reliab. Eng. Syst. Saf. **230**, 108936 (2023)
7. Yuan, H., Liu, K., Wu, X., et al.: GATransformer: A vessel trajectory prediction method based on attention algorithm in complex navigable waters. Ocean Eng. **326**, 120902 (2025)
8. Chen, Q., Xiao, C., Wen, Y., et al.: Ship intention prediction at intersections based on vision and bayesian framework. J. Mar. Sci. Eng. **10**(5), 639 (2022)
9. Ma, J., Liu, Q., Jia, C.: Data-driven model for ship encounter intention inference in intersection waters based on AIS data. Proc. Inst. Mech. Eng. Part M J. Eng. Marit. Environ. **236**(3), 701–712 (2022)
10. Chen, L., Huang, Y., Zheng, H., et al.: Cooperative multi-vessel systems in urban waterway networks. IEEE Trans. Intell. Transp. Syst. **21**(8), 3294–3307 (2019)
11. Weidong, X., et al.: Optimizing multi-vessel collision avoidance decision making for autonomous surface vessels: a colregs-compliant deep reinforcement learning approach. J. Mar. Sci. Eng. **12**(3), 372 (2024)
12. Cheng-Cheng, W., et al.: Scalable-MADDPG-based cooperative target invasion for a multi-USV system. IEEE Trans. Neural Netw. Learn. Syst. (2023)
13. Wenqiang, G., et al.: Collaborative optimization of vessel scheduling and tugboat allocation in seaports using a multi-action deep reinforcement learning framework. Eng. Appl. Artif. Intell. **156**, 111239 (2025)
14. Qi, W., et al.: Integrated scheduling optimization for automated container terminal: a reinforcement learning-based approach. IEEE Trans. Intell. Transp. Syst. (2025)
15. Xu, B., Li, S.E., Bian, Y., et al.: Distributed conflict-free cooperation for multiple connected vehicles at unsignalized intersections. Transp. Res. Part C Emerg. Technol. **93**, 322–334 (2018)

Multi-agent Task Allocation and Path Planning for Sustainable Synchronous Collaboration

Shaohao Zhai, Yifeng Zhou(✉), and Zhan Bu(✉)

School of Computer Science, Nanjing Audit University, Nanjing 211815, China
{yfzhou,zhanbu}@nau.edu.cn

Abstract. Recent sustainable synchronous collaboration (SSC) scenarios impose additional constraints on Multi-Agent Task Allocation and Path Planning (MATAPP), including agents' round-trip resource replenishment and collaboration consistency during task execution, requiring integrated optimization of round-trip paths and synchronous collaboration costs. Traditional methods struggle to solve this problem effectively or partially optimize the above objectives due to high complexity. To address this, this paper proposes a method for MATAPP in SSC scenarios. First, it introduces a multi-round task allocation framework guided by a dynamic resource-demand strategy, and uses a refinement mechanism based on path length prediction instead of computing exact paths to enhance solution quality without excessive computation. Subsequently, the method proposes an extended Conflict-Based Search path planning algorithm to compute conflict-free paths for agents in each task allocation round while ensuring collaboration consistency; it allows asynchronous agent arrivals at tasks to avoid path cost inflation from strict synchronization. Experimental results indicate that the method efficiently solves the MATAPP problem in SSC scenarios, achieving optimal solutions in small-scale maps and significantly outperforming benchmark algorithms in both small-scale and large-scale maps.

Keywords: Multi-Agent Systems · Path Planning · Task Allocation · Sustainable Synchronous Collaboration

1 Introduction

Multi-Agent Task Allocation and Path Planning (MATAPP) is a core problem in multi-agent collaboration, aiming to optimally assign tasks to agents, establish task-agent matching, generate global conflict-free paths for collaborative task completion while satisfying constraints and optimizing objectives like efficiency and resource balancing [1,2].

Unlike traditional MATAPP [3], this study focuses on sustainable synchronous collaboration (SSC) scenarios. Here, agents complete current and subsequent task sequences with time-consumed resources; a key feature is all agents

© The Author(s), under exclusive license to Springer Nature Singapore Pte Ltd. 2027
H. Sun et al. (Eds.): ChineseCSCW 2025, CCIS 2911, pp. 17–32, 2027.
https://doi.org/10.1007/978-981-92-0288-1_2

must gather at task vertices to trigger execution, though asynchronous arrivals are permitted (early agents wait) [9]. When resources deplete, agents return to a central depot for replenishment before resuming tasks, forming a core execution and replenishment cycle [7]. Previous research addresses temporal coordination constraints like task order or strict simultaneous arrival [10], but agents shuttle between depots and task vertices without precedence constraints in SSC. Asynchronous arrival boosts fault tolerance yet creates a trade-off between relaxed synchronization and more waiting or redundant paths, and traditional algorithms fail to balance resource consumption, round-trip replenishment, and asynchronous arrivals.

To address this, we propose a hierarchical optimization framework integrating a resource-demand-oriented dynamic task allocation strategy and an extended Conflict-Based Search (CBS) conflict resolution mechanism [12], balancing synchronization latency, path redundancy, and resource return constraints. The method employs a multi-round, dynamic resource-demand-guided framework with path length prediction in the allocation phase. It simplifies computations while matching tasks' multi-type resource needs to agent states, minimizing waiting and return costs. In the planning phase, the method adopts an extended Conflict-Based Search (CBS) algorithm, which allows asynchronous agent arrivals while ensuring collaboration consistency to avoid path cost inflation from strict synchronization. Experiments on small-scale (Random, Warehouse, Maze) [10] and large-scale (Warehouse, Dragon-age, Den520_d) [10] maps validate performance: in small-scale tests against LaCAM* [6], CBS-TA-MLA [7], and ITA-CBS-MLA [8], our method matches LaCAM*'s optimal solutions, with SOC and Makespan 38% better than CBS-TA-MLA and ITA-CBS-MLA; in large-scale scenarios, it outperforms LaCAM* by 10% in SOC and Makespan.

2 Related Work

2.1 Multi-agent Task Allocation and Path Planning

Existing MATAPP literature focuses on these core directions, path planning for pre-assigned tasks, joint and decoupled optimization of task allocation and path planning.

In pre-assigned scenarios, the key is to plan conflict-free paths for efficient multi-agent task completion. The classical Conflict-Based Search (CBS) algorithm [12] resolves vertex and edge conflicts via hierarchical constraint propagation but struggles with complex collaborative conditions (e.g., agents waiting at task points for all collaborators). Zhao et al. [4] proposed "Waitable Path Coordination" to allow sequential arrivals, reducing conflicts via controlled waiting but relaxing action consistency (unsuitable for high-precision simultaneous arrival needs). In contrast, Yan et al. [9] introduced "Strict Simultaneous Arrival Constraints" to ensure consistency, yet this significantly increases path costs and waiting overhead in dense task or large agent environments, leading to redundancy. These methods perform well in static or simple collaboration scenarios but lack adaptability for complex tasks, they neglect the coupling between task waiting and path planning (failing to balance consistency and efficiency) and ignore the impact of return-to-base replenishment paths, limiting applicability in resource-constrained settings.

Traditional decoupled strategies first assign tasks (e.g., market-based auctions [11], Ferreira et al.'s distributed framework [16]) then plan paths, offering modularity but risking suboptimal solutions, especially when agents converge on collaborative tasks (hard to balance allocation decisions and path costs). Joint optimization aims at global efficiency via integrated modeling of allocation and planning [13]. Recent coupled methods (e.g., Hu et al.'s RL-based conflict-resistant path planning [15], Brown et al.'s integrated framework [2]) address decoupled shortcomings but fail to model spatiotemporal coupling from collaborative waiting and return paths. This causes significant redundancy in resource-constrained, strictly synchronized scenarios. To balance quality and efficiency, this work adopts a semi-decoupled framework, it retains joint optimization's global awareness while reducing computation via staged allocation-planning, using predicted collaborative path lengths (not full exact paths) to guide task assignments.

2.2 Sustainable Multi-agent Synchronous Collaboration

A new class of synchronous collaboration problems has emerged, featuring multi-agent work at the same task point, repeated travel between depots and tasks, and "sustainability" (continuous task execution with replenishment only when resources are depleted). Existing studies are partially focused on sustained collaboration or synchronization constraints.

In sustainable multi-agent collaboration, research primarily centers on managing task waiting to ensure efficiency. For example, Hu et al. [15] optimized collaborative waiting via RL to reduce latency but overlooked the interplay between return paths and waiting times (limiting long-term efficiency). Traditional return path methods (e.g., Dantzig et al.'s TSP model [14] for VRP) work for single agents but not multi-agent collaboration—they ignore coupling between waiting and return paths. This study addresses this via a resource-oriented allocation mechanism that integrates return path costs into task-path planning based on task demands and agent states.

In multi-agent collaboration under synchronization constraints, research predominantly focuses on ensuring arrival consistency via temporal or synchronization mechanisms. Zhao et al. [4] and Wang et al. [18]'s temporal constraints allow independent subtask completion in order (reducing waiting but lacking high-precision consistency). Yan et al. [9] and Zhang et al. [19]'s simultaneous arrival constraints ensure consistency but increase redundancy. These methods lack practicality in complex settings (e.g., large-scale or dense tasks) where balancing efficiency and resource costs is challenging. This study's flexible synchronous waiting mechanism compromises by permitting asynchronous arrivals—early agents wait appropriately to ensure smooth execution while controlling redundancy and waiting losses.

3 Problem Formulation

3.1 System Environment Modeling

Map: The environment is a 2D $n \times n$ ($n \in \mathbb{N}$) 4-connected grid $G = \langle V, E\rangle$ (Fig. 1(a)). V denotes grid cells with coordinates $(x_v, y_v) \in \{1, \ldots, n\}^2$; $O \subseteq V$ is obstacles (agents cannot traverse). An undirected edge $(u, v) \in E$ exists if $u, v \in V \setminus O$ are 4-neighbors; $d(u, v)$ is the distance between u and v.

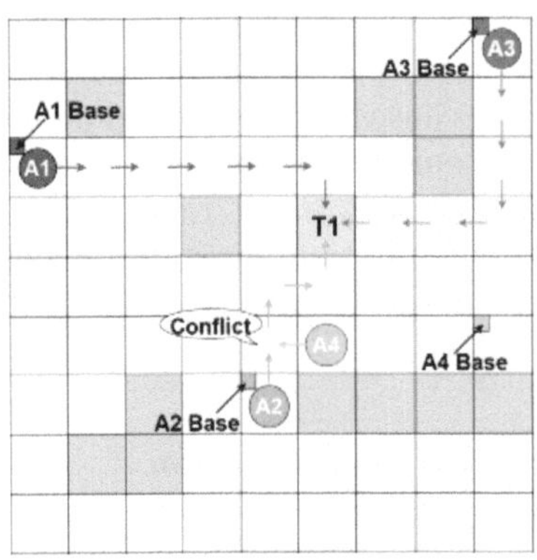

(a) Example map

(b) Synchronous collaboration

Fig. 1. An Example of System Environment Modeling for SSC

Base: Bases (starting points) are denoted as $S = \{\, s_i \mid i = 1, \ldots, base\_num \}$, each associated with a resource type $r_k \in R$ (set of all resources).

Resource: $R = \{r_1, \ldots, r_k\}$, an intrinsic property of bases and a requirement of tasks.

Task: Task set $M = \{\, m_j \mid j = 1, \ldots, n_t \}$ (n_t = total tasks). Each m_j has heterogeneous resource requirements $(R^{m_j}, k) = \left((R_1^{m_j}, k_1), \ldots, (R_i^{m_j}, k_i)\right)$, where $R_p^{m_j}$ is the p-th resource type and k_p is its quantity. m_j decomposes into i subtasks $\langle sm_{j_1}, \ldots, sm_{j_i}\rangle$, each corresponding to one resource type.

Agent: Agent set $A = \{\, a_i \mid i = 1, \ldots, base\_num \}$ (one agent per base). a_i is represented by $\langle w_i, s_i^{r_k}\rangle$, where w_i is load capacity and $s_i^{r_k}$ is the carried resource type. a_i can perform subtasks requiring r_k; its task queue is $\langle sm_{1_k}, \ldots, sm_{j_k}\rangle$.

Path: For a_i, $l_i^t \in V$ is its position at time t. Its complete path is $\Pi_i = \langle l_i^1, \ldots, l_i^t\rangle$, with $|\Pi_i|$ as path length. Conventions: l_i^0 is initial position; $l_i^t = l_i^{t+1}$ means waiting.

Conflict: Five conflict types exist in MAPF : vertex, edge, follow, loop, exchange conflicts [10] (Fig. 2). A special case—*synchronous collaboration conflict*—arises at task points: agents may overlap at task vertices (for collaboration) but incur edge conflicts when departing.

Synchronous Collaboration: For m_j at u (needing a_i, a_j, a_k), a_i, a_j occupy u at t, a_k arrives at $t + n$; a_i, a_j wait until a_k arrives. Formally, $\exists t, l_i^t = l_j^t$,

$\exists t+n, l_i^t = \cdots = l_i^{t+n} = l_k^{t+n}$. In SSC, agents execute task sequences (subsequent tasks wait until current done) and return to s_i for replenishment when resources are depleted. Synchronous collaboration conflict (Fig. 1(b)) is defined as $C = \langle a_i, a_j, u, v, t \rangle$, $\exists t, l_i^t = l_j^t$ (collaborating at u), $\exists t+1, t+2, l_i^{t+1} = l_j^{t+1}, l_i^{t+2} = l_j^{t+2}$.

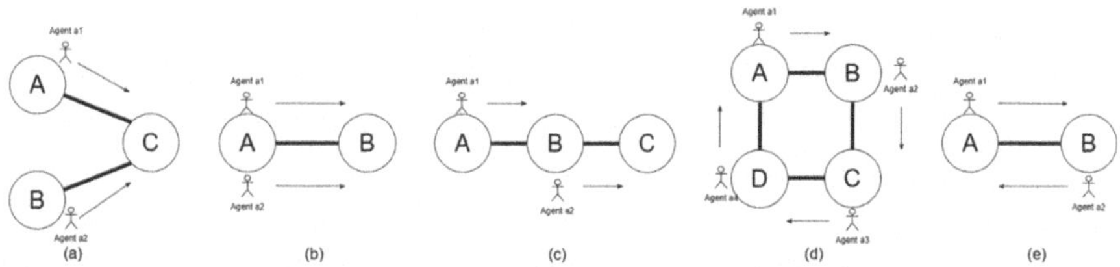

Fig. 2. Common conflict types [10]

3.2 Objective Function

This study optimizes system performance from three perspectives: Minimum Path Length, Shortest Return Path, and Minimum Waiting Time. It revises the classical definitions of Makespan and Sum of Costs, denoting the updated metrics as **Makespan*** and **SOC*** to represent the optimal solution under the proposed framework.

Minimum Path Length: This is a fundamental requirement of path planning, corresponding to the Sum of Costs in classical path planning. In this study, it refers to the path traversed by each agent to complete all assigned tasks. For each agent a_i, its task path is denoted as $\zeta(\Pi_i)$.

Shortest Return Path: Given the limited resources carried by each agent, agents must return to their starting points for replenishment occasionally. The length of these return paths directly affects both the system Makespan and Sum of Costs. Conceptually, a return path can be treated as a special type of task path, where the starting point serves as the "task point" for the return journey. For each agent a_i, its return path is denoted as $\xi(\Pi_i)$.

Thus, an agent's complete path consists of the combination of its task path and return path. The unified optimization objective for this requirement is expressed as:

$$p(i) = \min\left(\sum_{i=1}^{m} \zeta\left(\Pi_i\right) + \sum_{i=1}^{m} \xi(\Pi_i)\right), \forall a_i \in A \tag{1}$$

where $p(i)$ represents the complete path of agent a_i, $\zeta(\Pi_i)$ is the task path of a_i, and $\xi(\Pi_i)$ is the return path of a_i.

Minimum Waiting Time: This study requires multi-agent synchronous waiting for collaboration, agents stay at the task point to wait for other required agents to arrive. The objective of minimizing waiting time is described as:

$$\min \sum_{j=1}^{n} \Delta T_j, \forall m_j \in M \tag{2}$$

where $\Delta T_j = FT_j - ST_j$, ST_j denotes the start time of the task m_j, and FT_j denotes its completion time.

Integrated Objective Functions: The updated optimal metrics (Makespan* and SOC*) integrate the three components mentioned above. Their formal expressions are as follows:

$$\text{Makespan*} = \left[\max_{a_i \in A} p(i) + \sum_{m_j \in M} \Delta T_j \right] \tag{3}$$

where ΔT_j is the waiting time incurred by agents at task m_j, and $p(i)$ is the complete path of agent a_i.

$$\text{SOC*} = \left(\sum_{i=1}^{m} p(i) + \sum_{j=1}^{n} \Delta T_j \right), \forall a_i \in A, \forall m_j \in G \tag{4}$$

where $p(i)$ is the complete path of agent a_i, and ΔT_j is the waiting time associated with task m_j.

3.3 Problem Complexity Analysis

MATAPP extends the NP-hard MAPF problem [10]: task allocation has a search space of $O(m^{n_t})$; path planning constraints grow exponentially with agents and tasks; synchronous collaboration conflicts ($C = \langle a_i, a_j, u, v, t \rangle$) increase constraint complexity [15]. Additionally, synchronous waiting amplifies spatiotemporal coupling [9], return constraints interact with allocation and planning [14], resource constraints demand feasible matching [2], and multi-objective optimization requires balancing path and waiting trade-offs [15]. In summary, MATAPP complexity arises from allocation-planning coupling, synchronous waiting, return path dynamics, and resource constraint interactions.

Theorem 1. *NP-hard of the MATAPP Problem. Given a 2D grid $G = \langle V, E \rangle$, task set $M = \{m_j | j = 1, \ldots, n_t\}$, agent set $A = \{a_i | i = 1, \ldots, m\}$ (each m_j has (R^{m_j}, k), each a_i carries r_k with w_i), minimizing **Makespan*** (Eq. 3) and **SOC*** (Eq. 4) under synchronous waiting and backhaul constraints. The decision version (exists solution with **Makespan*** $\leq K$) is NP-hard.*

Proof. 1)*Reduction to MAPF*: MAPF is NP-hard [10]; fixed task allocation reduces MATAPP to MAPF (planning conflict-free paths for m agents). 2) *Task Allocation Complexity*: Assigning n_t tasks to m agents with resource and capacity constraints is NP-hard [2]. 3)*Synchronous Constraints*: Temporal coordination increases complexity exponentially [9]; optimizing ΔT_j further complicates the search space. 4)*Backhaul Constraints*: Return paths extend the NP-hard VRP [14], with coupling to allocation and waiting increasing constraints. By integrating these NP-hard subproblems, the MATAPP decision version is NP-hard.

4 Methods

4.1 Hierarchical Framework

To solve traditional flaws (joint: redundancy; decoupled: poor collaboration), a semi-decoupled framework is proposed: **Allocation Layer**: Assigns $m_j \in M$ to $a_i \in A$ via (R^{m_j}, k) and w_i, minimizing $\sum \Delta T_j$ and $\sum p(i)$. **Planning Layer**: Generates Π_i on $G = \langle V, E \rangle$, resolves conflicts, optimizes backhaul $\xi(\Pi_i)$. **Feedback**: Updates $\mathcal{A}$ via conflicts and ΔT_j, forming a closed loop. This ensures: $\text{Ma kespan}^* = \min\left[\max p(i) + \sum \Delta T_j\right], \quad \text{SOC}^* = \min\left(\sum p(i) + \sum \Delta T_j\right)$

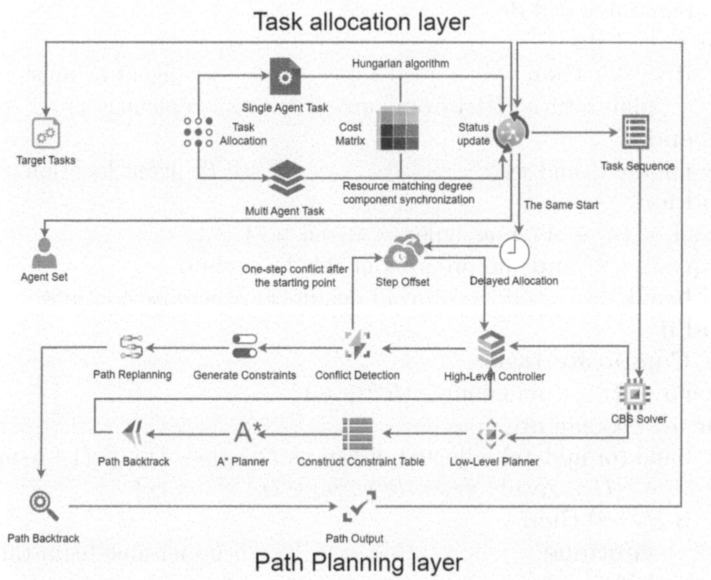

Fig. 3. Task allocation and path planning framework

For real-world adaptability, the *Dynamic Task Planner* splits agent execution into four phases. Agents adjust plans via real-time resource state w_i to keep $\mathcal{A}(m_j)$ feasible, using predicted collaborative path lengths to balance allocation quality and computational efficiency. The following is the iterative execution process: 1)Initialize agent states ($l_i^0 \in V$, resource type $s_i^{r_k} \in R$, capacity w_i), map $G = \langle V, E \rangle$, and task point locations $v_j \in V$; 2)dynamically generate each m_j's resource requirements (R^{m_j}, k) to obtain $\mathcal{A}(m_j) \subseteq A$; 3)use improved CBS for path planning (handle collaboration conflicts $C = \langle a_i, a_j, m_j, v, t \rangle$, optimize $\xi(\Pi_i)$); 4)update agent states and adjust next-stage $\mathcal{A}$ and Π_i (see Fig. 3).

4.2 Dynamic Task Allocation Based on Resource Demand Orientation

The proposed multi-round dynamic task allocation algorithm adapts to real-time resource consumption and replenishment, outperforming static methods that treat tasks as one-time decisions unable to respond to changes in agent resource status w_i. It monitors agents' resource levels, triggering backhaul replenishment when depleted and incorporating the backhaul path $\xi(\Pi_i)$ into global optimization.

Algorithm 1. Hierarchical Dynamic Task Allocation

Require: Map $G = \langle V, E \rangle$, Agents $A = \{a_i\}_{i=1}^{m}$, Tasks $M = \{m_j\}_{j=1}^{n_t}$, Threshold ϵ
Ensure: Allocation $\mathcal{A}$ and paths Π

remaining $\leftarrow M$; $\mathcal{A} \leftarrow \emptyset$; $\Pi \leftarrow \emptyset$
while remaining $\neq \emptyset$ **do**
  for $a_i \in A$ **do**
    if $w_i \leq \epsilon$ **then** ▷ agent a_i must resupply
      plan return $\xi(\Pi_i)$ from current l_i^t to s_i; replenish w_i
    end if
    update l_i^t and w_i ▷ l_i^t: agent location at time t
  end for
  Avail $\leftarrow \{a_i \in A \mid a_i.\text{assigned} = \varnothing,\ w_i > \epsilon\}$
  if Avail $= \emptyset$ **and** no progress in this loop **then**
    break ▷ avoid deadlock; otherwise continue next cycle
  end if
  // **Composite tasks**
  Comp $\leftarrow \{m_j \in \text{remaining} \mid |R^{m_j}| > 1\}$
  for $m_j \in$ Comp **do**
    build (or update) adjusted distances $D[i,j] \leftarrow D[i,j]\cdot(1+\alpha\cdot\text{penalty}_i)$
    $\mathcal{U}_j \leftarrow \{\mathcal{U} \subseteq \text{Avail} \mid \forall r_k \in R^{m_j}, \exists a_i \in \mathcal{U} : s_i^{r_k} = r_k\}$
    if $\mathcal{U}_j = \emptyset$ **then**
      continue ▷ no feasible team this round
    end if
    select $\mathcal{U}_j^\star = \arg\min_{\mathcal{U} \in \mathcal{U}_j} \left(\sum_{a_i \in \mathcal{U}} D[i,j] + \lambda\gamma_j(\mathcal{U})\right)$
    assign $\mathcal{U}_j^\star$ to m_j; $\mathcal{A} \leftarrow \mathcal{A} \cup \{(\mathcal{U}_j^\star, m_j)\}$
    remaining $\leftarrow$ remaining $\setminus \{m_j\}$; mark a_i.assigned $= m_j$ for $a_i \in \mathcal{U}_j^\star$
    optional: update $D[i,k] \leftarrow d(m_j, m_k) + d(m_k, s_i)$ for $a_i \in U_j^\star$
  end for
  // **Single-resource tasks**
  $S \leftarrow \{m_j \in \text{remaining} \mid |R^{m_j}| = 1\}$
  if $S \neq \emptyset$ **then**
    build cost matrix $C[i,j]$ for $a_i \in$ Avail, $m_j \in S$ from adjusted $D[i,j]$
    $\mathcal{A}_{\text{single}} \leftarrow$ Hungarian(C) ▷ optimal matching for single-resource tasks
    update a_i.assigned and remove assigned m_j from remaining
    $\mathcal{A} \leftarrow \mathcal{A} \cup \mathcal{A}_{\text{single}}$

    end if
    plan/update Π_i for newly assigned agents; resolve conflicts
    release finished bindings; keep ongoing assignments
end while
return $\mathcal{A}, \Pi$

Two-Tier Allocation Mechanism: To address resource constraints w_i and path optimization, the hierarchical algorithm (Algorithm 1) employs a two-tier mechanism based on task resource demands (R^{m_j}, k) (a uniform strategy would yield suboptimal results). First, the low-level A* algorithm [5] in path planning calculates conflict-free paths from agents a_i to task points m_j, recording distances in table D where $D[i,j] = d(l_i^t, m_j)$ (based on map $G = \langle V, E \rangle$). For composite tasks (requiring multiple R^{m_j} types), queues are built by required resources r_k; agents carrying r_k ($s_i^{r_k} = r_k$) are sorted by $D[i,j]$ (ascending); groups with the shortest total path and smallest intra-group time difference (γ_j) are selected. D is updated to include backhaul costs: $D[i,k] = d(m_j, m_k) + d(m_k, s_i)$. For single-resource tasks ($|R^{m_j}| = 1$), the Hungarian algorithm [17] optimizes D for allocation $\mathcal{A}(m_j)$ (solutions recorded). Assigned composite tasks are removed from M; the process repeats until no composite tasks remain, with complete allocation $\mathcal{A}$ formed by merging solutions.

Resource Status Monitoring Mechanism: Embedded in the algorithm cycle: when an agent's resources drop below $w_i < \epsilon$, backhaul replenishment is triggered, and $\xi(\Pi_i)$ is included in global conflict detection. A 3D cost model guides allocation: $\mathrm{Cost}(a_i, m_j) = d(l_i^t, m_j) + \beta \cdot d(m_j, s_i) + \alpha \cdot penalty_i$ (where $penalty_i = 1 - w_i/w_i^{\max}$ is the resource depletion penalty, α, β are weights). For low-resource agents, $D[i,j]$ is adjusted to $D[i,j] \cdot (1 + \alpha \cdot penalty_i)$ to prioritize tasks near start s_i; γ_j avoids excessive waiting ΔT_j for composite tasks.

Multi-round Allocation Execution Strategy: Traditional one-shot allocation causes long completion times for mixed tasks, so multi-round allocation is used: agent-task bindings are released after each round to allow re-participation. Each iteration records optimal allocation set $\mathcal{A}_t$ (minimizing $\sum p(i) + \sum \Delta T_j$), following the two-tier mechanism (forming composite groups first, then allocating single-resource tasks, updating D) until all composite tasks are allocated. The final $\mathcal{A}$ is the union of all $\mathcal{A}_t$ ($\mathcal{A} = \bigcup_t \mathcal{A}_t$) (Table 1).

Table 1. Table of formulae for calculating the corrected distance

Correction term	Calculation formula
Calculate the forward path distance	$d_{forward} = A^*(a.position, t.position)$
Calculate return path distance	$d_{return} = A^*(t.position, a.start\_position)$
Resource penalty factor	$penalty = (1 - a.current\_resource/a.resource\_amount)$
Combined correction	$corrected_{distance} = d_{forward} + penalty * d_{return}$
Collaboration add synchronisation cost term	$\gamma = (\max(d_{forward}) - \min(d_{forward}))$

Let $|A|$ be the number of agents, $|M|$ means the number of tasks. Each round uses the Hungarian algorithm [17] (per-round complexity $O(\max(|A|,|M|)^3)$); worst-case requires $O(|M|)$ iterations (especially for composite tasks). Total worst-case complexity: $O\left(|M| \cdot \max(|A|,|M|)^3\right)$. In practice, the semi-decoupled framework reduces redundant calculations, resulting in lower complexity than the theoretical bound.

4.3 Path Planning for Sustainable Synchronous Collaboration

The extended Conflict-Based Search (CBS) algorithm handles collaborative conflicts $C = \langle a_i, a_j, u, v, t\rangle$. Unlike conventional methods that avoid all conflicts, task point m_j conflicts here are acceptable and necessary for collaboration. Instead of eliminating all conflicts, we coordinate essential ones to optimize group waiting time ΔT_j and individual path cost $p(i)$.

Algorithm 2. Extended CBS Path Planning

Require: Agent set A (all a_i), Task set M (all m_j), start positions $S = \{s_i \mid a_i \in A\}$, constraint set $\mathcal{C}$ ▷ $\mathcal{C}$ stores vertex/edge/collaboration constraints for agents
Ensure: Path set $\Pi = \{\Pi_i \mid a_i \in A\}$
Initialization: Construct CBS root node n_0 with initial individual paths Π_i and empty constraint set $\mathcal{C}$
Insert n_0 into the open list $\mathcal{O}$ ▷ $\mathcal{O}$ is the priority queue for CBS nodes, ordered by cost
while $\mathcal{O} \neq \emptyset$ **do**
  Remove node n with the smallest cost from $\mathcal{O}$
  if n has no detected conflict **then**
    return Π of n
  else
    Identify conflict $C = \langle a_p, a_q, u, v, t\rangle$
    if $u = m_j$ for some $m_j \in M$ **then** ▷ Conflict at a task point
      If $a_p \in \mathcal{A}(m_j)$: add positive wait constraint $\{a_p, m_j, t\}$ to $\mathcal{C}$
      If $a_q \in \mathcal{A}(m_j)$: add positive wait constraint $\{a_q, m_j, t\}$ to $\mathcal{C}$
      Update Π_p and/or Π_q by inserting wait actions until $t = \max\{t_i \mid a_i \in \mathcal{A}(m_j)\}$
    else ▷ General path conflict
      Assign positive constraint $\{a_{\text{keep}}, u, t\}$ to the agent closer to its assigned task
      Assign negative constraint $\{a_{\text{yield}}, u, t\}$ to the other agent
    end if
    Generate child nodes of n based on updated $\mathcal{C}$ and insert into $\mathcal{O}$
  end if
end while
return No feasible solution found

Extended Conflict Detection Strategy: After task allocation $\mathcal{A}$, an enhanced CBS (Algorithm 2) is used. Conventional CBS only identifies vertex ($l_i^t = l_j^t \notin m_j$) and edge conflicts ($l_i^t = l_j^t, l_i^{t+1} = l_j^{t+1}$), failing to handle collaborative conflicts from synchronized waiting at m_j. We extend it to distinguish synchronous collaboration conflicts at task points from general movement conflicts. For conflicts at m_j: if agent a_i is in the assigned group $\mathcal{A}(m_j)$, a positive constraint $\{a_i, m_j, t\}$ requires waiting until all group agents arrive ($t = \max\{t_i \mid a_i \in \mathcal{A}(m_j)\}$) without blocking others. If not, standard resolution applies: the agent closer to its task gets a positive constraint $\{a_i, u, t\}$, the other a negative $\{a_j, u, t\}$. This targets both conflict types efficiently.

Asynchronous Movement Strategy: Synchronized collaboration creates new conflicts: agents must occupy m_j together but may collide when departing for next tasks (e.g., $l_i^{t+1} = l_j^{t+1} = v$). Conventional CBS would increase complexity, so we propose an asynchronous strategy for shared m_j departures. Embedded in conflict detection, it monitors co-located agents $a_i, a_j \in \mathcal{A}(m_j)$ scheduled to depart simultaneously, analyzing trajectories Π_i for post-departure overlaps. When found, the agent with the longest path ($a_{\text{delay}} = \arg\max_{a_i \in \mathcal{A}(m_j)} |\Pi_i|$) is delayed by one time step ($l_{\text{delay}}^{t+1} = m_j$), preventing collisions without re-planning full paths. Dynamic monitoring adjusts delays iteratively to avoid new conflicts ($\Pi_i \cap \Pi_j = \emptyset$), reducing costs while maintaining flexibility.

For map $G = \langle V, E \rangle$, extended CBS uses A* [5] at each Constraint Tree (CT) node with complexity $O(|E| + |V| \log |V|)$. Worst-case CT nodes grow exponentially with conflict depth d (branching factor b), giving complexity $O\left(b^d \cdot (|E| + |V| \log |V|)\right)$.

Computational Complexity: Combined with task allocation, overall worst-case complexity is $O\left(|M| \cdot \max |A|, |M|)^3 + b^d \cdot (|E| + |V| \log |V|)\right)$. Our semi-decoupled approach reduces redundant expansions, achieving lower practical complexity than theoretical bounds.

5 Experiments

5.1 Experimental Settings

Experimental Map and Environment: Experiments use 2D maps (*Random*, *Warehouse*, *Maze*, *Dragon − age*, *Den*520_*d*) from Stern et al.'s (2019) MAPF Benchmark [10], split into small and large-scale scenarios (due to CBS-TA-MLA/ITA-CBS-MLA scalability limits). Small-scale: *Random* (8 × 8, 5a/5t), *Warehouse* (31 × 31, 5a/5t), *Maze* (31 × 31, 5a/5t) – all four algorithms compared. Large-scale: *Warehouse* (31 × 31, 20a/15t), *Dragon − age* (81 × 65, 15a/15t), *Den*520_*d* (257 × 256, 15a/10t) – only vs. LaCAM* (others computationally intractable). Following the experimental setup outlined in Stern et al. (2019) [10], a run-time limit of 120 s (2 min) is imposed to evaluate both algorithm success rates and solution quality. The metrics include Sum of Costs (total steps of all agents), Makespan (max steps of all agents), Success Rate, Running Time. For LaCAM*, which adheres to the 120-second runtime limit is denoted as "–" to reflect this fixed constraint.

Benchmarks: We evaluated the performance of the proposed algorithm against three state-of-art methods: CBS-TA-MLA [7], ITA-CBS-MLA [8], and LaCAM* [6]; their core principles are summarized below.

CBS-TA-MLA [7]: Employs multiple high-level constraint trees to explore task allocations (via K-best algorithm) and a low-level Multi-Label A (MLA) planner (optimizing path cost, time steps, and conflicts). It enables robust agent coordination by evaluating diverse allocation-path combinations but has high computational complexity in large-scale scenarios.

ITA-CBS-MLA [8]: Uses a single constraint tree for iterative target assignment with sequential allocation validation, alongside a low-level MLA planner. It avoids the exhaustive evaluation overhead of CBS-TA-MLA, achieving a balance between computational efficiency and solution quality and proving ideal for time-critical or resource-limited environments.

LaCAM* [6]: Adopts a two-level search framework with lazy constraint generation (adding constraints only when conflicts arise, reducing search space) and enhanced successor generation. It integrates Priority Inheritance with Backtracking (PIBT) and randomized action selection to ensure completeness and optimality, efficiently solving large complex MAPF instances.

5.2 Results and Analyses

On small-scale maps (Random 8 × 8, Warehouse 31 × 31, Maze 31 × 31), Our algorithm and LaCAM* achieved optimal Sum of Costs and Makespan compared to CBS-TA-MLA and ITA-CBS-MLA. For example, both reached 117.90/23.58 (Random), 450.42/90.08 (Warehouse), and 801.2/200.3 (Maze), while CBS-TA-MLA and ITA-CBS-MLA scored 30–40% higher on Maze (1140.72/285.18 and 1132.08/283.02) (Table 2).

Table 2. Comparison of algorithms under small-scale map experiments

Map	Algorithm	sum of cost	makespan	running time
Random(8 × 8)	Our Algorithm	**117.90**	**23.58**	107.1 ms
	LaCAM*	**117.90**	**23.58**	–
	CBS-TA-MLA	191.8	38.36	45 ms
	ITA-CBS-MLA	195.1	39.02	**14.78 ms**
Warehouse (31 × 31) (5Agent-5Task)	Our Algorithm	**450.42**	**90.08**	901.42 ms
	LaCAM*	**450.42**	**90.08**	–
	CBS-TA-MLA	874.1	174.82	705.58 ms
	ITA-CBS-MLA	886.1	177.22	**322.99 ms**
Maze(31 × 31)	Our Algorithm	**801.2**	**200.3**	4024.82 ms
	LaCAM*	**801.2**	**200.3**	–
	CBS-TA-MLA	1140.72	285.18	2647.49 ms
	ITA-CBS-MLA	1132.08	283.02	**2382.29 ms**

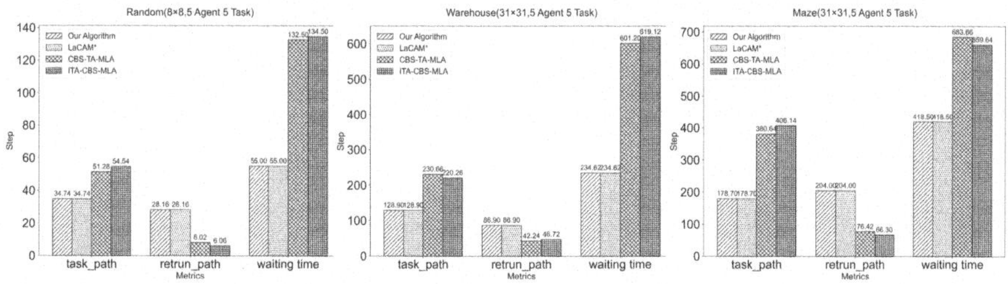

(a) Random (b) Warehouse (c) Maze

Fig. 4. Comparison of algorithms under small-scale map

Path decomposition shows improved CBS and LaCAM* maintained balanced task paths (178.7) and return paths (204.0) with waiting times of 418.5. In comparison, CBS-TA-MLA and ITA-CBS-MLA had shorter returns (76.42/66.3) but longer task paths (380.64/406.14) and higher waits (683.66/659.64). Their strategies—K-best allocation (CBS-TA-MLA) and iterative local optimization (ITA-CBS-MLA)—compress returns but inflate tasks, with shared-task conflicts worsening waits in complex topologies like Maze (see Fig. 4).

Our Algorithm uses asynchronous movement (single-step delays for longest-path agents at shared tasks) with dynamic monitoring ($\Pi_i \cap \Pi_j = \emptyset$), balancing paths and controlling waits. LaCAM* achieves similar balance via lazy constraints and two-level search. Results confirm balanced task path and return path planning reduces waits and improves efficiency, with the proposed method yielding optimal solutions across small-scale maps.

Table 3 and Fig. 5 compare Our Algorithm with LaCAM* on large-scale maps: $Warehouse$ (31 × 31, 20 agents/15 tasks), $Dragon-age$ (81 × 65, 15 agents/15 tasks), and $Den520\_d$ (257 × 256, 15 agents/10 tasks), measuring success rate, SOC, Makespan, runtime, task path and return paths ($\zeta(\Pi_{ij}), \xi(\Pi_{ij})$) with waiting times ΔT.

Table 3. Comparison of algorithms under large-scale map experiments

Map	Algorithm	success rate	sum of cost	makespan	running time
Warehouse	OurAlgorithm	**47/50**	**1202.38**	**60.12**	9918.5 ms
	LaCAM*	34/50	1774.48	88.72	–
Dragon-age (81 × 65)	OurAlgorithm	50/50	**1739.25**	**115.95**	9731.5 ms
	LaCAM*	50/50	1885.23	125.68	–
Den520_d (257 × 256)	OurAlgorithm	50/50	**5420.21**	**361.35**	11293.5 ms
	LaCAM*	50/50	6067.04	404.47	–

Our Algorithm outperforms LaCAM* across all metrics. On $Warehouse$, it achieves 47/50 successes (vs. 34/50) with SOC=1202.38 and Makespan=60.12

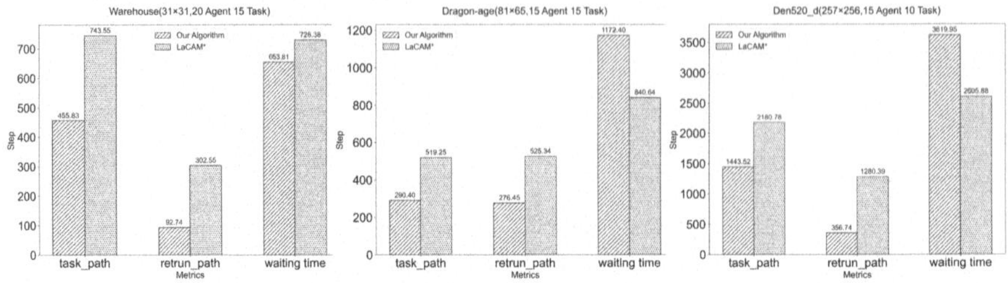

(a) Warehouse (b) Dragon-age (c) Den520d

Fig. 5. Comparison of algorithms under large-scale map

(vs. 1774.48/88.72, 20% better). *Dragon−age* sees 50/50 successes for both, but Our Algorithm has lower SOC (1739.25 vs. 1885.23) and Makespan (115.95 vs. 125.68, 6% better). On *Den*520*_d*, both hit 50/50 successes, with Our Algorithm showing SOC=5420.21 and Makespan=361.35 (vs. 6067.04/404.47, >20% better). Its runtimes (9918.5 ms, 9731.5 ms, 11293.5 ms) contrast with LaCAM*'s fixed 120 s limit ("–") and suboptimal results.

This edge stems from its asynchronous strategy: delaying longest-path agents at m_j ($l^{t+1}_{\text{delay}} = m_j$) avoids overlaps, with dynamic monitoring ($\Pi_i \cap \Pi_j = \emptyset$) reducing redundancy. Though ΔT rises in dense scenarios like *Den*520*_d*, shorter paths offset waits to lower SOC. LaCAM*'s lazy constraints reduce ΔT but lengthen paths, increasing SOC, confirming the proposed method's superiority.

6 Conclusion

This study proposes tailored Multi-Agent Task Allocation and Path Planning algorithms for Sustainable Synchronous Collaboration via a hierarchical framework. The task allocation layer uses a resource-demand-driven dynamic strategy: prioritizing cross-resource teams for multi-resource tasks and optimal matching for single-resource tasks to ensure coordinated assignments, reduce redundant trips and maintain efficiency. The path planning layer introduces an enhanced Conflict-Based Search (CBS) algorithm—extended conflict detection supports collaborative waiting constraints—and a dynamic execution mechanism for staged conflict resolution, lowering overhead from frequent conflicts. Compared to benchmarks ITA-CBS-MLA, CBS-TA-MLA and LaCAM*, the framework significantly improves success rate, total cost and execution time, achieving optimal solutions in small-scale scenarios and notable gains in large-scale SSC environments. Despite these advances, there are some limitations that exist, higher waiting times in large-scale scenarios, potential planning failures within the 120-second constraint for ultra-large agent–task configurations, and performance degradation in extreme map topologies (e.g., narrow conduits) with excessive, hard-to-resolve conflicts. Future research will focus on refining conflict resolution strategies, optimizing latency, and enhancing scalability under complex environmental constraints.

Acknowledgment. This research was partially supported by the National Key Research and Development Program of China under Grant 2024YFC3307900, and in part by the National Natural Science Foundation of China under Grants 72371133, and in part by the Qing Lan Project of Jiangsu Province, and in part by the MOE (Ministry of Education in China) Liberal arts and Social Sciences Foundation (No.24YJCZH472).

References

1. Felner, A., Stern, R.: Search-based optimal solvers for the multi-agent pathfinding problem: summary and challenges. In: Proceedings of the International Symposium on Combinatorial Search, pp. 1–8. AAAI Press (2017)
2. Brown, K., Peltzer, O.: Optimal sequential task assignment and path finding for multi-agent robotic assembly planning. In: 2020 IEEE International Conference on Robotics and Automation (ICRA), pp. 441–447. IEEE, Paris (2020)
3. Hou, Y., Ma, Z., et al.: Online multi-agent task assignment and path finding with kinematic constraint in the federated internet of things. IEEE Trans. Consum. Electron. **70**(1), 2586–2595 (2023)
4. Zhao, Y., Zhou, D., et al.: Cooperative multiple task assignment problem with target precedence constraints using a Waitable path coordination and modified genetic algorithm. IEEE Access **9**, 39392–39410 (2021)
5. Hart, P.E., Nilsson, N.J., Raphael, B.: A formal basis for the heuristic determination of minimum cost paths. IEEE Trans. Syst. Sci. Cybern. **4**(2), 100–107 (1968)
6. Okumura, K.: Engineering LaCAM*: towards real-time, large-scale, and near-optimal multi-agent pathfinding. arXiv preprint: arXiv:2308.04292 (2023)
7. Min, Z., Zhang, Y., et al.: Research on multi-agent pickup and delivery problem of non-fixed delivery locations. J. Comput.-Aided Des. Comput. Graph. (2023)
8. Xu, X., Yin, Q.: Solving multi-goal task assignment and path finding problem with a single constraint Tree. In: 2024 43rd Chinese Control Conference (CCC), pp. 5704–5709. IEEE, Kunming (2024)
9. Yan, F., Chu, J., et al.: Cooperative task allocation with simultaneous arrival and resource constraint for multi-UAV using a genetic algorithm. Expert Syst. Appl. **245**, 123023 (2024)
10. Stern, R., Sturtevant, N., et al.: Multi-agent pathfinding: definitions, variants, and benchmarks. In: Proceedings of the International Symposium on Combinatorial Search, vol. 10, no. 1, pp. 151–158 (2019)
11. Khamis, A., Hussein, A.: Multi-robot task allocation: a review of the state-of-the-art. In: Cooperative Robots and Sensor Networks, pp. 31–51. Springer (2015)
12. Sharon, G., Stern, R., et al.: Conflict-based search for optimal multi-Agent pathfinding. Artif. Intell. **219**, 40–66 (2015)
13. Hönig, W., Kiesel, S., et al.: Conflict-based search with optimal task assignment. In: Proceedings of the 17th International Conference on Autonomous Agents and MultiAgent Systems (AAMAS '18), pp. 757–765. IFAAMAS, Richland (2018)
14. Laporte, G.: The vehicle routing problem: an overview of exact and approximate algorithms. Eur. J. Oper. Res. **59**(3), 345–358 (1992)
15. Hu, H., Yang, X., et al.: Anti-conflict AGV path planning in automated container terminals based on multi-agent reinforcement learning. Int. J. Prod. Res. **61**(1), 65–80 (2021)

16. Ferreira, B.A., Petrović, T., Orsag, M., Bogdan, S.: Distributed allocation and scheduling of tasks with cross-schedule dependencies for heterogeneous multi-robot teams. IEEE Access **12**, 74327–74342 (2024)
17. Kuhn, H.W.: The Hungarian method for the assignment problem. Naval Res. Logistics Q. **2**(1–2), 83–97 (1955)
18. Wang, Y., Xiang, B.: Scrimp: scalable communication for reinforcement- and imitation-learning-based multi-agent pathfinding. In: 2023 IEEE/RSJ International Conference on Intelligent Robots and Systems (IROS), pp. 9301–9308. IEEE, Detroit (2023)
19. Wu, J., Zhang, J., et al.: Multi-UAV collaborative dynamic task allocation method based on ISOM and attention mechanism. IEEE Trans. Veh. Technol. **73**(5), 6225–6235 (2023)

Collaborative Learning Group Formation Considering Cognition-Emotion Coevolution

Yuling Li[1], Yanting Cao[2], Yifeng Zhou[1(✉)], and Zhan Bu[1]

[1] School of Computer Science, Nanjing Audit University, Nanjing 211815, China
yfzhou@nau.edu.cn

[2] Southeast University-Monash University Joint Graduate School, Southeast University, Suzhou 215123, China

Abstract. Studies on collaborative learning group formation often emphasize either the quantitative modeling of learning utility or the affective states of groups when designing group formation algorithms, but overlook the interaction mechanism and coevolution dynamics between learner's cognition and emotion states. To solve the problem, this paper proposes a duplex multiagent diffusion framework that models the cognition and emotion relations among learners as two distinct network layers, the cognition layer and the emotion layer, and captures their coevolution in collaborative learning through intra-layer diffusion and cross-layer influence. Considering the diffusion characteristics of knowledge in structured interactions, we introduce a learner influence analysis method for the cognitive-emotion duplex network. It can be employed to select core members with the highest influence scores as the initial group seeds and greedily incorporate potential group members. In response, a genetic optimization algorithm is proposed to refine the formed groups, further enhancing learners' cognition gains. Through experiments conducted on real-world and simulated learner networks, we validate the effectiveness of the proposed collaborative learning group formation algorithm.

Keywords: Collaborative Learning · Group Formation · Cognitive Diffusion · Emotion Evolution

1 Introduction

Collaborative learning is an efficient method where learners collaborate in groups to solve problems, complete tasks, or create products [1]. It emphasizes learners' subjectivity, facilitates group interaction, and allows learners to enhance personal abilities through mutual learning. Its effectiveness has been verified in numerous studies [2–4]. In practice, the rationality of group formation directly affects intragroup interaction quality and learners' academic performance [5]. How to effectively assign learners to suitable groups (forming teams with collaborative potential) has become a key issue in collaborative learning research [6].

© The Author(s), under exclusive license to Springer Nature Singapore Pte Ltd. 2027
H. Sun et al. (Eds.): ChineseCSCW 2025, CCIS 2911, pp. 33–48, 2027.
https://doi.org/10.1007/978-981-92-0288-1_3

Current researches mostly focus on matching learners' individual characteristics, personal traits or learning styles with collaborative tasks; it proposes group and system level optimization goals (e.g., homogeneity, heterogeneity) to ultimately develop group formation schemes [7]. In addition, some studies include emotional connections as one of the group formation goals, such as group cohesion [8], group trust [9], and member satisfaction [10].

However, these studies mainly focus on the group's macro-level cognitive levels and emotional states, but overlook the potential diffusion of individuals' cognitive and emotional states in group interactions [11], which may cause intragroup emotion spread and ultimately impact the collaborative learning effectiveness of the whole system. Furthermore, individuals' cognitive and emotional states can co-evolve in collaborative learning groups: group members tend to greatly increase the frequency and willingness of cognitive sharing when receiving positive emotions (e.g., trust, encouragement) [12]; conversely, if assimilated into negative emotions (e.g., anxiety, resistance), they will subconsciously reduce the scope and frequency of cognitive interactions [13]. Meanwhile, individuals' cognitive reserves feed back to their emotional systems via psychological efficacy: when learners improve their cognitive level through collaboration, the sense of achievement obtained is converted into emotional motivation, manifesting as greater interaction willingness and emotional openness in the group [14].

To capture the dynamic interaction process and form groups that facilitate diffusion of positive emotion and cognition, we first use a duplex network architecture to model cognition and emotion evolution processes. Next, collaborative coevolution is modeled by dynamically adjusting cognitive diffusion probability and emotion thresholds. Based on this model, we define the collaborative learning group formation problem with cognition-emotion coevolution, aiming to maximize learners' cognitive enhancement. We then propose a heuristic group formation algorithm based on duplex network influence maximization and genetic optimization, which identifies high-influence individuals in both networks as core members, greedily selects other learners to enhance intragroup influence potential, and finally updates groups iteratively via genetic optimization. Experiments on real-world and simulated datasets validate the performance of the proposed approach by comparing it with benchmark methods: uniform K-means based [29], balanced gain based [29] and graph partition algorithms [30].

The remainder of this paper is organized as follows. In Sect. 2, we present the related work on the group formation problem considering cognition and emotion. In Sect. 2, we model the coevolution process of cognition and emotion, then propose the collaborative learning formation problem to maximize cognition improvement. In Sect. 4, we introduce the heuristic grouping based on genetic optimization and duplex network influence maximization initialization. In Sect. 5, we present experimental results to validate our models and methods. Finally, we conclude our paper in Sect. 6.

2 Related Work

Collaborative learning group formation is critical to the effectiveness of collaborative activities, and its classification helps better address diverse learning scenarios [15]. Based on existing studies and differences in learners' core demands and task attributes, collaborative learning group formation problems fall into two typical types: cognition-driven and emotion-oriented collaborative learning group formation problems.

2.1 Cognition-Driven Collaborative Learning Group Formation

The main application scenarios of the cognition-driven collaborative learning group formation problem are cognition-intensive tasks (e.g., interdisciplinary competitions [16], academic research [17]). Researchers focusing on these scenarios aim to maximize learners' cognitive abilities via structured collaborative mechanisms that facilitate cognitive transfer and integration. For instance, considering learners' skill attribute heterogeneity [18], interdisciplinary research teams often form discipline-heterogeneous groups, where members leverage cognitive complementarity to complete research tasks faster and more efficiently. Zhang et al. [19] regard the cognitive level gap between group members and leaders as learners' gain expectation, and form groups that maximize learners' cognitive development by adjusting inter-member differentiation.

However, existing studies are based on the static perspective of learners' ability assessment. While they capture the initial cognitive distribution characteristics of groups, they fail to fully reveal the dynamic diffusion and evolution patterns of individuals' cognition in collaborative networks. Specifically, cognitive transfer is not just the superposition of heterogeneous elements, but a self-organization and reconstruction process triggered by continuous collaborative interactions. This dynamic evolutionary feature affects groups' dynamic cognitive learning efficiency, rendering the assumption of solidified cognitive states in traditional modeling hard to apply directly.

2.2 Emotion-Driven Collaborative Learning Group Formation

Emotion-driven collaborative learning group formation is mainly used in scenarios with prominent emotional support needs (e.g., online learning communities [20], mental health mutual support groups [21]). In these scenarios, researchers usually take optimizing members' emotional experience as the core goal and enhance the resilience of collaborative learning by adjusting emotion interactions among members. Here, theoretical modeling and quantitative analysis of members' emotions are the research focus. For existing studies like the "learning partner matching system" [22] on MOOC platforms, researchers mainly use MOOC platform data and quantify members' emotions via text analysis, facial recognition or questionnaires to divide learning groups; additionally, some researchers decompose individuals' emotions into key indicators using the dimension model [23] and group learners based on these indicators.

Existing emotion analysis frameworks can capture individuals' transient emotion traits, but fail to characterize emotion diffusion in interaction networks and its impact on individuals' cognition. Specifically, collective resonance of positive emotions stimulates cognitive engagement, while the diffusion of negative emotions inhibits cognitive sharing. The coupling mechanism between such dynamic emotion evolution and cognitive development is key to building stable learning groups, and it is the central focus of this paper.

3 Problem Formulation

To fill the gap of traditional collaborative learning group formation in cognition-emotion coevolution scenarios, this paper models the coevolution of these two dimensions via multi-agent group influence diffusion: cognition diffusion manifests as discrete episodic events and transient impacts, while emotion state transformation relies on gradual multi-source social signal input and psychological threshold-breaking. Their evolution is modeled through a duplex network–cognition dissemination follows the Independent Cascade model (IC) [24] (a probabilistic chain triggered by expert learners, with propagation probability regulated by current emotion), and emotion interaction uses the Linear Threshold model (LT) [24] (characterizing gradual changes), with cognition level indirectly regulating emotion propagation via emotion threshold. Under this framework, cognition and emotion form a two-way feedback loop, and the optimal coevolution solution is solved to meet collaborative learning's goals of cognitive efficacy and emotional stability.

Learner: Each learner v_i is defined by a quaternion $v_i =< c_i, \epsilon_i, x_i, y_i >$. $c_i \in [0,1]$ is the initial cognition level (higher value means higher level). $x_i \in \{0,1\}$ indicates whether the learner gains new cognition (described as activation/inactivation in this model). For emotion quantification, with reference to the PAD model [25], $\epsilon_i \in [-1,1]$ represents the emotion's P dimension (initial positive emotion level): $\epsilon_i \geq 0$ means positive emotion, $\epsilon_i < 0$ means negative emotion. $y_i \in \{0,1\}$ is the emotion's A dimension (emotion activation state): $y_i = 0$ means inactivated (not influenced by others), $y_i = 1$ means activated. $S^l = \{v_1^l, v_2^l, \cdots, v_n^l\}, |S^l| \leq n$ is the set of activated learners in the duplex network. At $t = 0$, learners in S^l are initially activated, i.e., *Core learners* (the set is also *Core Learner Set*). At $t > 0$, newly activated learners are added to S^l.

Collaborative Learning Groups: The formation scheme of learning groups is denoted by $G = \{g_1, g_2, \cdots, g_m\}$, where $g_i = \{v_1, v_2, \cdots, v_j\}$ denotes the set of members of the ith learning group.

Duplex Network: The cognition-emotion diffusion duplex network is denoted as $G_l = (V^l, E^l, P^l), l \in \{1,2\}$. Corresponding to learners' cognition and emotion diffusion relationships respectively. Learner set $V^l = \{v_1^l, v_2^l, \cdots, v_n^l\}, |V^l| = n$ means individuals in the two networks are one-to-one–learners with the same serial number across layers represent the same collaborative learning participant. E^l is the network's edge set, where each $e_{ij}^l \in E^l$ is the edge between learner i

and j in layer l, with weight $p^l_{ij} \in P^l$. p^l_{ij} denotes cognition influence probability (in cognition network) and emotion influence probability (in emotion network) respectively. N^l_i denotes learner v_i's neighbor set in layer l; Fig. 1 shows the cognition-emotion diffusion duplex network.

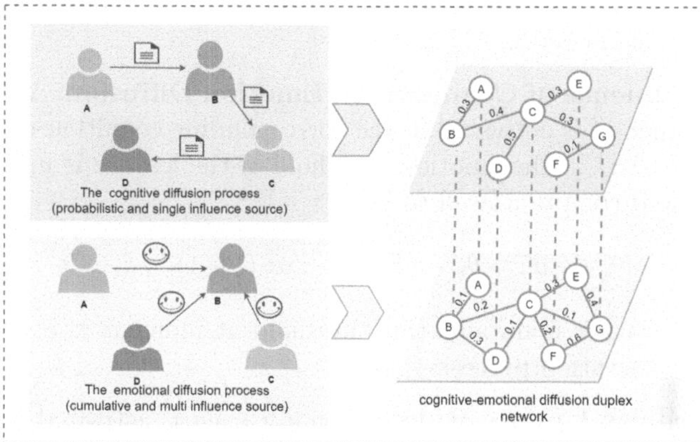

Fig. 1. the duplex cognition-emotion network.

Cognition Diffusion Model: In the cognition sharing network $G_1 = (V^1, E^1, P^1)$, referring to IC model [24], each learner has two states: activated and inactivated. Initially, all learners are inactive except those in the core learner set S^1_0. At $t > 0$, if learner v^1_i is activated at $t-1$ (i.e., $v^1_i \in S^1_{t-1} \backslash S^1_{t-2}$), it will attempt to activate its inactive neighbor v^1_j at t. The activation probability is the cognition sharing probability p^1_{ij} between v^1_i and v^1_j: on success, v^1_j is activated at t (i.e., $v^1_j \in S^1_t \backslash S^1_{t-1}$); on failure, if no other activated neighbors activate v^1_j at t, v^1_j remains inactive (i.e., $v^1_j \in V^1 \backslash S^1_t$). Each activated learner attempts to activate its inactive neighbors only once. The diffusion process ends when no new learners are activated.

Cross-layer Influence of Emotion on Cognition Diffusion: At $t-1$, if learner v^2_i (corresponding to v^1_i) is activated in the emotion network (i.e., $v^2_i \in S^2_{t-1} \backslash S^2_{t-2}$) and gains $\Delta\epsilon_i(t-1)$, and v^1_i is not activated in the cognition network at t, the cognitive sharing probability between v^1_i and its neighbors is adjusted by its emotion state, updated as:

$$p_{ij}{}^{1'} = p_{ij}{}^{1} \cdot (1 + \beta \cdot \Delta\epsilon_i(t-1)) \tag{1}$$

Here, p^1_{ij} is the initial cognitive sharing probability between v^1_i and v^1_j, and β is the cross-layer influence coefficient of emotion shift on cognitive sharing. A positive $\Delta\epsilon_i(t-1)$ (positive emotion shift from others) increases v^1_i's cognitive sharing probability with neighbors while a negative one decreases it. Subsequently, v^1_i uses the updated $p^{1'}_{ij}$ at t for subsequent cognitive diffusion.

Emotion Diffusion Model: In the emotion diffusion network $G_2 = (V^2, E^2, P^2)$, following the rule of LT model [24], each learner has a binary activation state (active/inactive) and is given an individual emotion threshold $\theta_v, \theta_v \in [0,1]$. At moment $t(t > 0)$, the cumulative effect on v_i^2 generated by all activated neighbors is more than this threshold value, i.e., $\theta_v \leq \sum_{v_j^2 \in N_i^2 \cap S_{t-1}^2} p_{ij}^2$, the learner v_i^2 is activated. The diffusion process ends when no more new learners are activated in the network.

Cross-layer Influence of Cognition on Emotion Diffusion: At the moment $t-1$, if the learner v_i^2 is activated in the corresponding cognition network layer, that is, $v_i^1 \in S_{t-1}^1 \backslash S_{t-2}^1$, the emotion threshold of the learner is updated by the learner's improved cognition level to be:

$$\theta_v' = \theta_v - (1-\beta) \cdot \Delta c_v(t-1) \tag{2}$$

After that, the learner maintains this threshold at moment t to participate in the subsequent activation process.

Learner Attribute Update Rule: When a learner is activated in any single-layer network, both its own cognition level and emotion state will be evolved by the cognition level $c_j(t)$ and emotion state $\epsilon_j(t)$ of the activated neighbor learners around that layer, and the learner's cognition level will be evolved when it is activated at the moment t in the cognition network:

$$c_i(t) = c_i(t-1) + \sum\nolimits_{j \in N_i^1 \cap S_{t-1}^1} p_{ij}^1 \cdot \Delta c_{ij}(t-1) \tag{3}$$

where $c_i(t-1)$ denotes the cognition level value of the learner in the previous moment, p_{ij}^1 denotes the cognition sharing probability between learner v_i^1 and learner v_j^1, and Δc_{ij} denotes the cognition level difference between learner v_i^1 and learner v_j^1. The learner's emotion state value in the emotion network also evolves under the influence of the activated neighbor learners in the layer:

$$\epsilon_i(t) = \epsilon_i(t-1) + \sum\nolimits_{j \in N_i^2 \cap S_{t-1}^2} p_{ij}^2 \cdot \epsilon_j(t-1) \tag{4}$$

where $\epsilon_i(t-1)$ denotes the emotion state value of learner v_i^2 in the previous moment, p_{ij}^2 denotes the probability of emotion contagion between learner v_i^2 and learner v_j^2.

Collaborative Learning Group Formation Problem: The set of learners is $S = \{s_1, s_2, \cdots, s_n\}$, which is divided into m groups with the number of members in each group differs by no more than one, which can be denoted as $\bar{G} = \{g_1, g_2, \cdots, g_m\}, |g_i| = n/m$. One of the learners can only join a collaborative learning group. We take the cognitive gains of learners in the collaborative learning process (including the number of activated cognition learners and the value of cognition level enhancement of individuals in the group) as the goal, i.e., our objective is to make the cognition and emotion diffusion in the whole system maximize the learners' cognitive gains:

$$max \sum_{i=1}^{m} \left(\frac{\sum_{v \in g_i} \Delta c_v \cdot \sum_{v \in g_i} x_v}{|g_i|} \right) \tag{5}$$

$$s.t. \quad g_i \cap g_j = \emptyset, \forall i, j \in \{1, 2, \cdots, m\}, i \neq j \tag{6}$$

$$||g_i| - |g_j|| \leq 1, \forall i, j \in \{1, 2, \cdots, m\} \tag{7}$$

4 Methodology

4.1 Group Formation Framework

To address the goal of maximizing collaborative learning groups' cognitive gain based on the aforementioned cognition-emotion diffusion model, this section designs a heuristic grouping algorithm (DIMGA) integrating genetic optimization and duplex network influence maximization, which is shown in Algorithm 1.

The algorithm first accounts for cognition and emotion diffusion in the duplex network, where learners' learning gains depend on received cognitive influence intensity and indirect cognitive gains from positive emotion influence. To promote cognition and positive emotion diffusion then maximize cognitive enhancement, it adopts the DIM Initialization method (referring to multi-network influence maximization [25]) to identify high-influence learners in both network layers as core members, generating initial populations (Lines 2–3, Algorithm 2).

Algorithm 1. The Genetic Group Formation Algorithm based on Duplex network Influence Maximization (DIMGA)

Input: $G_l(V^l, E^l, P^l)$, $mpop\_sizegenerationsR_C R_m$
Output: G^*
1: $G^* \leftarrow \varnothing$, $F_{best} \leftarrow -\infty$, $Pop \leftarrow \varnothing$
2: $Pop_{initial} \leftarrow DIM\_Initialization(G_l, m, group\_size, pop\_size)$
3: $Pop \leftarrow Pop_{initial}$
4: **for** $gen \leftarrow 1$ **to** $generations$ **do**
5: $Fit \leftarrow EvaluatePopulation(Pop)$
6: $maxFit \leftarrow \max(Fit)$
7: **while** $maxFit > F_{best}$ **do**
8: $F_{best} \leftarrow maxFit$
9: $G^* \leftarrow Pop[argmax(F_{best})]$
10: **end while**
11: $Parents \leftarrow SelectParents(Pop, Fit)$
12: $O \leftarrow Crossover(Parents, R_C)$
13: $O' \leftarrow Mutation(O, R_m)$
14: $Pop \leftarrow SelectSurvivors(Pop \cup O', pop\_size)$
15: **end for**
16: **return** G^*

After that, each grouping scheme in the current population is simulated by Monte Carlo method, which conducts the coevolution process. The fitness is evaluated according to the simulation results (line 5), Here is the definition of fitness:

$$fitness(P_{cur}) = \sum_{i=1}^{m} \sum\nolimits_{v \in g_i} (x_v \cdot \Delta c_v + y_v \cdot \Delta \epsilon_v) \tag{8}$$

where P_{cur} denotes the population in the current interaction round, and the fitness is related to the activation level and collaborative learning gains.

After selecting the maximum-fitness division scheme as the current iteration's best grouping scheme (lines 6–9), the genetic process proceeds as follows: high-fitness schemes (individuals) are preferentially selected as parents via elite retention and roulette strategy (line 11). To refine solutions and generate high-quality offspring, two core genetic operations *Crossover* and *Mutation* are then applied(lines 12–13), after which mutated offspring are merged with parents and optimal-fitness individuals are retained to ensure high-quality new generations (line 14). Multiple iterations ultimately yield the overall optimal grouping scheme.

4.2 DIM-Based Group Initialization

Algorithm 2 outlines the population initialization method. It first couples the duplex cognition-emotion network into a weighted coupled influence graph (line 3, shown in Algorithm 3). This coupling mechanism synthesizes learners' cognition and emotion interactions to construct a more comprehensive inter-individual relationship representation, aligning with real-world collaborative scenarios.

The algorithm then identifies "non-candidate learners" (those with low global network influence) via backpropagation in the coupled network. Starting from these low-influence learners, it backwardly accumulates each learner's potential influence on others. This reverse logic captures both direct effects and indirect impacts through intermediaries, holistically quantifying latent network impact. Finally, a learner list sorted by influence is obtained (line 4), highlighting individuals with significant potential to drive group dynamics.

Algorithm 2. $DIM\_Initialization(G_l, m, group\_size, pop\_size)$

Input: $G_l(V^l, E^l, P^l)$, m, $group\_size$, pop_size
Output: $Pop_{initial}$
1: $Pop_{initial} \leftarrow \emptyset$
2: **for** $i \leftarrow 1$ **to** pop_size **do**
3: $G_{coupled} \leftarrow CreateCoupledGraph(G_l)$
4: $Cand_{non} \leftarrow FindNonCandidates(G_{coupled})$
5: $S_{learners} \leftarrow ReverseBFSSearch(G_{coupled}, Cand_{non})$
6: $L_{core} \leftarrow S_{learners}[1 \cdots m]$
7: $groups \leftarrow GenerateGrouping(G_{coupled}, L_{core}, group\_size)$
8: $Pop_{initial} \leftarrow Pop_{initial} \cup groups$
9: **end for**
10: **return** $Pop_{initial}$

Based on the core learners, a BFS-based greedy selection strategy is employed for grouping: the learner with the highest remaining influence score is prioritized to join a collaborative group, and the group is expanded via breadth-first search to ensure internal connectivity. The influence score is defined as:

$$score(n, g_i) = \sum\nolimits_{v \in g_i} w_{coupled}(n, v) \tag{9}$$

where $w_{coupled}(n, v)$ represents the edge weight from learner v to learner n in the coupled graph, g_i denotes the set of members in the current group. The summation only includes members v in group g_i that have a direct edge connection with learner n.

The process continues until all remaining learners are divided into m groups (line 7). The resulting grouping scheme with tightly connected intragroup structures and core learner-driven collaboration serves as the genetic algorithm's initial population (line 8), avoiding random initialization drawbacks and providing high-quality, diverse starting solutions for subsequent optimization.

The Algorithm 3 first copies the attributes of the learners into the coupled graph (lines 1–4), traverses the edges and updates the influential probability between the learners (lines 5–14) by multiplying their difference of cognition level in the cognition network. While traversing the edges in the emotion network, since learners have both positive and negative emotion values, the influence potential is denoted as the probability multiplying the emotion value of out learners (lines 15–25). Through the weighted sum of the cognition influence potential and the emotion influence potential, we get the coupled influence graph (line 26).

4.3 GA-Based Group Optimization

While the DIM-based initialization efficiently forms initial groups with basic collaborative potential, it may settle into local optima due to heuristic biases. To address these limitations, we introduce a genetic algorithm (GA) [26] for global optimization. The specific design of the two core operations is detailed below.

Crossover operation focuses on integrating advantageous features from two parent schemes to explore better solutions in the solution space. It adopts a strategy based on group overlap and similarity: by constructing a cost matrix, it retains grouping substructures from parent individuals that exhibit high overlap and similarity–effectively preserving components proven effective in previous generations. New division schemes generated through matrix-based matching serve as offspring, and the algorithm returns the list of final offspring once all parent pairings and crossovers are completed.

To avoid local optima and enhance solution diversity, two targeted mutation strategies are designed: 1) *Negative emotion mutation*: For groups with excessive negative emotion learners, it exchanges such learners to mitigate negative impacts on collaboration (e.g., resolving eroded communication norms or

Algorithm 3. CreateCoupledGraph(G_l)

Input: $G_l(V^l, E^l, P^l)$
Output: G_{coupled}

Initialize G_{coupled} as an empty directed graph
for each learner n in G_l **do**
  add learner n to G_{coupled} with cognition and emotion
end for
for each edge e_{uv} in E^1 **do**
  Add edge e_{uv} to G_{coupled}, $P_{(u\to v)} \leftarrow \varnothing$, $p'^{1}_{(u\to v)} \leftarrow |c_u - c_v| \cdot p^1_{uv}$
  if edge e_{uv} in E^2 **then**
    if $\epsilon_u > 0$ **then**
      $p'^{2}_{u\to v} \leftarrow \epsilon_u \cdot p^2_{uv}$
    end if
    $p'^{2}_{u\to v} \leftarrow -|\epsilon_u| \cdot p^2_{uv}$, $p_{u\to v} \leftarrow p'^{1}_{u\to v} + p'^{2}_{u\to v}$
  else
    $p_{u\to v} \leftarrow p'^{1}_{u\to v}$
  end if
end for
for each edge e_{uv} in E^2 **do**
  Add edge e_{uv} to G_{coupled}, $p_{u\to v} \leftarrow \varnothing$
  if $\epsilon_u > 0$ **then**
    $p'^{2}_{u\to v} \leftarrow \epsilon_u \cdot p^2_{uv}$
  end if
  $p'^{2}_{u\to v} \leftarrow -|\epsilon_u| \cdot p^2_{uv}$
  if edge e_{uv} in E^1 **then**
    $p'^{1}_{u\to v} \leftarrow |c_u - c_v| \cdot p^1_{uv}$, $p_{u\to v} \leftarrow p'^{1}_{u\to v} + p'^{2}_{u\to v}$
  else
    $p_{u\to v} \leftarrow p'^{2}_{u\to v}$
  end if
end for
return G_{coupled}

reduced participation). 2) *Low connectivity mutation*: For groups where learners are weakly connected, it reallocates learners to improve overall intragroup influence, aligning with the core goal of optimizing collaborative effectiveness.

5 Experiments

5.1 Experimental Settings

Datasets: The real dataset is from Czech secondary school students' relationship and interaction dynamics data collected by Lintner T and šed'ová K et al. [27], covering 2021–2022 school year longitudinal interaction data. We built the duplex network based on the dataset's emotional relationship network (students' emotional connections) and classroom interaction network (cognitive communication), cleaned student attribute data, mapped proficiency levels to [0,1] and emotion states to [-1,1], and finally retained 114 learners' data for experiments. Students' cognition and emotion value distributions fit normal distributions ($\mu = 0.45$, $\sigma = 0.22$ for cognition; $\mu = 0.24$, $\sigma = 0.23$ for emotion).

The simulated dataset randomly generates 120 students' attribute data. Using NetworkX [28], we constructed three duplex networks: small-world network ($n = 120, k = 6, p = 0.1$) with high local clustering and short global paths; scale-free network ($n = 120, \theta = 2$) with power-law degree distribution; and randomized network ($n = 120, p = 0.05$) with random connections.

Benchmarks:

- K-means Based Grouping Algorithm (UKB) [29]: this algorithm utilizes K-means clustering to divide learners into several clusters based on their cognition level and emotion state values, and then randomly assigns learners to groups within each cluster. It ensures that the cognition and emotion characteristics are evenly distributed among different collaborative groups.
- Balanced Gain Based Algorithm (BGB) [29]: this algorithm first selects leaders into learning groups by learners' comprehensive ability ranking, then adds remaining learners to unfilled collaborative learning groups in ability ranking order until all learners join.
- Graph Partition (GP) [30]: the GP graph partition algorithm divides a weighted network into a specified number of non-overlapping subgraphs by minimizing inter-group cut edges. Here, we use metis' python interface to partition the composite influence graph into a given number of groups, taking diffusion propagation probabilities between learners as edge weights, to assign all learners to collaborative learning groups.

5.2 Results and Analyses

Effectiveness Analyses: To test the effectiveness and necessity of the initial and optimized grouping strategies, we conducted experiments on real datasets. DIMGA refers to grouping optimized via GA after DIM initialization; DIM groups solely by influence maximization; GA uses random initialization followed by GA-based optimization iterations. Table 1. shows the specific benefits of each strategy, DIMGA performs optimally in four evaluation metrics for cognition-emotion coevolution. Single DIM outperforms the strategy with genetic optimization after random initialization in all experiments, as the genetic algorithm's iteration solution space is insufficient to match DIM in finite experiments.

On the real dataset, different algorithms (DIMGA, UKB, BGB, GP) are tested. Table 2 presents the performance in average activation counts, where GP achieves the most activated emotion learners at $m = 3$ and $m = 6$ but activates both positive and negative emotion learners, thus failing to yield the most activated cognitive learners. Figure 2. displays average cognition and emotion gains, and it shows DIMGA's overall performance outperforms the others. This is because its grouping strategy identifies highly influential learners as initial

Table 1. The performance of different initial strategy with real dataset

Group number	Strategy	C-activation	E-activation	C-gains	E-gains
m = 3	**DIMGA**	**31.9**	**19.5**	**0.1388**	**0.1258**
	DIM	7.3	8.1	0.0211	0.0242
	GA	5.8	4.92	0.0036	-0.0027
m = 6	**DIMGA**	**30.9**	**16.9**	**0.1157**	**0.0756**
	DIM	23.7	12.6	0.0771	0.0369
	GA	7.8	7.34	0.0014	0.0007
m = 9	**DIMGA**	**30.8**	**15.4**	**0.1041**	**0.0719**
	DIM	28.3	14.3	0.0934	0.0694
	GA	10.5	10.06	0.0005	-0.0005

group cores and then builds groups by preferentially adding members along the cores' cognition and emotion diffusion paths. This ensures diffusion scope and positive enhancement of both dimensions, ultimately boosting collaborative benefits and confirming DIMGA's superior collaborative advantages.

Table 2. The performance of different algorithms on activation numbers

algorithm	m = 3		m = 6		m = 9	
	C-activation	E-activation	C-activation	E-activation	C-activation	E-activation
DIMGA	**31.9**	19.5	**30.9**	16.9	**30.8**	**15.4**
UKB	5.7	5.6	8.0	7.7	10.7	10.6
BGB	3.9	3.0	9.3	7.2	11.9	10.5
GP	21.8	**25.6**	24.4	**17.8**	14.1	14.1

Compared with UKB and BGB, GP's overall effectiveness is second only to DIMGA, because GP splits the network by interaction probability of edges between in-group learners, ensuring intragroup interaction frequency and thus expanding intragroup cognitive diffusion scope. In contrast, UKB and BGB mainly divide groups by learners' attribute differences, failing to preserve cognition-emotion diffusion paths; this leads to poor intragroup diffusion and lowers final collaborative benefits.

In order to verify the effect of network structure and group size where learners are located on the grouping algorithms, this paper also conducts experimental tests on simulated datasets, Fig. 3–Fig. 4 reveal the learning gains of different algorithms on duplex small-world networks(WS), duplex scale-free networks(BA), and duplex randomized networks(ER), respectively.

Figure 3 shows that DIMGA's cognition gains in the three network structures decrease as the number of subgroups increases. This is because more subgroups

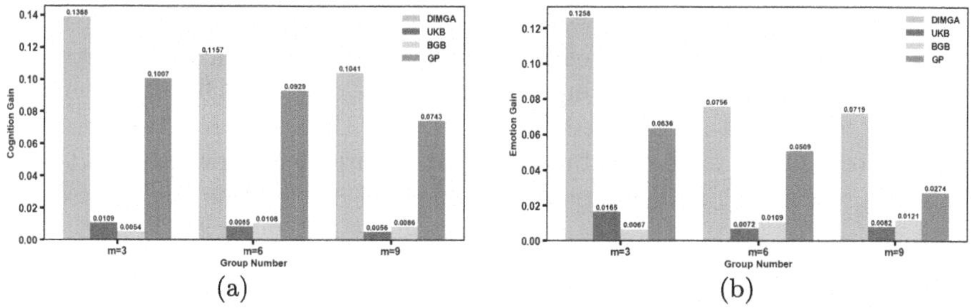

Fig. 2. The performance of different algorithms on learning gains with real dataset.

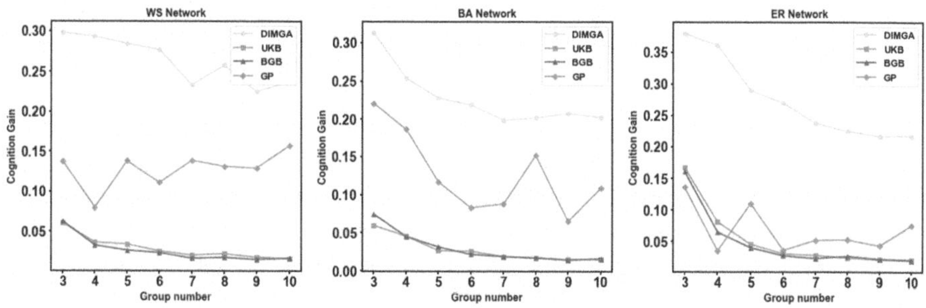

Fig. 3. Cognition gain of the algorithm with simulated dataset.

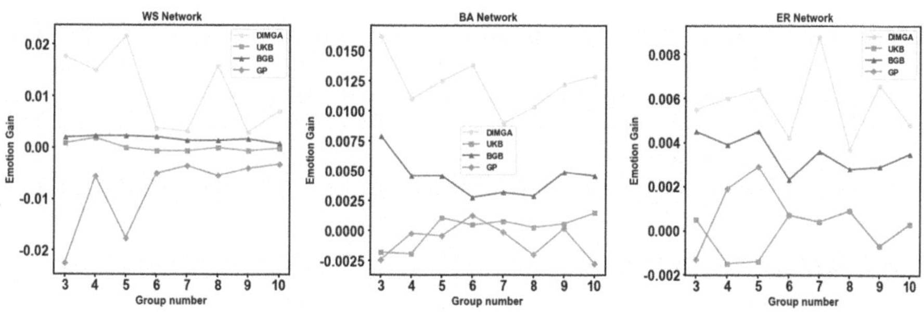

Fig. 4. Emotion gain of the algorithm with simulated dataset.

lead to fewer learners per group, dispersing member pairs with high diffusion probability across different groups by narrowing the overall cognition dissemination scope and reducing cognition gains. A comparison of network structures reveals that the algorithm's overall performance in small-world and scale-free networks is more stable than in random networks; this is due to the randomness of learner connections in random networks, which causes large differences in the algorithm's performance under different subgroup counts.

Figure 4 shows each algorithm's emotion gain. As seen, GP's emotion gain is lower than the other three algorithms across different network structures.

Because though GP's in-group learners are closely connected, it ignores learners' own attributes during grouping, easily causing negative influence diffusion within groups and lowering overall group emotion levels. Second, DIMGA's emotion gain is more obvious in the small-world network than in other two networks, which is because the small-world network's structure facilitates faster and wider emotion spread, and the comparison algorithms also show this same trend.

6 Conclusion

This paper focuses on solving collaborative learning group formation, with special emphasis on the autonomous diffusion and coevolution of cognition and emotion in groups. To this end, we first model cognition and emotion diffusion in collaborative learning groups using the IC and LT model, respectively; then consider their interactions to model cognition-emotion coevolution. Furthermore, to construct groups maximizing cognitive gains in group-oriented diffusion, we design a heuristic grouping algorithm based on duplex network influence maximization and genetic strategies that first identifies core learners via duplex network influence maximization to generate initial groups, then iterates new groups through genetic optimization. Finally, experimental evaluations on real and simulated datasets verify the algorithm's effectiveness, showing it has significant advantages in systematic learning gains for cognition-emotion coevolution in group-oriented diffusion scenarios.

Acknowledgment. This research was supported by the MOE (Ministry of Education in China) Liberal arts and Social Sciences Foundation (No.24YJCZH472), the National Key Research and Development Program of China under Grant 2024YFC3307900, the National Natural Science Foundation of China under Grants 72371133, and the Qing Lan Project of Jiangsu Province.

References

1. Yang, X.: A historical review of collaborative learning and cooperative learning. TechTrends **67**(4), 718–728 (2023)
2. Salma, N.: Collaborative learning: an effective approach to promote language development. Int. J. Soc. Sci. Educ. Stud. **7**(2), 57–61 (2020)
3. Chandra, R.: Collaborative learning for educational achievement. IOSR J. Res. Method Educ. (IOSR-JRME) **5**(3), 2320–7388 (2015)
4. Rutherford, S.M.: Collaborative Learning: Theory, Strategies and Educational Benefits. Nova (2014)
5. Chen, C.M., Kuo, C.H.: An optimized group formation scheme to promote collaborative problem-based learning. Comput. Educ. **133**, 94–115 (2019)
6. Amara, S., Macedo, J., et al.: Group formation in mobile computer supported collaborative learning contexts: a systematic literature review. J. Educ. Technol. Soc. **19**(2), 258–273 (2016)

7. Sánchez, O.R., Ordonez, C.A.C., et al.: Homogeneous group formation in collaborative learning scenarios: an approach based on personality traits and genetic algorithms. IEEE Trans. Learn. Technol. **14**(4), 486–499 (2021)
8. Lambić, D., Lazović, B., et al.: A novel metaheuristic approach for collaborative learning group formation. J. Comput. Assist. Learn. **34**(6), 907–916 (2018)
9. Poort, I., Jansen, E., et al.: Does the group matter? Effects of trust, cultural diversity, and group formation on engagement in group work in higher education. High. Educ. Res. Dev. **41**(2), 511–526 (2022)
10. Kooloos, J.G., Klaassen, T., et al.: Collaborative group work: effects of group size and assignment structure on learning gain, student satisfaction and perceived participation. Med. Teach. **33**(12), 983–988 (2011)
11. Polo, C., Lund, K., et al.: Group emotions: the social and cognitive functions of emotions in argumentation. Int. J. Comput.-Support. Collab. Learn. **11**(2), 123–156 (2016)
12. Yang, I.: Social sharing of private emotions within a group: the case of positive and negative emotions. Organisational Soc. Dyn. **14**(2), 285–321 (2014)
13. Stephan, W.G.: Intergroup anxiety: theory, research, and practice. Pers. Soc. Psychol. Rev. **18**(3), 239–255 (2014)
14. Wang, M.T., Eccles, J.S.: School context, achievement motivation, and academic engagement: a longitudinal study of school engagement using a multidimensional perspective. Learn. Instr. **28**, 12–23 (2013)
15. Kreijns, K., Kirschner, P.A., et al.: Identifying the pitfalls for social interaction in computer-supported collaborative learning environments: a review of the research. Comput. Hum. Behav. **19**(3), 335–353 (2003)
16. Konak, A., Kulturel-Konak, S., et al.: Enhancing student learning in innovation competitions and programs. Eur. J. Eng. Educ. **50**(2), 360–380 (2025)
17. Chang, C.C., Hwang, G.J.: Promoting students' real case-handling performance and higher order thinking in virtual contexts: a metaverse-facilitated collaborative learning approach. Interact. Learn. Environ. **33**(4), 2978–2993 (2025)
18. Asfani, K., Chen, H.L.: Problem or project-based computer-supported collaborative learning practices in computer education: a systematic review of SSCI articles published from 2014 to 2023. Educ. Inf. Technol. **30**(6), 7627–7658 (2025)
19. Zhang, J., Yu, P.S.: Enterprise employee training via project team formation. In: Proceedings of the Tenth ACM International Conference on Web Search and Data Mining, pp. 3–12. Springer, Heidelberg (2017)
20. Sun, N., Rosson, M.B.: Where is community among online learners? Identity, efficacy and personal ties. In: Proceedings of the 2018 CHI Conference on Human Factors in Computing Systems, pp. 1–13. Springer, Heidelberg (2018)
21. Dennis, C.L., Hodnett, E.: Effect of peer support on prevention of postnatal depression among high risk women: Multisite Randomised Controlled Trial. BMJ 338, (2009)
22. Aggarwal, K., Arora, A.: Influence maximization for MOOC learners using BAT optimization algorithm. Int. J. Fuzzy Syst. Appl. (IJFSA) **11**(2), 1–19 (2022)
23. Mehrabian, A.: Pleasure-arousal-dominance: a general framework for describing and measuring individual differences in temperament. Curr. Psychol. **14**, 261–292 (1996)
24. Shakarian, P., Bhatnagar, A.: The independent cascade and linear threshold models. Diffusion Soc. Netw. 35–48 (2015)
25. Singh, S.S., Singh, K., et al.: MIM2: multiple influence maximization across multiple social networks. Physica A: Stat. Mech. Appl. **526**, 120902 (2019)

26. Lotf, J.J., Azgomi, M.A., et al.: An improved influence maximization method for social networks based on genetic algorithm. Physica A: Stat. Mech. Appl. **586**, 126480 (2022)
27. Lintner, T., Šed'ová, K., et al.: Relational and interactional dynamic network data from Czech lower-secondary school students. Data Brief **51**, 109641 (2023)
28. Aric, A.H., Daniel, A.S.: Exploring network structure, dynamics, and function using NetworkX. In: Proceedings of the 7th Python in Science Conference, pp. 11–15 (2008)
29. Liu, Y., Liu, Q., et al.: Collaborative learning team formation: a cognitive modeling perspective. In: Database Systems for Advanced Applications: 21st International Conference, pp. 383–400 (2016)
30. Reddy, T.D.T., Kartikaaditya, S.: Efficient graph partitioning approaches for enhanced accident prediction. In: Proceedings of 6th International Conference on Smart Systems and Inventive Technology, pp. 432–444 (2024)

E-Motorcycle Multi-Task Assignment Method Based on E-CARGO and Deep Learning-Driven Bearing Health Assessment

Jin Zhang[1], Ruiling Gao[1], Wenyi Mao[2,3], Xuan Xu[1], Yingqi Hou[1], Wen'an Tan[1](✉), Tao He[1,2,3], and Liping Li[1]

[1] Shanghai Polytechnic University, Shanghai 201209, China
watan@sspu.edu.cn

[2] Shanghai Key Laboratory of Trustworthy Computing, East China Normal University, Shanghai 200062, China

[3] Guangzhou Muwei Technology Co., LTD, Guangzhou 211106, China

Abstract. In the context of smart cities, the study of how electric motorcycle fleets can perform tasks such as parallel path planning and vehicle-to-infrastructure cooperative communication within a given time frame has become a critical research topic. Bearing health directly determines the execution results of assignment instructions, but existing task allocation algorithms do not incorporate this key factor into real-time decision-making. Therefore, this paper introduces the E-CARGO (Environment-Class, Agent, Role, Group and Object) role-resource collaborative computing framework and innovatively proposes a Bearing Health Multi-Task Assignment (BHMTA) model with bearing health assessment. First, we evaluate the bearing health status of electric motorcycles based on deep learning methods as an explicit safety constraint for the assignment algorithm. Then, a task satisfaction conflict matrix is constructed to quantify the mutual exclusion relationship, and a rider preference matrix is introduced to characterize the subjective preferences. Finally, a mixed integer programming model is established to solve the problem with the goal of maximizing global satisfaction under health-aware constraints. Experiments show that rider satisfaction is 3.4% higher on average than the greedy algorithm. More critically, by embedding bearing health into the decision-making process as a mandatory constraint, BHMTA achieves no violations, while greedy methods cannot avoid high-risk assignments. BHMTA innovatively upgrades device health from a background maintenance indicator to a priori decision-making condition,providing highly reliable intelligent decision-making support for smart city development.

Keywords: Collaborative Computing · Deep Learning · Bearing Health · Multi-Task Assignment · Electric Motorcycle

1 Introduction

In the context of smart cities, electric motorcycle fleets have evolved from serving merely as "last-mile carriers" to becoming critical components in the collaborative ecosystem of "human–vehicle–infrastructure–cloud" systems [1]. Each motorcycle must perform

© The Author(s), under exclusive license to Springer Nature Singapore Pte Ltd. 2027
H. Sun et al. (Eds.): ChineseCSCW 2025, CCIS 2911, pp. 49–62, 2027.
https://doi.org/10.1007/978-981-92-0288-1_4

multiple heterogeneous tasks simultaneously within a single scheduling cycle, including path planning, battery coordination, edge computing, and more. The high task concurrency and stringent resource constraints, such as vehicle batteries, computing power, and load-bearing health, directly impact the safety of the fleet, the quality of service, and the efficiency of smart cities. Consequently, there is an urgent need for a highly reliable real-time multi-task allocation mechanism.

The field of collaborative computing has introduced numerous role-resource collaboration models, such as distributed multi-machine collaborative task allocation [2], privacy-enhanced online joint task allocation [3], and cloud-edge-end collaborative service delivery with resource optimization [4]. These models are based on the E-CARGO framework, which serves as the theoretical foundation for role-based collaboration (RBC) [5]. Precise matching of agents and roles is achieved through group role assignment (GRA). Additionally, this framework has given rise to several sub-models, including group multi-role assignment (GMRA), group role assignment with conflicting agents (GRACA), and group role assignment with cooperation and conflict factors (GRACCF) [6–9], to cater to collaboration requirements across various scenarios. However, most of these studies concentrate on general-purpose robots or human-robot interaction scenarios, viewing device health primarily as a backend maintenance metric rather than actively integrating health status as a binding constraint into real-time scheduling decisions. This renders them challenging to apply directly to high-reliability, high-load urban transportation environments.

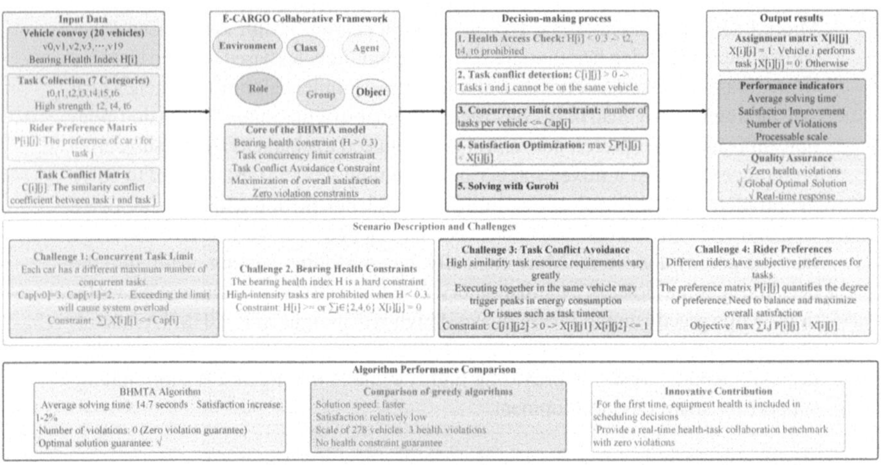

Fig. 1. BHMTA uses the E-CARGO framework as its input, taking as input the bearing health index, concurrency limit, task set, and rider preference matrix. When making decisions, it first filters high-risk tasks based on the health threshold, then checks for task conflicts and concurrency limits. Finally, it develops a mixed integer program with the goal of maximizing satisfaction and solves it in seconds using Gurobi.

To address these shortcomings, this paper proposes a BHMTA model with a bearing health index. The main contributions of this paper are as follows:

1. We implement BHMTA formal modeling by introducing the bearing health index H[i] as a safety constraint in the task allocation algorithm, classifying it as a Mixed-Integer Linear Programming (MILP) problem.
2. We construct an innovative "conflict-preference" joint representation mechanism to form an integrated matrix, where the task conflict matrix quantifies task exclusivity and the rider preference matrix captures subjective preferences, isolating overloaded combinations while enhancing rider personalization.
3. Under the safety constraint, we formulate an MILP problem to maximize satisfaction while achieving no violations. Using Gurobi, we obtain global optimal solutions for city-scale instances within an average of 14 s, with average satisfaction increasing by 3.4% compared to the greedy method, providing a reliable real-time task

2 BHMTA Formal Modeling

2.1 Bearing Health Assessment Based on Deep Learning

To assess the bearing health status of electric motorcycles and incorporate it as a safety constraint in task scheduling, this study employs a deep learning-based fault diagnosis model. The model utilizes vibration signals generated during bearing operation as the primary input and leverages a deep neural network to learn the complex mapping between fault characteristics and health conditions.First, a feature selector of the binary banyan tree growth optimization algorithm [10] is designed to screen and optimize the original features, remove redundant features, and extract the most representative feature subset. Secondly, the optimized features are input into the dual-tower recall model [11], in which the user tower encodes the operating status features of the bearing to generate an operating status feature vector, and the content tower encodes the known fault mode features to generate a fault mode feature vector. By calculating the similarity between the two feature vectors, the model can quickly identify potential fault modes. In the training stage, the contrast loss function is used to optimize the network parameters to improve the accuracy of fault diagnosis. The model was validated on multiple industrial bearing datasets, achieving high diagnostic accuracy (F1 value > 0.99) and low latency (average response time < 0.3 s). This ensures that the output H[i] reliably reflects the real-time health of the bearing, providing a key basis for subsequent scheduling decisions (such as determining vehicle is availability).

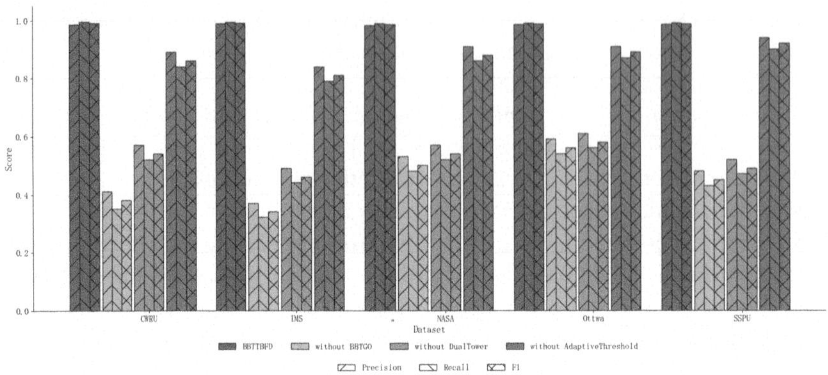

Fig. 2. A figure shows the training results of our model based on deep learning.

2.2 E-CARGO-Based Secondary Modeling

A city-level electric motorcycle fleet management platform needs to complete seven collaborative tasks (t_0-t_6) within the next scheduling cycle. The platform has 20 registered riders, each equipped with the same model of electric motorcycle (v_0-v_{19}), all equipped with a real-time bearing health monitoring module. Table 1 shows the task requirements and the basic satisfaction weights for each task. Table 2 shows the Concurrent task limit.

Table 1. Number of Vehicles Required for Various Tasks

No	Task Description	Number of Vehicles	Basic Satisfaction Weights
t_0	Real-Time Route Planning	3	0.9
t_1	Battery Replacement Collaboration	2	0.85
t_2	Edge Computing Offload	4	0.95
t_3	Vehicle-Road Collaborative Communication Relay	3	0.92
t_4	High-Precision Map Update	2	0.88
t_5	Traffic Incident Detection	4	0.93
t_6	Emergency Response Patrol	2	0.96

Table 2. Concurrent task limit

V_0	V_1	V_2	V_3	V_4	V_5	V_6	V_7	V_8	V_9	V_{10}	V_{11}	V_{12}	V_{13}	V_{14}	V_{15}	V_{16}	V_{17}	V_{18}	V_{19}
2	3	1	2	4	3	2	1	3	4	2	1	3	2	4	2	2	1	3	2

The real-time bearing health monitoring module uses an onboard lightweight deep learning model to obtain the bearing health index of each motorcycle in real time. Industry research indicates that when H[i]<0.3, , the vehicle must not be assigned to high-intensity tasks (t_2, t_3, t_6) to ensure system reliability and user safety. Continuing to perform high-intensity tasks increases the probability of failure. To strictly eliminate high-risk assignments, we explicitly introduce bearing health as a safety constraint into the assignment model. Therefore, the model imposes the following constraints:

$$\forall i \in \{0, 1..., 19\},\ H_i \in [0, 1];\ \forall i \in \{0, 1..., 19\}, \forall j \in \{2, 3, 6\}\, H[i] < 3 \Rightarrow T_{ij} = 0.$$

The bearing health index H[i] serves as a non-negotiable safety constraint in this paper. This threshold of 0.3 is based on the minimum acceptable level of bearing health in industry standards. Building on this threshold, we further incorporate a "health penalty" into the vehicle-mission satisfaction matrix B:

$$B_{i,j} = \begin{cases} 0 & ifj \in \{2, 3, 6\} \wedge H[i] < 0.3 \\ Originalsatisfaction & else \end{cases}, \forall i \in \{0, 1 \ldots, 19\}$$

Furthermore, tasks often have similar requirements. For example, CPU-intensive edge computing and I/O-intensive map updates, when executed on the same vehicle, have similar resource consumption patterns. Simultaneously assigning two highly similar tasks with significantly different resource requirements to the same vehicle will disrupt the overall fleet energy-latency balance, leading to battery discharge spikes or task timeouts. Therefore, the model introduces a constraint based on task similarity: when the task similarity exceeds a threshold, the difference in resource requirements between the two tasks assigned to the same vehicle must be limited to ensure execution stability and reliability. The similarity threshold of 0.5 was experimentally verified and effectively avoids resource conflicts while maintaining flexibility in task allocation.During assignment, bearing health and task weights are set to 1, and rider preference weights are set to 0.2. Thus, BHMTA, building on the GMRA framework, introduces a bearing health threshold and task similarity constraints, forming a reliable task allocation sub-model for electric motorcycle fleets.

Definition 1: Let m be the total number of electric motorcycles, or m=|A|; let n be the total number of tasks, or n=|R|. Let i be the index of an element in the vehicle set A, or $i \in \{0, 1, \ldots, m-1\}$, and let j be the index of an element in the task role set R, or $j \in \{0, 1, \ldots, n-1\}$.

Definition 2: The n-dimensional vector L gives the number of vehicles required for each task role j, where L[j] is the lower bound on the number of vehicles that must be assigned to task j.

Definition 3: The $m \times n$ dimensional matrix B records the "rider-task basic satisfaction", where the higher the value of B[i,j], the greater the initial satisfaction of vehicle i in performing task j. Original satisfaction is shown in Fig. 3, and the bearing health penalty is also introduced.

Definition 4: The assignment matrix T of shape $m \times n$ indicates whether vehicle i is assigned to task role j, where $T[i, j] \in \{0, 1\}$, as shown in Fig. 4; 0 indicates an unassigned vehicle, and 1 indicates an assigned vehicle.

$$B = \begin{pmatrix} 0.22 & 0.31 & 0.18 & 0.27 & 0.82 & 0.14 & 0.13 \\ 0.77 & 0.83 & 0.21 & 0.90 & 0.99 & 0.93 & 0.45 \\ 0.18 & 0.84 & 0.35 & 0.55 & 0.34 & 0.47 & 0.52 \\ 0.79 & 0.55 & 0.44 & 0.72 & 0.83 & 0.61 & 0.67 \\ 0.04 & 0.91 & 0.48 & 0.45 & 0.56 & 0.11 & 0.09 \\ 0.57 & 0.60 & 0.75 & 0.42 & 0.04 & 0.02 & 0.05 \\ 0.30 & 0.05 & 0.47 & 0.63 & 0.83 & 0.95 & 0.91 \\ 0.32 & 0.65 & 0.68 & 0.15 & 0.81 & 0.18 & 0.25 \\ 0.70 & 0.11 & 0.62 & 0.69 & 0.41 & 0.94 & 0.88 \\ 0.01 & 0.23 & 0.85 & 0.23 & 0.67 & 0.76 & 0.72 \\ 0.58 & 0.06 & 0.92 & 0.48 & 0.46 & 0.64 & 0.60 \\ 0.45 & 0.04 & 0.67 & 0.25 & 0.65 & 0.42 & 0.39 \\ 0.38 & 0.69 & 0.40 & 0.57 & 0.65 & 0.48 & 0.41 \\ 0.41 & 0.33 & 0.18 & 0.54 & 0.98 & 0.80 & 0.74 \\ 0.66 & 0.68 & 0.39 & 0.28 & 0.34 & 0.05 & 0.12 \\ 0.03 & 0.95 & 0.34 & 0.32 & 0.29 & 0.88 & 0.79 \\ 0.60 & 0.80 & 0.70 & 0.80 & 0.60 & 0.80 & 0.85 \\ 0.30 & 0.80 & 0.30 & 0.50 & 0.80 & 0.20 & 0.90 \\ 0.27 & 0.59 & 0.74 & 0.91 & 0.42 & 0.22 & 0.58 \\ 0.82 & 0.57 & 0.94 & 0.92 & 0.45 & 0.57 & 0.66 \end{pmatrix}$$

Fig. 3. Rider-Task Satisfaction Matrix

$$T = \begin{pmatrix} 0 & 0 & 0 & 0 & 0 & 0 & 0 \\ 0 & 0 & 0 & 1 & 0 & 0 & 0 \\ 0 & 0 & 0 & 1 & 0 & 0 & 0 \\ 1 & 0 & 0 & 0 & 0 & 0 & 0 \\ 0 & 1 & 0 & 0 & 0 & 0 & 0 \\ 0 & 0 & 1 & 0 & 0 & 0 & 0 \\ 0 & 0 & 0 & 0 & 0 & 0 & 1 \\ 0 & 0 & 0 & 0 & 0 & 0 & 0 \\ 0 & 0 & 0 & 1 & 0 & 0 & 0 \\ 0 & 0 & 1 & 0 & 0 & 0 & 0 \\ 0 & 0 & 1 & 0 & 0 & 0 & 0 \\ 0 & 0 & 0 & 0 & 0 & 0 & 0 \\ 0 & 0 & 0 & 0 & 0 & 0 & 0 \\ 0 & 0 & 0 & 0 & 0 & 1 & 0 \\ 1 & 0 & 0 & 0 & 0 & 0 & 0 \\ 0 & 1 & 0 & 0 & 0 & 0 & 0 \\ 0 & 0 & 1 & 0 & 0 & 0 & 0 \\ 0 & 0 & 0 & 0 & 1 & 0 & 0 \end{pmatrix}$$

Fig. 4. Allocation Matrix

Definition 5: The m-dimensional vector L_a gives the maximum number of task roles that each vehicle i can simultaneously assume within the same scheduling cycle, which is $L_a = [2, 3, 1, 2, 4, 3, 2, 1, 3, 4, 2, 1, 3, 2, 4, 3, 2, 1, 2, 3]$.

Definition 6: To ensure that task j is feasible in the system, a sufficient number of vehicles must be assigned to it, which is $\Sigma_{i=0}^{m-1} T[i, j] \geq L[j], \quad \forall j \in \{0, 1, \ldots, n-1\}$.

$$SIM = \begin{pmatrix} 1.0 & 0.60 & 0.75 & 0.88 & 0.77 & 0.73 & 0.80 \\ 0.60 & 1.0 & 0.65 & 0.76 & 0.70 & 0.62 & 0.78 \\ 0.75 & 0.65 & 1.0 & 0.78 & 0.77 & 0.75 & 0.82 \\ 0.88 & 0.76 & 0.78 & 1.0 & 0.87 & 0.90 & 0.85 \\ 0.77 & 0.70 & 0.77 & 0.87 & 1.0 & 0.85 & 0.79 \\ 0.73 & 0.62 & 0.75 & 0.90 & 0.85 & 1.0 & 0.81 \\ 0.80 & 0.78 & 0.82 & 0.85 & 0.79 & 0.81 & 1.0 \end{pmatrix}$$

Fig. 5. Similarity Matrix

$$P = \begin{pmatrix} 0.7 & 0.2 & 0.8 & 0.4 & 0.9 & 0.1 & 0.6 \\ 0.8 & 0.3 & 0.7 & 0.5 & 0.8 & 0.2 & 0.7 \\ 0.6 & 0.4 & 0.9 & 0.3 & 0.7 & 0.3 & 0.8 \\ 0.5 & 0.5 & 0.6 & 0.8 & 0.4 & 0.4 & 0.9 \\ 0.9 & 0.1 & 0.5 & 0.7 & 0.6 & 0.5 & 0.2 \\ 0.3 & 0.8 & 0.4 & 0.6 & 0.3 & 0.9 & 0.4 \\ 0.2 & 0.6 & 0.3 & 0.9 & 0.2 & 0.8 & 0.7 \\ 0.4 & 0.7 & 0.8 & 0.5 & 0.1 & 0.6 & 0.3 \\ 0.1 & 0.9 & 0.2 & 0.4 & 0.8 & 0.7 & 0.5 \\ 0.8 & 0.5 & 0.1 & 0.3 & 0.9 & 0.4 & 0.6 \\ 0.7 & 0.4 & 0.8 & 0.2 & 0.5 & 0.3 & 0.9 \\ 0.6 & 0.3 & 0.7 & 0.9 & 0.2 & 0.1 & 0.8 \\ 0.5 & 0.2 & 0.6 & 0.4 & 0.7 & 0.8 & 0.3 \\ 0.4 & 0.1 & 0.5 & 0.3 & 0.6 & 0.9 & 0.2 \\ 0.3 & 0.9 & 0.4 & 0.2 & 0.8 & 0.7 & 0.1 \\ 0.2 & 0.8 & 0.3 & 0.1 & 0.5 & 0.6 & 0.9 \\ 0.1 & 0.7 & 0.2 & 0.9 & 0.4 & 0.5 & 0.8 \\ 0.9 & 0.6 & 0.1 & 0.8 & 0.3 & 0.2 & 0.7 \\ 0.8 & 0.5 & 0.9 & 0.7 & 0.2 & 0.4 & 0.6 \\ 0.7 & 0.4 & 0.8 & 0.6 & 0.1 & 0.3 & 0.5 \end{pmatrix}$$

Fig. 6. Rider-task preference matrix

Definition 7: The task similarity matrix SIM is an matrix of shape$n \times n$, as shown in Fig. 5, where sim represents the degree of similarity between task j_1 and task j_2 in terms of resource demand patterns; the diagonal is always 1, which is$SIM[j, j] \equiv 1$; and $SIM[j_1, j_2] = SIM[j_2, j_1]$.

Definition 8: The rider-task preference matrix P is represented as shown in Fig. 6. If a rider is assigned to a task with a higher preference value, his riding style will be smoother and energy consumption will be lower, which will significantly improve his satisfaction.

Definition 9: Let $\alpha \in (0, 1)$ be the rider preference weight. Satisfaction ω is defined as the sum of the satisfaction of all assigned vehicle-task pairs:

$$\omega = \Sigma_{i=0}^{m-1} \Sigma_{j=0}^{n-1} (Q[j] + \alpha \cdot P[i, j]) \cdot H[i] \cdot T[i, j] \tag{1}$$

Where Q[j] is the basic satisfaction weight of task j; $P[i, j]$ is the preference of rider i for task j; $\alpha = 0.2$ is the preference weight; $T[i, j] = 1$ means assignment, and $T[i, j] = 0$ means no assignment.

$$B_{i,j} = \begin{cases} 0 & if j \in \{2, 3, 6\} \wedge H[i] < 0.3 \\ Originalsatisfaction & else \end{cases}, \forall i \in \{0, 1 \ldots, 19\} \tag{2}$$

$$T\left[i, j\right] \in \{0, 1\}(0 \leq i < m, 0 \leq j < n) \tag{3}$$

$$\sum_{i=0}^{m-1} T[i, j] = L[j] \quad (0 \leq j < n) \tag{4}$$

$$\sum_{j=0}^{n-1} T[i,j] \le L_a[i] \; (0 \le i < m) \tag{5}$$

$$T[i,j_1] + T[i,j_2] \le 1 \quad ((0 \le i < m, 0 \le j_1 < j_2 < n) \\ |B[i,j_1] - B[i,j_2]| > (1 - SIM[j_1][j_2]) \cdot 0.5) \tag{6}$$

Among them, (2) vehicles with poor bearing health are excluded from performing high-intensity tasks, (3) the assignment relationship is limited to binary decision, (4) the required number of vehicles for each type of task is guaranteed to be exactly met, (5) the number of concurrent tasks per vehicle is ensured not to exceed its capacity limit, and (6) resource conflicts are avoided by limiting task similarity.

2.3 Task Similarity Calculation

To measure the similarity between any two tasks [11], we directly reuse the "vehicle-task basic satisfaction matrix" B as the source of task features. Each column B[:, j] is considered as the "satisfaction profile" of task j on the 20 vehicles; the closer the profiles, the more similar the tasks. Therefore, the similarity between tasks j_1 and j_2 is defined as the cosine similarity of the two column vectors:

$$SIM(j_1, j_2) = \frac{\sum_{i=0}^{m-1} B[i,j_1] \cdot B[i,j_2]}{\sqrt{\sum_{i=0}^{m-1} B[i,j_1]^2}\sqrt{\sum_{i=0}^{m-1} B[i,j_2]^2}}, \quad 0 \le j_1, j_2 < n. \tag{7}$$

Algorithm 2: Task-Satisfaction-Profile Similarity Solver

```
Input:  m×n matrix B (vehicle-task base satisfaction)
Output: n×n symmetric matrix SIM
1: n ← number of columns of B
2: m ← number of rows of B
3: Initialize SIM[n][n] ← 0
4: for j1 ← 0 to n-1 do
5:   for j2 ← 0 to n-1 do
6:     if j1 == j2 then
7:       SIM[j1][j2] ← 1
8:     else
```

3 BHMTA Experimental Verification

3.1 Experimental Environment and Input

The BHMTA model inherits the feasibility condition of the underlying GMRA framework, namely: $\sum_i L_a[i] \geq \sum_j L[j]$.

All test cases are generated to satisfy this inequality, guaranteeing at least one feasible assignment. Table 3 summarizes the hardware, software, and solver configurations used throughout the experiment. To evaluate scalability, we partitioned the instance space into six incremental layers, maintaining a bearing health threshold $H[i] < 0.3$ for all vehicles. The following ratios were maintained to maintain feasibility: a capacity-to-demand ratio of $\max(L_a) : \max(L) = 5 : 3$ and a 4:1 ratio between the number of tasks and the number of available riders. The resulting ideal input scales are listed in Table 4.

Table 3. Experimental environment and solver library

Environment and Standard Library	Specifications
Hardware Environment	CPU Intel i7-8750H @ 2.20 GHz
	RAM 16.0 GB
Software Environment	OS Windows 10
	IDE PyCharm 2022.2.3
	Language Python 3.12
Solver Standard Library	gurobipy 12.0.2

Table 4. Ideal BHMTA input scale

Number of **Vehicles**	Number of **Tasks**	L random number upper limit	**L_a random number upper limit**
10 – 20	4 – 6	2	3
21 – 30	6 – 8	2	3
31 – 40	8 – 10	3	5
41 – 50	10 – 12	3	5
51 – 75	13 – 19	5	9
76 – 100	20 – 25	5	9
101 – 125	26 – 32	10	16
126 – 150	33 – 37	10	16
151 – 175	38 – 44	13	22
176 – 200	45 – 50	13	22
201 – 225	51 – 57	17	28
226 – 250	58 – 62	17	28

(*continued*)

Table 4. (*continued*)

Number of **Vehicles**	Number of **Tasks**	L random number upper limit	L_a **random number upper limit**
251 – 275	63 – 69	20	34
276 – 300	70 – 75	20	34

3.2 Simulation Experiment Comparison

In order to comprehensively measure the implementation value of BHMTA in actual operation, the experiment designed three core indicators:

- Satisfaction ω: used to measure the effect of different algorithms on improving the overall satisfaction of riders. The level of satisfaction directly corresponds to the platform user rating and repurchase rate;
- Average solution time: reflects whether the dispatching system can complete real-time decisions within the 30-s morning/evening peak window;
- Number of violations: positively correlated with the vehicle failure rate. One violation results in an average direct loss of 1,500 yuan and a brand reputation loss of 3–5 times;

On this basis, this paper compares the MILP solution with the classic greedy allocation method. In order to fit the urban background, the experimental scale strictly follows the smart city gridding [13] specifications. The number of electric motorcycles in the grid is usually lower than 300, and the task demand is based on a 3-h cycle. Therefore, this study sets the vehicle upper limit to 278 and the task upper limit to 71 orders, which can cover the entire "morning/evening peak + off-peak" period at the urban grid level. The experimental data recorded in Table 5 are satisfaction ω, average solution time (ms), number of bearing health violations, and effect improvement. The relevant calculation formulas are as follows:

$$\Delta\omega(\%) = \left(\frac{\omega_1 - \omega_2}{\omega_2}\right) \times 100\% \tag{8}$$

$$\Delta t(s) = \frac{t_1 - t_2}{1000} \tag{9}$$

where: ω_1 is the satisfaction score obtained using the MILP method, ω_2 is the satisfaction score obtained using the Greedy method, t_1 is the solution time (milliseconds) obtained using the MILP method, and t_2 is the solution time (milliseconds) obtained using the Greedy method.

The experimental results show that BHMTA achieves good results in terms of satisfaction, solution time, and number of violations, thus enabling city-level electric motorcycle fleets to save tens of millions of yuan in potential failure losses every day without increasing hardware investment.

(1) In the medium-sized scale (214 vehicles and 51 tasks), ω achieved the maximum improvement of 4.93%. As the fleet size increases, the MILP solution shows a

significant advantage, with an average satisfaction increase of 3.4% (total satisfaction increase of 47.6%/number of experimental groups 14 = 3.4%), thereby improving the platform's order completion rate.

(2) Although the solution time increases exponentially with the problem size (average 14 s), the 47.6% satisfaction gain is exchanged for a cumulative solution time increment of 208.127 s across all experiments, that is, an average of only 4.37 s is required for each 1% satisfaction increase, which means that the platform can obtain the satisfaction increase bonus at zero additional cost without adding hardware.

(3) By taking bearing health as an explicit safety constraint in the MILP formulation, BHMTA achieves no violations in all test cases, completely avoiding the costs of sudden downtime and road rescue caused by bearing failures; the greedy algorithm without this constraint resulted in 1–3 violations in all experiments.

Table 5. Comparison of experimental results

Number		MILP			Greedy			Effect improvement	
M	N	ω1	t1(ms)	Violations	ω2	t2(ms)	Violations	Δω(%)	Δt(s)
18	4	28.92	22.5	0	28.39	0	1	0.53	0.0225
28	6	44.26	27.6	0	44.26	0.1	1	0	0.0275
39	8	61.62	53	0	59.99	0.1	1	1.63	0.0529
46	11	76.94	55.5	0	75.38	0.3	2	1.56	0.0552
69	14	114.96	236.9	0	111.98	0.2	1	2.78	0.2367
78	23	213.87	816.5	0	206.61	0.5	1	7.26	0.816
113	26	255.09	1884.8	0	252.83	0.6	2	2.26	1.8842
127	33	335.27	2221.3	0	330.76	0.9	1	4.51	2.2204
175	39	292.06	9146	0	288.3	1.5	3	3.76	9.1445
188	45	454.25	9934.7	0	449.58	2.1	3	4.67	9.9326
214	51	448.97	17289.4	0	444.04	2.2	2	4.93	17.2872
245	58	549.96	26900.5	0	545.45	4.4	3	4.51	26.8961
268	67	608.44	42263.8	0	603.87	3.2	1	4.57	42.2606
278	71	639.17	97295.4	0	634.54	4.1	3	4.63	97.2913

4 Related Work

The coordination of electric motorcycle fleets can be formulated as a multi-service integration problem, necessitating the concurrent execution of path planning, battery swapping, edge computing, vehicle-to-road cooperative communication relaying, map updating, and emergency patrolling. Early work focused on the dual objectives of energy consumption and delay: Hu et al. [14] reviewed smart charging, emphasizing the coordination between operators and power grids; Biswas et al. [15] explored the potential for integration of the Internet of Things, edge intelligence, 5G and blockchain; Zhang et al. [16] analyzed the bottleneck of vehicle-road cooperative communication relay. These studies collectively show that delay-energy has become a key indicator for measuring large-scale fleet services. However, none of the above studies incorporate bearing health into the decision loop, resulting in the inability to quantify reliability risks. To fill this gap, this paper first sets the bearing health index H[i] evaluated by deep learning as a mandatory safety constraint of the scheduling algorithm, and based on this, formalizes BHMTA as an MILP problem.

In the field of collaborative computing, the E-CARGO framework and deep learning algorithms have been utilized to address a variety of complex problem scenarios, such as multi-robot fault recovery [17] and multi-task allocation [18]. In addition, research in the intersection of multi-task allocation and health management has gradually emerged in recent years. Khalatbarisoltani et al. [19] proposed an integrated thermal management and energy management system for hybrid electric vehicles based on multi-agent deep reinforcement learning. The system minimizes fuel consumption while taking into account driver comfort and battery life. Zhou et al. [20] proposed a health-aware adaptive energy management strategy based on variable horizon driving pattern recognition for fuel cell vehicles, which significantly reduced the total driving cost and alleviated the degradation of the fuel cell system and battery by optimizing driving pattern recognition and energy management.

Recent studies in vehicle health management have achieved notable advancements; however, they predominantly concentrate on individual vehicles or isolated application scenarios, while largely overlooking the coordinated scheduling requirements of large-scale electric motorcycle fleets. Furthermore, existing approaches exhibit three key limitations: (i) the assumption of sufficient energy availability, which fails to account for the battery constraints inherent to electric motorcycles; (ii) the neglect of real-time health thresholds, potentially allowing high-risk vehicles to be assigned to task execution; and (iii) the absence of task similarity penalties, which hampers the effective management of resource surges arising from concurrent multitasking. To address these challenges, this paper introduces a conflict-preference joint representation mechanism, which incorporates a cosine similarity-based task conflict matrix to prevent overload task combinations, and a rider preference matrix to enhance personalized service experiences. To the best of our knowledge, this is the first approach to quantitatively integrate both resource conflict and human–machine preference considerations into a unified framework. Building upon this, the proposed BHMTA method advances the field by embedding bearing health hard thresholds and cosine similarity-driven conflict rules into a generalized multi-role allocation (GMRA) model, thereby yielding the first health-aware, MILP-compatible role allocation framework specifically designed for cooperative electric vehicle fleets.

5 Conclusion and Future Work

This paper presents a bearing health-aware mixed-integer linear programming (MILP) model, termed BHMTA, which integrates the E-CARGO formalism with the Gurobi solver to enable reliable task allocation in cooperative electric vehicle fleets. By actively embedding bearing health as a mandatory safety constraint into the MILP formulation, we transform real-time health telemetry into enforceable decision rules, theoretically guaranteeing no violations for health-critical tasks. Experiments at increasing scales (18–278 vehicles) demonstrate that MILP achieves an average satisfaction improvement of 3.4% while strictly upholding no violations, while the Greedy approach exhibits 1–3 violations per instance, with the cost increasing with scale. Each 1% improvement in satisfaction requires only an additional 4.37 s on average—still within the 30-s scheduling window.

While BHMTA demonstrates impressive performance in several areas, including a 3.4% average satisfaction improvement while guaranteeing no violations, the current model still has room for improvement. For example, the static health threshold ($H[i] \geq 0.3$) fails to consider the dynamic decay patterns of different vehicle models and ages, nor does it analyze the threshold's sensitivity. Task similarity calculation is based solely on cosine similarity, failing to incorporate actual resource requirements such as battery capacity and onboard computing power. The comparison algorithm only includes greedy algorithms and does not compare with recent mainstream multi-task allocation algorithms. When the fleet is large, the MILP solution time exceeds the 30-s scheduling window.

Future work will improve and expand these aspects. We will expand the static health threshold to an online dynamic threshold, capturing the dynamic changes of the health curve through cross-fleet joint learning; improve the task similarity calculation method to incorporate more practical resource requirements; introduce mainstream multi-task allocation algorithms for comparison and comprehensively evaluate the performance of BHMTA; explore more efficient algorithm optimization methods to improve the efficiency of solving large-scale problems; expand application scenarios to include hybrid solutions with edge-cloud hierarchies and large fleets; and implement privacy-preserving joint optimization to ensure passenger data security. These improvements will make BHMTA more adaptable to complex vehicle conditions, enhancing its competitiveness and scalability in practical applications.

References

1. An, J., Cao, L., Wang, Y., Khan Jadoon, A., Wang, S.: Adaptive fault-tolerant optimized platoon cloud tracking control for heterogeneous vehicles via dual learning mechanism. In: IEEE Trans. Autom. Sci. Eng. **22**, 4382–4393(2025)
2. Luo, L., Chakraborty, N., Sycara, K. : Provably-good distributed algorithm for constrained multi-robot task assignment for grouped tasks. IEEE Trans. Robot. **31**(1), 19–30 (2025)
3. Zhang, C., Luo, X., Liang, J., Liu, X., Zhu, L., Guo, S.: POTA: privacy-preserving online multitask assignment with path planning. IEEE Trans. Mob. Comput. **23**(5), 5999–6011(2024)
4. Ju, Y., et al.: Joint secure offloading and resource allocation for vehicular edge computing network: a multi-agent deep reinforcement learning approach. IEEE Trans. Intell. Transp. Syst. **24**(5), 5555–5569 (2023)
5. Mao, W., Tan, J., Tan, W.: E-CARGO-based dynamic weight offload strategy with resource contention mitigation for edge networks. J. Ind. Inf. Integr. **42**, 100695 (2024)
6. Gao, R., et al.: Collaborative deep learning-based video stream face recognition with load balancing strategy via RBC and GPU scheduling.In: 2025 28th International Conference on Computer Supported Cooperative Work in Design (CSCWD), pp. 2557–2562 (2025)

7. Zhu, H.: E-CARGO and Role-Based Collaboration: Modeling and Solving Problems in the Complex World. John Wiley & Sons (2021)
8. Zhu, H., Liu, D., Ma, H., Sheng, Y., Zhang, L., Jiang, Q.: E- CARGO/RBC Research guide: a road map for researchers. IEEE Syst. Man Cybern. Mag. **10**(3), 64–75 (2024)
9. Gao, R., Zhang, W., Mao, W.: Method towards collaborative cloud and edge computing via RBC for joint communication and computation resource allocation, J. Ind. Inf. Integr. **44**, 100776 (2025)
10. Wu, X., Fei, M., Zhou, W., et al.: Binary Banyan tree growth optimization: a practical approach to high-dimensional feature selection. Knowl.-Based Syst. **315**, 113252 (2025)
11. Wang, J., Zhu, J., He, X.: Cross-batch negative sampling for training two-tower recommenders. In: Proceedings of the 44th International ACM SIGIR Conference on Research and Development in Information Retrieval, pp. 1632–1636(2021)
12. Xia, P., Zhang, L., Li, F.: Learning similarity with cosine similarity ensemble. Inf. Sci. **307**, 39–52 (2015)
13. Li, M., Mour, N., Smith, L.: Machine learning based on reinforcement learning for smart grids: predictive analytics in renewable energy management. Sustain. Cities Soc. **109**, 105510 (2024)
14. Hu, J., Morais, H., Sousa, T., et al.: Electric vehicle fleet management in smart grids: a review of services, optimization and control aspects. Renew. Sustain. Energy Rev. **56**, 1207–1226 (2016)
15. Biswas, A., Wang, H.C.: Autonomous vehicles enabled by the integration of IoT, edge intelligence, 5G, and blockchain. Sensors **23**(4), 1963 (2023)
16. Zhang, X., Li, J., Zhou, J., et al.: Vehicle-to-everything communication in intelligent connected vehicles: a survey and taxonomy. Autom. Innov. 1–33 (2025)
17. Wang, M., Zhang, P., Zhang, G., et al.: A resilient scheduling framework for multi-robot multi-station welding flow shop scheduling against robot failures. Robot. Comput.-Integr. Manuf. **91**, 102835 (2025)
18. Liu Z., Zhao Z.: Multiattribute E-CARGO task assignment model based on adaptive heterogeneous residual networks. IEEE Trans. Comput. Soc. Syst. **11**(3), 3826–3838 (2024)
19. Khalatbarisoltani, A., Han, J., Liu, W., et al.: Health-consciousness integrated thermal and energy management of connected hybrid electric vehicles using cooperative multi-agent deep reinforcement learning. IEEE Trans. Intell. Vehic. (2024)
20. Zhou, S., et al.: Health-aware adaptive energy management strategy for fuel cell vehicles based on variable horizon driving pattern recognition. IEEE Trans. Transp. Electr. **11**(5), 11463–11476 (2025)

Dual Graph Representation Learning

Huiling Zhu[1(✉)], Xin Luo[2], and Hankz Hankui Zhuo[2]

[1] South China Normal University, Guangzhou, China
zhuhl02@gmail.com
[2] Sun Yat-Sen University, Guangzhou, China

Abstract. Graph representation learning embeds nodes in large graphs as low-dimensional vectors and is of great benefit to many downstream applications. Most embedding frameworks, however, are inherently transductive and unable to generalize to unseen nodes or learn representations across different graphs. Inductive approaches neglect different contexts of nodes and cannot learn node embeddings dually. In this paper, we present a context-aware unsupervised dual encoding framework, **CADE**, to generate representations of nodes by combining real-time neighborhoods with neighbor-attentioned representation, and preserving extra memory of known nodes. We exhibit that our approach is effective by comparing to state-of-the-art methods.

Keywords: graph representation learning · unsupervised learning · dual learning

1 Introduction

The study of real world graphs, such as social network analysis ([5, 10]), molecule screening ([2]), knowledge base reasoning (DBLP:conf/icml/TrivediDWS17, [7]), and biological protein-protein networks analysis ([13]), evolves with the development of computing technologies. Learning vector representations of graphs is effective for a variety of prediction, such as link prediction ([9], [6]) and node clustering ([1, 8]).

There are mainly two approaches for graph representation learning. Transductive models ([3, 9, 11]) are able to learn representations of existing nodes but unable to generalize to new nodes. Inductive models were proposed to address this issue. GraphSAGE ([4]), leverages feature information to generate embeddings of new nodes. However, it samples all neighborhood nodes randomly and uniformly without considering the difference of nodes. GAT ([12]) uses given class labels to guide attention over neighborhoods to aggregate feature information. However, without ground-truth class labels, it is difficult for unsupervised approaches to build attention. In this paper, we introduce a **dual encoding** framework for unsupervised inductive representation learning of graphs. Instead of learning self-attention over neighborhoods of nodes, we exploit bi-attention between representations of two nodes that co-occur in a short random-walk.

© The Author(s), under exclusive license to Springer Nature Singapore Pte Ltd. 2027
H. Sun et al. (Eds.): ChineseCSCW 2025, CCIS 2911, pp. 63–74, 2027.
https://doi.org/10.1007/978-981-92-0288-1_5

Our contributions can be summarized as follows:

- we introduce a dual encoding framework to produce context-aware representation for nodes, and conduct experiments to demonstrate its efficiency and effectiveness;
- we apply bi-attention mechanism for graph representation dual learning, managing to learn dual representation of nodes more precisely;
- we combine the training of transductive global bias with inductive encoding process, as memory of nodes that are already used for training.

2 Model

Let $\mathcal{G} = \{V, E, \boldsymbol{X}\}$ be an undirected graph, where a set of nodes V are connected by a set of edges E, and $\boldsymbol{X} \in \mathbb{R}^{|V| \times f}$ is the attribute matrix of nodes. A global embedding bias matrix is denoted by $\boldsymbol{B} \in R^{|V| \times d}$, where a row of $\boldsymbol{B}$ represents the d-dimensional global embedding bias of a node. The hierarchical layer number, the embedding output of the l-th layer and the final output embedding are denoted by L, $\boldsymbol{h}^l$ and $\boldsymbol{z}$, respectively.

2.1 Context-Aware Inductive Embedding Encoding

The embedding generation process is described in Algorithm 1. Assume that the dual encoder is trained and parameters are fixed. After training, positive pairs are collected by random walks on the whole dataset. The features of each positive pair are passed through a dual-encoder. Embeddings of nodes are generated so that the components of a pair are related and adjacent to each other.

Algorithm 1. Context-Aware Dual-Encoding (**CADE**)

input: the whole graph $\mathcal{G} = (V, E)$; the feature matrix $\boldsymbol{X}$; the trained DualENC
output: learned embeddings $\boldsymbol{z}$;

Run random walks on $\mathcal{G}$ to gain a set of positive pair $\mathbb{P}$;
$\mathbb{Z}_v \leftarrow \emptyset, \forall v \in V$
for $(v, v_p) \in \mathbb{P}$ **do**
  $z_v, z_{v_p} = \mathrm{DualENC}(\mathrm{v}, \mathrm{v_p}, \mathcal{G}, \mathrm{X})$;
  $\mathbb{Z}_v \leftarrow \mathbb{Z}_v \cup z_v$
  $\mathbb{Z}_{v_p} \leftarrow \mathbb{Z}_{v_p} \cup z_{v_p}$
end for
for $v \in V$ **do**
  $\boldsymbol{z}_v = \mathrm{Mean}(\mathbb{Z}_{\mathrm{v}})$;
end for

2.2 Dual-Encoder with Multi-Sampling

In this subsection, we explain the dual encoder.

In Step 2 to Step 6 in Algorithm 2, we directly apply a **bi-attention layer** on the two sets of embedding outputs with different sampled neighborhood feature as input We use the hierarchical sampling and aggregating framework as a base encoder in our experiments, but it can also be designed in many other ways.

To train our encoder before using it to generate final representations of nodes, we apply a typical pair reconstruction loss function with negative sampling [4], where node v_p co-occurs with v on fixed-length random walk ([9]), σ is the sigmoid function, P_n is a negative sampling distribution, Q defines the number of negative samples. Note that z_v and z_{v_p} are dual representation to each other while z_{v_n} represents the direct encoder output of negative sample v_n.

$$J_{\mathcal{G}}(z_v) = -\log(\sigma(\boldsymbol{z}_v^T \boldsymbol{z}_{v_p})) - Q \cdot \mathbb{E}_{v_n \sim P_n(v)} \log(\sigma(-\boldsymbol{z}_v^T \boldsymbol{z}_{v_n})) \tag{1}$$

Algorithm 2. DualENC

input: Training graph $\mathcal{G}(V, E)$; node attributes $\boldsymbol{X}$; global embedding bias matrix $\boldsymbol{B}$; sampling times K; positive node pair (v, v_p);
output: adjacent embeddings z_v and z_{v_p};

1: For node v and v_p, generate K embeddings, $\boldsymbol{h}_v$, $\boldsymbol{h}_{v_p}$, using a base encoder SAGB
2: **for** $i, j \in \{1, ..., K\}$ **do**
3: $\quad S_{i,j} \leftarrow \alpha(\boldsymbol{h}_{vi}, \boldsymbol{h}_{v_pj})$
4: **end for**
5: softmax on flattened similarity matrix S: $S_{i,j} \leftarrow \frac{e^{S_{i,j}}}{\sum_{0,0}^{K,K} e^{S_{i,j}}}$
6: calculate attention a_v and a_{v_p}:
$\boldsymbol{a}_{vi} \leftarrow \sum_{j=1}^{K} S_{i,j}, \boldsymbol{a}_{v_pj} \leftarrow \sum_{i=1}^{K} S_{i,j}$
7: $\boldsymbol{z}_v \leftarrow \sum_{t=1}^{K} \boldsymbol{a}_{vk} \boldsymbol{h}_{vk}^L$
8: $\boldsymbol{z}_{v_p} \leftarrow \sum_{t=1}^{K} \boldsymbol{a}_{v_pk} \boldsymbol{h}_{v_pk}^L$

2.3 Dual-Encoder with Multi-Aggregating

Besides learning dual representation with multiple sampling, we introduce another version of our dual encoder with multiple aggregator function. The intuition is that through different perspective, a node can be represented differently corresponding to different kinds of positive nodes.

In Step 1 in Algorithm 2, for a node v, we sample neighborhood once and aggregate feature with K sets of parameters, gaining K different representations h_{vk} corresponding to K different character of v. Given a positive node pair, v and v_p, their dual representation are calculated by applying bi-attention as we described in the last section. There is but one difference that we use a weigh vector $\boldsymbol{A} \in R^{2d}$ as parameter instead of dot-product, to calculate the $K \times K$ attention matrix between node v and node v_p, where $\cdot^T$ represents transposition and $||$ is the concatenation operation. The rest of calculation of dual representation is the same as Sect. 2.2.

$$S_{ij} \leftarrow \frac{\exp(\boldsymbol{A}^\top[\boldsymbol{h}_{vi}||\boldsymbol{h}_{v_pj}])}{\sum_{0,0}^{K,K}\exp(\boldsymbol{A}^\top[\boldsymbol{h}_{vi}||\boldsymbol{h}_{v_pj}])} \tag{2}$$

Another difference is during training. With K sets of parameter for aggregating, negative sample v_n is now also represented by K different embeddings. We set $K = 5$ and use different shape to represent the embeddings of the positive node pair and the negative sampled nodes.

To make sure that any embeddings of node v_n as far away from any of node v as possible, it is equal to maximizing the distance between their **support embeddings**, which is the closest pair of embeddings of v and v_n. The support embedding can be calculated by the learned dual encoder. In conclusion, our loss function are as follows:

$$J_{\mathcal{G}}(z_v) = -\log(\sigma(\boldsymbol{z}_v^T \boldsymbol{z}_{v_p})) - Q \cdot \mathbb{E}_{v_n \sim P_n(v)} \log(\sigma(-\boldsymbol{z}_v'^{\top} \boldsymbol{z}_{v_n})) \tag{3}$$

$$\boldsymbol{z}_v, \boldsymbol{z}_{v_p} = \text{DualENC}(v, v_p, \boldsymbol{A}) \tag{4}$$

$$\boldsymbol{z}_v', \boldsymbol{z}_{v_n} = \text{DualENC}(v, v_p, \boldsymbol{A}^*) \tag{5}$$

where $\boldsymbol{A}^*$ representing that we stop the back-propagation through $\boldsymbol{A}$ in dual encoding for negative sample node, since $\boldsymbol{A}$ are supposed to learn bi-attention between the positive node pair and be reused only to capture the support embedding of v and its negative sample nodes.

2.4 Memorable Global Bias in Hierarchical Encoding

In this subsection, we explain the base encoder used in our proposed dual encoding framework, and introduce how memorable global bias is applied within this framework.

For generating embedding for one specific node u, we describe the process below. First, we construct a neighborhood tree with node u as the root, $\mathbb{N}_u$, by iteratively sampling immediate neighborhood of nodes of the last layer as children. Nodes at the lth layer are denoted by $\mathbb{N}_u^l$, $\mathbb{N}_u^0 = \{u\}$. At each iteration, each node i aggregates the representations of its children j, $\{h_j^{l-1}\}$, and of itself, h_i^{l-1}, into a single vector h_i^l, as representation of the next layer. After L iterations, we gain the Lth layer representation of v, as the final output. While this framework generates good representation for nodes, it cannot preserve sufficient embedding informations for known nodes. More specifically, for nodes that are known but trained less than average, the learned model would have treated them like nodes unmet before. Therefore, we intuitively apply distinctive and trainable global bias to each node, as follows:

$$h^{l-1}_{\mathcal{S}(i)} \leftarrow \text{AGGREGATE}_l(\{h^{l-1}_j, \forall j \in \mathcal{S}(i)\}) \tag{6}$$

$$h^l_i \leftarrow \sigma(W^l \cdot [h^{l-1}_i || h^{l-1}_{\mathcal{S}(i)}]) \tag{7}$$

$$h^l_i \leftarrow h^l_i + b_i, l < L \tag{8}$$

$$b_i \leftarrow one\_hot(i)^{\mathsf{T}} B \tag{9}$$

where $B \in R^{|V| \times d}$ is the trainable global bias matrix, $\mathcal{S}(i)$ represents the sampled neighborhood and also the children nodes of node i in the neighborhood tree, AGGREGATE represents the neighborhood aggregator function, and $||$ is a operator of concatenating vectors.

On one hand, B can be reused to produce embeddings for the known nodes or the unknown connected with the known, as supplement to the neural network encoder. On another hand, the global bias vectors can partially offset the uncertainty of the encoding brought by the random sampling not only during the training but also the final generation. Lastly but not least, we use only one set of global bias for all nodes, which means for any node, its representations of hidden layers are all added by the same bias vector. As a result of that, we are able to update parameters of aggregator function in the lowest layer with the global updated bias of nodes, highly increasing the training efficiency.

It is important for us to apply no global bias to the last layer of output, which is also the candidate of the dual-encoder output of nodes before applied with attention. The reason is that applying extra bias onto the last layer would directly change the embedding distribution of known nodes, making it unequal to the embedding distribution of unseen nodes. In general, the implementation of the base encoder with global bias is shown in Algorithm 3. The * in Step 8 means the children of node i in the neighborhood tree $\mathbb{N}_u$.

Algorithm 3. SAGB: sampling and aggregating with global bias

input: node u; hierarchical depth L; weight matrices W^l; non-linearity σ; differentiable neighbor aggregator AGGREGATE$_l$; fixed-size uniform sampler $\mathcal{S} : v \rightarrow 2^V$
output: embedding z_u;

1: $\mathbb{N}^0_u = \{u\}$;
2: **for** $l = 1...L$ **do**
3: $\quad \mathbb{N}^l_u \leftarrow \{\mathcal{S}(i), \forall i \in \mathbb{N}^{l-1}_u\}$;
4: **end for**
5: **for** l=1...L **do**
6: $\quad$ **for** $i \in \mathbb{N}^0_u \bigcup \mathbb{N}^1_u \bigcup ... \bigcup \mathbb{N}^{L-l}_u$ **do**
7: $\quad\quad h^{l-1}_{\mathcal{S}^*(i)} \leftarrow \text{AGGREGATE}_l(\{h^{l-1}_j, \forall j \in \mathcal{S}^*(i)\})$
8: $\quad\quad h^l_i \leftarrow \sigma(W^l \cdot [h^{l-1}_i || h^{l-1}_{\mathcal{S}^*(i)}])$
9: $\quad\quad$ **if** $l < L$: $h^l_i \leftarrow h^l_i + \text{one\_hot}(i)^{\mathsf{T}} B$
10: $\quad$ **end for**
11: **end for**
12: **return** $z_u \leftarrow h^L_u$

3 Experiments

In this section, we compare CADE against two strong baselines in an inductive and unsupervised setting, on challenging benchmark tasks of node classification and link prediction. We also perform further studies of the proposed model in Sect. 3.5.

3.1 Datasets

The following graph datasets are used in experiments and statistics are summarized in Table 1: Pubmed, Blogcatalog, Reddit, PPI.

Table 1. Dataset Statistics

Dataset	Nodes	Edges	Classes	Features	Avg Degree
Pubmed	19717	44324	3	500	4.47
Blogcatalog	5196	171743	6	8189	66.11
Reddit	232,965	11,606,919	41	602	100.30
PPI	56944	818716	121[4]	50	28.76

3.2 Experimental Settings

We compare CADE against the following approaches in a fully unsupervised and inductive setting: GraphSAGE and Graph2Gauss. GraphSAGE is a hierarchical neighbor sampling and aggregating encoder for inductive learning while G2G only uses the attributes of nodes to learn their representations.

Beside the above two models, we also include experiment results of raw features as baselines. In comparison, we call the version of dual-encoder with multiple sampling as **CADE-MS**, while the version with multiple aggregator function as **CADE-MA**. [1234]

For CADE-MS, CADE-MA and GraphSAGE, we set the depth of hierarchical aggregating as $L = 2$, the neighbor sampling sizes as $s_1 = 20, s_2 = 10$, and the number of random-walks for each node as 100 and the walk length as 4. The sampling time in CADE-MS or the number of aggregator in CADE-MA is set as $K = 10$. And for all emedding learning models, the dimension of embeddings is set to 256, as for raw feature, we use all the dimensions. Our approach is impemented in Tensorflow and trained with the Adam optimizer at an initial learning rate of 0.0001.

[1] Available at https://linqs.soe.ucsc.edu/data..
[2] http://www.blogcatalog.com/.
[3] http://www.reddit.com/.
[4] PPI is a multi-label dataset.

Table 2. Prediction results for Pubmed/Blogcatalog w.r.t different unseen ratio

Methods	Pubmed			Blogcatalog		
unseen-ratio	10%	30%	50%	10%	30%	50%
RawFeats	79.22	77.66	77.74	**90.00**	**89.05**	**87.08**
G2G	80.70	76.67	76.31	62.35	56.19	48.46
GraphSAGE	82.05	81.32	79.68	71.48	69.33	64.92
CADE-MS	**84.25**	**83.40**	**81.74**	77.35	73.71	70.88
CADE-MA	**84.56**	**83.03**	**82.40**	84.33	82.21	79.04

3.3 Inductive Node Classification

We evaluate the node classification performance of methods on the four datasets. On Reddit and PPI, we follow the same training/validation/testing split used in GraphSAGE. On Pubmed and Blogcatalog, we randomly selected 10%/20%/30% nodes for training while the rest remain unseen. We report the averaged results over 10 random split.

After spliting the graph dataset, the model is trained in an unsupervised manner, then the learnt model computes the embeddings for all nodes, a node classifier is trained with the embeddings of training nodes and finally the learnt classifier is evaluated with the learnt embeddings of the testing nodes, i.e. the unseen nodes.

We compare our method against 3 baselines: (i)a logistic-regression feature-based classifier (that ignores graph structure), (ii)Graph2Gauss as another unsupervised and inductive approach , (iii)the original hierarchical neighbor sampling and aggregating framework, GraphSAGE.

Comparation on node classification performance on Pubmed and Blogcatalog dataset with respect to varying ratios of unseen nodes, are reported in Table 2. CADE-MS and CADE-MA outperform other approaches on Pubmed. On Blogcatalog dataset, however, RawFeats performs best mainly because that, in Blogcatalog dataset, node features are not only directly extracted from a set of user-defined tags, but also are of very high dimensionality (up to 8,189). Hence extra neighborhood information is not needed. As shown in Table 2, CADE-MA performs better than CADE-MS, and both outperform GraphSAGE and G2G. CADE-MA is capable of reducing high dimensionality while losing less information than CADE-MS, CADE-MA is more likely to search for the best aggregator function that can focus on those important features of nodes. As a result, the 256-dimensional embedding learnt by CADE-MA shows the cloest node classification performance to the 8k-dimensional raw features.

3.4 Inductive Link Prediction

Link prediction task evaluates how much network structural information is preserved by embeddings. We preform the following steps: (1) mark some nodes as unseen from the training of embedding learning models. For Pubmed 20% nodes are marked as unseen; (2) randomly hide certain percentage of edges and equal-number of non-edges as testing edge set for link prediction, and make sure not to produced any dangling node; (3) the rest of edges are then used to form the input graph for embedding learning and with equal number of non-edges form the training edge set for link predictor; (4) after training and inductively generation of embeddings, the training edge set and their corresponding embeddings will help to train a link predictor; (5) finally evaluate the performance on the testing edges by the area under the ROC curve (AUC) and the average precision (AP) scores.

Comparation on performance with respect to varying percentage of hidden edges are reported in Table 3. CADE shows best link prediction performance on both datasets.

Table 3. Link prediction results for Pubmed/PPI w.r.t different percentage of hidden-edges

Dataset	Methods	90%:10%		80%:20%		60%:40%		40%:60%	
		AUC	AP	AUC	AP	AUC	AP	AUC	AP
Pubmed	RawFeats	57.61	54.72	58.51	56.19	54.47	52.82	52.41	50.77
	G2G	64.13	68.60	63.52	65.15	60.03	66.16	58.97	61.17
	GraphSAGE	85.49	82.79	87.64	83.35	81.07	77.47	79.34	74.92
	CADE-MS	**89.95**	**88.79**	**90.36**	**86.67**	**87.14**	**83.77**	**84.76**	**79.53**
	CADE-MA	**89.73**	**89.76**	**90.94**	**88.90**	**90.54**	**87.89**	**85.27**	**80.15**
PPI	RawFeats	57.46	56.99	57.34	56.86	57.35	56.75	56.83	56.36
	G2G	60.62	58.98	60.99	59.38	61.05	59.54	60.93	59.49
	GraphSAGE	82.74	81.20	82.21	80.66	82.11	80.51	82.07	80.70
	CADE-MS	**85.87**	**85.08**	**84.21**	**83.48**	**84.46**	**82.84**	**83.61**	**82.39**
	CADE-MA	**86.33**	**85.32**	**85.85**	**84.63**	**84.15**	**82.15**	81.98	79.54

3.5 Model Study

Sampling Complexity in CADE-MS.

Our proposed CADE-MS requires multiple neighborhood sampling, which increases the complexity of embedding learning. Yet by comparing CADE-MS against GraphSAGE with the same quantity of sampled neighborhood per node, the superiority of CADE model over existing models is still vast. In practice, we set the sampling layer $L = 2$ and the first-layer sampling size as 20. For the second layer, denote by s_2' the sampling size in GraphSAGE, and by s_2 and T the sampling size and sampling time in CADE-MS. We compare the two methods with $s_2' = s_2 * K$.

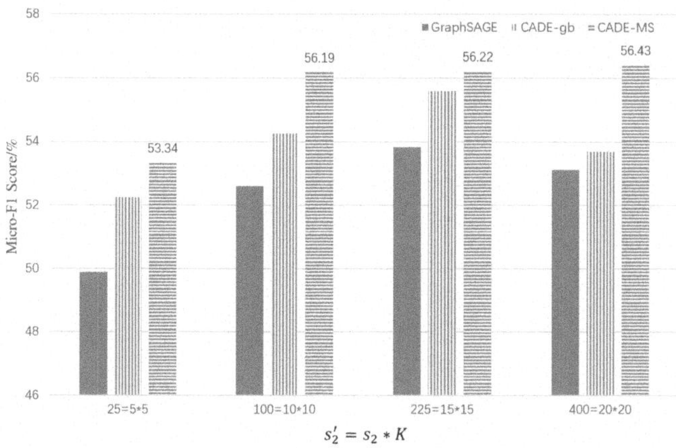

Fig. 1. node classification performance (micro-f1 score) w.r.t varying sampling sizes.

A variant of CADE, called CADE-gb, applies only memorable global bias and no dual-encoding framework, has the same sampling complexity as GraphSAGE. For the efficiency of experiment, we conduct experiments of node classification on a small subset of PPI, denoted by **subPPI**, which includes 3 training graphs plus one validation graph and one test graph. Results are reported in Fig. 1. With much smaller sampling width, CADE-MS still outperforms the original framework significantly.

It implicates that searching for the best representation match through multiple sampling and bi-attention is efficient to filtering userful neighbor nodes without supervision from any node labels, and that the context-aware dual-encoding framework is capable of improving the inductive embedding learning ability without increasing sampling complexity. We aslo observe that CADE-gb, the variant simply adding the memorable global bias, continually shows advance in different sampling sizes.

Sensitivity Study. To evaluate the parameter sensitivity of CADE-MS and CADE-MA, we conduct node classification experiments on two superparameters: dimensionality and dual learning parameter K.

For dimensionality sensitivity study, we compare GraphSAGE, CADE-MS and CADE-MA on PPI dataset, embedding vector dimension set as 50/100/200/300/400. Results are reported in Fig. 2. We observe that the node classification f1 scores of CADE-MS and CADE-MA both rise as the dimensionality increases, with a stable advance over GraphSAGE of about 5%. Also, the result curves shows that CADE-MA is less sensitive to embedding dimensionality and achieves the max performance at 300 embedding dimensions, while CADE-MS stably performs better and better with increasing embedding size, which indicates that CADE-MS relies more on the embedding dimensionality. And again, the fact that CADE with only 50 embedding dimensions outperforms

GraphSAGE with 400 embedding dimensions demonstrates the effectiveness of our proposed model.

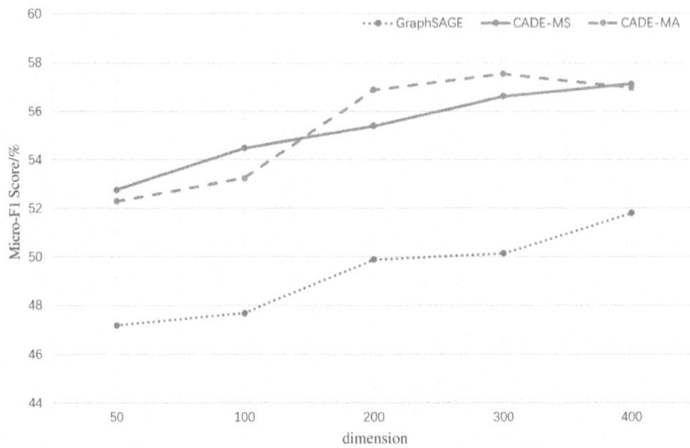

Fig. 2. Classification results w.r.t different embedding dimension on PPI.

The second sensitivity experiment is to study the influence of K, i.e. the number of candidate representation for dual encoding. We evaluate the node classification performance of CADE-MS/CADE-MA using different value of K. Experiments are conducted on subPPI in consideration of the huge memory cost caused by a large value of K, and we set $L - 2$ and $s_1 = 20$, $s_2 = 25$. In order to only measure the influence of different K, we remove the global bias in CADE-MA and CADE-MS. In addition, we also report the runtime of the model. The results are shown in Fig. 3.

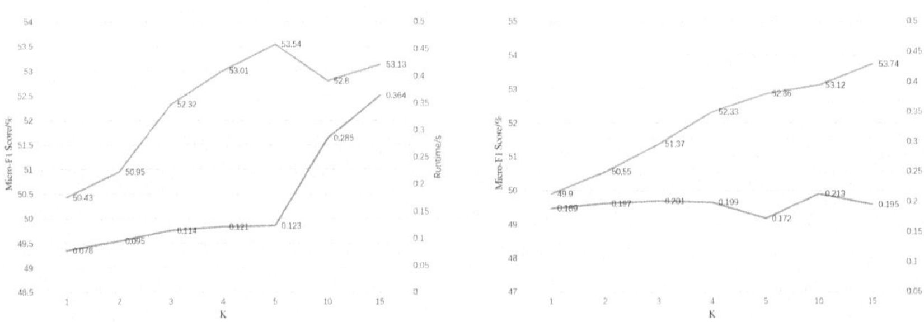

(a) Reddit (b) PPI

Fig. 3. Classification results (micro-averaged F1 scores) w.r.t different values of K on subPPI.

As we can see from Fig. 3a, the runtime of CADE-MS increases as K increases, while at K=5 the F1 scores already reach the highest value, which indicates that setting K as 5 is the most effective and efficient. In the implementation of CADE-MA, we calculate K aggregator functions parallelly, which is why we can see in Fig. 3b that the runtime of CADE-MA is independent of K, while the node classification performance of CADE-MS keeps improving as K increases.

Necessarity of Hidden Memory. We conduct a brief comparison experiment in this section to demonstrate the necessarity to not apply global bias to the encoder output, i.e. the last layer of hierarchical aggregating. We compare the original framework GraphSAGE, with the variants of our method: applying global bias to only the last layer, applying global bias to the former layers, and the full version of CADE.

Table 4. node classification performance (f1-micro score) with different way of applying global bias

method	F1-micro
GraphSAGE	50.22
CADE-gl	39.24
CADE-gb	54.13
CADE	58.22

As Table 4 shows, CADE-gl shows even worse performance than GraphSAGE, while CADE-gb demonstrates the great effect of keeping respective memory of the hidden representation for each node.

4 Conclusion

We proposed CADE, an unsupervised and inductive network embedding approach which is capable of preserving local connectiveness distinctively, as well as learning and memorizing global identities for seen nodes while generalizing to unseen nodes. We applied a bi-attention architecture upon hierarchical aggregating layers to capture the most relevant representations dually for any positive pair. We present an effective way of combining inductive and transductive ideas by allowing trainable global embedding bias to be retrieved in hidden layers within the hierarchical aggregating framework. Experiments demonstrate the superiority of CADE over baselines on unsupervised and inductive tasks. In the future, we would use dual encoding framework in supervised embedding learning, or combing dual encoding with G2G by learning distribution representations dually for positive pairs.

References

1. Ding, C.H., He, X., Zha, H., Gu, M., Simon, H.D.: A min-max cut algorithm for graph partitioning and data clustering. In: Proceedings of the 2001 IEEE International Conference on Data Mining, 29 November – 2 December 2001, San Jose, California, USA, pp. 107–114 (2001)
2. Duvenaud, D.K., et al.: Convolutional networks on graphs for learning molecular fingerprints. In: NIPS, pp. 2224–2232 (2015)
3. Grover, A., Leskovec, J.: node2vec: scalable feature learning for networks. In: KDD, pp. 855–864 (2016)
4. Hamilton, W.L., Ying, R., Leskovec, J.: Inductive representation learning on large graphs. In: NIPS (2017)
5. Hamilton, W.L., Ying, R., Leskovec, J.: Representation learning on graphs: methods and applications. IEEE Data Eng. Bull. **40**(3), 52–74 (2017)
6. Li, Y., Jingpeng, W., Zhang, Z.: NGLinker: link prediction for node featureless networks. Big Data Res. **41**, 100558 (2025)
7. Liu, X., Guo, X., Wen, G.: SecKG2vec: a novel security knowledge graph relational reasoning method based on semantic and structural fusion embedding. Comput. Secur. **149**, 104192 (2025)
8. Nie, F., Zhu, W., Li, X.: Unsupervised large graph embedding. In: Proceedings of the Thirty-First AAAI Conference on Artificial Intelligence, 4–9 February 2017, San Francisco, California, USA, pp. 2422–2428 (2017)
9. Perozzi, B., Al-Rfou, R., Skiena, S.: DeepWalk: online learning of social representations. In: KDD, pp. 701–710 (2014)
10. Singh, S.S., Muhuri, S., Mishra, S., Srivastava, D., Shakya, H.K., Kumar, N.: Social network analysis: a survey on process, tools, and application. ACM Comput. Surv. **56**(8), 1–39 (2024)
11. Tang, J., Qu, M., Wang, M., Zhang, M., Yan, J., Mei, Q.: LINE: large-scale information network embedding. In: WWW, pp. 1067–1077 (2015)
12. Velickovic, P., Cucurull, G., Casanova, A., Romero, A., Liò, P., Bengio, Y.: Graph attention networks. CoRR, abs/1710.10903 (2017)
13. Zitnik, M., Leskovec, J.: Predicting multicellular function through multi-layer tissue networks. Bioinformatics **33**(14), i190–i198 (2017)

A Joint Resource Security Allocation Scheme with Collaborative Interference and UAV Assistance

Taoshen Li[1,2(✉)], Junzhi Xu[2], and Xuling Zeng[2]

[1] Nanning University, No. 8 Longting Road, Nanning, China
tshli@gxu.edu.cn

[2] Guangxi University, No. 100 Daxue Road, Nanning, China

Abstract. This paper studied the problem of maximizing the security rate of a self-energy-recycling full-duplex UAV relay network, and proposed a joint resource security allocation scheme based on collaborative interference and UAV assistance for communication scenarios with eavesdroppers. This scheme jointly optimizes the transmission power and flight trajectory of relay UAVs and interference UAVs, as well as the SWIPT power splitting ratio, in order to maximize the relay security rate. For the non-convex original problem with multiple coupled variables, the problem was transformed into three approximately equivalent convex sub-problems using the first-order Taylor expansion and continuous convex approximation method. Simulation results show that the joint optimization scheme with collaborative interference can achieve secure transmission in a self-energy full-duplex UAV relay network, and the system transmission performance can also be improved to some extent.

Keywords: Collaborative Interference · Unmanned Aerial Vehicles (UAV) · Self Energy Recycling · Security Rate · Trajectory Optimization · Resource Allocation

1 Introduction

The limited energy of unmanned aerial vehicle (UAV) greatly restricts the improvement of network performance, and the contradiction between the high-performance requirements of networks and the limited energy of UAVs has become a key issue in the research of UAV relay communication. Simultaneous wireless information and power transfer(SWIPT) technology can harvest energy from the transmission power while transmitting information, which is a promising solution to alleviate the limited energy reserve of UAVs and improve network performance[1].

Many existing researches mainly optimize the performance of drone relay networks from the perspective of resource optimization algorithms. [2] studied energy-saving communication in multi-user UAV relay networks. In [3] and [4], the authors used probabilistic the line of sight(LoS) channel model to accurately describe the dynamic effects of factors such as distance, altitude, environmental type.

© The Author(s), under exclusive license to Springer Nature Singapore Pte Ltd. 2027
H. Sun et al. (Eds.): ChineseCSCW 2025, CCIS 2911, pp. 75–84, 2027.
https://doi.org/10.1007/978-981-92-0288-1_6

Transmission delay is one of the experience indicators in communication systems. [5] derived delay expressions for different types of users, and reduced user delay by optimizing transmission power. The author of [6] designed an adaptive transmission mechanism to ensure low latency transmission of sudden business. [7] minimized the total computing task delay by optimizing the UAV location and bandwidth allocation.

Information transmission security is another key issue in UAV communication networks. [8] provided a confidentiality capacity maximization strategy for unmanned aerial vehicle relay systems. [9] considered the physical layer security and fairness of UAV relay systems in multi node IoT scenarios. [10] used collaborative beamforming technology and improved evolutionary algorithms to reduce eavesdropping reception rates. [11] proposed an optimal interference layout scheme based on deep learning networks to overcome the instability of imperfect channel information. Based on artificial noise(AN) interference technology and statistical channel state information, [12] proposed a relay selection strategy for passive eavesdropping scenarios. [13] maximized the average confidentiality rate of the secondary relay network.

Aiming at the energy limitation problem in UAV relay systems, [14] combined successful convex approximation, particle swarm optimization, and other methods, optimized the total energy consumption of the UAV system; [15] adopted reinforcement learning methods to construct a charging and replacement mechanism for multiple UAVs; [16] used a distributed control strategy to optimize the allocation of target search tasks for multiple UAVs; [17] considered the large-scale machine class communication scenarios, and adopted a clustering based particle swarm optimization algorithm to optimize the clustering of communication devices.

This paper aims to optimize and improve the SWITP performance of UAV communication networks in energy limited scenarios, and proposes a trajectory optimization and resource allocation scheme to solve the security performance optimization problem of self energy recycling(SER) UAV relay network in collaborative interference.

2 System Model

Consider a double UAVs full-duplex(FD) relay communication network as shown in Fig. 1, which consists of a relay UAV, a interference UAV, a base station source node(BSSN), a regal user destination node(DN) and a eavesdropper node(EN). The relay UAV is equipped two antennas for transmitting and receiving information, and the interference UAV is equipped with one antenna for transmitting interference signals. Assumed that BSSN cannot directly communicate with DN, and a relay UAV is deployed to effectively transmit information from BSSN to DN at a tolerable level of interference. To ensure that DN information is not stolen by nearby EN and improve the information confidentiality of the secondary network, a interference UAV is deployed to send artificial noise (AN) to interfere with EN's information eavesdropping. The deployed UAV starts from the designated location and performs tasks within a work cycle of time T. The relay UAV adopts SWIPT technology with power splitting (PS) structure to divide the received RF signal power into two parts, which are used for self charging and information decoding, respectively. In addition, relay UAV also collect self interference signals to provide energy for themselves.

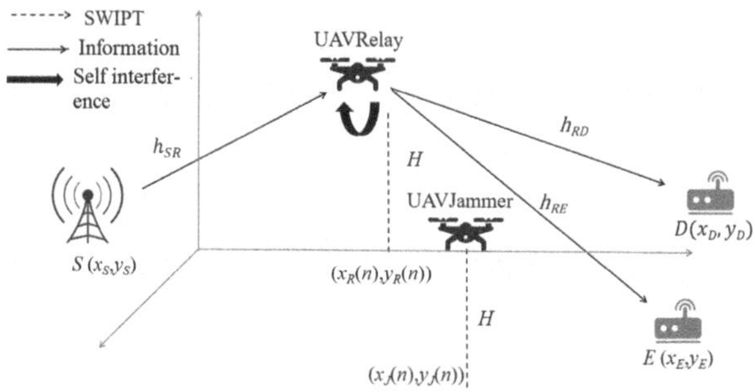

Fig. 1. The UAV security relay network model.

In Fig. 1, *S*, *D*, and *E* are the source node, legitimate destination node, and eavesdropping node respectively, and their positions are represented as $C_S = [{l_S}^T, 0]^T$, $C_D = [{l_D}^T, 0]^T$ and $C_E = [{l_E}^T, 0]^T$, where l_S, l_D and l_E represent as the horizontal coordinates of *S*, *D*, and *E*, respectively. Assuming that the UAV has obtained precise coordinates of the source and target nodes in advance, and ignores the takeoff and landing phases of the UAV, as well as the UAV flies horizontally at a fixed altitude H. Let ${I_R}^0 = [{x_R}^0, {y_R}^0]^T$, ${I_J}^0 = [{x_J}^0, {y_J}^0]^T$ be the starting horizontal positions of the relay UAV and the interference UAV, respectively, and ${I_R}^F = [{x_R}^F, {y_R}^F]^T$, ${I_J}^F = [{x_J}^F, {y_J}^F]^T$ be the ending horizontal positions of the relay UAV and the interference UAV, respectively. The time period T is divided into N equally long time slots ($T = Nt$). The coordinates of the relay UAV and the interference UAV in time slot n are represented as $C_R = [l_R[n]^T, H]^T$ $(0 \le n \le N)$, $C_J = [l_J[n]^T, H]^T$ $(0 \le n \le N)$, respectively. The trajectories of the relay UAV and the interference UAV during the working period T can be represented by sequences $l_R = [l_R[1], l_R[2], \ldots, l_R[N]]^T$ and $l_J = [l_J[1], l_J[2], \ldots, l_J[N]]^T$ of length N, respectively.

Figure 2 is a schematic diagram of relay communication including the receiving architecture of PS-SWIPT. Let the transmission power P_S of the source node be a constant value, and ρ $(0 \le \rho \le 1)$ be the PS ratio coefficient of the relay UAV. In time slot n, the signal received by the relay UAV from the source node S is divided into two parts: $\rho(n)P_S h_{SR}[n]$ and $(1- \rho(n))P_S h_{SR}[n]$. The former is the information part sent by the source node S to the relay UAV, and the latter is converted into battery energy and used for decoding the information from the relay UAV to the destination node D.

Considering the self interference in FD mode, the expression for the total energy collected during the working cycle T is:

$$\sum_{n=1}^{N} E(n) = \delta t \sum_{n=1}^{N} (1 - \rho(n))(P_S h_{SR}[n] + h_u p_R(n)) \tag{1}$$

where, $P_S h_{SR}[n]$ and $h_u p_R(n)$ respectively denote the energy harvesting by the relay from the source node and self interference at time n, h_u denotes the self interference channel, $\rho(n)$ denotes power splitting ratio, $p_R(n)$ is relay transmission power.

Assuming that the relay UAV can perfectly eliminate self interference signals, in the nth time slot, the transmission rate from the source node S to the UAV relay at time slot

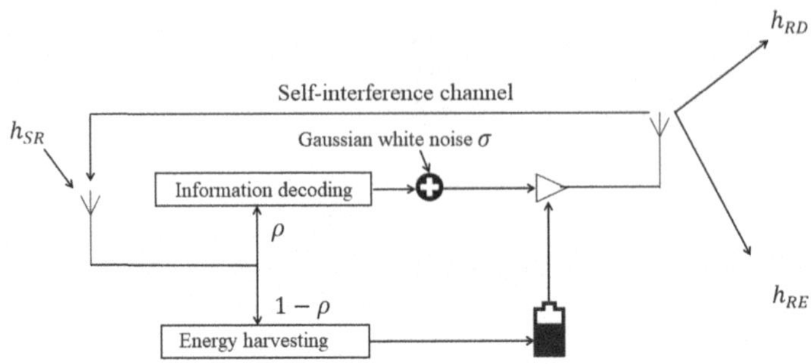

Fig. 2. The SWIPT structure of the relay.

n can be expressed as:

$$R_{SR}[n] = B\log_2(1 + \frac{\rho(n)P_S h_{SR}[n]}{\sigma^2}) \tag{2}$$

where, B is the channel bandwidth, σ^2 is the additive Gaussian white noise (AWGN) power at the receiver.

At time slot n, the transmission rate from the UAV to the target node D can be expressed as:

$$R_{RD}[n] = B\log_2(1 + \frac{p_R(n)h_{RD}[n]}{p_J(n)h_{JD}[n] + \sigma^2}) \tag{3}$$

where, $p_J(n)$ is interference UAV's transmission power.

The receiving rate of eavesdropping node E at time slot n is:

$$R_{RE}[n] = B\log_2(1 + \frac{p_R(n)h_{RE}[n]}{p_J(n)h_{JE}[n] + \sigma^2}) \tag{4}$$

The transmission rate from the source node S to the legal receiving node D in all N time slots can be expressed as:

$$R_{SD}[n] = \min(R_{SR}[n], R_{RD}[n]) \tag{5}$$

The security rate of the relay UAV at the nth time slot is represented as:

$$R_{\text{sec}}[n] = R_{SD}[n] - R_{RE}[n] \tag{6}$$

3 Problem Description and Joint Optimization Algorithm

3.1 Problem Description

Our optimization objective is to jointly optimize the trajectories of UAV and interference UAV, transmission power, power splitting coefficient, and noise power of relay UAV based on constraints such as information causality and energy harvesting, in order to maximize the average confidentiality rate of information transmission for relay UAV. The original optimization problem(P0) can be expressed as:

$$\text{P0}: \max_{\{p_R(n),p_J(n),\rho(n)\},\{l_R[n[,l_J[n]\}} \frac{1}{N}\sum_{n=1}^{N} R_{\text{sec}}[n] \tag{7a}$$

$$s.t. \sqrt{\|l_R[n]-l_J[n]\|^2} \leq d_{\min} \tag{7b}$$

$$\|l_R[n+1]-l_R[n]\|^2 \leq d_{\max}^2 \tag{7c}$$

$$\|l_J[n+1]-l_J[n]\|^2 \leq d_{\max}^2 \tag{7d}$$

$$\left\|l_J[N]-l_J^F\right\|^2 \leq d_{\max}^2 \tag{7e}$$

$$\left\|l_R[N]-l_R^F\right\|^2 \leq d_{\max}^2 \tag{7f}$$

$$I_R[1]=I_R^0, I_J[1]=I_J^0 \tag{7g}$$

$$0 \leq p_J(n) \leq p_{\max} \tag{7h}$$

$$0 \leq p_R(n) \leq p_{\max} \tag{7i}$$

$$0 \leq \rho(n) \leq 1 \tag{7j}$$

$$\sum_{i=1}^{n} p_R(i) \leq P_{ba} \leq \sum_{i=1}^{n} E(i) \tag{7k}$$

where, constraint (7b) indicates that the distance between two UAVs is not less than the minimum safe distance d_{min} to prevent mutual collision; (7c) - (7f) limit the flight distance of UAVs in each time slot to not exceed the specified maximum distance d_{max}; (7g) defined the starting point of the UAVs; (7h) and (7i) respectively ensure that the transmission power of the relay UAV and the interference UAV does not exceed the specified power threshold p_{max}; (7j) denotes the range of power splitting ratio; (7k) ensure that the relay UAV can only use the energy from the current and previous time slots for transmission in each time slot, P_{ba} represents the initial energy that the UAV can use for relay, and $\sum_{i=1}^{n} E(i)$ is the total energy harvested by the relay in time slot k. Obviously, problem P0 is a non convex problem with multiple coupled variables, which is difficult to solve directly.

3.2 Problem Solving and Joint Optimization Algorithm Design

To solve the problem of multi-variable coupling, P0 is decomposed into three optimization sub problems: relay UAV trajectory optimization, interference UAV trajectory optimization, and resource allocation optimization. Firstly, in the sub problem of optimizing the trajectory of relay UAVs, the first-order Taylor expansion method is used to perform continuous convex approximation on the non convex parts of the sub problem. Secondly, the same continuous convex approximation method is used to obtain the convex subproblem in the trajectory optimization of interference UAV. Next, in the sub problem of resource allocation optimization, a concave function is constructed to perform continuous convex approximation on the sub problem, and an alternating iterative algorithm is designed to solve the sub problem of resource allocation optimization. Finally, alternately solve three convex subproblems and update the objective function values until the function values converge.

To solve the above optimization problems, we use the constructor method to perform convex optimization on the objective function and constraints through the lemma proposed in [18].

Lemma 1 [18]: For any x³0, let $\varphi(t) = -tx + \ln t + 1$ be a concave function about t, we have:

$$-\ln x = \max_{t>0} \varphi(t) \tag{8}$$

If and only if $t = 1/x$, $-\ln x = \varphi(t)$. Lemma 1 provides a tight upper bound for $\varphi(t)$, where the maximum value $\varphi(t)$ coincides with $-\ln x$ when $t = 1/x$.

Introduce relaxation variables t_D and t_E. According to Lemma 1, given $p_J(n)$, $p_R(n)$ and $\rho(n)$, it is not difficult to derive the closed form of the optimal relaxation variables t_D and t_E as follows:

$$t_D^* = 1/(p_J(n)h_{JD}[n] + \sigma^2) \tag{9}$$

$$t_E^* = 1/(p_R(n)h_{RE}[n] + p_J(n)h_{JE}[n] + \sigma^2) \tag{10}$$

After performing convex optimization on the original problem, the block coordinate descent method can be used to gradually approximate the optimal solution of the original problem. The algorithm for alternating optimization solution is described as follows:

Algorithm 1: The algorithm for alternating optimization solution
Input: Given variables $l_J[n]$ and $l_R[n]$, initial variables $p_J^{(0)}(n)$, $p_R^{(0)}(n)$, $\rho^{(0)}(n)$;
Output: $p_J^*(n)$, $p_R^*(n)$, $\rho^*(n)$
(1) Assuming iteration times m=0 and threshold θ_1=10^{-6};
(2) Given $p_J^{(m)}(n)$, $p_R^{(m)}(n)$, and $\rho^{(m)}(n)$, find the optimal $t_D^{(m+1)}$ and $t_E^{(m+1)}$ based on equations (9) and (10);
(3) According to $t_D^{(m+1)}$ and $t_E^{(m+1)}$, solve for $p_J^{(m+1)}(n)$, $p_R^{(m+1)}(n)$, and $\rho^{(m+1)}(n)$;
(4) Update the value of objective function value of problem;
(5) m=m+1;
(6) Repeat Steps (2)-(5) until the objective function value is less than the threshold θ_1=10^{-6}.
(7) Update $p_R(n)$=$p_R^{(m)}(n)$, $p_J(n)$=$p_J^{(m)}(n)$, $\rho(n)$=$\rho^{(m)}(n)$;
(8) Return to joint optimization algorithm (Algorithm 2).

Based on the above solving process, the joint optimization algorithm proposed in this paper is described as follows:

Algorithm 2: The joint optimization algorithm
Input: Known parameters: $\beta_0,\eta,H,P_S,l_S[x_S,y_S]^T,l_D[x_D,y_D]^T,l_E[x_E,y_E]^T$;
Output: $l_J^*[n]$, $p_J^*(n)$, $p_R^*(n)$, $\rho^*(n)$;
(1) Assuming iteration times i=0 and $p_J^{(0)}(n)$, $p_R^{(0)}(n)$, $\rho^{(0)}(n)$, $l_J^{(0)}[n]$, $l_R^{(0)}[n]$, convergence accuracy of objective function θ=10^{-6};
(2) Given $p_J^{(i)}(n)$, $l_J^{(i)}[n]$, $p_R^{(i)}(n)$, and $\rho^{(i)}(n)$, find the optimal solution $l_R^{(i+1)}[n]$;
(3) Given $p_J^{(i)}(n)$,$p_R^{(i)}(n)$, $l_R^{(i+1)}[n]$, and $\rho^{(i)}(n)$, find the optimal solution $l_J^{(i+1)}[n]$;
(4) Given $l_R^{(i+1)}[n]$ and $l_J^{(i+1)}[n]$, find the optimal solution $p_R^{(i+1)}(n)$, $p_J^{(i+1)}(n)$, $\rho^{(i+1)}(n)$ by using algorithm 1;
(5) Update the value of objective function value;
(6) i=i+1;
(7) Repeat Steps (2)-(6) until the objective function value converges at the given accuracy θ or reaches the maximum number of iterations;
(8) Return the optimal solution $l_J^*[n]$=$l_J^{(i+1)}[n]$, $p_R^*(n)$=$p_R^{(i+1)}(n)$, $\rho^*(n)$=$\rho^{(i+1)}(n)$, $p_J^*(n)$=$p_J^{(i+1)}(n)$, $l_R^*[n]$=$l_R^{(i+1)}[n]$.

4 Simulation Experiment and Results Analysis

This section will evaluate and analyze the performance of the proposed scheme through simulation experiments.The simulation software adopts the Matlab software with R2018b version. The experimental scenario is set up as a simulated 1000M´1800M UAV communication network scenario(as shown in Fig. 3). Set the position of BSSN node S to (-300, 0), the position of legal receiving node D to (800, 200), the position of illegal eavesdropping node E to (200, -800). The relay UAV starts working at coordinates (430, 250), and the interference UAV starts outputting artificial noise interference at (-430, -250). The relay UAV and the interference UAV are moving towards each other.

The relevant initial parameters in the simulation experiment are set as follows: UAV's altitude H = 10m, unit path loss $\beta_0 = -30$db, AWGN power = -90dbm, flight time slot $N = 22$, source node transmission power $P_S = 0.1w$, relay UAV power threshold $P_R = 0.5w$, interference UAV power threshold $P_J = 0.5w$, relay UAV starting point $I_R{}^0 =$ (430, 250), interference UAV starting point $I_J{}^0 = (-430, -250)$, UAV remaining energy $P_{ba} = 0.01w$, energy harvesting efficiency $\delta = 0.9$, self interference channel coefficient $h_u = 0.7$, objective function threshold $\theta = 10^{-6}$.

The content of the simulation experiment is divided into two parts: one is to analyze the effectiveness and convergence of the proposed scheme, as well as the performance changes under different parameters; the second is to verify the superiority of the proposed scheme through performance comparison experiments. Two comparison schemes are: Scheme 1 is the proposed scheme with a fixed PS ratio of $\rho = 0.7$; Scheme 2 is a security optimization scheme without SWIPT technology.

Figure 3 shows the optimized trajectories of relay UAV and interference UAVs based on different work cycles in experiment. When the time slot N is set to 16, the relay UAV

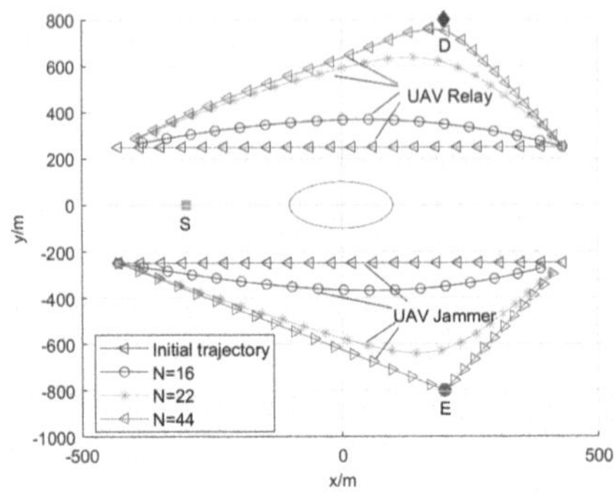

Fig. 3. The trajectory of UAV

is farthest from the receiving node D. When N = 44, the relay UAV's flight trajectory is closest to the node D. When the flight time is limited, the relay UAV cannot reach the optimal working position to perform the task. As the flight time increases, the relay UAV can approach the optimal service position to transmit more information to the node D. By comparing the optimized trajectories of interference UAV in three different time slot N, it can be observed that the more time the interference UAV obtains, the farther its trajectory is from the receiving node D and the relay UAV. At the same time, it is observed that with sufficient flight time, the optimized trajectory of the interference UAV is closer to the eavesdropping node E.

Figure 4 shows the average security rate iteration diagrams of the joint optimization scheme proposed in this paper for $N = 16$, 24, and 44. It can be seen that the average security rate increases with the given flight time. When the flight time is sufficient, the UAV can find the optimal working position to provide service to receiving node D.

Figure 5 shows the comparative experimental results of the average security rate between proposed scheme and scheme 2 under different remaining energy P_{ba}. It can be seen that when $P_{ba} = 0.4w$, scheme 2 gradually converges after the 50th iteration, while our scheme gradually converges to the extremum after the 40th iteration. When $P_{ba} = 0.04w$, the proposed scheme gradually converges after the 20th iteration, while scheme 2 only gradually converges after the 45th iteration, which indicate that the average security rate and convergence of proposed scheme are significantly better than scheme 2 under energy limitation.

Figure 6 shows the impact of P_S on the throughput of different relay networks. It can be seen that when the remaining energy is limited ($P_{ba} = 0.04w$), the average security rates in the three schemes increase with the increase of P_S. When the power P_S of the source node is the same, the average security rate of proposed scheme is better than the other two schemes, and the advantage expands with the increase of P_S.

Figure 7 analyzes the impact of UAV remaining energy P_{ba} on the security rate of different relay networks. It can be seen that as the P_{ba} decreases, the average security rate of the three schemes also significantly decreases.When there is more P_{ba}, the average security rate of both scheme 2 and proposed scheme is better than that of scheme 1. When P_{ba} is low, the average security rate of proposed scheme is better than the other two schemes.

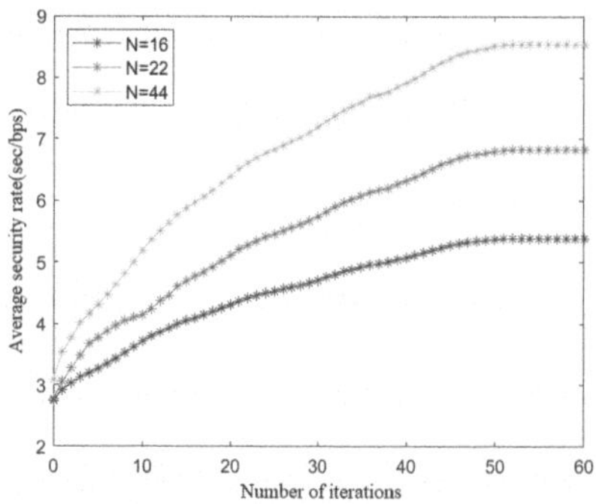

Fig. 4. Influence of different flight times on security rates

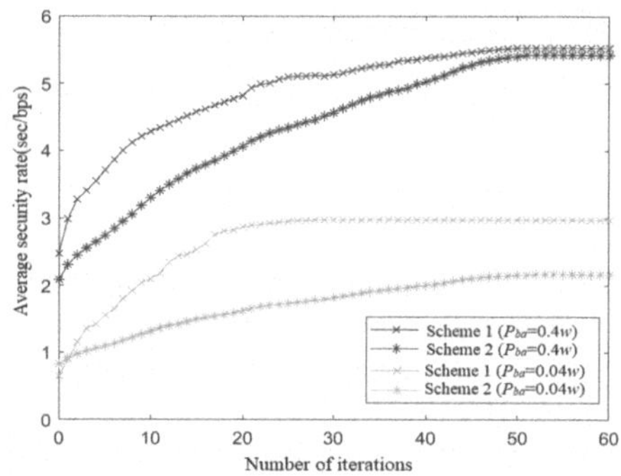

Fig. 5. Throughput iteration of joint optimization algorithm

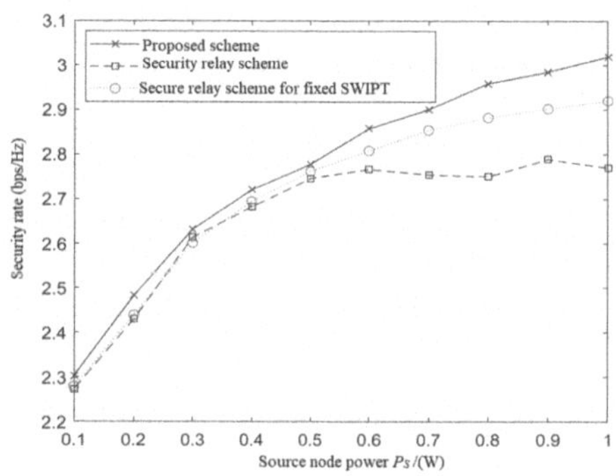

Fig. 6. Influence of P_S on the throughput under different relay systems.

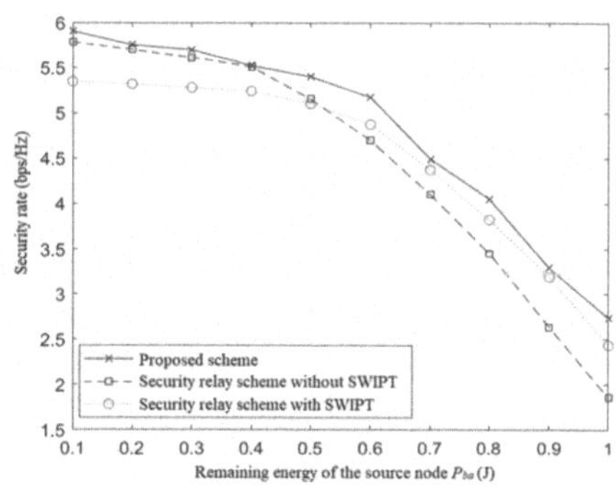

Fig. 7. The impact of self-energy recycling on the system throughput.

5 Conclusions

This paper investigates the transmission security problems in the UAVs relay network with self energy recycling under energy limitation. Aiming at communication scenarios with eavesdroppers and collaborative interference, a joint resource security allocation scheme based on collaborative interference and UAV assistance is proposed with the goal of maximizing security rate. Firstly, a secure transmission network framework for self energy recycling relay UAVs under collaborative interference is designed, and a mathematical optimization model is established under constraints such as safe transmission power threshold, maximum flight rate, and energy harvesting. Then, a resource allocation scheme based on continuous convex approximation is proposed for non convex secure rate optimization problems. In order to achieve maximum security rate, this scheme jointly optimizes the transmission power and flight trajectory of relay UAVs and interference UAVs, as well as the SWIPT PS ratio. The simulation experiment results show that the joint optimization scheme with collaborative interference can achieve secure transmission of self energy recycling and full duplex UAV relay network. In collaborative interference scenarios, the security performance of energy limited self energy recycling UAV relay networks is superior to conventional full duplex UAV relay networks.

References

1. Wang, W., Tang, J., Zhao, N., et al.: Joint precoding optimization for secure SWIPT in UAV-aided NOMA networks. IEEE Trans. Commun. **8**, 5028–5040 (2020)
2. İlhan, B.: Energy-efficient communication for UAV-enabled mobile relay networks. Comput. Netw. **213**, 10971 (2022)
3. Lyu, H., Jang, J., Lee, H., et al.: Non-Iterative optimization of trajectory and radio resource for aerial network. IEEE Trans. Wireless Commun. **24**, 1555–1567 (2025)
4. Zhou, J., Wang, M., Tian, D., et al.: Reliability-optimal UAV-assisted mobile edge computing: joint resource allocation, data transmission scheduling and motion control. IEEE Trans. Mob. Comput. **24**, 4217–4234 (2025)
5. Sabuj, S.R., Ahmed, A., Cho, Y., et al.: Cognitive UAV-aided URLLC and mMTC services: analyzing energy efficiency and latency. IEEE Access **9**, 5011–5027 (2021)
6. Senadhira, N., Durrani, S., Alvi, S.A., et al.: UAV-assisted IoT monitoring network: adaptive multiuser access for low-latency and high-reliability under bursty traffic. IEEE Trans. Commun. **73**, 5279–5294 (2025)
7. Wu, Q., Cui, M., Zhang, G., et al.: Latency minimization for UAV-enabled URLLC-based mobile edge computing systems. IEEE Trans. Wireless Commun. **23**, 3298–3311 (2024)
8. An Q., Pan Y., Han H., et al.: Secrecy capacity maximization of UAV-enabled relaying systems with 3D trajectory design and resource allocation. Sensors **22**, 4519 (2022)
9. Na, Z., Ji, C., Lin, B., et al.: Joint optimization of trajectory and resource allocation in secure UAV relaying communications for internet of things. IEEE Internet Things J. **9**, 16284–16296 (2022)
10. Sun G.,Li J.,Wang A.,Wu Q.,et al.: Secure and energy-efficient UAV relay communications exploiting collaborative beamforming. IEEE Trans. Commun. **70**, 5401–5416 (2022)
11. Tang, X., Liu, N., Zhang, R., et al.: Deep learning-assisted secure UAV-relaying networks with channel uncertainties. IEEE Trans. Veh. Technol. **71**, 5048–5059 (2022)
12. Duo, B., Luo, J., Li, Y., et al.: Joint trajectory and power optimization for securing UAV communications against active eavesdropping. China Commun. **18**, 88–99 (2021)
13. Wang, Z., Guo, J., Chen, Z., et al.: Robust secure UAV relay-assisted cognitive communications with resource allocation and cooperative jamming. J. Commun. Netw. **24**, 139–153 (2022)
14. Gong, H., Huang, B., Jia, B.: Energy-efficient 3-D UAV ground node accessing using the minimum number of UAVs. IEEE Trans. Mob. Comput. **23**, 12046–12060 (2024)
15. Tariq, Z.U.A., Baccour, E., Erbad, A., et al.: RL-Based adaptive UAV swarm formation and clustering for secure 6G wireless communications in dynamic dense environments. IEEE Access **12**, 125609–125628 (2024)
16. Yan, K., Xiang, L., Yang, K.: Cooperative target search algorithm for UAV swarms with limited communication and energy capacity. IEEE Commun. Lett. **28**, 1102–1106 (2024)
17. Shen, L., Wang, N., Zhang, D., et al.: Energy-aware dynamic trajectory planning for UAV-enabled data collection in mMTC Networks. IEEE Trans. Green Commun. Netw. **6**, 1957–1971 (2022)
18. Guan X., Wu Q., Zhang R.: Intelligent reflecting surface assisted secrecy communication: is artificial noise helpful or not?. IEEE Wireless Commun. Lett. **9**, 778–782 (2020)

An Angular Quantization-Guided Evolutionary Framework for Feature Selection in High-Dimensional Imbalanced Classification

Guanghua Lyu[1], Zefeng Lin[1], Yanzong Zheng[2], Genghui Li[1], and Yu Zhou[1](✉)

[1] College of Computer Science and Software Engineering, Shenzhen University, Shenzhen, China
{2400101051,2510103091}@mails.szu.edu.cn, ligh@szu.edu.cn, zhouyu_1022@126.com

[2] HKUST (Guangzhou) Information Hub, The Hong Kong University of Science and Technology (Guangzhou), Guangzhou, China
yzheng822@connect.hkust-gz.edu.cn

Abstract. High-dimensional imbalanced data are common in fields such as medical diagnosis and network security. Their complex feature spaces and skewed class distributions pose serious challenges to traditional classification methods. Feature selection is an effective way to alleviate these issues, but existing methods often struggle to balance classification performance and solution diversity. To address this, this paper proposes an angular quantization-guided non-dominated sorting genetic algorithm (AQ-NSGA) for many-objective feature selection. It leverages angular information to guide population evolution and maintain solution diversity by calculating the cosine similarity between new candidates and the population archive, determining whether to retain new individuals to prevent premature convergence. Moreover, AQ-NSGA employs a dynamically adjusted combined evolutionary operator to enhance exploration and convergence at different stages. Experiments on 10 real-world high-dimensional imbalanced datasets demonstrate that AQ-NSGA outperforms two state-of-the-art and two traditional algorithms in terms of balanced accuracy, g-mean, and recall. Ablation studies further confirm the effectiveness of the angular quantization component in improving classification performance.

Keywords: Feature selection · Angular quantization · Many-objective optimization · Classification

1 Introduction

Many real-world classification problems face challenges such as class imbalance (CI) and high-dimensionality (HD) of data, including microarray gene expression analysis [13] and medical image segmentation [10]. For instance, microarray

© The Author(s), under exclusive license to Springer Nature Singapore Pte Ltd. 2027
H. Sun et al. (Eds.): ChineseCSCW 2025, CCIS 2911, pp. 85–100, 2027.
https://doi.org/10.1007/978-981-92-0288-1_7

technology has played a significant role in cancer research involving thousands of features, where the class distribution is often highly imbalanced, with the majority class having far more samples than the minority class. Recently, feature selection (FS) has become increasingly important in the era of data explosion [21,27], showing great potential in addressing both CI and HD issues [25,26]. By extracting highly relevant information and removing redundant features, FS can significantly enhance both classification performance and computational efficiency [23].

Among these works, FS is often modeled as a multi-objective optimization problem (MOP) [6], where problems with four or more conflicting objectives are referred to as many-objective optimization problems (MaOPs) [8]. A general MOP with box constraints can be expressed as [4]:

$$\text{Minimize} \quad F(\mathbf{x}) = (f_1(\mathbf{x}), f_2(\mathbf{x}), \ldots, f_m(\mathbf{x}))^T, \quad \text{subject to} \quad \mathbf{x} \in \Omega, \tag{1}$$

where m is the number of objectives ($m \geq 4$ for MaOPs), and $\Omega = \prod_{i=1}^{n}[l_i, u_i] \subseteq \mathbb{R}^n$ defines the decision space bounded by l_i and u_i. The solution of an MOP is a Pareto-optimal set (PS) of nondominated solutions, whose objective vectors form the Pareto front (PF) [4], representing optimal trade-offs among objectives. Multi-objective evolutionary algorithms (MOEAs) can approximate multiple trade-off solutions in a single run without requiring convexity or continuity. Owing to their parallel search capability, MOEAs have been extensively applied to complex optimization tasks. Metaheuristic algorithms such as GAs, ACO, DE, ABC, and PSO have also shown strong global search ability in FS problems. Building on these, improved solution selection strategies have enhanced MOEA performance. For example, NSGA-II maintains diversity via crowding distance, while its variants NDCD and NSGA-II/SDR [14] refine this through dynamic crowding and strengthened dominance. However, as the number of objectives grows, maintaining diversity becomes harder. NSGA-III [3] mitigates this using reference point-based selection.

Despite the fact that the above algorithms have achieved some promising results, selecting the minimal and most precise set of key features from CI and HD datasets remains extremely challenging. Previous multi-objective FS methods often focus on improving classification accuracy and reducing the number of selected features, but they may struggle to balance these goals with maintaining solution diversity [5]. In contrast to the conventional MOEAs, recent studies revealed that angle-based evolutionary algorithms can effectively balance solution convergence and diversity by leveraging angular distance information as a global leader selection strategy to guide the population toward the PF [1,5,15,18]. Therefore, it is worthwhile to further explore multi-objective evolutionary algorithms that incorporate angular quantization.

To address the challenges posed by high-dimensional imbalanced data, this paper proposes an angular quantization-guided non-dominated sorting genetic algorithm (AQ-NSGA) for many-objective FS. By leveraging angular information to guide the evolutionary process, AQ-NSGA balances convergence toward the PF with solution diversity. Adaptive evolutionary operators and a weighted

KNN classifier further enhance exploration and classification performance in complex feature spaces. Overall, the proposed approach provides a promising framework for tackling many-objective FS problems in high-dimensional imbalanced data classification.

2 Related Works

2.1 Evolutionary Algorithms for FS

Many Pareto-based MOEAs struggle with many-objective optimization problems (MaOPs) due to dominance resistance (DR) and active diversity promotion (ADP) [17]. DR occurs when most solutions become mutually non-dominated in high-dimensional spaces, weakening selection pressure. ADP, meanwhile, preserves low-quality solutions merely for diversity, potentially slowing convergence. To mitigate DR, researchers have proposed relaxed dominance relations that enhance selection pressure toward the true Pareto front (PF), such as ϵ-dominance, CDAS-dominance, fuzzy Pareto dominance, and θ-dominance, all shown to outperform standard Pareto dominance. For ADP, tailored diversity mechanisms have been developed. For example, PS-NSGA [27] employs an accuracy-preferred dominance operator and quick bit mutation to favor individuals with higher classification accuracy. Saadatmand and Akbarzadeh-T [12] introduced JSEMO, a Jaccard Similarity-based method that jointly handles evolutionary feature selection and imbalanced classifier selection. Additionally, MOEA/D-SAS [2] balances convergence and diversity through decomposition-based sorting and angle-based selection, distinguishing it from conventional selection schemes.

While the aforementioned studies have advanced FS, challenges remain in handling HD and CI data. Some methods emphasize convergence at the expense of diversity, while others tend to retain low-quality solutions for diversity maintenance. Consequently, it is still difficult to achieve a good balance between classification accuracy and population diversity. These challenges highlight the need for explainable strategies, such as angular quantization-guided mechanisms, to preserve diverse and high-quality solutions in HD space.

2.2 Imbalanced FS

In recent years, Class-Imbalanced Feature Selection (CIFS) has attracted considerable attention due to its prevalence in real-world applications and importance in security domains. Multi-objective CIFS approaches generally fall into two categories: ensemble learning with sample space partitioning and weighting mechanisms. Ensemble methods partition the sample space into subregions and combine predictions from regional classifiers [22,24]. For example, some approaches integrate evolutionary undersampling with feature selection, optimizing F1-score and G-mean via multi-objective algorithms [9,11,25]. In contrast, weighting mechanisms offer a simpler alternative by adjusting feature or instance weights to handle imbalance [7], with methods like JSEMO leveraging similarity measures and dual-weighted classifiers.

These studies demonstrate the potential of evolutionary CIFS, but many still rely on fixed metrics and standard classifiers, limiting adaptability and potentially biasing the search. Partitioning-based methods can also worsen imbalance in certain subspaces. In this paper, we focus on weighting mechanisms for their simplicity and stability, and adopt a many-objective setting to jointly optimize accuracy, class balance, and feature reduction, providing a more comprehensive treatment of HD and CI problems.

3 The Proposed Method

3.1 Overall Framework

In the NSGA domain, random population initialization often results in individuals that are either too similar or overly different, leading to premature convergence or poor convergence, respectively. To address this, we propose an angular quantization-guided NSGA framework (AQ-NSGA) for class prediction on HD and CI data, as illustrated in Fig. 1. Components shaded in dark indicate our key innovations. Angular quantization is incorporated into both initialization and offspring generation to enhance population diversity, and further embedded in environmental selection by introducing an angular similarity-based penalty to the crowding distance. Moreover, individuals are real-valued encoded within bounded ranges, mitigating quality bias among them. The major components of the AQ-NSGA framework are detailed as follows:

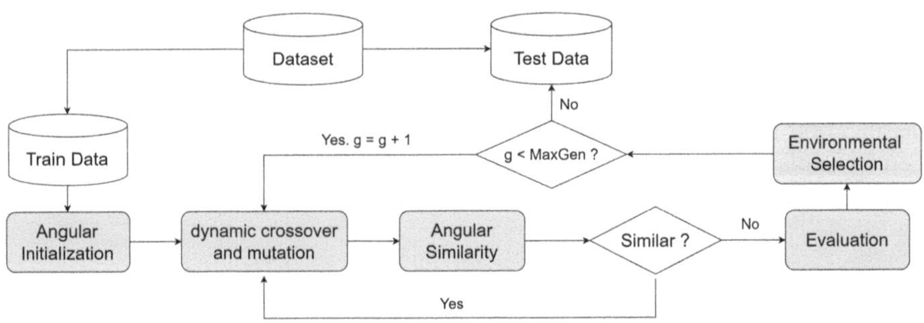

Fig. 1. The workflow of the proposed AQ-NSGA.

1. Population Initialization: Each individual is encoded as a real-valued vector. The first candidate is directly evaluated, while subsequent ones compute cosine similarity with existing individuals. A dynamic threshold determines whether the new solution is accepted, ensuring controlled diversity.

2. Offspring Generation: Parents are randomly selected, and offspring are produced via BLX-α crossover, which broadens the search region. Gaussian mutation introduces strong early perturbations, while non-uniform mutation in later stages refines convergence. An angle-based similarity check filters overly similar offspring to preserve diversity.
3. Fitness Evaluation: Each individual is evaluated by k-fold cross-validation over the selected features. Given the confusion matrix with true positives (TP), true negatives (TN), false positives (FP), and false negatives (FN), four objectives are optimized simultaneously: Accuracy (Acc), Sensitivity (Sen), Specificity (Sep), and the Number of Selected Features (NSF):

$$Acc = \frac{TP + TN}{TP + TN + FP + FN}, \quad Sen = \frac{TP}{TP + FN} \tag{2}$$

$$Sep = \frac{TN}{TN + FP}, \quad NSF = \frac{\mathcal{S}}{D} \tag{3}$$

where $\mathcal{S}$ and D denote the number of selected and total features, respectively. These metrics jointly form the objective vector for optimization.
4. Environmental Selection: The next generation is obtained using fast non-dominated sorting and crowding distance to ensure convergence and diversity. Duplicate solutions are removed. Within each PF, an angle-based penalty adjusts crowding distance, discouraging redundant individuals and enhancing the spread of the PF.

3.2 Angular Quantization Strategy

To preserve both quality and diversity while optimizing classification accuracy, we design an evolutionary framework guided by angular information. This idea not only directs population initialization and offspring generation, but also introduces a screening mechanism for selecting diverse, high-quality individuals. In environmental selection, angular information helps identify non-dominated individuals with greater diversity, ensuring that the most informative offspring drive exploration in the decision space. The inclusion of diverse offspring benefits the target task by broadening search directions.

Here, cosine similarity is used to measure angular relations among individuals in the decision space, owing to its robustness to outliers and focus on vector direction rather than magnitude [20]. It is defined as

$$\cos(\mathbf{x}, \mathbf{y}) = \frac{\mathbf{x} \cdot \mathbf{y}}{|\mathbf{x}|, |\mathbf{y}|} = \frac{\sum_{i=1}^{d} x_i y_i}{\sqrt{\sum_{i=1}^{d} x_i^2}, \sqrt{\sum_{i=1}^{d} y_i^2}}, \tag{4}$$

where $\mathbf{x}, \mathbf{y} \in \mathbb{R}^d$ are two vectors in the decision space. Larger values indicate greater directional similarity. In evolutionary optimization, this enables quantifying alignment among individuals in high-dimensional spaces, capturing structural redundancy while remaining scale-invariant.

For the population initialization and offspring generation stages, as written in Algorithm 1, each new offspring's cosine similarity with existing individuals is evaluated, and the maximum similarity guides evolution. In environmental selection, the cosine similarity between PF individuals is incorporated as a penalty term in crowding distance calculation to maintain diversity.

Algorithm 1. Angular Similarity Calculation

Input: Population archive A, new individual x_{new}
Output: $MaxScore$: the maximum similarity
1: Compute similarity scores between x_{new} and all individuals in A
2: Identify the individual with the highest score
3: Set $MaxScore$ as this score
4: **return** $MaxScore$

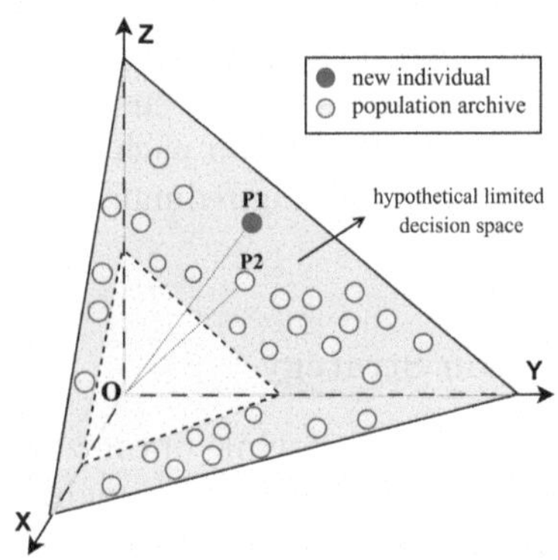

Fig. 2. A simple application example of cosine similarity in three-dimensional space. Obviously, the decision space dimension of the dataset is much higher, but the angluar quantization is still valid. (Color figure online)

As illustrated in Fig. 2, we assume a simple decision space where the red dot denotes a newly generated offspring and light-colored dots represent archived individuals. The offspring computes its cosine similarity with all archived individuals and records the maximum value. If this value is below a dynamic threshold, the offspring is retained; otherwise, it is discarded. During initialization (Algorithm 2), individuals are randomly generated as real-valued vectors within bounded ranges. When the archive is non-empty, cosine similarity is evaluated, and the threshold gradually tightens with iterations to ensure appropriate diversity. In the offspring generation stage, new individuals are produced through crossover and mutation, followed by the same angular filtering mechanism used in initialization.

In the environmental selection stage, an angle-based penalty is incorporated into the crowding distance to complement objective-space dispersion. Cosine similarity between individuals in the same PF is computed, and highly similar solutions are penalized to maintain diversity. Formally, let $s(x_i, x_j)$ denote the angular similarity defined in Eq. (4). If $s(x_i, x_j)$ exceeds a threshold τ, the adjusted crowding distance is:

$$CD'(x_i) = CD(x_i) - \lambda s(x_i, x_j), \tag{5}$$

where λ controls the penalty strength. This adjustment discourages redundant solutions and preserves diversity in the final population.

Algorithm 2. Population Initialization

Input: PopSize N, dimension D, threshold parameter θ
Output: Initialized population P

Initialize empty population P
for $i \leftarrow 1$ **to** N **do**
    Generate random vector $x \in [0.3, 0.7]^D$
    if $i > 1$ **then**
        Compute similarity s between x and P
        Set dynamic threshold $\tau = (1 - i/N) + \theta$
        if $s \geq \tau$ **then**
            Reject x and regenerate
    Evaluate fitness and objectives of x
    Store x and its attributes in P
return P

3.3 Adaptive Evolutionary Operators

A major advantage of real-value encoding in group evolutionary algorithms is its ability to directly represent and compute periodic continuous variables such as angles without extra discretization or mapping, greatly simplifying problems involving directions, rotations, or phases. It also aligns the solution representation with the natural expression of the problem, avoiding discrepancies between chromosome encoding and the search space. Real-coded genetic operations, such as crossover and mutation, can thus manipulate parameters directly and semantically—crossover produces intuitive intermediate solutions, while mutation (e.g., Gaussian perturbation) enables fine-grained local exploration. Consequently, the search becomes a more direct and efficient exploration of the true problem space, free from the constraints of binary encoding.

In this work, the BLX-α crossover operator is adopted to enhance exploration. Given two parent vectors p_1 and p_2, let $c_{\min} = \min(p_1, p_2)$, $c_{\max} = \max(p_1, p_2)$, and $I = c_{\max} - c_{\min}$. Each offspring c_k is generated by:

$$c_k = c_{\min} - \alpha I + (1 + 2\alpha) \cdot r \cdot I, \quad k = 1, 2, \tag{6}$$

where $\alpha \geq 0$ controls extrapolation and $r \sim U(0,1)$ is uniformly distributed. A larger α promotes global exploration, while a smaller one emphasizes local exploitation, effectively balancing diversity and convergence in the search.

We adopt a hybrid mutation strategy that applies Gaussian mutation in early generations and switches to non-uniform mutation later. Before mutation, each gene is decoded, perturbed, clipped to the feasible range, and re-encoded. Gaussian mutation introduces zero-mean perturbations to encourage global exploration:

$$\text{gene}_{\text{new}} = \text{gene}_{\text{original}} + \mathcal{N}(0, \sigma^2), \tag{7}$$

where σ is proportional to the gene range, ensuring appropriate mutation scales across dimensions.

As evolution progresses, non-uniform mutation performs finer, generation-dependent adjustments:

$$\text{gene}_{\text{new}} = \text{gene}_{\text{original}} + \Delta(g, r_1) \cdot (r - 0.5), \tag{8}$$

with $r, r_1 \sim U(0,1)$ and

$$\Delta(g, r_1) = (1 - r^{(1-g/g_{\max})^b}) \times \begin{cases} 1 - \text{gene}_{\text{original}}, & r_1 < 0.5, \\ \text{gene}_{\text{original}}, & r_1 \geq 0.5. \end{cases} \tag{9}$$

Here $b > 0$ controls the non-uniformity profile: large Δ at early stages enables wide exploration, while $\Delta \to 0$ as $g \to g_{\max}$ supports fine local search. The algorithm switches from Eq. (7) to Eq. (8) at a predefined generation. This hybrid design combines the global search ability of Gaussian mutation with the local refinement of non-uniform mutation, enhancing both diversity and convergence.

3.4 KNN Weighted Classifier

KNN is well-known for its simplicity, low computational cost, and effectiveness. However, its performance is suboptimal when dealing with high-dimensional imbalanced data. In contrast, KNN2W demonstrates superior performance. Similarly, following the approach in [12], we also adopt a weighted KNN algorithm with two metrics: label frequency of the data and the distance between the test point and its nearest neighbors. To enhance classification fairness and accuracy, in this paper, label frequency is assigned a higher weight to address imbalanced class distributions, ensuring that underrepresented classes receive adequate attention. Distance-based weights, maintain the influence of geometric proximity, ensuring that local structures are respected. To balance classification performance and efficiency, the number of nearest neighbors in KNN2W is fixed at 5, as supported by prior studies [16,19]. This setting strikes a balance between computational cost and the algorithm's capacity to generalize across datasets.

4 Experimental Setup and Result

4.1 Parameter Settings and Datasets

To achieve the fairest possible comparison, we have tried our best to keep the parameter settings of NSGA-II/SDR, NSGA-III, PS-NSGA, JSEMO, and AQ-NSGA consistent under a unified standard. The specific parameters are summarized in Table 2.

Table 1. Dataset

No.	Dataset	#Features	#Ins.	#Class	%Smallest	%Largest	Imbalance Ratio
1	SRBCT	2,308	83	4	13	35	2.69
2	Leukemia 1	5,327	72	3	13	53	4.08
3	DLBCL	5,469	77	2	25	75	3.00
4	9Tumor	5,726	60	9	3	15	5.00
5	Brain Tumor 1	5,920	90	5	4	67	16.75
6	Brain Tumor 2	10,367	50	4	14	30	2.14
7	Prostate	10,509	102	2	49	51	1.04
8	Leukemia 2	11,225	72	3	28	39	1.39
9	11Tumor	12,533	174	11	4	16	4.00
10	Lung Cancer	12,600	203	5	4	84	21.00

Table 2. Parameter settings for NSGA-II/SDR, NSGA-III, PS-NSGA, JSEMO, and AQ-NSGA. ($*$ indicates parameters specific to AQ-NSGA)

Parameter	Value
Population size (N)	100
Max iterations ($MaxIt$)	100
Number of objectives (M)	4
K-fold cross validation (k)	5
Convergence/selection threshold (Th)	0.98
Crossover $probability^*$ (p_c)	1
Mutation $probability^*$ (p_m)	1
Similarity threshold τ^*	$\tau = (1 - i/N) + \theta$

As shown in Table 2, the number of optimization objectives for all algorithms is unified to four to enable fair comparison in many-objective optimization. The parameters of the dynamic similarity threshold for AQ-NSGA are detailed in Algorithm 2. Since different algorithms emphasize distinct aspects, it is neither possible nor necessary to standardize classifiers, evolutionary operators, or diversity mechanisms. Ten real-world high-dimensional datasets with varying imbalance ratios (1.04–21.00) are selected, as listed in Table 1. These datasets cover a broad range of feature dimensions (hundreds to tens of thousands) and class numbers, representing diverse and challenging CI scenarios commonly used in prior studies [12,27]. To ensure robustness, each experiment is conducted using 10 runs of 5-fold cross-validation, maximizing data utilization and mitigating overfitting for more objective performance evaluation.

4.2 Benchmark Methods and Performance Metrics

To evaluate the effectiveness of the proposed AQ-NSGA, we compared it with several representative NSGA-based algorithms, including NSGA-II/SDR, NSGA-III, PS-NSGA, and JSEMO. These methods respectively emphasize similarity-driven diversity, reference point-based selection, problem-specific enhancement, and similarity-based diversity via Jaccard distance. Such comparisons allow a comprehensive assessment of how our angular quantization mechanism improves population diversity, convergence, and classification performance across different high-dimensional scenarios. The classification measures are Balanced Accuracy (BAC), Geometric Mean (G-mean), and Recall, while the optimization indicators include Hypervolume (HV). The classification metrics evaluate the predictive quality of selected feature subsets, and HV assesses the convergence and diversity of the obtained Pareto front. A Wilcoxon significance test with a 0.05 confidence level is applied to compare methods, where "+" and "−" denote results significantly better or worse than AQ-NSGA, respectively, and "≈" indicates no significant difference.

Let TP, TN, FP, and FN represent true positives, true negatives, false positives, and false negatives, respectively. The classification metrics are defined as follows:

$$\text{Recall} = \frac{TP}{TP + FN}, \quad \text{Specificity} = \frac{TN}{TN + FP}, \tag{10}$$

$$\text{BAC} = \frac{\text{Recall} + \text{Specificity}}{2}, \quad \text{G-mean} = \sqrt{\text{Recall} \times \text{Specificity}}. \tag{11}$$

BAC and G-mean are adopted to provide balanced evaluation of both majority and minority classes, mitigating the bias that often occurs in imbalanced datasets. Recall is further included to emphasize the detection capability of minority classes, which is critical in imbalanced scenarios. Beyond classification performance, the quality of the Pareto front (PF) is assessed using the Hypervolume (HV) indicator. HV measures the volume of the objective space dominated by the obtained solutions relative to a reference point, where larger values indicate better convergence and diversity. The reference point is defined by slightly extending the maximum values of the final PF to ensure all solutions are covered.

Table 3. Comparison of HV for Different Algorithms.

No.	NSGA-II/SDR	NSGA-III	PS-NSGA	JSEMO	AQ-NSGA
1	$0.6462 \pm 0.2560^{\approx}$	$0.7396 \pm 0.2679^{\approx}$	$0.3997 \pm 0.4365^{\approx}$	$0.5564 \pm 0.2258^{\approx}$	$\mathbf{0.7610 \pm 0.7164}$
2	$0.6535 \pm 0.3261^{\approx}$	$0.6041 \pm 0.1850^{\approx}$	$0.5620 \pm 0.4719^{\approx}$	$0.5548 \pm 0.2353^{\approx}$	$\mathbf{0.9813 \pm 0.6242}$
3	$\mathbf{0.8625 \pm 0.3611}^{+}$	$0.8484 \pm 0.2831^{+}$	$0.4082 \pm 0.5485^{\approx}$	$0.6458 \pm 0.3544^{+}$	0.1988 ± 0.0828
4	$3.2016 \pm 0.9830^{+}$	$3.2690 \pm 0.4193^{+}$	$\mathbf{50.8971 \pm 12.6509}^{+}$	$3.3722 \pm 0.6295^{+}$	1.2546 ± 1.2900
5	$1.6601 \pm 0.7150^{\approx}$	$1.5464 \pm 0.4885^{\approx}$	$\mathbf{13.7622 \pm 9.2547}^{+}$	$1.6954 \pm 0.4803^{\approx}$	1.3481 ± 0.6778
6	$\mathbf{1.3493 \pm 0.8714}^{+}$	$1.0917 \pm 0.4631^{\approx}$	$0.6346 \pm 0.7316^{\approx}$	$1.0716 \pm 0.5563^{\approx}$	0.7410 ± 0.4687
7	$0.6674 \pm 0.1471^{-}$	$0.6716 \pm 0.2076^{-}$	$0.0827 \pm 0.0537^{-}$	$0.6116 \pm 0.1801^{-}$	$\mathbf{1.6336 \pm 0.7318}$
8	$\mathbf{0.6882 \pm 0.5966}^{\approx}$	$0.4127 \pm 0.1257^{\approx}$	$0.0750 \pm 0.0735^{-}$	$0.5269 \pm 0.2138^{\approx}$	0.6079 ± 0.3282
9	$2.2897 \pm 0.2598^{+}$	$1.9272 \pm 0.3546^{+}$	$\mathbf{22.9532 \pm 16.0205}^{+}$	$2.6731 \pm 0.6106^{+}$	1.0308 ± 0.4554
10	$1.2121 \pm 0.2742^{\approx}$	$1.2707 \pm 0.5711^{\approx}$	$\mathbf{2.9693 \pm 2.6872}^{+}$	$1.2705 \pm 0.3610^{\approx}$	1.0376 ± 0.4604

Table 4. Comparison of BAC for Different Algorithms.

No.	NSGA-II/SDR	NSGA-III	PS-NSGA	JSEMO	AQ-NSGA
1	$0.9004 \pm 0.0329^{-}$	$0.8967 \pm 0.0408^{-}$	$0.8937 \pm 0.0376^{-}$	$0.9072 \pm 0.0251^{-}$	$\mathbf{0.9835 \pm 0.0056}$
2	$0.8954 \pm 0.0369^{-}$	$0.8998 \pm 0.0265^{-}$	$0.8853 \pm 0.0429^{-}$	$0.8724 \pm 0.0378^{-}$	$\mathbf{0.9671 \pm 0.0063}$
3	$0.8904 \pm 0.0284^{+}$	$0.8838 \pm 0.0418^{\approx}$	$\mathbf{0.8963 \pm 0.0245}^{+}$	$0.8902 \pm 0.0336^{+}$	0.8674 ± 0.0192
4	$0.6261 \pm 0.0323^{-}$	$0.6573 \pm 0.0310^{-}$	$0.6917 \pm 0.0559^{\approx}$	$0.6145 \pm 0.0274^{-}$	$\mathbf{0.6978 \pm 0.0159}$
5	$0.7814 \pm 0.0610^{-}$	$0.8002 \pm 0.0212^{-}$	$0.8800 \pm 0.0390^{\approx}$	$0.7762 \pm 0.0352^{-}$	$\mathbf{0.8719 \pm 0.0287}$
6	$0.8422 \pm 0.0582^{-}$	$0.8658 \pm 0.0281^{\approx}$	$\mathbf{0.8979 \pm 0.0287}^{+}$	$0.8570 \pm 0.0320^{\approx}$	0.8738 ± 0.0128
7	$0.8727 \pm 0.0262^{\approx}$	$0.8766 \pm 0.0382^{\approx}$	$\mathbf{0.9379 \pm 0.0143}^{+}$	$0.8695 \pm 0.0182^{\approx}$	0.8834 ± 0.0108
8	$0.9363 \pm 0.0377^{-}$	$0.9414 \pm 0.0213^{-}$	$0.9373 \pm 0.0144^{-}$	$0.9319 \pm 0.0177^{-}$	$\mathbf{0.9640 \pm 0.0108}$
9	$0.7939 \pm 0.0236^{-}$	$0.8167 \pm 0.0134^{-}$	$0.8875 \pm 0.0394^{-}$	$0.7903 \pm 0.0388^{-}$	$\mathbf{0.9161 \pm 0.0097}$
10	$0.8861 \pm 0.0249^{-}$	$0.8797 \pm 0.0238^{-}$	$0.9593 \pm 0.0148^{\approx}$	$0.8912 \pm 0.0278^{-}$	$\mathbf{0.9708 \pm 0.0022}$

4.3 Many-Objective Optimization Performance Analysis

Table 3 reports the HV values across all datasets. Overall, AQ-NSGA demonstrates competitive performance compared with other algorithms. On several datasets, such as Dataset 1 and Dataset 7, it achieves the highest HV values (0.7610 ± 0.7164 and 1.6336 ± 0.7318), indicating superior convergence and diversity. Even when not attaining the best results, AQ-NSGA maintains small variance and stable performance, reflecting its robustness and ability to avoid premature convergence. The Wilcoxon signed-rank test further supports these findings, showing that AQ-NSGA performs significantly better or comparably to most competitors on multiple instances. Although it may not dominate across all datasets, its stable and balanced behavior highlights a strong trade-off between exploration and convergence.

In summary, the results demonstrate that AQ-NSGA consistently delivers reliable Pareto fronts with good convergence–diversity balance, making it a robust and practical approach for high-dimensional feature selection tasks.

Table 5. Comparison of GM for Different Algorithms.

No.	NSGA-II/SDR	NSGA-III	PS-NSGA	JSEMO	AQ-NSGA
1	$0.8888 \pm 0.0401^-$	$0.8807 \pm 0.0558^-$	$0.8808 \pm 0.0475^-$	$0.8934 \pm 0.0412^-$	$\mathbf{0.9835 \pm 0.0056}$
2	$0.8852 \pm 0.0424^-$	$0.8863 \pm 0.0357^-$	$0.8641 \pm 0.0639^-$	$0.8534 \pm 0.0536^-$	$\mathbf{0.9669 \pm 0.0064}$
3	$0.8639 \pm 0.0546^{\approx}$	$0.8523 \pm 0.0681^{\approx}$	$\mathbf{0.8729 \pm 0.0469}^{\approx}$	$0.8715 \pm 0.0442^{\approx}$	0.8521 ± 0.0240
4	$0.3681 \pm 0.0616^-$	$0.4415 \pm 0.0745^-$	$0.4798 \pm 0.1255^-$	$0.3530 \pm 0.0559^-$	$\mathbf{0.5717 \pm 0.0333}$
5	$0.6820 \pm 0.1142^-$	$0.7285 \pm 0.0421^-$	$0.8265 \pm 0.0683^-$	$0.6680 \pm 0.0675^-$	$\mathbf{0.8536 \pm 0.0483}$
7	$0.8562 \pm 0.0319^-$	$0.8628 \pm 0.0485^{\approx}$	$\mathbf{0.9359 \pm 0.0146}^+$	$0.8473 \pm 0.0246^-$	0.8791 ± 0.0118
8	$0.9311 \pm 0.0494^-$	$0.9404 \pm 0.0220^-$	$0.9363 \pm 0.0148^-$	$0.9308 \pm 0.0182^-$	$\mathbf{0.9638 \pm 0.0109}$
9	$0.6991 \pm 0.0506^-$	$0.7436 \pm 0.0317^-$	$0.8379 \pm 0.0808^-$	$0.6885 \pm 0.0809^-$	$\mathbf{0.9125 \pm 0.0105}$
10	$0.8613 \pm 0.0365^-$	$0.8531 \pm 0.0352^-$	$0.9472 \pm 0.0265^-$	$0.8531 \pm 0.0530^-$	$\mathbf{0.9707 \pm 0.0023}$

Table 6. Comparison of RECALL for Different Algorithms.

No.	**NSGA-II/SDR**	**NSGA-III**	**PS-NSGA**	**JSEMO**	**AQ-NSGA**
1	$0.8501 \pm 0.0504^-$	$0.8425 \pm 0.0646^-$	$0.8392 \pm 0.0577^-$	$0.8591 \pm 0.0431^-$	$\mathbf{0.9649 \pm 0.0060}$
2	$0.8532 \pm 0.0491^-$	$0.8604 \pm 0.0357^-$	$0.8394 \pm 0.0641^-$	$0.8274 \pm 0.0554^-$	$\mathbf{0.9445 \pm 0.0079}$
3	$0.9486 \pm 0.0149^+$	$\mathbf{0.9538 \pm 0.0161}^+$	$0.9345 \pm 0.0182^+$	$0.9203 \pm 0.0176^+$	0.6981 ± 0.0328
4	$0.3121 \pm 0.0581^-$	$0.3746 \pm 0.0608^-$	$0.4313 \pm 0.1105^-$	$0.2958 \pm 0.0532^-$	$\mathbf{0.4696 \pm 0.0830}$
5	$0.6268 \pm 0.1076^-$	$0.6621 \pm 0.0385^-$	$\mathbf{0.7922 \pm 0.0714}^+$	$0.6135 \pm 0.0640^-$	0.7597 ± 0.0336
6	$0.7565 \pm 0.1009^-$	$0.7967 \pm 0.0501^-$	$0.8073 \pm 0.0491^{\approx}$	$0.7799 \pm 0.0593^-$	$\mathbf{0.8123 \pm 0.0111}$
7	$0.8381 \pm 0.0382^{\approx}$	$0.8543 \pm 0.0566^{\approx}$	$\mathbf{0.9374 \pm 0.0149}^+$	$0.8254 \pm 0.0301^-$	0.8469 ± 0.0360
8	$0.9135 \pm 0.0557^-$	$0.9213 \pm 0.0293^-$	$0.9166 \pm 0.0190^-$	$0.9097 \pm 0.0240^-$	$\mathbf{0.9578 \pm 0.0021}$
9	$0.6155 \pm 0.0461^-$	$0.6595 \pm 0.0261^-$	$0.7895 \pm 0.0770^-$	$0.6096 \pm 0.0745^-$	$\mathbf{0.8461 \pm 0.0433}$
10	$0.8141 \pm 0.0432^-$	$0.8052 \pm 0.0406^-$	$0.9361 \pm 0.0276^-$	$0.8201 \pm 0.0534^-$	$\mathbf{0.9625 \pm 0.0096}$

4.4 Classification Performance Analysis

Tables 4, 5 and 6 summarize the classification results across ten datasets. Overall, AQ-NSGA achieves consistently strong and stable performance, particularly on imbalanced datasets.

In terms of BAC and G-mean, AQ-NSGA frequently attains the best or near-best results, demonstrating its robustness in balancing majority and minority class performance. For instance, on Dataset 1, Dataset 2, Dataset 8, and Dataset 10, both BAC and G-mean exceed 0.96, clearly surpassing other methods. Even on more challenging datasets such as Dataset 4, AQ-NSGA still provides noticeable improvements (BAC: 0.6978 ± 0.0159, G-mean: 0.5717 ± 0.0333), indicating its resilience in severe imbalance conditions. Recall results further confirm AQ-NSGA's ability to capture minority-class patterns. On several datasets (e.g., Dataset 1, Dataset 2, Dataset 8, and Dataset 10), recall values remain above 0.94, showing that the algorithm effectively enhances sensitivity toward underrepresented samples. Although recall may decline slightly in certain datasets (e.g., Dataset 3), the corresponding BAC and G-mean remain competitive, reflecting a balanced trade-off between sensitivity and specificity. Significance tests verify that AQ-NSGA outperforms most competitors across BAC, G-mean, and Recall with statistically significant advantages in the majority of cases.

In summary, AQ-NSGA demonstrates robust and well-balanced classification capability, excelling especially in imbalanced scenarios while maintaining stability and strong generalization across diverse datasets.

4.5 Ablation Study

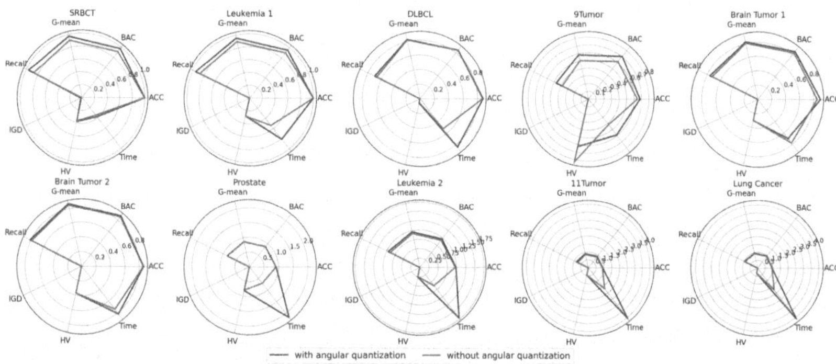

Fig. 3. Comparison of mean results of ablation experiments on angular quantization components.

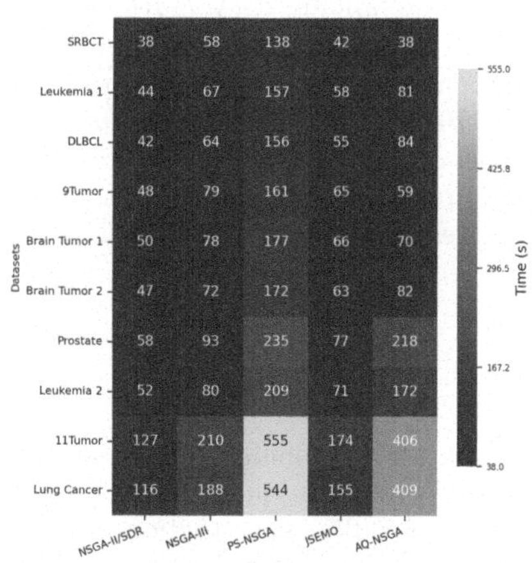

Fig. 4. Average computational cost (seconds) across datasets.

To evaluate the contribution of angular quantization, we performed an ablation experiment where it was removed from initialization, offspring generation, and environmental selection. The modified algorithm was tested on the same datasets and metrics, and results are summarized in Fig. 3. All indicators were normalized to ensure comparable scales. As shown in Fig. 3, AQ-NSGA consistently achieves higher BAC, G-mean, and Recall, confirming that angular quantization improves classification balance and robustness on imbalanced data. It also enhances convergence and diversity of the obtained PF, reflected by better HV performance. The corresponding time-cost comparison in Fig. 4 indicates a slight increase in runtime due to additional similarity computations, but this overhead is marginal compared to the notable gains in optimization and classification quality.

5 Conclusion

In this work, we propose AQ-NSGA, a many-objective FS method for high-dimensional and imbalanced data. The algorithm employs angular quantization to guide the evolutionary process, and adaptive operators to enhance the search efficiency. In addition, a weighted KNN classifier is incorporated to better handle class imbalance during evaluation. With these components, AQ-NSGA maintains population diversity and reduces classification bias. Experimental evaluations on ten real-world datasets demonstrate that AQ-NSGA consistently outperforms both traditional and advanced baselines, particularly on BAC, G-mean, and recall. The ablation study further confirms that angular quantization is an indispensable component, as removing it leads to clear performance degradation. Although the method entails a modest increase in runtime, the improvement in both classification quality and optimization stability makes the trade-off favorable. In the future, we aim to adapt this framework to broader data types and application domains, further enhancing its versatility and impact.

Acknowledgments. This work was supported by grants from the Guangdong Science and Technology Programme 2024B0101120003, the Natural Science Foundation China 72271168, the Shenzhen Science and Technology Program KJZD20230923114111021, the Guangdong Basic and Applied Basic Research Foundation 2024A1515012485, and the Shenzhen Fundamental Research Program JCYJ20220810112354002.

References

1. Alndiwee, M., Al-Mahairi, M.M., Hamdan, R.: A novel bundle adjustment approach based on guess-aided and angle quantization multiobjective particle swarm optimization (GAMOPSO) for 3D reconstruction applications. IEEE Access **10**, 71508–71520 (2022)
2. Cai, X., Yang, Z., Fan, Z., Zhang, Q.: Decomposition-based-sorting and angle-based-selection for evolutionary multiobjective and many-objective optimization. IEEE Trans. Cybern. **47**(9), 2824–2837 (2016)
3. Deb, K., Jain, H.: An evolutionary many-objective optimization algorithm using reference-point-based nondominated sorting approach, part i: solving problems with box constraints. IEEE Trans. Evol. Comput. **18**(4), 577–601 (2013)

4. Deb, K., Sindhya, K., Hakanen, J.: Multi-objective optimization. In: Decision Sciences, pp. 161–200. CRC Press (2016)
5. Han, F., Wang, T., Ling, Q.: An improved feature selection method based on angle-guided multi-objective PSO and feature-label mutual information. Appl. Intell. **53**(3), 3545–3562 (2023)
6. Jiao, R., Nguyen, B.H., Xue, B., Zhang, M.: A survey on evolutionary multiobjective feature selection in classification: approaches, applications, and challenges. IEEE Trans. Evol. Comput. (2023)
7. Kundu, R., Chattopadhyay, S., Cuevas, E., Sarkar, R.: AltWOA: altruistic whale optimization algorithm for feature selection on microarray datasets. Comput. Biol. Med. **144**, 105349 (2022)
8. Li, B., Li, J., Tang, K., Yao, X.: Many-objective evolutionary algorithms: a survey. ACM Comput. Surv. (CSUR) **48**(1), 1–35 (2015)
9. Liu, Y., Wang, Y., Ren, X., Zhou, H., Diao, X.: A classification method based on feature selection for imbalanced data. IEEE Access **7**, 81794–81807 (2019)
10. Medley, D.O., Santiago, C., Nascimento, J.C.: CyCoSeg: a cyclic collaborative framework for automated medical image segmentation. IEEE Trans. Pattern Anal. Mach. Intell. **44**(11), 8167–8182 (2021)
11. Qing, Y., Ma, C., Zhou, Y., Zhang, X., Xia, H.: Cooperative coevolutionary multi-objective genetic programming for microarray data classification. In: Proceedings of the Genetic and Evolutionary Computation Conference, pp. 804–811 (2021)
12. Saadatmand, H., Akbarzadeh-T, M.: Many-objective jaccard-based evolutionary feature selection for high-dimensional imbalanced data classification. IEEE Trans. Pattern Anal. Mach. Intell. **01**, 1–16 (2024)
13. Shah, M., Marchand, M., Corbeil, J.: Feature selection with conjunctions of decision stumps and learning from microarray data. IEEE Trans. Pattern Anal. Mach. Intell. **34**(1), 174–186 (2011)
14. Tian, Y., Cheng, R., Zhang, X., Su, Y., Jin, Y.: A strengthened dominance relation considering convergence and diversity for evolutionary many-objective optimization. IEEE Trans. Evol. Comput. **23**(2), 331–345 (2018)
15. Wang, C., Chen, Q., Xue, B., Zhang, M.: Semantics-guided multi-task genetic programming for multi-output regression. Pattern Recogn. **161**, 111289 (2025)
16. Wang, Z., Gao, S., Zhou, M., Sato, S., Cheng, J., Wang, J.: Information-theory-based nondominated sorting ant colony optimization for multiobjective feature selection in classification. IEEE Trans. Cybern. **53**(8), 5276–5289 (2022)
17. Xiang, Y., Zhou, Y., Li, M., Chen, Z.: A vector angle-based evolutionary algorithm for unconstrained many-objective optimization. IEEE Trans. Evol. Comput. **21**(1), 131–152 (2016)
18. Xiong, Z., Yang, J., Hu, Z., Zhao, Z., Wang, X.: Evolutionary many-objective optimization algorithm based on angle and clustering. Appl. Intell. **51**, 2045–2062 (2021)
19. Xue, B., Zhang, M., Browne, W.N.: Particle swarm optimization for feature selection in classification: a multi-objective approach. IEEE Trans. Cybern. **43**(6), 1656–1671 (2012)
20. Zhang, H., Chen, Q., Xue, B., Banzhaf, W., Zhang, M.: A semantic-based hoist mutation operator for evolutionary feature construction in regression. IEEE Trans. Evol. Comput. **28**(6), 1689–1703 (2023)
21. Zhang, Y., Wang, Y.H., Gong, D.W., Sun, X.Y.: Clustering-guided particle swarm feature selection algorithm for high-dimensional imbalanced data with missing values. IEEE Trans. Evol. Comput. **26**(4), 616–630 (2021)

22. Zhou, Y., Gao, L., Wang, D., Wu, W., Zhou, Z., Ye, T.: Imbalanced multi-fault diagnosis via improved localized feature selection. IEEE Trans. Instrum. Meas. (2023)
23. Zhou, Y., Kang, J., Kwong, S., Wang, X., Zhang, Q.: An evolutionary multi-objective optimization framework of discretization-based feature selection for classification. Swarm Evol. Comput. **60**, 100770 (2021)
24. Zhou, Y., Qiu, Y., Kwong, S.: Region purity-based local feature selection: a multiobjective perspective. IEEE Trans. Evol. Comput. **27**(4), 787–801 (2022)
25. Zhou, Y., Yang, N., Huang, X., Lee, J., Kwong, S.: A novel multiobjective genetic programming approach to high-dimensional data classification. IEEE Trans. Cybern. (2024)
26. Zhou, Y., Yang, N., Wang, R.: An embedded unlabeled data partitioning PU-learning method based on genetic programming. IEEE Trans. Comput. Soc. Syst. (2024)
27. Zhou, Y., Zhang, W., Kang, J., Zhang, X., Wang, X.: A problem-specific non-dominated sorting genetic algorithm for supervised feature selection. Inf. Sci. **547**, 841–859 (2021)

Optimizing Task Allocation Under Cold-Start Conditions: A Reputation-Based Approach for Complex Crowdsourcing

Shaohang Qi[1], Tao Bi[1], Hualei Yu[1], Zhan Bu[2], Weicheng Shao[1], and Jiuchuan Jiang[1(✉)]

[1] School of Computer and Artificial Intelligence, Nanjing University of Finance and Economics, Nanjing 210023, China
{1120230542,1120241398,1120251352}@stu.nufe.edu.cn, {9120231068,jcjiang}@nufe.edu.cn

[2] School of Computer Science, Nanjing Audit University, Nanjing 211815, China
zhanbu@nau.edu.cn

Abstract. In crowdsourcing platforms, complex tasks often require multiple skills and impose stringent quality requirements. Therefore, requesters tend to select workers with high reputations and extensive experience to increase the likelihood of successful task completion. However, this preference leads to a cold-start problem, as new workers with low reputations struggle to obtain tasks, while the limited number of reputable workers hampers overall task allocation efficiency. To address these challenges, this paper proposes a novel task allocation mechanism designed to alleviate the cold-start problem for new workers and enhance overall allocation performance. The proposed mechanism consists of three components: First, tasks are divided into two parts, with one part assigned to experienced workers and the other to new workers, allowing the latter to participate without compromising task quality. Second, a reputation update mechanism is introduced to adjust a worker's reputation based on their actual contributions, thus promoting the reputation growth of new workers. Finally, experimental results on a real-world crowdsourcing dataset demonstrate that the proposed method significantly improves task allocation success rates and the participation of new workers. It also increases the number of workers and tasks actually assigned, while achieving a more balanced allocation between different types of workers and tasks.

Keywords: Crowdsourcing · Cold start · Reputation · Worker Collaboration · Task Allocation

---

The work was supported in part by the National Natural Science Foundation of China under Grant (62476121 and 72371133), in part by the National Social Science Funds of China (22BGL261), and in part by Qing Lan Project of Jiangsu Province.

© The Author(s), under exclusive license to Springer Nature Singapore Pte Ltd. 2027
H. Sun et al. (Eds.): ChineseCSCW 2025, CCIS 2911, pp. 101–111, 2027.
https://doi.org/10.1007/978-981-92-0288-1_8

1 Introduction

The concept of crowdsourcing was first introduced by American writer Jeff Howe in 2006, referring to the use of collective intelligence to address problems [1]. In recent years, crowdsourcing has developed rapidly, leading to task allocation platforms that can be broadly divided into two categories: micro-task platforms, such as Amazon Mechanical Turk and Lionbridge [2], and complex-task platforms, such as Freelancer and Upwork [3]. Compared to micro-tasks, complex tasks are larger in scale, demand higher expertise and reputation, and often require collaborative teamwork for completion [4,5].

Current research on complex-task crowdsourcing primarily emphasizes task quality [6]. To ensure reliable outcomes, task requesters tend to prefer experienced workers with high reputations [7–9]. However, this practice excludes new workers with no prior reputation, creating a cold-start dilemma [10]. Without a track record, newcomers are often perceived as risky, making it difficult for them to gain trust and obtain assignments. This not only limits their participation and professional growth but also weakens the platform's ability to attract fresh talent, ultimately hindering sustainable development [11]. Moreover, the pool of experienced workers is limited. When demand surges, they cannot fully meet requesters' needs, leading to low allocation rates and inefficient resource utilization [12]. Thus, a critical challenge for complex-task crowdsourcing is how to effectively integrate new workers while maintaining task quality [13].

Several approaches have been proposed to mitigate the cold-start problem, yet they face notable limitations. SocialTransfer, for example, models worker skills by transferring knowledge from social networks, but its reliance on interpretable and consistent social data limits applicability to complex collaborative tasks [14]. Gong et al. [15] employed cross-platform influence estimation to identify potential candidates, but ignored the skill adaptation issues inherent to the tasks themselves. The GRLM model inferred the distribution of expertise from the worker relationship graph, which improved recommendation accuracy but assumed that some new workers already possessed expert skills—making it hard to address the cold-start issue for all new workers [16].

In summary, most existing studies focus on individual capability assessment and recommendation optimization [17], but rarely exploit collaboration to ease the cold-start problem. Furthermore, many methods are tailored to micro-tasks and are less applicable to complex tasks requiring multi-person cooperation [18]. To address this gap, this paper proposes a novel approach for integrating new workers with zero reputation into complex-task crowdsourcing. First, tasks are decomposed into components jointly executed by experienced and new workers, enabling participation without compromising quality. This collaborative task mechanism reduces exclusion risks and fosters reputation building. Second, we introduce a worker competitiveness metric, which quantifies a worker's relative advantage in securing assignments and prioritizes competitive workers during allocation, thereby lowering assignment failure rates. In addition, a reputation update mechanism adjusts workers' reputations based on their actual contributions, further alleviating the cold-start challenge. Finally, experiments on a real-world crowdsourcing dataset demonstrate that the proposed method outperforms existing approaches in task assignment success rate, new worker participation, and reputation growth.

The rest of this paper is structured as follows: Sect. 2 defines the problem; Sect. 3 presents the proposed allocation algorithm; Sect. 4 reports and analyzes experimental results; and Sect. 5 concludes the study.

2 Problem Description

In a crowdsourcing environment for complex tasks, new workers often struggle to secure opportunities to participate because they lack historical task records and have no reputation—leading to a cold-start problem. To help new workers overcome this cold-start dilemma and smoothly enter the task assignment process, this paper assigns tasks to teams of experienced and new workers, who complete them collaboratively. This ensures task quality while providing new workers with participation opportunities. This paper also introduces a reputation update mechanism. After a task is completed, a worker's reputation is updated according to their actual contributions to the task, thereby alleviating the cold-start problem faced by new workers with no reputation. This chapter is structured as follows: Sect. 2.1 covers the reputation update mechanism, and Sect. 2.2 outlines this paper's optimization objectives.

2.1 Reputation Update Mechanism

This paper enables experienced and new workers to collaborate on tasks, which ensures task quality while also granting new workers opportunities to participate. Once a task is completed, a worker's reputation is updated according to their actual contributions to the task. The reputation update mechanism primarily influences three key factors: a worker's actual workload, a task's required reputation threshold, and a task's required workload. It is defined as the number of workers needed to complete the task. Specifically, the required reputation for task t is $R_t \in [0, 1.0]$, the reputation of worker w_i is $R_{w_i} \in [0, 1.0]$, the required workload for task t is $workload_t \in [0, 1000]$, and the maximum workload a worker can take on at one time is $workload_{w_i} \in [0, 100]$. Therefore, the mechanism is defined as follows:

$$R_{w_i} = R_{w_i} + Enhance_{w_i \to t} \tag{1}$$

$$Enhance_{w_i \to t} = (1 - R_{w_i}) \left(1 - e^{-k\left(\frac{workload_{w_i,t}}{workload_t} + R_t\right)}\right) \tag{2}$$

Specifically, R_{w_i} represents a worker's reputation, $Enhance_{w_i \to t}$ denotes the increase in a worker's reputation after successful task completion, $\text{workload}_{w_i,t}$ is the actual workload that worker w_i undertakes in task t, workload_t is the workload required for task t, R_t is the reputation required for task t, k controls the rate of reputation growth. Here, k is assigned different values for experienced and new workers to achieve distinct growth rates, which prevents extreme scenarios. Examples include experienced workers' reputation approaching 1 after completing only a few tasks, or new workers gaining minimal reputation from one task and thus being unable to participate in subsequent tasks.

$$R_{w_i} = R_{w_i} - Down_{w_i \to t} \tag{3}$$

$$Down_{w_i \to t} = R_{w_i} \left(1 - e^{-k\left(\frac{workload_{w_i,t}}{workload_t} + R_t\right)}\right) \tag{4}$$

Specifically, R_{w_i} represents a worker's reputation, $Down_{w_i \to t}$ denotes the decline in a worker's reputation if a task fails, $workload_{w_i,t}$ is the actual workload that worker w_i undertakes in task t, $workload_t$ is the workload required for task t, R_t is the reputation required for task t, k controls the rate of reputation growth.

In addition, the actual workload $workload_{w_i,t}$ that worker w_i undertakes in task t falls into two categories: the actual workload taken on by experienced workers, and that taken on by new workers. The factors influencing a worker's actual workload are as follows: the maximum workload a worker can take on at one time; the total maximum workload that experienced workers in the selected worker group for task t can take on at one time; the workload required for the task; and a threshold. This threshold is defined as the proportion of task t workload that can be allocated to new workers. The specific formula is as follows:

$$workload_{w_k,t} = \frac{workload_{w_k}}{\sum_{\forall w_k \in W_t} workload_{w_k}} \cdot workload_t (1 - \tau_t) \tag{5}$$

In this context, $workload_{w_k,t}$ represents the actual workload that an experienced worker undertakes in task t, $workload_{w_k}$ denotes the maximum workload an experienced worker can take on at one time, $\sum_{\forall w_k \in W_t} workload_{w_k}$ is the total maximum workload that experienced workers in the selected group for task t can take on at one time, $workload_t$ is the workload required for task t, τ_t is the workload fraction (threshold) that can be allocated to new workers.

$$workload_{w_j,t} = \frac{workload_{w_j}}{\sum_{\forall w_j \in W_t} workload_{w_j}} \cdot workload_t \cdot \tau_t \tag{6}$$

In this context, $workload_{w_j,t}$ represents the actual workload of a new worker in task t, $workload_{w_j}$ denotes the maximum workload a new worker can take on at one time, $\sum_{\forall w_j \in W_t} workload_{w_j}$ is the total maximum workload that new workers in the selected group for task t can take on at one time, $workload_t$ is the workload required for task t, τ_t is the workload fraction (threshold) that can be allocated to new workers.

2.2 Optimization Objective

By introducing a reputation update mechanism, this paper establishes the following optimization objectives: 1) Maximize the team's overall reputation upon task completion; 2) Minimize the total wages paid to the team's workers. Additionally, the team must satisfy the following constraints: 1) The total salary of the team's workers must not exceed the task budget; 2) The team's total workload capacity must be greater than the workload required for the task; 3) The total workload assigned to new workers in the team must be less than or equal to the threshold percentage of the task's total workload; 4) For each skill required by the task, there must be at least one worker with a high reputation in that skill. Thus, the objective function for this paper's complex task allocation model can be formalized as:

$$W_t = \arg\max_{W_t \subseteq W} \left(\frac{\sum\limits_{\forall w_i \in W_t} Enhance_{w_i \to t}}{\sum\limits_{\forall w_i \in W_t} \gamma_{w_i}} \right)$$

$$\begin{aligned} \text{s.t.} \quad & \sum_{\forall w_i \in W_t} \gamma_{w_i} \leq b_t \\ & \sum_{\forall w_i \in W_t} workload_{w_i} \geq workload_t \\ & \sum_{\forall w_j \in W_t} workload_{w_j} \leq workload_t \cdot \tau_t \\ & \forall S_t(j) \in S_t, \exists w_i \in W_{S_t(j)}, R_{w_i} \geq R_t \end{aligned} \tag{7}$$

In this context, $\sum\limits_{\forall w_i \in W_t} Enhance_{w_i \to t}$ represents the total increase in the team's overall reputation after task completion, $\sum\limits_{\forall w_i \in W_t} \gamma_{w_i}$ is the total salary of the team's workers, b_t denotes the task budget, $\sum\limits_{\forall w_i \in W_t} workload_{w_i}$ is the total workload capacity of the team's workers, $workload_t$ is the workload required for task t, $\sum\limits_{\forall w_j \in W_t} workload_{w_j}$ is the total workload assigned to new workers in the team, τ_t is the workload fraction (threshold) allocable to new workers, $W_{S_t(j)}$ is the set of workers possessing individual skills required for task t, R_{w_i} represents a worker's reputation, R_t is the reputation required for task t.

3 Task Allocation Model Based on the Algorithm for Maximizing Team Reputation Improvement

This chapter introduces a worker competitiveness metric, which gauges a worker's advantage over others in securing tasks. By comprehensively considering both task and worker attributes, the most suitable worker is selected for each task. The structure of this chapter is outlined below: Sect. 3.1 presents the worker selection mechanism, which prioritizes workers with high competitiveness for team inclusion. Section 3.2 designs an algorithm to maximize the team's overall reputation increase. This algorithm comprehensively accounts for team composition, reputation growth, and cost control to form an optimal worker team that meets all constraints.

3.1 Worker Selection Mechanism

Workers differ in their credibility, maximum workload capacity, salary, and task coverage. This means their competitiveness relative to a given task also varies. In practical task allocation, teams often face skill shortages or insufficient workload capacity among existing workers to meet task requirements. To address this issue, we propose that a worker will be more conducive to the smooth completion of a task if they possess either skills currently lacking in the team, or skills the team already has but for which existing workload capacity is insufficient to meet task demands. Thus, the competitiveness of worker w_i relative to task t can be formalized as follows:

$$V_{w_i \to t} = \frac{\dfrac{workload_{w_i}}{workload_t} + \dfrac{|S_{w_i} \cap (S_t - S_{W_t})|}{|S_t|}}{\gamma_{w_i}} \cdot R_{w_i} \tag{8}$$

In this context, $workload_{w_i}$ represents the maximum workload a worker can undertake, $workload_t$ denotes the lack of workload for the task t, $\left|\frac{S_{w_i} \cap (S_t - S_{W_t})}{S_t}\right|$ is the extent to which a worker covers the skills currently lacking for task t, R_{w_i} is a worker's reputation (for experienced workers, R_{w_i} reflects their actual reputation, while new workers are assigned a default value of R_t, the reputation required for the task, to enable their participation in task competition), γ_{w_i} is the worker's salary.

3.2 Algorithm for Maximizing Team's Overall Reputation Improvement

In Sect. 3.1, this paper presents a worker selection mechanism designed to identify highly competitive workers and form an optimal competitive team. Specifically, the algorithm first partitions the task workload into two segments based on the task threshold, assigning each segment to experienced workers and new workers respectively. Following this workload division, the mechanism evaluates two key aspects: skills currently lacking in the team, and existing skills whose current capacity is insufficient to meet task requirements. It then selects workers who both satisfy task demands and demonstrate high competitiveness to join the team. Under the constraint of budget limitations, workers are continuously screened and incorporated until all task requirements are fully met. The task allocation algorithm is detailed as follows:

4 Experimental Verification and Analysis

4.1 Experimental Parameter Settings

This experiment is based on the Freelancer crowdsourcing dataset. The dataset includes two types of information: worker-related details (skills, salary, maximum one-time workload capacity, and reputation) and task-related details (required skills, required reputation, budget, workload, and threshold the proportion of workload allocable to new workers). Each worker can possess up to five distinct skills, and each task requires up to five distinct skills. For this experiment, key parameters are set as follows: the required reputation for a task $R_t \in [0.8, 0.9]$, the required workload $workload_t$ ranges from 0 to 500, the threshold τ_t ranges

---

Algorithm 1. Team Reputation Growth Maximization Algorithm (TRGM)

Require: Task set T, Worker set W
Ensure: Task allocation results

$W_{S_t(j)} \leftarrow \varnothing$ ▷ Initialize the skill matching worker set
for $t \in T$ **do** ▷ Screening experienced and new workers who meet task skill requirements
  for $w_i \in W$ **do**
    if $(S_t(j) \in S_{w_i}) \wedge (R_{w_i} \geq R_t || R_{w_i} == 0)$ **then**
      $W_{S_t(j)} = W_{S_t(j)} \cup \{w_i\}$
    end if
  end for
  while $b_t \geq 0$ **and** $\sum_{\forall w_i \in W_t} workload_{w_i} \leq workload_t$ **do**
    for $S_t(j) \in S_t$ **do**
      for $w_i \in W_{S_t(j)}$ **do** ▷ Calculating worker competitiveness
        $$V_{w_i \to t} = \frac{1}{\gamma_{w_i}} \cdot \left(\frac{workload_{w_i}}{workload_t} + \frac{|S_{w_i} \cap (S_t - S_{W_t})|}{|S_t|} \right) \cdot R_{w_i}$$
      end for
      if $(V_{w_i \to t} == \max\{w_i \in W_{S_t(j)} \mid V_{w_i \to t}\}) \wedge (b_t \geq \gamma_{w_i}) \wedge (\sum_{\forall w_j \in W_t} workload_{w_j} \leq workload_t \cdot \tau_t)$ **then**
        $W_t = W_t \cup \{w_i\}$ ▷ Select the best workers to join the team
        $b_t = b_t - \gamma_{w_i}$ ▷ Update remaining budget
      end if
      for $S_t(j) \in W_{S_t(k)}$ **do**
        $W_{S_t(k)} = W_{S_t(k)} - \{w_i\}$
      end for
    end for
  end while
  if success **then**
    for $w_i \in W_t$ **do**
      $R_{w_i} = R_{w_i} + Enhance_{w_i \to t}$ ▷ Update worker reputation value
    end for
  end if
end for

---

from 0.3 to 0.5, the reputation of experienced workers w_k ranges from 0.8 to 1.0, each worker's maximum work-load capacity ranges from 50 to 100. In the reputation update mechanism, the value of k is set to 1 for experienced workers and 2 for new workers. The experiment was implemented in Python 3.9, running on a system equipped with an AMD Ryzen 5 5600H with Radeon Graphics (3.30 GHz) and 16 GB of memory.

4.2 Evaluation and Comparison Methods

Under the same worker pool conditions, this paper compares the proposed method with alternative approaches using four key metrics. These metrics are designed to fully demonstrate its performance, including: number of successfully assigned tasks, number of newly hired workers assigned successfully, average reputation increase of new workers, and budget savings. These metrics comprehensively reflect task assignment success rate, new worker participation rate, new worker reputation growth, and cost reduction. The specific comparison method is outlined below.

- **Cost Minimization-Based Task Allocation** (CMB): This approach prioritizes workers with lower costs, provided that the selected workers meet the task requirements.
- **Reliability-Based Task Allocation** (RB): This approach prioritizes workers with higher reputation, with the prerequisite that the workers satisfy the task's basic requirements.
- **Randomized Task Allocation** ($RANDOM$): This approach randomly selects workers from the candidate pool, as long as the selected workers meet the task requirements.
- **First-Come-First-Served Task Allocation** ($FCFS$): This approach gives priority to workers who submit applications first, on the condition that the workers meet the task's requirements.

4.3 Experimental Results

Impact of Task Number Variations on Allocation Outcomes. In crowdsourcing platforms, variations in task number often exert a significant impact on task allocation. To analyze this impact, we fixed the number of workers at 8,000 and gradually increased the number of tasks from 200 to 1,000, then compared changes in the four key metrics across different task numbers. As shown in Fig. 1, as task number increases, our approach outperforms the four benchmark algorithms across all four key metrics: number of successfully assigned tasks, number of newly hired workers assigned successfully, average reputation increase of new workers, and budget savings. This is mainly because our method comprehensively considers both task attributes and worker capabilities. By introducing a worker competitiveness metric, we achieve more accurate worker selection and avoid the mismatch issue caused by the one-sided considerations of traditional algorithms. In contrast, while the CMB and RB algorithms can optimize task

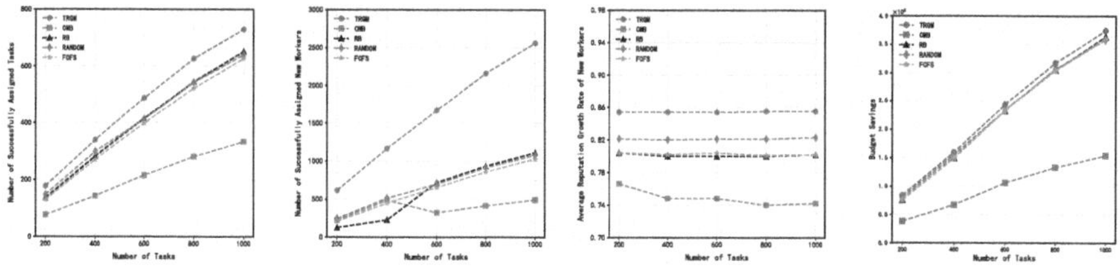

(a) Number of Successfully Assigned Tasks (b) Number of Successfully Assigned New Workers (c) Average Reputation Growth Rate of New Workers (d) Budget Savings

Fig. 1. Impact of Task Number Variations on Key Metrics.

costs or ensure task completion quality to some degree, they fail to account for new workers' participation. The *RANDOM* and *FCFS* algorithms, due to their random selection and first-come-first-served logic, easily lead to unfair allocation—ultimately resulting in low task allocation rates and worker utilization. Overall, our approach demonstrates greater stability and adaptability in response to task number changes.

Impact of Task Budget Variations on Allocation Outcomes. In addition to total task number, task budgets also exert a significant impact on task allocation performance. To explore how budget variations affect allocation performance, we fixed the number of workers at 8,000 and task number at 1,000 in the experiment. We then gradually increased the task budget from 50% to 150% of the original amount and observed trends in the various metrics. As shown in Fig. 2, the task allocation success rate of all algorithms generally rises with increasing task budgets. However, our method consistently outperforms the other algorithms in two key metrics: number of successfully allocated tasks and number of successfully allocated new workers. This advantage stems from the fact the fact that our method does not only focus on individual worker characteristics (e.g., cost or reputation) but also incorporates the multidimensional traits of both new and experienced workers by constructing a worker competitiveness index, thus enabling a more adaptive worker selection strategy. Furthermore, our method outperforms the comparison approaches in terms of average reputation increase for new workers and budget savings. In contrast, the *CMB* and *RB* algorithms prioritize local optima (e.g., cost minimization or reputation maximization) and fail to fully account for new workers, leading to lower new worker allocation success rates. The *RANDOM* and *FCFS* algorithms lack regulatory mechanisms for selection strategies and are highly random, resulting in moderately inferior performance.

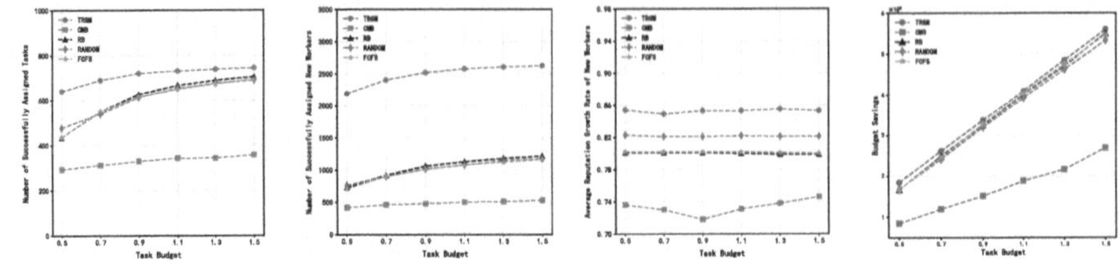

(a) Number of Successfully Assigned Tasks (b) Number of Successfully Assigned New Workers (c) Average Reputation Growth Rate of New Workers (d) Budget Savings

Fig. 2. Impact of Task Budget Variations on Key Metrics.

5 Conclusion

To address the challenge in existing crowdsourcing research on complex tasks, where new workers remain idle for extended periods due to their initial zero reputation, this paper proposes a three-part solution. First, we divide tasks by their threshold and assign them to experienced and new workers for collaborative completion. This approach provides new workers with participation opportunities while ensuring task quality. Second, we introduce a worker competitiveness metric that comprehensively considers both worker and task attributes. This metric helps select highly competitive workers for tasks, reducing the probability of task assignment failure. Third, we propose a reputation update mechanism that adjusts workers' reputations based on their actual contributions to tasks. This alleviates the cold-start problem faced by new workers due to their initial zero reputation.

To validate the effectiveness of our proposed method, we conducted experiments on a real crowdsourcing dataset and compared its performance with existing methods across multiple dimensions. The experimental results show that our method outperforms other approaches in task assignment success rate and budget savings, which fully demonstrates its effectiveness and applicability.

Conflict of Interest. The authors declare that they have no conflict of interest.

References

1. Lenart-Gansiniec, R., Czakon, W., Sułkowski, Ł, et al.: Understanding crowdsourcing in science. RMS **17**(8), 2797–2830 (2023)
2. Maddalena, E., Ibáñez, L.D., Reeves, N., et al.: Qrowdsmith: enhancing paid micro-task crowdsourcing with gamification and furtherance incentives. ACM Trans. Intell. Syst. Technol. **14**(5), 1–26 (2023)
3. Jiang, J., Zhou, Y., Jiang, Y., et al.: Batch allocation for decomposition-based complex task crowdsourcing e-markets in social networks. Knowl.-Based Syst. **194**, 105522 (2020)

4. Jiang, J., An, B., Jiang, Y., et al.: Group-oriented task allocation for crowdsourcing in social networks. IEEE Trans. Syst. Man Cybern.: Syst. **51**(7), 4417–4432 (2021)
5. Jiang, J., Di, K., An, B., et al.: Batch crowdsourcing for complex tasks based on distributed team formation in e-markets. IEEE Trans. Parallel Distrib. Syst. **33**(12), 3600–3615 (2022)
6. Jiang, J., An, B., Jiang, Y., et al.: Batch allocation for tasks with overlapping skill requirements in crowdsourcing. IEEE Trans. Parallel Distrib. Syst. **30**(8), 1722–1737 (2019)
7. Jiang, J., An, B., Jiang, Y., et al.: Context-aware reliable crowdsourcing in social networks. IEEE Trans. Syst. Man Cybern.: Syst. **50**(2), 617–632 (2020)
8. Li, J., Jiang, L., Zhang, W.: Label consistency-based ground truth inference for crowdsourcing. IEEE Trans. Neural Netw. Learn. Syst. **36**(5), 9408–9421 (2024)
9. Garaus, C., Garaus, M., Wagner, U.M.: Getting users involved in idea crowdsourcing initiatives: an experimental approach to stimulate intrinsic motivation and intention to submit. IEEE Trans. Eng. Manag. **71**, 3700–3711 (2024)
10. Han, L., Checco, M.E., A.: Crowd worker strategies in relevance judgment tasks. In: Proceedings of the 13th International Conference on Web Search and Data Mining, vol. 2020, pp. 241–249
11. Suyal, H., Singh, A.: Multilabel classification using crowdsourcing under budget constraints. Knowl. Inf. Syst. **66**(2), 841–877 (2024)
12. Bazaluk, O., Rahman, M.A., Zayed, N.M., et al.: Crowdsourcing review: the crowd workers' perspective. J. Ind. Bus. Econ. **51**(3), 647–666 (2024)
13. Lian, R., Zheng, Y., Wang, C.: Privro: a privacy-preserving crowdsourcing service with robust quality awareness. IEEE Trans. Serv. Comput. **17**(4), 1682–1697 (2024)
14. Zhao, Z., Cheng, J., Wei, F., et al.: Socialtransfer: transferring social knowledge for cold-start crowdsourcing. In: Proceedings of the 23rd ACM International Conference on Information and Knowledge Management, pp. 779–788 (2014)
15. Gong, Q., Chen, Y., He, X., et al.: Cross-site prediction on social influence for Cold-Start users in online social networks. ACM Trans. Web (TWEB) **15**(2), 1–23 (2021)
16. Zhao, Z., Wei, F., Zhou, M., et al.: Cold-Start expert finding in community question answering via graph regularization. In: Database Systems for Advanced Applications: 20th International Conference, DASFAA 2015, Hanoi, Vietnam, 20–23 April 2015, Proceedings, Part I. Springer, pp. 21–38 (2015)
17. Jiang, X., Zhang, J., Wu, M., et al.: TiFedCrowd: federated crowdsourcing with time-controlled incentive. IEEE Trans. Emerg. Top. Comput. Intell. **9**(2), 1514–1526 (2024)
18. Jiang, J., An, B., Jiang, Y., et al.: Understanding crowdsourcing systems from a multiagent perspective and approach. ACM Trans. Auton. Adaptive Syst. (TAAS) **13**(2), 1–32 (2018)

ACRO-NEEP: A Hierarchical Cooperative Optimization Framework for Symbolic Regression

Fan Yang[1], Shuangrong Liu[1(✉)], Ao Peng[1], Lin Wang[1(✉)], Bo Yang[1], and Xutong Wang[2]

[1] Shandong Key Laboratory of Ubiquitous Intelligent Computing, University of Jinan, Jinan 250022, China
ise_liusr@ujn.edu.cn, liusr.constant@gmail.com
[2] School of Statistics and Mathematics, Yunnan University of Finance and Economics, Kunming 650221, China

Abstract. The neural encoding expression programming (NEEP) has recently emerged as a promising direction in symbolic regression, but existing methods face two key limitations: 1) Poor coefficient optimization: coefficients in mathematical expressions often come from predefined constant pools or random initialization, rather than being adaptively tuned according to given data. This limitation causes inadequate coefficient optimization, thereby hindering the quality of the generated expression. 2) Unstable updates of the expression structure: The mapping from neural network to symbolic expressions is highly nonlinear, meaning that small perturbations in the weights of the neural network may lead to significant structural changes in the generated expressions. This instability hinders the robustness of NEEP. To solve these limitations, a hierarchical co-optimization framework, ACRO-NEEP is proposed in this study, which can adaptively optimize the structure and coefficients of expressions simultaneously. In addition, a multidimensional similarity-guided search strategy is designed to dynamically guide the optimization process by evaluating symbolic, structural, and functional similarities. This strategy mitigates the instability caused by nonlinear mapping and improves the robustness and convergence efficiency of the ACRO-NEEP. Experimental results demonstrate that ACRO-NEEP significantly outperforms mainstream comparative algorithms on the vast majority of problems, particularly exhibiting notable advantages on high-dimensional and complex tasks.

Keywords: Symbolic Regression · Neural Encoding Expression Programming · Coefficient Optimization · Covariance Matrix Adaptation Evolution Strategy

1 Introduction

Automatically discovering the mathematical relationship between variables from observational data is the core problem in scientific discovery and engineering

© The Author(s), under exclusive license to Springer Nature Singapore Pte Ltd. 2027
H. Sun et al. (Eds.): ChineseCSCW 2025, CCIS 2911, pp. 112–126, 2027.
https://doi.org/10.1007/978-981-92-0288-1_9

modeling [15,16]. Symbolic Regression (SR) [30] is able to automatically discover mathematical expressions that describe the relationship between variables. One of its key advantages is that it does not require the structure of mathematical expressions to be specified a priori, allowing it to capture complex nonlinear relationships and reveal underlying physical laws [25] or intricate patterns [9]. Compared to traditional regression techniques, expressions generated through symbolic regression are more interpretable and concise [20]. SR has found widespread application in diverse fields such as fluid dynamics [31], materials science [40], financial modeling [40], and control systems [21].

Traditional symbolic regression methods predominantly rely on evolutionary computation, such as Genetic Programming (GP) [14] and its variants. GP evolves tree-based models using genetic operations such as selection and mutation, while Gene Expression Programming (GEP) [7] similarly evolves expressions but with a linear representation. Grammatical Evolution (GE) [29] and Linear GP [5] encode genotypes into valid expressions through specific encoding rules, offering a more flexible approach to expression generation. Despite their success, these methods face a main limitations. This limitation comes from the discrete nature of the search space, which leads to oscillations in the search process, making it difficult for algorithms to explore large solution spaces effectively.

Neural network (NN)-based methods have recently garnered significant attention in the field of symbolic regression (SR), with Neural Encoding Expression Programming (NEEP) [1] being a representative approach in this direction. NEEP takes advantage of the ability of recurrent neural networks (RNNs) to capture contextual information in sequences, using them to generate mathematical expressions. This transforms the discrete search space of expressions into a continuous space of RNN weight vectors, effectively smoothing the search landscape and enhancing the capability to discover more accurate expressions [3].

Despite mitigating the discrete search space problem inherent in traditional methods, NEEP faces a core limitation: the numerical coefficients in the generated expressions are typically derived from a predefined constant pool or random initialization, rather than through a dedicated optimization process. Suboptimal coefficients can distort the performance of potentially high-quality expression structures, limiting further improvements in accuracy. Additionally, the mapping from the continuous weight space to the discrete expression space is highly nonlinear [17]. Small perturbations in the weight vector can lead to significant structural changes in the output expressions, thus reducing the stability and robustness of NEEP when applied to complex tasks.

To address the aforementioned challenges of coefficient optimization and the nonlinearity in weight-to-expression mapping, we propose an innovative approach called Adaptive Coefficient Refinement Optimization for Neural Encoding Expression Programming (ACRO-NEEP). Initially, ACRO-NEEP introduces a hierarchical cooperative optimization framework, where the upper-level NEEP module explores promising expression structures, while the lower-level CMA-ES module fine-tunes the coefficients within these expressions. These two levels interact through a feedback mechanism based on fitness evaluation, thereby achieving simultaneous optimization of both structure and coefficients. Furthermore,

ACRO-NEEP designed a multi-dimensional similarity search strategy(MSS). By evaluating structural, symbolic, and functional similarities, this strategy dynamically steers the search process, effectively balancing exploration and exploitation capabilities while mitigating oscillations caused by mapping discontinuities.

The main contributions of this paper are summarized as follows:

1) An innovative framework called ACRO-NEEP was proposed. Through the cooperative mechanism of NEEP and CMA-ES algorithms, the fine adjustment of the optimized expression structure and coefficients is realized at the same time. By designing a similarity search strategy, the stability of the NEEP method is effectively enhanced.
2) Aiming at the nonlinear problem in weight expression mapping, a multi-dimensional similarity search strategy is proposed. By considering similarity metrics for Symbol Distribution, Structure, and Function, this strategy mitigates the instability caused by nonlinear mapping. It balances exploration and development in the optimization process, enhancing the search process.

The remainder of this paper is organized as follows: Sect. 2 reviews related work on symbolic regression. Section 3 details the design and implementation of the proposed ACRO-NEEP method. Experimental results and analysis are presented in Sect. 4. Finally, Sect. 5 concludes the study, discussing future research directions.

2 Related Works

2.1 Symbolic Regression and Evolutionary Computation

Traditional symbolic regression methods are primarily based on evolutionary computation, particularly Genetic Programming (GP), which evolves mathematical expressions represented as tree structures through genetic operations such as selection, crossover, and mutation. These methods, since Koza's seminal work [14], uncover hidden relationships in data without prior model assumptions, making GP a widely adopted approach. To enhance GP's performance, various adaptations have been proposed, including Linear GP [4] for improved efficiency, Cartesian GP [24] for better local search, and Grammatical Evolution and Gene Expression Programming, which balance exploration and exploitation. Additionally, multi-objective optimization [26] and constant optimization techniques help mitigate code bloat [18] and refine coefficient optimization [34]. Despite these advancements, traditional methods still face a fundamental problem: the discrete search space causes shocks in the search process, limiting the effectiveness of algorithms in high-dimensional tasks [35].

2.2 Neural Network-Based Methods for Symbolic Regression

Recent research has shifted towards continuous optimization in symbolic regression by using neural networks to map expression generation into a continuous weight space. These approachs smooth the search landscape and improve efficiency. Notably, Neural Encoding Expression Programming (NEEP) [1] methods employ recurrent neural networks (RNNs) to generate expression sequences, optimizing the RNN's weights using continuous algorithms like Particle Swarm Optimization (PSO), which avoids the disruptive operations of traditional methods and improves the syntactic structure of expressions. Variants of this approach include DICO-NEEP [17], which integrates distance information and constant optimization; NEEP-ADF [19], which employs automatically defined functions for improved expression generation; and NEEP-RLAO [33], which incorporates reinforcement learning-assisted optimization for enhanced search efficiency. Despite these advancements, two key issues remain: poor optimization of numerical coefficients [12,32,38] and instability due to the nonlinear mapping between weight space and expression structure [17].

2.3 Numerical Optimization Techniques

Symbolic regression aims to discover both the structure and parameters of mathematical expressions, with coefficient optimization being critical for model accuracy. This inherently nonlinear, non-convex task presents significant challenges, especially in applications like medical radiotherapy [37], where accurate coefficient optimization enhances both prediction accuracy and biological interpretability [11]. Coefficient optimization methods fall into two categories: local optimization algorithms, like nonlinear least squares (NLS) and Levenberg-Marquardt [13], which are fast but sensitive to initial values [36], and global optimization algorithms such as genetic algorithms (GA) [10], particle swarm optimization (PSO) [22,39], and covariance matrix adaptation evolution strategy (CMA-ES) [8]. CMA-ES stands out for its adaptive nature, as it estimates the distribution of candidate solutions and dynamically adjusts the search step size, direction, and population size based on the problem's landscape. Its ability to handle ill-conditioned, high-dimensional, and noisy problems [28], makes it particularly effective in challenging optimization tasks.

3 Methodology

3.1 General Framework

ACRO-NEEP is a hierarchical optimization framework designed to tackle the challenges of symbolic regression. By decoupling structure search and coefficient optimization, ACRO-NEEP efficiently explores both the expression structure E and its corresponding coefficients c in a hybrid search space$\mathcal{S} = \mathcal{G} \times R^K$. The framework consists of two layers (see Fig. 1): (1) **structure search** using particle swarm optimization (PSO) in the continuous RNN weight space to generate promising candidate expressions, and (2) **coefficient optimization** using covariance matrix adaptation evolution strategy (CMA-ES) to refine the coefficients of each structure.

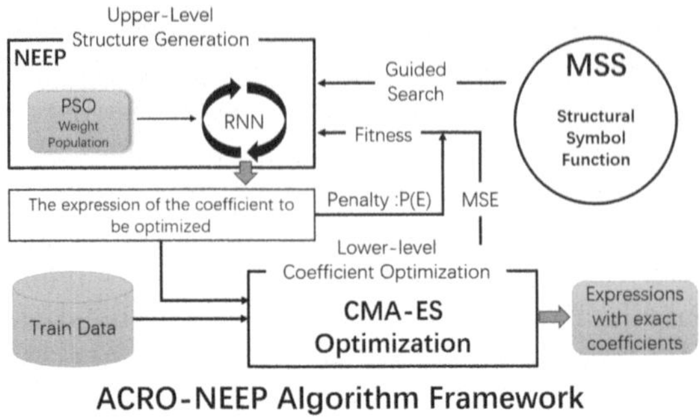

Fig. 1. The ACRO-NEEP framework uses PSO in the upper level to generate symbolic expressions via RNN weight exploration, CMA-ES in the lower level to fine-tune their coefficients, and a similarity-based strategy to balance exploration and exploitation by comparing with past solutions.

A closed-loop feedback mechanism links the layers, where the CMA-ES-optimized coefficients guide the PSO-driven structure search, leading to a more efficient and robust optimization process. To address the nonlinearity and instability of the mapping from RNN weights to discrete expressions, a stability-oriented local search strategy is introduced to balance exploration and exploitation.

The optimization objective is to jointly minimize the mean squared error (MSE) over the dataset, seeking the optimal structure E^* and coefficients c^*. ACRO-NEEP effectively addresses two core challenges: (1) **structure-coefficient coupling**, decoupling the two processes for efficient optimization; and (2) **mapping nonlinearity**, smoothing the search landscape.

3.2 Collaborative Optimization Mechanism

Upper-Level Structure Generation. The framework uses Neural Encoding Expression Programming (NEEP) as the expression generator. An RNN network treats its hidden states, $h_t \in R^H$,as intermediate representations of expressions and autoregressively generates prefix expression sequences, $S = (s_1, s_2, \ldots, s_T)$. Each symbol is selected from a dictionary containing operators, variables, and coefficients. The RNN's generation process is parameterized by the output layer weights, $Wout \in R^{H\times|\mathbb{V}|}$.

We formulate the optimization problem for the RNN's output weights as a continuous black-box optimization problem and solve it using Particle Swarm Optimization (PSO). For each particle in the PSO population, θ_i. Represents a set of weight parameters for RNNs. Its speed position update formula is as Eq. 1, Eq. 2.

$$v_i^{t+1} = \omega v_i^t + \phi_1 r_1 \left(p_i^t - \theta_i^t\right) + \phi_2 r_2 \left(g^t - \theta_i^t\right) \tag{1}$$

$$\theta_i^{t+1} = \theta_i^t + v_i^{t+1} \tag{2}$$

where v_i is the particle velocity, p_i is the historical optimal position of the particle, g is the global historical optimal position, and ω is the inertia weight, ϕ_1, ϕ_2 is the learning factor,$r_1, r_2 \sim U(0,1)$.

To inherently control the complexity of the generated expressions, we integrate a coefficient number constraint mechanism during the decoding process. Let the maximum allowed number of coefficients be K_{max}. When generating a symbol, if the number of coefficients already generated is less than K_{max}, the probability of selecting a coefficient symbol is forced to zero, and the probability distribution is renormalized. This mechanism ensures that the generated candidate expression structure satisfies the coefficient constraint, providing valid input for the lower-level optimization.

Lower-Level Coefficient Optimization. For each expression structure E_i generated by the upper-level PSO particles θ_i, the lower-level optimizer treats it as a parameterized function $f_{E_i}(x, c)$, where $c = (c_1, c_2, \ldots, c_K)$ represents the vector of coefficients to be optimized. The coefficient optimization problem is formulated as a non-linear least-squares problem in the continuous space, which can be expressed as Eq. 3.

$$c^* = \arg min \text{MSE}(c) = \arg min \frac{1}{N} \sum_{j=1}^{N} (y_j - f_{E_i}(x_j, c))^2 \tag{3}$$

To solve this problem, we use the Covariance Matrix Adaptation Evolution Strategy (CMA-ES). CMA-ES is a stochastic optimization algorithm based on distribution estimation. Its core idea is to adaptively update the mean and covariance matrix of the search distribution to approach the optimal region of the objective function. At each generation, the algorithm samples a population from a multivariate normal distribution, updates the mean and covariance matrix, and moves the distribution center accordingly. CMA-ES benefits from its strong robustness in handling non-linear and non-convex optimization problems, especially for fine-tuning coefficients in symbolic regression.

It is noteworthy that, to balance computational efficiency and optimization precision, CMA-ES adopts an approximate optimization strategy with a limited number of iterations (e.g., 50 generations). The theoretical rationale is that a high-quality expression structure should exhibit significantly better performance than an inferior structure, even when its coefficients are not fully optimized.

Fitness Function Design. To further guide the search process toward generating mathematically meaningful expressions, we introduce a structural penalty term based on operator ratio into the fitness function. This design is grounded in an inductive bias: a symbolic regression model with explanatory value typically requires a certain number of operators to capture nonlinear relationships in the data. Avoiding the generation of overly simplistic expressions (e.g., nearly constant functions) also serves as a regularization technique to enhance the model's generalization ability. The overall fitness function is defined as Eq. 4

$$Ftotal = MSE + P(E) \tag{4}$$

where the structural penalty term $P(E)$ is calculated as Eq. 5.

$$P(E) = \begin{cases} \lambda \cdot (\tau - r(E)), \text{ if } r(E) < \tau; \\ 0, \qquad\qquad\qquad \text{otherwise} \end{cases} \tag{5}$$

Here, $r(E) = |\mathcal{F}_{\mathcal{E}}| / |E|$ represents the operator ratio in expression E, $\tau = 0.2$ is the ratio threshold, and $\lambda = 1000$ is the penalty coefficient. This design ensures that the algorithm, while optimizing MSE, tends to discover mathematical expressions with a certain level of complexity and interpretability.

3.3 Multi-dimensional Similarity Search Strategy

The mapping $M : \Theta \to \mathcal{G}$ from the RNN weight spaceΘ to the expression space $\mathcal{G}$ is nonlinear, meaning that a minor perturbation in θ can cause a structural drastic change in $M(\theta)$. This discontinuity in the mapping limits the search stability of PSO in the continuous weight space.

To mitigate this problem, we designed a lightweight multi-dimensional similarity search strategy. The core idea of this strategy is to use the multi-dimensional similarity between the current expression and the historical global best expression to guide the perturbation of PSO particles, rather than constructing computationally expensive global similarity graphs.

Multi-Dimensional Similarity Metric. We define a comprehensive similarity function $Sim : \mathcal{G} \times \mathcal{G} \to [0, 1]$to quantify the closeness between two expressions E_i and E_j. Sim is a weighted sum of the following three metrics:

Symbol Distribution Similarity: Based on the Jaccard coefficient, measuring the overlap in symbol usage, as Eq. 6.

$$Sim_{\text{symbol}}(E_i, E_j) = \frac{|\mathcal{V}(E_i) \cap \mathcal{V}(E_j)|}{|\mathcal{V}(E_i) \cup \mathcal{V}(E_j)|} \tag{6}$$

where $\mathcal{V}(E)$ denotes the set of symbols in expression E.

Structural Similarity: Based on the Longest Common Subsequence (LCS), measuring the similarity in syntactic structure, as Eq. 7.

$$Sim_{\text{struct}}(E_i, E_j) = \frac{2 \cdot |\text{LCS}(E_i, E_j)|}{|E_i| + |E_j|} \tag{7}$$

where $|E|$ represents the length of the expression.

Functional Similarity: Based on the type distribution of operators and operands, indirectly assessing functional similarity, as Eq. 8.

$$Sim_{\text{func}}(E_i, E_j) = 1 - \frac{1}{|\mathcal{T}|} \sum_{t \in \mathcal{T}} \left| \frac{N_t(E_i)}{|E_i|} - \frac{N_t(E_j)}{|E_j|} \right| \tag{8}$$

where $\mathcal{T} = \{\text{operator}, \text{variable}, \text{coefficient}, \text{constant}\}$, and $N_t(E)$ is the number of symbols of type t in expression E.

The final comprehensive similarity is Eq. 9.

$$Sim(E_i, E_j) = \alpha \cdot Sim_{\text{symbol}} + \beta \cdot Sim_{\text{struct}} + \gamma \cdot Sim_{\text{func}} \tag{9}$$

where α, β, γ are weight hyper-parameters, and $\alpha + \beta + \gamma = 1$.

Similarity-Guided Perturbation. During the PSO iteration process, every 50 generations, for each particle θ_i, the comprehensive similarity $s = Sim(E_i, E_g)$ between its current expression E_i and the historical global best expression E_g is calculated. Depending on the value of s, different Gaussian perturbation strategies are adopted to fine-tune its position, balancing exploration and exploitation between iterations: $s = Sim(E_i, E_g)$, and the perturbation intensity σ_s is dynamically adjusted based on the similarity threshold.

This strategy ensures local fine-grained search in high-similarity regions while encouraging the exploration of new structures in low-similarity regions, effectively smoothing the search landscape.

3.4 Algorithm Workflow and Implementation

The overall workflow of ACRO-NEEP forms a closed-loop system that integrates structure generation, coefficient optimization, and feedback regulation. As illustrated in Fig. 2, the algorithm operates as follows: First, the NEEP module initializes a population of RNN weight vectors. In each iteration, the upper-level module decodes these weights into symbolic expressions and checks their validity (e.g., number of coefficients). For valid expressions, the lower-level module launches a CMA-ES instance to fine-tune their numerical parameters. The evaluation module computes a fitness score combining the CMA-ES-optimized mean squared error (MSE) and a structural penalty. This fitness is fed back to update the individual and global best solutions in the NEEP module.

Meanwhile, a similarity-guided module compares the current expression with historical best solutions across multiple dimensions and adaptively adjusts the perturbation intensity based on their similarity. This balances exploration and exploitation, enhancing search stability. By tightly coupling structure and parameter optimization—unlike traditional two-phase approaches—ACRO-NEEP enables efficient, accurate, and robust symbolic regression.

4 Experiments

This section aims to systematically validate the performance of the proposed ACRO-NEEP framework. The experimental design revolves around two core objectives: in Sect. 4.2, to compare ACRO-NEEP with state-of-the-art algorithms on diverse symbolic regression benchmarks, thereby evaluating its overall competitiveness; in Sect. 4.3, to analyze the contribution of the key innovative

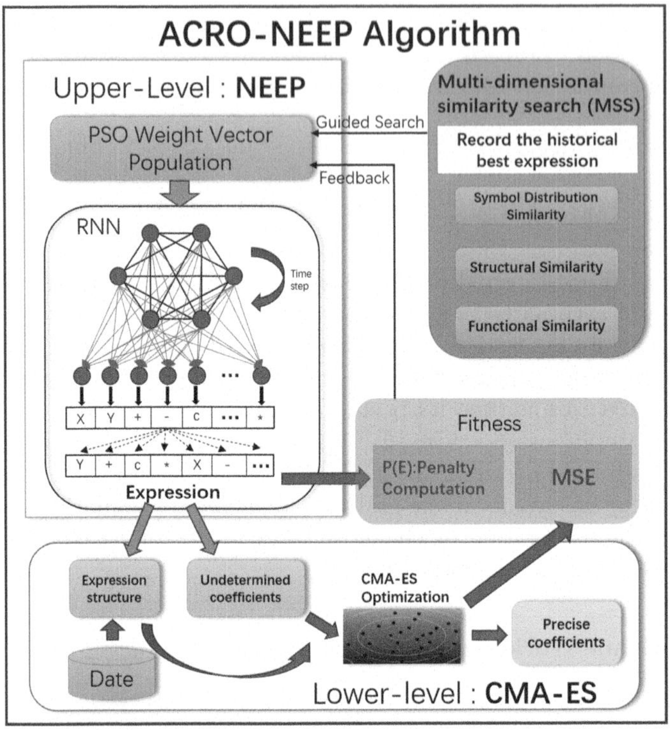

Fig. 2. Overall Workflow of the ACRO-NEEP Algorithm.

Table 1. Test problems used in this paper. U[a,b,c] is c samples uniformly randomized in [a,b] for the variable. E[a,b, c] are mesh points which are spaced equally with an interval of c, from a to b inclusive.

Name	Variables	Function	Trainingset	Testingset
Dic1	10	$x_1 + x_2 + x_3 + x_4 + x_5$	U[1,11,1000]	U[1,11,1000]
Dic3	10	$x_1 + \frac{x_2 x_3}{x_4} + \frac{x_3 x_4}{x_5}$	U[1,11,1000]	U[1,11,1000]
Dic4	10	$x_1 x_2 + x_2 x_3 + x_3 x_4 x_5 + x_5 x_6$	U[1,11,1000]	U[1,11,1000]
Dic5	10	$\sqrt{x_1 + \sin(x_2) + \log_e(x_3)}$	U[1,11,1000]	U[1,11,1000]
Nico9	2	$x_1^4 - x_1^3 + \frac{x_2^2}{2} - x_2$	U[−5,5,1000]	U[−5,5,1000]
Nico14	6	$\frac{x_5 x_6}{\frac{x_1}{x_2}\frac{x_3}{x_4}}$	U[−5,5,1000]	U[−5,5,1000]
Nico16	4	$32 - 3\frac{\tan(x_1)}{\tan(x_2)}\frac{\tan(x_3)}{\tan(x_4)}$	U[−5,5,1000]	U[−5,5,1000]
Nguyen6	1	$\sin(x) + \sin(x + x^2)$	U[−1,1,20]	U[−1,1,20]
Nguyen7	1	$\ln(x + 1) + \ln(x^2 + 1)$	U[0,2,20]	U[0,2,20]
Vlad3	2	$e^{-x}x^3(\cos x \sin x)(\cos x \sin^2 x - 1)(y - 5)$	x:E[0.05,10,0.1] y:E[0.05,10.05,2]	x:E[−0.5,10.5,0.05] y:E[−0.5,10.5,0.5]
Energy	8	Energy efficiency of buildings		
Concrete	8	Concrete compressive strength		

module—the multi-dimensional similarity metric—through ablation studies. All experiments are conducted under identical computational environments, with each algorithm executed independently for multiple runs to ensure statistical significance of the results, thus guaranteeing rigor and fairness in the evaluation.

Table 2. Comparison of Hyperparameter Settings

Algorithm Category	Algorithm Name	Key Hyperparameters and Settings
Traditional EA	GP	Tournament Size: 3 Max Tree Depth: 10 Max Tree Nodes: 61 Crossover Max Depth: 10 Mutation Max Depth: 4
	GEP	Head Length: 30 Crossover Rate: 0.7 Mutation Rate: 0.1 IS Transposition Rate: 0.1 RIS Transposition Rate: 0.1 Inversion Rate: 0.1
Neural-Based SR Methods	GA-NEEP, PSO-NEEP, CMAES-NEEP	Head Length: 30 Hidden Neurons: 40 Time Steps: 10 Fixed Weight Sparsity: 0.5 Optimization Weight Range: -2,2
	DICO-NEEP, NEEP-RLAO	Share the same parameter configuration as the Neural SR Methods above
	ACRO-NEEP(our method)	Max Coefficients: 5 Coefficient Optimization Range: [0, 5] CMA-ES Max Iterations: 50 CMA-ES Tolerance: 1e-6 Similarity Threshold: 0.6

4.1 Benchmark and Configuration of Experiment

To comprehensively evaluate algorithm performance, we selected a total of 12 standard symbolic regression benchmark problems, including Dic1, Nico9, Nguyen6, Vlad3, Energy, and others. These benchmarks cover low-dimensional synthetic functions, high-dimensional complex systems, and real-world datasets [2,6,23,27], exhibiting considerable diversity in variable dimensionality, non-linear complexity, and data sources (detailed characteristics are provided in Table 1). Together, these datasets form a comprehensive testing benchmark sufficient to evaluate the algorithm's overall performance in terms of mathematical accuracy, high-dimensional scalability, and practical generalization capability.

To comprehensively evaluate the performance of ACRO-NEEP, we compared it with three categories of algorithms: 1) **Traditional evolutionary algorithms**, including Genetic Programming (GP) and Gene Expression Programming (GEP), representing classical symbolic regression methods; 2) **Neural-Based SR Methods**, such as GA-NEEP, PSO-NEEP, CMAES-NEEP, DICO-NEEP and NEEP-RLAO, which use neural networks for optimization, representing the latest advancements in the field. This selection ensures a broad comparison with both traditional and modern approaches. The parameter configuration details of the comparison algorithm are shown in Table 2. The experimental results for the compared methods are drawn directly from the original publications of the respective studies.

The specific settings for ACRO-NEEP were: a maximum of 5 coefficients, with the coefficient optimization range set to [0, 5], covering typical symbolic regression problems; the maximum CMA-ES iterations were set to 50, optimized for accuracy and efficiency through preliminary testing; the similarity threshold was set to 0.6, empirically effective for distinguishing search regions; and perturbation intensities were set at 0.05, 0.1, and 0.2, for high, medium, and low similarity regions, respectively. These parameter values were determined through extensive preliminary experiments. Each algorithm was executed 20 times per problem, with the median mean squared error (MSE) used as the performance metric.

Table 3. Comparison of Eight Algorithms

	GEP	GP	GA-NEEP	PSO-NEEP	CMAES-NEEP	DICO-NEEP	NEEP-RLAO	ACRO-NEEP
Dic1	6.00e+02	1.55e+01	2.04e+01	2.83e+00	**4.97e-30**	4.6e+01	1.01e+01	9.01e-30
Dic3	4.96e+02	1.29e+02	1.44e+02	1.18e+02	1.20e+02	1.36e+02	1.18e+02	**7.41e+01**
Dic4	7.00e+04	6.68e+03	3.01e+04	5.12e+03	3.62e+03	1.39e+04	1.19e+04	**2.08e+03**
Dic5	6.80e+00	8.96e-01	1.00e+00	5.99e-01	5.54e-01	2.00e+00	8.71e-01	**5.21e-01**
Nico9	4.80e+04	3.64e+02	1.32e+04	1.27e+03	2.65e+03	5.53e+03	3.75e+01	**2.85e+01**
Nico14	1.18e+07	1.20e+07	1.18e+07	1.18e+07	1.18e+07	–	2.26e+06	**1.78e+06**
Nico16	4.47e+09	4.48e+09	4.46e+09	4.91e+09	4.46e+09	–	–	**5.95e+07**
Nguyen6	2.10e-01	1.54e-01	1.10e-01	1.40e-02	4.41e-03	7.72e-02	1.24e-02	**5.44e-17**
Nguyen7	2.63e-01	3.92e-02	3.30e-02	2.19e-03	1.15e-03	6.98e-04	1.40e-02	**9.10e-07**
Vlad3	7.63e+00	1.22e+00	9.47e-01	1.05e+00	1.01e+00	1.34e+00	**8.51e-01**	1.16e+00
Energy	1.06e+02	2.58e+01	4.52e+01	2.17e+01	2.34e+01	**1.34e+00**	8.65e+01	1.21e+01
Concrete	3.39e+02	2.26e+02	2.21e+02	1.80e+02	1.66e+02	2.28e+02	2.61e+02	**1.32e+02**
Better	0	0	0	0	1	1	1	9

4.2 Results and Analysis

The overall performance comparison results (Table 3, the Better term in the table represents the number of times the algorithm achieved the first place) demonstrate that ACRO-NEEP exhibits superior performance on the vast majority of test problems. It achieved the top ranking in 9 out of the 12 problems, significantly outperforming other comparative algorithms. Notably, its advantage is particularly pronounced on high-dimensional complex problems (e.g., the Dic and Nico series). For instance, on the Dic1 problem, its MSE reached a near-perfect magnitude (9.01×10^{-30}); on the highly challenging Nico16 problem, it reduced the error by nearly two orders of magnitude. These results fully validate the effectiveness of the hierarchical cooperative optimization mechanism it employs: the upper-level PSO is responsible for exploring promising expression structures, while the lower-level CMA-ES focuses on fine-tuning coefficients. Through fitness feedback, they form a closed loop, collectively overcoming the search challenges caused by structure-coefficient coupling.

4.3 Ablation Study

To further investigate the necessity of the innovative components in the framework, an ablation study was designed to dissect the role of the multi-dimensional similarity search strategy (MSS). The experiment was independently conducted 20 times on six datasets, comparing the convergence performance of the average best training error between the full version of ACRO-NEEP and a version with the MSS module disabled (ACRO-NEEP-w/o-MSS). The experimental results, shown in Fig. 3, demonstrate that the multi-dimensional similarity search strategy (MSS) significantly improves convergence across all six datasets with diverse characteristics fully validating its effectiveness.

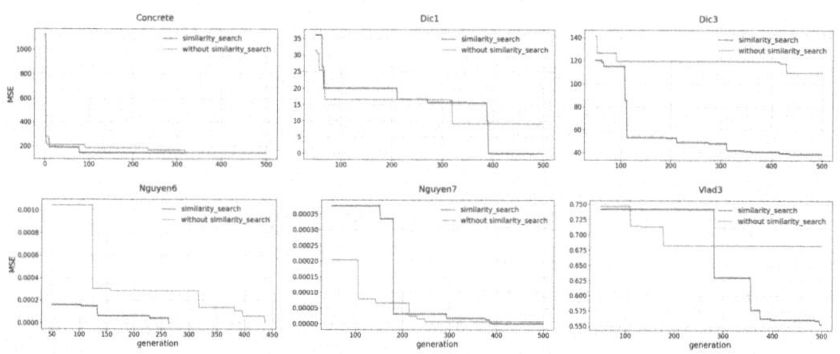

Fig. 3. Evolution of the average best MSE of 20 independent trials for ACRO-NEEP and a version with the MSS module disabled (ACRO-NEEP-w/o-MSS).

For high-dimensional problems such as Dic1 and Dic3, MSS effectively mitigates search instability in weight-space mapping through functional similarity metrics, suppressing search oscillations. For problems involving complex nonlinear combinations, such as Nguyen6, Nguyen7, and Vlad3, its structure-similarity-guided search intelligently directs the algorithm to escape local optima, avoiding blind random exploration. On the real-world dataset Concrete, MSS enhances robustness to noise and improves generalization capability by balancing structural compactness and functional similarity. This ablation study confirms that the MSS strategy is a critical component enabling ACRO-NEEP to achieve efficient and stable search.

5 Conclusion

This paper proposes ACRO-NEEP to address the critical issue of insufficient coefficient optimization in symbolic regression. The framework decouples structure search from parameter tuning: the upper-level PSO explores RNN weights to generate diverse symbolic expressions, while the lower-level CMA-ES fine-tunes their coefficients, achieving joint optimization of structure and parameters. To alleviate the instability caused by mapping continuous weights to discrete expressions, we further propose MSS, which leverages historical optimal solutions to enhance robustness and convergence. In standard benchmark experiments, ACRO-NEEP significantly outperforms existing state-of-the-art methods on high-dimensional problems (Dic, Nico, etc.) and real-world datasets (Concrete, Energy, etc.), demonstrating its effectiveness, advantages, and generalization capability.

Despite its strong performance, ACRO-NEEP has some limitations. First, it incurs high computational cost, as running CMA-ES for every candidate expression can become a bottleneck on complex problems. Second, the RNN decoder struggles to generate certain expression types. Future work will explore lightweight coefficient optimization—such as sharing CMA-ES instances or using surrogate models—and replace the RNN with more powerful generative architectures like Transformers to improve expression representation. We also plan to build a knowledge base of high-quality expression patterns to better preserve diversity during search. These improvements aim to enhance the framework's efficiency and scalability, further advancing symbolic regression for scientific discovery and engineering applications.

Acknowledgment. This work was supported by National Natural Science Foundation of China under Grant No. 61872419, No. 62072213, in part by the Shandong Provincial Natural Science Foundation No. ZR2022JQ30, No. ZR2022ZD01, No. ZR2023LZH015, in part by the Taishan Scholars Program of Shandong Province, China, under Grant No. tsqn201812077, in part by the "New 20 Rules for University" Program of Jinan City under Grant No. 2021GXRC077, in part by the Key Research Project of Quancheng Laboratory, China under Grant No. QCLZD202303, in part by the Research Project of Provincial Laboratory of Shandong, China under Grant No. SYS202201, in part by the University of Jinan Disciplinary Cross-Convergence Construction Project 2023 No. XKJC-202303, in part by the University of Jinan Disciplinary Cross-Convergence Construction Project 2024 No. XKJC-202402, in part by the Key Research and Development Program of Shandong Province (2024CXPT084).

References

1. Anjum, A., Sun, F., Wang, L., Orchard, J.: A novel neural network-based symbolic regression method: Neuro-encoded expression programming. In: International Conference on Artificial Neural Networks, pp. 373–386. Springer, Cham (2019)
2. Asuncion, A., Newman, D.: UCI machine learning repository (2007)
3. Bowman, S., Vilnis, L., Vinyals, O., Dai, A., Jozefowicz, R., Bengio, S.: Generating sentences from a continuous space. In: Proceedings of the 20th SIGNLL Conference on Computational Natural Language Learning, pp. 10–21 (2016)
4. Brameier, M.F., Banzhaf, W.: Linear Genetic Programming, Springer, Heidelberg (2007)
5. Dantzig, G.B.: Linear programming. Oper. Res. **50**(1), 42–47 (2002)

6. Dick, G.: Sensitivity-like analysis for feature selection in genetic programming. In: Proceedings of the Genetic and Evolutionary Computation Conference, pp. 401–408 (2017)
7. Ferreira, C.: Gene expression programming: a new adaptive algorithm for solving problems. arXiv preprint cs/0102027 (2001)
8. Hansen, N., Ostermeier, A.: Adapting arbitrary normal mutation distributions in evolution strategies: the covariance matrix adaptation. In: Proceedings of IEEE International Conference on Evolutionary Computation, pp. 312–317. IEEE (1996)
9. Hien, N.T., et al.: Genetic programming for storm surge forecasting. Ocean Eng. **215**, 107812 (2020)
10. Holland, J.H.: Genetic algorithms. Sci. Am. **267**(1), 66–73 (1992)
11. Hu, A., Zhou, W., Qiu, R., Li, J.: Symbolic regression: a versatile approach for constructing phenomenological models of radiobiological effects. Radiat. Res. **203**(5), 333–340 (2025)
12. Kamienny, P.A., d'Ascoli, S., Lample, G., Charton, F.: End-to-end symbolic regression with transformers. Adv. Neural. Inf. Process. Syst. **35**, 10269–10281 (2022)
13. Kommenda, M., Burlacu, B., Kronberger, G., Affenzeller, M.: Parameter identification for symbolic regression using nonlinear least squares. Genet. Program Evol. Mach. **21**(3), 471–501 (2020)
14. Koza, J.R.: Genetic programming as a means for programming computers by natural selection. Stat. Comput. **4**(2), 87–112 (1994)
15. La Cava, W., et al.: Contemporary symbolic regression methods and their relative performance. Adv. Neural. Inf. Process. Syst. **2021**(DB1), 1 (2021)
16. Larose, D.T., Larose, C.D.: Discovering Knowledge in Data: An Introduction to Data Mining. Wiley, Hoboken (2014)
17. Liu, C., Pang, C., Wang, L., Yang, B.: Dico-neep: Neep with distance information and constant optimization. In: 2024 International Joint Conference on Neural Networks (IJCNN), pp. 1–8. IEEE (2024)
18. Luke, S., Panait, L.: A comparison of bloat control methods for genetic programming. Evol. Comput. **14**(3), 309–344 (2006)
19. Ma, J., et al.: NEEP-ADF: neuro-encoded expression programming with automatically defined functions. Inf. Sci. **704**, 121957 (2025)
20. Makke, N., Chawla, S.: Interpretable scientific discovery with symbolic regression: a review. Artif. Intell. Rev. **57**(1), 2 (2024)
21. Makke, N., Chawla, S.: Symbolic regression: a pathway to interpretability towards automated scientific discovery. In: Proceedings of the 30th ACM SIGKDD Conference on Knowledge Discovery and Data Mining, pp. 6588–6596 (2024)
22. Marini, F., Walczak, B.: Particle swarm optimization (PSO). a tutorial. Chemometr. Intell. Lab. Syst. **149**, 153–165 (2015)
23. McDermott, J., et al.: Genetic programming needs better benchmarks. In: Proceedings of the 14th Annual Conference on Genetic and Evolutionary Computation, pp. 791–798 (2012)
24. Miller, J., Turner, A.: Cartesian genetic programming. In: Proceedings of the Companion Publication of the 2015 Annual Conference on Genetic and Evolutionary Computation, pp. 179–198 (2015)
25. Murari, A., Spolladore, L., Rossi, R., Gelfusa, M.: Combining dimensional and statistical analysis for efficient data driven modelling of complex systems. Inf. Sci. **644**, 119243 (2023)
26. Neumann, F.: Computational complexity analysis of multi-objective genetic programming. In: Proceedings of the 14th Annual Conference on Genetic and Evolutionary Computation, pp. 799–806 (2012)

27. Nicolau, M., Agapitos, A., O'Neill, M., Brabazon, A.: Guidelines for defining benchmark problems in genetic programming. In: 2015 IEEE Congress on Evolutionary Computation (CEC), pp. 1152–1159. IEEE (2015)
28. Nomura, M., Akimoto, Y., Ono, I.: CMA-ES with learning rate adaptation: can CMA-ES with default population size solve multimodal and noisy problems? In: Proceedings of the Genetic and Evolutionary Computation Conference, pp. 839–847 (2023)
29. O'Neill, M., Ryan, C.: Grammatical evolution. IEEE Trans. Evol. Comput. **5**(4), 349–358 (2002)
30. Orzechowski, P., La Cava, W., Moore, J.H.: Where are we now? A large benchmark study of recent symbolic regression methods. In: Proceedings of the Genetic and Evolutionary Computation Conference, pp. 1183–1190 (2018)
31. Quade, M., Abel, M., Shafi, K., Niven, R.K., Noack, B.R.: Prediction of dynamical systems by symbolic regression. Phys. Rev. E **94**(1), 012214 (2016)
32. Reis, L., Caminha, V., Penna, T.: Benchmarking symbolic regression constant optimization schemes, (2024). arXiv:2412.02126
33. Shan, H., et al.: NEEP-RLAO: neural encoded expression programming with reinforcement learning-assisted optimization. In: International Conference on Intelligent Computing. pp. 375–387. Springer, Cham (2025)
34. Topchy, A., Punch, W.F.: Faster genetic programming based on local gradient search of numeric leaf values. In: Proceedings of the Genetic and Evolutionary Computation Conference (GECCO-2001), vol. 155162, Morgan Kaufmann, San Francisco, CA (2001)
35. Tran, B., Xue, B., Zhang, M.: Genetic programming for feature construction and selection in classification on high-dimensional data. Memetic Comput. **8**(1), 3–15 (2016)
36. Transtrum, M.K., Sethna, J.P.: Improvements to the levenberg-marquardt algorithm for nonlinear least-squares minimization (2012). arXiv:1201.5885
37. Virgolin, M., Alderliesten, T., Bel, A., Witteveen, C., Bosman, P.A.: Symbolic regression and feature construction with gp-gomea applied to radiotherapy dose reconstruction of childhood cancer survivors. In: Proceedings of the Genetic and Evolutionary Computation Conference, pp. 1395–1402 (2018)
38. Virgolin, M., Bosman, P.A.: Coefficient mutation in the gene-pool optimal mixing evolutionary algorithm for symbolic regression. In: Proceedings of the Genetic and Evolutionary Computation Conference Companion, pp. 2289–2297 (2022)
39. Wang, L., Yang, B., Orchard, J.: Particle swarm optimization using dynamic tournament topology. Appl. Soft Comput. **48**, 584–596 (2016)
40. Wang, Y., Wagner, N., Rondinelli, J.M.: Symbolic regression in materials science. MRS Commun. **9**(3), 793–805 (2019)

NoiseMap: Visual Analytics for Interpreting Noise Scheduling Strategies in Diffusion Models for Multivariate Time Series Forecasting

Qiang Lu[1,2(✉)], Zilong Wang[1,2], Hongfeng Wu[1,2], Sangui Jian[1,2], Xueyu Luo[1,2], and Ye Yu[1,2]

[1] School of Computer Science and Information, Hefei University of Technology, Hefei, China
{2023170756,2023170694,jsg,2024111590}@mail.hfut.edu.cn, {luqiang,yuye}@hfut.edu.cn

[2] Intelligent Interconnected Systems Laboratory of Anhui Province, Hefei University of Technology, Hefei, China

Abstract. Diffusion models are increasingly used for multivariate time-series forecasting, most studies optimize architectures and metrics while overlooking how schedules shape representation learning and temporal structure. Motivated by the successful use of visual analytics (VA) in AI, we argue that interactive visualization can markedly enhance comparative analyses across diverse noise schedules. In this paper, we present NoiseMap, an interactive VA framework for multivariate time series that makes schedule effects observable and comparable by providing coordinated and linked views. These views enable users to align and compare schedules and noise-parameter settings side by side, select temporal segment, and trace schedule-induced changes across latent space. NoiseMap provides diffusion trajectories in latent space, supports temporal segment selection, and focuses on key latent dimensions to reveal how different noise schedules and their noise-parameter settings influence trends and periodicity. Evaluations on one real world multivariate time series dataset, combined with user interviews, demonstrate that NoiseMap effectively supports comparative analysis of noise schedules and provides actionable insights for model interpretation.

Keywords: Diffusion Model · Time-series forecasting · Visual analytics · Dimensionality reduction

1 Introduction

Diffusion models have achieved strong generative performance in images, audio, and video [1,2]. They corrupt data with gradually increasing noise and learn the reverse process to sample from the data distribution. This mechanism is well-suited to complex multivariate time series whose temporal dynamics and

© The Author(s), under exclusive license to Springer Nature Singapore Pte Ltd. 2027

H. Sun et al. (Eds.): ChineseCSCW 2025, CCIS 2911, pp. 127–140, 2027.
https://doi.org/10.1007/978-981-92-0288-1_10

noise characteristics often challenge traditional models. Continuous-time formulations (continuous noise schedules) [3] better respect temporal continuity, non-autoregressive diffusion models [4] can generate the entire forecast horizon in a single pass, mitigating error accumulation and facilitating comparison across variables. These properties make diffusion models a promising approach for multivariate time-series forecasting.

Motivated by the successful use of VA in explainable AI, we argue that VA approach based on latent space is well suited for comparing different noise schedules in diffusion models [5]. In this work, we present NoiseMap, a VA framework for systematic comparison of noise schedules. The framework first uses a Temporal Fusion Transformer (TFT) to extract compact and comparable embeddings from the high-dimensional intermediates of the diffusion process, and then applies UMAP to project these embeddings into 2D latent space, thereby revealing differences across stages, schedules, and parameter settings. NoiseMap provides coordinated and linked views with interactive operations, users can select temporal segment and dimensions of interest to explore and to understand differences among strategies in time series trends and seasonality. To preserve sequence structure and better express latent dynamics [6], our UMAP design incorporates temporal information. Case study on one real world time series dataset and user study demonstrate that NoiseMap helps users compare and interpret different noise schedules effectively in practice.

In summary, our contributions are as follows:

(1) We introduce NoiseMap, an interactive VA framework for interpreting and comparing noise schedules in diffusion-based multivariate time-series forecasting, making their impact on predictive behavior explicit.
(2) We propose a Time-Aware UMAP with three temporal constraints: direction-consistency, trend-preservation, and periodicity regularization—that preserves sequential structure and stabilizes schedule-induced trajectories for side-by-side comparison.
(3) We conduct case study on one real world time series dataset and perform user interviews, demonstrating the practicality and effectiveness of NoiseMap for comparing and explaining different noise schedules.

2 Related Work

Our framework focuses on explaining and comparing the impact of noise schedules in diffusion-based multivariate time series models. This section reviews related work on diffusion models for multivariate time-series forecasting, latent space in time series analysis and VA for explainable AI.

2.1 Diffusion for Multivariate Time-Series Forecasting

Diffusion models learn a denoising reverse process p_θ to approximate the data distribution $p_{\text{data}}(x)$ by inverting a forward noising process q [1]. Recent works extend this paradigm to multivariate time series to enable multi-step forecasting

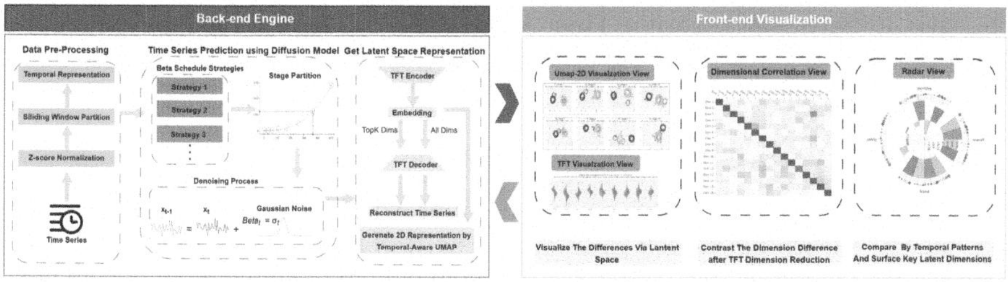

Fig. 1. The system pipeline of NoiseMap includes both backend and frontend components. The back-end engine utilizes diffusion models under multiple β-schedules for time-series forecasting, partitions the process into stages, embeds them with a Temporal Fusion Transformer (TFT), and projects the latent states to 2D using Time-Aware UMAP. On the front-end visualization, we offer five interactive views, including the Prediction Comparison View, facilitating a comprehensive assessment of different diffusion scheduling strategies and noise parameters.

while maintaining temporal coherence and cross-variable dependencies. Across forecasting, imputation, and generation, both discrete DDPM-style and continuous score-based (SDE) formulations have shown strong accuracy and calibrated uncertainty on complex datasets—for example, time-series forecasting with TimeGrad [4] and TimeDiff [7], imputation with CSDI [8], and controllable generation with Diffusion-TS [9] (Fig. 1).

Despite these advances, diffusion models still face limited interpretability in practical settings [10], which constrains their use in critical applications such as energy scheduling [11]. In particular, the noise-scheduling strategy, a key design factor, has a marked impact on predictive behavior and generalization [12], yet it has not been studied systematically and mechanistically. This gap makes it difficult to diagnose and tune model behavior under different strategies. To address this, we focus on DDPM-based time series methods and propose an interactive analysis framework that combines latent-space visualization to support interpretable comparisons of noise schedules [13].

2.2 Latent Space in Time Series Analysis

Dimensionality reduction (DR) maps high-dimensional representations to latent space, enabling visualization, pattern discovery, and clustering, on learned features of deep models. For multivariate time series, latent space visualization has been used to examine hidden states and model behaviors, improving qualitative understanding and interpretability in forecasting tasks [14].

Applying off-the-shelf DR directly to time series remains challenging: strong temporal dependencies and cross-variable coupling mean that projecting raw sequences or high-dimensional latent vectors can conflate temporally distant states, induce trajectory crossings and neighbor mixing [15]. UMAP preserves local neighborhoods and may retain some global structure, but its default pipeline is not time-aware and does not explicitly encode seasonality or trend, making stage-wise and cross-schedule differences difficult to reveal consistently

[16]. Accordingly, we develop a Time-Aware UMAP that incorporates temporal constraints to preserve temporal structure in the latent space.

2.3 Visual Analytics for Model Interpretability

VA has become an important means to improve the interpretability of complex machine-learning models [13]. With the development of deep neural networks, a series of model-specific VA systems emerged: Smilkov et al. [17] present the Embedding Projector to explore learned representations; Strobelt et al. [14] develop LSTMVis to inspect hidden-state dynamics in sequence models; and Kahng et al. [18] design GAN Lab for interactive experimentation with deep generative models.

In contrast, VA for diffusion models in time-series forecasting, especially for comparing noise schedules, has received limited attention. Diffusion involves multi-step sampling and noise scheduling, whose stage-wise dynamics are hard to trace; multivariate time series additionally bring strong temporal dependencies and cross-variable interactions, further complicating process-level explanations. Current evaluations largely rely on point-forecast metrics (RMSE, MAE) and, for probabilistic quality, the continuous ranked probability score (CRPS), which provide limited insight into how different schedules affect temporal components [19].

To address this gap, we present NoiseMap, a VA framework for diffusion-based multivariate time series that focuses on the dynamic evolution under different noise schedules. We analyze intermediate latent representations, adopt TFT and time-aware UMAP, and use coordinated views with linked interactions to depict stage-aligned trajectories for side-by-side comparison across schedules and noise-schedule parameters.

3 Design Overview

This section introduces the research background, followed by requirement analysis and analytical tasks.

3.1 Background

We follow the standard diffusion formulation: a forward process that gradually adds noise and a reverse process that learns to denoise. Let the noise schedule be $\{\beta_t\}_{t=1}^{T}$ with $\beta_t \in (0,1)$, and define $\alpha_t = 1 - \beta_t$ and $\bar{\alpha}_t = \prod_{s=1}^{t} \alpha_s$; $\mathbf{I}$ is the identity matrix.

The forward (noising) process [1] is:

$$q(\mathbf{x}_t \mid \mathbf{x}_{t-1}) = \mathcal{N}\big(\sqrt{\alpha_t}\,\mathbf{x}_{t-1},\,(1-\alpha_t)\mathbf{I}\big)\,. \tag{1}$$

where $\mathbf{x}_t$ is the noised sample at step t and α_t controls the injected noise.

The reverse (denoising) process is:

$$p_\theta(\mathbf{x}_{t-1} \mid \mathbf{x}_t) = \mathcal{N}\big(\boldsymbol{\mu}_\theta(\mathbf{x}_t, t),\,\sigma_t^2\mathbf{I}\big)\,. \tag{2}$$

where μ_θ is predicted by a neural network and σ_t is a fixed or learned standard deviation.

The training objective is:

$$\mathcal{L}_{\text{simple}} = \mathbb{E}_{t,\mathbf{x}_0,\epsilon}\left[\left\|\epsilon - \epsilon_\theta\big(\sqrt{\bar{\alpha}_t}\,\mathbf{x}_0 + \sqrt{1-\bar{\alpha}_t}\,\epsilon,\, t\big)\right\|_2^2\right]. \tag{3}$$

where $\epsilon \sim \mathcal{N}(\mathbf{0}, \mathbf{I})$ is injected noise and ϵ_θ denotes the predicted noise; the expectation is over t, $\mathbf{x}_0$, and ϵ.

The noise schedule $\{\beta_t\}_{t=1}^{T}$ determines the per-step noise injection and thus affects the latent-space trajectory and the learning difficulty. Common schedules include Linear, Cosine, Exponential, Quadratic, and Sigmoid. These schedules have been widely explored in image generation, but systematic comparisons for time-series forecasting remain scarce. To analyze their effects, we implement each schedule in a parametric form. Linear/Exponential/Quadratic schedules are produced by interpolating β_t over the interval $[\beta_{\text{start}}, \beta_{\text{end}}]$. For the Cosine schedule we use the smoothed form:

$$\alpha_{\text{cumprod}}(t) = \cos^2\left(\frac{t/T + s}{1+s}\cdot\frac{\pi}{2}\right). \tag{4}$$

where $s \in (0, 1)$ controls the early-stage disturbance rate (a larger s yields a smoother start). Each schedule uses parameter ranges consistent with its design; our goal is to make the temporal profile of noise injection controllable and observable, so that differences in dynamic-structure modeling and predictive performance can be examined more clearly.

3.2 Requirement Analysis

Given the importance of noise scheduling for applying diffusion models to time-series forecasting, we aim to build a VA framework that supports interactive comparative analysis of intermediate representations across multiple noise schedules during the diffusion process. To clarify the research gaps and design goals, we conducted a focused survey of recent work on diffusion models for time-series forecasting [3,20,21]and on VA for model interpretability [22–24]. From this survey, we found the following requirements:

R1: Stage Alignment and Unified Comparison. Provide schedule-aware stage partitioning of the diffusion process so that intermediate states under different schedules are semantically comparable.

R2: Path Presentation and Evolution. Visualize diffusion trajectories and structural aggregation in latent space to reveal how schedules shape the morphology of generation paths.

R3: Emphasis on Temporal Components. In the TFT representation space, identify dimensions that exhibit the most pronounced differences, and support reconstruction along these dimensions to distinguish each schedule's modeling preferences on different temporal components.

R4: Local Time-Segment Analysis. Support interactive comparisons starting from time segments or key samples to facilitate scenario-specific analysis.

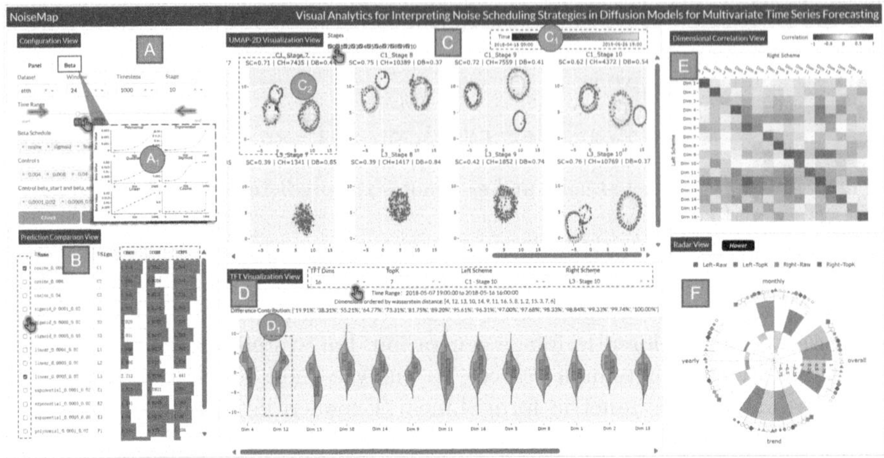

Fig. 2. The interface of NoiseMap. Configuration View (A) configures noise-schedule parameters and includes a stage-reference inset (A1). Prediction Comparison View (B) compares schedules by RMSE, CORR, and CRPS. UMAP-2D Visualization View (C) and TFT Visualization View (D) compare schedules in latent space. Dimensional Correlation View (E) inspects correlations among TFT dimensions. Radar View (F) summarizes temporal components and modeling preferences to contrast schedules. (Color figure online)

3.3 Analytical Tasks

We summarize the following tasks based on the aforementioned requirements. The tasks follow an overview-to-detail progression from global comparison to local, scenario-specific analysis.

T1: Global Comparison. Under a unified stage-partition rule, provide an overview and side-by-side comparison across noise schedules. Analysts focus on:

- *What evolutionary structures and aggregation patterns do different schedules form in latent space?* **(R1)**
- *Where do stage-wise performance differences emerge?* **(R2)**

T2: Key Dimensions and Structural Components. In the TFT representation space, identify dimensions with the most pronounced cross-schedule differences, and use them for reconstruction and interpretation:

- *Which dimensions differ most across schedules?* **(R3)**
- *How do these dimensions correspond to temporal components such as trend and seasonality?* **(R3)**

T3: Fine-Grained Analysis from Local Segments. Starting from local temporal segments or key samples, conduct interactive comparison and alignment:

– *How do diffusion paths and modeling behaviors change within specific periods, enabling scenario-specific analysis?* **(R4)**

4 NoiseMap

4.1 Noise Scheduling and Stage Partition

Let the noise schedule be $\{\beta_t\}_{t=1}^{T}$ with $\beta_t \in (0,1)$, $\alpha_t = 1-\beta_t$, and $\bar{\alpha}_t = \prod_{s=1}^{t} \alpha_s$.

Classes of Noise Schedules. We parameterize common noise schedules:

$$\beta_t = \beta_{\text{start}} + (\beta_{\text{end}} - \beta_{\text{start}})\, w_t, \qquad t = 1, \ldots, T. \tag{5}$$

where $w_t \in [0,1]$ specifies the time profile. We use

$$w_t = \begin{cases} \dfrac{t}{T}, & \text{Linear schedule,} \\ \dfrac{e^{\kappa t/T} - 1}{e^{\kappa} - 1}, & \text{Exponential schedule,} \\ \left(\dfrac{t}{T}\right)^{p}, & \text{Polynomial / Quadratic schedule,} \\ \sigma\left(a\left(\dfrac{t}{T} - 0.5\right)\right), & \text{Sigmoid schedule.} \end{cases} \tag{6}$$

where $\kappa \in \mathbb{R}$ controls the curvature of the exponential profile; $p > 0$ is the power exponent for the polynomial profile; $\sigma(x) = 1/(1 + e^{-x})$ denotes the logistic function; and $a > 0$ sets its slope around $t/T = 0.5$. The normalization ensures $w_0 = 0$ and $w_T = 1$.

For the Cosine schedule (defined on $\bar{\alpha}$), we use the smoothed form

$$\bar{\alpha}(t) = \cos^2\left(\frac{t/T + s}{1 + s} \cdot \frac{\pi}{2}\right), \quad s \in (0,1). \tag{7}$$

where s is a smoothing constant, users can inspect the schedule-specific stage-partition details in Fig. 2 A1.

4.2 Evaluation Protocol

We assess forecasts using a composite protocol comprising three complementary criteria—point accuracy (RMSE), temporal consistency (CORR), and probabilistic calibration (CRPS).

Standard UMAP implicitly assumes independent and identically distributed (i.i.d.) samples and thus ignores temporal dependencies, which can break evolutionary continuity, We augment the UMAP objective with three structure-aware regularizers to preserve temporal properties in the latent embedding: direction consistency loss (DCL), trend preservation loss (TPL), and periodicity regularization loss (PRL). Intuitively, DCL encourages locally smooth latent directions, TPL aligns the dominant trend between the original sequence and the latent trajectory, and PRL enforces consistency between points.

5 Visual Analytics Framework

5.1 UMAP-2D Visualization View

This view (Fig. 2 C) compares latent structures across noise schedules and diffusion stages. We adopt a small-multiples matrix: rows are schedules and columns are stages. Each panel shows a 2D projection; points correspond to the selected temporal segment. Colors are encoded according to the legend (Fig. 2 C_1) to represent time; the resulting trajectories reveal their direction and continuity (Fig. 3).

Users can hover to see tooltips (time index and latent coordinates)(Fig. 2 C_2), drag the time-range slider to highlight a temporal segment across all panels, synchronize views via the slider, and zoom/pan for local inspection.

For quantitative guidance, the top of each panel displays three cluster-structure indices: Silhouette Coefficient (SC), Calinski–Harabasz (CH), and Davies–Bouldin (DB), which update with schedules and stages to quantify cohesion and separation;their stage-wise variation, together with the time-encoded trajectories, helps reveal differences in latent evolution across schedules.

5.2 TFT Visualization View

This view (Fig. 2 D) enables side-by-side analysis of two selected schemes by visualizing the distributions of TFT-encoder latent dimensions within the selected temporal segment. Users first set four options: **TFT Dims** d (how many latent dimensions to extract), **TopK** K (how many key dimensions to focus on), and the two configurations via **Left Scheme** and **Right Scheme** (each a schedule–stage pair to compare). Given these settings, the view renders paired violin plots for the d dimensions (one row per dimension): the left violin shows the **Left Scheme** in blue and the right violin shows the **Right Scheme** in red.

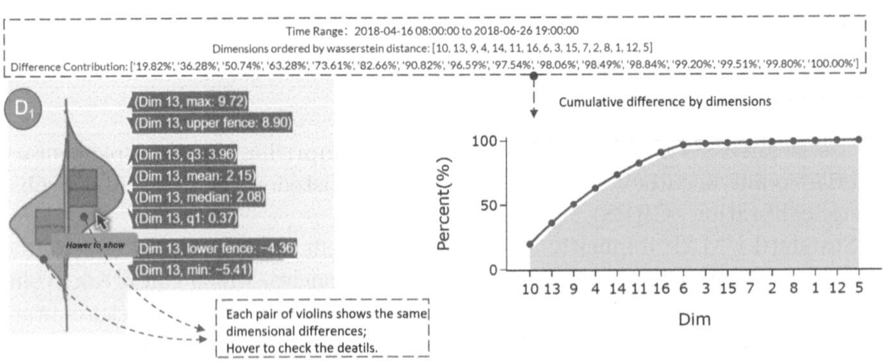

Fig. 3. Each violin pair in the TFT Visualization View shows the dimension-wise distribution difference; dimensions are ordered by the Wasserstein distance. Hover to inspect the distribution of each violin plot.

Each violin summarizes the kernel density of latent values; optional boxplots overlay the min–max whiskers, the Q1/Q3 box, and the mean. By comparing location and spread, users assess representation stability and distributional shifts across dimensions. All samples that form the violins correspond exactly to the temporal segment covered by the time-range slider, ensuring temporal consistency with other views.

5.3 Dimensional Correlation View

This view (Fig. 2 E) reveals how noise schedules shape the latent structure by visualizing inter–dimension correlations within the selected temporal segment.

Both axes enumerate latent dimensions (Dim 1, ..., Dim d); the heatmap is a $d \times d$ correlation matrix. Let $z_i^L, z_i^R \in \mathbb{R}^N$ be the i-th TFT latent series for the **Left** and **Right** schemes over the selected temporal segment All correlations are Pearson coefficients (range $[-1, 1]$; color mapping per legend).

- **Main diagonal** ($i{=}j$): cross–scheme alignment of the same-index dimensions, $C_{ii} = \mathrm{corr}\big(z_i^L,\, z_i^R\big)$.
- **Upper triangle** ($i{<}j$): within–scheme correlations for the **Right scheme**, $C_{ij} = \mathrm{corr}\big(z_i^R,\, z_j^R\big)$.
- **Lower triangle** ($i{>}j$): within–scheme correlations for the **Left scheme**, $C_{ij} = \mathrm{corr}\big(z_i^L,\, z_j^L\big)$.

Hovering a cell shows the triple (i, j, corr) . An approximately diagonal–dominant pattern indicates disentanglement; persistent off–diagonal bands/blocks indicate intra–scheme coupling, while small values on the main diagonal suggest semantic drift between schemes at the same dimension index.

5.4 Radar View

The Radar View (Fig. 2 F) compares **Left Scheme** and **Right Scheme** on trend, seasonality(monthly, yearly), and an across-variable overall correlation score. The time span is synchronized with the global time–range slider.

Using a unified TFT encode–decode pipeline, we produce two reconstructions: *Raw* decodes from the full latent vector; **TopK** keeps only the K key latent dimensions selected in the TFT Visualization view (others are zeroed in the same normalized space) and decodes. Each reconstruction is then decomposed by Prophet into trend, monthly, yearly, and an across-variable correlation is computed as the overall metric.

Dimension Contribution. To quantify the marginal effect of a single latent dimension on each aspect, for scheme s and aspect in trend, monthly, yearly, and overall, let $\rho^{(s)}_{a,\mathrm{all}}$ be the correlation using all dimensions and $\rho^{(s)}_{a,-k}$ the correlation after removing dimension k. With the Fisher-z transform for stable comparison,

$$\Delta^{(s)}_{k,a} = z\left(\rho^{(s)}_{a,\mathrm{all}}\right) - z\left(\rho^{(s)}_{a,-k}\right), \qquad z(\rho) = \tfrac{1}{2}\ln\frac{1+\rho}{1-\rho}. \tag{8}$$

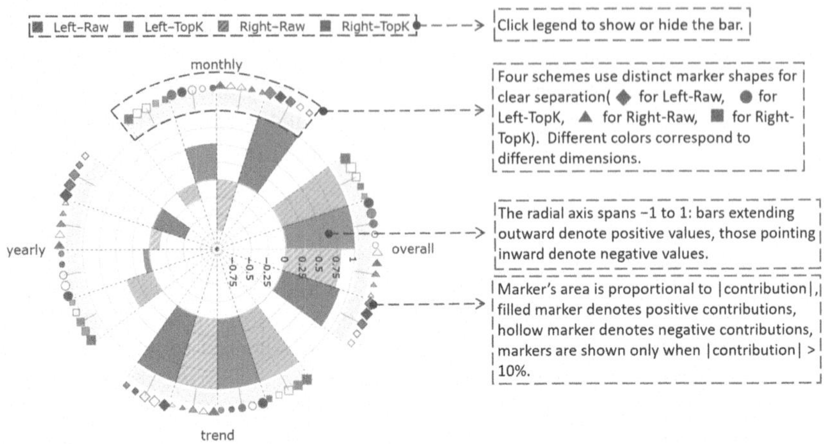

Fig. 4. Radar View, shows differences between the left and right schedules across different temporal components, TopK overlays reconstructions using the selected K dimensions, revealing modeling preferences. Hover to inspect each dimension's contribution on each component.

We normalize positive contributions across dimensions for visualization (Fig. 4):

$$w_{k,a}^{(s)} = \frac{\max\left(0, \Delta_{k,a}^{(s)}\right)}{\sum_j \max\left(0, \Delta_{j,a}^{(s)}\right) + \varepsilon}, \tag{9}$$

with a small $\varepsilon > 0$ for numerical stability. In this view, marker area is proportional to $w_{k,a}^{(s)}$ (contribution strength) and fill/outline encodes the sign($\Delta_{k,a}^{(s)}$).

Radial values are mapped to $[-1, 1]$: outward bars denote positive values, inward bars denote negative values. The four series (Left-Raw, Left-TopK, Right-Raw, Right-TopK) use distinct colors and marker styles. The legend toggles series visibility; tooltips show scheme, value and contribution.

6 Evaluation

6.1 Case Study: ETTh

In this case, Mike selected a real world multivariate time series dataset, ETTh. The dataset comprises hourly measurements from a Chinese power grid, combining transformer operation logs and meteorological observations, spanning July 2016 to July 2018 (about 17,000 records). To emulate a realistic long-term forecasting scenario, the data were split chronologically into training and test sets at a 9:1 ratio. The goal is to forecast and to examine how different noise schedules affect modeling behavior and predictive performance.

First, he set the window to 24 and partitioned the diffusion process into 10 stages. He then loaded all noise schedule in Configuration View (Fig. 2 A) and conducted an overall comparison in the Prediction Compare View (Fig. 2 B). The initial assessment shows that Cosine is the most balanced and overall strongest across the three metrics; Polynomial excels in RMSE but is clearly weaker in CORR and CRPS, indicating better point accuracy but poorer stability and calibration; Exponential ranks near the top on CORR yet lags on RMSE and CRPS; by contrast, Linear underperforms Cosine on all metrics (Fig. 5).

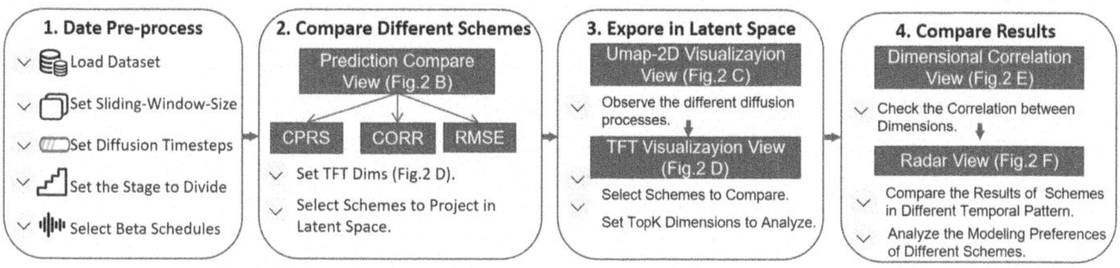

Fig. 5. Workflow of the case study.

Next, Mike set TFT Dims in TFT Visualization View (Fig. 2 D) to 16 and switched to the UMAP-2D Visualization View(Fig. 2 C) to compare the latent structural evolution under different schedules. As illustrated in the figure, the Cosine schedule (first row in Fig. 2 C, **C1**) quickly exhibits clear partitioning in mid-to-late stages (Stage 7 to Stage 10), reaching high structural quality at Stage 8 (SC=0.75, CH=10389, DB=0.37), indicating that well-separated latent representations emerge earlier. In contrast, the Linear schedule (second row in Fig. 2 C, **L3**) remains dense and undifferentiated at the same stages, showing noticeable separation by Stage 10 (SC=0.76, CH=10769, DB=0.37). This difference suggests that **C1** converges earlier to semantically meaningful latent structure, whereas **L3** requires more diffusion steps to achieve effective modeling. Mike then focused on Stage 10 and highlighted the 30%–42.5% time slice to examine key samples that transition smoothly from one cluster to another, probing the high-dimensional mechanisms behind changes in the diffusion path. To this end, he applied a TFT-based dimensionality-reduction step to project the predictions and visualize their aggregate distribution patterns.

In the Dimensional Correlation View(Fig. 2 E), Mike analyzed pairwise correlations. The upper and lower triangles visualize, respectively, the within-schedule Pearson correlations for Linear and Cosine. He observed that the lower triangle (**C1**) concentrates closer to zero, indicating better decoupling across dimensions and more independent temporal signals; the upper triangle (**L2**) shows broadly higher positive correlations, implying more pronounced coupling in the high-dimensional representation. This decoupling difference suggests that, compared with **L3**, **C1** forms more separable temporal-structure representations in latent space, providing clearer support for components such as trend and yearly cycles.

To verify whether this difference affects temporal-component modeling, Mike proceeded to the Radar View to compare performance on the original components using **TopK** dimensions. The Radar View (Fig. 2 F) presents, for each schedule, the modeling correlations across multiple temporal components. The results show that **C1** achieves noticeably higher correlations than **L3** on all four components in the selected temporal segment, further confirming that its latent-space decoupling advantage contributes positively to modeling performance. Mike then examined dimension-level contributions and found that most of the component gaps are driven by the top three dimensions in Wasserstein distance, which directly reflects the two schemes' modeling preferences over temporal components.

6.2 User Study

Interview Participants. This study targets graduate-level machine learning practitioners. Our sample (7 male, 3 female; mean age 24 years) covers diverse subfields and varying prior exposure to diffusion models, which increases heterogeneity. Participation was voluntary (Fig. 6).

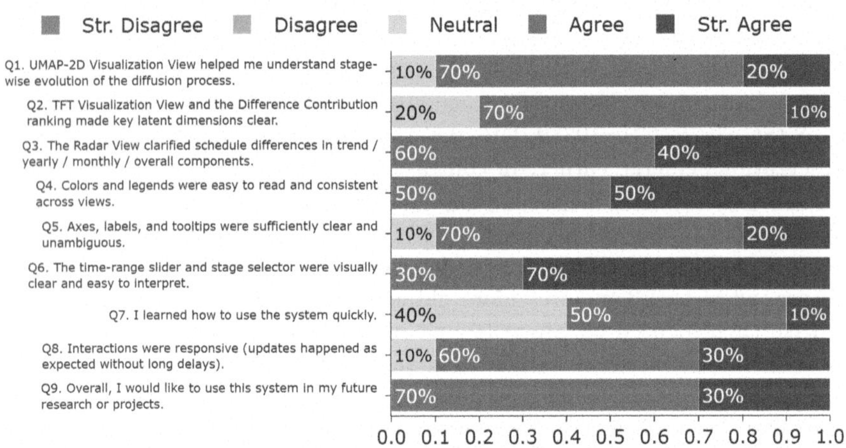

Fig. 6. Questions and results of the user interview. The left are the questions, the right are the scores given by ten users corresponding to each question, users are asked to rate by a point Likert scale (from strongly disagree to strongly agree).

Interview Process. The study followed a three-step protocol: (1) brief tutorial (~5 min) introducing the system goals, the coordinated views, and key controls (time-range slider, stage selector, *TopK*); (2) free exploration (~15–20 min) on NoiseMap; (3) questionnaire & short interview (~10–15 min). The questionnaire contained **9** five-point Likert items covering Interpretability, Visual Design, and Usability. Response distributions are summarized in Fig. 6.

Results. We summarize findings by item blocks :

- **Q1–Q3 (Interpretability).** Most participants agreed that NoiseMap supports stage-wise evolution tracing, surfaces key latent dimensions, and enables component-level comparison—confirming its effectiveness for comparative, explanation-oriented analysis.
- **Q4–Q6 (Visual Design).** The visual design was consistently clear and coherent, indicating low reading effort and stable cross-view alignment.
- **Q7–Q9 (Usability).** Participants learned the interface quickly, reported responsive interactions, and indicated strong willingness to reuse.

Overall, the study shows that NoiseMap supports understanding and comparison of diffusion schedules, offers a coherent and readable design, and achieves practical usability for research workflows.

7 Conclusion

We present NoiseMap, a VA framework for comparing and interpreting noise schedules in multivariate diffusion-based forecasting. Evidence from the ETTh case and the user study indicates that NoiseMap helps users quickly localize influential dimensions and time segments, improving schedule selection and model tuning. Future work will extend to broader models and scenarios, and further enhance scalability and analytical depth.

Acknowledgments. This work is supported by grants of the National Natural Science Foundation of China (No. 62372153) and the Anhui Provincial Natural Science Foundation (No. 2308085MF216).

References

1. Ho, J., Jain, A., Abbeel, P.: Denoising diffusion probabilistic models. Adv. Neural. Inf. Process. Syst. **33**, 6840–6851 (2020)
2. Blattmann, A., et al.: Align your latents: high-resolution video synthesis with latent diffusion models. In: Proceedings of the IEEE/CVF Conference on Computer Vision and Pattern Recognition, pp. 22563–22575 (2023)
3. Guo, Z., Lang, J., Huang, S., Gao, Y., Ding, X.: A comprehensive review on noise control of diffusion model. arXiv preprint arXiv:2502.04669 (2025)
4. Rasul, K., Seward, C., Schuster, I., Vollgraf, R.: Autoregressive denoising diffusion models for multivariate probabilistic time series forecasting. In: International Conference on Machine Learning, pp. 8857–8868. PMLR (2021)
5. Liu, Y., Jun, E., Li, Q., Heer, J.: Latent space cartography: visual analysis of vector space embeddings. In: Computer Graphics Forum, vol. 38, pp. 67–78. Wiley Online Library (2019)
6. Poličar, P.G., Zupan, B.: Uncovering temporal patterns in visualizations of high-dimensional data. Mach. Learn. **114**(2), 35 (2025)

7. Shen, L., Kwok, J.: Non-autoregressive conditional diffusion models for time series prediction. In: International Conference on Machine Learning, pp. 31016–31029. PMLR (2023)
8. Tashiro, Y., Song, J., Song, Y., Ermon, S.: CSDI: conditional score-based diffusion models for probabilistic time series imputation. Adv. Neural. Inf. Process. Syst. **34**, 24804–24816 (2021)
9. Yuan, X., Qiao, Y.: Diffusion-TS: interpretable diffusion for general time series generation. arXiv preprint arXiv:2403.01742 (2024)
10. Zhao, Z., Shi, Y., Wu, S., Yang, F., Song, W., Liu, N.: Interpretation of time-series deep models: a survey. arXiv preprint arXiv:2305.14582 (2023)
11. Peng, H., et al.: Diffusion-based conditional wind power forecasting via channel attention. IET Renew. Power Gener. **18**(3), 306–320 (2024)
12. Nichol, A.Q., Dhariwal, P.: Improved denoising diffusion probabilistic models. In: International Conference on Machine Learning, pp. 8162–8171. PMLR (2021)
13. Hohman, F., Kahng, M., Pienta, R., Chau, D.H.: Visual analytics in deep learning: an interrogative survey for the next frontiers. IEEE Trans. Visual Comput. Graphics **25**(8), 2674–2693 (2018)
14. Strobelt, H., Gehrmann, S., Pfister, H., Rush, A.M.: LSTMVis: a tool for visual analysis of hidden state dynamics in recurrent neural networks. IEEE Trans. Visual Comput. Graphics **24**(1), 667–676 (2017)
15. Rauber, P.E., Falcao, A.X., Telea, A.C., et al.: Visualizing time-dependent data using dynamic t-SNE (2016)
16. McInnes, L., Healy, J., Melville, J.: UMAP: uniform manifold approximation and projection for dimension reduction. arXiv preprint arXiv:1802.03426 (2018)
17. Smilkov, D., Thorat, N., Nicholson, C., Reif, E., Viégas, F.B., Wattenberg, M.: Embedding projector: interactive visualization and interpretation of embeddings. arXiv preprint arXiv:1611.05469 (2016)
18. Kahng, M., Thorat, N., Chau, D.H., Viégas, F.B., Wattenberg, M.: GAN lab: understanding complex deep generative models using interactive visual experimentation. IEEE Trans. Visual Comput. Graphics **25**(1), 310–320 (2018)
19. Hyndman, R.J., Athanasopoulos, G.: Forecasting: principles and practice. OTexts (2018)
20. Multi-resolution diffusion models for time series. In: ICLR (2024)
21. Diffusion-TS: time series diffusion for probabilistic forecasting. In: ICLR (2024)
22. Schlegel, U., Keim, D.A., et al.: State of the art of visual analytics for explainable deep learning. In: Computer Graphics Forum (2023). STAR report
23. Wang, J., et al.: Visual analytics for machine learning: a data perspective. IEEE Trans. Vis. Comput. Graph. (2024)
24. Liu, M., et al.: VA+embeddings: visual analysis of embeddings – a star. Comput. Graph. Forum (2023)

Topic D: Collaborative Data, Software and Services

SHindex: A Two-Tier Distributed Index for Road-Network Trajectory Data

Hao Li, Na Tang(✉), Jingjing Li, and Yong Tang

College of Computer Science, South China Normal University, Guangzhou, China
tangna@scnu.edu.cn

Abstract. With the continuous advancement of Internet of Vehicles (IoV) technology and the widespread adoption of mobile device positioning, historical trajectory data from road networks have experienced explosive growth. Characterized by large volume, frequent updates, and significant noise, these data pose serious challenges to efficient storage management and fast query processing. To address these issues, this paper proposes SHindex, a distributed index based on the underlying HBase database and the Spark distributed computing framework. The structure of SHindex consists of three main components: data partitioning, a global index, and a local index. Data partitioning employs a time-slicing strategy combined with a Z2-index-based quadtree partitioning method to achieve preliminary data aggregation and fast positioning. The global index, built upon S2 mapping, projects spherical surfaces into a one-dimensional space to form a efficient lookup table, enabling coarse-grained spatio-temporal indexing. The local index uses a hybrid structure of a trinomial line-ordered tree and a Ball-tree to accomplish fine-grained spatio-temporal indexing. Furthermore, this paper introduces the ND (Next-Door) algorithm for trajectory outlier detection and a trajectory segmentation strategy as part of the preprocessing pipeline, significantly improving data quality. A data partitioning strategy is also designed to mitigate data skew and ensure load balancing across partitions. Finally, through comprehensive comparative experiments with 3DR-tree and TrajSpark, the results demonstrate that SHindex achieves superior performance in both spatio-temporal range queries and K-nearest neighbor (KNN) query scenarios.

Keywords: Distributed trajectory indexing · Spatio-temporal indexing · K-nearest neighbor query · Trajectory query

1 Introduction

With the rapid advancement of intelligent transportation systems, the historical trajectory data generated in the road network shows explosive growth. However, trajectory data contains rich information with mining value, but also has a huge amount of data, high update frequency, 'noise' and other characteristics, so it is necessary to efficiently store and manage these massive historical trajectory data, and establish a specific index to improve the efficiency of trajectory query.

© The Author(s), under exclusive license to Springer Nature Singapore Pte Ltd. 2027
H. Sun et al. (Eds.): ChineseCSCW 2025, CCIS 2911, pp. 143–154, 2027.
https://doi.org/10.1007/978-981-92-0288-1_11

This paper proposes a distributed index named SHindex for historical trajectory data in road networks, based on the HBase distributed storage and Spark computing framework. The index adopts a hierarchical architecture design: the upper-layer global index slices massive data by time dimension through a time-slicing partitioning strategy, and constructs quadtree partitions based on Z2 indexing within each time slice. The lower-layer local index utilizes a combined structure of a trident linear order tree and a Ball-tree within quadtree partitions to perform fine-grained indexing for time and space dimensions, respectively. Finally, multi-dimensional comparative experiments with 3DR-tree [1] and TrajSpark [2] show that SHindex demonstrates superior performance in scenarios such as spatio-temporal range queries and K-nearest neighbor queries.

2 Related Work

In the realm of distributed indexing, Summit [3] and HadoopTrajectory [4] are all built upon the Hadoop framework. Summit [3] adopts a two-level indexing architecture: the global index partitions trajectory data across different data nodes based on temporal information, while the local index utilizes R-trees, quadtrees, or KD-trees. HadoopTrajectory [4] extends the core layer of Hadoop to enable MapReduce programs to directly process trajectory data, storing index files in the HDFS file system. However, due to their reliance on the Hadoop framework, these indexes incur significant disk I/O overhead, leading to suboptimal efficiency.

Spark-based indexing systems include GeoSpark [5], DITA [6], TrajSpark [2], Dragoon [7], and RP-Tree [8]. GeoSpark [5] supports multiple spatial partitioning methods. DITA [6] effectively identifies central points and constructs tree index structures for these points to facilitate subsequent pruning operations. TrajSpark [2] features a Hash index at the head of each partition to map trajectories to moving object IDs. Dragoon [7] introduces a mutable RDD model to address the issue of RDD updates. RP-Tree [8] improves upon DITA by enabling hierarchical partitioning of road networks based on the traffic flow carried by each road segment. Spark-based indexes significantly accelerate data processing through in-memory computing. However, when spatio-temporal indexes exceed available memory capacity, query performance may degrade due to increased data spilling and memory management overhead.

NoSQL-based indexes include MD-HBase, GeoMesa [9], TrajMesa [10], TMan [11] and LevelDBST [12]. Both MD-HBase and GeoMesa use Z-Ordering curves to transform multi-dimensional data into one-dimensional space, supporting spatio-temporal range queries and nearest neighbor searches. TrajMesa [10] introduces a horizontal storage model and innovatively proposes a composite key-value encoding structure to support complex queries. TMan [11] develops the TShape index to represent the spatial features of trajectories. LevelDBST [12] introduce the Dual-Key Encoding (DKE) scheme within the spatio-temporal Layer. However, these indexes do not consider the mutation problem of Z-curve encoding, and their management is complex. They require designing different key-values for different trajectory queries, leading to data redundancy.

Learning-Based Indexes. SLBRIN [13] integrates traditional BRIN (Block Range Index) with neural networks for efficient one-dimensional key-value queries in columnar databases. Patil [14] boosts training efficiency by transferring pre-trained model structures across datasets based on distribution similarity. However, these methods face challenges in two or higher dimensions, such as uneven data distribution, dimensional coupling, and high-dimensional sparsity [15]. It is currently primarily used in read-only analysis or hot-cold data tiering scenarios, with the future trend lying in its combined use with traditional indexes.

3 SHIndex Model

3.1 Overall Introduction

SHindex employs HBase as its underlying data storage. The trajectory index is structured into three modules: data partitioning, local index, and global index. Prior to building the trajectory index, data preprocessing is essential. The main purpose of data preprocessing is to clean, transform, and optimize raw trajectory data, ensuring the accuracy and efficiency of subsequent processing and analysis. Data partitioning distributes the data evenly across storage nodes through specific partitioning algorithms to achieve load balancing. The global index provides coarse-grained retrieval, narrowing queries down to a relatively broad yet accurate spatial range. In contrast, the local index performs finer-grained retrieval, enabling more precise data localization. The system supports various trajectory queries, including but not limited to K-Nearest Neighbor (KNN) queries and spatio-temporal range queries. The entire system is driven by Spark as the execution engine. Leveraging its in-memory computation capability, Spark significantly reduces disk I/O and accelerates data processing speed. Meanwhile, its parallel processing capacity further enhances the overall query performance of the system (Fig. 1).

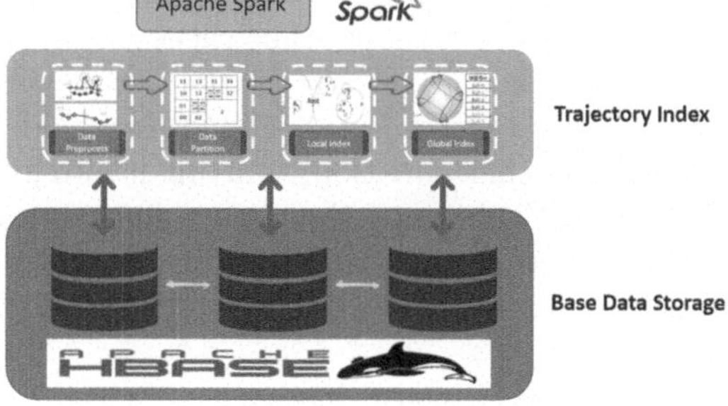

Fig. 1. Overall Architecture Diagram.

3.2 Data Preprocessing

During data collection, numerous outliers emerge due to various factors. As illustrated in Fig. 2, points ain trajectory tr1and point bin tr2are identified as outliers, since the segments connecting them to adjacent points deviate markedly from the overall trajectory direction. If retained, such outliers would adversely affect subsequent steps like data partitioning and index construction. To address this, we propose the ND (Next-Door) algorithm, which calculates the number of adjacent points for each GPS location and removes those with abnormal neighbor counts.

For trajectory segmentation, a multi-criteria strategy is introduced, incorporating thresholds for time, distance, direction angle, and instantaneous velocity. If the difference between consecutive points along a trajectory exceeds any of these thresholds, the point is designated as a segmentation point, reflecting a significant change in motion state and triggering subdivision of the trajectory (Fig. 3).

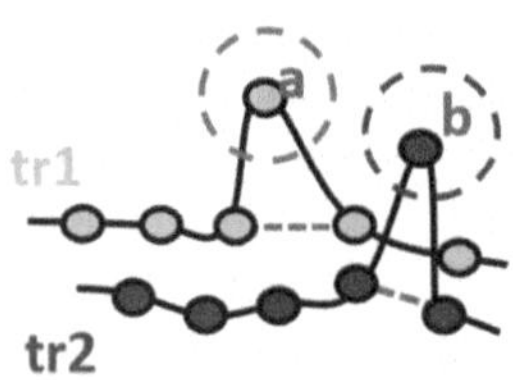

Fig. 2. Trajectory Outliers.

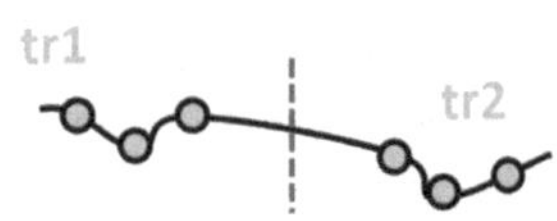

Fig. 3. Trajectory Segmentation.

3.3 Data Partitioning

To improve the efficiency of data management and query processing, trajectory data within the same partition should adhere to the principles of temporal locality and spatial locality. This paper proposes a time-first, space-second partitioning method. For the temporal Partitioning, time slices are divided according to a fixed time interval (year, month, day); for the spatial Partitioning, when the data volume within a Z2 partition exceeds a predefined threshold, the system triggers a dynamic subdivision of that partition, splitting it into four sub-partitions. This process continues recursively until the data volume in each sub-partition reaches a balanced state. This ensures that even in areas with extremely high data density, the system can effectively distribute the workload through finer grid granularity (Fig. 4).

3.4 Global Index

The global index is stored on the master node of the cluster, maintaining metadata about partitioned data across all slave nodes. To address this, this paper

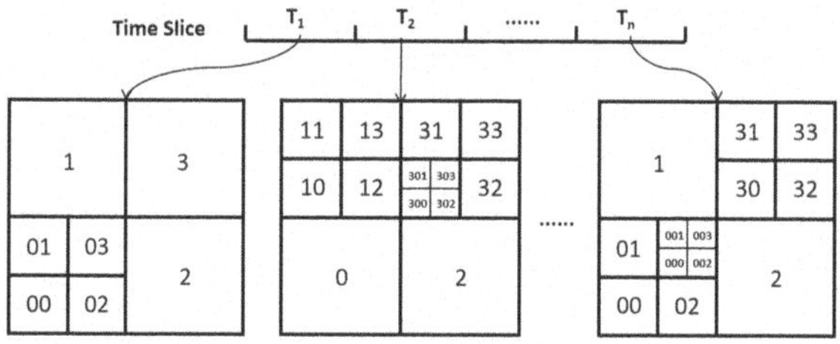

Fig. 4. Data Partitioning.

proposes a SHIndex inspired by the S2 indexing system. Specifically: Given longitude and latitude coordinates, a sphere ID can be computed along with its corresponding Hilbert curve encoding. By integrating temporal information, the combined spatio-temporal key can be used to query the SHIndex table and retrieve the corresponding partition ID (Fig. 5).

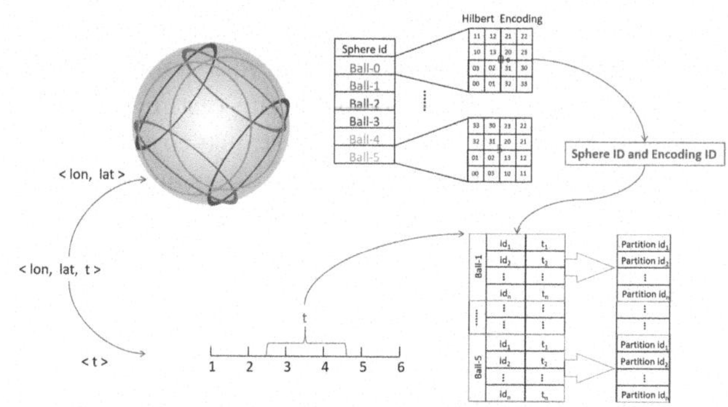

Fig. 5. Global Index.

3.5 Local Index

For each partition, a corresponding TB-Tree is constructed. The TB-Tree consists of an upper-layer time index and a lower-layer space index. For the upper-layer time index, a bucketing strategy is adopted for construction, whose core goal is to determine an optimal time split point to balance the subsequent ternary ordinal tree and facilitate subsequent pruning operations. This process is divided into three steps: time interval bucketing, in-bucket average midpoint calculation, and global equilibrium split point calculation. For example, given the time intervals{[1,3],[1,4],[1,5],[1,6],[2,3],[2,4],[2,5],[3,4],[4,5],[4,6],[4.5,5.5],[5,6],[5,7],[5,8], [6,7], [6,9],[7,8],[7,9]}, the final midpoint is calculated as 4.75. Based on the global equilibrium split point, a balanced trinomial line-ordered tree can be constructed, as shown in Fig. 6.

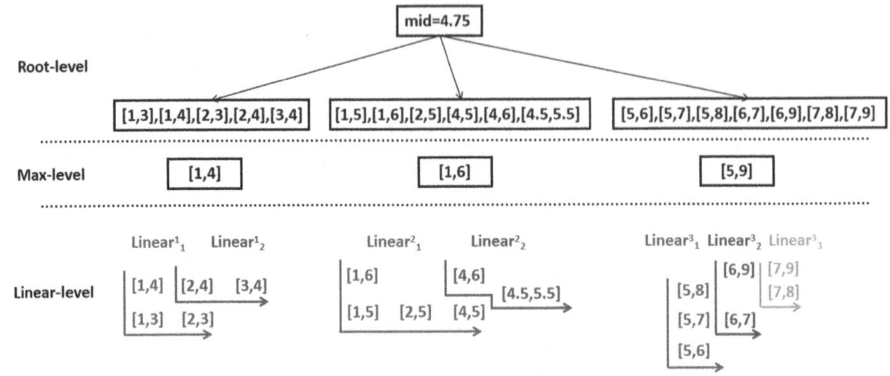

Fig. 6. Trinomial Line-ordered Tree.

When constructing the lower-layer spatial index, the process begins by identifying the two points with the maximum Euclidean distance in the target spatial region, denoted as points a and b. The midpoint of the line segment connecting these two points is calculated and defined as the root node Root. Based on this, Region A and Region B are partitioned using the distances from points a and b to Root. For a given point set, if a point's distance to point a is smaller than its distance to point b, it is assigned to Region A; otherwise, it is assigned to Region B. After the initial partitioning, the above steps are recursively applied to each region until the predefined maximum resolution is achieved. This process is illustrated in Fig. 7.

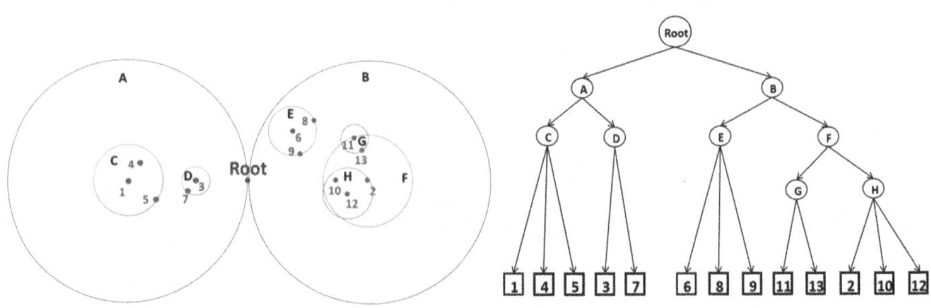

Fig. 7. Local Spatial Index.

Algorithm 1 Construction of Local Index TB-Tree

Input: *Data Partition*
Output: *Local Index*

/*Stage 1: Constructing the Upper-Layer Temporal Index*/
For the current partition, group individual trajectories into time buckets based on their initial timestamp (first_time).
Compute a globally balanced temporal split point (final_mid) from the aggregated data of all buckets. This point aims to create balanced subsets for efficient query pruning.
Construct a balanced trinomial-linear tree using final_mid as the root split value. This tree structure provides an ordered index for the temporal dimension, enabling fast filtering of trajectories based on time ranges.
/*Stage 2: Constructing the Lower-Layer Spatial Index*/
For the spatial data within the partition, recursively build a Ball-tree:
While the current region's resolution is finer than the preset maximum resolution and the region is not empty.
Identify the two points with the maximum Euclidean distance within the current region.
Calculate the midpoint between these two farthest points.
Partition all points in the current region into two sub-regions (Domain_A, Domain_B) based on which of the two farthest points they are closer to (using Euclidean distance).

In Algorithm 1, assuming the number of partitions is m, the average number of trajectories per partition is n, and the number of buckets is b (typically a small constant), the time complexity of Stage 1 (constructing the upper-layer temporal index) can be approximated as $O(nm)$, while the time complexity of Stage 2 (constructing the lower-layer spatial index) is $O(mn^2)$.

4 SHIndex Query Operation

Spatio-Temporal Range Query. Spatio-temporal range query refers to returning all data that lies within both a specified spatial region and a specified temporal interval. The detailed algorithm for spatiotemporal range queries is presented in Algorithm 2.

Algorithm 2 Spatio-temporal range query

Input: The query requires a temporal range Qt and a spatial range Qs
Output: $Presult$:Collection of points which match the query range
1: **Global index query**: According to the query spatial range Qs,calculate the corresponding spherical surface number id and the corresponding Hilbert code;According to the query temporal range Qt,search for the eligible partitions Partition through the spatiotemporal hash index table.
2: **Local index query**: Within the partitions that match Qt, find the sequence set related to Qt in the ternary line order tree;Search spherical spaces of line sequences meeting time conditions, then find spatial points satisfying Qs.
3: **Integrate the query result sets**: Deduplicate the obtained spatial points and store them in point set $Presult$.

K-Nearest Neighbor Query. K-nearest neighbor query refers to finding the K points closest to a query point q given an integer K. The specific algorithm for K-nearest neighbor queries is presented in Algorithm 3.

Algorithm 3 K-nearest neighbor query

Input: The central point q of the $MBRi$ represented by the query trajectory segment Tri, and the value of K
Output: Query result set $Presult$
1: **Use the global index**: Get query point q's temporal range Qt and spatial range Qs;Search eligible partitions via the spatiotemporal hash index table using Qs and Qt.
2: **Use the local index**: Use the trinomial line-ordered tree in the partition to find the set of line sequences related to Qt;Search the set of spherical spaces corresponding to the line sequences that meet the time conditions, and find the spatial points containing the query point q.
3: **Find the K points nearest to the query point q**: If current spatial region has $\geq K$ points, return top K; else expand search to upper layer and return top K.(Backtracking search ensures complete nearest neighbor recall by leveraging the parent node's full containment of all descendant nodes.)

5 Experimental

The road network dataset is derived from Guangzhou, while the trajectory dataset is generated using the Thomas-Brinkhoff [16]. This paper uses a 3-node cluster for experiments, with 3DR-tree and TrajSpark as baselines. 3DR-tree integrates temporal info as the 3rd dimension, mapping trajectories to 3D space via 3D MBRs to address traditional indexing limits. TrajSpark adopts a 3-layer hybrid index (temporal, quadtree, B+ tree) for fast object localization and query.

5.1 SHindex Construction Experiments

This subsection compares the index construction costs (spatial in Fig. 8 and time in Fig. 9) of SHindex, 3DR-tree, and TrajSpark. As the experimental data volume increases from 300K to 1.8M, all three methods show a linear upward trend in spatio-temporal costs. In terms of spatial overhead, SHindex requires higher resources to build both global and local indexes, while TrajSpark uses a three-layer global index structure but only a simple hash table for local indexing, resulting in lower spatial costs than SHindex. In terms of time, SHindex incurs higher costs than the other two due to its complex local index construction, which involves building both an upper-layer trinomial line-ordered tree and a lower-layer spatial index.

5.2 SHindex Queries Experiments

Spatio-Temporal Range Queries. The performance evaluation of spatio-temporal range queries can be divided into the following three scenarios.

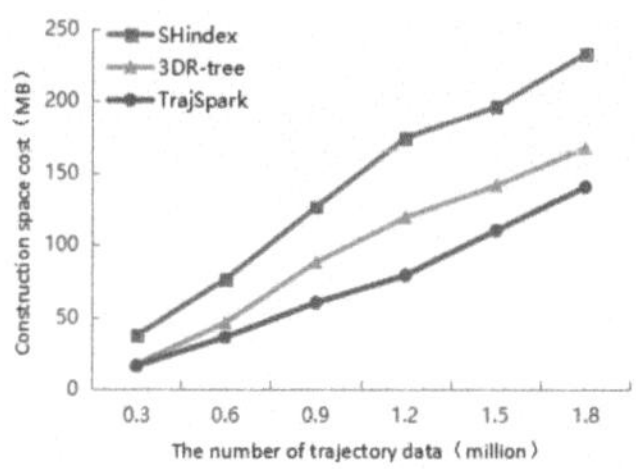

Fig. 8. Spatial Costs of Index.

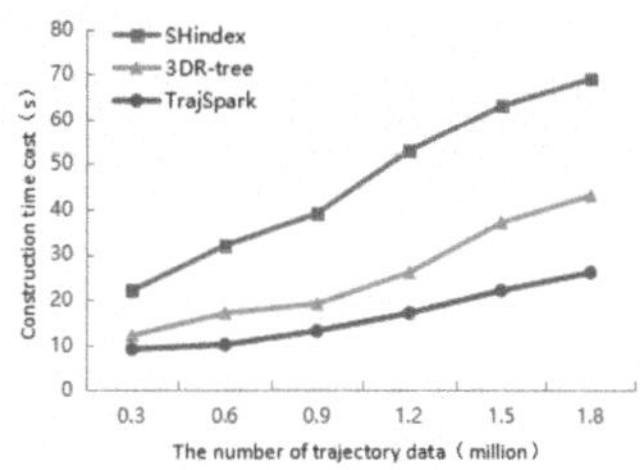

Fig. 9. Time Costs of Index.

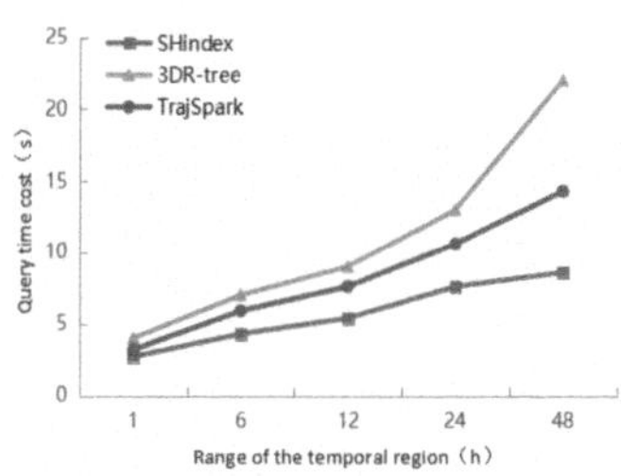

Fig. 10. Only changing time regions.

(1) For the queries with only changing time ranges. Results in Fig. 10.
(2) For the queries with only changing spatial ranges. Results in Fig. 11.
(3) For the queries with fixed spatio-temporal range and changing data volume. Results in Fig. 12.

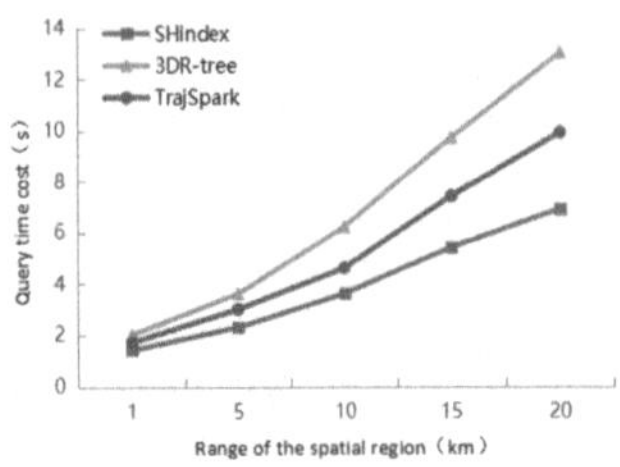

Fig. 11. Only changing spatial regions.

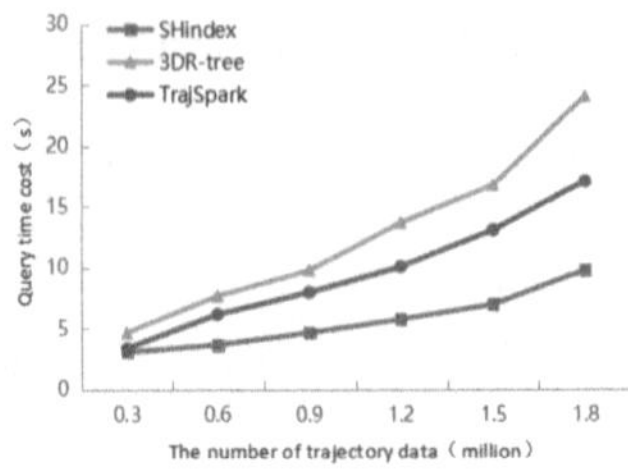

Fig. 12. Fixed spatio-temporal range and changing data volume.

Experimental results show that 3DR-tree has significantly higher query overhead than other methods in all three query scenarios, with exponential growth as query conditions change. TrajSpark uses a three-level hierarchy to boost data positioning efficiency, but its local index relies on lightweight hash mapping, lacking deep spatio-temporal indexing. This forces TrajSpark to perform global scans for spatio-temporal range queries instead of targeted filtering. By contrast, SHindex combines a global index with a two-layer local index for efficient irrelevant data filtering. Despite high index construction costs, SHindex delivers superior query performance in spatio-temporal range query scenarios.

K-Nearest Neighbor Queries. The performance evaluation of K-nearest neighbor (KNN) queries can be categorized into two scenarios.

(1) For the queries with fixed data volume and adjusted K values. Results in Fig. 13.
(2) For the queries with fixed K value and expanded data volume. Results in Fig. 14.

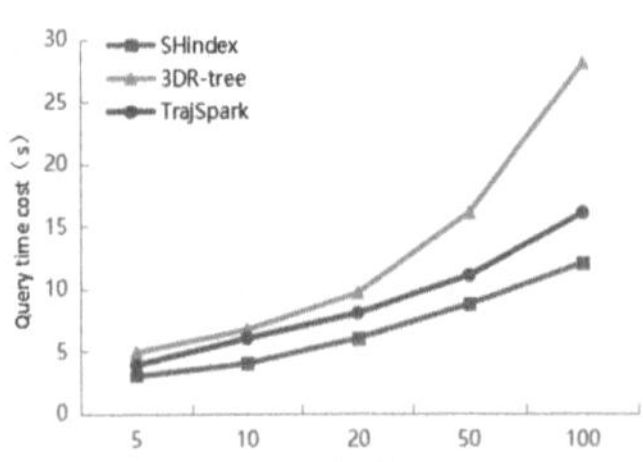

Fig. 13. Fixed data volume and adjusted K values.

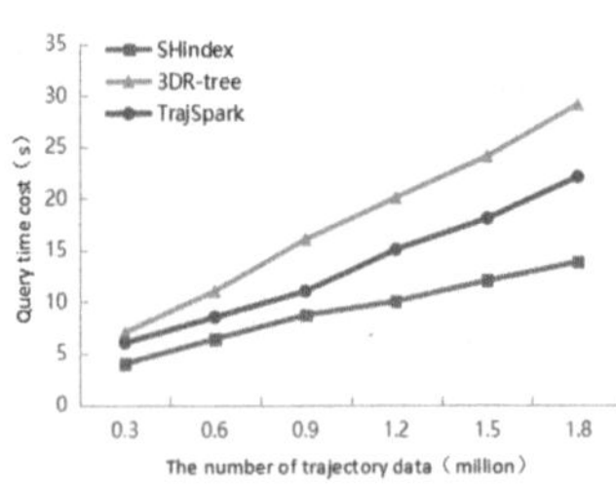

Fig. 14. Fixed K value and expanded data volume.

Experimental results show that the time overhead of the three indexes gradually increases for both query types. As the K value increases, 3DR-tree needs to traverse more MBR nodes, causing the number of invalid traversals to grow exponentially, while TrajSpark requires collecting more trajectory data and calculating distances for KNN queries, with its global sorting time positively correlated with the K value—SHindex, however, reduces invalid node traversal via its lower-layer spatial ball tree. When the data volume increases, the depth of 3DR-tree rises, leading to more hierarchical node traversals, and TrajSpark's hash table entries grow, requiring more trajectory data scans for KNN; although SHindex's global index partitions also increase, it prunes candidates through the global index and filters irrelevant data via spatio-temporal-aware local indexing, maintaining efficient query performance.

6 Conclusion

This paper proposes a hierarchical distributed index SHindex. The upper-layer global index, based on an improved S2 index, maps 2D space to 1D Hilbert curve and integrates time dimension for fast data-to-partition ID mapping via spatio-temporal hash table. The lower-layer local index uses TB-Tree for intra-partition search. After data denoising and trajectory segmentation preprocessing, a time-first then space partitioning method is proposed for load balancing. It supports spatio-temporal range and KNN queries. Experiments against 3DR-tree and TrajSpark show SHindex outperforms in query performance. Future work will explore complex query types.

References

1. Theodoridis, Y., Vazirgiannis, M., Sellis, T.: Spatio-temporal indexing for large multimedia applications. In: Proceedings of the Third IEEE International Conference on Multimedia Computing and Systems, pp. 441–448. (1996)
2. Zhang, Z., Jin, C., Mao, J., et al.: TrajSpark: a scalable and efficient in-memory management system for big trajectory data. In: Chen, L., Jensen, C., Shahabi, C., Yang, X., Lian, X. (eds.) Web and Big Data. APWeb-WAIM 2017. LNCS, vol. 10366, pp. 11–26. Springer, Cham (2017). https://doi.org/10.1007/978-3-319-63579-8_2
3. Alarabi, L.: Summit: a scalable system for massive trajectory data management. Sigspatial Spec. **10**(3), 2–3 (2018)
4. Bakli, M., Sakr, M., Soliman, T.H.A.: HadoopTrajectory: a Hadoop spatiotemporal data processing extension. J. Geogr. Syst. **21**(2), 211–235 (2019)
5. Yu, J., Wu, J., Sarwat, M.: Geospark: a cluster computing framework for processing large-scale spatial data. In: Proceedings of the 23rd SIGSPATIAL International Conference on Advances in Geographic Information Systems, pp. 1–4 (2015)
6. Shang, Z., Li, G., Bao, Z.: DITA: distributed in-memory trajectory analytics. In: Proceedings of the 2018 International Conference on Management of Data, pp. 725–740. (2018)
7. Fang, Z., Chen, L., Gao, Y.: Dragoon: a hybrid and efficient big trajectory management system for offline and online analytics, pp. 287–310 (2021)
8. Wang, Y., Li, K., Li, G., et al.: Road-aware indexing for trajectory range queries. IEEE Trans. Knowl. Data Eng. 8476–8489 (2023)

9. Fox, A., Eichelberger, C., Hughes, J.: Spatio-temporal indexing in non-relational distributed databases. In: IEEE International Conference on Big Data, pp. 291–299 (2013)
10. Li, R., He, H., Wang, R., et al.: Trajmesa: a distributed nosql-based trajectory data management system. IEEE Trans. Eng. Manag. **35**(1), 1013–1027 (2023)
11. He, H., Xu, Z., Li, R., et al.: TMan: a high-performance trajectory data management system based on key-value stores. In: 2024 IEEE 40th International Conference on Data Engineering (ICDE), pp. 4951–4964 (2024)
12. Zhao, X., Lam, K.Y., Kuo, T.W.: Indexing spatiotemporal trajectory data streams on key-value storage. Computing **106**(8), 2707–2735 (2024)
13. Wang, L., Hu, L., Fu, C., et al.: SLBRIN: a spatial learned index based on brin. ISPRS Int. J. Geo-Inf. **12**(4), 171 (2023)
14. Patil, M., Ravishankar, C.V.: Model reuse in learned spatial indexes. In: Proceedings of the 36th International Conference on Scientific and Statistical Database Management, pp. 1–12 (2024)
15. Al-Mamun, A., Wang, J., Aref, W.G.: Learned indexes from the one-dimensional to the multi-dimensional spaces: challenges, techniques, and opportunities. In: Proceedings of the Companion of the 2025 International Conference on Management of Data, pp. 788–796 (2025)
16. Brinkhoff, T.: Generating network-based moving objects. In: Proceedings of the 12th International Conference on Scientific and Statistica Database Management, pp. 253–255 (2000)

Adaptive Cognitive Evolution for Dynamic Knowledge Tracing with Time-Aware Temporal Representation

Yingxin Chen[1], Feiyi Tang[2], Luming Zhang[1], Zhijie Zhong[1], Zhisheng Zheng[1], Ronghua Lin[1(✉)], and Chengjie Mao[1]

[1] South China Normal University, Guangzhou 510631, China
rhlin@m.scnu.edu.cn
[2] GuangZhou Polytechnic University, Guangzhou 511483, China

Abstract. In recent years, dynamic graph-based Knowledge Tracing (KT) has emerged as a promising approach to model student learning states. However, most existing knowledge tracing methods address only a single temporal dimension, emphasizing long-term intervals or focusing exclusively on short-term intervals. In addition, they lack a unified mechanism to dynamically model student cognitive changes in response to various learning behaviors. We propose TACE-KT, a novel dynamic graph-based knowledge tracing framework that introduces two key modules to address these challenges. Firstly, the Time-Aware Temporal Representation Module (TATR) employs LSTM for long-term modeling and Transformer for short-term analysis, thereby obtaining multigranular temporal representations. Secondly, the Adaptive Cognitive Evolution Module (ACE) integrates a response evaluation, a knowledge acquisition estimation, and a forgetting mechanism, which dynamically and accurately update the cognitive states of students to capture their evolving knowledge levels effectively. Experimental results on four real-world educational datasets demonstrate that TACE-KT significantly improves the accuracy of knowledge state tracking and future performance prediction.

Keywords: Knowledge tracing · Dynamic graph · Time sequence · Cognitive evolution

1 Introduction

Currently, online education platforms are widely employed in the educational domain and have collected extensive records of student questions. Knowledge Tracing (KT) utilizes these records to monitor the underlying knowledge states of the students, providing educators with valuable information.

Figure 1 illustrates the core idea of KT with Dynamic Graph, which aims to model the evolving mastery of the underlying concepts of the students based on their interactions with questions at different timestamp. By leveraging the association between questions and required knowledge components, KT dynamically infers each student's latent knowledge state and predicts future performance.

© The Author(s), under exclusive license to Springer Nature Singapore Pte Ltd. 2027
H. Sun et al. (Eds.): ChineseCSCW 2025, CCIS 2911, pp. 155–169, 2027.
https://doi.org/10.1007/978-981-92-0288-1_12

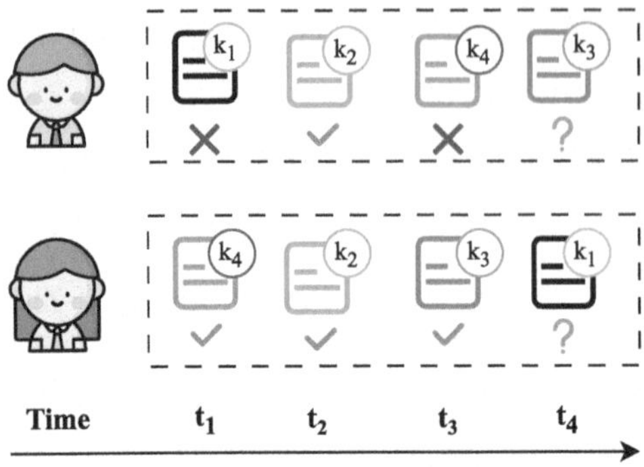

IDs	KC
k_1	Addition
k2	Subtraction
k3	Multiplication
k4	Division

Fig. 1. An example of knowledge tracing with Dynamic Graph.

Traditional KT methods are based on Bayesian inference and factor analysis. With the development of machine learning techniques, deep learning has demonstrated the ability to effectively trace students' cognitive state. The first deep learning model applied to KT was the DKT [1], which uses RNNs or LSTMs to predict future student performance. Since DKT [1] overlooks the importance of each problem, later models introduced attention mechanisms. SAKT [2] utilizes self-attention to assign different weights based on the relevance of the current problem to past problems. AKT [3] employs both single and adaptive attention mechanisms to adjust problem weights dynamically. SAINT [4] uses interactive self-attention to model the relationship between students and problems. With the development of graph neural networks, GKT [5] was the first to apply graphs to KT, converting knowledge structures into graphs for prediction. GIKT [6] models the interactions between students' problems and their skills. DGEKT [7] constructs a dual-graph structure to model student learning interactions, capturing heterogeneous question-concept associations and interaction transitions through hypergraphs and directed graphs. DyGKT [8] advances the field by utilizing dynamic graph structures that adapt continuously to evolving learning trajectories.

However, most existing knowledge tracing methods address only a single temporal dimension, emphasizing long-term intervals or focusing exclusively on short-term intervals. These models often neglect factors such as forgetting and the varying effects of different questions on students' knowledge states. To address these limitations, we introduce TACE-KT, which comprises two key modules, the Time-Aware Temporal Representation Module(TATR) and the Adaptive Cognitive Evolution module (ACE). The TATR leverages both short-term and long-term intervals dependencies to obtain rich temporal representations, enabling effectively utilize temporal information when updating students' knowledge states. Moreover, considering that different questions have varying effects on students' knowledge state updates and students may forget knowledge over time during the learning process, we propose the ACE to dynamically and accurately update each student's cognitive state. Through the collaboration of these two modules, TACE-KT effectively captures students' knowledge states across different periods, thereby enabling more precise prediction of future performance.

In short, a novel framework TACE-KT is presented for attaining the goal, and the main contributions are as follows.

- TATR effectively combines LSTM-based long-term evolution tracing with Transformer-driven local window analysis, generating multi-granular temporal representations.
- ACE module integrates response evaluation, knowledge acquisition estimation, and forgetting mechanism component to trace and update the student's cognitive state.
- Empirical results on four real-world datasets indicate that TACE-KT offers a competitive predictive performance.

2 Related Work

2.1 Knowledge Tracing

Knowledge tracing aims to predict the probability of a student answering a new problem correctly based on a given sequence of questions, $X = \{x_1, x_2, \ldots, x_n\}$. Traditional KT models rely on Bayesian inference [9] and factor analysis and often struggle to capture the complex cognitive dynamics involved in learning processes adequately. DKT [1] employs RNNs to estimate the probability of a correct response at each time step, effectively modeling intricate learning behaviors. The DKVMN [10] incorporates an external memory module that explicitly stores and updates knowledge mastery. Subsequent innovations, such as SAKT [2], AKT [3], and SAINT [4], integrate attention mechanisms to overcome DKT's limitation of treating all historical interactions uniformly. Graph-based methods, including GKT [5], GIKT [6], GRKT [11], and SKT [12], represent the propagation of concept-level influences by capturing structural dependencies within knowledge graphs. STHKT [13] constructs a tripartite heterogeneous graph to depict relationships among concepts, questions, and students. MIKT [14] introduces a multi-scale framework for tracing knowledge states, combining broad patterns with specific interactions while enhancing interpretability through Item Response Theory. HD-KT [15] improves the robustness of model by explicitly addressing anomalous interactions, and QDCKT [16] uses difficulty-aware embeddings instead of question IDs.

Most graph-based knowledge tracing methods are static and less suited for dynamic changes in students' knowledge states. However, DyGKT [8] was the first to apply dynamic graphs to knowledge tracing, enabling more accurate tracking of students' evolving knowledge states.

2.2 Dynamic Graphs

A dynamic graph refers to a complex graph structure that involves temporal evolution. Dynamic graphs can be divided into Discrete-Time Dynamic Graphs

(DTDGS) and Continuous-Time Dynamic Graphs (CTDGS) [17]. In continuous dynamic graphs, each event has a timestamp, allowing for smoother tracking of the evolution of graph structures and providing a more accurate analysis of the temporal relationships and dependencies between events. This is particularly well-suited for knowledge tracing.

The Know-Evolve [18] model uses knowledge graphs as interactive networks, using a temporal process to model the occurrence of events. Based on strategies similar to Know-Evolve, Dyrep [19] introduces a method for modeling multiple types of graphs. The GHNN [20] uses the Hawkes process to model temporal dependencies between nodes and learns evolving node representations through intensity functions. DGNN [21] utilizes an update component to maintain the freshness of node information and a propagation component to disseminate new interaction information to affected nodes. In Jodie [22], the update operation refreshes node embeddings, while the predict operation forecasts their future embedding trajectories. TGAT [23] introduces a specially designed temporal graph attention layer to aggregate feature data from the historical neighbors of target nodes. TGN [24] integrates methods from TGAT, Jodie, and Dyrep to propose a unified approach that aggregates local neighbor information to update node representations.

3 Methodology

This section presents our proposed method in detail. As shown in Fig. 2, our framework models student–question interactions as a dynamic, temporally evolving bipartite graph where red nodes denote students and blue nodes represent questions annotated with knowledge component tags. The framework comprises two primary modules: the Time-Aware Temporal Representation Module(TATR) and the Adaptive Cognitive Evolution Module(ACE). The TATR captures multi-scale temporal information using LSTM for long-term modeling and Transformer for short-term analysis. Meanwhile, the ACE dynamically updates the students' cognitive state. It integrates three key components: a response evaluation, a knowledge acquisition estimation, and a forgetting mechanism. This design effectively models the processes of knowledge mastery, acquisition, and decay, leading to more accurate predictions of students' future performance.

3.1 Preliminaries

Dynamic graph-based knowledge tracing aims to model the evolution of students' knowledge state through their sequence of interactions with questions. Let $\mathcal{S}$ denotes the set of students, $\mathcal{Q}$ denotes the set of questions, and $\mathcal{K}$ denotes the set of knowledge components, for each student $s \in \mathcal{S}$, the learning history is represented as a time-ordered sequence $\{(q_i, t_i, r_i, k_i)\}_{i=1}^{l}$, where $q_i \in \mathcal{Q}$ is the question at time t_i, $r_i \in \{0, 1\}$ indicates the corresponding response (0 for incorrect, 1 for correct), and $k_i \in \mathcal{K}$ is the knowledge component associated with the

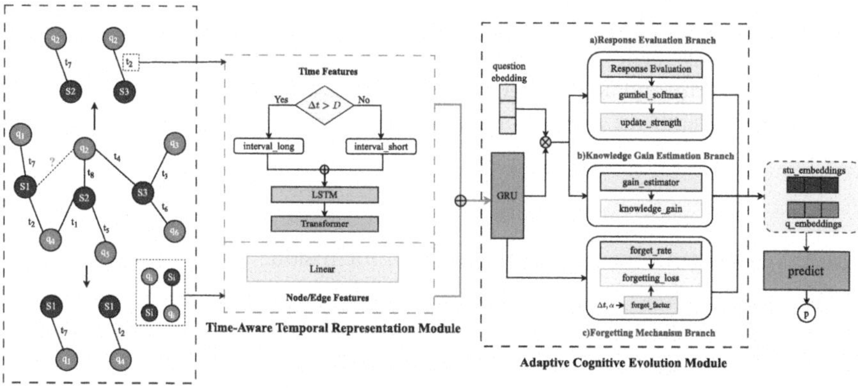

Fig. 2. The overall framework of the proposed TACE-KT.

question. The model's primary objective is to infer the student's latent knowledge state and estimate the probability of a correct response to the subsequent question.

3.2 Time-Aware Temporal Representation Module

To capture the evolving behavioral patterns of students over time, this module employs advanced encoding techniques on sequential data to model both short-term and long-term intervals comprehensively.

Dual Time Encoder. Let $\boldsymbol{t} = [t_1, t_2, \ldots, t_N]$ denotes the input timestamp sequence, the difference between consecutive timestamps is computed as $\Delta t_i = t_{i+1} - t_i, \quad i = 1, 2, \ldots, N-1$. To maintain a consistent sequence length, the difference for the final timestamp is defined as $\Delta t_N = t_{N-1}$. To differentiate between short-term and long-term intervals, We take one day as the dividing line and define the threshold D is 86400 s. Any time interval exceeding D is a long time interval, and any interval below D is a short time interval. The short-term and long-term time masks are defined as follows:

$$m_i^s = 1\{\Delta t_i \leq D\}, m_i^l = 1\{\Delta t_i > D\} \tag{1}$$

Obtained time masks allow the model to differentiate between short-term and long-term intervals. By feeding the masked differences through a linear layer followed by a ReLU activation,we obtain a d-dimensional representation.The short-term time encoding is given by

$$s_i = \mathrm{ReLU}\big(W_{\mathrm{s}}\,(\Delta t_i \cdot m_i^{\mathrm{s}})\big) \tag{2}$$

and the long-term time encoding is given by

$$\ell_i = \mathrm{ReLU}\big(W_{\mathrm{l}}\,(\Delta t_i \cdot m_i^{\mathrm{l}})\big) \tag{3}$$

where $W_s, W_l \in \mathbb{R}^{d\times 1}$ are the encoding weights, and $m_i^s, m_i^l \in \{0,1\}$ are the short-term or long-term time masks.

The short-term and long-term time encoding are fused by summation and then passed through an additional linear transformation to generate the time encoding:

$$X_i = W_o(s_i + \ell_i), \quad W_o \in \mathbb{R}^{d\times d} \tag{4}$$

where W_o is the transformation matrix used for fusion.

LSTM Layer. After obtaining the fused time encoding X_i, an LSTM layer is applied to model the sequential data. For an input encoding at time t, denoted by X_t, the LSTM updates the hidden state as follows:

$$h_t = \text{LSTM}(X_t, h_{t-1}) \tag{5}$$

where h_t represents the current hidden state that captures local temporal dependencies, thereby contributing to a coherent temporal feature representation.

Transformer Encoder. After performing local temporal smoothing, we feed the LSTM's hidden state sequence into a multi-layer Transformer encoder to further capture global dependencies across time steps. Specifically, let

$$H = \left[h_1, h_2, \ldots, h_L\right]^{\top} \in \mathbb{R}^{L\times d}, \tag{6}$$

denote the LSTM output sequence, where L is the sequence length and d is the dimensionality of the time encoding. By leveraging a self-attention mechanism, the Transformer encoder captures global temporal dependencies among all time steps, resulting in the final feature representation:

$$Z = \text{TransformerEncoder}(H) \tag{7}$$

This approach effectively integrates both local and global temporal information to produce a rich encoding that enhances the model's ability to trace and predict students' evolving behaviors. We adopt the Dual Time Encoder proposed in DyGKT [8] to capture the temporal dependency between interactions, due to its proven effectiveness in knowledge tracing.

3.3 Adaptive Cognitive Evolution Module

In this section, we present an ACE specifically designed to capture the evolution of students' knowledge states accurately. The TATR generates raw representations for edge, timestamp, student nodes, and question nodes, which are then passed to the ACE module's GRU-based sequential encoder to extract each student's initial knowledge state. We denote this initial state as $\mathbf{K}_t \in \mathbb{R}^d$, where d represents the dimensionality of the node features.

Following this, the hidden state is combined with the corresponding question embedding $\mathbf{q} \in \mathbb{R}^d$ to create a composite input $s = [\mathbf{K}_t; \mathbf{q}] \in \mathbb{R}^{2d}$, which directs the update of the knowledge state. This update process is regulated by three closely integrated sub-modules: the Response Evaluation, the Knowledge Acquisition Estimation, and the Forgetting Mechanism.

Response Evaluation. The Response Evaluation is designed to quantify the importance of the current interaction in updating the student's knowledge state and produce an update strength indicator. Specifically, we first construct the strategy input vector:

$$\mathbf{s} = \left[\mathbf{K}_t; \mathbf{q}\right] \in \mathbb{R}^{2d}, \tag{8}$$

where $\mathbf{K}_t \in \mathbb{R}^d$ denotes the current knowledge state and $\mathbf{q} \in \mathbb{R}^d$ represents the question embedding. The vector $\mathbf{s}$ is then passed through a two-layer fully-connected network. In the first layer, a ReLU activation function is applied, and in the second layer the network outputs logits corresponding to two discrete actions (low strength and high strength). Formally, the transformation is defined as:

$$\mathbf{l} = f_{\text{resp}}(\mathbf{s}) = \text{FC}_2\big(\text{ReLU}(\text{FC}_1(\mathbf{s}))\big), \tag{9}$$

where $\mathbf{l} \in \mathbb{R}^2$ denotes the unnormalized logits for the two update actions. To enable differentiable learning while simulating discrete decision-making, we apply the Gumbel-Softmax trick with a temperature parameter τ=0.5 to obtain a normalized probability distribution:

$$\text{GumbelSoftmax}(\mathbf{l}, \tau) = [p_0, p_1]. \tag{10}$$

Finally, the update strength u is defined as the probability of selecting the high update action:

$$u = p_1, \quad u \in [0, 1]. \tag{11}$$

This design enables the model to automatically learn the relative importance of each interaction, thereby providing a dynamic modulation factor for the subsequent knowledge acquisition.

Knowledge Acquisition Estimation. The goal of the Knowledge Acquisition Estimation is to capture the potential positive change in the student's knowledge induced by the current interaction. This component also takes the strategy input $\mathbf{s}$ as its basis and maps the interaction information into a vector space that characterizes knowledge acquisition. In this paper, this component is composed of a two-layer fully-connected network. The first layer employs a ReLU activation function to extract intermediate features, while the second layer uses a Tanh activation function to constrain the output within the interval $[-1, 1]$. This ensures that the estimated acquisition, denoted by $\mathbf{g} \in \mathbb{R}^d$, can reflect both positive and negative adjustments. The computation is formalized as:

$$\mathbf{g} = f_{\text{acquisition}}(\mathbf{s}) = \tanh\Big(W_{g2}\,\text{ReLU}\big(W_{g1}\,\mathbf{s} + \mathbf{b}_{g1}\big) + \mathbf{b}_{g2}\Big). \tag{12}$$

where W_{g1} and W_{g2} are learnable weight matrices, while $\mathbf{b}_{g1}$ and $\mathbf{b}_{g2}$ are the corresponding bias vectors. These parameters transform the input strategy vector and enable the network to model knowledge acquisition effectively. To ensure that each interaction contributes proportionally to the knowledge acquisition process, we perform an element-wise product of $\mathbf{g}$ by the update strength u, resulting in the final knowledge acquisition:

$$\mathbf{G} = u \cdot \mathbf{g}. \tag{13}$$

This mechanism guarantees that meaningful interactions yield a corresponding impact on knowledge acquisition, enabling the model to dynamically adjust the intensity of the knowledge state update based on the current interaction.

Forgetting Mechanism. The Forgetting Mechanism is designed to model the decay of the student's knowledge over time, thereby simulating the natural forgetting process observed in real-world learning. In this, the current knowledge state $\mathbf{K}_t$ is first processed through a Sigmoid-gated network to obtain the forgetting rate vector:

$$\mathbf{r} = f_{\text{forget}}(\mathbf{K}_t) = \sigma\big(W_f\, \mathbf{K}_t + \mathbf{b}_f\big), \tag{14}$$

where W_f is the learnable weight matrix and $\mathbf{b}_f$ is the bias vector. They transform the current knowledge state $\mathbf{K}_t$ into a forgetting rate vector, controlling how much knowledge decays over time. And the Sigmoid function $\sigma(\cdot)$ restricts the output values to the interval $[0, 1]$, effectively measuring the propensity of each knowledge dimension to decay. Recognizing that the time interval Δt plays a critical role in modulating the forgetting effect, we introduce a nonlinear time factor defined as:

$$\phi(\Delta t) = \Big(\log(1 + \Delta t)\Big)^{\alpha}, \tag{15}$$

where α is a learnable parameter that adjusts the nonlinear response of the forgetting curve. The overall forgetting loss is then determined by combining the forgetting rate, the time factor, and a compensation term $(1 - u)$, as expressed by:

$$\mathbf{F} = \mathbf{r} \cdot \phi(\Delta t) \cdot (1 - u). \tag{16}$$

This indicates that interactions characterized by low update strength incur a greater degree of forgetting, whereas those with high update strength serve to reinforce and preserve the accumulated knowledge.

Knowledge State Update Equation. Integrating the contributions of the three components, the update of the knowledge state is formally given by:

$$\mathbf{K}_{t+1} = \mathbf{K}_t + \mathbf{G} - \mathbf{F}. \tag{17}$$

In this equation, G denotes the gain in knowledge resulting from the current interaction, whereas F represents the loss of knowledge due to temporal decay and the relatively low importance of the interaction. This design balances knowledge accumulation and decay, enabling a dynamic and fine-grained tracing of the knowledge state of students over time.

After the sequential updater produces the updated knowledge state $\mathbf{K}_t \in \mathbb{R}^d$, we derive both student and question embeddings via a shared output layer. The student embedding at time t is given by

$$\mathbf{x}_s^t = \mathbf{W}_{\text{out}} \mathbf{K}_t + \mathbf{b}_{\text{out}}, \tag{18}$$

where $\mathbf{W}_{\text{out}} \in \mathbb{R}^{d \times d}$ and $\mathbf{b}_{\text{out}} \in \mathbb{R}^d$ are learnable parameters that project the latent knowledge state into the prediction. To obtain the question embedding, we first fuse the student's current state with the static question representation $\text{Emb}(q_t) \in \mathbb{R}^d$ via element-wise addition, then apply the same projection:

$$\mathbf{x}_q^t = \mathbf{W}_{\text{out}}\big(\mathbf{K}_t + \text{Emb}(q_t)\big) + \mathbf{b}_{\text{out}}. \tag{19}$$

Both $\mathbf{x}_s^t$ and $\mathbf{x}_q^t$ are concatenated and passed through a two-layer MLP f with ReLU activation in the hidden layer and a Sigmoid output unit, yielding the probability of a correct response:

$$\hat{y}_i = \sigma\big(f(\mathbf{x}_s^t, \mathbf{x}_q^t)\big). \tag{20}$$

Training is performed by minimizing the Binary Cross-Entropy loss over a batch of N interactions:

$$\mathcal{L} = -\frac{1}{N}\sum_{i=1}^{N}\big[y_i \log(\hat{y}_i) + (1 - y_i)\log(1 - \hat{y}_i)\big], \tag{21}$$

where $y_i \in \{0, 1\}$ is the ground-truth correctness label. We use the Adam optimizer with gradient clipping to ensure stable convergence.

4 Experiments

4.1 Datasets

We conduct experiments on four real-world datasets. Detailed statistics of these datasets are summarized in Table 1.

ASSISTment12.[1] This dataset was collected from the free online tutoring platform ASSISTments and comprises mathematical question data from the 2012–2013 academic year.

ASSISTment17.[2] Derived from a 2017 data mining competition, this dataset contains student problem-solving records from middle school mathematics and science courses.

Slepemapy.cz.[3] Provided by the open online system slepemapy.cz, this dataset encompasses data on students' geographic knowledge acquisition.

EdNet-KT1.[4] This large-scale dataset was compiled by Santa, an AI-powered multi-platform self-learning solution for tutoring, and consists of records of question-answer pairs.

1 https://sites.google.com/site/assistmentsdata/datasets/2012-13-school-data-with-affect

2 https://sites.google.com/view/assistmentsdatamining/dataset

3 https://www.fi.muni.cz/adaptivelearning/a=data

4 https://github.com/riiid/ednet

Table 1. Statistics of all datasets.

Dataset	Students	questions	Concepts	Interactions
ASSISTment12	46.7k	180.0k	198	6123.3k
ASSISTment17	1.7k	3.2k	102	942.8k
Slepemapy.cz	91.3k	1.5k	1454	10087.3k
EdNet-KT1	20.0k	12.3k	189	18813.8k

4.2 Baseline

We adopt a range of representative deep knowledge tracing models for baseline comparisons, including DKT, IEKT, LPKT, CT-NCM, QIKT, AKT, and SimpleKT. We also include several dynamic graph learning approaches, such as TGN, TGAT, and DyGFormer. Moreover, we consider DyGKT, a dynamic graph-based knowledge tracing method, to provide a direct comparison within the same problem setting.

DKT [1] uses a Recurrent Neural Network to predict student responses, estimating the probability of a correct answer at each time step.
IEKT [25] models students' cognition before predictions and evaluates their sensitivity to knowledge acquisition before updating knowledge states.
LPKT [26] considers changes in knowledge states during the interval since the last interaction when making predictions.
CT-NCM [27] integrates knowledge forgetting dynamics by combining a neural Hawkes process with a scalable learning function.
QIKT [28] models knowledge transitions through question-sensitive cognitive representations from a knowledge acquisition and problem-solving module.
AKT [3] applies a monotonic attention mechanism that decays with time, reducing the impact of earlier interactions.
SimpleKT [29] adopts the Rasch model to capture question variations and uses dot-product attention to extract temporal learning patterns.
TGN [24] maintains a memory module for node histories and updates it upon new events, generating real-time embeddings.
TGAT [23] maps continuous time into vectors via a time encoder and models temporal features using graph attention.
DyGFormer [30] designs a Transformer-based architecture to learn from nodes' first-hop historical interactions.
DyGKT [8] introduces dynamic graph learning into knowledge tracing, capturing evolving relationships among students, questions, and concepts.

4.3 Evaluation Metrics

We employ Average Precision (AP) and Area Under the Curve (AUC) to evaluate students' future performance. AP measures the average precision across recall levels on the Precision–Recall curve, while AUC represents the area under the

Table 2. Average Precision (AP) results on different datasets

Dataset	ASSISTment12	ASSISTment17	Slepemapy.cz	EdNet-KT1
DKT	80.79	61.58	83.94	86.59
IEKT	83.70	64.34	87.16	86.43
LPKT	79.50	57.44	84.22	71.08
CT-NCM	77.58	60.16	83.27	82.18
QIKT	83.73	62.61	87.19	86.73
AKT	80.29	59.86	86.55	86.94
simpleKT	84.12	59.81	87.49	70.71
TGN	86.25	62.98	85.56	85.65
TGAT	86.03	63.21	85.86	85.94
DyGFormer	86.22	68.39	88.24	87.44
DyGKT	87.37	72.43	88.63	87.53
TACE-KT	**87.66**	**73.47**	**89.21**	**88.75**

ROC curve, reflecting the ranking quality of predictions.Both metrics are widely used in dynamic graph literature [8,23,24,30]. For experiments, the dataset is split into training (0.8), validation (0.1), and test (0.1) sets (Table 2).

4.4 Implementation Details

We employ the Adam optimizer for all our experiments.We choose learning rate at 0.01, and fixed the batch size at 2000 for training,validation, and testing.The embedding and hidden dimension numbers were fixed at 128.The dropout rate was set at 0.1.

4.5 Performance Comparision

The experimental results show that TACE-KT consistently outperforms both classical sequence-based methods and recent dynamic-graph approaches in terms of average precision on every benchmark. Compared with the best performing static models, TACE-KT delivers clear and uniform gains across all datasets. At the same time, it further improves upon state-of-the-art dynamic-graph methods, demonstrating its ability to capture evolving student–question interactions more effectively than prior graph-based strategies.

A similar trend is observed for AUC evaluation. TACE-KT achieves higher AUC values than all classical sequence models, reflecting stronger overall ranking quality, and it maintains an edge over Transformer-based graph architectures as well. These findings confirm that our integration of multi-scale temporal fusion and adaptive cognitive evolution yields substantial and robust improvements over both families of baselines (Table 3).

Table 3. AUC results on different datasets

Dataset	ASSISTment12	ASSISTment17	Slepemapy.cz	EdNet-KT1
DKT	68.24	71.27	65.42	71.01
IEKT	73.17	73.36	71.03	70.38
LPKT	69.08	68.37	69.78	61.71
CT-NCM	63.15	70.25	67.12	70.15
QIKT	73.24	71.92	71.01	70.38
AKT	66.43	68.55	70.19	71.57
simpleKT	73.62	67.33	71.53	70.42
TGN	76.86	73.45	73.40	76.89
TGAT	76.63	71.37	67.86	71.76
DyGFormer	76.96	77.60	70.73	74.67
DyGKT	78.46	80.58	73.58	78.61
TACE-KT	**78.83**	**81.40**	**74.59**	**79.39**

4.6 Ablation Study

In this ablation study, we design several degraded variants of the TACE-KT model by removing key modules to evaluate their individual contributions to overall performance. As shown in Fig. 3, we report the AUC results across four datasets: ASSISTment12, ASSISTment17, Slepemapy.cz, and EdNet-KT1.

First, to verify the effectiveness of the TATR in capturing both short-term and long-term intervals, we construct three variants: w/o LSTM (without LSTM), w/o Transformer (without Transformer), and w/o LSTM+Transformer (without both LSTM and Transformer). The results demonstrate that removing either LSTM or Transformer leads to noticeable performance degradation, particularly on datasets with highly dynamic interactions such as Slepemapy.cz and EdNet-KT1. This indicates that TATR plays a crucial role in modeling local temporal patterns. Moreover, the joint use of LSTM and Transformer consistently outperforms using either component alone, highlighting their complementary strengths in temporal modeling.

Next, we evaluate the impact of the ACE by removing it from the model (w/o ACE). The results show a consistent performance drop across all datasets. Without ACE, the model cannot adaptively trace students' knowledge acquisition and forgetting processes, and cannot accurately evaluate their responses. This leads to reduced prediction accuracy. ACE refines cognitive representations by capturing subtle state changes and long-term effects, enhancing both the flexibility and precision of the model's understanding of student cognition. In conclusion, integrating both TATR and ACE enables TACE-KT to effectively capture temporal learning dynamics and cognitive evolution. This comprehensive modeling capability results in significant performance improvements across diverse educational datasets (Fig. 4).

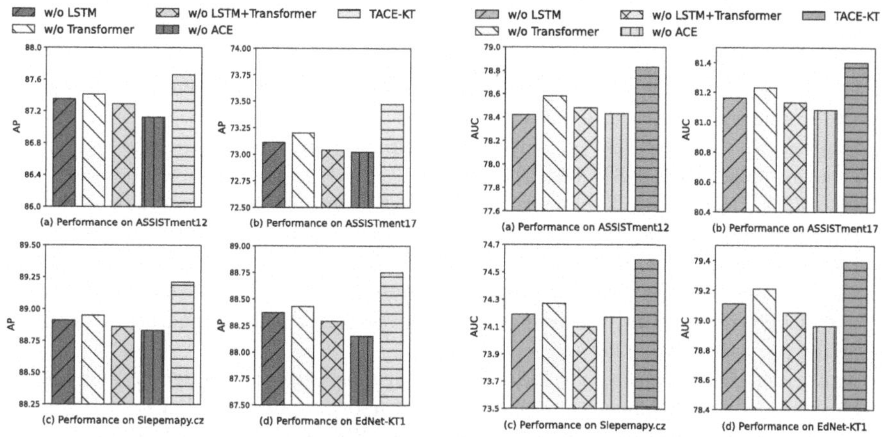

(a) AP for ablation study of TACE-KT. (b) AUC for ablation study of TACE-KT.

Fig. 3. Ablation study for TACE-KT.

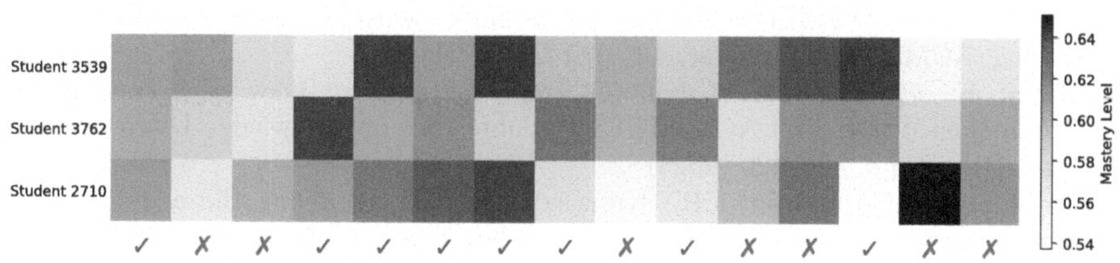

Fig. 4. The evolution process of three students' knowledge states traced by TACE-KT.

5 Conclusion

This paper proposes TACE-KT, a dynamic knowledge tracing framework that addresses limitations in temporal granularity and cognitive state modeling. It comprises two modules: the Time-Aware Temporal Representation (TATR) module, which uses an LSTM and a Transformer to capture long- and short-term dependencies; and the Adaptive Cognitive Evolution (ACE) module, which dynamically updates students' cognitive states via response evaluation, knowledge acquisition, and forgetting mechanisms. Experiments on four real-world datasets show that TACE-KT consistently outperforms dynamic graph baselines, validating the effectiveness of its multi-scale temporal representation and adaptive cognitive modeling.

Acknowledgements. This work was partly supported by the National Key Research and Development Program of China (Research and Demonstration Application of Key Technologies for Personalized Learning Driven by Educational Big Data) under Grant 2023YFC3341200.

References

1. Piech, C., et al.: Deep knowledge tracing. In: Advances in Neural Information Processing Systems, vol. 28 (2015)
2. Pandey, S., Karypis, G.: A self-attentive model for knowledge tracing. arXiv preprint arXiv:1907.06837 (2019)
3. Ghosh, A., Heffernan, N., Lan, A.S.: Context-aware attentive knowledge tracing. In: Proceedings of the 26th ACM SIGKDD International Conference on Knowledge Discovery & Data Mining, pp. 2330–2339 (2020)
4. Choi, Y., et al.: Towards an appropriate query, key, and value computation for knowledge tracing. In: Proceedings of the Seventh ACM Conference on Learning@ Scale, pp. 341–344 (2020)
5. Nakagawa, H., Iwasawa, Y., Matsuo, Y.: Graph-based knowledge tracing: modeling student proficiency using graph neural network. In: 2019 IEEE/WIC/ACM International Conference on Web Intelligence (WI), pp. 156–163 (2019)
6. Yang, Y., Shen, J., Qu, Y., Liu, Y., Wang, K., Zhu, Y., Zhang, W., Yu, Y.: GIKT: a graph-based interaction model for knowledge tracing. In: Hutter, F., Kersting, K., Lijffijt, J., Valera, I. (eds.) ECML PKDD 2020. LNCS (LNAI), vol. 12457, pp. 299–315. Springer, Cham (2021). https://doi.org/10.1007/978-3-030-67658-2_18
7. Cui, C., et al.: DGEKT: a dual graph ensemble learning method for knowledge tracing. ACM Trans. Inf. Syst. **42**(3), 1–24 (2024)
8. Cheng, K., et al.: DyGKT: dynamic graph learning for knowledge tracing. In: Proceedings of the 30th ACM SIGKDD Conference on Knowledge Discovery and Data Mining, pp. 409–420 (2024)
9. Corbett, A.T., Anderson, J.R.: Knowledge tracing: modeling the acquisition of procedural knowledge. User Model. User-Adap. Inter. **4**, 253–278 (1994)
10. Zhang, J., et al.: Dynamic key-value memory networks for knowledge tracing. In: Proceedings of the 26th International Conference on World Wide Web, pp. 765–774 (2017)
11. Cui, J., et al.: Leveraging pedagogical theories to understand student learning process with graph-based reasonable knowledge tracing. In: Proceedings of the 30th ACM SIGKDD Conference on Knowledge Discovery and Data Mining, pp. 502–513 (2024)
12. Tong, S., et al.: Structure-based knowledge tracing: an influence propagation view. In: 2020 IEEE International Conference on Data Mining (ICDM), pp. 541–550. IEEE (2020)
13. Li, S., et al.: STHKT: spatiotemporal knowledge tracing with topological Hawkes process. Expert Syst. Appl. **259**, 125248 (2025)
14. Sun, J., et al.: Interpretable knowledge tracing with multiscale state representatio. In: Proceedings of the ACM Web Conference 2024, pp. 3265–3276 (2024)
15. Ma, H., et al.: HD-KT: advancing robust knowledge tracing via anomalous learning interaction detection. In: Proceedings of the ACM Web Conference 2024, pp. 4479–4488 (2024)
16. Liu, G., Zhan, H., Kim, J.: Question difficulty consistent knowledge tracing. In: Proceedings of the ACM Web Conference 2024, pp. 4239–4248 (2024)
17. Zheng, Y., Yi, L., Wei, Z.: A survey of dynamic graph neural networks. Front. Comp. Sci. **19**(6), 1–18 (2025)
18. Trivedi, R., et al.: Know-evolve: deep temporal reasoning for dynamic knowledge graphs. In: International Conference on Machine Learning, pp. 3462–3471. PMLR (2017)

19. Trivedi, R., et al.: Dyrep: learning representations over dynamic graphs. In: International Conference on Learning Representations (2019)
20. Wei, J., et al.: GHNN: graph harmonic neural networks for semi-supervised graph-level classification. Neural Netw. **151**, 70–79 (2022)
21. Ma, Y., et al.: Streaming graph neural networks. In: Proceedings of the 43rd International ACM SIGIR Conference on Research and Development in Information Retrieval, pp. 719–728 (2020)
22. Kumar, S., Zhang, X., Leskovec, J.: Predicting dynamic embedding trajectory in temporal interaction networks. In: Proceedings of the 25th ACM SIGKDD International Conference on Knowledge Discovery & Data Mining, pp. 1269–1278 (2019)
23. Xu, D., et al.: Inductive representation learning on temporal graphs. arXiv preprint arXiv:2002.07962 (2020)
24. Rossi, E., et al.: Temporal graph networks for deep learning on dynamic graphs. arXiv preprint arXiv:2006.10637 (2020)
25. Long, T., et al.: Tracing knowledge state with individual cognition and acquisition estimation. In: Proceedings of the 44th International ACM SIGIR Conference on Research and Development in Information Retrieval, pp. 173–182 (2021)
26. Shen, S., et al.: Learning process-consistent knowledge tracing. In: Proceedings of the 27th ACM SIGKDD Conference on Knowledge Discovery & Data Mining, pp. 1452–1460 (2021)
27. Ma, H., et al.: Reconciling cognitive modeling with knowledge forgetting: a continuous time-aware neural network approach. In: IJCAI, pp. 2174–2181 (2022)
28. Chen, J., et al.: Improving interpretability of deep sequential knowledge tracing models with question-centric cognitive representations. In: Proceedings of the AAAI Conference on Artificial Intelligence, vol. 37, pp. 14196–14204 (2023)
29. Liu, Z., et al.: simpleKT: a simple but tough-to-beat baseline for knowledge tracing. arXiv preprint arXiv:2302.06881 (2023)
30. Le, Y., et al.: Towards better dynamic graph learning: new architecture and unified library. Adv. Neural. Inf. Process. Syst. **36**, 67686–67700 (2023)

Beamforming for Reconfigurable Intelligence Surface Assisted Collaborative System of Communication and Sensing

Tianfang Luo[1], Zihan Li[1,2], Chao Liu[1,2], Pei Xiao[3], Tong Wang[1,2](✉), and Min Ouyang[1,2]

[1] Harbin Engineering University, Harbin 150001, China
wangtong@hrbeu.edu.cn

[2] Innovative Research Center for Intelligent Perception and Crowd Intelligence Computing of Heilongjiang Province, Harbin, China

[3] Institute for Communication Systems (ICS), Home for 5GIC and 6GIC, University of Surrey, Guildford, UK

Abstract. The collaboration between communication and sensing has emerged as an important technology for sixth-generation (6G) wireless communication networks. In this paper, we investigate the beamforming for the collaborative system of communication and sensing via the collaboration between reconfigurable intelligent surfaces (RIS) and multiple-input single-output (MISO) base stations (BS) in multi-user MISO systems. In order to promote the sum communication rate for all users while ensuring the radar sensing performance, we formulate a non-convex optimization problem to maximize the sum rate for all users under the constraints of the radar signal-to-noise ratio (SNR). To address the non-convex optimization, we propose a hybrid approach combining fractional programming and the alternating direction method of multipliers (ADMM) to optimize acceptance filter coefficients, the beamforming and the RIS reflection coefficients matrix. The simulation results indicate that the proposed scheme is able to enhance the communication capability while ensuring the radar performance. Furthermore, compared to the scheme without RIS collaboration, our scheme achieves more accurate alignment with target directions for sensing, while also providing good communication performance.

Keywords: Collaborative system of communication and sensing · reconfigurable intelligent surface · multiple-input single-output · alternating direction method of multipliers

1 Introduction

With the rapid development of the Internet of Things (IoT), the sixth-generation (6G) wireless communication network is poised to drive the society to holographic communication and digital twin [1–3]. These advancements also promote the continuous emergence of emerging technologies such as autonomous vehicles, smart healthcare, intelligent manufacturing [4, 5], etc. Therefore, the collaboration of sensing and communication capabilities has become essential for modern network.

© The Author(s), under exclusive license to Springer Nature Singapore Pte Ltd. 2027
H. Sun et al. (Eds.): ChineseCSCW 2025, CCIS 2911, pp. 170–183, 2027.
https://doi.org/10.1007/978-981-92-0288-1_13

Nowadays, many advanced techniques have been applied in the research of collaborative systems for communication and sensing [6]. Although these advanced techniques can significantly improve both communication and sensing performance of the system, its effectiveness will degrade in harsh propagation environments such as blocking and multipath fading. In order to deal with these limitations, reconfigurable intelligent surfaces (RIS) have been proposed as a promising solution [7, 8]. Reconfigurable intelligent surfaces (RIS), comprising planar arrays of metamaterial elements, is a transformative technology in the field of wireless communication [9]. It can be deployed to reliable connectivity between base stations and users through intelligent signal reflection under non-line-of-sight (NLoS) conditions while enhancing the coverage of the base station. For this capability, RIS has been widely used in wireless communication and sensing.

Influenced by the widespread adoption of RIS in various communication systems and sensing systems, the system performance when applying RIS in systems has been significantly enhanced. Researcher have systematically investigated the RIS schemes for radar sensing and communication performance metrics in different scenarios. As demonstrated in [10, 11], RIS effectively mitigates multi-user interference (MUI) through adaptive beamforming, enhancing the communication performance by minimizing the MUI. [10] proposes a joint optimization approach based on RIS, combining constant-modulus waveform design with discrete phase shift control. [10] employs an alternating optimization algorithm and an exact penalty function to minimize MUI. It leads to a significant increase in overall user throughput. [11] proposes a joint waveform design and passive beamforming method based on RIS. An alternating manifold optimization algorithm is used to balance radar beam alignment with communication performance. This approach significantly improves overall system throughput. [12] addresses the limitations of active beamforming performance under harsh channel conditions by proposing a joint active-passive beamforming alternating optimization algorithm based on manifold optimization. The method achieves a significant increase in the sum-rate of communication users. The comm-RIS architecture in [13] is used to assist communication system, optimizing joint beamforming and reflection coefficients. However, these studies only focus on communication-centric optimizations. In order to utilize the advantages of RIS in radar perception, [14] addresses the problem of performance degradation in NLoS environments. It proposes RIS deployment at line-of-sight (LoS) link blockages to enhance perception performance. In [10], SNR is employed as a dual metric for sensing and communication Quality of Service (QoS), but its single-user model does not consider the possible propagation paths of transmitted waveform for practical deployments. [15] proposes a line-of-sight angle estimation method based on RD-MUSIC and a RIS angle estimation approach maximizing angular diversity. In [15], alternating projection gradient–manifold optimization (AO-PGMO) algorithm is developed to achieve centimeter-level positioning accuracy for both targets and users, while jointly enhancing communication rates and radar mutual information.

Building on these foundations, we investigate the beamforming for collaborative systems of communication and sensing achieved through the collaboration of RIS and multiple-input single-output (MISO) base station. Our approach employs RIS to collaborate with a multi-antenna base station to detect multiple targets while communicating with multiple single-antenna users. The primary objective is to design an optimal beamforming strategy that maximizes the sum communication rate while maintaining adequate radar sensing performance. The key contributions of this paper are as follows:

1. We establish comprehensive signal models for both base station reception and user equipment under RIS collaboration in a multi-target, multi-user scenario, employing sum communication rate as the primary performance metric for communications and SNR as the sensing performance metric.
2. We formulate and solve a non-convex optimization problem that maximizes user sum-rate under joint constraints of radar SNR and transmission power. To address computational challenges, we develop a hybrid algorithm combining fractional programming with the Alternating Direction Method of Multipliers (ADMM) to derive the optimal beamforming matrix and RIS reflection coefficients.
3. We demonstrate that the proposed solution achieves superior communication performance without compromising radar detection capabilities through extensive simulations.

2 System Models

2.1 Signal Model

We consider an RIS-assisted collaborative system with J reflective elements, as illustrated in Fig. 1. The dual-function base station (BS) serves as both a radar transmitter and communication hub, equipped with N transmit/receive antennas arranged in a half-wavelength spaced uniform linear array (ULA). The BS simultaneously transmits detection signals to surveillance targets and data streams to M single-antenna mobile users (MU). Let $\tilde{M} = \{1, 2, ..., M\}$ denote the MU set, with the direction-of-arrival (DOA) of target assumed to be known at both the RIS and BS.

To enable effective integrated communication and sensing capabilities, let $\mathbf{z}[t]$ denote the signal. The composite transmitted signal at time t can be formulated as:

$$\mathbf{z}[t] = \mathbf{F}_c\mathbf{x}_c[t] + \mathbf{F}_R\mathbf{x}_R[t] = \mathbf{F}\mathbf{x}[t], \tag{1}$$

while $\mathbf{x}_c[t] \in \mathbb{C}^M$ and $\mathbf{x}_R[t] \in \mathbb{C}^N$ represent the communication symbols for M single-antenna users and the independent radar waveforms, respectively. $\mathbf{x}_c[t]$ and $\mathbf{x}_R[t]$ satisfy the constraints defined by $E\{\mathbf{x}_c[t]\mathbf{x}_c^H[t]\} = \mathbf{I}_M$, $E\{\mathbf{x}_R[t]\mathbf{x}_R^H[t]\} = \mathbf{I}_N$ and $E\{\mathbf{x}_c[t]\mathbf{x}_R^H[t]\} = 0$. $\mathbf{F}_c \in \mathbb{C}^{N\times M}$ denotes the beamforming matrix for communication, while $\mathbf{F}_R \in \mathbb{C}^{N\times N}$ denotes the beamforming matrix for radar. For ease of reference in the following sections, we define vector $\mathbf{x}[t] \triangleq \left[\mathbf{x}_c^T[t]\ \mathbf{x}_R^T[t]\right]^T$ and matrix $\mathbf{F} \triangleq \left[\mathbf{F}_c\ \mathbf{F}_R\right]$. Accordingly, the received signal of the m-th mobile MU is as follows [16]

$$y_m[t] = (\mathbf{h}_{B,m}^T + \mathbf{h}_{R,m}^T\Psi\mathbf{G})\mathbf{x}[t] + n_m[t], \tag{2}$$

where $\mathbf{h}_{B,m} \in \mathbb{C}^N$ and $\mathbf{h}_{R,m} \in \mathbb{C}^J$ denote the channels from the BS to the user, and from the RIS to the user, respectively. $\boldsymbol{\Psi}$ represents the reflection matrix of the RIS, expressed as $\boldsymbol{\Psi} \triangleq diag\{\varphi\}$, where $\varphi \triangleq [\varphi_1, \varphi_2, \varphi_3, ..., \varphi_J]^T$, satisfying $\|\varphi_j\| = 1, \forall j$. $n_m[t] \sim \mathcal{CN}(0, \sigma_m^2)$ denotes the additive white Gaussian noise (AWGN) at the user's receiver. The channel between the BS and RIS, denoted G, which conforms to Rice fading along with both of the other two channels mentioned above. It can be modeled as: $\mathbf{G} = \beta\sqrt{\kappa/\kappa+1}\mathbf{G}_{LoS} + \beta\sqrt{1/\kappa+1}\mathbf{G}_{NLoS}$, where β represents path loss and κ is the Rician factor. $\mathbf{G}_{NLoS}$ is the NLoS component modeled by Rayleigh fading. The LoS component $\mathbf{G}_{LoS}$ is constructed based on the arrival of direction and the direct of departure (DoD), represented by θ_{RB} and θ_{BR}, respectively. Specially, $\mathbf{G}_{LoS} = \mathbf{a}_R(\theta_{RB})\mathbf{a}_M^T(\theta_{BR})$, where $\mathbf{a}_R(\theta_{RB}) \triangleq \left[1, e^{-j\pi \sin\theta_{RB}}, \ldots, e^{-j(J-1)\pi \sin\theta_{RB}}\right]^T$.

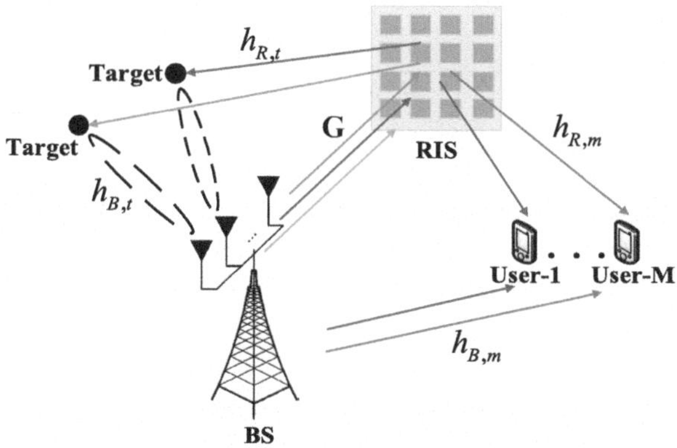

Fig. 1. RIS-assisted collaborative systems.

The signals transmitted by the BS propagate to the target through the LoS path and RIS-reflected path, then return to the BS through the same routes. As the RIS is consists of entirely passive components, it inherently avoids the self-interference problem. The baseband signal received by the BS's antenna array from the target-reflected signals can be expressed as:

$$\mathbf{y}_r[t] = \alpha_t\left(\mathbf{h}_{B,t} + \mathbf{G}^T\Psi\mathbf{h}_{R,t}\right)\left(\mathbf{h}_{B,t}^T + \mathbf{h}_{R,t}^T\Psi\mathbf{G}\right)\mathbf{F}\mathbf{x}[t] + \mathbf{n}_r[t], \tag{3}$$

where $\alpha_t \sim \mathcal{CN}\left(0, \sigma_t^2\right)$ denotes the radar cross-section (RCS). The BS-to-target channel is denoted as $\mathbf{h}_{B,t} \in \mathbb{C}^N$, while the RIS-to-target channel is denoted as $\mathbf{h}_{R,t} \in \mathbb{C}^J$. $n_r[t] \sim \mathcal{CN}\left(0, \sigma_r^2 I_M\right)$ is also the AWGN. We assume that the path between RIS and target is LoS, and $\mathbf{h}_{B,t} = \alpha_{B,t}\mathbf{a}_M(\theta_1)$, $\mathbf{h}_{R,t} = \alpha_{R,t}\mathbf{a}_R(\theta_2)$, where θ_1 and θ_2 are target references to the DoA of the BS/RIS, respectively. These DoA parameters can be estimated using a maximum likelihood algorithm. Beamforming optimization at the BS further enhances target detection accuracy. The $\mathbf{G}$ can be estimated using a dual time-scale framework that accounts for the fast fading and slow fading time scale channel. Radar sensing needs to analyze the reflected echo signals from the T samples observations. The combination of these samples is denoted as:

$$\mathbf{Y}_r = \alpha_t\mathbf{H}_t(\varphi)\mathbf{F}\mathbf{X} + \mathbf{N}_r, \tag{4}$$

where $\mathbf{H}_t(\varphi)$ denotes $\mathbf{H}_t(\varphi) = \left(\mathbf{h}_{B,t} + \mathbf{G}^T\Psi\mathbf{h}_{R,t}\right)\left(\mathbf{h}_{B,t}^T + \mathbf{h}_{R,t}^T\Psi\mathbf{G}\right)$, $\mathbf{X} = [\mathbf{x}[1], \mathbf{x}[2], \ldots, \mathbf{x}[T]]$, $\mathbf{N}_r \triangleq [\mathbf{n}_r[1], \ldots, \mathbf{n}_r[T]]$ [17]. It is worth notice that $H_t(\varphi)$ from the BS perspective is known, while we assume that the reflective RCS is uniform in all directions relative to the target.

2.2 Multi-user Communication Sum-Rate

The multi-user communication sum-rate acts as a fundamental performance measure in multi-user communication systems. Building on the above analysis, the signal-to-interference-plus-noise ratio (SINR) for the m-th user is defined as:

$$SINR_m = \frac{|\mathbf{h}_m^T(\varphi)\mathbf{f}_m|^2}{\sum_{z=m+1}^{M+N} |\mathbf{h}_m^T(\varphi)\mathbf{f}_z|^2 + \sigma_m^2}, \tag{5}$$

where $\mathbf{h}_m(\varphi) \triangleq \mathbf{h}_{B,m} + \mathbf{G}^T\Psi\mathbf{h}_{R,m}$ denotes the communication channel between the base station and users. For analytical clarity, we define $\mathbf{F} = [\mathbf{f}_1, \mathbf{f}_2, ..., \mathbf{f}_{M+N}]$, where $\mathbf{f}_z$ denotes the z-th column of the matrix $\mathbf{F}$, then the sum-rate of all communicating users can be expressed as:

$$SR = \sum_{m=1}^{M} \log_2(1 + SINR_m) \tag{6}$$

2.3 Low Bound of SNR in Rader Sensing

In radar sensing, target detection is a very important task, where SNR serves as a key performance metric. In order to improve the SNR of radar sensing, a matched filter $\mathbf{S}$ is used to process the echo signal and the signal is converted to a vector form by using the Kronecker product property. Then we process the vector signal through receiver filter $\mathbf{v} \in \mathbb{C}^{N\times(M+N)}$ to yield:

$$\mathbf{v}^H\tilde{y}_r = \alpha_t\mathbf{v}^H\left(\mathbf{S}\mathbf{S}^H \otimes \mathbf{H}_t(\varphi)\right)\mathbf{f} + \mathbf{v}^H\tilde{n}_r, \tag{7}$$

where $\mathbf{S}$ denote the orthogonal transmit waveform employed in the matched filter, $q \triangleq vec\{\mathbf{F}\}$, $\tilde{n}_r \triangleq \{N_r\mathbf{S}^H\}$.

Based on the preceding analysis, we can determine the following hypothesis test structure:

The null hypothesis (H_0): under the null hypothesis, where no target is present, the received signal comprises solely noise components. These noise follows a complex Gaussian distribution, formally expressed as $H_0 \sim \mathcal{CN}(0, \gamma_0)$, where $\gamma_0 = T\sigma_r^2\mathbf{v}^H\mathbf{v}$.

The target hypothesis (H_1): under the target hypothesis, the received signal constitutes a superposition of the target-reflected waveform and additive noise. These signal follows a complex Gaussian distribution, formally expressed as $H_1 \sim \mathcal{CN}(0, \gamma_1)$, where $\gamma_1 = \sigma_t^2 E\{|\mathbf{v}^H(\mathbf{S}\mathbf{S}^H \otimes \mathbf{H}_t(\varphi))\mathbf{f}|^2\} + T\sigma_r^2\mathbf{v}^H\mathbf{v}$.

We construct statistics L based the Neyman-Pearson detector:

$$L \sim \begin{cases} \gamma_0\chi_2^2, H_0 \\ \gamma_1\chi_2^2, H_1 \end{cases} \tag{8}$$

where L follows a chi-square distribution with 2 degrees of freedom. The decision rule for target detection is formulated as: when $L = |y|^2 > \ell$, L conforms to the H_1 model. The detection threshold ℓ is determined by the prescribed false-alarm probability. Thus, we derive the expression for the detection probability P_D:

$$P_D \propto \gamma_1/\gamma_0 = \frac{\sigma_t^2 \mathbb{E}\{|\mathbf{v}^H(\mathbf{S}\mathbf{S}^H \otimes \mathbf{H}_t(\varphi))\mathbf{f}|^2\}}{T\sigma_r^2 \mathbf{v}^H \mathbf{v}} + 1 \tag{9}$$

The detection probability exhibits a strong positive correlation with radar SNR. This fundamental relationship allows the radar SNR to be expressed through the following expression:

$$SNR = \frac{\sigma_t^2 \mathbb{E}\{|\mathbf{v}^H(\mathbf{S}\mathbf{S}^H \otimes \mathbf{H}_t(\varphi))\mathbf{f}|^2\}}{T\sigma_r^2 \mathbf{v}^H \mathbf{v}} + 1 \tag{10}$$

Applying the Jensen's inequality to the preceding formulation enables derivation of a lower bound for the radar SNR. This bound is formalized by the following inequality:

$$SNR > \frac{T\sigma_t^2 |\mathbf{v}^H(\mathbf{I}_{N+M} \otimes \mathbf{H}_t(\varphi))\mathbf{f}|^2}{\sigma_r^2 \mathbf{v}^H \mathbf{v}} \tag{11}$$

3 Beamforming Optimization Design

We propose a joint communication and sensing beamforming design. In particular, it is to combine the FP algorithm with the ADMM algorithm to optimize the transmit beamforming matrix, the receive filter, and the reflection matrix of the RIS, so as to maximize the sum rate of users while maintaining sensing performance. The optimization is formulated as:

$$\begin{aligned} &\max_{\mathbf{F},\mathbf{v},\psi} SR \\ &C_1 : \frac{T\sigma_t^2 |\mathbf{v}^H(I_{N+M} \otimes H_t(\varphi))\mathbf{f}|^2}{\sigma_r^2 \mathbf{v}^H \mathbf{v}} \geq S_{\min} \\ &C_2 : \|\mathbf{F}\|^2 \leq P_t, \\ &C_3 : |\varphi_j| = 1, \forall j. \end{aligned} \tag{12}$$

where constraint C_1 indicates that SNR must exceed a lower-bound threshold $S_{\min}$ under all operational conditions; constraint C_2 is a power constraint; and constraint C_3 is a RIS reflection coefficient constraint.

The analysis of the problem structure reveals non-convexity due to the complex objective function and the presence of coupled variables as well as unit modulus in the constraints. To resolve this non-convex optimization problem, we propose a hybrid approach combining FP and ADMM. This method decomposes the original problem into three solvable subproblems: receiver filter updates, beamforming matrix optimization, and the RIS reflection coefficients configuration.

3.1 Fractional Programming Algorithm

To address the complexity of the original objective function, we use FP by introducing auxiliary variables $\mathbf{g} = [g_1, g_2, ..., g_M]$ and $\mathbf{d} = [d_1, d_2, ..., d_M]$. We implement the Lagrangian dual transformation from FP to restructure the original objective function and perform a quadratic term expansion to obtain the following equivalent expression:

$$\begin{aligned}\mathcal{F}(\mathbf{f}, \varphi, \mathbf{g}, \mathbf{d}) \triangleq \sum_{m=1}^{M} \log_2(1 + g_m) - \sum_{m=1}^{M} g_m - \sum_{m=1}^{M} |d_m|^2 \sigma_m^2 \\ + \sum_{m=1}^{M} 2\sqrt{1 + g_m} \Re\left\{d_m^* \mathbf{h}_m^T(\varphi)\mathbf{f}_m\right\} - \sum_{m=1}^{M} |d_m|^2 \sum_{z=1}^{M+N} |\mathbf{h}_m^T(\varphi)\mathbf{f}_z|^2\end{aligned} \tag{13}$$

Meanwhile, for subsequent algorithmic improvement, we further simplify the objective function:

$$\mathcal{F}(\mathbf{f}, \varphi, \mathbf{g}, \mathbf{d}) = \Re\left\{\mathbf{b}^H \varphi\right\} - \varphi^H \mathbf{C} \varphi + \lambda_1 \tag{14}$$

where $\mathbf{b}$, $\mathbf{C}$,λ_1 can be obtained using matrix calculations. After completing the simplification of the objective function, we are able to observe that the optimization of variables $\mathbf{g}$, $\mathbf{d}$, and $\mathbf{f}$ is convex, while the optimization of variable φ is non-convex by given the other variables. Therefore, the subsequent optimization procedure is divided into two separate parts.

3.2 Optimization of Beamforming Matrix

Update g and d. By fixing all variables except $\mathbf{g}$ or $\mathbf{d}$, we decompose the original problem into convex subproblems through variable isolation, which can be solved by $\frac{\partial F}{\partial \mathbf{g}} = 0$. The optimization of the auxiliary variable $\mathbf{v}$ can be expressed as:

$$\mathbf{g}_m^\star = \frac{|\mathbf{h}_m^T(\varphi)\mathbf{f}_m|^2}{\sum_{z=m+1}^{N+M} |\mathbf{h}_m^T(\varphi)\mathbf{f}_z|^2 + \sigma_m^2 + \tau}, \forall m \tag{15}$$

Similarly, the optimization problem with auxiliary variable $\mathbf{d}$ can be expressed as:

$$\mathbf{d}_m^\star = \frac{\sqrt{1 + \mathbf{g}_m} |\mathbf{h}_m^T(\varphi)\mathbf{f}_m|^2}{\sum_{z=1}^{N+M} |\mathbf{h}_m^T(\varphi)\mathbf{f}_z|^2 + \sigma_m^2 + \tau}, \forall m \tag{16}$$

where $\tau = \max\left(10^{-6}, 0.01 \sum_{z=m+1}^{N+M} |h_m^T(\varphi)\mathbf{f}_z|^2 + \sigma_m^2\right)$ serves as a regularization component within the optimization framework, ensuring stability throughout the iterative process.

Update Receiver Filter v. By fixing all other parameters, the receiver filter is optimized through SNR maximization. The optimization problem is given by the following mathematical expression:

$$\max_{\mathbf{v}} \frac{T\sigma_t^2|\mathbf{v}^H(\mathbf{I}_{N+M} \otimes \mathbf{H}_t(\varphi))\mathbf{f}|^2}{\sigma_r^2\mathbf{v}^H\mathbf{v}} \tag{17}$$

The optimal solution of the receiver filter can be obtained through the Rayleigh entropy optimal solution:

$$\mathbf{v}^\star = \frac{(\mathbf{I}_{N+M} \otimes \mathbf{H}_t(\varphi))\mathbf{f}}{\mathbf{f}^H\left(\mathbf{I}_{N+M} \otimes \mathbf{H}_t^H(\varphi)\mathbf{H}_t(\varphi)\right)\mathbf{f}} \tag{18}$$

Following the receiver filter update, we reconfigure the radar SNR lower bound:

$$\Re\left\{\mathbf{v}^H(\mathbf{I}_{N+M} \otimes \mathbf{H}_t(\varphi))\mathbf{f}\right\} \geq \lambda_2 \tag{19}$$

During the formula refinement phase, we impose a non-negativity constrain $\mathbf{v}^H(\mathbf{I}_{N+M} \otimes \mathbf{H}_t(\varphi))\mathbf{f}$. Concurrently, we define λ_2 as $\lambda_2 \triangleq \sqrt{S_{\min}\sigma_r^2\mathbf{v}^H\mathbf{v}/\left(T\sigma_t^2\right)}$.

Update Beamforming Matrix f. After obtaining the determination of auxiliary variable **g**, **d** and receiver filter **v**, the beamforming matrix optimization reduces to a standard convex problem. This optimization is formulated as follows:

$$\begin{aligned} &\min_{\varphi} \varphi^H\mathbf{C}\varphi - \Re\{\mathbf{b}^H\varphi\} \\ &C_1 : \Re\{\mathbf{v}^H(\mathbf{I}_{N+M} \otimes \mathbf{H}_t(\varphi))\mathbf{f}\} \geq \lambda_2 \\ &C_2 : |\varphi| = 1 \end{aligned} \tag{20}$$

3.3 Optimization of RIS Reflection Coefficients

Update RIS Reflection Coefficients. φ. Upon determining auxiliary variable **g**, **d**, receiver filter **v**, and beamforming matrix **f**, the optimization of the RIS reflection coefficients can be expressed as follows:

$$\begin{aligned} &\min_{\varphi} \varphi^H\mathbf{C}\varphi - \Re\left\{\mathbf{b}^H\varphi\right\} \\ &C_1 : \Re\left\{\mathbf{v}^H(\mathbf{I}_{N+M} \otimes \mathbf{H}_t(\varphi))\mathbf{f}\right\} \geq \lambda_2 \\ &C_2 : |\varphi| = 1 \end{aligned} \tag{21}$$

The non-convexity of Constraint C_1 and the unit-modulus requirements in Constraint C_2 preclude direct optimization. In order to resolve this problem, we utilize the properties of the Kronecker product and the basic properties of matrices to rearrange and expand $\mathbf{H}_t(\varphi)$ as:

$$\begin{aligned} \mathbf{H}_t(\varphi) &= \left(\mathbf{h}_{B,t} + \mathbf{G}^T diag\{\mathbf{h}_{R,t}\}\varphi\right)\left(\mathbf{h}_{B,t}^T + \varphi^T diag\{\mathbf{h}_{R,t}\}^T\mathbf{G}\right) \\ &= \mathbf{h}_{B,t}\mathbf{h}_{B,t}^T + \mathbf{h}_{B,t}\varphi^T diag\{\mathbf{h}_{R,t}\}^T\mathbf{G} + \mathbf{G}^T diag\{\mathbf{h}_{R,t}\}\varphi\mathbf{h}_{B,t}^T \\ &\quad + \mathbf{G}^T diag\{\mathbf{h}_{R,t}\}\varphi\varphi^T diag\{\mathbf{h}_{R,t}\}^T\mathbf{G} \end{aligned} \tag{22}$$

The final term in the above expression is a non-convex, posing significant challenges for subsequent optimization. Therefore, we implement successive convex approximation for the quadratic components through the first-order Taylor expansion at the iteration point $\varphi(k)$:

$$\begin{aligned} \mathbf{G}^T diag\left\{\mathbf{h}_{R,t}\right\}\varphi\varphi^T diag\left\{\mathbf{h}_{R,t}\right\}^T\mathbf{G} \approx \mathbf{G}^T diag\left\{\mathbf{h}_{R,t}\right\}\varphi(k)\varphi(k)^T diag\left\{\mathbf{h}_{R,t}\right\}^T\mathbf{G} \\ +\mathbf{G}^T diag\left\{\mathbf{h}_{R,t}\right\}\left(\varphi'(k)\varphi(k)^T + \varphi(k)\varphi'(k)^T\right)diag\left\{\mathbf{h}_{R,t}\right\}^T\mathbf{G}(\varphi - \varphi(k)) \end{aligned} \tag{23}$$

The condition for the validity of the Taylor expansion is $\|\varphi - \varphi(k)\| << 1$. Substituting the Taylor expansion terms into the original formulation yields a linear function of φ:

$$\begin{aligned} \tilde{H}_t(\varphi) \approx \mathbf{h}_{B,t}\mathbf{h}_{B,t}^T + \mathbf{h}_{B,t}\varphi^T diag\left\{\mathbf{h}_{R,t}\right\}^T\mathbf{G} + \mathbf{G}^T diag\left\{\mathbf{h}_{R,t}\right\}\varphi\mathbf{h}_{B,t}^T \\ +\mathbf{G}^T diag\left\{\mathbf{h}_{R,t}\right\}\varphi(k)\varphi(k)^T diag\left\{\mathbf{h}_{R,t}\right\}^T\mathbf{G} \\ +\mathbf{G}^T diag\left\{\mathbf{h}_{R,t}\right\}\left(\varphi'(k)\varphi(k)^T + \varphi(k)\varphi'(k)^T\right)diag\left\{\mathbf{h}_{R,t}\right\}^T\mathbf{G}(\varphi - \varphi(k)) \end{aligned} \tag{24}$$

Bringing the linearized function to the original constraints, it can be transformed into:

$$\Re\left\{-\mathbf{v}^H\left(\mathbf{I}_{N+M} \otimes \tilde{H}_t(\varphi)\right)\mathbf{f}\right\} \le -\lambda_2 \tag{25}$$

It is clear that (24) is a linear constraint. In order to optimize the objective function under the unit-modulus requirements as well as the new constraints, we employ the ADMM algorithm. This requires introducing an auxiliary variable $\mathbf{O} \triangleq [o_1, o_2, ..., o_3]^T$ to satisfy the unit modulus constraint of the RIS reflection coefficient, and then we transform the optimization framework as:

$$\begin{aligned} &\min_{\varphi,o} \varphi^H\mathbf{C}\varphi - \Re\left\{\mathbf{b}^H\varphi\right\} \\ &C_1 : \Re\left\{-\mathbf{v}^H\left(\mathbf{I}_{N+M} \otimes \tilde{H}_t(\varphi)\right)\mathbf{f}\right\} \le -\lambda_2 \\ &C_2 : |\varphi_n| \le 1, \quad \forall n \\ &C_3 : |o_n| = 1, \quad \forall n, \\ &C_4 : \varphi = \mathbf{O} \end{aligned} \tag{26}$$

According to the ADMM algorithm, we construct an augmented Lagrangian function with Lagrange multipliers and penalty factor $\mu > 0$ to solve the above optimization problem, expressed as:

$$\min_{\varphi,\mathbf{o}} \varphi^H\mathbf{C}\varphi - \Re\left\{\mathbf{b}^H\varphi\right\} + \frac{\mu}{2}\|\varphi - \mathbf{O} + \frac{\lambda_3}{\mu}\|^2 \tag{27}$$

where $\lambda_3 \in \mathbb{C}^J$ is the dyadic variable in the ADMM algorithm, and the penalty factor μ is dynamically updated in accordance with (27).

$$\mu^{t+1} = \begin{cases} \min\left(1.5\mu^t, \mu_{\max}\right), \|\varphi - O\|_2 > 10\|\lambda_3\|_2 \\ \max\left(\dfrac{\mu^t}{1.5}, \mu_{\min}\right), \|\varphi - O\|_2 < 10\|\lambda_3\|_2 \\ 1.5\mu^t else \end{cases} \tag{28}$$

Update the RIS reflection coefficients φ*:* With other variables fixed, the optimization problem for the reflection coefficient is transformed into a convex optimization problem, which can be solved by a convex optimization algorithm.

Iterate auxiliary variable $\mathbf{O}$*:* During each iteration step, elements are projected onto the unit circle through normalization:

$$\begin{cases} \varphi_a^k = \varphi^k + \dfrac{k}{k+3}\left(\varphi^k - \varphi^{k-1}\right) \\ \mathbf{O}_n^{k+1} = \dfrac{\varphi_a^k + \frac{\lambda_3^k}{\mu}}{|\varphi_a^k + \frac{\lambda_3^k}{\mu}|} \end{cases} \tag{29}$$

Iterate dyadic variable λ_3*:* Upon determining the reflection coefficients φ, auxiliary variable $\mathbf{O}$, we can iteratively update λ_3 by the following expression:

$$\lambda_3^{k+1} = \lambda_3^k + (\varphi - \mathbf{O})\mu \tag{30}$$

3.4 Algorithm Summary

Building on the preceding analysis, Algorithm 1 outlines the beamforming and reflection design of the multi-objective framework with multi-user systems under worst-case radar SNR constraints. After the algorithm adopts the initialization strategy, it iteratively optimizes the individual variables by means of cyclic iteration until convergence. Meanwhile, we can conclude that the overall algorithmic complexity is $O\left((K \cdot (K+M))^3 + J^3\right)$ (Table 1).

Table 1. Procedure for FP-ADMM Alternating Algorithm

Algorithm 1: FP-ADMM Alternating Algorithm for Optimization
Input: $T, \mathbf{H}_t(\varphi), P_t, \mu, S_{\min}$
Output: $\mathbf{F}$, $\mathbf{v}$, φ
1. Initialize $\mathbf{F}$ and φ
2. **while** $\Delta > 10^{-4}$ **do**
3. Calculate the unique solution set of the auxiliary variables in equations (15) and (16)
4. Update receive filter $\mathbf{v}$ using equation (18)
5. Obtain $\mathbf{F}$ by solving the convex optimization problem (20)
6. Obtain φ by minimizing equation (27) using CVX toolbox
7. Update $\mathbf{O}$ and λ_3 sequentially using equations (29) and (30)
8. Set the step size according to (28)
9. Calculate $\Delta = \left(SR^k - SR^{k-1}\right) / SR^{k-1}$
10. **end while**
11. Return $\mathbf{F}$, $\mathbf{i}$, φ

4 Experimental Simulation

4.1 Simulation Scenario

We validate the efficacy of beamforming design under worst-case radar SNR constraints through comprehensive simulations. We set $N = 8$, $M = 4$, $\sigma_r = \sigma_m = -60dBm$, $\sigma_t^2 = 1$,$T = 2048$. Then we set the RIS at a distance of 10m from MU and the target, while the distance between the base station and RIS is 100m. The angle between BS and RIS is set to $\theta_{BR} = \frac{\pi}{4}$. In addition, we use the classical distance-based path loss model. We set the loss coefficients to $\varpi_{BR} = \varpi_{Rt} = 2.4$ for the links from the RIS to both the base station and the target, to $\varpi_{RM} = 2.6$ for the link between the RIS and users. We also set the loss coefficient to $\varpi_{Bt} = 2.9$ for the link between the BS and the target, to $\varpi_{BM} = 3.6$ for the link between the BS and users. Finally, the Rician factor for the links between the user and both the BS and the RIS is set to 3 dB.

4.2 Results Analysis

Convergence of the Algorithm. Figures 2 present the convergence behavior of the FP-ADMM algorithm. By varying the number of reflecting elements, transmit power, we obtained curves showing the sum-rate of communication users as a function of the iteration count. This figure demonstrates the convergence performance of our proposed algorithm under different predefined conditions. In Figs. 2(a), (b), we respectively set different reflection elements $J = [49, 60, 100]$, transmit power $P = [25, 30, 35]$. By comparing Figs. 2(a), (b), we observe that the communication sum-rate improvement becomes marginal after approximately 50 iterations, thereby validating the convergence of the proposed algorithm.

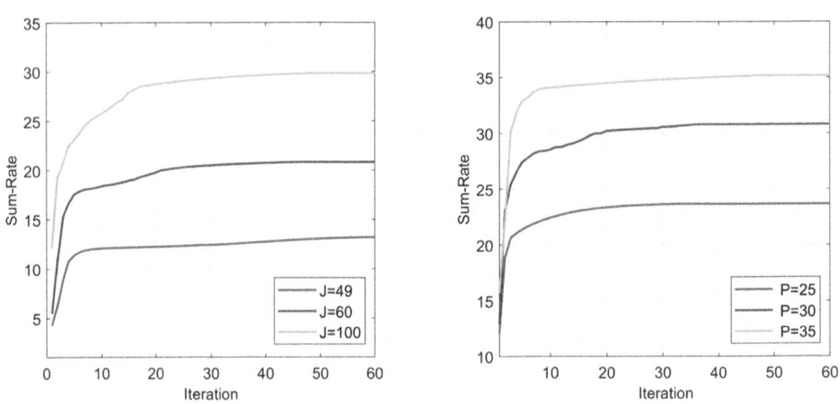

(a) (b)

Fig. 2. Comparison of the algorithm's convergence under different predefined conditions. (a)Reflection elements. (b)Transmit power.

Transmit Power and Reflecting Elements. Figure 3 illustrates the relationship between sum-rate and the number of elements, between sum-rate and the transmit power in the joint beamforming design under the radar SNR constraint. It also compares our approach with communication-only optimization scheme, and the scheme without RIS assistance, highlighting the superiority of our design. In Fig. 3(a), communication performance improves as the number of RIS elements increases. This is because increasing the number of reflecting elements allows for more precise control over the directionality and shape of the transmit beam, thereby enhancing beamforming capability. Moreover, in comparison to the systems without RIS assistance, our design demonstrates good communication performance. In Fig. 3(b), as the transmit power increases, so does the sum rate of communication users. Our approach improves communication functionality with the same transmit power by incorporating RIS reflection matrix optimization. Furthermore, as transmit power increases, the gap in communication and rate between our approach and the communication-only scheme gradually narrows. This suggests that, while maintaining a certain level of radar sensing capability, we can allocate more transmit power to enhance communication performance.

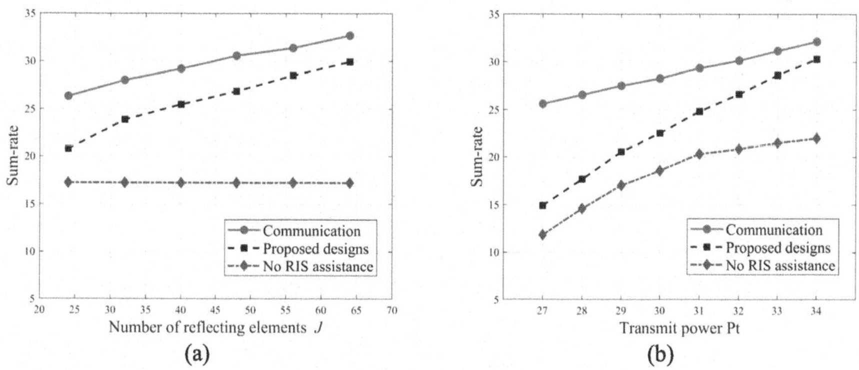

Fig. 3. The impact of reflecting elements and transmit power on the sum-rate. (a)Reflecting Elements. (b)Transmit Power.

5 Conclusion

In this paper, we investigated the beamforming for collaborative systems of communication and sensing achieved through the collaboration between RIS and MISO base stations. Communication performance was evaluated using the sum-rate, while radar performance was measured by the sensing SNR. To maximize the number of users and data rate under radar SNR, transmit power, and unit-modulus constraints, we proposed an alternating optimization algorithm that combines FP and ADMM to jointly optimize acceptance filter coefficients, beamforming and the RIS reflection coefficient matrix. Simulation results demonstrated the effectiveness and superiority of the proposed approach. Compared to existing methods, our approach achieves better communication performance while maintaining a required level of radar sensing through collaboration between the RIS and base stations.

Acknowledgments. This work was supported in part by the National Natural Science Foundation of China under Grant 62372131, the Key Research and Development Program of Heilongjiang Province under Grant 2023ZX01A20.

References

1. Wei, Z., Qu, H., Wang, Y., et al.: Integrated sensing and communication signals toward 5G-A and 6G: a survey. IEEE Internet Things J. **10**(13), 11068–11092 (2023)
2. Wollschlaeger, M., Sauter, T., Jasperneite, J.: The future of industrial communication: automation networks in the era of the internet of things and industry 4.0. IEEE Ind. Electron. Maga. **11**(1), 17–27 (2017)
3. Akpakwu, G.A., Silva, B.J., Hancke, G.P., et al.: A survey on 5G networks for the Internet of Things: communication technologies and challenges. IEEE access **6**, 3619–3647 (2017)
4. Liu, F., Cui, Y., Masouros, C., et al.: Integrated sensing and communications: toward dual-functional wireless networks for 6G and beyond. IEEE J. Sel. Areas Commun. **40**(6), 1728–1767 (2022)
5. Yang, P., Xiao, Y., Xiao, M., et al.: 6G wireless communications: vision and potential techniques. IEEE Network **33**(4), 70–75 (2019)
6. Zhang, J.A., Liu, F., Masouros, C., et al.: An overview of signal processing techniques for joint communication and radar sensing. IEEE J. Sel. Topics Signal Process. **15**(6), 1295–1315 (2021)
7. He, Y., Cai, Y., Mao, H., et al.: RIS-assisted communication radar coexistence: Joint beamforming design and analysis. IEEE J. Sel. Areas Commun. **40**(7), 2131–2145 (2022)
8. Sankar, R.S.P., Chepuri, S.P.: Beamforming in hybrid RIS assisted integrated sensing and communication systems. In: 2022 30th European Signal Processing Conference (EUSIPCO), pp. 1082–1086. IEEE (2022)
9. Buzzi, S., Grossi, E., Lops, M., et al.: Foundations of MIMO radar detection aided by reconfigurable intelligent surfaces. IEEE Trans. Signal Process. **70**, 1749–1763 (2022)
10. Wang, X., Fei, Z., Huang, J., et al.: Joint waveform and discrete phase shift design for RIS-assisted integrated sensing and communication system under Cramer-Rao bound constraint. IEEE Trans. Veh. Technol. **71**(1), 1004–1009 (2021)
11. Wang, X., Fei, Z., Zheng, Z., et al.: Joint waveform design and passive beamforming for RIS-assisted dual-functional radar-communication system. IEEE Trans. Veh. Technol. **70**(5), 5131–5136 (2021)
12. Luo, H., Liu, R., Li, M., et al.: Joint beamforming design for RIS-assisted integrated sensing and communication systems. IEEE Trans. Veh. Technol. **71**(12), 13393–13397 (2022)
13. Sankar, R.S.P., Chepuri, S.P., Eldar, Y.C.: Beamforming in integrated sensing and communication systems with reconfigurable intelligent surfaces. IEEE Trans. Wirel. Commun. **23**(5), 4017–4031 (2023)
14. Song, X., Qin, X., Xu, J., et al.: Cramér-rao bound minimization for IRS-enabled multiuser integrated sensing and communications. IEEE Trans. Wirel. Commun. (2024)
15. Ma, T., Xiao, Y., Lei, X., et al.: Integrated sensing and communication with reconfigurable intelligent surfaces. IEEE Trans. Veh. Technol. (2024)

16. Jiang, C., Zhang, C., Huang, C., et al.: Exploiting RIS in secure beamforming design for NOMA-assisted integrated sensing and communication. IEEE Internet Things J. **11**(17), 28123–28136 (2024)
17. Yu, Y., Li, D., Wang, B., et al.: NOMA-ISAC via IRS: a joint beamforming and reflecting optimization approach. In: 2024 IEEE/CIC International Conference on Communications in China (ICCC), pp. 1793–1798. IEEE (2024)

Short Video Rumor Detection Method Integrating Multimodal Information

Zeyu Liu[2], Jun Zhang[1], Donglin Cao[1,2,3,4(✉)], and Dazhen Lin[1]

[1] School of Informatics, Xiamen University, Xiamen 361005, China
[2] Institute of Artificial Intelligence, Xiamen University, Xiamen 361102, Fujian, China
[3] Pingtan Research Institute, Xiamen University, Pingtan 350400, China
[4] Fujian Key Laboratory of Big Data Application and Intellectualization for Tea Industry, Wuyi University, Wuyishan 354300, China

another@xmu.edu.cn

Abstract. With the rapid development of short video platforms, the widespread spread of short video rumors poses a serious threat to social security. However, existing studies face the problem of insufficient video rumor datasets. For this reason, this paper constructs the largest Chinese rumor video dataset, which contains 4542 video samples. It uses stratified sampling to divide the dataset into training set, validation set and test set, so as to maintain the consistency of data distribution. To address the challenge of multimodal information fusion, a hierarchical feature conversion and cross-modal alignment method is proposed. Specifically, optical character recognition (OCR) and CogVideoX are used to extract visual text; the Whisper model converts audio into text; combined with the title and time features in metadata, multimodal information is unified into a Chinese text representation. A detection model is trained based on the BERT model, and Focal Loss is adopted to alleviate the data imbalance problem. Experimental results show that the model achieves an accuracy of 93.51% and an F1-score of 0.6324 on the test set. Its performance is better than that of comparison models such as MDFEND and SV-FEND.

Keywords: Short Videos · Multimodal Fusion · Rumor Detection · BERT Model · Information Propagation

1 Introduction

With the rapid development of short video platforms, short videos have become one of the primary channels for information acquisition and dissemination among Chinese internet users. As of December 2024, the number of domestic short video users has exceeded 1 billion, accounting for over 90% of the total internet user base.

With advantages such as vivid content and efficient dissemination, short videos are widely used in scenarios like news reporting, health popularization,

© The Author(s), under exclusive license to Springer Nature Singapore Pte Ltd. 2027

H. Sun et al. (Eds.): ChineseCSCW 2025, CCIS 2911, pp. 184–197, 2027.
https://doi.org/10.1007/978-981-92-0288-1_14

and social event recording. However, due to their low production threshold and high review difficulty, they have also become an important carrier for rumor propagation. For example, during the COVID-19 pandemic, typical rumors such as "drinking alcohol can kill viruses" and "high-temperature environments can inhibit COVID-19" spread on a large scale through short videos, causing significant negative impacts. Therefore, the detection work targeting short video rumors holds great practical significance.

Although existing studies have established various rumor databases, they face the problem of insufficient video rumor datasets. Most existing rumor datasets are derived from text-based social platforms such as Weibo and Twitter. While these datasets have laid a foundation for rumor detection research, their data format is all text, which cannot support the development of multimodal rumor detection models. With the rapid rise of short video platforms such as Douyin and Kuaishou, video rumors have become a new challenge that urgently needs to be addressed, and there is an urgent need to construct a rumor dataset containing video content [1].

We aim to construct a rumor detection model suitable for Chinese short videos and have made the following contributions:

- We have constructed the largest Chinese rumor video dataset to date, alleviating the data shortage problem in multimodal rumor detection.
- To address the technical challenge of multimodal data fusion, we propose a hierarchical feature conversion and cross-modal alignment method. This method converts information from visual, auditory, and textual dimensions into a unified Chinese text representation through hierarchical feature modal conversion, realizing the standardized processing of multimodal information features.
- Experimental verification shows that the BERT model trained based on this method exhibits excellent rumor detection performance, with an accuracy rate of up to 93.51% on the test set.

2 Related Work

2.1 Unimodal Rumor Detection

In unimodal rumor detection, text-based methods have long dominated. Early studies, such as Castillo et al. [18], used decision tree algorithms to fuse text features, sentiment labels, and user attributes for credibility verification. Qazvinian et al. [19] adopted Bayesian classifiers to analyze lexical statistical features. With the popularization of deep learning, researchers have gradually shifted to more complex model architectures. Ma et al. [3] proposed a tree-structured recursive neural network (RvNN) to capture non-sequential propagation structures, improving early identification capabilities. Li et al.'s [4] BERT-DPCNN model combined pre-training with deep pyramid convolutions to extract multi-layer features. However, a single text modality struggles to handle cross-modal semantic conflicts. Pure text models lag by an average of more than 15% in F1-score in multimodal scenarios [5], and cannot address the image-text gap [6] or dynamic propagation patterns.

Unimodal detection based on visual features and user attributes faces greater challenges. In the image modality, overfitting is severe due to data sparsity. VGG-19 [2] achieves only 50%-60% accuracy on Twitter datasets. Papadopoulou et al. [7] used SVM to fuse video metadata and text features, but their manually designed features lack robustness. User attributes have discriminative power in specific scenarios but show poor cross-platform generalization. Although some unimodal models outperform certain multimodal methods on specific datasets, they still cannot handle multi-image tweets or modality-missing scenarios. Studies indicate that unimodal approaches suffer from incomplete semantic coverage, and their real-time advantages are offset by efficiency optimizations in multimodal methods. For example, the limited information of unimodal data makes it hard to identify metaphorical expressions in complex scenarios [21], while multimodal frameworks can improve accuracy through methods like cross-modal alignment [6] and composite convolution fusion [20]. In summary, despite local advantages in computational efficiency and interpretability, unimodal methods have significantly lagged behind multimodal frameworks in overall performance.

2.2 Multimodal Rumor Detection

In recent years, various deep learning models have emerged in multimodal rumor detection, improving detection performance by fusing multimodal information such as text, vision, and audio. Early models like EANN [8] extracted event-invariant features through adversarial training, but multimodal features were simply concatenated without effectively modeling cross-modal semantic interactions, and showed poor robustness in modality-missing scenarios. MVAE [9] used variational autoencoders to learn shared latent representations, but its generative architecture led to high computational complexity, making it difficult to capture fine-grained modality differences.

After 2022, researchers introduced more complex fusion mechanisms. TMIF [10] aligned text and image features through cross-modal attention, but relied on pre-trained modality alignment assumptions and was sensitive to spatio-temporal inconsistencies in heterogeneous data. MAFN [11] fused features using affine transformations; however, affine parameter learning was limited by local semantic associations, struggling to handle global semantic conflicts. AMFNN (Attention-based Multimodal Fusion Network) designed attention mechanisms at the word-visual object level, improving fine-grained interaction capabilities but limiting real-time performance due to the high computational overhead of cross-modal alignment. The multi-hop multimodal fusion model proposed in 2023 combined RGCN (Relational Graph Convolutional Network) with multi-hop attention, which could capture long-distance dependencies but significantly increased inference latency due to its multi-layer graph propagation structure. MMRDF [12] fused multi-level features through composite convolutions but still required separate processing of text and visual sub-networks, resulting in high resource consumption and inability to effectively handle audio modalities.

3 Construction of the Dataset

3.1 Data Collection

To obtain rumor video data with wide coverage and accurate annotations as much as possible, we first crawled 985 rumor-refuting articles published from February 2021 to December 2024 from the China Internet Joint Rumor Refutation Platform. Subsequently, based on the keywords of each rumor-refuting article, we searched and crawled videos on the Douyin platform corresponding to the themes, and extracted video links for subsequent data construction and processing. Finally, a total of 4542 valid video links were obtained. Each piece of data includes the following multi-dimensional features:

1. Multimodal raw data: video frame sequences (25fps), audio waveforms (16kHz), and ASR-transcribed text;
2. Metadata: title, release time, and source platform;
3. Label system: binary classification labels (rumor/non-rumor).

3.2 Data Annotation and Analysis

Although the database contains 4542 videos and 985 rumor-refuting articles after data collection, not all videos are rumor videos. The identification of rumors still requires manual work. For this reason, we conducted manual data annotation and adopted a cross-annotation mode with 3 annotators to ensure the reliability of annotation results. Meanwhile, since short video rumors are often more misleading, and rumor-refuting articles may not accurately target misleading information, we clearly defined that "misleading information" must meet any of the following conditions: factual errors, misleading statements, false associations, or emotionally incendiary misleading content. Only when such obvious misleading information appears in a video will it be annotated as a "rumor". Among the data, there are 552 rumor samples, accounting for approximately 11% of the total dataset, and 3990 non-rumor samples, accounting for approximately 89% of the total dataset.

Figure 1 shows the data distribution proportion of rumors by year. Among them, the data from 2024 accounts for approximately 57% of the total data volume, followed by 2023 and 2022, which account for approximately 23% and 12% respectively. The main data of this dataset (accounting for 92%) comes from the past three years, which has a timeliness advantage compared with datasets established by previous scholars.

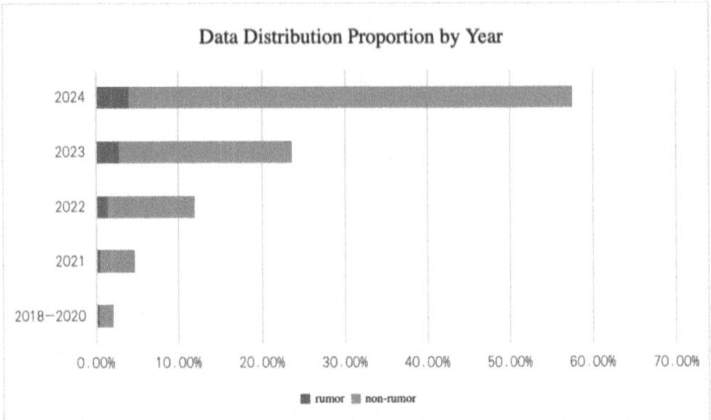

Fig. 1. Data Distribution Proportion by Year.

3.3 Dataset Division

Due to the sample imbalance of the dataset (the ratio of positive samples to negative samples is 1:9), it is necessary to ensure that the training set, validation set, and test set all contain a certain number of negative samples when dividing the dataset. We adopt the stratified sampling method to ensure that the training set, validation set, and test set all contain equal proportions of positive and negative samples. Specifically, the training set accounts for 64% of the total samples (0.8×0.8), the validation set accounts for 16% (0.8×0.2), and the test set accounts for 20%.

Table 1. Comparison of Data Distribution Before and After Division

Data	Total Number	Number of Rumors	Number of Non-Rumors	Average Text Length
Original Dataset	4,542	552	3,990	420.2
Training Set	2,906	348	2,558	414.1
Validation Set	726	87	639	424.4
Test Set	910	109	801	436.3

The comparison of the dataset before and after division is shown in Table 1. Each subset after division strictly maintains the distribution characteristics of the original data. Among them, the proportions of positive and negative samples in the training set, validation set, and test set are 12% and 88% respectively, which is consistent with the proportion of positive and negative samples in the original dataset. We train the rumor detection model by converting multiple modalities into text information; therefore, the length of the converted text is also one of the factors affecting model training. In the table above, the statistics of the average text length of the dataset before and after division are also presented. The text length includes the release date, video title, audio text, and visual text.

According to statistics, the average text length of the original dataset is 420.2 characters, while the average text lengths of the training set, validation set, and test set are 414.1, 424.4, and 436.3 characters respectively. The difference between the average text length of each subset after division and that of the original dataset does not exceed 20 characters. This indicates that the dataset division not only maintains the proportion of positive and negative samples but also does not have a significant impact on the text length distribution. Such a division strategy effectively preserves the statistical distribution characteristics of the original dataset and provides a reliable data foundation for model training and evaluation.

4 Multimodal Text-Based Rumor Detection Algorithm

4.1 Overall Framework of the Algorithm

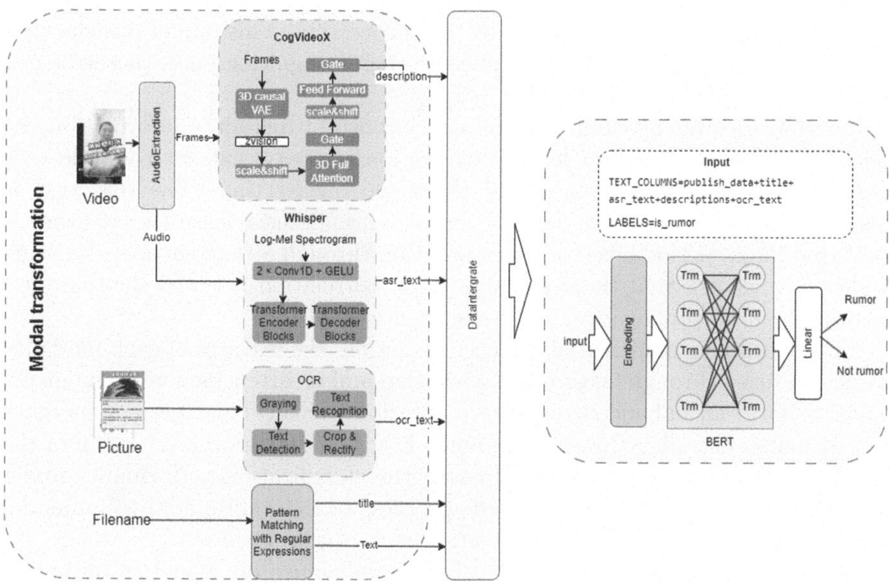

Fig. 2. Algorithm Framework.

The overall framework of the algorithm is shown in Fig. 2. The multimodal rumor detection framework we designed mainly includes the following core modules. First, we construct a multimodal data feature extraction and fusion module. Its core task is to unify the heterogeneous multi-source data of rumor videos into structured text features through cross-modal conversion technology, providing processable semantic input for subsequent deep learning models.

The valid information contained in the original data is mainly distributed in three dimensions: visual modality, auditory modality, and metadata. We have designed targeted multimodal feature extraction schemes:

In terms of visual feature extraction, we implement differentiated processing strategies for visual data in different formats in the dataset: (1) For static image sets in JPEG format, considering that such data mainly uses text-image layout as the information carrier and the background music is mostly irrelevant to semantics, we adopt Optical Character Recognition (OCR) technology to accurately extract text elements from images; (2) For dynamic video data in MP4 format, to fully capture the temporal semantic information in continuous frames, we introduce the CogVLM2-caption video description generation model based on the multi-scale spatiotemporal attention mechanism. This model shares the underlying multimodal architecture with the CogVideoX [13] model and generates coherent visual semantic description text through hierarchical feature decoding.

In the aspect of auditory feature processing, we construct an audio semantic analysis pipeline: first, extract independent audio tracks from videos through the FFmpeg multimedia framework; then, use the Whisper-large-v3 speech recognition model for end-to-end speech-to-text processing. This model has shown a 95.2% character accuracy rate in Chinese speech recognition tasks (according to the official test set).

For the video file attributes containing important metadata information, we specially design a metadata feature extraction strategy: extract the title text encoded in the video file name and the video release time. The title text is used as a key semantic feature after denoising, and the release time feature is converted into a periodic vector representation through a time encoder. Existing studies have shown that there is a significant correlation between the temporal pattern of rumor propagation and its authenticity [14].

After the above multimodal feature extraction, the features of each modality are deeply fused through feature concatenation and an attention weighting mechanism to form an enhanced text representation vector. This vector undergoes deep semantic encoding through the multi-head self-attention mechanism of the BERT-base-Chinese model. By comparing the classification performance under different feature combinations, the effectiveness of the multimodal-to-unimodal conversion method in the rumor detection task can be verified.

To alleviate the negative impact of data imbalance on model training and improve learning efficiency, we use Focal Loss as the loss function, and its calculation formula is as follows:

$$FL(p_t) = -\alpha_t(1 - p_t)^\gamma \log(p_t) \tag{1}$$

Among them, α_t is the weight factor, and we set the weight factor for positive classes to 0.25; p_t is the probability predicted for the correct class; γ is the focusing parameter, which is set to 2 in this experiment and used to control the degree of weight suppression for easily classified samples.

The overall algorithm is described as follows:

In the algorithm pseudocode, the Extra_audio() function is used to separate the audio stream Audio from videos. Subsequently, the audio is converted into

Algorithm 1. Multimodal Text-based Rumor Detection Algorithm

Input: Video files Videos, image set Pictures, file names Filename, labels Labels, pre-trained model bert
Output: Trained model parameters

```
Audio ← Extra_audio(Videos)
A_T ← Whisper(Audio)
V_t ← CogVideos(Videos)
O_t ← OCR(Pictures)
PD, Title ← Paras_filename(Filename)
Datas ← (PD + Title + A_T + V_t + O_t, Label)
for data, label in Datas do
    output ← bert.forward(data, label)
    loss ← Focalloss(output)
    loss.backward()
end for
Save(bert)
```

audio text information $\boldsymbol{A}_T$ via the Whisper model. Visual information is converted through the CogVideo model and OCR library, resulting in visual text information $\boldsymbol{V}_t$ and $\boldsymbol{O}_t$ respectively. Finally, the publication date PD and video title Title are extracted from formatted file names.

During model training, PD, Title, $\boldsymbol{O}_t$, $\boldsymbol{A}_T$, and $\boldsymbol{V}_t$ are concatenated to form the Context part of the data Datas, and the input label Label is used as the data label label. After the data is combined, it is input into the pre-trained BERT model for training. The Focal loss is used to calculate the loss, and parameters are updated through backpropagation. Finally, the model parameters with the highest F1 score are saved.

4.2 Evaluation Metrics

We use Accuracy, Recall, Precision, and F1-Score as evaluation metrics, with their calculation formulas as follows:

Accuracy measures the overall classification correctness of the model:

$$\text{Accuracy} = \frac{TP + TN}{TP + TN + FP + FN} \tag{2}$$

Precision represents the reliability of the model's predictions of rumors:

$$\text{Precision} = \frac{TP}{TP + FP} \tag{3}$$

Recall reflects the model's ability to detect actual rumor samples:

$$\text{Recall} = \frac{TP}{TP + FN} \tag{4}$$

F1-Score, as the harmonic mean of Precision and Recall, comprehensively evaluates the model's robust performance on class-imbalanced data:

$$F1 = \frac{2TP}{2TP + FP + FN} \tag{5}$$

Among them, True Positives (TP) refers to the number of rumor videos correctly identified as rumors; True Negatives (TN) refers to the number of non-rumor videos accurately classified as non-rumors; False Positives (FP) reflect the misclassification where non-rumor videos are incorrectly judged as rumors; and False Negatives (FN) refer to the missed detection where rumor videos are incorrectly categorized as non-rumors.

5 Experiments

5.1 Data Preprocessing

The most critical part of the method is converting the multimodal information of rumor videos into unified Chinese text information. The specific processing methods are as follows:

Auditory Feature Information: For the input data in MP4 format, we use the FFmpeg tool to extract high-quality audio streams from videos with the parameter `(-q:a 0 -map a)`, and temporarily save them as MP3 files with the same name. Subsequently, the Whisper model is used to transcribe the audio, outputting the corresponding text information. After processing, the average length of the audio text for 4542 short videos is 351.17 characters.

Visual Feature Information: For static image sets in JPEG format, we convert the original images into grayscale images. This method eliminates color interference while highlighting text regions in the images, which can improve the robustness and accuracy of OCR text recognition. For dynamic video data in MP4 format, we use the CogVideoX model, sampling one frame per second from the input videos and selecting a maximum of 24 frames as the model input. In the text generation stage, we set the maximum generation length to `max_new_tokens=2048` to avoid generating redundant content that wastes resources. Meanwhile, to ensure the generation of relatively accurate video description text, we set the generation temperature to `temperature=0.1` (a smaller value makes the generated content more conservative and deterministic), and set the nucleus sampling `top_p` and top-k sampling `top_k` to 0.1 and 1 respectively to prevent the model from generating text that deviates from the video content. After processing, the average length of the text generated from visual feature information (including `descriptions` and `ocr_text`) is 218.10 characters, which is shorter than the audio text.

Video File Attributes: When saving data, important metadata is stored in file names. The file name format for videos is "Release Date - Type (Image Set/Video) - Video Title", where the release date and video title are useful information. We extract the structured information from file names using regular expressions and save the release date and video title in JSON format. The average text length of the title (`title`) is 40.80 characters.

To better adapt to short video rumor detection, we also perform data cleaning: when inputting data, we remove content commonly found in short videos, such as "#", "@username", and multiple spaces to improve the quality of text data.

5.2 Parameter Settings

We use `bert-base-chinese` as the pre-trained model, where the maximum length of text tokens is set to 512 by default, and the DROPOUT rate is set to 0.5. During training, the `BATCH_SIZE` is 32, and the maximum number of epochs is 100; training stops if the validation F1-score does not improve for 5 consecutive epochs. The AdamW optimizer is used, with an initial learning rate of 0.00002 and a weight decay of 0.01, combined with a cosine annealing learning rate scheduler with a warm-up period accounting for 10% of the total steps. Hyperparameters include a classification threshold of 0.2 and downsampling the majority class (i.e., non-rumor samples) to 3000 samples.

5.3 Baseline Methods

MDFEND [16]: Constructed Weibo21, a multi-domain fake news dataset covering 9 domains. Meanwhile, it proposed the multi-domain detection model MDFEND. This model aggregates representations extracted by the domain-gated expert network to address domain shift.

SV-FEND [17]: Constructed FakeSV, a large-scale Chinese fake news short video dataset. It used cross-modal transformers to enhance interactions between different modalities. It also integrated content features with social context features through the self-attention mechanism.

GenFEND [15]: Proposed to use large language models to simulate diverse user-generated comments. This aims to solve the problem of insufficient diversity of actual comments in fake news detection. It also designed the GenFEND framework, which enhances detection performance through multi-perspective comment generation, multi-subgroup feedback understanding, and cross-perspective aggregation (Table 2).

5.4 Experimental Results and Analysis

We conducted multiple experiments to obtain results. Through comparison of the experimental results, the proposed method achieves good performance on the constructed dataset. Its accuracy of 0.9351 and F1 score of 0.6324 both rank the best among the comparative methods. Based on this result, the analysis of why other models perform worse than the proposed method on this dataset is as follows:

Table 2. Experimental Results and Comparison

Model	Accuracy	Recall	Precision	F1 Score
MDFEND	0.8638	0.7953	0.3741	0.5088
SV-FEND	0.9026	0.7348	0.4526	0.5937
GenFEND	0.8184	**0.8031**	0.3027	0.4397
Ours	**0.9351**	0.6299	**0.6349**	**0.6324**

1. Both GenFEND and MDFEND are single-text rumor detection models built based on the Weibo21 rumor dataset. However, the current comparative experiment uses video rumors. Thus, these two models can only use video titles as rumor data for training. They lack video frames and audio information, leading to limited data features obtained by the models. This makes it difficult for them to achieve good detection performance.
2. Although the SV-FEND model is a multi-modal rumor detection method, it directly encodes audio information and frame information before model training. This may lead to model misinterpretation: the model learns redundant information in images (e.g., background information) while ignoring the contained semantic information. As a result, it fails to identify rumor information in videos.

5.5 Ablation Experiments

To further explore which features in the experiment have a significant impact on the experimental results, we also conducted ablation experiments. We discussed separately the title (title), publication date (publish_date), audio text (asr_text), and visual information (descriptions and ocr_text) involved in the conversion of multi-modal data features. The experimental results are shown in the following table:

Table 3. Results of Ablation Experiments

Method	Accuracy	Recall	Precision	F1 Score
Without Removing Features	0.9351	0.6299	0.6349	0.6324
w/o `title`	0.9169	0.5118	0.5328	0.5221
w/o `publish_date`	0.9323	0.6119	0.6457	0.6284
w/o `asr_text`	0.9113	0.6850	0.5000	0.5781
w/o `description/ocr_text`	0.9372	0.6614	0.6412	0.6512

From the results in Table 3, it can be seen that in all ablation studies, removing the publication time has the least impact on the model, while removing the title has the greatest effect. Notably, removing visual information yields better results than the baseline.

Our analysis is as follows:

1. Although time may influence rumor detection, rumors here have lower temporal relevance compared to more time-sensitive types like political or entertainment rumors. Thus, removing publication time has minimal impact.
2. Removing the title has the largest effect on results. Although titles are typically short, they summarize video content concisely and contain rich semantic information, which greatly aids rumor detection.
3. Removing visual information leads to better performance than the baseline. This may be because visual information has low correlation with rumor content, or the model-generated video descriptions are inaccurate. Also, the description text has a shorter average length than audio, indicating lower importance. Considering generation quality and information content, visual information may slightly harm model performance. For example, if a doctor spreads a rumor, the description might label it as science popularization, misleading detection. Additionally, unclear video frames can produce inaccurate descriptions, hindering performance improvement.

6 Conclusions and Future Work

This study focuses on short-video rumor detection. We constructed a dataset containing 4542 Douyin samples, annotated by the China Internet Joint Rumor Refuting Platform. We integrated audio, visual, and textual information, titles, and publication times into a unified textual representation. A multimodal information transformation and fusion method was proposed. Based on the BERT pre-trained model, we established a detection model. Experiments confirm that our model outperforms traditional methods.

Current research has three main limitations for future improvement: First, the dataset requires expansion in size and sources, incorporating data from platforms like Kuaishou, Bilibili, and YouTube (including long videos), and enhancing model capability to process longer videos and texts. Second, annotation accuracy needs improvement through professional annotators to enhance objectivity. Third, the multimodal-to-text conversion process requires refinement to reduce the loss of key information (e.g., emotional cues) and improve both text generation quality and data cleaning.

Acknowledgments. This work is supported by the National Key Research and Development Program of China (No. 2023YFC3503001, 2023YFC3503004) and the Open Project Program of Fujian Key Laboratory of Big Data Application and Intellectualization for Tea Industry, Wuyi University (No. FKLBDAITI202401).

References

1. Jiang, F., Liang, G., Yang, J., Chen, L.: MMRDF: an improved multitask multimodal rumor detection framework. Electron. Lett. **59**(10), e12811 (2023)
2. Wen, L., Li, X., Li, X., Gao, L.: A new transfer learning based on VGG-19 network for fault diagnosis. In: 2019 IEEE 23rd International Conference on Computer Supported Cooperative Work in Design (CSCWD), pp. 205–209 (2019)
3. Ma, J., Gao, W., Wong, K.F.: Rumor detection on twitter with tree-structured recursive neural networks. In: Association for Computational Linguistics (2018)
4. Li, Y.-J., Zhang, H.-J., Pan, W.-M., Feng, R.-J., Zhou, Z.-Y.: Microblog rumor detection based on Bert-DPCNN. In: Artificial Intelligence in China: Proceedings of the 2nd International Conference on Artificial Intelligence in China, pp. 524–530 (2021)
5. Zhang, L., Ibrahim, S., Fadzil, A.F.A.: Rumor detection based on deep learning techniques: a systematic review. TELKOMNIKA (Telecommun. Comput. Electron. Control) **22**(4), 869–886 (2024)
6. Georgiev, P., et al.: Gemini 1.5: unlocking multimodal understanding across millions of tokens of context (2024). Gemini Team, arXiv preprint arXiv:2403.05530
7. Papadopoulou, O., Zampoglou, M., Papadopoulos, S., Kompatsiaris, I.: A corpus of debunked and verified user-generated videos. Online Inf. Rev. **43**(1), 72–88 (2019)
8. Wang, Y., et al.: Eann: event adversarial neural networks for multi-modal fake news detection. In: Proceedings of the 24th ACM SIGKDD International Conference on Knowledge Discovery & Data Mining, pp. 849–857 (2018)
9. Khattar, D., Goud, J.S., Gupta, M., Varma, V.: Mvae: multimodal variational autoencoder for fake news detection. In: The World Wide Web Conference, pp. 2915–2921 (2019)
10. Lv, J., Wang, X., Shao, C.: TMIF: transformer-based multi-modal interactive fusion for automatic rumor detection. Multimedia Syst. **29**(5), 2979–2989 (2023)
11. Fu, B., Sui, J.: Multi-modal affine fusion network for social media rumor detection. PeerJ Comput. Sci. **8**, e928 (2022)
12. Qi, L., Wan, S., Tang, B., Xu, Y.: Multimodal fusion rumor detection method based on attention mechanism. Comput. Eng. Appl. **58**(19), 209–217 (2022)
13. Yang, Z., Teng, J., Zheng, W., et al.: Cogvideox: text-to-video diffusion models with an expert transformer. arXiv preprint arXiv: 2408.06072 (2024)
14. Liu, Z., Yang, K., Hovy, E., Ananiadou, S.: Rumor Detection by Multi-task Suffix Learning based on Time-series Dual Sentiments (2025). arXiv:2502.14383 arXiv preprint
15. Nan, Q., Sheng, Q., Cao, J., Hu, B., Wang, D., Li, J.: Let silence speak: enhancing fake news detection with generated comments from large language models. In: Proceedings of the 33rd ACM International Conference on Information and Knowledge Management, pp. 1732–1742 (2024)
16. Nan, Q., Cao, J., Zhu, Y., Wang, Y., Li, J.: MDFEND: multi-domain fake news detection. In: Proceedings of the 30th ACM International Conference on Information & Knowledge Management, pp. 3343–3347 (2021)
17. Qi, P., et al.: Fakesv: a multimodal benchmark with rich social context for fake news detection on short video platforms. In: Proceedings of the AAAI Conference on Artificial Intelligence, vol. 37, no. 12, pp. 14444–14452 (2023)
18. Qazvinian, V., Rosengren, E., Radev, D., Mei, Q.: Rumor has it: identifying misinformation in microblogs. In: Proceedings of the 2011 Conference on Empirical Methods in Natural Language Processing, pp. 1589–1599 (2011)

19. Castillo, C., Mendoza, M., Poblete, B.: Information credibility on Twitter. In: Proceedings of the 20th International Conference on World Wide Web, pp. 675–684 (2011)
20. Wu, K., Lin, Y., Cao, D., Lin, D.: Interpretable short video rumor detection based on modality tampering. In: Proceedings of the 2024 Joint International Conference on Computational Linguistics, Language Resources and Evaluation (LREC-COLING 2024), pp. 9180–9189 (2024)
21. Zhang, H., Qian, S., Fang, Q., Xu, C.: Multi-modal meta multi-task learning for social media rumor detection. IEEE Trans. Multimed. **24**, 1449–1459 (2021)

Semantic Planning Meets Structural Retrieval: Knowledge Graph Subgraph Retrieval Collaboration for Robust LLM Reasoning

Shijie Chen[1], Jia Zhu[1(✉)], and Changqin Huang[2]

[1] Zhejiang Normal University, Jinhua 321004, China
jiazhu@zjnu.edu.cn
[2] Zhejiang University, Hangzhou 310058, China

Abstract. Large language models (LLMs) have demonstrated remarkable reasoning capabilities in complex tasks. However, their performance and trustworthiness are compromised by the lack of up-to-date knowledge and the tendency to hallucinate during reasoning, which can lead to incorrect reasoning processes. Knowledge graphs (KGs) encode vast amounts of factual knowledge in a structured format, and KG-based Retrieval-Augmented Generation(RAG) provides a reliable knowledge source for reasoning. Existing KG-based reasoning methods for LLMs, however, primarily treat KGs as static factual repositories and overlook the crucial role of their structural information in reasoning. In this paper, we introduce CoSubGraph-RAG, a novel framework that integrates LLMs with KGs to enhance reasoning performance. Our framework leverages the complementary strengths of LLMs and KGs by enabling the LLM to generate semantic relation paths and a subgraph retriever to extract relevant KG paths based on structural relevance. These components work synergistically to guide multi-hop reasoning, ensuring both semantic alignment and structural coherence. Extensive experiments on benchmark knowledge graph question answering datasets demonstrate that our approach significantly outperforms existing methods, achieving superior performance and cross-domain generalization capabilities.

Keywords: GraphRAG · KGQA · LLM reasoning

1 Introduction

Large language models (LLMs) have emerged as powerful tools, exhibiting exceptional reasoning abilities across a multitude of domains [1,3,4,14,21,41,42]. Despite their prowess, these models often encounter challenges such as hallucinations [15,16], outdated knowledge [8,20], and a dearth of domain-specific expertise [23]. To address these limitations, recent research has explored the synergistic integration of knowledge graphs (KGs) with LLMs [25,29,33]. Retrieval-augmented generation (RAG) has become a promising approach to leverage the

© The Author(s), under exclusive license to Springer Nature Singapore Pte Ltd. 2027
H. Sun et al. (Eds.): ChineseCSCW 2025, CCIS 2911, pp. 198–213, 2027.
https://doi.org/10.1007/978-981-92-0288-1_15

structured and up-to-date factual information encapsulated within KGs to bolster the reasoning fidelity and interpretability of LLMs.

Fig. 1. The issues of lack of knowledge and hallucination in LLMs reasoning and how they can be addressed by KGs.

As illustrated in Fig. 1, LLMs without knowledge augmentation may misinterpret relationships and produce incorrect answers. For instance, an LLM might mistakenly identify a daughter as a brother due to a lack of contextual knowledge. By integrating retrieved subgraphs from KGs, LLMs gain the necessary information to reason correctly, thereby significantly improving answer accuracy and reliability.

In this paper, we introduce **CoSubGraph-RAG**, a novel framework designed to seamlessly integrate Large Language Models (LLMs) with Knowledge Graphs (KGs) to achieve reliable and interpretable reasoning. Our approach is predicated on a *plan-and-solve* paradigm, where the LLM initially generates KG-grounded relation paths as trustworthy plans through a specialized planning module. These plans serve as blueprints for the subsequent retrieval of valid reasoning paths from the KG, effectively breaking down intricate reasoning tasks into a series of more manageable sub-tasks.

Traditional text-based retrieval methods, despite their demonstrated efficacy, face limitations in capturing the structural nuances of knowledge. Graph structures, in contrast, offer a more optimized approach for organizing knowledge, facilitating explicit relationship representation, minimizing redundancy, and supporting agile updates [5,32]. The research community has increasingly recognized the potential of graph-structured knowledge, particularly KGs, as dependable external resources [29,30]. However, the challenge of developing effective frameworks for extracting and utilizing information from the intricate structures of KGs persists.

To address these challenges, CoSubGraph-RAG incorporates a lightweight subgraph retriever, complemented by parallel triple-scoring and customized structural positional encoding. This enables the extraction of pertinent KG subgraphs that encompass critical evidence while remaining compatible with the processing capabilities of LLMs. Our framework ensures both semantic alignment and proper KG connectivity, enabling efficient multi-hop reasoning. Our contributions are summarized as follows:

- **Collaborative LLM-Retriever Architecture:** We propose CoSubGraph-RAG, which synergizes LLMs and a lightweight graph retriever to extract and validate reasoning paths. The LLM generates semantic relation sequences to guide retrieval, while the retriever dynamically scores and extracts KG subgraphs based on structural relevance. This collaboration ensures both semantic alignment and proper KG connectivity, enabling efficient multi-hop reasoning.
- **Efficient Graph-Based Reasoning:** We design a subgraph retriever that leverages parallel triple scoring and structural positional encoding, significantly enhancing computational efficiency while maintaining high retrieval accuracy.
- **State-of-the-Art Performance and Generalization:** Extensive experiments on benchmark Knowledge Graph Question Answering (KGQA) datasets demonstrate that CoSubGraph-RAG significantly outperforms existing KG-enhanced LLM methods. Moreover, it can be seamlessly integrated with various LLM architectures, showcasing excellent cross-domain potential.

2 Related Work

Recent advances have focused on improving the reasoning capabilities of Large Language Models (LLMs) for complex tasks through innovative prompting strategies. The work by Wei et al. [41] and Yao et al. [42] demonstrated that structured prompting can guide LLMs to decompose tasks and perform multi-step reasoning. Wang et al. [40] further proposed generating explicit reasoning plans to enhance procedural validity, while He et al. [11] developed task decomposition frameworks for hierarchical problem-solving. However, inherent limitations such as knowledge gaps and hallucination persist in LLM-based reasoning. To address these challenges, Yao et al. [43] conceptualized LLMs as interactive agents that dynamically acquire environmental knowledge, and Hong et al. [13] introduced FAME, a Monte Carlo planning-based framework that ensures verifiable reasoning trajectories.

Building on recent prompting innovations, Knowledge Graph-Enhanced LLM Reasoning has emerged as a promising paradigm that anchors language model outputs in structured knowledge while systematically integrating factual evidence to address knowledge gaps and hallucinations. Du et al. [9]proposed a contrastive learning framework to enhance the reasoning performance of the model. KD-CoT [39] enhanced CoT prompting for LLMs with relevant knowledge from KGs. StructGPT [17] retrieved KG facts for RAG. KB-BINDER [22] improved LLM reasoning by generating logical forms of the questions. ToG [33] leveraged a powerful LLM to select relevant facts hop-by-hop, and RoG [25] utilized the LLM to generate relation paths for better planning. These methods have lost flexibility and narrowed the space of possible subgraphs that can be retrieved, thereby affecting the quality of the final retrieval.

Complementing these knowledge-grounded approaches, semantic parsing methods translate natural language into executable formal queries. Early systems [11,44] used sequence models and graph networks for representation learning, while recent advances leverage LLMs for query generation [34] and hybrid validation [46]. Despite improved robustness, these methods remain constrained by their dependency on syntactic precision – any parsing failure inevitably terminates the reasoning process.

In summary, while existing approaches have made significant strides in enhancing LLM reasoning through structured prompting, KG integration, and semantic parsing, they still grapple with issues such as inflexible subgraph retrieval, insufficient capture of structural nuances, and over-reliance on syntactic precision. Our method employs two modules for information retrieval, enabling the LLM to integrate structure and semantics for reasoning, thereby achieving superior KGQA performance.

3 Preliminary

Knowledge graphs (KGs) store abundant factual knowledge as a collection of triples:

$$G = \{(e, r, e') \mid e, e' \in E,\ r \in R\}$$

where E and R denote the sets of entities and relations, respectively.

Knowledge Graph Question Answering (KGQA) is a typical reasoning task based on KGs. Given a natural language question q, its answer a_q, and a KG G, the task aims to design a function f to predict answers $a \in A_q$ based on knowledge from G, i.e., $a = f(q, G)$.

Reasoning paths are verbalized in the following format:

question entity → *relation* → *entity* → ... → *relation* → *answer entity.*

Here is a concrete example: Albert Einstein → place of birth → Ulm → located in → Germany.

4 The Framework of CoSubGraph-RAG

The central goal of our framework, **CoSubGraph-RAG**, is to enable efficient reasoning over large-scale KGs by retrieving a subgraph that is most likely to contain the correct answer for a given query. Formally, given a query q with the expected answer A_q, we aim to identify the optimal subgraph $G_q^* \subseteq G$ by maximizing the likelihood:

$$G_q^* = \arg\max_{G_q \subseteq G} P(A_q \mid G_q, q). \tag{1}$$

Direct optimization of this objective is computationally intractable due to the combinatorial nature of subgraph selection. To address this challenge, we decompose the process into two complementary modules: a *subgraph retriever* and an *LLM planning module*. These modules work in tandem to ensure both structural coherence and semantic alignment in the reasoning process.

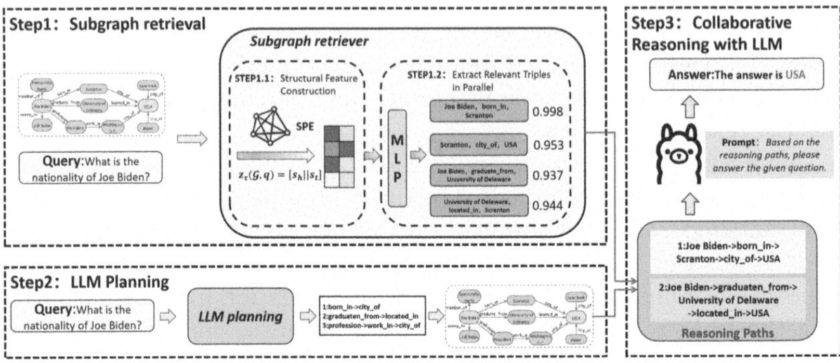

Fig. 2. The framework of CoSubGraph-RAG.

As illustrated in Fig. 2, our framework employs a collaborative reasoning process that integrates the efficiency of the subgraph retriever with the semantic capabilities of the LLM planning module. The subgraph retriever enhances efficiency by leveraging parallel triple scoring and encoding query-specific structural positions from the subject entity as features. It identifies key triples and assembles them into coherent reasoning paths. Simultaneously, the LLM planning module generates reasoning paths based on its learned reasoning strategies. These retrieved and generated reasoning paths are then merged and reformatted to meet the input requirements of the LLM, which conducts the final inference. This collaborative approach enables the model to effectively integrate structural and semantic reasoning, leading to more accurate and robust KGQA performance.

- **Subgraph Retriever:** We introduce a subgraph retriever $Q_\theta(G_q \mid q, G)$ parameterized by θ, designed to efficiently score candidate triples and assemble them into coherent reasoning paths. Specifically, the retriever leverages parallel triple scoring to evaluate the relevance of each candidate triple to the query q and encodes query-specific structural distances to capture the relational structure of the subgraph. Given a training dataset $\mathcal{D}$ and heuristically extracted surrogate subgraphs $\tilde{G}_q$ (e.g., shortest paths between topic entities T_q and answer entities A_q), the retriever is optimized via:

$$\max_{\theta} \mathbb{E}_{(q,A_q)\sim\mathcal{D}} Q_\theta(\tilde{G}_q \mid G, q). \tag{2}$$

A key innovation of our approach is the flexibility in subgraph structure: unlike prior methods that constrain subgraphs to fixed structures (such as trees or paths), our formulation allows for greater flexibility in capturing diverse reasoning patterns. This design choice is crucial for handling complex reasoning tasks that may involve multiple hops or non-linear relational structures.

- **LLM Planning Module:** The LLM planning module works in tandem with the subgraph retriever to generate candidate reasoning paths based on learned semantic and reasoning strategies. By leveraging its generative capabilities, the LLM planning module enhances the retrieval process by incorporating broader contextual understanding and human-like reasoning steps. This ensures that both structural and semantic information contribute to the final reasoning process. Specifically, the LLM planning module generates KG-grounded relation paths as trustworthy plans. This collaborative interaction ensures semantic alignment and proper KG connectivity, enabling efficient multi-hop reasoning.

The synergistic integration of the subgraph retriever and the LLM planning module is a core innovation of our framework. The subgraph retriever provides a flexible and efficient mechanism for capturing essential relational structures from the KG, while the LLM planning module ensures that the reasoning process is semantically aligned with the query context. This integration addresses the limitations of traditional text-based retrieval methods, which often fail to capture the structural nuances of knowledge graphs. By combining these two components, CoSubGraph-RAG achieves efficient multi-hop reasoning while maintaining high accuracy and interpretability. This synergy is particularly effective for complex reasoning tasks that require both structural coherence and semantic understanding. We will describe more technical details of each module in the next sections.

4.1 Subgraph Retrieval

Contemporary approaches to subgraph retrieval in knowledge graph applications have predominantly relied on heuristic-driven frameworks that emphasize specific subgraph typologies. These frameworks are primarily manifested in three categories of constrained search paradigms. The first category employs connectivity-constrained subgraph exploration [12]. The second paradigm focuses on path-based enumeration from topic entities, with strict cardinality and length restrictions [24–26,33,47]. The third strategy adopts a two-phase entity-centric approach, where subgraph construction is limited to the neighborhood expansion of selected entities [37,44].

However, these architectural constraints fundamentally restrict the explorable hypothesis space through their rigid structural priors and predefined expansion rules. Consequently, they compromise the retrieval effectiveness of graph-augmented systems by leading to suboptimal subgraph sampling. To address these limitations and achieve both efficiency and scalability in subgraph selection, we propose a novel approach that models the distribution over subgraphs by factorizing it over individual triples.

Triple Factorization. We factorize the retriever distribution as follows:

$$Q_\theta(G_q \mid G, q) = \prod_{\tau \in G_q} p_\theta(\tau \mid z_\tau, q) \times \prod_{\tau \in G \backslash G_q} (1 - p_\theta(\tau \mid z_\tau, q)) \tag{3}$$

where $z_\tau(G, q)$ encodes the latent relationship between triple τ and query q. This factorization offers several advantages:

- **Training Efficiency**: The objective decomposes into:

$$\max_\theta \mathbb{E}_{(q,A_q)\sim\mathcal{D}} \left[\sum_{\tau \in \tilde{G}_q} \log p_\theta(\tau \mid z_\tau, q) + \sum_{\tau \in G \backslash \tilde{G}_q} \log (1 - p_\theta(\tau \mid z_\tau, q)) \right] \tag{4}$$

  This decomposition allows each triple to be treated as an independent binary decision, significantly reducing computational complexity. As a result, it enables efficient parallel computation and gradient updates, thereby enhancing the scalability of the retrieval process.
- **Sampling Efficiency**: Our method enables independent scoring and selection of individual triples, which is particularly advantageous for large-scale knowledge graphs. This independence allows for dynamic subgraph selection, optimizing computational resource allocation by focusing only on relevant triples. This efficiency is crucial for handling the vast amounts of data present in real-world knowledge graphs.
- **Flexibility and Scalability**: Our approach supports arbitrary subgraph structures formed by triples, which is highly beneficial for adaptive reasoning with large language models (LLMs). Unlike previous methods that constrain subgraphs to specific structures (e.g., paths or trees), our framework allows for diverse reasoning patterns. By adjusting the K value in Top-K selection, the resulting subgraphs can be tailored to accommodate LLMs with varying reasoning capabilities. This ensures both scalability and adaptability, making our method suitable for a wide range of applications.

In practice, Q_θ can be further optimized by considering only subgraphs originating from topic entities T_q, as shown in prior work [18]. This simplification not only reduces computational overhead but also enhances the relevance of retrieved subgraphs by focusing on entities directly related to the query.

Structured Positional Encoding. To capture the structural information of the knowledge graph (KG), prior works have employed Graph Neural Networks (GNNs) to obtain latent representations of entities [19,26]. However, GNNs are known to have limited representation power due to issues such as over-smoothing and fixed receptive fields [6]. To address these limitations, we introduce *Structured Positional Encoding* (SPE), a novel method for encoding structural information in a KG.

Starting from a set of topic entities T_q, SPE propagates structural information via iterative message passing in both forward and reverse propagation processes. Specifically, the propagation rules are defined as:

$$\text{Forward propagation:} \quad s_e^{(f,l+1)} = \frac{1}{|\{e' \mid (e', \cdot, e) \in G\}|} \sum_{(e', \cdot, e) \in G} s_{e'}^{(f,l)} \tag{5}$$

$$\text{Reverse propagation:} \quad s_e^{(r,l+1)} = \frac{1}{|\{e' \mid (e, \cdot, e') \in G\}|} \sum_{(e, \cdot, e') \in G} s_{e'}^{(r,l)} \tag{6}$$

where $s_e^{(r,0)} = s_e^{(f,0)}$. We concatenate the results across all rounds and both directions to obtain the final entity encodings $s_e = [s_e^{(0)} \| s_e^{(f,1)} \| \cdots \| s_e^{(r,1)} \| \cdots]$. The final representation of a triple τ is then obtained by concatenating the encodings of its head and tail entities:

$$z_\tau(G, q) = [s_h \| s_t]. \tag{7}$$

The design of the SPE method can effectively capture the directional structural relationships in a KG, overcoming the limitations of traditional GNNs and one-hot encodings.

Efficient Retriever Implementation. To ensure scalability and efficiency, our retriever employs a lightweight binary classifier to compute the probability $p_\theta(\tau \mid z_\tau, q)$, integrating both structural (via SPE) and semantic embeddings. Following previous approaches [10], we leverage off-the-shelf pre-trained text encoders to embed all entities and relations in the KG based on their text attributes. To further enhance efficiency, pre-computed entity and relation embeddings are stored in a vector database. The inference procedure is as follows:

1. Embed the query q into a vector representation z_q.
2. Retrieve the pre-computed embeddings z_h, z_r, and z_t for the entities and relations comprising the triple τ.
3. Concatenate the vectors into a single representation and feed it into a multi-layer perceptron (MLP) to obtain a score:

$$s_\tau = \text{MLP}\big([z_q \| z_h \| z_r \| z_t \| z_\tau]\big) \tag{8}$$

This design ensures that the retriever scales efficiently to large KGs and can rapidly evaluate unseen triples. By combining structural and semantic information in a lightweight yet effective manner, our retriever achieves both high accuracy and computational efficiency, making it suitable for real-world applications.

4.2 LLM Planning

Our planning model training methodology employs subgraph-based data adaptation to address annotation challenges. While reasoning-based KGQA annotations are less resource-intensive than semantic parsing labels, acquiring precise relation chain annotations remains non-trivial. Prior approaches attempt to overcome this through weak supervision using question-answer pairs, where initial training data derives from extracting minimal-length paths between topic entities and answer candidates [25,47]. However, empirical analysis reveals significant noise contamination in these baseline path extraction methods. A notable failure mode occurs when entities share common attributes (e.g., both being male), creating spurious paths through neutral nodes (e.g., topic $\rightarrow$ gender $\rightarrow$ Male $\leftarrow$ gender $\leftarrow$ answer). Training on such unprocessed paths risks teaching the model irrelevant relational patterns.

To address this, we introduce directional path filtering, preserving only unidirectionally consistent paths from source to target entities. This approach maintains training signal integrity by leveraging Freebase's bidirectional relation properties, ensuring inverse relations preserve semantic meaning while eliminating circular references.

To further enhance training signal quality, we implement a GPT-4 knowledge distillation pipeline. Our methodology involves prompting GPT-4 with candidate paths from raw data, using specialized query templates to identify semantically relevant chains. This generates refined training instances that simultaneously mitigate noise exposure from raw data while recovering potentially valuable signals inadvertently discarded by strict path filtering.

The prompt provided to GPT-4 for path filtering is structured as follows:

> Select the most relevant reasoning path for answering the question. Return only the numbers of the chosen path separated by commas, without any additional text.
> **Paths:** $\{path\_list\}$
> **Question:** $\{Question\}$

We use the data filtered by GPT-4 to train the planning model. Specifically, we design a special prefix token for the planning task, where `[Planning]` denotes a path retrieval task. Figure 3 illustrates the training process of the planning model. Each question in the path-retrieval task can correspond to multiple paths.

4.3 Collaborative Reasoning with LLM

Our framework facilitates collaborative reasoning by integrating reasoning paths from two complementary sources: the subgraph retrieval module and the LLM planning module. Specifically, the subgraph retriever identifies the top-k relevant triples from the knowledge graph and converts them into structured reasoning paths. Simultaneously, the LLM planning module generates reasoning paths based on its internal planning strategy and the graph data. By merging

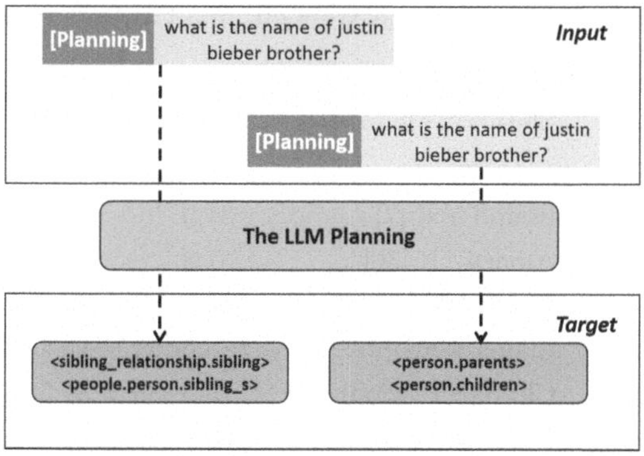

Fig. 3. An illustration of the Planning model training process. Each dark blue box represents a special token in our Planning model. (Color figure online)

these paths, we create a unified input for the LLM, enabling it to leverage both structured and semantically rich information for more accurate reasoning.

The prompt provided to the LLM is structured as follows:

> Based on the reasoning paths, please answer the given question. **Reasoning Paths:** {*Reasoning Paths*}
> **Question:** {*Question*}

This collaborative reasoning approach combines the efficiency of subgraph retrieval with the advanced semantic capabilities of the LLM planning module. This integration is particularly effective for complex reasoning tasks that require both structural coherence and deep semantic understanding, thereby enhancing the overall performance and robustness of the system.

5 Experiments

5.1 Datasets and Evaluation Metrics

We experiment with two widely used KGQA benchmarks: WebQuestionsSP (WebQSP) [45], Complex WebQuestions(CWQ) [35]. WebQSP contains 4,737 natural language questions that are answerable using a subset Freebase KG [2]. The questions require up to 2-hop reasoning within this KG. CWQ contains 34,699 total complex questions that require up to 4-hops of reasoning over the KG.

For evaluation metrics, we adopt Hit@1 and F1 metrics. H@1 is the accuracy of the top/first predicted answer. F1 takes into account the recall (number of true answers found) and the precision (number of false answers found) of the generated answers.

Table 1. Results of various methods on WebQSP and CWQ datasets. Metrics include Hit and F1.

Type	Method	WebQSP		CWQ	
		Hit@1	F1	Hit@1	F1
LLM	Flan-T5-xl [7]	31.0	–	14.7	–
	Alpaca-7B [36]	51.8	–	27.4	–
	LLaMA2-7B [38]	56.4	36.5	28.4	21.4
	Llama-3-8B [27]	55.5	34.8	28.1	22.4
	ChatGPT+CoT [41]	73.5	38.5	47.5	31.0
	GPT-4o-mini [28]	63.8	40.5	63.8	40.5
KG+LLM	KD-CoT [39]	68.6	52.5	55.7	–
	StructGPT [17]	72.6	–	54.3	–
	KB-BINDER [22]	74.4	–	–	–
	ToG+LLaMA2-7B [33]	68.9	–	57.6	–
	ToG+ChatGPT [33]	76.2	–	58.9	–
	ToG+GPT-4 [33]	82.6	–	69.5	–
	RoG [25]	85.7	70.8	62.6	56.2
	(Ours)	90.2	74.8	68.7	60.4

Table 2. Ablation studies of CoSubGraph-RAG

Method	WebQSP		CWQ	
	Hit@1	F1	Hit@1	F1
CoSubGraph-RAG	**90.2**	**74.8**	**68.7**	**60.4**
CoSubGraph-RAG w/o LLM planning	74.5	56.4	56.1	48.9
CoSubGraph-RAG w/o subgraph retriever	86.2	70.6	61.4	53.4

5.2 KGQA Performance Comparison

KGQA Baselines. We include results from other LLM-based KGQA methods due to their state-of-the-art performance, such as KD-CoT [39], StructGPT [17], ToG [33], and RoG [25]. These methods have consistently demonstrated their robustness and high accuracy on challenging KGQA benchmarks. In addition, we have selected these techniques to provide a comprehensive comparison with our approach, ensuring that the evaluation covers the most competitive strategies in the current literature. We do not compare with semantic parsing methods [46] because these approaches rely on additional training data—specifically, SPARQL annotations—which are both labor-intensive to produce and difficult to obtain in real-world scenarios. This reliance on extra annotated data not only increases the complexity of the training process but also limits the practical applicability of semantic parsing methods in many real-world applications.

Implementation Details. We employ SentenceBert [31] as the pre-trained text encoder for both the cosine similarity baseline and Subgraph retriever. For supervision signals, there are no ground-truth relevant subgraphs for a query q. Previous methods [25] for subgraph retrieval utilize the shortest paths connecting the topic and answer entities as weak supervision signals. However, this approach introduces significant noise and may filter out valuable information. To address this issue, we adopt the GPT-4-selected shortest paths from Sect. 4.2 as supervision signals, ensuring higher quality training data. For the LLM planning module, we build upon the Llama3-8B [27] model. We further fine-tune Llama3-8B using a curated dataset of filtered reasoning path examples.

Main Results. Table 1 presents performance results of different KGQA methods. CoSubGraph-RAG is the method that performs overall the best, achieving state-of-the-art results on the two KGQA benchmarks in almost all metrics. Additionally, the hybrid architecture achieves strong performance efficiency without relying on excessively large foundation models, demonstrating a balanced advancement in both accuracy and computational practicality. In particular, when compared with pure LLM approaches such as ChatGPT and ChatGPT+CoT, which struggle with handling both simple and complex queries, our method's integration of subgraph retrieval significantly enhances answer correctness and semantic alignment. Moreover, against KG+LLM baselines like RoG and ToG variants, CoSubGraph-RAG not only surpasses them in Hit@1 scores but also maintains competitive F1 values, highlighting its robust performance across different query complexities. Our collaborative approach enables the model to effectively integrate structural and semantic reasoning, thereby achieving more accurate and robust KGQA performance. Furthermore, its modular design allows for independent optimization and flexible adaptation to various tasks. We also illustrate case studies in Table 3. In Table 3, we can see that ChatGPT+CoT exhibits hallucinations and generates incorrect answers, whereas our method retrieves the correct reasoning path and enhances the faithfulness of the LLM.

Ablation Study. We conducted an ablation study to analyze the effectiveness of the relation paths generated by the LLM and the subgraph paths retrieved by the subgraph retriever in our method (CoSubGraph-RAG). We compare two variants: 1) w/o LLM planning, where we remove the LLM planning module and perform reasoning solely using the reasoning paths retrieved by the subgraph retriever; 2) w/o subgraph retriever, where we remove the subgraph retriever and perform reasoning solely using the reasoning paths obtained directly from the KG by the LLM. The experimental results are shown in Table 2.

From the ablation results, it is evident that both the LLM planning module and the subgraph retriever are integral to the effectiveness of the CoSubGraph-RAG framework. When the planning module is removed, the framework loses its ability to generate structured and trustworthy reasoning plans, leading to a noticeable decline in performance. This is because the reasoning process lacks

Table 3. Example of the hallucination of ChatGPT + CoT and how CoSubGraph-RAG improves the faithfulness of LLMs

Question:
Paul Ryan is owner of radio station WAMU and which college did he attend?
Answer:
American University
ChatGPT + CoT:
Step 1: Identify the owner of radio station WAMU. WAMU is a public radio station licensed to American University in Washington, D.C. It is not owned by Paul Ryan, the former Speaker of the U.S. House of Representatives. There seems to be a misunderstanding in the question. **Step 2:** Determine which college Paul Ryan attended. Paul Ryan attended Miami University in Oxford, Ohio. **Conclusion:** Since Paul Ryan is not the owner of WAMU, but we still need to answer the latter part of the question, the correct answer is: Miami University.
Reasoning Paths:
Paul Ryan → people.person.nationality → United States of America → location.location.containedby → University of California, Berkeley.
Paul Ryan → people.person.nationality → United States of America → location.location.containedby → American University.
Paul Ryan → education.education.student → m.0ktt9qt → education.education.institution → American University.
Ours:
Based on the provided reasoning paths, Paul RyanâĂŹs educational background is linked as follows: Paul Ryan → education.education.student → m.0ktt9qt → education.education.institution → American University. Therefore, the college Paul Ryan attended is American University. While other paths mention associations like nationality or geographic containment, the direct link to his education explicitly points to American University. Information about his ownership of radio station WAMU is not included in the given reasoning paths and would require additional data to confirm.

the guided, step-by-step blueprint that the planning module provides, making it harder to navigate complex tasks effectively. On the other hand, removing the subgraph retriever results in a less efficient retrieval process, as the framework struggles to extract and organize relevant knowledge subgraphs that contain critical evidence for reasoning. While the framework can still function without one of these components, the absence of either leads to a significant drop in performance, highlighting their complementary roles.

6 Conclusion and Future Work

In this work, we propose CoSubGraph-RAG, a novel LLM-retriever collaborative framework that synergizes semantic guidance from language models with structured knowledge graph retrieval. By dynamically coupling LLM-generated relation sequences with a graph-aware retriever employing parallel triple scoring and structural positional encoding, our method achieves joint optimization of semantic relevance and path validity. It achieves state-of-the-art performance on multi-hop KGQA tasks, demonstrating superior accuracy, interpretability, and computational efficiency compared to existing graph-based RAG approaches.

For future work, we plan to further improve the generalization capabilities of CoSubGraph-RAG and explore its applications in knowledge-intensive tasks such as recommendation systems and scientific literature analysis.

References

1. Bang, Y., et al.: A multitask, multilingual, multimodal evaluation of chatgpt on reasoning, hallucination, and interactivity. arXiv preprint arXiv:2302.04023 (2023)
2. Bollacker, K., Evans, C., Paritosh, P., Sturge, T., Taylor, J.: Freebase: a collaboratively created graph database for structuring human knowledge. In: Proceedings of the 2008 ACM SIGMOD International Conference on Management of Data, pp. 1247–1250 (2008)
3. Brown, T., et al.: Language models are few-shot learners. In: Advances in Neural Information Processing Systems, vol. 33, pp. 1877–1901 (2020)
4. Bubeck, S., et al.: Sparks of artificial general intelligence: Early experiments with GPT-4. arXiv preprint arXiv:2303.12712 (2023)
5. Chein, M., Mugnier, M.L.: Graph-Based Knowledge Representation: Computational Foundations of Conceptual Graphs. Springer (2008)
6. Chen, Z., Chen, L., Villar, S., Bruna, J.: Can graph neural networks count substructures? Adv. Neural. Inf. Process. Syst. **33**, 10383–10395 (2020)
7. Chung, H.W., et al.: Scaling instruction-finetuned language models. J. Mach. Learn. Res. **25**(70), 1–53 (2024)
8. Dhingra, B., Cole, J.R., Eisenschlos, J.M., Gillick, D., Eisenstein, J., Cohen, W.W.: Time-aware language models as temporal knowledge bases. Trans. Assoc. Comput. Linguist. **10**, 257–273 (2022)
9. Du, H., et al.: A contrastive framework for enhancing knowledge graph question answering: alleviating exposure bias. Knowl.-Based Syst. **280**, 110996 (2023)
10. Gao, Y., et al.: Retrieval-augmented generation for large language models: a survey. arXiv preprint arXiv:2312.10997 (2023)

11. He, G., Lan, Y., Jiang, J., Zhao, W.X., Wen, J.R.: Improving multi-hop knowledge base question answering by learning intermediate supervision signals. In: Proceedings of the 14th ACM International Conference on Web Search and Data Mining, pp. 553–561 (2021)
12. He, X., et al.: G-retriever: retrieval-augmented generation for textual graph understanding and question answering. Adv. Neural. Inf. Process. Syst. **37**, 132876–132907 (2025)
13. Hong, R., Zhang, H., Zhao, H., Yu, D., Zhang, C.: Faithful question answering with Monte-Carlo planning. In: ACL 2023 (2023)
14. Huang, J., Chang, K.C.C.: Towards reasoning in large language models: a survey. In: ACL 2023 (2023)
15. Huang, L., et al.: A survey on hallucination in large language models: principles, taxonomy, challenges, and open questions. arXiv preprint arXiv:2311.05232 (2023)
16. Ji, Z., et al.: Survey of hallucination in natural language generation. ACM Comput. Surv. **55**(12), 1–38 (2023)
17. Jiang, J., Zhou, K., Dong, Z., Ye, K., Zhao, W.X., Wen, J.R.: Structgpt: a general framework for large language model to reason over structured data. arXiv preprint arXiv:2305.09645 (2023)
18. Jiang, J., Zhou, K., Zhao, X., Wen, J.R.: Unikgqa: unified retrieval and reasoning for solving multi-hop question answering over knowledge graph. In: The Eleventh International Conference on Learning Representations (2022)
19. Kang, M., Kwak, J.M., Baek, J., Hwang, S.J.: Knowledge graph-augmented language models for knowledge-grounded dialogue generation. arXiv preprint arXiv:2305.18846 (2023)
20. Kasai, J., et al.: Realtime QA: what's the answer right now? In: Advances in Neural Information Processing Systems, vol. 36 (2024)
21. Kojima, T., Gu, S.S., Reid, M., Matsuo, Y., Iwasawa, Y.: Large language models are zero-shot reasoners. Adv. Neural. Inf. Process. Syst. **35**, 22199–22213 (2022)
22. Li, T., Ma, X., Zhuang, A., Gu, Y., Su, Y., Chen, W.: Few-shot in-context learning for knowledge base question answering. arXiv preprint arXiv:2305.01750 (2023)
23. Li, X., et al.: Are chatgpt and gpt-4 general-purpose solvers for financial text analytics? a study on several typical tasks. arXiv preprint arXiv:2305.05862 (2023)
24. Liu, G., Zhang, Y., Li, Y., Yao, Q.: Explore then determine: a GNN-LLM synergy framework for reasoning over knowledge graph. arXiv preprint arXiv:2406.01145 (2024)
25. Luo, L., Li, Y.F., Haffari, G., Pan, S.: Reasoning on graphs: faithful and interpretable large language model reasoning. In: International Conference on Learning Representations (2024)
26. Mavromatis, C., Karypis, G.: GNN-RAG: graph neural retrieval for large language model reasoning. arXiv preprint arXiv:2405.20139 (2024)
27. Meta: Build the future of ai with meta llama 3 (2024). https://llama.meta.com/llama3/. Accessed 31 July 2024
28. OpenAI: Hello gpt-4o (2024). https://openai.com/index/hello-gpt-4o/. Accessed 1 Aug 2025
29. Pan, S., Luo, L., Wang, Y., Chen, C., Wang, J., Wu, X.: Unifying large language models and knowledge graphs: a roadmap. IEEE Trans. Knowl. Data Eng. (2024)
30. Peng, B., et al.: Graph retrieval-augmented generation: a survey. arXiv preprint arXiv:2408.08921 (2024)
31. Reimers, N.: Sentence-bert: sentence embeddings using siamese bert-networks. arXiv preprint arXiv:1908.10084 (2019)

32. Robinson, I., Webber, J., Eifrem, E.: Graph databases: new opportunities for connected data. O'Reilly Media, Inc. (2015)
33. Sun, J., et al.: Think-on-graph: deep and responsible reasoning of large language model with knowledge graph. In: International Conference on Learning Representations (2024)
34. Sun, Y., Zhang, L., Cheng, G., Qu, Y.: Sparqa: skeleton-based semantic parsing for complex questions over knowledge bases. In: Proceedings of the AAAI Conference on Artificial Intelligence, vol. 34, pp. 8952–8959 (2020)
35. Talmor, A., Berant, J.: The web as a knowledge-base for answering complex questions. arXiv preprint arXiv:1803.06643 (2018)
36. Taori, R., et al.: Stanford alpaca: an instruction-following llama model (2023)
37. Taunk, D., Khanna, L., Kandru, S.V.P.K., Varma, V., Sharma, C., Tapaswi, M.: Grapeqa: graph augmentation and pruning to enhance question-answering. In: Companion Proceedings of the ACM Web Conference 2023, pp. 1138–1144 (2023)
38. Touvron, H., et al.: Llama 2: open foundation and fine-tuned chat models. arXiv preprint arXiv:2307.09288 (2023)
39. Wang, K., et al.: Knowledge-driven cot: exploring faithful reasoning in LLMs for knowledge-intensive question answering. arXiv preprint arXiv:2308.13259 (2023)
40. Wang, L., et al.: Plan-and-solve prompting: improving zero-shot chain-of-thought reasoning by large language models. arXiv preprint arXiv:2305.04091 (2023)
41. Wei, J., et al.: Chain-of-thought prompting elicits reasoning in large language models. Adv. Neural. Inf. Process. Syst. **35**, 24824–24837 (2022)
42. Yao, S., et al.: Tree of thoughts: deliberate problem solving with large language models. arXiv preprint arXiv:2305.10601 (2023)
43. Yao, S., et al.: React: synergizing reasoning and acting in language models. In: The Eleventh International Conference on Learning Representations (2022)
44. Yasunaga, M., Ren, H., Bosselut, A., Liang, P., Leskovec, J.: QA-GNN: reasoning with language models and knowledge graphs for question answering. In: Proceedings of the 2021 Conference of the North American Chapter of the Association for Computational Linguistics: Human Language Technologies, pp. 535–546 (2021)
45. Yih, W.T., Richardson, M., Meek, C., Chang, M.W., Suh, J.: The value of semantic parse labeling for knowledge base question answering. In: Proceedings of the 54th Annual Meeting of the Association for Computational Linguistics (Volume 2: Short Papers), pp. 201–206 (2016)
46. Yu, D., et al.: Decaf: joint decoding of answers and logical forms for question answering over knowledge bases. In: The Eleventh International Conference on Learning Representations (2022)
47. Zhang, J., et al.: Subgraph retrieval enhanced model for multi-hop knowledge base question answering. arXiv preprint arXiv:2202.13296 (2022)

CGSDP: Attention-Based Defect Prediction Combining Source Code Semantic and Directed Class Dependency Network

Weitao Liu[1], Zhichao Sun[1], Ningjiang Chen[1,2,3,4(✉)], and Chengyue Shi[1]

[1] School of Computer and Electronic Information, Guangxi University, Nanning 530004, China

[2] Guangxi Center of Technology Innovation for Intelligent Digital Services, Nanning, China
chnj@gxu.edu.cn

[3] Key Laboratory of Parallel, Distributed and Intelligent Computing (Guangxi University), Education Department of Guangxi Zhuang Autonomous Region, Nanning 530004, China

[4] Guangxi Academy of Artificial Intelligence, Nanning 530004, China

Abstract. As software scales up, the number and complexity of defects also increase, posing significant challenges and costs for testing and maintenance. Current software defect prediction methods are inadequate in extracting code contextual semantics, and methods based on software semantics often fail to consider the complex dependency relationships in software. To address these issues, this paper proposes Code-Graph Software Defect Prediction (CGSDP), a defect prediction approach that combines source code semantic and directed class dependency network. It uses deep learning and attention mechanisms to automatically extract representative features at low cost. Experimental results based on 7 open-source projects show that compared with baseline methods, CGSDP's F1 score has an average improvement in both within-project defect prediction and cross-project defect prediction, achieving better results than existing methods.

Keywords: Software Defect Prediction · Software Reliability · Deep Learning · Graph Neural Network · Source Code Semantic

1 Introduction

Software defect prediction (SDP) serves as a crucial fault-prevention technique within Artificial Intelligence for IT Operations (AIOps) [15], enabling the identification of potential defects and guiding maintainers to focus on vulnerable components for proactive failure mitigation. Recently, enterprises have increasingly adopted SDP to enhance software quality and reliability due to its demonstrated

© The Author(s), under exclusive license to Springer Nature Singapore Pte Ltd. 2027
H. Sun et al. (Eds.): ChineseCSCW 2025, CCIS 2911, pp. 214–229, 2027.
https://doi.org/10.1007/978-981-92-0288-1_16

business value [17]. Traditional SDP approaches rely on manually designed product metrics, which struggle to cope with the complexity of modern software systems and fail to satisfy AIOps requirements for fast and efficient failure prevention. To overcome the limitations of hand-crafted features, researchers have turned to extracting more comprehensive features directly from source code using Abstract Syntax Trees (ASTs), a tree-structured representation that captures code semantics through nodes corresponding to syntactic constructs. Compared to manual features, AST-derived features better represent code semantics and improve a model's understanding of contextual meaning. As illustrated in Fig. 1, even code segments with identical hand-crafted features may carry entirely different semantics depending on functional context. Deep learning techniques, capable of automatically learning complex and high-dimensional features, have been employed in AST-based SDP models, with several studies validating their effectiveness on public datasets [10,18,27]. However, as code complexity and scale grow, the resulting ASTs become increasingly large, making semantic feature extraction more challenging and computationally intensive.

```
public static int func(int input){ //local_variable_declaration
    int sum = 0; // local_variable_declaration
    int i = 1; // local_variable_declaration
    while (i<10){ // while_statement
        shout(); // method_invocation
        sum += i++; // assignment_expression
    }
    return sum; // return_statement
}
```

```
public static int func(int input){ //local_variable_declaration
    int sum = 0; // local_variable_declaration
    int i = 1; // local_variable_declaration
    shout(); // method_invocation
    while (i<10){ // while_statement
        sum += i++; // assignment_expression
    }
    return sum; // return_statement
}
```

Fig. 1. An example of code, AST nodes are provided in the comments.

Based on the preceding analysis, a novel software defect prediction approach named Code-Graph Software Defect Prediction (CGSDP) is proposed. The method introduces a lightweight architecture that integrates a CNN [9] with a Transformer [25], leveraging self-attention mechanisms to enhance contextual code semantics understanding while maintaining low computational overhead. Unlike existing hybrid AST-graph models such as CGCN [26], CGSDP addresses several critical limitations: whereas CGCN employs an undirected GCN that ignores dependency directionality (e.g., parent→child inheritance relationships), CGSDP incorporates direction-aware attention (DCDN-GAT) to prioritize influential neighboring nodes; furthermore, while CGCN's CNN-based encoder tends to lose long-range contextual information, the combined CNN-Transformer design in CGSDP reduces computational cost (averaging 109.43 ms/epoch) while preserving broader semantic context. Additionally, structural features are extracted from a Directed Class Dependency Network (DCDN) via a Graph Attention Network (GAT) [19]. By combining semantic features, structural features, and traditional product metrics, CGSDP provides a multi-view software representation that effectively improves defect prediction performance. The main contributions of this paper are summarized as follows:

- A self-attention-based method for software semantic feature extraction is proposed, which integrates CNNs for capturing local features and self-attention mechanisms for modeling global dependencies, thereby enhancing source code representation in a computationally efficient manner.
- It constructs a directed class dependency network from software dependencies in CGSDP, and employs graph attention to learn node attributes and structural information, thereby deriving structural features that compensate for semantic features' limitations in modeling complex software dependencies.
- A software defect prediction approach integrating semantic, structural, and handcrafted features is proposed. By leveraging deep learning for automated feature extraction, CGSDP achieves comprehensive software characterization through code semantics, internal dependencies, and product metrics, enabling efficient and effective defect prediction.

The remaining sections of this paper are organized as follows: Sect. 2 introduces the related work. Section 3 explains the method proposed in this paper. Section 4 describes the experimental environment and experimental settings. Section 5 validates the proposed method through experiments. Section 6 concludes the work and discusses future work.

2 Related Work

Software defect prediction (SDP), a key research area in software engineering, employs diverse techniques broadly categorized by code representation into: product metrics-based methods, AST-based representation, and network embedding approaches [6]. Manually designed product metrics rely on expert-defined features from code and development processes, e.g., Yu et al. [22] and Ardimento et al. [1] proposed process metrics, while Majd et al. [12] defined sentence-level metrics trained via LSTM, yet they exhibit limited defect characterization capability and require high expertise. In contrast, AST-based methods automatically capture semantic features using deep learning: Wang et al. [21] and Zhang et al. [24] employed DBN and transformers on AST-derived tokens, Malhotra et al. [13] applied multi-head CNN, and Wang et al. [20] introduced gated hierarchical LSTM, improving interpretability and semantic utilization but often losing contextual and dependency information. Network embedding, widely studied [4,5,23], represents software dependencies as graphs. Qu et al. [16] used node2vec, Zhou et al. [26] combined CNN and GCN, and Ma et al. [11] applied GraphSAGE, capturing global structural influences like function calls but facing high computational cost and low interpretability. Although some work such as Zhou et al. [26] integrates semantic and structural features, their model is constrained to undirected graphs and loses contextual semantics. CGSDP solves this with DCDN-GAT and CNN-Transformer, outperforming CGCN in cost and accuracy. Combining AST-based semantics with network-based structure offers a more comprehensive solution for enhancing SDP performance.

3 Method

3.1 Framework

The overall framework of the proposed method, illustrated in Fig. 2, consists of three key components: (1) Extracting semantic features from source code ASTs using a self-attention mechanism to capture long-range dependencies and enhance code representation quality [18]; (2) Building a software DCDN to model program dependencies and generate structural features via graph attention networks, thereby complementing semantic representations; (3) Integrating product metrics with semantic and structural features for defect prediction in downstream tasks, enabling efficient failure prevention in AIOps for software maintenance.

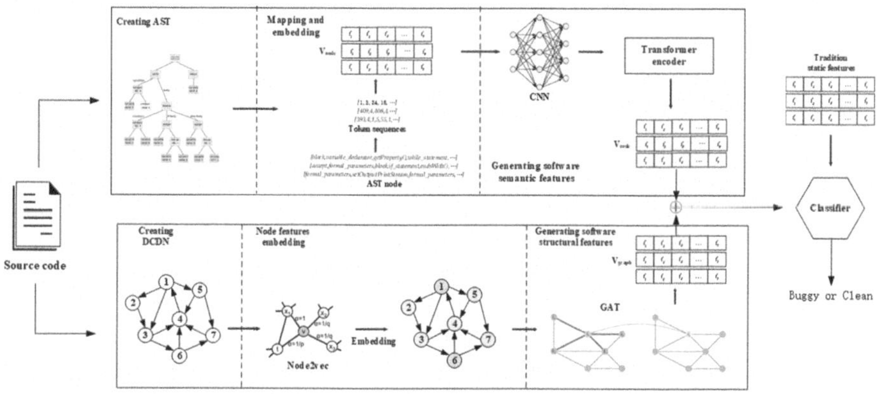

Fig. 2. The framework of CGSDP.

3.2 Self-attention Based Software Semantic Feature Extraction

As illustrated in Fig. 3, CGSDP extracts semantic features through three stages: source code parsing, mapping and embedding, and feature generation. While both Javalang and Tree-sitter were evaluated for AST construction, Javalang was selected as the primary parser due to its established usage in software engineering research. Statistical analysis via Wilcoxon signed-rank tests ($\alpha = 0.05$) confirmed no significant difference between their performance outcomes, supporting this methodological choice. The parsed ASTs undergo node extraction focusing on three categories: (a) method invocation and object creation nodes, (b) declaration nodes (e.g., InterfaceDeclaration, EnumDeclaration), and (c) control-flow statements (e.g., WhileStatement, ForStatement), with complete details provided in Table 1. Though Javalang serves as our main tool, Tree-sitter demonstrates advantages in active maintenance and cross-language parsing (e.g.,

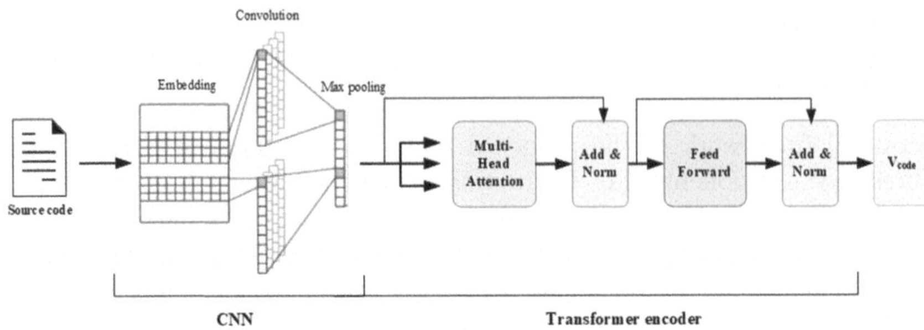

Fig. 3. Software semantic feature extraction method based on self-attention.

Table 1. Extracted AST nodes

Type	AST nodes
Node(a)	MethodInvocation, SuperMethodInvocation, ClassCreator
Node(b)	TypeDeclaration, InterfaceDeclaration, ClassDeclaration, MethodDeclaration, EnumDeclaration, ConstructorDeclaration, VariableDeclarator, FormalParameter, CatchClauseParameter, ReferenceType, BasicType
Node(c)	TryResource, IfStatement, WhileStatement, DoStatement, ForStatement, AssertStatement, BreakStatement, ContinueStatement, ReturnStatement, ThrowStatement, SynchronizedStatement, TryStatement, SwitchStatement, CatchClause, BlockStatement, StatementExpression, ForControl, SwitchStatementCase, EnhancedForControl

C++, Python), suggesting potential for extending CGSDP to multi-language defect prediction in future work.

Mapping and Embedding. The extracted AST sequences are transformed into word vectors to better represent node semantics. The Continuous Bag of Words (CBOW) model from Word2Vec [14] is employed to generate embeddings $f = \{\overrightarrow{f_1}, \overrightarrow{f_2}, \cdots, \overrightarrow{f_N}\}$ from the node set $N_{extract}$. To prevent the dilution of significant patterns by rare elements, only nodes occurring more than three times are included in the embedding process. Each node is mapped to an integer index and embedded into a vector, forming the original semantic feature sequence $V_{node} = \{\overrightarrow{f_1}, \overrightarrow{f_2}, \cdots, \overrightarrow{f_n}\}$. The sequence is zero-padded to a consistent length to meet the input requirements of subsequent neural networks.

Generating Software Semantic Features. The processed V_{node} is first passed through a CNN [8] for local feature integration and sequence length reduction, thereby decreasing computational complexity, before being fed into the transformer encoder. The encoder utilizes self-attention mechanisms to capture contextual semantics and salient code features, which is formulated as:

$$\text{Attention}(Q, K, V) = \text{softmax}\left(\frac{QK^T}{\sqrt{d_k}}\right) V, \tag{1}$$

where Q, K, and V represent the query, key, and value matrices, respectively, and d_k denotes the dimension of the key vectors. The self-attention output is obtained by computing the similarity between queries and keys, then using these similarity scores as weights to aggregate the corresponding values. After processing through the CNN and transformer modules, V_{node} is transformed into the semantic feature vector V_{code}.

3.3 Software Structural Feature Extraction Method Based on Graph Attention Networks

The extraction of software structural features follows three sequential steps: (1) Creating Directed Class Dependency Network. (2) Node features embedding. (3) Generating software structural features.

Creating Directed Class Dependency Network. Based on the work of Qu et al. [16], the following three dependency types are considered when constructing the DCDN: (1) Inherit: If class c_1 inherits from class c_2, there exists a directed edge $e_{(12)} =< c_1, c_2 >$. (2) Aggregation: If class c_1 contains class c_2, there exists a directed edge $e_{(12)} =< c_1, c_2 >$. (3) Method usage: If class c_1 uses methods from class c_2, there exists a directed edge $e_{(12)} =< c_1, c_2 >$. The multiple edges between the same pair of nodes are merged into a single edge, forming the resulting DCDN denoted as G_{code}.

Node Features Embedding. The initial features for each node consist of the traditional product metrics. To capture the structural characteristics of DCDN, Node2vec generates vector representations for each node based on the structure of DCDN. The process of generating network embedding features is shown in Fig. 4. Finally, the generated network embedding features are concatenated with the initial features to serve as attributes for each node.

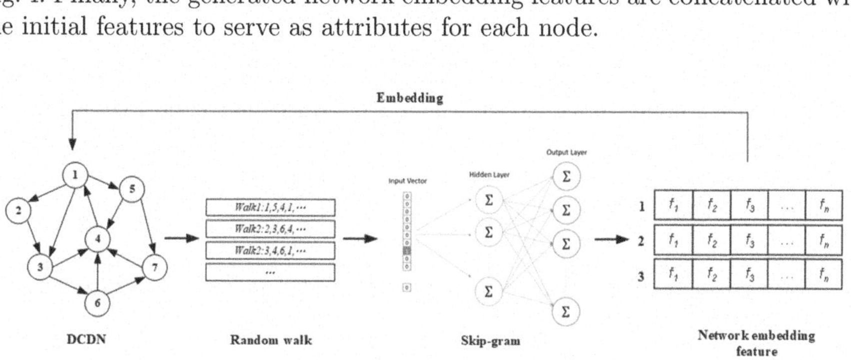

Fig. 4. Process of generating network embedding features.

Generating Software Structural Features. After G_{code} is constructed and embedded, CGSDP employs Graph Attention Networks (GAT) to extract structural features from the code graph. The GAT takes as input a set of node features $h = \{\vec{h_1}, \vec{h_2}, \cdots, \vec{h_N}\}$, where $\vec{h_i} \in \mathbb{R}^F$ denotes the feature vector of node i, N represents the total number of nodes in the graph, and F indicates the feature dimension of each node. The GAT produces as output a transformed set of node features $h' = \{\vec{h'_1}, \vec{h'_2}, \cdots, \vec{h'_N}\}$, where $\vec{h'_i} \in \mathbb{R}^{F'}$ represents the updated feature vector of node i. In GAT, the importance of neighboring node j to the central node i is computed through an attention mechanism. The attention score e_{ij} is calculated using equation:

$$e_{ij} = \alpha([W\vec{h_i} || W\vec{h_j}]), \quad j \in \mathcal{N}_i \tag{2}$$

where $W \in \mathbb{R}^{F' \times F}$ represents a learnable weight matrix, $||$ denotes the concatenation operation of the transformed node features, $\alpha(\cdot) : \mathbb{R}^{2F'} \to \mathbb{R}$ is a single-layer feedforward network that maps the concatenated features to a scalar attention score, and $\mathcal{N}_i$ represents the set of neighboring nodes of node i.

Subsequently, the normalized attention coefficient α_{ij} is obtained by applying the softmax function to the attention scores, as shown in equation:

$$\alpha_{ij} = \frac{\exp\left(\text{LeakyReLU}(e_{ij})\right)}{\sum_{k \in \mathcal{N}_i} \exp\left(\text{LeakyReLU}(e_{ik})\right)} \tag{3}$$

where LeakyReLU$(\cdot)$ denotes the Leaky Rectified Linear Unit activation function with a negative slope of 0.2, and the denominator sums over all neighbors k of node i to ensure normalization.

To enhance the stability of the attention learning process, GAT employs a multi-head attention mechanism. The final output features are computed by concatenating the outputs from K independent attention heads, as formulated in equation:

$$\vec{h'_i} = \Big\Vert_{k=1}^{K} \sigma\left(\sum_{j \in \mathcal{N}_i} \alpha_{ij}^k W^k \vec{h}_j\right) \tag{4}$$

where $||$ represents the concatenation operation across multiple attention heads, K denotes the number of attention heads, α_{ij}^k represents the normalized attention coefficient for the k-th attention head, $W^k \in \mathbb{R}^{F'/K \times F}$ denotes the weight matrix corresponding to the k-th attention head, and $\sigma(\cdot)$ represents a non-linear activation function (typically ELU).

3.4 Integration of Semantic and Structural Features for Software Defect Prediction

Following the comprehensive extraction of semantic features from source code and structural features from the Directed Class Dependency Network (DCDN), CGSDP integrates these complementary representations to form a unified feature vector for defect prediction. This integration strategy enables the model to simultaneously leverage both the contextual semantics of code constructs and the architectural dependencies within the software system.

After the aforementioned processing steps, the code semantic feature vector V_{code} and the graph structural feature vector V_{graph} are integrated into a unified representation $V_{\text{integrate}}$, which comprehensively captures both semantic and structural characteristics. The integration is performed through element-wise addition:

$$V_{\text{integrate}} = V_{\text{code}} \oplus V_{\text{graph}}, \tag{5}$$

where $\oplus$ denotes the element-wise addition operation between V_{code} and V_{graph}. This additive fusion approach ensures dimensional consistency while allowing complementary information to reinforce relevant feature dimensions. The integrated feature vector $V_{\text{integrate}}$ is subsequently concatenated with traditional product metrics and utilized for downstream prediction tasks.

During the training phase, a Softmax layer processes the enhanced feature representation to predict the defect propensity of each file. The model is optimized using the backpropagation algorithm with Adam optimizer, which minimizes the cross-entropy loss for defect classification. The loss function is defined as:

$$Loss = -\frac{1}{N}\sum_{i=1}^{N}\left[y_i \log(Z_i) + (1 - y_i)\log(1 - Z_i)\right], \tag{6}$$

where N denotes the total number of samples, $y_i \in \{0, 1\}$ represents the ground-truth label of the i-th sample (0 for non-defective, 1 for defective), and Z_i indicates the predicted probability of the i-th sample being defective. The training employs early stopping with a patience of 10 epochs to prevent overfitting and ensure generalization capability.

4 Experiments and Evaluation

4.1 Experiment Setup

Seven open-source projects from the PROMISE repository are evaluated [24], which is a standard benchmark in defect prediction research. Table 2 details their characteristics across versions, including file counts, DCDN edges, and defect rates. This diverse dataset with varying complexity levels provides a comprehensive testbed for approach validation.

Based on established experimental configurations [6], the F1-score, precision, and Area Under the ROC Curve (AUC) are selected as evaluation metrics. True positive (TP) represents correctly predicted positive instances, false positive (FP) represents incorrectly predicted positive instances, true negative (TN) represents correctly predicted negative instances, and false negative (FN) represents incorrectly predicted negative instances. The definitions are as follows: $Precision = \frac{TP}{TP+FP}$, $Recall = \frac{TP}{TP+FN}$, $F1\ score = \frac{2 \times Precision \times Recall}{Precision+Recall}$.

The performance comparison is conducted using the Win/Tie/Loss indicator following prior work [20], supplemented by the Wilcoxon signed-rank test

Table 2. Dataset information

Project	Version	Files	Edges	Defect rate
Ant	1.4	177	853	23.2
	1.6	350	1798	26.6
	1.7	741	3678	22.4
Camel	1.2	606	2668	35.6
	1.4	848	3731	17.1
	1.6	934	4322	20.0
Jedit	4.0	293	1546	25.6
	4.1	300	1638	26.3
	4.2	355	2061	13.5
Lucene	2.0	186	756	48.9
	2.2	234	947	60.7
	2.4	330	1482	61.5
Poi	2.0	309	1318	12.0
	2.5	380	1693	65.3
	3.0	438	2194	64.2
Velocity	1.4	195	1016	75.4
	1.5	214	1127	66.3
	1.6	229	1219	34.1
Xalan	2.4	676	4258	16.3
	2.5	762	4567	50.8
	2.6	875	4806	47.0

and Cliff's delta test. The Wilcoxon test is a nonparametric statistical hypothesis test used to assess whether two matched samples originate from the same distribution, with a p-value below 0.05 indicating a statistically significant difference. Complementing this, Cliff's delta test quantifies the effect size between two sample sets via the $|\delta|$ value, whose interpretation levels are provided in Table 3. Results are reported as p-value (effect level), where $p < 0.05$ is marked as such. A result is classified as 'win' if $p < 0.05$ and the effect level is positive, 'loss' if $p < 0.05$ and the effect level is negative, and 'tie' otherwise.

Table 3. The effective levels of the Cliff's delta test

Cliff's delta value	Effective level
$\|\delta\| < 0.147$	Negligible
$0.147 \leq \|\delta\| < 0.33$	Small
$0.33 \leq \|\delta\| < 0.474$	Medium
$0.474 < \|\delta\|$	Large

To validate the effectiveness of CGSDP, a comparative analysis was conducted against three baseline methods: (1) the Traditional Approach [7] using 20 manual product metrics; (2) CNN [9] integrating CNN-extracted semantic features with product metrics; and (3) CGCN [26] modeling code as undirected graphs and combining CNN with GCN to capture semantic-structural features, outperforming CNN, BiLSTM, and Node2Vec. Experiments ran in Python 3.7 on an Intel i7-11700 CPU and NVIDIA GTX 1080 GPU with 32 GB RAM, using Keras 2.9.0 and TensorFlow 2.9.1. Models trained for 300 epochs with Adam (lr = 0.001); Word2Vec produced 32-dim word embeddings, Node2Vec (p = 0.25, q = 2) 16-dim structural embeddings. All CNNs used 32 filters; GCN and GAT had two layers (64, 32 units); self-attention and graph attention employed 5 heads, with early stopping to prevent overfitting. Each code file was represented as a 32-dim vector post-feature extraction. To address class imbalance [2], SMOTEENN [3] was applied unless the defect rate fell within 0.4–0.6.

4.2 Results and Analyses

To evaluate the effectiveness of CGSDP, the evaluation focuses on addressing the following three research questions:

- RQ1. How well does CGSDP perform in within-project defect prediction?
- RQ2. How well does CGSDP perform in cross-project defect prediction?
- RQ3. What is the impact of the attention mechanism on the prediction task of CGSDP?

The aim of RQ1 and RQ2 is to evaluate the performance of CGSDP in various software defect prediction tasks, while RQ3 aims to investigate the effect of the self-attention mechanism and the graph attention network introduced by CGSDP on the efficiency of defect prediction tasks.

Table 4. Comparison of the performance of different classifiers

Project	LR			MLP			RF		
	F1	AUC	Pre	F1	AUC	Pre	F1	AUC	Pre
Ant1.7	0.713	0.895	0.619	0.705	0.895	0.612	**0.748**	**0.926**	**0.686**
Camel1.6	0.666	0.918	0.567	0.637	0.891	0.538	**0.727**	**0.943**	**0.639**
Jedit4.2	0.611	0.930	0.475	0.559	0.892	0.424	**0.797**	**0.971**	**0.706**
Lucene2.4	0.875	0.922	0.913	0.844	0.884	0.888	**0.888**	**0.936**	**0.930**
Poi3.0	0.902	0.930	0.933	0.884	0.906	0.928	**0.936**	**0.964**	**0.969**
Velocity1.6	0.843	0.929	0.821	0.674	0.789	0.559	**0.875**	**0.941**	**0.889**
Xalan-2.6	**0.897**	0.955	**0.925**	0.868	0.929	0.880	0.895	**0.957**	0.922
AVG	0.787	0.926	0.750	0.739	0.884	0.690	**0.838**	**0.948**	**0.820**

RQ1. How well does CGSDP perform in within-project defect prediction?

Within-Project Defect Prediction (WPDP), the most common defect prediction scenario, utilizes both source and target data from the same project and can be divided into two categories: Within Version Defect Prediction (WVDP) and Cross Version Defect Prediction (CVDP), as detailed in the following sections.

Figure 5 present the experimental results of CGSDP compared to baseline methods in the WVDP task. The bottom row of each table displays the average values of each evaluation metric across all tasks. CGSDP achieved an AUC greater than 0.8 in all tasks, indicating outstanding predictive performance across all projects. Except for Ant1.6, Jedit4.0, and Poi2.0, CGSDP outperformed other baseline methods in F1 scores across all projects, with an average F1 score of 0.792, improving by 37.4%, 12.9%, and 4.2% over the other baseline methods, respectively. In terms of accuracy, CGSDP also surpassed other baseline methods in most tasks, achieving an average accuracy of 0.752, which represents improvements of 39.3%, 13.8%, and 5.6% over the respective baseline methods.

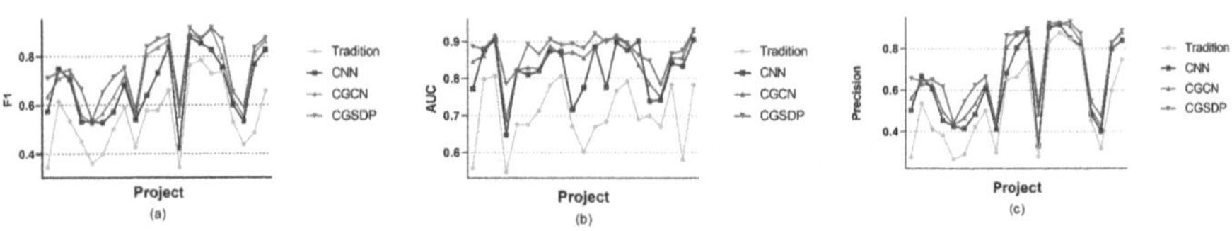

Fig. 5. Comparation of CGSDP and the baseline methods in WVDP (a) Comparison of F1 score between CGSDP and the baseline methods (b) Comparison of AUC between CGSDP and the baseline methods (c) Comparison of precision between CGSDP and the baseline methods.

The performance of classifiers for Within-project Defect Prediction (WVDP) was compared using the latest project versions, with Logistic Regression (LR), Multilayer Perceptron (MLP), and Random Forest (RF) being evaluated. Experimental results presented in Table 4 indicate that RF significantly outperforms the other classifiers, improving F1 by 6.4 %, AUC by 2.3%, and Accuracy by 9.3% over LR, and by 13.3%, 7.2%, and 18.8% over MLP, respectively. However, RF requires more than ten times longer for grid search and classification compared to LR and MLP. Considering the performance-time trade-off, LR was selected as the final classifier.

RQ2. How well does CGSDP perform in cross-project defect prediction?

In CVDP tasks, the latest version of each project is selected as the test set, while the latest versions of other projects are utilized as the training set. To ensure statistical reliability, 50 repeated experiments are conducted with average values reported.

Table 5 shows the Win/Tie/Lose indicators of CGSDP's F1 compared to baseline methods. Among the 42 tasks, CGSDP achieves the highest F1 score in 18 tasks. Compared to baseline methods, CGSDP improves the F1 score by 8%,

Table 5. Performance of CGSDP and the baseline methods in CVDP

Project	Tradition			CNN			CGCN			CGSDP		
	F1	AUC	Pre	F1	AUC	Pre	F1	AUC	Pre	F1	AUC	Pre
Ant1.4 ⇒ Ant1.6	0.384	0.565	0.342	0.395	0.565	0.295	0.403	0.568	0.296	**0.559**	**0.747**	**0.451**
Ant1.6 ⇒ Ant1.7	0.564	0.807	0.461	**0.609**	**0.851**	**0.544**	0.534	0.699	0.467	0.498	0.832	0.343
Camel1.2 ⇒ Camel1.4	0.334	0.656	0.222	0.351	0.736	0.455	0.353	0.652	0.272	**0.477**	**0.778**	**0.548**
Camel1.4 ⇒ Camel1.6	0.402	0.661	0.312	0.377	0.662	0.344	0.453	0.720	**0.367**	**0.474**	**0.781**	0.339
Jedit4.0 ⇒ Jedit4.1	0.565	0.785	0.454	0.560	0.794	0.444	0.579	0.788	0.483	**0.638**	**0.854**	**0.529**
Jedit4.1 ⇒ Jedit4.2	0.425	0.828	0.283	0.442	0.842	0.299	0.442	0.816	0.315	**0.476**	**0.875**	**0.321**
Lucene2.0 ⇒ Lucene2.2	0.682	0.657	0.664	0.677	**0.739**	**0.792**	**0.732**	0.657	0.620	0.718	0.547	0.603
Lucene2.2 ⇒ Lucene2.4	0.668	**0.701**	**0.782**	0.629	0.650	0.759	0.667	0.693	0.777	**0.676**	0.646	0.681
Poi2.0 ⇒ Poi2.5	0.454	0.479	0.627	0.736	0.751	0.798	0.811	0.765	0.767	**0.846**	**0.838**	**0.851**
Poi2.5 ⇒ Poi3.0	0.712	0.696	**0.797**	0.607	0.546	0.664	**0.753**	**0.730**	**0.776**	0.741	0.656	0.708
Velocity1.4 ⇒ Velocity1.5	0.581	0.389	0.584	0.646	0.593	0.717	0.606	0.403	0.594	**0.646**	**0.679**	**0.792**
Velocity1.5 ⇒ Velocity1.6	0.553	0.692	0.426	0.600	0.747	0.468	0.552	0.687	0.426	**0.619**	**0.748**	**0.520**
Xalan2.4 ⇒ Xalan2.5	0.562	0.634	**0.649**	0.553	0.540	0.518	0.449	0.582	0.601	**0.620**	**0.638**	0.607
Xalan2.5 ⇒ Xalan2.6	0.539	0.630	0.567	0.636	0.704	0.497	**0.689**	**0.803**	**0.587**	0.653	0.725	0.528
AVG	0.530	0.656	0.512	0.559	0.694	0.542	0.573	0.683	0.525	**0.617**	**0.739**	**0.559**

5.5%, and 4.3% respectively. According to the Win/Tie/Lose indicators of F1 score, CGSDP has good performance for Camel and Xalan but performs poorly for Ant and Lucene. The average AUC of CGSDP is 0.677, indicating good classifier performance. In terms of precision, CGSDP has an average decrease of 4% compared to traditional method. CGCN also shows similar patterns, with lower precision to CNN but improved F1 score.

RQ3. What is the impact of the attention mechanism on the prediction task of CGSDP?

To evaluate the performance improvement of CGSDP attributed to the two attention mechanisms, an ablation study is conducted by performing the WVDP task on 6 versions of the data. The method without any attention mechanism is denoted as CNN, the method incorporating graph attention is referred to as CNN-GAT, and the method utilizing self-attention is designated as CNN-ATT. Table 6 show the experimental results. The results indicate that both self-attention and graph attention enhance the performance on most tasks. The effects of these two attention mechanisms are comparable. CGSDP leverages the self-attention mechanism to understand the software semantics and the graph attention mechanism to capture the software structure features, achieving better performance.

Table 6. Performance of different settings of CGSDP in WVDP

Project	CNN			CNN-ATT			CNN-GAT			CGSDP		
	F1	AUC	Pre	F1	AUC	Pre	F1	AUC	Pre	F1	AUC	Pre
Ant1.7	0.669	0.898	0.559	**0.757**	**0.937**	**0.667**	0.717	0.916	0.623	0.737	0.924	0.637
Camel1.6	0.545	0.815	0.438	0.576	0.837	0.466	0.538	0.798	0.435	**0.646**	**0.886**	**0.532**
Jedit4.2	0.509	0.847	0.376	0.487	0.851	0.360	0.535	0.875	0.404	**0.535**	**0.870**	**0.404**
Lucene2.4	0.722	0.755	0.802	0.786	0.812	0.835	0.797	0.826	0.835	**0.822**	**0.849**	**0.850**
Poi3.0	0.855	0.875	0.910	**0.869**	**0.882**	**0.915**	0.830	0.858	0.901	0.857	0.869	0.913
Velocity1.6	0.625	0.756	0.506	0.641	0.768	0.524	0.624	0.749	0.519	**0.648**	**0.783**	**0.523**
Xalan-2.6	0.831	0.907	0.852	0.845	0.916	0.860	0.861	0.929	0.881	**0.874**	**0.934**	**0.893**
AVG	0.679	0.836	0.635	0.709	0.858	0.661	0.700	0.850	0.657	**0.731**	**0.874**	**0.679**

Table 7. Parameters and training time of CGSDP with different settings

Project	Max length of token vector	Edges	CNN (ms/epoch)	CGSDP-GAT (ms/epoch)	CGSDP-ATT (ms/epoch)	CGSDP (ms/epoch)
Ant1.4	1389	853	28	46	40	53
Ant1.6	1749	1798	40	56	54	65
Ant1.7	1975	3687	68	83	90	103
Camel1.2	911	2668	38	55	57	73
Camel1.4	1557	3731	63	78	84	99
Camel1.6	1868	4322	77	90	100	118
Jedit4.0	7994	1546	107	114	121	139
Jedit4.1	8080	1638	110	120	125	142
Jedit4.2	6527	2061	104	116	126	133
Lucene2.0	1458	756	29	42	39	53
Lucene2.2	1591	947	34	46	43	57
Lucene2.4	3225	1482	56	70	72	83
Poi2.0	3426	1318	56	70	71	85
Poi2.5	3427	1693	66	79	80	91
Poi3.0	3435	2194	71	84	86	100
Velocity1.4	4240	1016	50	61	60	72
Velocity1.5	4702	1127	54	70	68	82
Velocity1.6	4880	1219	60	72	74	84
Xalan2.4	3658	4258	101	115	122	136
Xalan2.5	2085	4567	73	86	91	106
Xalan2.6	2125	4806	78	93	101	116

Although the attention mechanisms improve the feature representation, they also increase model complexity and training time. Table 7 shows the average training time per epoch for CGSDP with different settings. The average training time per epoch for CGSDP is 109.43 ms, which is about 29.85 ms longer than CNN. This is due to the self-attention (an average increase of 16.24 ms) and the graph attention (an average increase of 13.48 ms). It is worth noting that the self-attention mechanism only slightly increases the processing time, ranging from 9 to 23 ms. This is because the inputs have similar sizes after CNN processing, and thus there is no significant increase in processing time due to the input token sequence.

5 Conclusion

This paper presents CGSDP, a novel software defect prediction approach that integrates both semantic and structural features from source code. CGSDP constructs Abstract Syntax Trees (ASTs) to represent software semantics, embeds token sequences into word vectors, and employs a CNN-enhanced Transformer to extract semantic features efficiently with reduced computational cost. A self-attention mechanism is applied to capture both local and global semantic information while minimizing contextual loss. To address the limitations of ASTs in structural modeling, we utilize network embedding and Graph Attention Networks (GAT) to encode global software dependencies. By combining product metrics with semantic and structural features, CGSDP comprehensively characterizes programs and enables multi-faceted defect prediction for efficient AIOps. Experimental evaluations on seven open-source PROMISE datasets in within-project and cross-project settings demonstrate that CGSDP outperforms state-of-the-art methods, improving average F1 scores by 5.4%, 7.7%, and 4.3%, respectively. Future work will focus on AST sequence segmentation for improved efficiency, incorporating domain adaptation to enhance cross-project transferability, and extending the framework to cross-language defect prediction using unified parsers.

Acknowledgments. This work is supported by the National Natural Science Foundation of China (No. 62162003) and the Central Guiding Local Technology Development Fund (No. 2024ZYZX4030).

Disclosure of Interests. The authors have no relevant financial or non-financial interests to disclose.

References

1. Ardimento, P., Aversano, L., Bernardi, M.L., Cimitile, M., Iammarino, M.: Just-in-time software defect prediction using deep temporal convolutional networks. Neural Comput. Appl. **34**(5), 3981–4001 (2022)
2. Brownlee, J.: Imbalanced classification with Python: better metrics, balance skewed classes, cost-sensitive learning. Machine Learning Mastery (2020)
3. Cetiner, M., Sahingoz, O.K.: A comparative analysis for machine learning based software defect prediction systems. In: 2020 11th International Conference on Computing, Communication and Networking Technologies (ICCCNT), pp. 1–7. IEEE (2020)
4. Chen, J., Wang, X., Xu, X.: GC-LSTM: graph convolution embedded LSTM for dynamic network link prediction. Appl. Intell. **52**(7), 7513–7528 (2022)

5. Dhelim, S., Aung, N., Kechadi, M.T., Ning, H., Chen, L., Lakas, A.: Trust2vec: large-scale IoT trust management system based on signed network embeddings. IEEE Internet Things J. **10**(1), 553–562 (2022)
6. Giray, G., Bennin, K.E., Köksal, Ö., Babur, Ö., Tekinerdogan, B.: On the use of deep learning in software defect prediction. J. Syst. Softw. **195**, 111537 (2023)
7. He, Z., Peters, F., Menzies, T., Yang, Y.: Learning from open-source projects: an empirical study on defect prediction. In: 2013 ACM/IEEE International Symposium on Empirical Software Engineering and Measurement, pp. 45–54. IEEE (2013)
8. Li, B., Zhang, Y., Sainath, T., Wu, Y., Chan, W.: Bytes are all you need: end-to-end multilingual speech recognition and synthesis with bytes. In: ICASSP 2019-2019 IEEE International Conference on Acoustics, Speech and Signal Processing (ICASSP), pp. 5621–5625. IEEE (2019)
9. Li, J., He, P., Zhu, J., Lyu, M.R.: Software defect prediction via convolutional neural network. In: 2017 IEEE International Conference on Software Quality, Reliability and Security (QRS), pp. 318–328. IEEE (2017)
10. Liu, Q., Xiang, J., Xu, B., Zhao, D., Hu, W., Wang, J.: Aging-related bugs prediction via convolutional neural network. In: 2020 7th International Conference on Dependable Systems and Their Applications (DSA), pp. 90–98. IEEE (2020)
11. Ma, J., Sun, Y.Y., He, P., Zeng, Z.F.: Gsage2defect: an improved approach to software defect prediction based on inductive graph neural network. In: SEKE, pp. 45–50 (2023)
12. Majd, A., Vahidi-Asl, M., Khalilian, A., Poorsarvi-Tehrani, P., Haghighi, H.: Sldeep: statement-level software defect prediction using deep-learning model on static code features. Expert Syst. Appl. **147**, 113156 (2020)
13. Malohtra, R., Yadav, H.S.: An improved CNN-based architecture for within-project software defect prediction. In: Reddy, V.S., Prasad, V.K., Wang, J., Reddy, K.T.V. (eds.) Soft Computing and Signal Processing. AISC, vol. 1325, pp. 335–349. Springer, Singapore (2021). https://doi.org/10.1007/978-981-33-6912-2_31
14. Mikolov, T., Chen, K., Corrado, G., Dean, J.: Efficient estimation of word representations in vector space. arXiv preprint arXiv:1301.3781 (2013)
15. Notaro, P., Cardoso, J., Gerndt, M.: A survey of AIOps methods for failure management. ACM Trans. Intell. Syst. Technol. (TIST) **12**(6), 1–45 (2021)
16. Qu, Y., et al.: node2defect: using network embedding to improve software defect prediction. In: Proceedings of the 33rd ACM/IEEE International Conference on Automated Software Engineering, pp. 844–849 (2018)
17. Stradowski, S., Madeyski, L.: Industrial applications of software defect prediction using machine learning: a business-driven systematic literature review. Inf. Softw. Technol. **159**, 107192 (2023)
18. Uddin, M.N., Li, B., Ali, Z., Kefalas, P., Khan, I., Zada, I.: Software defect prediction employing BiLSTM and BERT-based semantic feature. Soft. Comput. **26**(16), 7877–7891 (2022)
19. Velickovic, P., Cucurull, G., Casanova, A., Romero, A., Lio, P., Bengio, Y., et al.: Graph attention networks. Stat **1050**(20), 10-48550 (2017)
20. Wang, H., Zhuang, W., Zhang, X.: Software defect prediction based on gated hierarchical LSTMs. IEEE Trans. Reliab. **70**(2), 711–727 (2021)
21. Wang, S., Liu, T., Nam, J., Tan, L.: Deep semantic feature learning for software defect prediction. IEEE Trans. Software Eng. **46**(12), 1267–1293 (2018)
22. Yu, Q., Jiang, S., Qian, J., Bo, L., Jiang, L., Zhang, G.: Process metrics for software defect prediction in object-oriented programs. IET Software **14**(3), 283–292 (2020)

23. Zhang, P., Chen, J., Che, C., Zhang, L., Jin, B., Zhu, Y.: IEA-GNN: anchor-aware graph neural network fused with information entropy for node classification and link prediction. Inf. Sci. **634**, 665–676 (2023)
24. Zhang, Q., Wu, B.: Software defect prediction via transformer. In: 2020 IEEE 4th Information Technology, Networking, Electronic and Automation Control Conference (ITNEC), vol. 1, pp. 874–879. IEEE (2020)
25. Zheng, W., Tan, L., Liu, C.: Software defect prediction method based on transformer model. In: 2021 IEEE International Conference on Artificial Intelligence and Computer Applications (ICAICA), pp. 670–674. IEEE (2021)
26. Zhou, C., He, P., Zeng, C., Ma, J.: Software defect prediction with semantic and structural information of codes based on graph neural networks. Inf. Softw. Technol. **152**, 107057 (2022)
27. Zhu, K., Ying, S., Zhang, N., Zhu, D.: Software defect prediction based on enhanced metaheuristic feature selection optimization and a hybrid deep neural network. J. Syst. Softw. **180**, 111026 (2021)

An Emoticon-Aware Autoencoder Method for Face Replacement in Images from Videos

Yifei Wang[1], Zheng Qin[2], Rhibull Tang[3], Yueqian Li[4], Sichuang Xu[4], Yan Zhou[1(✉)], and Junyang Chen[4(✉)]

[1] School of Mathematical Sciences, Shenzhen University, Shenzhen, China
zhouy1016@szu.edu.cn
[2] School of Business, The University of Sydney, Sydney, Australia
[3] Shenzhen Middle School, Shenzhen, China
[4] College of Computer Science and Software Engineering, Shenzhen University, Shenzhen, China
junyangchen@szu.edu.cn

Abstract. This paper presents a robust single-image-to-video face replacement framework that integrates facial expression generation with identity transfer. Traditional approaches often suffer from facial distortion and limited generalization under data scarcity. To overcome these challenges, we propose an emoticon-aware autoencoder with a co-training mechanism that jointly learns expression synthesis and face replacement. A StarGAN-based expression generator expands a single image into eight basic emotion classes, supplemented by geometric augmentations to create about 1,000 samples, enhancing model robustness. The framework adopts a three-stage architecture: (1) pre-processing via MTCNN and a VGG-11–enhanced encoder for precise mask generation; (2) a dual-branch autoencoder with a shared encoder and independent decoders for feature extraction and reconstruction; and (3) inference through source–target feature decoupling and dynamic fusion for seamless identity transfer. Experimental results show that the proposed method effectively reduces facial distortion and improves temporal consistency, offering a reliable solution for single-sample video face replacement.

Keywords: Face Replacement · Emoticon-awaring · Generative Adversarial Networks · Video Synthesis

1 Introduction

Face replacement technology, a generative AI technique based on deep learning and computer vision algorithms [10], transfers identity and expression features from a source image to a specified facial region in target videos or images while preserving scene-specific illumination, pose, and background consistency. Its core applications span three domains: 1) **Privacy protection** [19], where high-fidelity anonymization replaces traditional pixelation for sensitive individuals in news media and public

Y. Wang and Z. Qin—Equal contribution.

© The Author(s), under exclusive license to Springer Nature Singapore Pte Ltd. 2027
H. Sun et al. (Eds.): ChineseCSCW 2025, CCIS 2911, pp. 230–245, 2027.
https://doi.org/10.1007/978-981-92-0288-1_17

surveillance data desensitization; 2) **Film production** [12], addressing actor unavailability and reducing reshoot costs for high-risk action scenes; and 3) **Immersive entertainment** [16], enabling single-image virtual avatar creation for cross-temporal identity interaction experiences. Early approaches relied on parametric models or image databases. Database-based methods [1] achieved offline replacement via prebuilt face libraries but suffered from poor occlusion adaptation, weak extreme expression handling, and inability for targeted replacement.

In general, parametric models partially mitigated these issues: 2D frameworks [11] enabled static replacement through shape alignment but faltered under varying illumination or viewpoints, while 3D models improved pose robustness at the cost of high computational complexity and multi-angle data dependency. With the proliferation of deep learning in visual media, current methods predominantly adopt two paradigms: GAN-based frameworks [13] and conventional convolutional architectures [6]. However, most existing techniques require multi-angle/expression source images or videos to handle diverse facial poses in target videos, leading to facial distortion such as feature distortion when limited to single-view source data—a critical limitation termed **data-model dynamic mismatch**.

To address this challenge, we propose a **robust, distortion-free video face replacement framework** for single-image-driven scenarios, overcoming data dependency constraints inherent in existing methods. Our solution centers on two innovations:

a. Multi-modal data augmentation: Leveraging StarGAN [3], we design an 8-category base expression generator combined with rotation, translation, and geometric distortion operations to synthesize 1,000+ augmented samples, significantly enhancing model generalization.

b. Modular processing architecture: We further propose an end-to-end efficient processing framework, which consists of three key components: pre-processing, model construction, and generation: In the pre-processing stage, MTCNN [20] performs high-precision face detection and boundary localization, while FAN [2] extracts facial landmarks, and a pretrained VGG-11 network [5] replaces the traditional U-Net [15] encoder to generate accurate facial masks through deep semantic feature extraction. During model construction, a dual-branch autoencoder is developed with a shared encoder for feature extraction and independent decoders for identity-preserving facial reconstruction. In the generation stage, target images are passed through the trained encoder and source-specific decoder for seamless face conversion, and the resulting frames are blended sequentially to synthesize the final video.

Main contributions: This work systematically addresses the data–model dynamic mismatch in single-image video face replacement, arising from the inherent misalignment between monocular source images and multi-expression target videos. To mitigate this issue, we propose a distortion-minimized framework that integrates adversarial optimization with dynamic feature disentanglement, achieving high-fidelity results even under limited data conditions. Overall, this study establishes a new paradigm for robust video face replacement, effectively bridging the gap between practical deployment needs and the constraints of data-intensive algorithms.

2 Proposed Model

The proposed method can be divided into three main stages: data augmentation, data pre-processing and model construction, and face generation and replacement.

2.1 Data Augmentation

To address the single-sample problem, we propose a two-stage data augmentation method based on StarGAN. The specific process is as follows: (1) Input a single photograph containing the target face and a source video with the faces to be replaced. Perform frame extraction on the source video to obtain multiple source face images, (2) Due to the lack of multi-angle and multi-expression data for the target face, pre-train StarGAN [4] on the RaFD dataset [7] (containing labeled images with eight expressions $\times$ three angles, specifically including: anger, disgust, fear, happiness, sadness, surprise, contempt, and neutral). Use the pre-trained model to generate eight expression variants of the target face, and expand them to approximately 1000 samples through geometric transformations (rotation/translation/distortion) in the subsequent face swapping stage, achieving the expansion from a single sample to multiple samples.

The pre-training involves three key loss functions:

$$\mathcal{L}_{adv} = \mathbb{E}_I[\log D_{src}(I)] + \mathbb{E}_{I,e}[\log(1 - D_{src}(G(I,e)))] \tag{1}$$

where $\mathcal{L}_{adv}$ represents the adversarial loss function, $\mathbb{E}_I[\cdot]$ denotes the expectation over original input images I sampled from the RaFD dataset, D_{src} is the source domain discriminator function distinguishing real from generated images, $D_{src}(I)$ is the probability output of the discriminator D_{src} for a real image I, $\mathbb{E}_{I,e}[\cdot]$ denotes the expectation over original images I and target domain labels e, $e \in \mathbb{R}^8$ represents the target domain's emotion label vector, G is the generator function, $G(I,e)$ is the image generated by the generator given the input image I and target label e, $D_{src}(G(I,e))$ is the probability output of the discriminator D_{src} for the generated image $G(I,e)$. The generator $G(I,e)$ aims to produce realistic data to deceive the discriminator D_{src}, while the discriminator is trained adversarially by maximizing the log-likelihood of recognizing real data ($\log D_{src}(I)$) and minimizing the log-likelihood of misjudging generated data ($\log(1-D_{src}(G(I,e)))$), ultimately compelling the generator to improve its generation quality.

The second is the domain classification loss, which differs when training the generator G and the discriminator D: when training the generator G, the goal is to classify the generated image into the target domain, as shown in Eq. 2:

$$\mathcal{L}^r_{cls} = \mathbb{E}_{I,e'}[-\log D_{cls}(e'|I)] \tag{2}$$

where $\mathcal{L}^r_{cls}$ is the domain classification loss for real images, used for training the discriminator D, $\mathbb{E}_{I,e'}[\cdot]$ denotes the expectation over real images I and their original domain labels e', I is a real image sampled from the RaFD dataset, e' is the original domain (emotion) label of the real image I, D_{cls} is the domain classification function within the discriminator D, $D_{cls}(e'|I)$ represents the probability distribution over domain labels predicted by the classifier D_{cls} for the real image I, specifically computed as the negative log-likelihood of the true label e'.

When training the discriminator D, the goal is to correctly classify the real image into its original domain, given by Eq. 3:

$$\mathcal{L}_{cls}^{f} = \mathbb{E}_{I,e}[-\log D_{cls}(e|G(I,e))] \tag{3}$$

where $\mathcal{L}_{cls}^{f}$ is the domain classification loss for fake (generated) images, used for training the generator G, $\mathbb{E}_{I,e}[\cdot]$ denotes the expectation over original images I and target domain labels e, I is an original image sampled from the RaFD dataset, e is the target domain's emotion label vector, G is the generator function, $G(I,e)$ is the image generated by the generator, D_{cls} is the domain classification function within the discriminator D, $D_{cls}(e|G(I,e))$ represents the probability distribution over domain labels predicted by the classifier D_{cls} for the generated image $G(I,e)$, specifically computed as the negative log-likelihood of the target label e.

Finally, the reconstruction loss ensures that the domain-independent parts of the input image remain unchanged, while only the domain-related parts are altered. That is, after the input image I is converted into the target domain image $G(I,e)$ by the generator G, and then restored to the original domain image $G(G(I,e),e')$ by G again, it is expected that the resulting image is consistent with the original input image I (the domain-independent parts remain unchanged, and the domain-related parts change and then change back). The formula is shown in Eq. 4:

$$\mathcal{L}_{rec} = \mathbb{E}_{I,e,e'}[\|I - G(G(I,e),e')\|_1] \tag{4}$$

where $\mathcal{L}_{rec}$ represents the reconstruction loss (or cycle consistency loss), $\mathbb{E}_{I,e,e'}[\cdot]$ denotes the expectation over original images I, target domain labels e, and original domain labels e', I is the original input image, e is the target domain label, e' is the original domain label of I, G is the generator function, $G(I,e)$ is the image generated by translating I to the target domain e, $G(G(I,e),e')$ is the reconstructed image obtained by translating the generated image $G(I,e)$ back to the original domain e', $\|\cdot\|_1$ denotes the L1 norm, calculating the sum of absolute differences between the pixel values of the original image I and the reconstructed image $G(G(I,e),e')$.

The final objective functions are shown as follow:

$$\mathcal{L}_D = -\mathcal{L}_{adv} + \lambda_{cls}\mathcal{L}_{cls}^{r} \tag{5}$$

$$\mathcal{L}_G = \mathcal{L}_{adv} + \lambda_{cls}\mathcal{L}_{cls}^{f} + \lambda_{rec}\mathcal{L}_{rec} \tag{6}$$

where $\mathcal{L}_D$ is the total loss function for training the discriminator D, $\mathcal{L}_G$ is the total loss function for training the generator G, $\mathcal{L}_{adv}$ is the adversarial loss (Eq. 1), $\mathcal{L}_{cls}^{r}$ is the domain classification loss for real images (Eq. 2), $\mathcal{L}_{cls}^{f}$ is the domain classification loss for fake images (Eq. 3), $\mathcal{L}_{rec}$ is the reconstruction loss (Eq. 4), λ_{cls} and λ_{rec} are hyperparameters used to adjust the weights of the classification loss and reconstruction loss, respectively.

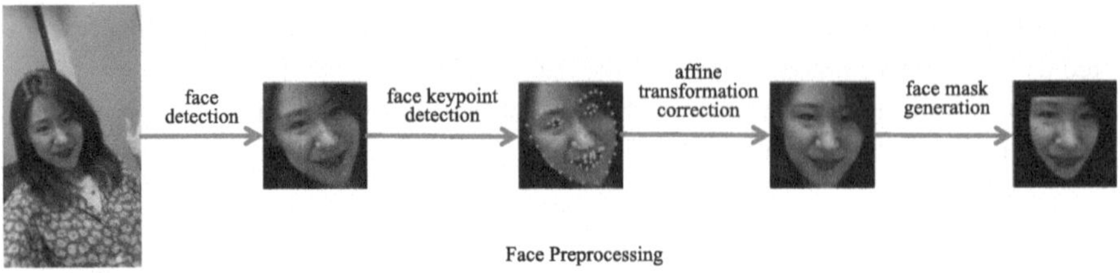

Fig. 1. Face preprocessing comprises three steps: 1) face detection to roughly eliminate background regions devoid of faces, 2) face alignment to adjust facial size and orientation, 3) face mask generation to remove hair, ears, and other elements within the detected facial region that are not required as model inputs.

2.2 Data Pre-processing and Model Contruction

In face replacement tasks, input images require preprocessing to ensure that the autoencoder model receives exclusively facial regions. **This selective processing is critical,** as the autoencoder's reconstruction must focus on facial features while preserving non-target peripheral regions (e.g., hair, ears) and background elements. **To address complex background interference in video frame extractions and non-facial artifacts in StarGAN-generated images,** our preprocessing framework implements a three-phase standardization protocol Fig. 1: (1) preliminary coarse background removal via facial bounding box localization, (2) spatial normalization through affine transformations to unify facial scale and orientation, and (3) pixel-level segmentation for precise elimination of non-target areas within detected regions while retaining essential facial attributes. **The proposed framework** achieves standardized model inputs by eliminating irrelevant visual components while maintaining geometric consistency across facial samples.

Face Detection. Since face swapping tasks typically target single-face replacement, the demand for multi-face detection is relatively low. This paper does not require high precision for small face detection but prioritizes speed. Among lightweight models, MTCNN [20] achieves the fastest inference speed. Although its multi-face detection performance lags behind S3FD [9] and DSFD [8], its overall performance remains above average, making it suitable for our requirements.

MTCNN produces a bounding box and five facial landmarks as final outputs. The model employs three cascaded networks for efficient face detection: P-Net, R-Net, and O-Net. The fundamental concept involves preliminary screening using simpler shallow networks for speed, followed by processing candidate regions through more accurate but computationally intensive networks.

- **P-Net**: Constructs an image pyramid to handle multi-scale faces, using a fully convolutional network to rapidly generate candidate regions (12×12 input). Outputs face probability, bounding box offsets, and 5-point landmark coordinates.
- **R-Net**: Incorporates fully connected layers for detection refinement (24×24 input), enhancing screening accuracy through feature reinforcement.

– **O-Net**: Employs a deeper network for precise localization (48×48 input), generating final bounding boxes and landmarks.

MTCNN adopts a multi-task joint training strategy with objective functions comprising classification and regression losses. For face classification (face/non-face), the cross-entropy loss is defined as Eq. 7:

$$L_i^{det} = -\left(y_i^{det}\log(p_i) + (1 - y_i^{det})(1 - \log(p_i))\right) \tag{7}$$

where y_i^{det} denotes the ground truth label and p_i represents the predicted face probability.

Bounding box regression and landmark localization employ L2 losses:

$$L_i^{box} = \left\|\hat{y}_i^{box} - y_i^{box}\right\|_2 \tag{8}$$

$$L_i^{landmark} = \left\|\hat{y}_i^{landmark} - y_i^{landmark}\right\|_2 \tag{9}$$

where $\hat{y}_i^{box}$ and $\hat{y}_i^{landmark}$ denote the network-corrected coordinates, while y_i^{box} and $y_i^{landmark}$ represent ground truth values.

The total loss combines weighted averages of these components. For P-Net and R-Net, higher weights are assigned to face detection since these networks primarily filter face-containing regions. In contrast, O-Net increases the weight for landmark localization to emphasize precise final positioning. The optimization objective L_{total} is formulated as:

$$L_{total} = min\sum_{i=1}^{n}\sum_{j\in det,box,landmark}\alpha_i\beta_i^j L_i^j. \tag{10}$$

where N denotes the number of training samples, α_j represents loss weights, and $\beta_i^j \in \{0, 1\}$ indicates sample type. The selected parameters are: $\alpha_{\text{det}} = 1$, $\alpha_{\text{box}} = 0.5$, $\alpha_{\text{landmark}} = 0.5$ for P/R-Net, $\alpha_{\text{det}} = 1$, $\alpha_{\text{box}} = 0.5$, $\alpha_{\text{landmark}} = 1$ for O-Net.

Face Alignment. Face alignment effectively mitigates intra-class feature shifts caused by variations in pose, expression, and imaging angle by mapping the key point coordinates of the input face to a standard space, ensuring geometric consistency of the model input data, thereby enhancing the robustness of deep feature extraction, reducing facial distortion or boundary artifacts resulting from geometric mismatches between source and target domain faces during subsequent face replacement, and establishing a geometric constraint benchmark for cross-domain feature mapping, ensuring anatomical rationality during identity feature transfer. This study utilizes FAN [2] as the face alignment network. Due to its foundation on an improved HourGlass architecture, FAN enables the precise detection of 68 keypoints, thereby establishing a high-accuracy basis for pose alignment through affine transformation.

The FAN architecture accepts cropped facial regions as input (resized to 256×256) and outputs 68 facial landmark coordinates in absolute image coordinates. The network employs a stacked Hourglass backbone with enhanced residual blocks, where each hourglass module performs bottom-up/top-down processing to capture multi-scale contextual features. The loss function combines heatmap regression with Normalized Mean Error (NME):

$$\text{NME} = \frac{1}{N}\sum_{k=1}^{68}\frac{\|\hat{y}_k - y_k\|_2}{d}, \quad d = \sqrt{w_{\text{bbox}} \cdot h_{\text{bbox}}} \tag{11}$$

where $\hat{y}_k$ and y_k denote predicted/ground-truth landmarks, w_{bbox} and h_{bbox}represent the face bounding box dimensions. The normalization factor d ensures scale-invariant error measurement across varying face sizes.

After processing through the FAN network, a matrix of 68 facial key points, denoted as $P_{origin} \in \mathbb{R}^{68\times 2}$, is obtained. Subsequently, an affine transformation is applied to transform the original key point matrix into a standard face template key point matrix, P_{ref}, as defined by Eq. 12:

$$P_{origin}^{\top} \cdot C^{\top} = P_{ref}^{\top}, \tag{12}$$

$$C = \begin{pmatrix} \alpha & -\beta & t_x \\ \beta & \alpha & t_y \\ 0 & 0 & 1 \end{pmatrix} \tag{13}$$

where α represents the scaling factor (controlling face size), β represents the rotation factor (controlling face angle), and t_x, t_y represent the translation factors (controlling face position). The C matrix is solved using the least squares method, with the objective function defined in Eq. 14. Finally, the obtained C matrix is used to perform affine transformation on each pixel of the original image, as shown in Eq. 15.

$$\min_{a,b,t_x,t_y} \sum_{i=1}^{68} \left\| C \begin{bmatrix} x_i \\ y_i \\ 1 \end{bmatrix} - \begin{bmatrix} x_i' \\ y_i' \\ 1 \end{bmatrix} \right\|^2 \tag{14}$$

$$\begin{bmatrix} x_{\text{new}} \\ y_{\text{new}} \\ 1 \end{bmatrix} = C \cdot \begin{bmatrix} x_{\text{orig}} \\ y_{\text{orig}} \\ 1 \end{bmatrix} \tag{15}$$

Facial Mask Generation. This study employs a U-Net architecture for image segmentation. Inspired by [5], we enhance the U-Net's segmentation accuracy by integrating a pre-trained VGG11 model: replacing the original U-Net encoder with a VGG11 network pre-trained on ImageNet. The refined network takes the affine-transformed image I_{AT} as input and outputs a binary mask I_{mask}. The final segmentation result I_u is obtained by element-wise multiplication:

$$I_u = I_{AT} \odot I_{mask} \tag{16}$$

where $\odot$ denotes element-wise multiplication. The loss function is defined as shown in Eq. 17:

$$
\begin{aligned}
L &= H - \log J \\
H &= -\frac{1}{n}\sum_{i=1}^{n}\left[y_i \log(\hat{y}_i) + (1 - y_i)\log(1 - \hat{y}_i)\right] \\
J &= \frac{1}{n}\sum_{i=1}^{n}\left(\frac{y_i\hat{y}_i}{y_i + \hat{y}_i - y_i\hat{y}_i}\right)
\end{aligned}
\tag{17}
$$

where y_i represents the ground truth label of pixel i, $\hat{y}_i$ is the predicted mask value, and n is the total number of image pixels.

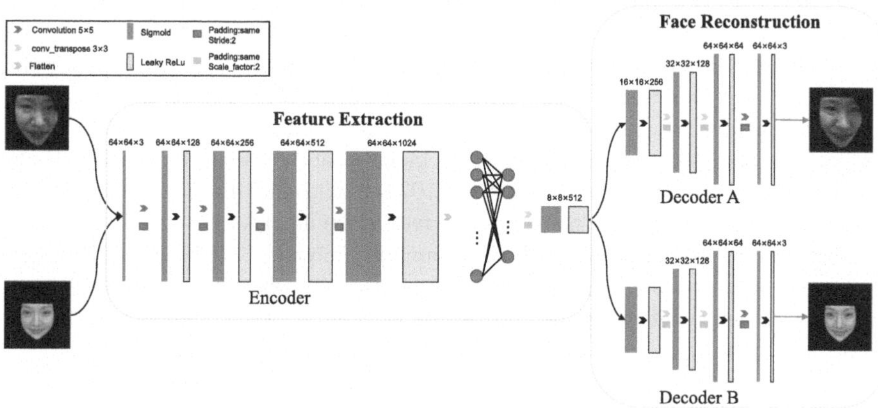

Fig. 2. Autoencoder architecture with 1 encoder and 2 decoders. The encoder extracts deep common features across faces through convolutional downsampling and filters identity-related shallow features. Two independent decoders undertake the task of feature reconstruction respectively: decoder A restores the common features to the personalized features of face A, and decoder B corresponds to the restoration of face B.

2.3 Face Generation and Replacement

Following the acquisition of two preprocessed face datasets, data augmentation is employed to enhance the model's generalization ability. Prior to inputting the data into the autoencoder, image augmentation techniques including random translations, rotations, and scaling are applied. This enhances data diversity, compelling the model to overlook superficial individual variations (e.g., shallow features like facial feature positions) and concentrate on extracting deep semantic features representing the common facial structure (e.g., fundamental architecture of the face).

During the training phase, an autoencoder architecture comprising one encoder and two decoders is utilized (see Fig. 2). The encoder employs convolutional downsampling to extract deep common features shared across different faces (e.g., the basic morphology of eyes, nose, and mouth), while filtering out identity-specific shallow features.

Two separate decoders are responsible for the feature reconstruction task: Decoder A maps the common features back to the personalized features of face A, and Decoder B performs the analogous mapping for face B. This dual-decoder design achieves the decoupling of common and personalized features, establishing a foundational feature space for the face swapping task.

The encoder, designed specifically to extract common facial features, consists of four 5×5 convolutional layers, one flatten layer, two fully connected layers, and one upsampling layer. The leaky ReLU activation function is used throughout these layers. The initial four convolutional layers perform downsampling operations, progressively extracting deeper semantic features. Innovatively, fully connected layers are employed at the bottleneck stage, a departure from traditional autoencoders that typically use convolutional layers in this position. The rationale is that while the parameter sharing mechanism of convolutional layers excels at capturing local features (e.g., eye size, lip thickness), it struggles to acquire holistic global features. In contrast, fully connected layers, possessing a larger number of parameters, can effectively fuse deep semantic features, thereby enhancing model stability. To mitigate potential difficulties in decoding overly abstract deep features, an upsampling step is included at the end of the encoder. It utilizes transposed convolution to upscale the 1024-dimensional 4×4 feature map to a 512-dimensional 8×8 feature map, which serves as the input for the decoders.

Each decoder is composed of three upsampling modules. Each module employs 3×3 transposed convolutions to perform dimensionality expansion, ultimately outputting a face image with the same dimensions as the input. The complete autoencoder architecture is illustrated in Fig. 2.

Its loss function is designed with two core objectives: reconstruction loss (reconstructing face A from input face A) and swapping loss (transforming input face A into face B). The reconstruction loss emphasizes pixel-level fidelity, whereas the swapping loss focuses on addressing the realism of the swapped output, such as unnatural boundaries or distorted facial features.

Image quality assessment (IQA) metrics can be broadly categorized into two types: low-level metrics based on pixel-wise errors, such as Mean Squared Error (MSE), Peak Signal-to-Noise Ratio (PSNR), and Mean Absolute Error (MAE), and high-level metrics that consider global information, such as the SSIM [17] and GMSD [18]. The formulas for the basic metrics are:

$$MSE = \frac{1}{N} \sum_{p \in P} \|x(p) - y(p)\|_2^2 \tag{18}$$

$$PSNR = 10 \log_{10} \left(\frac{MAX_I^2}{MSE} \right) \tag{19}$$

$$MAE = \frac{1}{N} \sum \|x(p) - y(p)\|_2 \tag{20}$$

where N is the total number of pixels, and $x(p)$ and $y(p)$ are the pixel values of the original and reconstructed images at position p, respectively. MAX_I represents the maximum possible pixel value (e.g., 255 for 8-bit grayscale images). Although these metrics quantify pixel-level differences, they do not fully capture the nuances of human visual perception and often correlate poorly with subjective quality assessments.

The SSIM metric assesses image similarity based on three components: luminance (l), contrast (c), and structure (s):

$$l(x,y) = \frac{2\mu_x\mu_y + c_1}{\mu_x^2 + \mu_y^2 + c_1} \tag{21}$$

$$c(x,y) = \frac{2\sigma_x\sigma_y + c_2}{\sigma_x^2 + \sigma_y^2 + c_2} \tag{22}$$

$$s(x,y) = \frac{\sigma_{xy} + c_3}{\sigma_x\sigma_y + c_3} \tag{23}$$

$$SSIM(x,y) = [l(x,y)]^\alpha [c(x,y)]^\beta [s(x,y)]^\gamma \tag{24}$$

where μ_x and μ_y are the pixel means of the original and reconstructed images, respectively. σ_x and σ_y are the standard deviations of the original and reconstructed images, respectively. σ_{xy} denotes the covariance between the two images. c_1, c_2, c_3 are stability constants employed to prevent the denominator from becoming zero. The exponents α, β, γ are utilized to adjust the relative importance of the three components, the specific settings are detailed in Sect. 3.2. An SSIM value approaching 1 signifies a greater similarity between the two images. Although computationally more demanding than GMSD, SSIM demonstrates greater stability across diverse datasets compared to the potential variability of GMSD.

The final loss function integrates the global perceptual advantages of SSIM with the luminance preservation characteristic of MSE:

$$L_{final}(P_{orig}, P_{gen}) = \lambda_1 \cdot MSE(P_{orig}, P_{gen}) - \lambda_2 \cdot SSIM(P_{orig}, P_{gen}) \tag{25}$$

where $\lambda_1, \lambda_2$are hyperparameters, and $P_{trans}$and P_{gen}represent the original and generated image blocks/pixel, respectively. This combination effectively balances structural integrity and color fidelity and alleviates problems such as color shift or structural distortion that may occur when relying on only a single metric. Experimental results show that the hybrid loss function significantly enhances the visual quality of the generated images while preserving the naturalness of face replacement.

After training, the model comprises an encoder and two decoders (A/B). The encoder extracts common deep semantic features, while the decoders reconstruct these features into corresponding faces (A/B). By inputting face A into the encoder to obtain deep features and then passing them through decoder B, a composite image is generated, possessing the identity features (appearance) of face B and the deep semantic features (expression and pose) of A, thereby completing face swapping. This operation replaces only the masked region within the face detection bounding box, resulting in a black background that requires fusion with the original image A.

3 Experiments

3.1 Datasets

- **RaFD Dataset** [7]**:** The Radboud Faces Database (RaFD) is a dataset containing high-quality facial images of Caucasian adults and children, systematically controlled for facial expressions. It is used for training during the StarGAN pre-training

phase, and three faces with different expressions (happy, sad, neutral) are extracted as target faces for experiments during the face swapping phase.
- **Web-Collected Dataset** [14]**:** In the face swapping phase, face images collected from the web were used (as shown in the first image of the first row in Fig. 3), and the source video (the video to be replaced) in the face swapping phase also originated from the web.

3.2 Experiment Settings

In the pre-training phase, StarGAN was trained on the RaFD dataset (containing 8 expressions, 90% training set + 10% test set, 256×256 resolution) for 200,000 epochs. The adversarial loss λ_{adv} was set to 1, while the domain classification loss λ_{cls} and reconstruction loss λ_{rec} were set to 10. The Adam optimizer was employed for optimization. During the training of the autoencoder, an encoder with 4 convolutional layers (5×5 kernel, channel count progressively increased from 64 to 512) was used, followed by a 1024-dimensional fully connected layer and transposed convolutional layers to upsample the features to $8 \times 8 \times 512$. The decoder consisted of two independent branches, each containing 3 transposed convolutional layers with 3×3 kernels (channel count progressively decreased from 512 to 64) and residual blocks. The final output matched the input dimensions. L1 reconstruction loss ($\lambda_1 = 10$) was used to constrain pixel-level errors, combined with SSIM structural similarity loss ($\lambda_2 = 5$) to maintain global structural consistency. The Adam optimizer was used for training over 200 epochs. The hyperparameters for the Structural Similarity Index (SSIM) are specifically set as $\alpha = \beta = \gamma = 1$, $c_1 = 0.01^2$, and $c_2 = 0.03^2$.

3.3 Replacement Result

As shown in Fig. 3, the first column displays the keyframe sequence of the original video, and the second column shows the face swapping results of the source video after training with different expression data generated by the StarGAN method. Observations indicate: (1) When the camera shake is minimal and the facial angle is moderate, the system can effectively preserve the identity features of the source image, and the output results have high clarity; (2) When the video frames experience severe shaking or extreme facial angles, issues such as edge distortion, detail blurring, and local replacement failure occur; (3) In the RaFD cross-dataset test (last three columns), the method demonstrates good generalization ability across different genders and individuals, achieving the expected balance between maintaining the expression features of the target video and the identity information of the source. However, handling scenes with violent motion and extreme angles remains a technical bottleneck.

3.4 Ablation Study

We initially compare our approach (face swapping after generating diverse expression images using StarGAN) against a method that directly replicates a single image 1,000 times before performing face swapping. As depicted in Fig. 4, regardless of the angle or

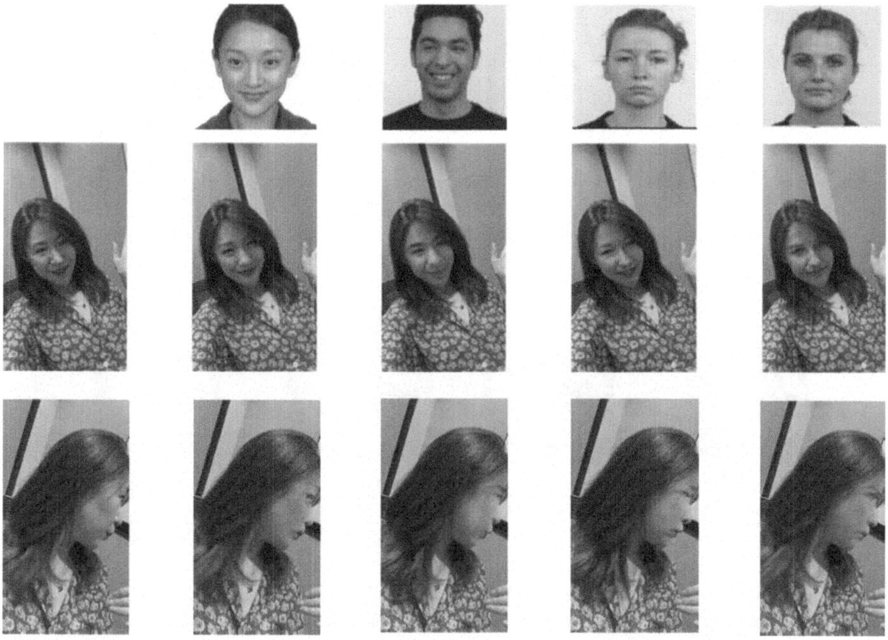

Fig. 3. Experimental Results. The first column displays source images extracted from the source video. The first image in the second column is the target face (sourced from the internet), while the subsequent two images are the replacement results. Columns three to five follow a similar format, with target faces sourced from the RaFD dataset.

expression, our method more effectively preserves the identity information of image B (i.e., it resembles face B more closely) and the expression information of image A, while also achieving higher resolution (i.e., greater clarity). Specifically, the varied expression images generated by StarGAN, when subjected to face swapping, not only maintain the original person's identity features remarkably well but also seamlessly integrate new expression information, resulting in synthesized images that appear more realistic and natural. In contrast, although the method of directly replicating images and then performing face swapping can produce face-swapped results, it is noticeably inferior to our method in terms of expression naturalness and image clarity. Furthermore, our method exhibits enhanced robustness and adaptability when handling different angles and expressions, enabling the generation of high-quality face-swapped images across a wide range of scenarios.

3.5 Comparative Analysis

This study further presents a comparative analysis between the proposed method and GANimation, a generative face replacement approach based on Action Unit (AU)-conditioned GANs. **GANimation** performs anatomically guided expression synthesis from a single image by continuously parameterizing AU activations. Its framework

Fig. 4. The source video face image is compared with the replaced face image, the first one is the source video face image, and the second one is the replaced face image

Fig. 5. Comparison of the proposed method and GANimation in face replacement effect.

adopts an unsupervised learning strategy incorporating attention mechanisms that focus the generator on key facial regions, using color transformation and spatial attention masks to achieve localized expression editing while preserving background and illumination consistency. The discriminator constrains anatomical plausibility through an AU regression branch, and together with Wasserstein GAN-GP adversarial training, cycle-consistency loss, and attention smoothness regularization, the method enables fine-grained and continuously controllable expression manipulation. However, results show that GANimation often produces severe visual artifacts such as tearing and stretching, particularly when the subject exhibits large movements in the original video. As illustrated in Fig. 5, these distortions degrade expression fidelity and fine details, whereas the proposed method effectively preserves subtle facial features and integrates target expressions more naturally. It also demonstrates stronger robustness and adaptability across diverse poses and expressions, achieving more stable results.

To further evaluate performance differences, a Mean Opinion Score (MOS) test was conducted comparing the proposed method with GANimation in terms of video quality and face replacement accuracy. Ten participants—four computer vision practitioners and six related-field students—rated each method on a 0–5 scale (details in

Table 1. Comparison of the Mean Opinion Score (MOS) between the proposed method and GANimation on the face replacement task. The scoring is performed from two dimensions: video quality (clarity, coherence) and face replacement accuracy (whether the expression pose is like the source face A, and whether the identity information is like the target face B), and the scoring standard is 0–5.

Rater	Our method		GANimation	
	Video quality	Face swapping accuracy	Video quality	Face swapping accuracy
Rater 1	4	4	1	1
Rater 2	4	3	1	1
Rater 3	4	4	1	2
Rater 4	3	2	1	1
Rater 5	4	4	2	1
Rater 6	4	3	1	1
Rater 7	3	3	1	1
Rater 8	4	3	1	1
Rater 9	4	4	2	2
Rater 10	3	3	1	1
Average Score	3.7	3.3	1.2	1.2

the Appendix). As summarized in Table 1, the proposed method achieved an average MOS of 3.7 for video quality and 3.3 for replacement accuracy, significantly surpassing GANimation's respective scores of 1.2 in both aspects. These findings confirm that the proposed approach not only maintains greater visual clarity and temporal coherence but also preserves identity fidelity while synthesizing accurate expressions and poses, thereby producing substantially higher-quality face replacement results.

4 Conclusion

In summary, this work introduces a novel single-image-to-video face-swapping framework that integrates expression generation with face synthesis to overcome the data scarcity of single-image inputs. By employing StarGAN to expand a single image into diverse expression samples, the framework transforms face swapping into a tractable multi-image task. Leveraging MTCNN and FAN for precise alignment and a VGG-enhanced U-Net for high-quality mask generation, the model effectively encodes, reorganizes, and transfers facial features through a shared-encoder, multi-decoder design. Experimental results show that our method achieves superior identity preservation and visual fidelity compared to existing GAN-based approaches, demonstrating significant progress in single-image video face swapping.

Acknowledgement. This work is supported by Stable Support Project of Shenzhen (2023 1120161634002), Shenzhen Science and Technology Program (JCYJ20240813141417023), Natural Science Foundation of Guangdong Province of China (2025A1515010233), Guangdong Provincial Department of Education (2024KTSCX060), Open Project of State Key Lab. for Novel Software Technology of Nanjing University (KFKT2025B22), Tencent "Rhinoceros Birds" - Scientific Research Foundation for Young Teachers of Shenzhen University, the Intelligent Computing Center of Shenzhen University.

References

1. Bitouk, D., Kumar, N., Dhillon, S., Belhumeur, P., Nayar, S.K.: Face swapping: automatically replacing faces in photographs. In: ACM SIGGRAPH 2008 Papers. SIGGRAPH 2008. Association for Computing Machinery, New York, NY, USA (2008). https://doi.org/10.1145/1399504.1360638
2. Bulat, A., Tzimiropoulos, G.: How far are we from solving the 2D & 3D face alignment problem? (and a dataset of 230,000 3D facial landmarks). In: Proceedings of the IEEE International Conference on Computer Vision (ICCV) (2017)
3. Choi, Y., Choi, M., Kim, M., Ha, J.W., Kim, S., Choo, J.: Stargan: unified generative adversarial networks for multi-domain image-to-image translation. In: Proceedings of the IEEE Conference on Computer Vision and Pattern Recognition (CVPR) (2018)
4. Choi, Y., Uh, Y., Yoo, J., Ha, J.W.: Stargan v2: diverse image synthesis for multiple domains. In: Proceedings of the IEEE/CVF Conference on Computer Vision and Pattern Recognition (CVPR) (2020)
5. Iglovikov, V., Shvets, A.: Ternausnet: U-net with vgg11 encoder pre-trained on imagenet for image segmentation. arXiv preprint arXiv:1801.05746 (2018)
6. Korshunova, I., Shi, W., Dambre, J., Theis, L.: Fast face-swap using convolutional neural networks. In: Proceedings of the IEEE International Conference on Computer Vision, pp. 3677–3685 (2017)
7. Langner, O., Dotsch, R., Bijlstra, G., Wigboldus, D.H., Hawk, S.T., Van Knippenberg, A.: Presentation and validation of the radboud faces database. Cogn. Emot. **24**(8), 1377–1388 (2010)
8. Li, J., et al.: DSFD: dual shot face detector. In: Proceedings of the IEEE/CVF Conference on Computer Vision and Pattern Recognition, pp. 5060–5069 (2019)
9. Li, Y., Lyu, X., Gu, Y., Zhang, M., Li, J.: Face detection algorithm based on improved S3FD network. Laser Technol. **45**(6), 722–728 (2021)

10. Melnik, A., et al.: Face generation and editing with stylegan: a survey. IEEE Trans. Pattern Anal. Mach. Intell. **46**(5), 3557–3576 (2024). https://doi.org/10.1109/TPAMI.2024.3350004
11. Min, F., Sang, N., Wang, Z.: Automatic face replacement in video based on 2D morphable model. In: 2010 20th International Conference on Pattern Recognition, pp. 2250–2253 (2010). https://doi.org/10.1109/ICPR.2010.551
12. Murphy, G., Ching, D., Twomey, J., Linehan, C.: Face/off: changing the face of movies with deepfakes. PLoS ONE **18**(7), e0287503 (2023)
13. Natsume, R., Yatagawa, T., Morishima, S.: Rsgan: face swapping and editing using face and hair representation in latent spaces. arXiv preprint arXiv:1804.03447 (2018)
14. News, E.: 10 female celebrities who still look stunning in id photos (2019). https://k.sina.cn/article_6426370535_17f57286700100q1k9.html. Accessed 20 Aug 2023
15. Ronneberger, O., Fischer, P., Brox, T.: U-Net: convolutional networks for biomedical image segmentation. In: Navab, N., Hornegger, J., Wells, W.M., Frangi, A.F. (eds.) MICCAI 2015. LNCS, vol. 9351, pp. 234–241. Springer, Cham (2015). https://doi.org/10.1007/978-3-319-24574-4_28
16. Walczyna, T., Piotrowski, Z.: Fast fake: easy-to-train face swap model. Appl. Sci. **14**(5), 2149 (2024)
17. Wang, Z., Bovik, A.C., Sheikh, H.R., Simoncelli, E.P.: Image quality assessment: from error visibility to structural similarity. IEEE Trans. Image Process. **13**(4), 600–612 (2004)
18. Xue, W., Zhang, L., Mou, X., Bovik, A.C.: Gradient magnitude similarity deviation: a highly efficient perceptual image quality index. IEEE Trans. Image Process. **23**(2), 684–695 (2013)
19. Yang, Y., Huang, Y., Shi, M., Chen, K., Zhang, W.: Invertible mask network for face privacy preservation. Inf. Sci. **629**, 566–579 (2023)
20. Zhang, K., Zhang, Z., Li, Z., Qiao, Y.: Joint face detection and alignment using multitask cascaded convolutional networks. IEEE Signal Process. Lett. **23**(10), 1499–1503 (2016). https://doi.org/10.1109/LSP.2016.2603342

Trajectory Similarity Detection Based on Graph Contrastive Learning

Zhiqiang Li[1,2], Jing Gao[1,2], and Guiling Wang[1,2(✉)]

[1] School of Artificial Intelligence and Computer Science, North China University of Technology, Beijing, China
lizhiqiang@mail.ncut.edu.cn, {gaojing,wangguiling}@ncut.edu.cn
[2] Beijing Key Laboratory on Integration and Analysis of Large-Scale Stream Data, Beijing, China

Abstract. The discovery of similar trajectories aims to efficiently and accurately identify trajectories that are spatially similar to a given one within massive trajectory datasets. Traditional similarity measures such as DTW, Hausdorff distance, and EDR directly compare raw trajectory points without leveraging intrinsic data features and suffer from high computational costs, making them unsuitable for large-scale datasets. To address these issues, this paper proposes a contrastive learning framework based on a dual graph attention mechanism that learns trajectory representations in a latent space for efficient similarity computation. Two trajectory augmentation strategies are designed to construct positive samples. Trajectories are then mapped onto a regular grid to build a global grid graph, and both global and local Graph Attention Networks (GATs) are used to extract spatial features. Finally, a Transformer module is employed to further model the contextual relationships of the trajectories and obtain the final trajectory representations. Based on the learned trajectory representations, similar trajectory queries can be efficiently performed.

Keywords: Similar trajectories · Trajectory similarity computation · Graph attention network · Contrastive learning

1 Introduction

With the widespread adoption of GPS-enabled devices and the rapid development of location-based services, a massive amount of trajectory data is being continuously collected, encompassing vehicle routes, pedestrian movements, and animal migration paths. Leveraging this large-scale trajectory data, researchers have conducted extensive studies in areas such as traffic planning, flow analysis, and similar trajectory discovery. The objective of similar trajectory discovery is to identify trajectories from large datasets that resemble a target trajectory in terms of spatial shape, movement patterns, or semantics. This task holds significant value in applications such as intelligent traffic scheduling, route recommendation, and abnormal behavior detection.

Similar trajectory discovery methods are typically categorized into index-based, heuristic-based, and learning-based approaches. Index-based methods rely on building

© The Author(s), under exclusive license to Springer Nature Singapore Pte Ltd. 2027
H. Sun et al. (Eds.): ChineseCSCW 2025, CCIS 2911, pp. 246–260, 2027.
https://doi.org/10.1007/978-981-92-0288-1_18

spatial index structures for trajectory databases, such as R-trees, R*-trees, and Quadtrees. Heuristic-based methods employ traditional distance measures such as Hausdorff distance [1], dynamic time warping (DTW) [3], Fréchet distance [4], and edit distance with real penalty (ERP) [5]. These approaches generally depend on point-to-point matching between trajectories, requiring the comparison of all points from both trajectories to compute similarity. Consequently, traditional similarity computation methods incur high time costs and are unsuitable for large-scale datasets.

To overcome these limitations, recent research has increasingly adopted neural network-based approaches to learn trajectory representations. These methods encode trajectory data into low-dimensional vector embeddings and measure similarity via vector distance metrics. Such approaches not only improve computational efficiency but also enhance the capacity to capture latent trajectory features.

While existing learning-based studies [6–8] have significantly reduced the computational cost of similarity computation, fail to capture the interaction between global spatial structures and individual trajectory behaviors, often neglecting the interaction between global regional characteristics and individual trajectory features. In practice, trajectories are shaped not only by individual behavioral patterns but also by the spatial distribution and characteristics of the regions they traverse. Factors such as road structure, functional zoning, and traffic density can substantially influence movement patterns. Modeling trajectories solely from temporal or spatial perspectives fails to capture these coupled effects comprehensively.

To address this gap, we propose a global–local trajectory modeling framework that simultaneously captures shared regional structural features and trajectory-specific variations. For global regional features, we partition the geographical space into regular grids and map GPS trajectory points to their corresponding grid cells. By counting the number of connections (edges) between grids, we construct a global grid flow graph and design a global graph attention network (GAT) encoder to learn shared spatial patterns. Prior research [12–14] has validated the effectiveness of transforming GPS trajectories into grid sequences as model input. This grid-based representation reduces the impact of GPS noise while preserving rich location information. However, the same grid cell may carry different significance for different trajectories. To account for this, we construct local trajectory graphs for individual trajectories and employ a local GAT to capture trajectory-specific features. Our main contributions are as follows:

(1) We propose two trajectory augmentation algorithms to construct similar trajectories from different perspectives for training.
(2) We design a dual-level trajectory graph using a global weighted GAT and a local GAT to learn trajectory embeddings, which not only capture hidden features of the entire grid region but also provide personalized trajectory representations.

2 Related Work

2.1 Similarity Measurement Methods for Trajectories

Trajectory similarity measurement methods can be broadly categorized into heuristic-based and learning-based approaches.Heuristic methods typically involve point-to-point comparisons between trajectories, which are computationally expensive. For example,

Dynamic Time Warping (DTW) [3] seeks an optimal alignment path between two trajectories such that the cumulative distance (typically Euclidean) along this path is minimized, thus quantifying their similarity. The Hausdorff distance [10] is a max-min distance measure between two sets, where each trajectory is treated as a set of points, and the distance measures how far the points of one trajectory are from the other. The Fréchet distance [11] is similar to the Hausdorff distance but treats trajectories as ordered curves during computation.

Learning-based methods typically use neural networks to encode input trajectories and learn an embedding space that approximates specific distance metrics. In this way, trajectories are mapped into low-dimensional representations, enabling efficient similarity computation.Li et al. proposed t2vec [12], which employs an RNN-based encoder-decoder model to minimize the spatial distance perception loss between the original and reconstructed trajectories. This method accounts for the effects of noise and low sampling rates, addressing the high computational cost of traditional methods.T3S [13] introduces spatial and structural features for trajectory similarity and adaptively learns the weights of these features to approximate various heuristic measures.

2.2 Trajectory Contrastive Learning

Trajectory contrastive learning is a self-supervised learning technique. Its core idea is to learn a discriminative representation space by pulling together similar samples and pushing apart dissimilar ones. In recent years, with the widespread availability of trajectory data and the increasing cost of manual annotation, contrastive learning has been increasingly applied to trajectory similarity modeling. These methods automatically generate positive sample pairs through algorithms, enabling effective trajectory representation learning without the need for extensive manual labeling.Tong et al. proposed STT-CL [13], which extracts rich multi-scale features from trajectories using spatiotemporal grids and incorporates temporal information into the learning of similar trajectories.Chang et al. introduced TrajCL [15], a model that captures trajectory features from both spatial and structural perspectives. They designed a dual-feature fusion encoder to generate the final trajectory representation.

3 Preliminaries

3.1 Definitions

Definition 1 (GPS Trajectory): A GPS trajectory is typically represented as a sequence of sampled points obtained through discrete sampling by a positioning device, denoted as $T^{gps} = \{p_1, p_2, \ldots, p_n\}$ $\mathrm{T}^{\mathrm{gps}} = \{\mathrm{p}_1, \mathrm{p}_2, \ldots, \mathrm{p}_\mathrm{n}\}$ $\mathrm{T}^{\mathrm{gps}} = \{\mathrm{p}_1, \mathrm{p}_2, \ldots, \mathrm{p}_\mathrm{n}\}$ where each sampled point $p_i = (x_i, y_i, t_i)$. Here, x_i and y_i represent the longitude and latitude of the point, respectively, and t_i denotes the timestamp, indicating the location of the moving object at time t_i.

Definition 2 (Grid Trajectory): The region covered by a trajectory is divided into regular grids, and each grid is assigned a unique ID. A grid trajectory is formed by mapping each point in the GPS trajectory to its corresponding grid based on location information, replacing the point's coordinates with the grid ID. It is denoted as $T^g = (\tau_1, \tau_2, \ldots, \tau_n)$, where $\tau_i = \{g_i, t_i\}$, g_i represents the grid ID, and t_i is the timestamp of the point. If multiple consecutive points in a trajectory are mapped to the same grid ID, only one representative point is retained.

Definition 3 (Trajectory Length): The length of a GPS trajectory refers to the number of points in T^{gps}.The length of a grid trajectory refers to the number of points in the grid trajectory T^g.

Definition 4 (Global Grid Flow Graph): Given a set of historical vehicle trajectories S, for $\forall T^{gps} \in S$, we convert T^{gps} to a grid trajectory T^g. By aggregating the grid IDs g_i from each T^g, we construct a global grid flow graph $G_w = (N_{G_w}, E_{G_w}, \mathrm{w})$, where:

- N_{G_w} is the set of nodes, representing all grids involved in the grid trajectories;
- E_{G_w} is the set of edges, where an edge is formed between two adjacent grids;
- w is the weight of the edge, where the weight $w_{i,j}$ of edge $e_{i,j}$ corresponds to the number of times this edge appears across all grid trajectories.

3.2 Problem Statement

Similar trajectory discovery aims to learn a trajectory encoder $\mathcal{F}\mathrm{T} \rightarrow \mathrm{h} \in R^d$, which maps a trajectory to a low-dimensional vector representation. In the embedding space, similar trajectories are mapped to vectors that are close to each other, while dissimilar ones are mapped farther apart. This enables efficient retrieval of the most similar trajectories from a large-scale trajectory database for a given query trajectory.

4 The Model

The structure of the proposed dual graph attention-based contrastive learning model for trajectory similarity is shown in Fig. 1.

Our model design, as illustrated in Fig. 1, follows the dual-branch structure of the MoCo [15] contrastive learning framework. Given a trajectory dataset S, we divide the underlying space using a regular grid and map GPS trajectory points to their corresponding grid cells. Each trajectory point is then replaced by the ID of its grid cell, converting the original GPS point sequence into a sequence of grid IDs. By counting the number of connections between adjacent grids, we construct the global grid flow graph G_w For each training trajectory T, it is first passed through the trajectory augmentation module, which implements two trajectory augmentation algorithms to generate a similar trajectory T'. We consider (T,T') as a similar trajectory pair, serving as a positive sample pair for training.In the local trajectory graph construction module, we extract key features from each trajectory point in both T and T', and construct local trajectory graphs to capture individual trajectory characteristics.In the global-local feature extraction module, we design a global GAT and a local GAT to capture trajectory features from two perspectives. The extracted global and local features are then concatenated with positional encodings and fed into a Transformer encoder to obtain the final trajectory representation vectors z and z'.We train our model using the InfoNCE loss function: $\mathcal{L} = -\log \frac{\exp(\frac{sim(z,z')}{\tau})}{\sum_{k=1}^{|Qneg|} \exp(\frac{sim(z,z_k^-)}{\tau})}$ which encourages similar trajectories to be closer in the embedding space while pushing dissimilar trajectories farther apart. Here, τ is the temperature coefficient, and z_k^- denotes negative samples stored in a fixed-size queue maintained by the MoCo framework, representing samples from previous training steps.

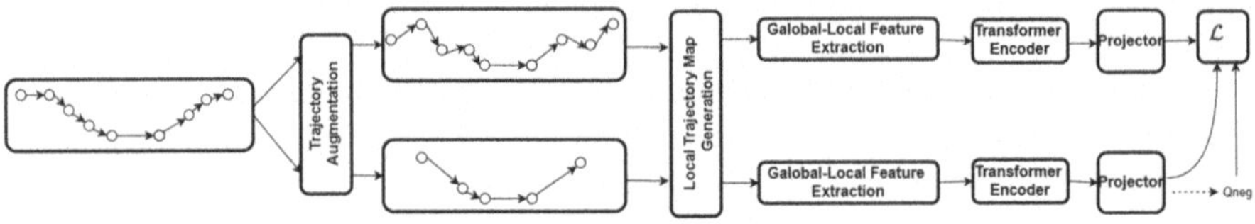

Fig. 1. A contrastive learning framework based on dual graph attention mechanisms.

4.1 Trajectory Augmentation Method

The trajectory augmentation module generates trajectory variants from the input trajectories, which serve as positive samples for the original trajectories. The generated variants should retain some characteristics of the original trajectories while also introducing differences. This enables the encoder to learn to capture both the common and distinguishing features from the variants. We have designed two similar-trajectory generation algorithms.

(1) Partial Trajectory Point Offset: To simulate trajectories that are slightly different in spatial position but similar in overall path, we design the partial trajectory point offset method, which generates similar trajectories by applying a random offset to some points in the trajectory. Given a trajectory T, the algorithm produces a similar trajectory $\tilde{T}$ through partial trajectory point offset.

$$\tilde{\mathrm{T}} = \left[p'_1, p', \ldots, p'_n\right], \forall p_i = (x_i, y_i) \in \mathrm{T}$$

$$p'_i = (x_i + \Delta x_i, y_i + \Delta y_i), \Delta x_i \sim X_n, \Delta y_i \sim X_n$$

Here, Δx_i and Δy_i are random offsets sampled from a bounded Gaussian distribution.

(2) Random Trajectory Point Deletion: Randomly remove some points from the trajectory to simulate scenarios of missing data or different sampling rates. To better preserve the structure of the original trajectory, we avoid deleting n (n = 5) consecutive points. Given a trajectory T, the random trajectory point deletion algorithm generates the trajectory $\tilde{T}$ as follows: $\tilde{T} = [p'_i, p'_{i+1}, \ldots, p'_{n-n\rho}]$. ρ is the probability of random removal.

4.2 Local Trajectory Graph Construction

For the trajectories T and T' generated by the trajectory augmentation algorithms, we construct them as graph structures to capture the local spatial structural features between trajectory points. Since trajectory data is inherently sequential, we connect adjacent points in their temporal order; that is, for each pair of adjacent points (p_i, p_{i+1}), we create an edge. For each node, we construct the feature vector $g_i = [x_i, y_i, d_i, r_i]$, where $x_i andy_i$ are the coordinates obtained by converting the point's longitude and latitude into Mercator projection coordinates, d_i? denotes the average distance between the current point and its two neighboring points,$d_i = 0.5 * (|\overline{p_{i-1}, p_i}| + |\overline{p_i, p_{i+1}}|)$,and r_i is the angle between the two trajectory segments adjacent to p_i, $r_i = \angle p_{i-1}p_ip_{i+1}$. Finally, we transform trajectory T into the local graph structure G^{loc} =(V, E, X), where V is the set of all nodes in the graph, Eis the set of all edges, and X represents the features of the trajectory points.

4.3 Global-Local Feature Extraction

The design of the global–local feature extraction module is shown in Fig. 2.We design a global weighted GAT and a local GAT to capture trajectory features. The underlying space is divided into regular grids, and GPS points are mapped to the grid cells in which they are located, with each trajectory point represented by the ID of its enclosing grid cell. Compared with GPS trajectories, grid trajectories preserve location information while capturing richer shape information. We construct a global grid flow graph from the grid trajectories to learn global-level grid embeddings.

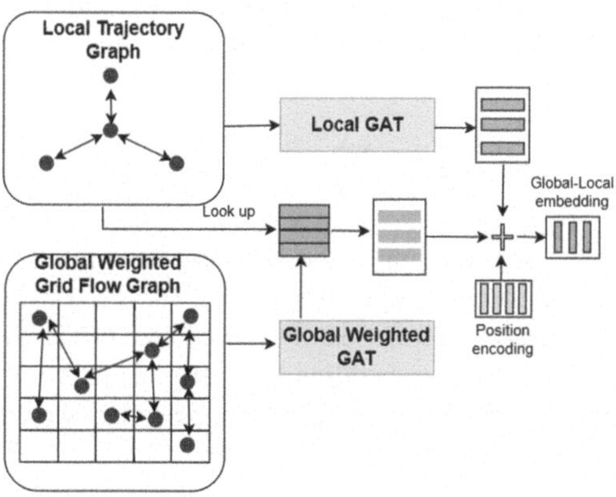

Fig. 2. Global-Local Feature Extraction Module Structural Diagram.

Given the global grid flow graph G_w, we design a global GAT model to learn the global representation of each grid, enabling more effective capture of the spatial dependencies between regional grids. Specifically, when computing the attention scores, we take into account both the positional features of the current grid and its connected grids, as well as the occurrence frequency weights. The attention computation is formulated as follows:

$$\alpha_{nn'}^{Global} = \frac{\exp(\text{LeakyReLu}(a_{nn'}^T(\beta_{nn'}))}{\sum_{n'' \in N_n^{Global}} \exp(LeakyReLu(a_{nn''}^T(\beta_{nn''}))} \tag{1}$$

Here, $\alpha_{nn'}^{Global} \in$ R denotes the attention weight of the neighboring grid n' with respect to the current grid n, and $a^T \in R^d$ is a trainable parameter matrix.

$$\beta_{nn'} = [v_n; v_{n'}; w]W_s \tag{2}$$

Here, $\beta_{nn'} \in$ R is the importance score, and $v_n, v_n' \in R^M$ are the coordinate values of grids n and n'. W $\in$ R denotes the number of occurrences of the edge $e_{nn'}$ formed between grids n and n', and $W_s \in R^{(2M+1)\times 1}$. Based on the above formula, we incorporate the frequency weight into the calculation of the importance score, which can affect the importance value in the following way: vehicles tend to choose more convenient and smoother routes; for example, roads in areas such as supermarkets or hospitals may be congested, and vehicles usually avoid passing through these areas. As a result, the transition frequency weights between different regions in trajectories may lead to different importance scores. Finally, by computing the weighted sum of the domain-intersection features and the attention weights, we obtain the embedding representation of grid n.

$$h_n = \sum\nolimits_{n' \in N_n^{Global}} \alpha_{nn'} v_{n'} \tag{3}$$

$v_{n'} \epsilon R^M$ is the embedding representation of grid n', and $h_n \in R^M$. To improve the generalization capability of the attention mechanism, we adopt multi-head attention, which means using H independent single-head attention layers in the GAT and then concatenating their results:

$$h_n^H = \Big\|_{j=1}^H (\sum\nolimits_{n' \in N_n^{Global}} \alpha_{nn''}^j, v_{n'}^j \tag{4}$$

$h_n^H \epsilon R^{M\times H}$ represents the aggregation of the H single-head attention layers. The final global grid embedding for grid nnn is given by: $emb_n^{Global} = \sigma(h_n^H)$, where $emb_n^{Global} \in R^{M\times L}$ and σ denotes the activation function of the weighted GAT's single-head attention layer. Thus, we obtain the global embeddings for all grids as $X^g \in R^d$, which we use as the grid embedding table. By looking up X^g via grid IDs, we convert grid IDs into embeddings. Therefore, the grid trajectory $T^g = (\tau_1^g, \tau_2^g, \ldots, \tau_{|T^g|}^g)$ can be transformed into a grid embedding sequence $E^g = \left(e_1^g, e_2^g, \ldots, e_{|T^g|}^g\right)$.

Although grid embeddings contain rich regional information, the same grid embedding carries identical information across different trajectories. However, the same grid ID can have different semantics depending on the trajectory. To address this issue, we design a local GAT to capture individual trajectory features. For each trajectory T^{gps}, we construct it as a graph structure. Since trajectory points have an inherent sequential order, we create an edge between every pair of adjacent trajectory points. For each node, we build the feature vector $g_i = [x_i, y_i, d_i, r_i]$, where x_i, y_i are the Mercator projection coordinates converted from the point's longitude and latitude, d_i represents the average distance between the current point and its two neighbors, and r_i? is the angle between the two trajectory segments adjacent to p_i, Since neighbors in the local trajectory graph have varying importance, we leverage an attention mechanism to learn the weights between different nodes.

$$
\begin{aligned}
r_i &= \angle p_{i-1} p_i p_{i+1} \\
d_i &= 0.5 * (|\overline{p_{i-1}, p_i}| + |\overline{p_i, p_{i+1}}|) \\
\alpha_{ij} &= \frac{\exp(\text{LeakyReLu}(a^T (Wg_i || Wg_j))}{\sum_{k \in \mathcal{N}(i)} \exp(LeakyReLu(a^T (Wg_i || Wg_k))}
\end{aligned} \tag{5}
$$

where $\alpha_{ij} \in$ R represents the attention score of the neighboring node jj with respect to the current node i, and $a^T \in R^d$ is a trainable parameter matrix. The final node representation of the local trajectory is given by:

$$
emb_n^{local} = \left(\sum\nolimits_{\mathrm{j} \in \mathcal{N}(\mathrm{i})} \alpha_{ij} W g_j \right) \tag{6}
$$

Here, $emb_n^{local} \in R^M$. We combine the global and local embeddings of the trajectory and add positional encoding as follows:

$$
s_i = \text{emb}_n^{Global} + \text{emb}_n^{Local} + p_i^g, s_i \in R^M \tag{7}
$$

where $s_i \in R^M$, and p_i^g is the positional encoding of the global grid embedding. The dimension of the spatial grid embedding is d_p, The positional encoding formula is as follows.

$$
e_{i,j} = \begin{cases} \sin\left((i/10000^{j/d_p}\right), j \text{ is even} \\ \cos\left(i/10000^{j/d_p}\right), j \text{ is odd} \end{cases} \tag{8}
$$

4.4 Transformer Encoder

The Transformer is a sequence modeling architecture based on self-attention mechanisms, capable of efficiently capturing dependencies between any positions in a sequence. It offers strong global modeling capabilities and structural scalability, making it especially suitable for handling long sequences and complex structures. In trajectory modeling, it can simultaneously preserve temporal features and spatial structural information, and is widely used in representation learning and contrastive learning tasks. We use the Transformer to model the relationships between trajectory points and generate a global representation vector z $\in R^M$ for the entire trajectory through weighted average pooling.

$$
\text{S} = \text{TransformerEncoder}([s_1, s_2, \ldots, s_l]) \tag{9}
$$

$$
\text{z} = \frac{1}{l} \sum\nolimits_{i=1}^{L} m_i.S \tag{10}
$$

5 Experiments

5.1 Experimental Data

Our experiments utilized the following two datasets:

Porto: The Porto dataset contains over 1.7 million vehicle trajectory records, collected from 442 taxis in Porto, Portugal.

Beijing Taxi Dataset: The Beijing dataset comes from the T-Driver project and includes one week of travel trajectories from 10,375 taxis in Beijing, China, spanning from February 2 to February 8, 2008.

Table 1. Statistics of the experiment datasets.

Dataset	Trajectories	Mean Length(km)
Porto	1,615,421	7.12
Beijing	846,922	5.26

5.2 Baseline Methods

To evaluate our model, we compare it with the following four state-of-the-art methods:

t2vec: An unsupervised representation learning method that models trajectory temporal information using a bidirectional RNN and employs triplet loss to ensure similar trajectories have closer representations while dissimilar ones are farther apart.

TrjSR: A deep learning approach for the "similar trajectory search" task, which embeds trajectories using convolutional neural networks (CNN). It constructs local trajectory segment contrastive learning and uses an offset-based data augmentation strategy to generate negative samples, enabling fine-grained semantic modeling of trajectories.

SRN: A time series similarity calculation model based on recurrent neural networks.

STT-CL: A framework that leverages contrastive learning to evaluate spatiotemporal trajectory similarity, extracting rich features at multiple scales using spatiotemporal grids.

5.3 Experiment Settings

Based on previous studies [13–15], we conduct experiments evaluating the methods from two perspectives: self-similarity and k-nearest neighbor search tasks.

(1) Top-k Similarity Search:First, we use the Top-k Hit Rate (HR@k), which measures the percentage overlap between the top-k retrieved results and the ground truth. The second metric is Recall@50 for the top 10 ground truth trajectories (R10@50), which counts how many of the top 10 ground truth trajectories are found within the top 50 retrieved trajectories for a query. For HR@k, given a query set Q, for each trajectory.

T_q in Q, we retrieve the top-k most similar trajectories from the database D. If the top-k retrieved results contain k' true similar trajectories, then

$$\text{HR@K} = k'/\text{k} \tag{11}$$

For R10@50, for each trajectory in Q,we retrieve the top 50 most similar trajectories. If among these top 50 results there are k' trajectories from the top-10 ground truth set, then

$$R10@50 = k'/10 \tag{12}$$

We conducted related experiments using four common trajectory distance measures: Hausdorff distance, DTW (Dynamic Time Warping) distance, Fréchet distance, and EDR (Edit Distance on Real sequence).The experimental results are shown in Table 1 and Table 2.In this section, we compare our model with four other state-of-the-art learning models on the top-k similar trajectory search task using DTW, Hausdorff, Fréchet, and EDR distances. The results are shown in Tables 1 and 2. Across all four distance measures, we highlight the best-performing models, and our model outperforms the others on nearly all evaluation metrics.Specifically, in the R10@50 task, our model achieves the best performance under all four distances, with a notable improvement of nearly 10% in hit rate over t2vec under the DTW distance. By leveraging graph neural networks, our model effectively captures the structural information of individual trajectories, leading to high-quality trajectory representations.The performance results in Table 2 and Table 3 demonstrate the effectiveness of our proposed model.

Table 2. Similarity comparison on the Porto dataset using DTW, Hausdorff, Fréchet, and EDR distances

Porto								
Model	DTW				Hausdorff			
	HR@5	HR@10	HR@50	R10@50	HR@5	HR@10	HR@50	R10@50
t2vec	0.068	0.106	0.125	0.254	0.055	0.072	0.116	0.173
TrjSR	0.138	0.194	0.217	0.382	0.136	0.148	0.281	0.334
SRN	0.173	0.261	0.391	0.411	0.217	0.472	0.593	0.776
STT-CL	0.162	0.315	0.395	0.571	0.218	0.351	0.437	0.627
ours	0.197	0.377	0.409	0.581	0.227	0.559	0.792	0.814
	Fréchet				EDR			
t2vec	0.104	0.562	0.611	0.695	0.047	0.047	0.071	0.120
TrjSR	0.271	0.338	0.474	0.572	0.061	0.082	0.157	0.232
SRN	0.113	0.361	0.491	0.679	0.271	0.412	0.506	0.742
STT-CL	0.284	0.437	0.537	0.616	0.114	0.271	0.472	0.622
ours	0.292	0.566	0.631	0.731	0.210	0.329	0.617	0.735

Table 3. Similarity comparison on the Beijing dataset using DTW, Hausdorff, Fréchet, and EDR

Beijing								
Model	DTW				Hausdorff			
	HR@5	HR@10	HR@50	R10@50	HR@5	HR@10	HR@50	R10@50
t2vec	0.117	0.139	0.275	0.314	0.097	0.114	0.208	0.286
TrjSR	0.109	0.227	0.429	0.504	0.271	0.412	0.544	0.651
SRN	0.183	0.207	0.441	0.307	0.259	0.371	0.409	0.522
STT-CL	0.027	0.114	0.236	0.277	0.197	0.206	0.374	0.492
ours	0.277	0.397	0.402	0.517	0.202	0.355	0.573	0.673
	Fréchet				EDR			
t2vec	0.169	0.202	0.411	0.417	0.076	0.119	0.274	0.399
TrjSR	0.204	0.231	0.483	0.515	0.039	0.174	0.409	0.517
SRN	0.137	0.219	0.433	0.519	0.103	0.197	0.317	0.429
STT-CL	0.114	0.193	0.361	0.429	0.081	0.127	0.481	0.509
ours	0.192	0.497	0.681	0.637	0.112	0.261	0.449	0.519

(2) Self-Similarity:

We randomly sample some trajectories from the test data to construct a query set Q and a database D. For each sampled trajectory T_q? in the query set, we create two sub-trajectories: one composed of the odd-indexed points of T_q?, denoted as $T_q^a = [p_1, p_3, p_5, \ldots]$, and the other composed of the even-indexed points, denoted as $T_q^b = [p_2, p_4, p_6, \ldots]$.We place T_q^a? into the query set Q and T_q^b? into the database D, treating T_q^b? as the most similar trajectory to T_q^a?. For each query $T_q^a \in Q$, we compute the similarity between T_q^a? and all trajectories in D using different methods, then rank the database trajectories in descending order of similarity. Ideally, the trajectory T_q^b should be ranked first among the similar trajectories retrieved for T_q^a.

We set databases D of varying sizes to evaluate the ranking of self-similar trajectory retrieval by different methods under different database capacities. The database size ranges from 10k to 80k. When the database is small, the ranking of the query results should be low (a ranking closer to 1 indicates better performance; a smaller rank means the retrieved self-similar trajectory appears earlier in the results, reflecting better recognition ability of the model in the self-similarity experiment). As the database size increases, the number of samples grows, potentially introducing trajectories more similar to T_q^a, which increases the difficulty for the model to find T_q^b. The experimental results are shown in Table 4. On the Porto dataset, as the database size increases from 10k to 80k, the ranking variation of our method increases by only 0.194. Among all compared methods, our method exhibits the smallest fluctuation as the database grows. This demonstrates that our model can stably and effectively capture trajectory features, indicating that in the vector embedding space, distances between similar trajectories are effectively pulled closer, showcasing strong representation capability.

Table 4. Self-Similarity query results on Porto and Beijing datasets

DataSet	Method	10K	20K	40K	60K	80K
Porto	t2vec	1.192	1.514	2.173	2.594	2.771
	TrjSR	2.015	1.927	2.531	3.001	3.886
	SNR	1.729	2.335	2.518	2.791	3.401
	STT-CL	1.213	1.008	1.317	1.022	1.032
	Ours	1.107	1.008	1.114	1.217	1.301
Beijing	t2vec	1.241	1.197	1.513	1.183	1.394
	TrjSR	1.916	2.013	2.437	2.971	3.019
	SNR	1.608	2.077	2.491	2.813	3.391
	STT-CL	1.013	1.092	1.194	1.226	1.731
	Ours	1.009	1.073	1.096	1.177	1.291

5.4 Ablation Study

We conducted ablation experiments to evaluate the impact of each component on the final performance of the model. Specifically, we conducted a complete experiment and two ablation experiments on the Porto dataset: 1) We did not use the global GAT based on the global area grid flow map to learn trajectory representation input; 2) Not using local GAT based on local individual trajectories to learn trajectory representations; In each experiment, the parameter settings remain unchanged from the complete model, with only one component removed. The results are shown in Table 5.

Table 5. Ablation study: Comparing the full model with 2 variants

	DTW				Hausdorff			
Method	HR@5	HR@10	HR@50	R10@50	HR@5	HR@10	HR@50	R10@50
w/o 1	0.182	0.311	0.382	0.497	0.214	0.543	0.788	0.799
w/o 2	0.191	0.329	0.397	0.579	0.221	0.552	0.789	0.811
Full Model	0.197	0.377	0.409	0.581	0.227	0.559	0.792	0.814
	Fréchet				EDR			
w/o 1	0.289	0.498	0.622	0.729	0.177	0.321	0.599	0.721
w/o 2	0.291	0.564	0.629	0.730	0.198	0.327	0.616	0.732
Full Model	0.292	0.566	0.631	0.731	0.210	0.329	0.617	0.735

5.5 Model Training

The training time of the model is also crucial, especially in today's era of large-scale data. In this section, we compare the training of different models on the Porto dataset, as shown in Fig. 3.To evaluate the training time cost of different models, we constructed three training sets of varying sizes on the Porto dataset, containing 100K, 200K, and 400K trajectories respectively, and conducted experiments accordingly. We recorded the average training time per epoch for the four compared methods. The experimental results show that among the compared methods, our model achieves the lowest training time when training on 400K samples, while t2vec has the longest training time at the largest sample size (400K). This demonstrates the training efficiency advantage of our model on large-scale data. However, when the training dataset is small, our method incurs higher training time mainly because it requires constructing the global grid flow graph, which is less advantageous at smaller data scales.

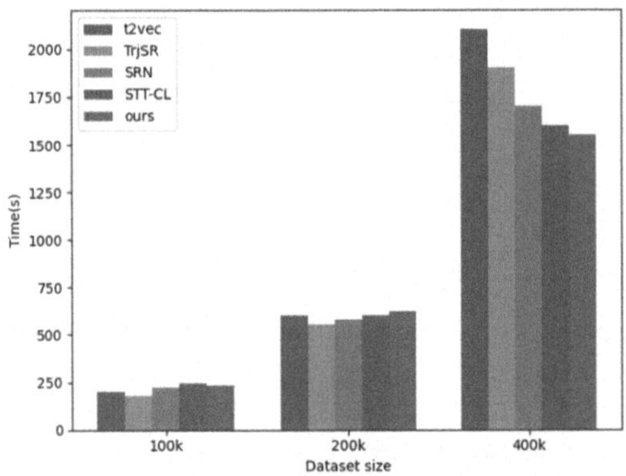

Fig. 3. Model Training Time.

6 Conclusion

This paper proposes a trajectory similarity computation model based on a dual graph attention mechanism, which captures the latent features of trajectories from both global and local perspectives. It effectively extracts rich positional information from the global grid graph as well as structural features of the trajectories. This enables the generated representations of similar trajectories to be closer in the embedding space, while dissimilar trajectories are farther apart. Experimental results demonstrate that our model performs excellently in handling large-scale trajectory data and outperforms the best baseline methods across a range of key evaluation metrics. These findings highlight the importance of extracting trajectory features from both global and local views and underscore the advantages of contrastive learning in computing trajectory similarity.

References

1. Atev, S., Miller, G., Papanikolopoulos, N.P.: Clustering of vehicle trajectories. TITS **11**(3), 647–657 (2010)
2. Yi, B.K., Jagadish, H.V., Faloutsos, C.: Efficient retrieval of similar time sequences under time warping. In: ICDE, pp. 201–208 (1998)

3. Alt, H., Godau, M.: Computing the fréchet distance between two polygonal curves. Int. J. Comput. Geom. Appl. **5**, 75–91 (1995)
4. Chen, L., Özsu, M.T., Oria, V.: Robust and fast similarity search for moving object trajectories. In: Proceedings of the 2005 ACM SIGMOD International Conference on Management of Data,. SIGMOD '05, pp. 491–502 (2005)
5. Agarwal, P.K., Fox, K., Munagala, K., Nath, A., Pan, J., Taylor, E.: Subtrajectory clustering: models and algorithms. In: PODS, pp. 75–87. ACM (2018)
6. Agrawal, R., Faloutsos, C., Swami, A.N.: Efficient similarity Search in sequence databases. In: FODO (Lecture Notes in Computer Science), vol. 730, pp. 69–84. Springer, Heidelberg (1993)
7. Fang, Z., Du, Y., Chen, L., Hu, Y., Gao, Y., Chen, G.: E2DTC: an end to end deep trajectory clustering framework via self-training. In: ICDE, pp. 696–707. IEEE (2021)
8. Han, P., Wang, J., Yao, D., Shang, S., Zhang, X.: A graph-based approach for trajectory similarity computation in spatial networks. In: KDD, pp. 556–564. ACM (2021)
9. Alt, H.: The computational geometry of comparing shapes. In: Efficient Algorithms, pp. 235–248 (2009)
10. Alt, H., Godau, M.: Computing the Fréchet distance between two polygonal curves. Int. J. Comput. Geom. Appl. **5**(01n02), 75–91 (1995)
11. Sakurai, Y., Yoshikawa, M., Faloutsos, C.: FTW: fast similarity search under the time warping distance, pp. 326–337 (2005)
12. Yang, P., Wang, H., Zhang, Y., Qin, L., Zhang, W., Lin, X.: T3S: effective representation learning for trajectory similarity computation. In: 2021 IEEE 37th International Conference on Data Engineering (ICDE). IEEE, 2183–2188 (2021)
13. He, K., Fan, H., Wu, Y., Xie, S., Girshick, R.: Momentum contrast for unsupervised visual representation learning. In: CVPR 2020, pp. 9729–9738 (2020)
14. Wang, S., Bao, Z., Culpepper, J.S., et al.: A survey on trajectory data management, analytics, and learning. ACM Comput. Sur. (CSUR). **54**(2), 1–36 (2021)
15. Chang, Y., Qi, J., Liang, Y., et al.: Contrastive trajectory similarity learning with dual-feature attention. In: 2023 IEEE 39th International Conference on Data Engineering (ICDE), pp. 2933–2945. IEEE (2023)
16. Yao, D., Hu, H., Du, L., Cong, G., Han, S., Bi, J.: Traj-GAT: a graph-based long-term dependency modeling approach for trajectory similarity computation. In: KDD, pp. 2275–2285 (2022)
17. Yang, C., Chen, L., Wang, H., Shang, S.: Towards efficient selection of activity trajectories based on diversity and coverage. In: AAAI, pp. 689–696 (2021)
18. Lan, T., et al.: MM-DAG: multi-task DAG Learning for multi-modal data - with application for traffic congestion analysis. In: KDD, pp. 1188–1199 (2023)
19. Li, X., Zhao, K., Cong, G., Jensen, C.S., Wei, W.: Deep representation learning for trajectory similarity computation. In: ICDE, pp. 617–628 (2018)
20. Kipf, T.N., Welling, M.: Semi-supervised classification with graph convolutional networks (2017). https://arxiv.org/abs/1609.02907
21. Devlin, J., Chang, M.W., Lee, K., Toutanova, K.: BERT: pre-training of deep bidirectional transformers for language understanding. In: NAACL, pp. 4171–4186 (2019)
22. Liu, X., Liang, Y., Huang, C., et al.: When do contrastive learning signals help spatio-temporal graph forecasting?. In: Proceedings of the 30th international conference on advances in geographic information systems. 1–12, (2022)
23. Vlachos, M., Kollios, G., Gunopulos, D.: Discovering similar multidimensional trajectories. In: ICDE, pp. 673–684 (2002)
24. Fang, Z., Du, Y., Chen, L., Hu, Y., Gao, Y., Chen, G.: E2DTC: an end to end deep trajectory clustering framework via self-training. In: ICDE, pp. 696–707 (2021)

25. Xu, Z., Wu, Y., Zhou, H., et al.: Spatio-temporal meta-learning for trajectory representation learning. Knowl.-Based Syst. 114141 (2025)
26. Chen, W., Liang, Y., Zhu, Y., et al.: Deep learning for trajectory data management and mining: a survey and beyond. arXiv preprint arXiv:2403.14151 (2024)
27. Xie, Z., Bai, X., Xu, X., et al.: An anomaly detection method based on ship behavior trajectory. Ocean Eng. **293**, 116640 (2024)
28. Guffanti, T., Gammelli, D., D'Amico, S., et al.: Transformers for trajectory optimization with application to spacecraft rendezvous. In: 2024 IEEE Aerospace Conference, pp. 1–13. IEEE (2024)
29. Zheng, X., Zhu, J.: Traj-lo: In defense of lidar-only odometry using an effective continuous-time trajectory. IEEE Rob. Autom. Lett. **9**(2), 1961–1968 (2024)
30. Zhu, Y., Yu, J.J., Zhao, X., et al.: Controltraj: controllable trajectory generation with topology-constrained diffusion model. In: Proceedings of the 30th ACM SIGKDD Conference on Knowledge Discovery and Data Mining, pp. 4676–4687 (2024)

LLM-Driven Multi-agent Simulation for Teaching Dynamics and Peer Effects

Kedi Wang[1,2], Jianye Yang[1,2], Guiling Wang[1,2](✉), Hongying Qian[1,2], Yunhe Zhu[1,2], Yuan Liu[1,2], Wenhui Zhao[3], and Jingting Xu[3]

[1] School of Artificial Intelligence and Computer Science, North China University of Technology, Beijing 100144, China
{2024322040114,yangjye,zyh18253962138,liuan}@mail.ncut.edu.cn

[2] Beijing Key Laboratory on Integration and Analysis of Large-scale Stream Data, Beijing, China
wangguiling@ncut.edu.cn

[3] China National Institute of Standardization, Beijing 100191, China
{zhaowh,xujingt}@cnis.ac.cn

Abstract. Traditional educational simulations typically model learners in isolation, neglecting two critical classroom dynamics: peer interaction and adaptive teaching. This limits their ability to capture the complexity of real classrooms. To bridge this gap, we present an LLM-driven multi-agent simulation that systematically models teaching dynamics and peer effects. Our model innovatively integrates an adaptive teacher agent, a cohort of student agents within a dynamic social network, and an automated evaluation system. A key contribution is the teacher agent's feedback-driven content selection mechanism, which adjusts teaching difficulty based on group performance, forming a closed "teach-learn-evaluate-adjust" loop. Student social connections are modeled using a Watts-Strogatz network that evolves towards homophilous clustering. Simulations show that peer interaction significantly boosts students' cognitive growth, with the learning curve following an inverted-U-shaped. By integrating a dynamic social network to model peer relationships, our work validates peer-effects theory and informs the optimization of intelligent teaching strategies.

Keywords: LLM · Multi-Agent System (MAS) · Dynamic Social Network · Feedback Mechanism · Peer Effect

1 Introduction

As AI reshapes education, computer-based simulations of teaching and learning have become a key research area. However, most models focus on individual learners, neglecting the critical roles of social interaction and adaptive teaching. The "peer effect"—where students influence each other's learning—and a

© The Author(s), under exclusive license to Springer Nature Singapore Pte Ltd. 2027
H. Sun et al. (Eds.): ChineseCSCW 2025, CCIS 2911, pp. 261–267, 2027.
https://doi.org/10.1007/978-981-92-0288-1_19

teacher's ability to adjust strategies based on class feedback are fundamental to real classroom dynamics but are often absent in simulations [1].

Existing research leveraging Multi-Agent Systems (MAS) [4], Large Language Models (LLMs) for feedback [3], and social network analysis [7] have explored these components in isolation. A significant gap remains in integrating these elements into a unified system with a closed feedback loop, where teacher behavior dynamically responds to group performance and social structures co-evolve with learning. This work addresses this gap by proposing an LLM-driven multi-agent simulation that models teaching dynamics, peer effects, and teacher adaptation. Our main contributions are: (1) A feedback-driven topic selection mechanism for the teacher agent that enables adaptive teaching by dynamically adjusting content based on group performance. (2) An LLM-powered multi-agent simulation with a heterogeneous agent population on a dynamic social network. (3) An experimental framework that systematically validates how peer influence shapes group learning outcomes, offering theoretical support for AI-driven pedagogical optimization.

2 Related Work

Research in educational simulation has progressed on several fronts. Multi-Agent Systems (MAS) have been used to model teacher and student behaviors [4], but often lack dynamic social structures and adaptive teacher agents. LLMs have shown great potential for generating personalized feedback [3], yet this feedback rarely informs the teacher agent's subsequent actions to close the teaching loop. Concurrently, studies on social learning, often using static network models like the Watts-Strogatz model [2,7], have demonstrated the strong link between social centrality and academic performance. Recent work has begun exploring LLMs for adaptive tutoring and collaborative learning [3,5], but a holistic simulation environment that integrates teacher adaptation with dynamic peer interactions remains an open challenge. Our work bridges these gaps by creating a unified simulation where an adaptive teacher, dynamic social networks, and LLM-based evaluation are fully integrated.

3 Simulation Method for Multi-agent Educational Scenarios

Our model is designed around a cyclical "Teach-Learn-Evaluate-Adjust" process, as illustrated in Fig. 1. In each round, the Teacher Agent delivers a lecture, which Student Agents learn from and summarize. An Evaluation System then scores these summaries, and the feedback drives adjustments in both student cognitive levels and the teacher's future strategy, forming a closed feedback loop. This entire workflow is detailed below, following the four core phases of the simulation.

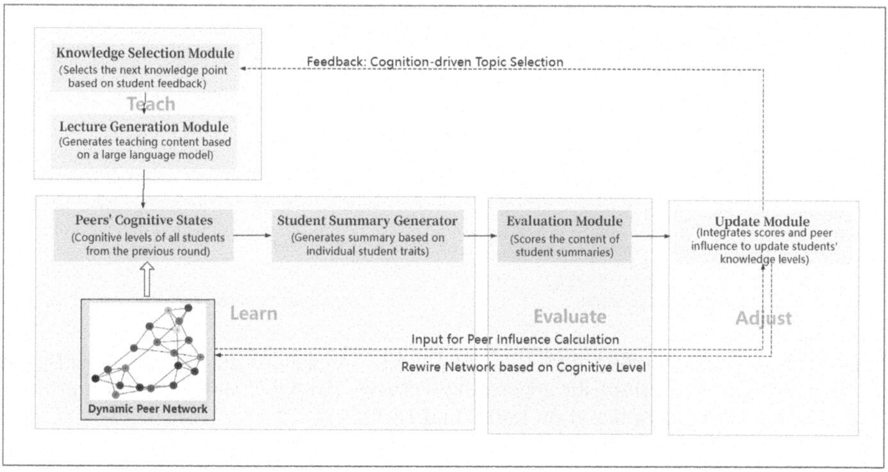

Fig. 1. The "Teach-Learn-Evaluate-Adjust" feedback loop in the LLM-driven multi-agent simulation.

3.1 Teach Phase: Adaptive Content Generation

This phase is driven by the Teacher Agent, which performs two main tasks corresponding to the modules in Fig. 1:

- **Knowledge Selection:** Based on the class's average performance from the previous round (feedback), the teacher selects the most relevant topic from a structured knowledge base that is within a manageable difficulty range.
- **Lecture Generation:** The agent then uses an LLM to generate a lecture on the selected topic, guided by the prompt template shown in Fig. 2.

A key feature is the teacher's adaptive mechanism, where the teaching difficulty for the next round, d_{t+1}, is adjusted based on the students' average score $\overline{F_t}$:

$$d_{t+1} = d_t + \eta(\overline{F_t} - F_{\text{target}}) \tag{1}$$

where η is the adjustment rate and F_{target} is the desired performance level. This allows the teacher to dynamically cater to the group's learning pace.

3.2 Learn Phase: Student Interaction and Network Dynamics

In this phase, each Student Agent processes the lecture and interacts with its peers. This involves:

- **Student Summary Generation:** Each student generates a summary of the lecture, guided by a prompt template that incorporates their individual traits (Fig. 2). This process is influenced by their cognitive level (R_i) and key non-cognitive traits such as confidence, curiosity, and attention span.

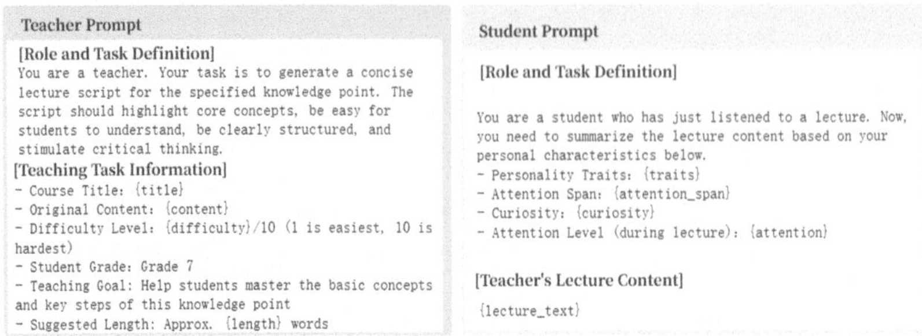

(a) Teacher Prompt Template (b) Student Prompt Template

Fig. 2. The prompt templates used to guide the LLM in generating agent behaviors. (a) The Teacher Agent's prompt for generating lectures. (b) The Student Agent's prompt for generating summaries based on individual traits.

- **Peer Interaction:** Students are embedded in a dynamic social network. Their learning is influenced by the cognitive states and performance of their connected peers.

The update to a student's cognitive level is the core of our peer effect model, integrating individual learning, forgetting, social influence from neighbors N(i), and a fatigue factor that simulates performance fluctuations over time:

$$R_i^{(t+1)} = (1 - \lambda_i)R_i^t + \alpha_i \cdot S_i^t + \beta_i \cdot (\text{Score}_{N(i)}^t - R_i^t) + \epsilon_t \tag{2}$$

Here, λ_i is a forgetting factor, α_i is the learning rate, S_i^t is the student's own score, $\text{Score}_{N(i)}^t$ is the average score of neighbors, and β_i is the peer influence coefficient, and ϵ_t is a random noise term.

3.3 Evaluate Phase: LLM-Based Assessment

The student summaries generated in the Learn phase are passed to the Evaluation Module. This module uses an LLM (e.g., GPT-3.5-turbo) to score each summary against the original lecture. It provides a holistic score (0–100) based on criteria like conceptual coverage, accuracy, and logical coherence. The resulting scores serve as quantitative feedback for the final phase.

3.4 Adjust Phase: The Dual-Feedback Loop

This final phase closes the simulation loop by processing the evaluation feedback in the Update Module. The adjustments occur in a dual loop:

- **Student-Level Adjustment:** Each student's cognitive level is updated using their own score and the average score of their peers, as defined in Eq. (2).
- **Teacher-Level Adjustment:** The average class score is fed back to the Teacher Agent to adjust the difficulty for the next round, as defined in Eq. (1).

- **Network-Level Adjustment:** The social network is dynamically rewired based on students' cognitive levels to simulate the principle of homophily. Periodically (e.g., every 3 rounds), existing connections are re-evaluated, and new links are preferentially formed between students with similar cognitive levels, encouraging the formation of homogeneous clusters.

This integrated feedback mechanism ensures that the teacher, students, and their social structure co-evolve throughout the simulation.

4 Experiments

4.1 Experimental Setup

We conducted simulations using three LLMs (GPT-3.5-turbo, DeepSeek, Qwen-MAX) for robustness. Each run featured one teacher and 20 student agents over 10 teaching rounds. The teaching content was based on a Grade 7 math curriculum. The student social network was initialized as a Watts-Strogatz small-world network (avg. degree=4, rewiring prob=0.1) and rewired every 3 rounds. This network is chosen for its ability to model real-world social structures, exhibiting both local clustering (student cliques) and short average path lengths (cross-group connections). Key parameters are in Table 1.

Table 1. Key Agent Parameters.

Student Agent Parameter	Value
Initial Learning Level	$N(60, 10^2)$
Learning Efficiency α	$[0.3, 0.5]$
Knowledge Forgetting Rate λ	$[0.1, 0.2]$
Peer Influence Coefficient β	$\{0, 0.2, 0.5, 0.8\}$ (for diff. groups)
Teacher Agent Parameter	**Value**
Initial Teaching Complexity	3 (out of 10)
Adaptive Adjustment Coefficient η	0.2

To isolate the peer effect, we established four experimental groups by varying the peer influence coefficient β: **Control Group** ($\beta = 0$), **Low-Peer Group** ($\beta = 0.2$), **Mid-Peer Group** ($\beta = 0.5$), and **High-Peer Group** ($\beta = 0.8$).

5 Analysis of Experimental Results

Our experiments consistently demonstrate the significant positive impact of peer interaction on learning. As shown in Table 2, the average final learning level of the class systematically increases with a higher peer influence coefficient across all three LLMs. This confirms the core hypothesis that the peer effect facilitates

Table 2. Average Final Class Learning Levels Under Different Peer Influence Strengths.

Model	No-Peer	Low-Peer	Mid-Peer	High-Peer
Qwen-MAX	67.32 ± 0.5	80.27 ± 0.4	83.01 ± 0.3	85.91 ± 0.4
DeepSeek	68.53 ± 0.3	80.55 ± 0.3	82.73 ± 0.2	85.14 ± 0.2
GPT-3.5-turbo	67.53 ± 0.3	80.33 ± 0.2	82.51 ± 0.2	85.47 ± 0.2

cognitive gains, aligning with social learning theories. The differences between all experimental groups and the control group were found to be statistically significant ($p < 0.01$).

The dynamic learning trajectory, however, reveals a more nuanced pattern. Figure 3 illustrates that the group's average learning level follows an inverted-U trend: an initial phase of rapid growth followed by a plateau or even a slight decline. This suggests that while peer effects are initially beneficial, factors like cognitive overload may emerge over time, limiting further gains [6].

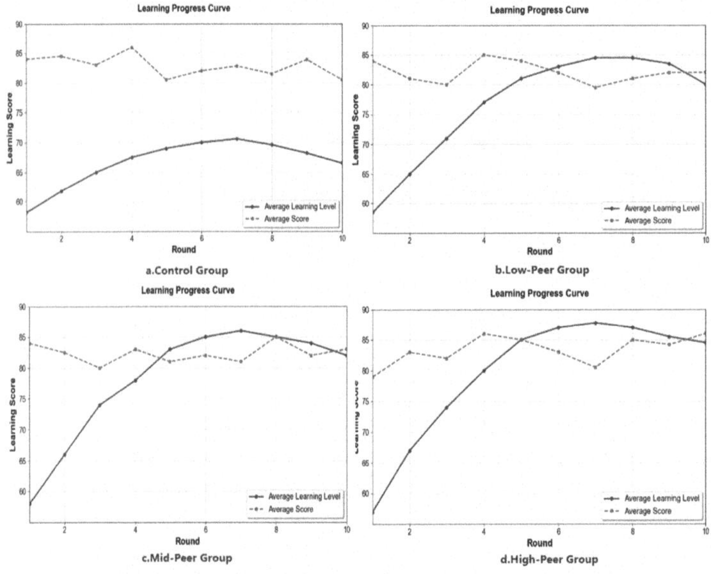

Fig. 3. Learning evolution curves for the four experimental groups (using Qwen-MAX).

Furthermore, we observed a dynamic evolution in the social network structure. The network, initially a small-world graph, progressively shifted toward "homophilous clustering," where students of similar cognitive levels formed tighter clusters (Fig. 4). This self-organization, while promoting deep collaboration within homogeneous groups, may also create silos that hinder knowledge transfer between students of different ability levels.

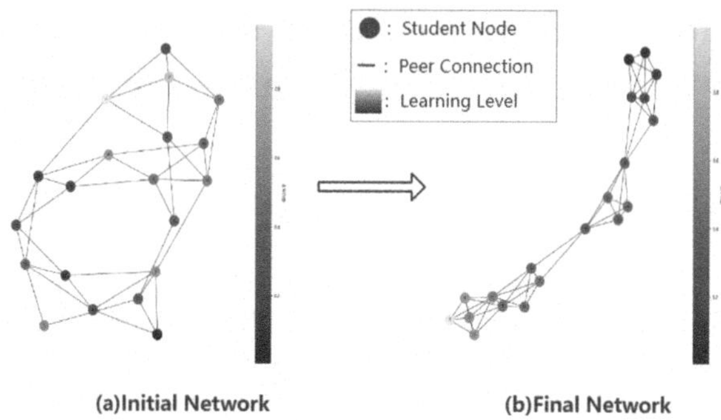

Fig. 4. Network evolution from (a) an initial small-world structure to (b) a state of homophilous clustering.

6 Conclusion

In this paper, we developed and validated an LLM-driven multi-agent simulation to study teaching dynamics and peer effects by integrating an adaptive teacher agent with interacting student agents on a dynamic social network. Our findings confirm that moderate peer influence significantly boosts cognitive gains but also reveal an inverted-U-shaped learning trajectory, suggesting potential cognitive overload. While this work provides a powerful tool for exploring pedagogical strategies, it has limitations, including its reliance on preset parameters and the need for validation with real-world data. Future research should also compare adaptive and static teaching strategies to further isolate their effects. Nevertheless, our simulation offers key theoretical insights for designing AI-assisted teaching systems that effectively harness social dynamics.

References

1. Akers, R.L., Jennings, W.G.: Social learning theory. In: Piquero, A.R. (ed.) The Handbook of Criminological Theory, pp. 230–240. John Wiley & Sons (2015)
2. Cruz-Benito, J., Borras-Gene, O., Garcia-Penalvo, F.J., Blanco, A.F., Theron, R.: Learning communities in social networks and their relationship with the MOOCs. IEEE Revista Iberoamericana de Tecnologias del Aprendizaje **12**(1), 24–36 (2017)
3. Kinder, A., et al.: Effects of adaptive feedback generated by a large language model: a case study in teacher education. Comput. Educ. Artif. Intell. **8**, 100349 (2025)
4. Park, M., et al.: Empowering personalized learning through a conversation-based tutoring system with student modeling. In: Extended Abstracts of the 2024 CHI Conference on Human Factors in Computing Systems, pp. 1–10 (2024)
5. Steinert, S., Avila, K.E., Ruzika, S., Kuhn, J., Küchemann, S.: Harnessing large language models to develop research-based learning assistants for formative feedback. Smart Learn. Environ. **11**(1), 62 (2024)
6. Sweller, J.: Cognitive load during problem solving: effects on learning. Cogn. Sci. **12**(2), 257–285 (1988)
7. Watts, D.J., Strogatz, S.H.: Collective dynamics of 'small-world' networks. Nature **393**(6684), 440–442 (1998)

Automatic Feature Interaction Learning via Attention-Free Neural Networks

Ting Bi[1,2,3], Meng Xu[4(✉)], Meiru Wang[1,2], and Yuanbo Xu[1,2,3(✉)]

[1] Software College, Jilin University, Changchun, China
[2] MIC Lab (Mobile Intelligent Computing Lab), Jilin University, Changchun, China
yuanbox@jlu.edu.cn
[3] Key Laboratory of Symbolic Computation and Knowledge Engineering of Ministry of Education, Changchun, China
[4] Changchun Jinyang Hi-tech Co., Ltd, Changchun, China
xumengzl@ccjinyang.com.cn

Abstract. Collaborative filtering learns users' preferences from transactions but faces cold-start problems and data sparsity in large-scale scenarios. We propose an efficient framework using only side information to model connections among high-dimensional features. Categorical, numerical, and unstructured textual features are mapped into a unified low-dimensional space to retain semantic information. Inspired by attention-free transformers, we adapt multi-head self-attention to automatically capture feature interactions, avoiding manual feature engineering. Residual connections model high-order combinations, and a feed-forward network captures implicit interactions. Experiments on public datasets show our model outperforms state-of-the-art methods in Click-Through Rate prediction and reduces RMSE in rating prediction. Analysis further demonstrates that effective feature interaction improves both recommendation accuracy and interpretability.

Keywords: Feature interactions · Attention-free · Recommendation · CTR prediction · Rating prediction

1 Introduction

With the rapid development of mobile Internet and large-scale data, providing users with personalized services has become crucial for enhancing experience and increasing revenue [1–3]. Recommendation systems (RSs), as a bridge between information producers and consumers, play an essential role in e-commerce, advertising, and personalized search. In particular, Click-Through Rate (CTR) prediction aims to estimate users' interests from historical data and predict future behaviors [9,16]. Typically, data are represented in tabular form after normalization and discretization through feature engineering [10].

The evolution of CTR models mainly focuses on feature interaction and model enhancement. Early methods depended on manual feature design, while

© The Author(s), under exclusive license to Springer Nature Singapore Pte Ltd. 2027
H. Sun et al. (Eds.): ChineseCSCW 2025, CCIS 2911, pp. 268–281, 2027.
https://doi.org/10.1007/978-981-92-0288-1_20

deep learning enabled automatic extraction. Attention-based models such as AFM [27], AutoInt [38], and InterHAt [19] improve interpretability and capture high-order dependencies. However, their quadratic attention cost limits scalability. To overcome this, AFT and its simplified variant AFT-simple approximate dot-product attention with linear complexity while maintaining modeling power.

Traditional RSs relying solely on user-item interactions suffer from sparsity and cold start issues [15] To address these problems, recent works introduce side information such as user profiles and item attributes [11,12,17]. Inspired by this and AFT-simple, we propose a feature interaction model that leverages side information to predict user preferences efficiently. The model embeds user and item features into low-dimensional spaces and employs a multi-head AFT-simple mechanism with residual connections to model diverse high-order interactions.

The main contributions are summarized as follows:

- We propose a model that utilizes side information to handle large-scale, sparse data with categorical, numerical, and textual features.
- We design an AFT-simple-based attention layer to capture explainable high-order feature interactions.
- The model can predict for unseen users or items without interaction records, alleviating the cold start problem.
- Experiments on real-world datasets show that our model surpasses state-of-the-art CTR and rating prediction methods.

2 Related Work

Prediction, as a core task in recommendation systems, faces challenges mainly in three aspects: collaborative filtering, cold start, and deep learning.

Collaborative Filtering. It assumes that similar users share similar preferences, predicting unknown ratings from behavioral similarity [22,25]. Early memory-based methods [21] suffered from high computational cost, prompting model-based techniques such as MF, CMF, and BPR [23,24,28] that learn latent representations. Later, NCF [22] introduced deep nonlinear modeling, and SIF [29] further improved efficiency through adaptive interaction search.

Cold Start. This problem arises when recommending for new users or items lacking sufficient interactions. Solutions typically exploit side information or balance exploration and exploitation. LinUCB [20,30] applies contextual bandits for exploration, and PGCR [31] uses Bayesian dropout for balance. Meta-learning methods, such as Meta-Embedding [32] and Melu [35], adapt embeddings from few samples, while MWUF [33] and MetaHIN [36] map cold features to warm spaces using heterogeneous information networks.

Deep Learning. The success of neural networks in vision and NLP has extended to recommendation tasks [37]. Deep models capture high-level semantics via convolutional, graph, or autoencoder architectures. SR-GNN [38] models user sessions as graphs, and UBR [39] retrieves relevant behaviors by search. However, excessive model complexity may cause overfitting and inefficiency [40]. Lightweight architectures such as NFNet [41] and AFT-simple [27] improve both performance and efficiency by simplifying normalization or attention mechanisms.

3 Preliminaries

In this section, we first define the prediction tasks considered in our work, followed by brief introductions to the key models used.

3.1 Problem Definition

Definition 1 (CTR Prediction). *In CTR prediction, the original data usually include multiple categories, such as categorical, numerical, and unstructured textual features. These original features are first transformed into the same low-dimensional space and then concatenated as the final feature vector x. In addition, the label $y \in \{0, 1\}$ corresponding to each instance indicates user click behavior. CTR prediction is defined to predict the probability of a user clicking according to the input feature vector x.*

Definition 2 (Rating Prediction). *Consistent with CTR prediction, the preprocessing work is the same. With the concatenation of user features and item features, the problem of rating prediction is defined to predict the rating that the user may give to an item.*

3.2 Multi-Head Attention and Residual Network

Multi-Head Attention (MHA). Since AFT-simple serves as a simplified alternative to MHA, we briefly review MHA here. Given input $X \in R^{m \times d}$ with m feature fields and h heads, the representation of head i is:

$$H_i = \sigma \left(\frac{Q_i (K_i)^T}{\sqrt{d_k}} \right) V_i \tag{1}$$

$$s.t.\ Q_i = XW_i^Q, K_i = XW_i^K, V_i = XW_i^V \tag{2}$$

where σ is the softmax function and $W_i^Q, W_i^K, W_i^V \in R^{d \times d_k}$ are learnable parameters with $d_k = d/h$. MHA concatenates all H_i to maintain the same dimension as X.

Residual Network. Residual networks [43] address the degradation problem in deep models by introducing identity mapping, formulated as $y = F(x) + x$. This skip connection alleviates gradient vanishing and enhances representation ability in deep architectures.

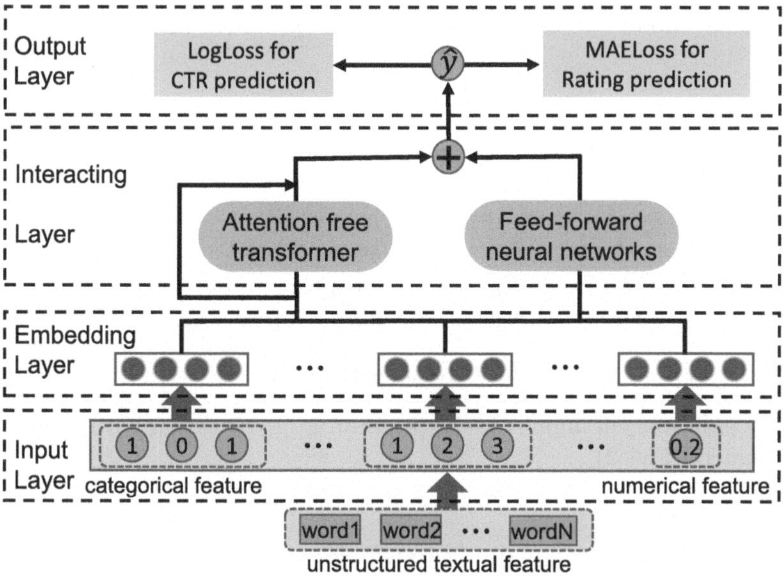

Fig. 1. Structure diagram of our proposed model FIAfN.

4 Automatic Feature Interaction Learning via Attention-Free Neural Networks

In this section, we describe the proposed model FIAfN in detail. The motivation is to leverage side information to automatically accomplish high-order feature interactions, avoiding manual feature engineering and alleviating the cold start problem. The overall framework is illustrated in Fig. 1.

4.1 Input Layer

The input layer receives preprocessed user and item features, concatenated as:

$$x = [x_1; x_2; \cdots; x_m] \tag{3}$$

where m is the total number of feature fields and x_i represents the i-th field. Numerical features are scalars, categorical ones are one-hot or multi-hot codes, and textual features are mapped from words to integer sequences via a constructed dictionary.

4.2 Embedding Layer

Categorical features are first embedded by multiplying an embedding matrix M_i:

$$e_i = M_i x_i \tag{4}$$

For multi-hot inputs, we take the mean of multiple embeddings:

$$e_i = \frac{1}{n} M_i x_i \tag{5}$$

where n is the number of active values. Numerical features are projected into the same embedding space via:

$$e_i = m_i x_i \tag{6}$$

For unstructured textual features, a dynamic recurrent neural network (dynamic_rnn) with LSTM cells is applied to capture semantic information:

$$h_t = f(Ux_t + Wh_{t-1}) \tag{7}$$

where x_t indicates the input of t-th position, U is transition matrix and W is weight matrix (Fig. 2).

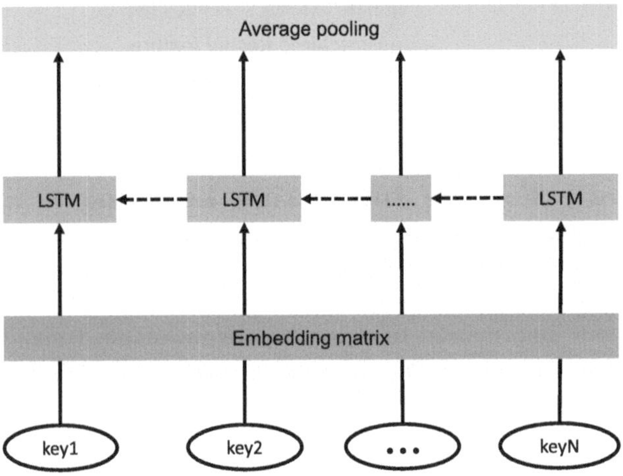

Fig. 2. Frame diagram of embedding layer for textual feature.

All feature embeddings are concatenated to form the input of the interacting layer.

4.3 Interacting Layer

After embedding, all features lie in a shared low-dimensional space. To model feature dependencies, we integrate AFT-simple with a two-layer feed-forward neural network to capture explicit and implicit interactions simultaneously. AFT-simple replaces traditional attention with a simplified yet efficient formulation:

$$H_i = \sigma_q(Q_i) \odot \frac{\sum_{t=1}^{d} exp(K_i^t) \odot V_i^t}{\sum_{t=1}^{d} exp(K_i^t)}, \tag{8}$$

where $\odot$ denotes element-wise multiplication and σ_q is the sigmoid function. This design offers speed and memory efficiency compared with standard Transformers.. To model correlations between feature a and feature b, the attention weight under head h is:

$$I_{a,b}^{(h)} = \frac{exp(\Psi^{(h)}(e_a, e_b))}{\sum_{i=1}^{m} exp(\Psi^{(h)}(e_a, e_i))}, \tag{9}$$

$$\Psi^{(h)}(e_a, e_b) = \langle W_Q^{(h)} e_a, W_K^{(h)} e_b \rangle, \tag{10}$$

where $\Psi^{(h)}(\cdot)$ measures pairwise similarity using element-wise product. Each feature a is updated by aggregating its related features:

$$\hat{e}_a^{(h)} = \sum_{b=1}^{m} I_{a,b}^{(h)} (W_V^{(h)} e_b). \tag{11}$$

Concatenating outputs of all heads gives:

$$\hat{e_a} = \hat{e}_a^{(1)} \oplus \cdots \oplus \hat{e}_a^{(h)}. \tag{12}$$

A residual connection is added to preserve learned features:

$$e_a^{res} = ReLU(\hat{e_a} + W_{res} e_a), \tag{13}$$

where W_{res} aligns dimensions. Stacking multiple AFT-simple blocks enables higher-order feature modeling. The final combination is obtained by:

$$\hat{y}_A = w(e_1^{res} \oplus e_2^{res} \oplus \cdots \oplus e_m^{res}) + b. \tag{14}$$

4.4 Output Layer

For CTR prediction, we apply a sigmoid activation:

$$\hat{y} = sigmoid(\hat{y}_A + \hat{y}_F), \tag{15}$$

and use Logloss as the objective. For rating prediction, the output is scaled to $(0, 5)$ and optimized by MAELoss. Model parameters are updated via gradient descent.

5 Experiments and Discussions

5.1 Data Sets and Evaluation Metric

Data Sets. We evaluate FIAfN on three real-world datasets: Criteo, MovieLens-1M, and MovieLens-100k. Tables 1 and 2 summarize their statistics after preprocessing. Following prior work, we randomly split data into 80% training and 10% validation/testing. For the highly unbalanced Criteo dataset, we apply Stratified-KFold sampling to preserve label distribution.

Table 1. Statistics of Criteo

Dataset name	Instances	Fields	Features	Positive Ratio
Criteo	45,840,617	39	3,725,160	26%

- **Criteo**. The industry benchmark for CTR prediction, including 13 numerical and 26 categorical features. Rare features (frequency <10) are replaced with "$< UNK >$", and numerical features are normalized by $\log^2(z)$ if $z > 2$.
- **MovieLens-1M & 100k**. Contain user–item rating records. Ratings higher than 3 are treated as positive (label 1), below 3 as negative (label 0). After binarization, MovieLens-1M remains 739,012 instances with 96.85% sparsity. These datasets allow us to verify FIAfN's performance on sparse and small-scale recommendation scenarios.

Table 2. Statistics of MovieLens

Dataset name	Instances	Fields	Users	Items	Sparsity
MovieLens-1M	739,012	8	6039	3883	96.85%
Movielens-100k	100,000	8	943	1682	93.69%

Evaluation Criterion. For CTR prediction, we report **AUC** and **Logloss** as standard metrics. AUC reflects ranking quality, while Logloss (binary cross-entropy) measures prediction accuracy. A small gain (e.g., 0.001) in AUC or Logloss is considered significant in industrial applications [1,18,42]. For rating prediction, **MAE** and **RMSE** are adopted.

Baselines. We compare FIAfN with three categories of models:

Shallow Models: LR (linear combination of raw features); **FM** (second-order interactions via factorized parameters); **HOFM** (extends FM to arbitrary-order interactions).

Deep Models: NFM (Bi-interaction layer + DNN), **DeepCrossing** (residual fully connected layers), **DCN** (explicit high-order interactions via cross layers).

Attention-Based Models: AFM (weights feature interactions via attention), **AutoInt+** (multi-head self-attention + feed-forward layers).

5.2 Experimental Settings

All models are implemented in TensorFlow (Python3, CUDA 8). For CTR prediction, embedding dimension $d = 16$, batch size 1024 (512 for FIAfN), and three interaction layers are used. Each AFT-simple block contains two attention heads. Dropout is tuned by grid search from $\{0.1–0.9\}$.

Baseline configurations follow the best-performing AutoInt: three MHA layers, hidden size 32. For NFM, DCN, and DeepCrossing, we use standard settings from their papers (e.g., NFM hidden=200, DCN=3 layers, DC=4 layers).

For rating prediction, $d = 10$, batch size 4096, 500 epochs are used to prevent overfitting. Adam optimizer is adopted for all deep models.

Baselines. We compare FIAfN with three types of baselines. **Shallow models**: LR, FM, HOFM. **Deep learning models**: NFM, DeepCrossing, DCN. **Attention-based models**: AFM, AutoInt+.

5.3 Experimental Settings

All methods are implemented in TensorFlow (Python3, CUDA 8). For baselines, embedding dimension $d = 16$ and batch size 1024. FIAfN adopts three interaction layers, hidden units $n = 16$, 2 attention heads, and batch size 512. Dropout is selected by grid search (not used for Criteo). Deep models follow default settings in AutoInt. For rating prediction, $d = 10$, batch size 4096, epoch 500. All networks are optimized with Adam.

5.4 Performance Comparison

Comparison of Different Methods. We evaluate FIAfN and baselines on CTR (Criteo, Movielens-1M) and rating prediction (Movielens-100k, Movielens-1M). Results are shown in Tables 3 and 4.

Table 3. Comparison of Different Methods in CTR Prediction

model	Criteo		Movielens-1M	
	AUC	Logloss	AUC	Logloss
LR	0.7858	0.4474	0.7716	0.4424
FM	0.7933	0.4464	0.8252	0.3998
HOFM	0.8005	0.4508	0.8304	0.4013
NFM	0.7968	0.4537	0.8357	0.3883
DeepCrossing	0.8009	0.4513	0.8448	0.3814
DCN	0.8067	0.4419	0.7968	0.4266
AFM	0.7965	0.4541	0.8227	0.4048
AutoInt+	0.8083	0.4434	0.8488	0.3753
FIAfN	**0.8109**	**0.4388**	**0.8875**	**0.3290**

From the results, FIAfN achieves the best overall performance on all datasets. On Movielens-1M, it outperforms AutoInt+ by 4.56% (AUC) and 11.46% (Logloss), verifying its strong ability to model high-order nonlinear feature interactions. The moderate gain on Criteo may relate to its undisclosed semantics.

Analysis of Time Complexity. We first analyze the time complexity and then present runtime results in Fig. 3. The computation cost mainly comes from three parts.

First, in the embedding layer, assuming the hidden unit u and sequence length s in dynamic_rnn, the complexity is $O(s^2u + su^2)$. Second, for the attention-free transformer, similar to MHA with h heads and $d_k = \frac{d}{h}$, the complexity of one interaction layer is $O(md^2 + m^2h + md)$, while our attention-free mechanism reduces it to $O(md)$ by removing dot products. Third, the two-layer feed-forward network with N neurons costs $O(N^2)$. Therefore, the total complexity of FIAfN is $O(s^2u + su^2 + md + N^2)$, where most time is spent in the interaction layer.

Table 4. Comparison of Different Methods in Rating Prediction

model	Movielens-100k		Movielens-1M	
	MAE	RMSE	MAE	RMSE
LR	0.5086	0.5518	0.4658	0.4780
FM	0.4863	0.5099	0.4164	0.4454
NFM	0.4670	0.4874	0.3658	0.4270
DCN	0.4684	0.4984	0.3627	0.4285
AFM	0.4941	0.5036	0.4609	0.4716
AutoInt	0.4669	0.4841	0.3663	0.4273
FIAfN	**0.4258**	**0.4562**	**0.3409**	**0.4145**

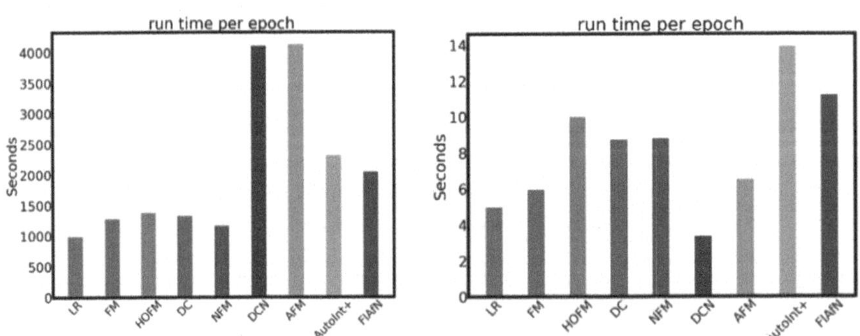

(a) Criteo (b) Movielens-1M

Fig. 3. Runtime results of different algorithms

As shown in Fig. 3, Criteo contains more features than Movielens-1M, causing deeper models (e.g., DCN, AFM) to spend more time exploring high-order interactions. Although FIAfN replaces MHA and theoretically reduces complexity, the dynamic_rnn slightly increases runtime due to textual feature integration. Nevertheless, this addition enhances performance, and the trade-off is reasonable for handling high-dimensional and sparse data. Overall, FIAfN achieves the best efficiency-performance balance among all methods.

Impact of Model Structure. To validate the contribution of each component, we conduct an ablation study comparing FIAfN with two variants (Table 5).

Table 5. Comparison Results of Different Variants

Metrics	FIAfN	no_RNN	no_FNN	AutoInt+
AUC	0.8875	0.8602	0.8557	0.8488
Logloss	0.3304	0.3592	0.3642	0.3753

Removing dynamic_rnn (no_RNN) or feed-forward network (no_FNN) both reduce performance, showing that textual information and implicit feature interaction are crucial. Notably, no_RNN still surpasses AutoInt+, confirming the advantage of the attention-free mechanism. The complete FIAfN achieves the best results, proving that each module complements the others and ensures robust modeling of user–item relations.

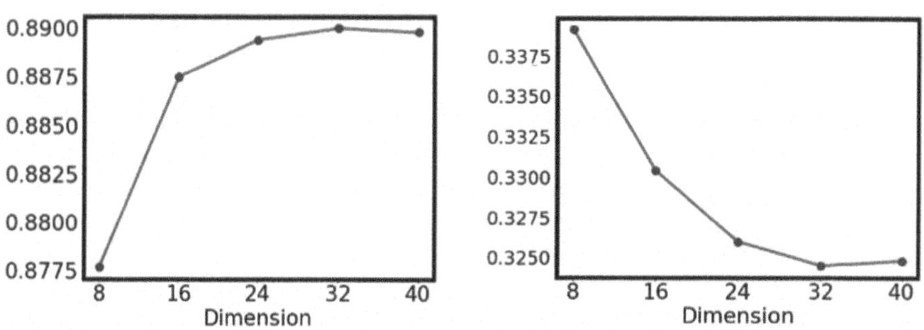

(a) CTR (b) Rating

Fig. 4. Visualization of feature interactions

We further analyze the effect of embedding dimension d, which also equals the LSTM unit number. As shown in Fig. 4, performance improves as d increases and saturates around $d = 16$. Considering efficiency and accuracy, we set $d = 16$ as the default.

Interpretability of Model. Finally, we demonstrate the interpretability of FIAfN via visualization on the MovieLens-1M dataset, since Criteo data is encrypted. Figure 5 highlights representative learned feature combinations, indicating that FIAfN not only achieves superior accuracy but also provides explainable recommendations.

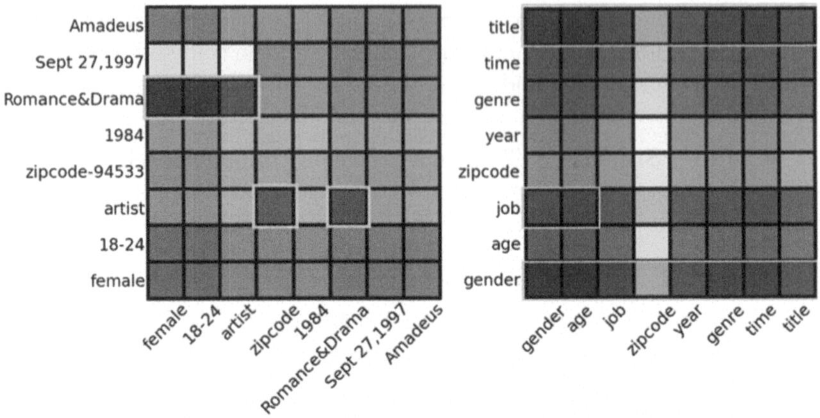

(a) One case with CTR=0.9 (b) Overall feature interactions

Fig. 5. Heat map of attention score

6 Conclusion

In this paper, we propose an effective model FIAfN to model user–item relationships solely based on side information, addressing the cold-start problem without relying on historical interactions. Experimental results demonstrate that FIAfN effectively captures high-order feature interactions and achieves strong performance.

In the future, we plan to further improve model efficiency while maintaining accuracy, as current parameters remain relatively large. We also aim to integrate capsule neural networks with temporal components to better capture users' evolving interests.

To illustrate the interpretability of FIAfN, Fig. 5(a) shows one prediction case with CTR=0.9. The model correctly identifies the meaningful combinatorial feature <*Gender=female, Age=[18,24), Job=artist, MovieGenre=Romance & Drama*>, which reflects realistic user preferences.

Furthermore, Fig. 5(b) summarizes global feature correlations based on average attention scores. The strong relationships among <*Job, Gender, Age*> and the importance of textual information confirm that FIAfN can model interpretable and high-order feature interactions effectively, ensuring both accuracy and explainability in recommendation tasks.

Acknowledgment. This work is supported by the Natural Science Foundation of China No. 62472196, Jilin Science and Technology Research Project 20230101067JC

References

1. Cheng, H.-T., et al.: Wide & deep learning for recommender systems. In: Proceedings of the 1st Workshop on Deep Learning for Recommender Systems, pp. 7–10. ACM (2016)
2. Graepel, T., Candela, J.Q., Borchert, T. Her-brich, R.: Web-scale Bayesian click-through rate prediction for SponsoredSearch advertising in Microsoft's Bing search engine. In: Proceedings of the 27th International Conference on International Conference on Machine Learning, pp. 13–20 (2010)
3. He, X., et al.: Practical lessons from predicting clicks on ads at facebook. In: Proceedings of the Eighth International Workshop on Data Mining for Online Advertising, pp. 1–9. ACM (2014)
4. Fan, H., Poole, M.S.: What is personalization? Perspectives on the design and implementation of personalization in information systems. J. Organ. Comput. Electron. Commer. **16**(3), 179–202 (2006)
5. Pan, Z., et al.: Sparse factorization machines for click-through rate prediction. In: Proceedings of the 2016 IEEE 16th International Conference on Data Mining (ICDM), pp. 400–409. IEEE (2016)
6. Qu, Y., et al.: Product-based neural networks for user response prediction. In: Proceedings of the 2016 IEEE 16th International Conference on Data Mining, pp. 1149–1154. IEEE (2016)
7. Zhang, K., et al.: Multi-interactive attention network for fine-grained feature learning in CTR prediction. In: Proceedings of the 14th ACM International Conference on Web Search and Data Mining, pp. 984–992 (2021)
8. Zhou, G., et al.: Deep interest network for click-through rate prediction. In: Proceedings of the 24th ACM SIGKDD International Conference on Knowledge Discovery & Data Mining, pp. 1059–1068 (2018)
9. Agarwal, D., Long, B., Traupman, J., Xin, D., Zhang, L.: LASER: a scalable response prediction platform for online advertising. In: Proceedings of the 7th ACM international conference on Web search and data mining (WSDM '14). Association for Computing Machinery, New York, NY, USA, pp. 173–182 (2014)
10. Juan, Y., Zhuang, Y., Chin, W.-S., Lin, C.-J.: Field-aware factorization machines for CTR prediction. In: Proceedings of the 10th ACM Conference on Recommender Systems (RecSys '16). Association for Computing Machinery, New York, NY, USA, pp. 43–50 (2016)
11. Guo, Q., Sun, Z., Theng, Y.-L.: Exploiting side information for recommendation. In: Proceedings of the International Conference on Web Engineering, Berlin-Heidelberg, Germany: Springer, pp. 569–573 (2019)
12. Jiang, Y., et al.: TriMLP: a foundational MLP-like architecture for sequential recommendation. ACM Trans. Inf. Syst. **42**(6), 157:1–157:34 (2024). https://doi.org/10.1145/3670995
13. Guo, G., Zhang, J., Thalmann, D.: A simple but effective method to incorporate trusted neighbors in recommender systems. In: Proceedings of the International Conference on User Modeling, Adaptation, and Personalization, Berlin-Heidelberg, Germany, pp. 114–125. Springer (2012)
14. Yang, B., Lei, Y., Liu, D., Liu, J.: Social collaborative filtering by trust. In: Proceedings of the International Joint Conference on Artificial Intelligence, Menlo Park: AAAI Press, pp. 1633–1647 (2013)
15. Yuanbo, X., Yang, Y., Wang, E., Zhuang, F., Xiong, H.: Detect professional malicious user with metric learning in recommender systems. IEEE Trans. Knowl. Data Eng. **34**(9), 4133–4146 (2022). https://doi.org/10.1109/TKDE.2020.3040618

16. Yuanbo, X., Wang, E., Yang, Y., Chang, Y.: A unified collaborative representation learning for neural-network based recommender systems. IEEE Trans. Knowl. Data Eng. **34**(11), 5126–5139 (2022)
17. Sun, Z.: Research commentary on recommendations with side information: a survey and research directions. Electron. Commer. Res. Appl. **37**, 100879 (2019)
18. Guo, H., Tang, R., Ye, Y., Li, Z., He, X.: Deep FM: a factorization-machine based neural network for CTR prediction. In: Proceedings of the 26th International Joint Conference on Artificial Intelligence, AAAI Press, pp. 1725–1731 (2017)
19. Yuanbo, X., Zhuang, F., Wang, E., Li, C., Jie, W.: Learning without missing-at-random prior propensity: a generative approach for recommender systems. IEEE Trans. Knowl. Data Eng. **37**(2), 754–765 (2025). https://doi.org/10.1109/TKDE.2024.3490593
20. Yuanbo, X., Wang, E., Yang, Y., Xiong, H.: GS-RS: a generative approach for alleviating cold start and filter bubbles in recommender systems. IEEE Trans. Knowl. Data Eng. **36**(2), 668–681 (2024). https://doi.org/10.1109/TKDE.2023.3290140
21. Sarwar, B., Karypis, G., Konstan, J., Riedl, J.: Item-based collaborative filtering recommendation algorithms. In: Proceedings of the International World Wide Web Conference (WWW), pp. 285–295 (2001)
22. Jiang, Y., Yang, Y., Yuanbo, X., Wang, E.: Spatial-temporal interval aware individual future trajectory prediction. IEEE Trans. Knowl. Data Eng. **36**(10), 5374–5387 (2024)
23. Koren, Y.: Factorization meets the neighborhood: a multifaceted collaborative filtering model. In: Proceedings of the ACM SIGKDD Conference on Knowledge Discovery and Data Mining (KDD), pp. 426–434 (2008)
24. Hsieh, C.-K., Yang, L., Cui, Y., Lin, T.-Y., Belongie, S., Estrin, D.: Collaborative metric learning. In: Proceedings of the 26th International Conference on World Wide Web, pp. 193–201 (2017)
25. Xue, H.-J., Dai, X., Zhang, J., Huang, S., Chen, J.: Deep matrix factorization models for recommender systems. In: Proceedings of the Twenty-Sixth International Joint Conference on Artificial Intelligence, IJCAI-17, pp. 3203–3209 (2017)
26. Ning, X., Karypis, G.: Slim: sparse linear methods for top-n recommender systems. In: Proceedings of the 2011 IEEE 11th International Conference on Data Mining, pp. 497–506. IEEE (2011)
27. Bi, T., Xu, H., Xu, Y.: Invariant and environment-specific preference learning with auxiliary information for unbiased recommendation. In: Proceedings of the IEEE International Conference on Data Mining (ICDM) (2025)
28. Rendle, S., Freudenthaler, C., Gantner, Z., Schmidt-Thieme, L.: BPR: Bayesian personalized ranking from implicit feedback. In: Proceedings of the Conference on Uncertainty in Artificial Intelligence (UAI), pp. 452–461 (2009)
29. Yao, Q., Chen, X., Kwok, J.T., Li, Y., Hsieh, C.-J.: Efficient neural interaction function search for collaborative filtering. In: Proceedings of the Web Conference 2020 (WWW'20), Association for Computing Machinery, New York, NY, USA, pp. 1660–1670 (2020)
30. Li, L., Chu, W., Langford, J., Schapire, R.E.: A contextual-bandit approach to personalized news article recommendation. In: Proceedings of the 19th International Conference on World Wide Web, (WWW'10), pp. 661–670 (2010)
31. Wang, E., et al.: Zone-enhanced Spatio-Temporal representation learning for urban POI recommendation. IEEE Trans. Knowl. Data Eng. **35**(9), 9628–9641 (2023). https://doi.org/10.1109/TKDE.2023.3243239

32. Pan, F., et al.: Warm up cold-start advertisements: Improving CTR predictions via learning to learn ID embeddings. In: Proceedings of the 42nd International ACM SIGIR Conference on Research and Development in Information Retrieval, pp. 695-704 (2019)
33. Zhu, Y., et al.: Learning to warm up cold item embeddings for cold-start recommendation with meta scaling and shifting networks. In: Proceedings of the 44th International ACM SIGIR Conference on Research and Development in Information Retrieval (SIGIR'21). Association for Computing Machinery, New York, NY, USA, pp. 1167–1176 (2021)
34. Wang, H., et al.: Knowledge-aware graph neural networks with label smoothness regularization for recommender systems. In: Proceedings of the 25th ACM SIGKDD International Conference on Knowledge Discovery & Data Mining, pp. 968–977 (2019)
35. Lee, H., et al.: Melu: meta-learned user preference estimator for cold-start recommendation. In: Proceedings of the 25th ACM SIGKDD International Conference on Knowledge Discovery & Data Mining, pp. 1073–1082 (2019)
36. Lu, Y., Fang, Y., Shi, C: Meta-learning on heterogeneous information networks for cold-start recommendation. In: Proceedings of the 26th ACM SIGKDD International Conference on Knowledge Discovery & Data Mining, pp. 1563–1573 (2020)
37. Xu, H., Xu, Y., Li, C., Zhuang, F.: Causal structure representation learning of unobserved confounders in latent space for recommendation. ACM Trans. Inf. Syst. (2025). https://doi.org/10.1145/3731447
38. Wu, S., et al.: Session-based recommendation with graph neural networks. In: Proceedings of the Thirty-Third AAAI Conference on Artificial Intelligence (AAAI-19), pp. 346–353 (2019)
39. Qin, J., et al.: User behavior retrieval for click-through rate prediction. In: Proceedings of the 43rd International ACM SIGIR Conference on Research and Development in Information Retrieval, pp. 2347-2356 (2020)
40. He, X., Chua, T.S.: Neural factorization machines for sparse predictive analytics. In: Proceedings of the 40th International ACM SIGIR Conference on Research and Development in Information Retrieval, pp. 355-364 (2017)
41. Brock, A., et al.: High-performance large-scale image recognition without normalization. arXiv preprint arXiv:2102.06171 (2021)
42. Wang, R., Fu, B., Fu, G., Wang, M.: Deep & Cross Network for Ad Click Predictions. In: Proceedings of the ADKDD'17. Association for Computing Machinery, New York, NY, USA, pp. 12:1–12:7 (2017)
43. He, K., Zhang, X., Ren, S., Sun, J.: Deep residual learning for image recognition. In: Proceedings of the IEEE conference on computer vision and pattern recognition, pp. 770–778 (2016)

Identifying Collaborative Enterprise Communities in Multi-chain Industrial Networks via Incomplete Multi-view Clustering

Xianghui Hu[1], Kai Di[1], Yichuan Jiang[2], Jie Chen[2], Zhengyi An[3], and Pan Li[1](✉)

[1] School of Automation, Zhejiang Normal University, Hangzhou 311231, China
{dikai,lipan}@seu.edu.cn

[2] School of Computer Science and Engineering, Southeast University, Nanjing 211189, China
{yjiang,220224297}@seu.edu.cn

[3] School of Cyber Science and Engineering, Southeast University, Nanjing 211189, China
230239729@seu.edu.cn

Abstract. As industrial ecosystems evolve toward more interconnected and dynamic architectures, multi-chain collaborative networks are emerging as a vital paradigm in service computing, enabling flexible enterprise partnerships and resource sharing across supply chains. In such settings, enterprise data are inherently multi-view, integrating diverse attribute features and network topologies. However, these datasets often suffer from missing information due to privacy concerns, fragmented data collection, and limited sharing practices, hindering accurate analysis of collaboration patterns and community structures crucial for strategic decision-making. Existing methods for incomplete multi-view clustering typically focus on either attribute features or topological information in isolation and often rely on simple, one-time imputations that fail to capture complex interdependencies among enterprises. To address these limitations, we propose Cyclic Reconstruction with Topological Constraints for Incomplete Multi-View Clustering (CRTC-IMVC), a novel framework that iteratively reconstructs missing attributes guided by network structure. By introducing topological supervision into the reconstruction process, CRTC-IMVC ensures that the recovered data reflect both intrinsic attributes and inter-enterprise connections. Additionally, it incorporates global constraints via graph Laplacian regularization to maintain consistency across views and avoid fragmented representations. Extensive experiments on both a real-world multi-chain industrial network dataset and two public multi-view benchmarks demonstrate that CRTC-IMVC significantly outperforms existing approaches in clustering accuracy and robustness under varying levels of data incompleteness. Remarkably, CRTC-IMVC sustains high performance even as missing rates increase, underscoring its potential for practical applications in collaborative analytics and industrial network analysis.

© The Author(s), under exclusive license to Springer Nature Singapore Pte Ltd. 2027
H. Sun et al. (Eds.): ChineseCSCW 2025, CCIS 2911, pp. 282–296, 2027.
https://doi.org/10.1007/978-981-92-0288-1_21

Keywords: Incomplete Multi-View Clustering · Collaborative Enterprise Communities · Industrial Networks · Topological Constraints

1 Introduction

In service-oriented industrial ecosystems, enterprises interact across multiple supply chains via heterogeneous services, forming complex inter-organizational networks. These networks are naturally modeled as multi-view graphs, where each view corresponds to a distinct type of service interaction or data source. Accurate modeling of such multi-view data is crucial for service discovery, collaboration optimization, and efficient resource allocation in industrial service platforms.

However, a key challenge in real-world service-oriented computing scenarios is data incompleteness. Due to proprietary technologies, siloed enterprise systems, and privacy-preserving constraints, service-related information is often fragmented and inconsistently available across views. These issues hinder comprehensive understanding of enterprise behaviors and disrupt critical tasks such as service-based community detection.

Traditional single-view clustering methods [1,6] fall short in capturing the multi-relational nature of service interactions, while standard multi-view clustering approaches assume full data availability—an assumption that rarely holds in decentralized industrial service environments. Existing joint representation learning [2,4,15] and graph-based techniques [3,5] are susceptible to distorted latent spaces or structural misalignment when facing missing data across views.

Incomplete multi-view clustering in service computing introduces several technical challenges: heterogeneity of missing patterns across service views, inconsistent dimensionality, and increased noise from partial observations. Naive imputation or mean-filling often introduces bias, while early matrix factorization-based methods [9,18] lack flexibility to handle multi-relational and topological dependencies in complex service systems.

To tackle these issues, we propose **Cyclic Reconstruction with Topological Constraints for Incomplete Multi-View Clustering (CRTC-IMVC)**, a novel framework designed for service-oriented industrial networks. CRTC-IMVC processes multi-view enterprise datasets that contain both incomplete attribute features and service network structures. We adopt non-negative matrix factorization to construct a shared latent subspace and iteratively reconstruct missing data via a topology-supervised cyclic optimization process.

A key innovation is the incorporation of service topology information as supervisory signals during the reconstruction process. Unlike prior approaches that rely solely on either attribute features [8,14] or network links [13,17], CRTC-IMVC jointly leverages both, capturing the latent dependencies among service providers and consumers. This reflects the core goals of service-oriented computing—integrating heterogeneous service components for coherent decision support.

We further introduce adaptive view weighting and graph Laplacian regularization to preserve global consistency across views, extending techniques from [10] to the incomplete multi-view setting. This enables our model to maintain robust service clustering even under significant data sparsity.

Our main contributions include:

- **A cyclic reconstruction framework** that incorporates service topology into representation learning, enabling structure-aware data imputation in service-oriented multi-view settings.
- **A topological supervision mechanism** that ensures semantically related service entities are embedded similarly, enhancing service community detection.
- **Global consistency preservation** through Laplacian regularization and view-adaptive integration, facilitating robust clustering in complex service networks.
- **Extensive experimental validation** on real-world industrial datasets and public service graphs, demonstrating superior performance across varying levels of incompleteness compared to state-of-the-art multi-view clustering methods.

2 Problem Definition and Model Formulation

We first formally define the incomplete multi-view clustering problem in multi-chain industrial networks, then present our CRTC-IMVC framework.

2.1 Problem Definition

Definition 1. ***(Incomplete Multi-View Industrial Network).*** *An incomplete multi-view industrial network consists of N enterprise nodes observed across m views, represented as $\mathcal{G} = (\mathcal{X}, \mathcal{W})$, where:*

- $\mathcal{X} = \{\mathbf{X}^{[1]}, \mathbf{X}^{[2]}, \ldots, \mathbf{X}^{[m]}\}$ *is the collection of enterprise attribute matrices with $\mathbf{X}^{[k]} \in \mathbb{R}^{d_k \times N}$ representing the k-th view, and d_k is the feature dimension of that view.*
- $\mathcal{W} = \{\mathbf{W}^{[1]}, \mathbf{W}^{[2]}, \ldots, \mathbf{W}^{[m]}\}$ *contains the adjacency matrices encoding topological connections, where $w_{ij}^{[k]} = 1$ indicates a connection between enterprises i and j in view k.*
- *For each view k, the attribute matrix $\mathbf{X}^{[k]}$ can be partitioned into observed components $\mathbf{X}_E^{[k]} \in \mathbb{R}^{d_k \times N_E^{[k]}}$ and missing components $\mathbf{X}_M^{[k]} \in \mathbb{R}^{d_k \times N_M^{[k]}}$, where $N = N_E^{[k]} + N_M^{[k]}$.*

Definition 2. ***(Enterprise Community Detection).*** *Given an incomplete multi-view industrial network $\mathcal{G}$, the enterprise community detection task aims to partition the N enterprises into C disjoint communities $\Upsilon_1, \Upsilon_2, \ldots, \Upsilon_C$ such that:*

- *Enterprises within the same community exhibit high similarity in terms of both attribute features and topological connections.*
- *The partitioning maximizes intra-community cohesion and inter-community separation despite incomplete observations.*

2.2 The CRTC-IMVC Framework

Our CRTC-IMVC framework addresses enterprise community detection through topology-supervised cyclic reconstruction of incomplete multi-view data. The key intuition is that missing attributes can be more accurately reconstructed by leveraging both observed attributes and topological relationships.

Shared Latent Representation. Following multi-view learning principles, we assume all views share an underlying latent subspace that captures essential enterprise characteristics. For each view k, we model the relationship between the attribute matrix $\mathbf{X}^{[k]}$ and this latent space through non-negative matrix factorization (NMF):

$$\mathbf{X}^{[k]} \approx \mathbf{U}^{[k]}\mathbf{P} \tag{1}$$

where $\mathbf{U}^{[k]} \in \mathbb{R}^{d_k \times r}$ is the view-specific basis matrix, and $\mathbf{P} \in \mathbb{R}^{r \times N}$ is the shared latent representation across all views. To ensure non-negativity, we normalize the input matrices using min-max scaling:

$$x_{id}^{[k]} = \frac{x_{id}^{[k]} - \min_{1\leq j\leq N} x_{jd}^{[k]}}{\max_{1\leq j\leq N} x_{jd}^{[k]} - \min_{1\leq j\leq N} x_{jd}^{[k]}}, \quad d = 1, \ldots, d_k \tag{2}$$

Cyclic Reconstruction with Constraints. To jointly model attributes and topology while handling missing data, we formulate the CRTC-IMVC objective function:

$$\begin{aligned}
&\min J\big(\mathbf{X}^{[k]}, \mathbf{U}^{[k]}, \mathbf{P}, \mathbf{S}, \varpi^{[k]}\big) \\
&= \sum_{k=1}^{m} \left[\varpi^{[k]} \left(\left|\mathbf{X}^{[k]} - \mathbf{U}^{[k]}\mathbf{P}\right|^2 + \lambda \left|\mathbf{U}^{[k]}\right|^2 + \alpha \operatorname{tr}(\mathbf{P}\mathbf{L}^{[k]}\mathbf{P}^T)\right)\right] \\
&\quad + \beta \operatorname{tr}(\mathbf{PLsP}^T) + \gamma \left|\mathbf{S}\right|^2 + \delta \sum_{k=1}^{m} \varpi^{[k]} \ln \varpi^{[k]} \\
&\text{s.t.} \quad \mathbf{X}_E^{[k]} = \mathbf{X}^{[k]}\mathbf{C}E^{[k]}, \quad \varpi^{[k]} \in [0,1], \quad \sum k = 1^m \varpi^{[k]} = 1, \\
&\mathbf{S}_i^T\mathbf{1} = 1, \quad \mathbf{U}^{[k]}, \mathbf{P}, \mathbf{S} \geq 0
\end{aligned} \tag{3}$$

where:

- $\mathbf{C}_E^{[k]}$ is a column selection matrix that identifies observed samples in view k
- $\mathbf{L}^{[k]} = \mathbf{D}^{[k]} - \mathbf{W}^{[k]}$ is the Laplacian matrix for view k
- $\mathbf{L}_S$ is the Laplacian matrix derived from the similarity matrix $\mathbf{S}$
- $\varpi^{[k]}$ represents the adaptive weight for view k

3 Optimization Algorithm

We now present an efficient optimization procedure for the CRTC-IMVC framework. The objective function in Eq. (3) involves multiple variables that are coupled in a non-convex manner. To solve this challenging optimization problem, we adopt an alternating minimization approach that iteratively updates each variable while fixing the others.

3.1 Alternating Optimization Framework

Let $\mathbf{X}_t^{[k]}$, $\mathbf{U}_t^{[k]}$, $\mathbf{P}_t$, $\mathbf{S}_t$, and $\varpi_t^{[k]}$ denote the variables at iteration t. Our optimization procedure decomposes the original problem into five subproblems that are solved sequentially:

- Update incomplete data matrices $\mathbf{X}^{[k]}$ by reconstructing missing values
- Update view-specific basis matrices $\mathbf{U}^{[k]}$ using multiplicative updates
- Update shared latent representation $\mathbf{P}$ with topological constraints
- Update similarity matrix $\mathbf{S}$ to maintain global consistency
- Update view weights $\varpi^{[k]}$ to adaptively balance multiple views

This alternating strategy guarantees non-negative solutions while progressively minimizing the objective function until convergence.

3.2 Optimization Steps

Missing Data Reconstruction. With all other variables fixed, we update each view's attribute matrix $\mathbf{X}^{[k]}$ by preserving observed values while reconstructing missing entries using the current basis matrices and latent representation:

$$\mathbf{X}_{t+1}^{[k]} = \mathbf{U}_t^{[k]}\mathbf{P}_t\mathbf{C}_M^{[k]}\mathbf{F}_M^{[k]} + \mathbf{X}_E^{[k]}\mathbf{F}_E^{[k]} \tag{4}$$

Here, $\mathbf{C}_M^{[k]}$ selects columns corresponding to missing samples, while $\mathbf{F}_M^{[k]}$ and $\mathbf{F}_E^{[k]}$ are reassembly matrices that map reconstructed and observed data back to their original positions:

$$\mathbf{C}_E^{[k]} = \mathbf{I}[:, E_k], \quad E_k \subseteq 1, \ldots, N : \text{indices of observed samples} \tag{5}$$

$$\mathbf{C}_M^{[k]} = \mathbf{I}[:, M_k], \quad M_k \subseteq 1, \ldots, N : \text{indices of missing samples} \tag{6}$$

$$\mathbf{F}_E^{[k]} = [\mathbf{I}_E^{[k]} \quad \mathbf{O}_E^{[k]}] \in \mathbb{R}^{N_E^{[k]} \times N} \tag{7}$$

$$\mathbf{F}_M^{[k]} = [\mathbf{O}_M^{[k]} \quad \mathbf{I}_M^{[k]}] \in \mathbb{R}^{N_M^{[k]} \times N} \tag{8}$$

This update ensures that observed values remain unchanged while missing values are reconstructed based on the current latent representation, preserving data integrity throughout the optimization process.

Basis Matrix Update. For each view k, we update the basis matrix $\mathbf{U}^{[k]}$ by minimizing:

$$\mathcal{L}_1(\mathbf{U}^{[k]}) = \varpi^{[k]}(|\mathbf{X}^{[k]} - \mathbf{U}^{[k]}\mathbf{P}|_F^2 + \lambda|\mathbf{U}^{[k]}|_F^2) \tag{9}$$

Taking the gradient and applying a multiplicative update rule to ensure non-negativity, we derive:

$$\mathbf{U}_{t+1}^{[k]} = \mathbf{U}t^{[k]} \odot \frac{\mathbf{X}t + 1^{[k]}\mathbf{P}_t^T}{\mathbf{U}_t^{[k]}\mathbf{P}_t\mathbf{P}_t^T + \lambda\mathbf{U}_t^{[k]}} \tag{10}$$

where $\odot$ denotes element-wise multiplication and division is also performed element-wise. This multiplicative update automatically maintains the non-negativity constraint while adaptively adjusting the learning rate.

Latent Representation Update. The latent representation $\mathbf{P}$ integrates information from all views and incorporates topological constraints. We update it by minimizing:

$$\mathcal{L}_2(\mathbf{P}) = \sum_{k=1}^{m} \varpi^{[k]}(|\mathbf{X}^{[k]} - \mathbf{U}^{[k]}\mathbf{P}|_F^2 + \alpha \mathrm{tr}(\mathbf{P}\mathbf{L}^{[k]}\mathbf{P}^T)) + \beta \mathrm{tr}(\mathbf{P}\mathbf{L}_S\mathbf{P}^T) \tag{11}$$

Using the Laplacian decomposition $\mathbf{L}^{[k]} = \mathbf{D}^{[k]} - \mathbf{W}^{[k]}$ and applying multiplicative updates, we obtain:

$$\mathbf{P}_{t+1} = \mathbf{P}_t \odot \frac{\sum_{k=1}^{m} \varpi_t^{[k]}((\mathbf{U}_{t+1}^{[k]})^T\mathbf{X}_{t+1}^{[k]} + \alpha\mathbf{P}_t\mathbf{W}^{[k]}) + \frac{1}{2}\mathbf{P}_t(\mathbf{S}_t + \mathbf{S}_t^T)}{\sum_{k=1}^{m} \varpi_t^{[k]}((\mathbf{U}_{t+1}^{[k]})^T\mathbf{U}_{t+1}^{[k]}\mathbf{P}_t + \alpha\mathbf{P}_t\mathbf{D}^{[k]}) + \mathbf{P}_t\mathbf{D}_S} \tag{12}$$

This update incorporates both reconstruction fidelity and topological smoothness, ensuring that the latent representation captures both attribute similarities and network structure.

Similarity Matrix Update. The similarity matrix $\mathbf{S}$ captures relationships between enterprises in the latent space. We update it by solving:

$$\min_{\mathbf{S}} \beta \mathrm{tr}(\mathbf{P}\mathbf{L}_S\mathbf{P}^T) + \gamma|\mathbf{S}|_F^2 \quad \text{s.t.} \quad \mathbf{S}_i^T\mathbf{1} = 1, \mathbf{S} \geq 0 \tag{13}$$

This constrained optimization problem can be reformulated row-wise as:

$$\min_{\mathbf{S}_i} |\mathbf{S}_i + \mathbf{Q}_i|^2 \quad \text{s.t.} \quad \mathbf{S}_i^T\mathbf{1} = 1, \mathbf{S}_i \geq 0 \tag{14}$$

where $\mathbf{Q}_{ij} = \frac{\beta}{2\gamma}|\mathbf{p}_i - \mathbf{p}_j|^2$. Using KKT conditions, we derive the closed-form solution:

$$\mathbf{S}_{ij,t+1} = \left(\frac{1 + \sum_{j=1}^{l} \widetilde{\mathbf{Q}}_{ij,t+1}}{l} - \mathbf{Q}_{ij,t+1}\right)_+ \tag{15}$$

where $\widetilde{\mathbf{Q}}_i$ contains the l smallest elements from $\mathbf{Q}_i$ and $(x)_+ = \max(x, 0)$.

View Weight Update. Finally, we update the view weights $\varpi^{[k]}$ to adaptively balance multiple views based on their reconstruction quality and topological consistency:

$$\min_{\varpi^{[k]}} \sum_{k=1}^{m} \varpi^{[k]} T^{[k]} + \delta \sum_{k=1}^{m} \varpi^{[k]} \ln \varpi^{[k]} \quad \text{s.t.} \quad \sum_{k=1}^{m} \varpi^{[k]} = 1, \varpi^{[k]} \geq 0 \tag{16}$$

where $T^{[k]} = |\mathbf{X}^{[k]} - \mathbf{U}^{[k]}\mathbf{P}|_F^2 + \lambda|\mathbf{U}^{[k]}|_F^2 + \alpha \mathrm{tr}(\mathbf{P}\mathbf{L}^{[k]}\mathbf{P}^T)$. This yields the softmax-style update:

$$\varpi_{t+1}^{[k]} = \frac{\exp(-T_{t+1}^{[k]}/\delta)}{\sum_{k=1}^{m} \exp(-T_{t+1}^{[k]}/\delta)} \tag{17}$$

3.3 Algorithm Summary

The complete CRTC-IMVC optimization procedure is summarized in Algorithm 1. The algorithm iteratively updates all variables until convergence or reaching the maximum number of iterations.

Algorithm 1: The CRTC-IMVC Optimization Procedure

Input: Incomplete multi-view enterprise attribute and topology matrices $(\mathbf{X}_E^{[k]}, \mathbf{W}^{[k]})$ for $k = 1, \ldots, m$; Number of collaboration clusters C; Regularization parameters λ, α, β, γ, and δ; Maximum number of iterations $t_{\max}$.

Output: Completed multi-view attribute matrices $\{\mathbf{X}^{[k]}\}$ for $k = 1, \ldots, m$; Optimal latent representation matrix $\mathbf{P}^*$; Adaptive view weights $\{\varpi^{[k]}\}$ for $k = 1, \ldots, m$; Enterprise collaboration group partition $\{\Upsilon_i\}$ for $i = 1, \ldots, C$.

$t \leftarrow 0$;
Randomly initialize $\mathbf{U}_t^{[k]}$, $\mathbf{P}_t$, $\mathbf{S}_t$, and $\varpi_t^{[k]}$;
Compute Laplacian matrices $\mathbf{L}^{[k]}$ from $\mathbf{W}^{[k]}$;
repeat
  $t \leftarrow t + 1$;
  Update $\mathbf{X}_t^{[k]}$ via Eq. (4);
  Update $\mathbf{U}_t^{[k]}$ via Eq. (10);
  Update $\mathbf{P}_t$ via Eq. (12);
  Update $\mathbf{S}_t$ via Eq. (15);
  Update $\varpi_t^{[k]}$ via Eq. (17);
  Compute objective function value J_t via Eq. (3);
until $\left|\frac{J_{t+1} - J_t}{J_t}\right| < \epsilon$ *or* $t = t_{\max}$
Apply K-means on $\mathbf{P}^* = \mathbf{P}_t$ to obtain community partition $\{\Upsilon_i\}_{i=1}^{C}$;
return $\mathbf{P}^*$, $\{\Upsilon_i\}_{i=1}^{C}$.

3.4 Time and Space Complexity Analysis

Let $d_{\max} = \max\{d^{[1]}, \ldots, d^{[m]}\}$. As shown in Algorithm 1, the time complexity of the proposed CRTC-IMVC framework mainly comprises the following components:

- **Multi-view Data Completion:** Involving matrix multiplication and imputation operations, with a time complexity of $O(md_{\max}N^2)$.
- **Basis Matrix Update:** Involving matrix multiplications, with a time complexity of $O(md_{\max}rN)$.
- **Latent representation update:** Entailing multi-view matrix operations and Laplacian regularization, with a complexity of $O(m(d_{\max}rN + rN^2) + rN^2)$.
- **Similarity Matrix Update:** Involving pairwise distance computation and sorting, with a time complexity of $O(N^2 \log N)$.
- **View Weight Update:** Including matrix norm and trace computations for $T^{[k]}$, yielding a complexity of $O(m(d_{\max}rN + rN^2 + r^2N))$.

Given that $r \ll N$ and $r < d_{\max}$ typically hold in practice, the overall time complexity across t iterations is $O(t(md_{\max}N^2 + N^2 \log N))$, and the total space complexity is approximately $O(mN^2)$.

4 Experiments

To validate the performance of the proposed CRTC-IMVC algorithm in real-world scenarios, we conduct extensive experiments covering the following aspects: clustering performance comparison on a real-world multi-chain industrial network dataset and two public multi-view datasets, and robustness to missing data rates.

4.1 Experimental Setup

Datasets. We evaluate our method on both industrial and public benchmark datasets:

Multi-chain Industrial Network (MCIN) consists of enterprise data from the Jinan Industrial Development Park with three views: (1) Business Performance (6 features including sales and operating metrics), (2) Financial Structure (8 features including assets and production capacity), and (3) Energy Consumption (4 features). Each view includes topological relationships based on market similarity, financial complementarity, and energy efficiency synergy, with natural missing values due to privacy constraints.

Public Benchmark Datasets include WebKB (3 views, 203 samples, 3 classes) and Caltech101-7 (6 views, 1474 samples, 7 classes), as summarized in Table 1. Since these datasets lack explicit network structure, we construct topological connections using a class-informed strategy with sparsity parameter $\tau = 10/N$, creating sparse networks that simulate enterprise connections.

Table 1. Summary of Public Real-World Datasets

Dataset	#Views	#Samples	#Classes	#Topology Edges	# Features
WebKB	3	203	3	609	170
				1015	230
				609	230
Caltech101-7	6	1474	7	5896	48
				4422	40
				5896	254
				4422	1984
				2948	512
				5896	928

Comparison Methods We compare CRTC-IMVC against eight state-of-the-art methods for incomplete multi-view clustering:

- **PVC** [9]: Partial multi-view clustering using NMF to learn a shared subspace
- **IMG** [18]: Graph-regularized multimodal grouping with adaptive manifold regularization
- **DAIMC** [7]: Double-aligned incomplete multi-view clustering with consensus basis matrices
- **OPIMC** [8]: One-pass incomplete multi-view clustering using weighted matrix factorization
- **IMSR** [12]: Incomplete multi-view subspace representation learning with imputation
- **DCP** [11]: Deep contrastive clustering with entropy-based view recovery
- **IMCRV** [16]: Incomplete multi-view clustering with reciprocal-view reconstruction
- **CSGR** [10]: Consensus spectral graph regularization for multi-layer networks

For PVC and IMG (which only handle two views), we evaluate all pairwise view combinations and report the best result. For fair comparison, we simulate missing data by removing entries such that missing instances are mutually exclusive across views, as some baselines cannot handle overlapping missingness patterns.

Evaluation Metrics. We use four metrics to evaluate clustering performance: Accuracy (ACC), Normalized Mutual Information (NMI), Calinski-Harabasz Index (CHI), and Davies-Bouldin Index (DBI). Higher values of ACC, NMI, and CHI indicate better performance, while lower DBI values are preferred. For the industrial network dataset where ground truth is unavailable, we use CHI and DBI as internal validation metrics.

Implementation Details. We implement all experiments in MATLAB. The latent space dimension is set equal to the number of clusters for all methods. We tune parameters via grid search: $\lambda \in \{10^{-3}, 10^{-2}, ..., 10^{3}\}$, $\alpha \in$

$\{10^{-1}, 10^0, ..., 10^3\}$, $\beta \in \{10^{-2}, 10^{-1}, ..., 10^2\}$, $\gamma \in \{10^{-3}, 10^{-2}, ..., 10^3\}$, and $\delta \in \{10^3, 10^4, ..., 10^6\}$. Each experiment is repeated 20 times with different random initializations, and average results are reported.

4.2 Enterprise Community Detection in Industrial Networks

We first evaluate CRTC-IMVC on the industrial network dataset to assess its effectiveness in real-world enterprise community detection. Since ground truth labels are unavailable for this proprietary dataset, we use internal validation metrics (CHI and DBI) to evaluate clustering quality.

To isolate the contribution of topological supervision, we perform an ablation study comparing the full CRTC-IMVC framework against a variant without topological constraints (setting $\alpha = 0$). We test both methods with cluster numbers ranging from 4 to 8 based on domain knowledge of typical enterprise coalition sizes in the industrial park.

Table 2. Clustering performance on the industrial network dataset

Method	CHI ↑					DBI ↓				
	C=4	C=5	C=6	C=7	C=8	C=4	C=5	C=6	C=7	C=8
No Topology	15.67	21.87	48.98	38.72	34.09	6.90	5.84	5.47	7.94	7.77
CRTC-IMVC	**33.94**	**73.70**	**76.83**	**56.45**	**46.44**	**3.52**	**3.48**	**2.56**	**2.90**	**3.23**

Table 2 shows that CRTC-IMVC consistently outperforms the non-topological variant across all cluster configurations. The improvements are substantial—averaging 117% higher CHI and 55% lower DBI—demonstrating that topological supervision significantly enhances clustering quality. The optimal performance occurs with C=6 clusters, yielding the highest CHI (76.83) and lowest DBI (2.56), which aligns with domain experts' understanding of the industrial park's natural community structure.

These results validate our core hypothesis that incorporating network topology into reconstruction significantly improves enterprise community detection under incomplete data conditions. By guiding attribute reconstruction with structural constraints, CRTC-IMVC captures complementary patterns that would be missed by methods relying solely on attributes.

4.3 Performance on Public Benchmark Datasets

To evaluate robustness under varying degrees of incompleteness, we simulate missing data at rates from 10% to 70% on WebKB and Caltech101-7 datasets. Tables 3 and 4 present detailed ACC and NMI results for all comparison methods across different missing rates.

Based on these experimental results, we observe several key findings:

Table 3. ACC comparison on WebKB and Caltech101-7 datasets

Method	WebKB				Caltech101-7			
	10%	30%	50%	70%	10%	30%	50%	70%
PVC	0.764	0.655	0.527	0.527	0.397	0.369	0.289	0.253
IMG	0.788	0.719	0.616	0.532	0.481	0.486	0.407	0.351
DAIMC	0.754	0.759	0.714	0.660	0.585	0.588	0.545	0.518
OPIMC	0.729	0.714	0.709	0.576	*0.733*	*0.725*	*0.721*	*0.717*
IMSR	0.636	0.596	0.517	0.507	0.570	0.552	0.520	0.502
DCP	0.493	0.478	0.468	0.384	0.697	0.649	0.638	0.583
IMCRV	0.754	0.709	0.581	0.522	0.601	0.599	0.487	0.400
CSGR	*0.857*	*0.857*	*0.857*	*0.857*	0.596	0.596	0.596	0.596
CRTC-IMVC	**0.956**	**0.951**	**0.926**	**0.877**	**0.895**	**0.856**	**0.839**	**0.823**

Table 4. NMI comparison on WebKB and Caltech101-7 datasets

Method	WebKB				Caltech101-7			
	10%	30%	50%	70%	10%	30%	50%	70%
PVC	0.499	0.327	0.072	0.023	0.221	0.132	0.069	0.024
IMG	0.541	0.378	0.158	0.032	0.238	0.163	0.099	0.032
DAIMC	0.438	0.421	0.297	0.227	0.581	0.583	0.378	0.271
OPIMC	0.298	0.295	0.293	0.135	0.554	0.540	0.536	0.534
IMSR	0.232	0.223	0.199	0.196	0.581	0.577	0.543	0.533
DCP	0.031	0.025	0.023	0.022	0.453	0.411	0.402	0.397
IMCRV	0.410	0.366	0.227	0.161	0.400	0.384	0.332	0.285
CSGR	*0.706*	*0.706*	*0.706*	*0.706*	*0.666*	*0.666*	*0.666*	*0.666*
CRTC-IMVC	**0.956**	**0.938**	**0.927**	**0.800**	**0.795**	**0.757**	**0.751**	**0.736**

1) Superior Performance: CRTC-IMVC consistently outperforms all comparison methods across both datasets and all missing rates. On WebKB, it achieves 95.6% ACC and 95.6% NMI at 10% missing rate, surpassing the second-best method by 9.9% points in ACC and 25.0% points in NMI. On Caltech101-7, it reaches 89.5% ACC and 79.5% NMI, exceeding the second-best performer by 16.2 and 12.9% points, respectively.

2) Robustness to Missing Data: As the missing rate increases from 10% to 70%, CRTC-IMVC demonstrates remarkable resilience. On WebKB, its ACC drops by only 7.9% points (from 95.6% to 87.7%), while other attribute-based methods show much steeper declines—for example, IMG drops by 25.6% points (from 78.8% to 53.2%) and IMCRV by 23.2% points (from 75.4% to 52.2%).

Similarly, on Caltech101-7, CRTC-IMVC maintains 82.3% ACC even at 70% missing rate, representing only a 7.2% point decrease from its performance at

10% missing rate. In contrast, most other methods show severe degradation—IMCRV drops by 20.1% points and DCP by 11.4% points.

3) Method-Specific Insights: OPIMC shows relatively stable performance on Caltech101-7 (only 1.6% point drop in ACC from 10% to 70% missing rate), making it the second-best performer on this dataset. However, it performs considerably worse on WebKB, suggesting its effectiveness varies by data characteristics.

CSGR, which relies solely on topological information, maintains constant performance across all missing rates (85.7% ACC on WebKB and 59.6% ACC on Caltech101-7). While this stability is advantageous at high missing rates, it limits performance at low missing rates where attribute information is abundant.

Traditional incomplete multi-view methods (PVC, IMG) that don't effectively integrate structural information show the steepest performance drops as missing rates increase, highlighting the importance of topology-guided reconstruction.

Deep learning-based DCP performs well on Caltech101-7 at low missing rates but degrades significantly as missingness increases, suggesting limited effectiveness of its imputation strategy under severe data loss.

4) Dataset-Specific Observations: The performance gap between CRTC-IMVC and other methods is particularly pronounced on WebKB, where our method maintains over 87% ACC even at 70% missing rate. This may be attributed to WebKB's well-defined community structure, which our topology-guided approach effectively leverages. On Caltech101-7, which has more complex and heterogeneous features, CRTC-IMVC still demonstrates superior performance, confirming its adaptability to different data characteristics.

These results validate that CRTC-IMVC's topology-guided reconstruction approach effectively leverages complementary information sources across different dataset scales and characteristics. The consistent performance advantage, especially under high missing rates, confirms the method's suitability for real-world industrial applications where incomplete data is common.

4.4 Parameter Sensitivity Analysis

We analyze five key parameters in CRTC-IMVC: λ (basis matrix complexity), α (local topology regularization), β (global consistency), γ (similarity matrix regularization), and δ (view weight balancing). Tests are conducted on WebKB and Caltech101-7 with 50% missing data.

Analysis of Topology Parameters α and β. Fig. 1 shows how topology parameters affect clustering performance. Larger values of α (local topology regularization) generally improve results, particularly in the range $10^0, 10^1, 10^2$, highlighting the importance of view-specific topological constraints. However, when α exceeds 10^3, performance degrades, suggesting excessive constraints reduce model flexibility.

For β (global regularization), smaller values ($10^{-2}, 10^{-1}, 10^0$) produce better results, indicating global consistency plays a less dominant role than local topological supervision. Optimal performance occurs with strong local constraints

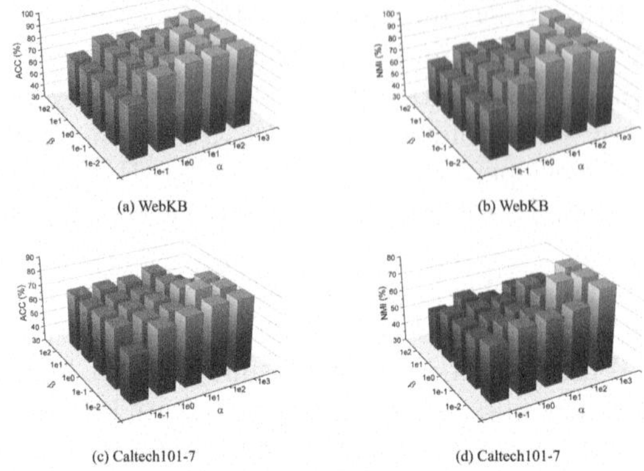

Fig. 1. Parameter sensitivity analysis of topology parameters α and β on WebKB and Caltech101-7 datasets (50% missing rate)

(high α) and moderate global constraints (low to medium β). Caltech101-7 shows greater sensitivity to parameter changes, likely due to its larger scale and complex feature space.

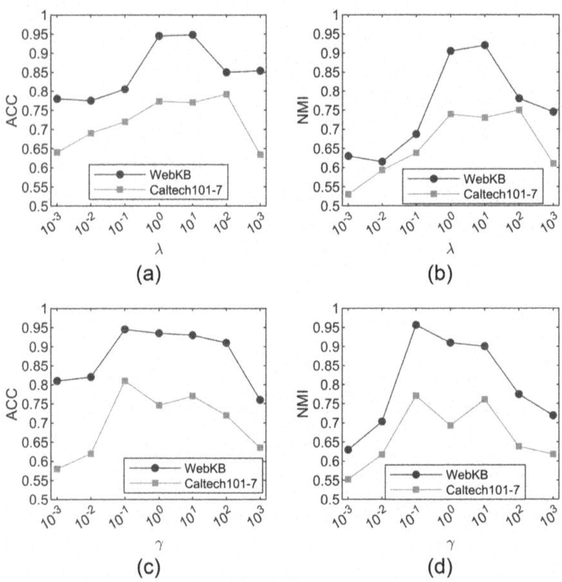

Fig. 2. Parameter sensitivity analysis of regularization parameters λ and γ on WebKB and Caltech101-7 datasets (50% missing rate)

Analysis of Regularization Parameters λ and γ. Fig. 2 shows the effects of λ and γ on clustering performance. Moderate values (10^{-2} to 10^2) consistently yield optimal results, with WebKB showing greater robustness to parameter changes than Caltech101-7.

When λ is too small ($<10^{-2}$), the model may overfit to observed data; when too large ($> 10^2$), excessive regularization constrains the basis matrices' expressiveness. Similarly, extreme γ values either make the similarity matrix too sparse (low values) or too uniform (high values), degrading performance.

Overall, CRTC-IMVC shows robustness to parameter variations within reasonable ranges. Based on our experiments, we recommend starting with $\alpha \in 10^0, 10^1$, $\beta \in 10^{-1}, 10^0$, $\lambda \in 10^0, 10^1$, and $\gamma \in 10^0, 10^1$ for new datasets.

For view weight parameter δ, optimal values typically scale with dataset size: smaller datasets perform better with $\delta \approx 10^3$, while larger datasets benefit from higher values (10^4-10^5) to ensure more uniform view contributions.

5 Conclusion

We tackle the critical challenge of enterprise community detection in service-oriented industrial supply chains with incomplete multi-view data. To this end, we propose a novel method, CRTC-IMVC, which integrates network topology as supervisory signals to guide the reconstruction of missing attributes while ensuring global consistency in the shared latent space.

Extensive experiments on both real-world industrial service networks and public benchmark datasets validate the effectiveness of our approach. On the industrial dataset, CRTC-IMVC achieved substantial improvements over non-topological baselines, including a 117% increase in CHI and a 55% reduction in DBI. On public datasets, our method consistently outperformed state-of-the-art techniques across a wide range of missing data scenarios, maintaining robust clustering performance even with 70% missing attributes.

These results confirm that topology-guided reconstruction is a powerful strategy for managing incomplete multi-view information in enterprise service networks, offering significant practical implications for service-based collaboration, supply chain intelligence, and industrial network optimization. Future work will explore scalability to large-scale service ecosystems and extend the framework to support dynamic and evolving inter-enterprise relationships.

Acknowledgement. This work was supported by the National Key Research and Development Program of China (No. 2024YFB3309400), the National Natural Science Foundation of China (Nos. 62576088, 62303111, 62476121, 62076060), the Guangxi Science and Technology Major Program, China (No. AA24206003), and the Key Research and Development Program of Guangxi, China (No. AB2410317).

References

1. Bedzek, J., Ehrlich, R., Full, W.: The fuzzy c-means clustering algorithm. Comput. Geosci. **10**(1), 191–203 (1984)
2. Benjamin, J.B.M., Yang, M.S.: Weighted multi-view possibilistic c-means clustering with L2 regularization. IEEE Trans. Fuzzy Syst. **30**(5), 1357–1370 (2022)
3. Chen, M.S., Wang, C.D., Lai, J.H.: Low-rank tensor based proximity learning for multi-view clustering. IEEE Trans. Knowl. Data Eng. **35**(5), 5076–5090 (2022)
4. Deng, Z.: Multi-view clustering with the cooperation of visible and hidden views. IEEE Trans. Knowl. Data Eng. **34**(2), 803–815 (2022)
5. Fang, S.G., et al.: Efficient multi-view clustering via unified and discrete bipartite graph learning. IEEE Trans. Neural Netw. Learn. Syst. **35**(8), 11436–11447 (2024)
6. Hartigan, J.A., Wong, M.A.: Algorithm as 136: a k-means clustering algorithm. J. Roy. Stat. Soc.: Ser. C (Appl. Stat.) **28**(1), 100–108 (1979)
7. Hu, M., Chen, S.: Doubly aligned incomplete multi-view clustering. IJCAI, 2262–2268 (2019)
8. Hu, M., Chen, S.: One-pass incomplete multi-view clustering. In: Proceedings of the AAAI Conference on Artificial Intelligence, vol. 33, pp. 3838–3845. AAAI (2019)
9. Li, S.Y., Jiang, Y., Zhou, Z.H.: Partial multi-view clustering. In: Proceedings of the AAAI Conference on Artificial Intelligence, vol. 28, AAAI (2014)
10. Li, X., et al.: Consensus subspace graph regularization based on prior information for multiplex network clustering. Eng. Appl. Artif. Intell. **135**(1), 108851 (2024)
11. Lin, Y., et al.: Dual contrastive prediction for incomplete multi-view representation learning. IEEE Trans. Pattern Anal. Mach. Intell. **45**(4), 4447–4461 (2022)
12. Liu, J., et al.: Self-representation subspace clustering for incomplete multi-view data. In: Proceedings of the ACM International Conference on Multimedia, pp. 2726–2734. ACM (2021)
13. Pio-Lopez, L., Valdeolivas, A., Tichit, L., Remy, É., Baudot, A.: Multiverse: a multiplex and multiplex-heterogeneous network embedding approach. Sci. Rep. **11**(1), 8794 (2021)
14. Shao, W., He, L., Yu, P.S.: Multiple incomplete views clustering via weighted nonnegative matrix factorization with regularization. In: Proceedings of the Joint European Conference on Machine Learning and Knowledge Discovery in Databases, pp. 318–334. Springer (2015)
15. Yang, Z., Michailidis, G.: A non-negative matrix factorization method for detecting modules in heterogeneous omics multi-modal data. Bioinformatics **32**(1), 1–8 (2016)
16. Yin, J., Sun, S.: Incomplete multi-view clustering with reconstructed views. IEEE Trans. Knowl. Data Eng. **35**(3), 2671–2682 (2021)
17. Zhang, H., Qiu, L., Yi, L., Song, Y.: Scalable multiplex network embedding. In: Proceedings of the International Joint Conference on Artificial Intelligence, vol. 18, pp. 3082–3088. IJCAI (2018)
18. Zhao, H., Liu, H., Fu, Y.: Incomplete multi-modal visual data grouping. In: Proceedings of the International Joint Conference on Artificial Intelligence, pp. 2392–2398. IJCAI (2016)

Family-Aware Graph Neural Networks with Loss Function Optimization for Android Malware Classification

Ximeng Wu[1], Wan Zhang[1], Bohan Zhang[2], Xiang Li[1], and Jing Zhang[1](✉)

[1] School of Cyber Science and Engineering, Southeast University, Nanjing 211189, China
{220235471,zhangwan,lixiang_15,jingz}@seu.edu.cn

[2] College of Liberal Arts and Sciences, University of Illinois Urbana-Champaign, Urbana, IL 61801, USA
bohanz5@illinois.edu

Abstract. Android malware increasingly evolves through family-driven variants, challenging conventional detectors under obfuscation and polymorphism. We propose a family-aware graph framework that integrates static function call graph (FCG) modeling with a connectivity-aware multi-head dynamic pooling (MH-DP) to adaptively select family-critical subgraphs from permission, opcode, and topology views. A momentum-updated prototype clustering module and prototype-guided aggregation enhance intra-family compactness, while a contrastive-enhanced family loss (CE-FAR) jointly optimizes cross-entropy with family-level constraints to increase inter-family margins. Our method achieves 84.16% category accuracy and 75.60% family accuracy on CICAndMal2017, and 94.8% accuracy on Drebin, outperforming traditional baselines and remaining competitive. Ablation experiments show that removing MH-DP or family-aware regularization leads to consistent drops across datasets, whereas CE-FAR yields the most balanced robustness and discriminability without extra inference cost. Overall, the design effectively mines family-common semantics and improves resilience to obfuscation for Android malware classification.

Keywords: Android malware · Graph neural networks · Family-aware representation · Discriminative loss · Malware classification

1 Introduction

Static methods (e.g., permissions, opcodes, Manifest, and DEX features) are lightweight and scalable, but are prone to feature drift due to API renaming, reflection, packing, and junk code, and struggle to capture cross-function and component attack chains. Dynamic methods observe temporal behaviors through sandboxing of sensitive APIs, system calls, and network traffic, but incur high runtime costs, are easily bypassed by sensor, GPS, and time-zone environment

© The Author(s), under exclusive license to Springer Nature Singapore Pte Ltd. 2027
H. Sun et al. (Eds.): ChineseCSCW 2025, CCIS 2911, pp. 297–311, 2027.
https://doi.org/10.1007/978-981-92-0288-1_22

checks, and often fail to meet real-time requirements due to complex triggers. The field has seen the development of dedicated neural architectures for graphs, represented by Graph Convolutional Networks (GCNs) [5] and Graph Attention Networks (GATs) [13], and temporal graph networks (TGNs) [11] on FCGs and control flow graphs (CFGs) [14] model structural relationships. However, uniform aggregation and fixed pooling ratios often result in the dilution of critical subgraphs, while node encodings remain susceptible to obfuscation. Additionally, the absence of family-commonality-aware weighting restricts family-level generalization and reduces robustness against variants.

In response to these challenges, we present a novel Android malware detection framework centered on malware families. It seamlessly integrates a dual strategy of dynamic perception and hierarchical reinforcement to tackle the critical tasks of uncovering family commonality and countering polymorphism. The pipeline is fully static: Apktool/smali with "invoke-*" scanning constructs a semantics-preserving function call graph FCG. Dual-modality node features, comprising a PSCout/APK Explorer permission bit-vector concatenated with a Dalvik opcode histogram, are then input into a GCN backbone. Building on this foundation, we introduce three key mechanisms: (i) Multi-head dynamic scoring with connectivity-constrained top-k pooling, which jointly selects critical subgraphs based on permission, opcode, and topology views; (ii) Family prototype clustering with momentum updates, and prototype-guided cosine-weighted aggregation, which emphasizes family-shared malicious logic while suppressing noisy subgraphs; (iii) A family loss function trained jointly with cross-entropy to enforce intra-family compactness and inter-family separation. Additionally, we present Contrastive-Enhanced FAR (CE-FAR), which introduces contrastive objectives at the graph, subgraph, and prototype levels to stabilize representations and enhance robustness against small samples and obfuscation, without incurring additional inference-time complexity. Evaluations on CICAndMal2017 and Drebin show category accuracy of 84.16% and family accuracy of 75.60%, outperforming traditional baselines, with Drebin results also exceeding those of classical methods. The key contributions of this paper are outlined below:

(1) A connectivity-aware multi-head dynamic pooling mechanism that fuses permissions, opcodes, and topology to select family-critical subgraphs adaptively;
(2) A prototype-guided family refiner with momentum-updated family prototypes, cosine-weighted aggregation, and a family loss function that jointly strengthens intra-family compactness and inter-family separability;
(3) CE-FAR, a three-level contrastive training strategy (graph, subgraph, and prototype) that improves robustness to obfuscation and small-sample challenges without increasing inference complexity.

2 Related Work

2.1 Graph-Based Android Malware Detection

The graph-based approach to Android malware detection represents static or dynamic APK information as graph structures, such as FCG, and learns structural and semantic patterns for malware classification [10,17]. Wang et al. [15] proposed FAGnet, which introduces a family-aware representation refinement mechanism within a GNN framework to promote cohesion within families while enforcing a clearer separation between them, and validated its effectiveness on benchmark datasets. Ou and Xu [10] proposed S3Feature, which mines sensitive subgraphs via static analysis as discriminative features, thus improving Android malware detection with subgraph-level evidence. Xu et al. [17] constructed call graphs from DEX files and employed graph convolutional networks (GCNs) to learn behavior-level features, achieving effective Android malware detection.

2.2 Android Malware Family Classification

Android malware family classification refers to assigning malicious samples to specific families using static, dynamic, or network-traffic cues, thereby capturing cross-variant attack templates and behavioral patterns [1,6,20]. Abuthawabeh and Mahmoud [1] employed conversation-level network traffic features to build a unified detection and family-classification framework, modeling both statistical and temporal properties of communication sessions to improve family separability. Fan et al. [20] proposed FamDroid, which uses static analysis to extract structural and semantic features from APKs systematically and applies learning-based methods for family attribution, demonstrating the effectiveness of static features for family-level modeling. Kim et al. [6] designed features from built-in and custom permissions and combined them with multiple machine-learning classifiers to categorize samples into families, indicating that permission signals provide stable and scalable cues for family discrimination.

3 Methodology

3.1 Overall Architecture

The overall architecture is schematically shown in Fig. 1. The pipeline consists of four stages: (i) The Global Graph Encoder & Readout generates a global embedding from the constructed FCG. (ii) The Connectivity-Aware Multi-Head Dynamic Pooling mechanism scores nodes from permission, opcode, and topology perspectives, applying connectivity constraints to select candidate subgraphs. (iii) Subgraph Readout & Aggregation module maps each subgraph to a fixed-length vector and performs cross-subgraph weighted aggregation to produce a bag-level representation. (iv) Prototype-Guided Family Refinement aligns this representation with momentum-updated family prototypes via cosine-weighted aggregation to yield a more discriminative feature. Subsequently, the global and refined features are fused and input into a classifier to generate family scores. During the training process, cross-entropy and family loss are jointly optimized. Additionally, contrastive enhancements are introduced at the graph, subgraph, and prototype levels to strengthen intra-family cohesion and expand inter-family separability. These contrastive objectives are applied exclusively during training, resulting in no additional inference-time cost [4].

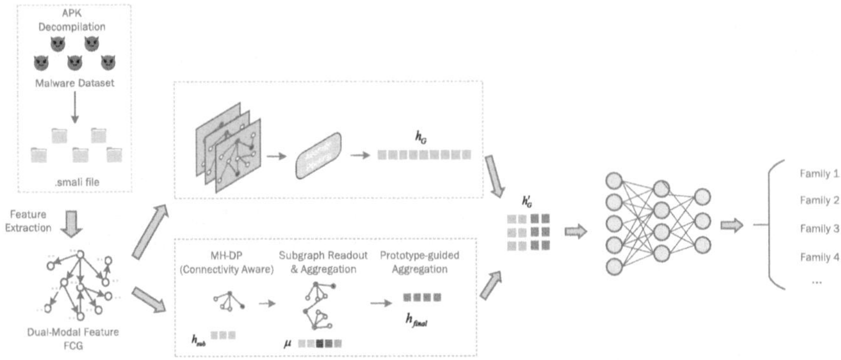

Fig. 1. Architectural overview of the proposed system.

3.2 Feature Extraction Module

In malware family classification tasks, extracting representative semantic and structural features is crucial for accurately distinguishing between different families [19]. Building on FAGnet [15], our approach leverages a static analysis-based feature extraction module. Each malware sample is first decompiled to smali code using Apktool, from which an FCG is constructed to model the program's execution logic. This process effectively removes interference caused by code obfuscation while preserving the semantic integrity of malicious behaviors.

FCG is represented as $G = (V, E)$. Each node $v \in V_G$ (where $|V_G| = n$) represents an API in the call graph. And $e_{i,j} = (v_i, v_j) \in E$ represents the invocation relationship from node v_i to v_j. The node feature matrix is denoted by X, in which each node i is represented by a dual-modal feature vector x_i, formed by concatenating its permission attributes and opcode features, as shown in Fig. 2. Permission features $p_i \in \{0, 1\}^P$ are obtained from existing API-permission mapping systems (e.g., PSCout, APK Explorer). APIs involving sensitive permissions (e.g., `SEND_SMS`, `READ_CONTACTS`) are encoded as binary vectors of dimension P, while non-sensitive APIs are represented as zero vectors. Opcode features $o_i \in \mathbb{R}^O$ are obtained by traversing the smali files and counting the occurrences of Dalvik bytecode instructions within each API function, resulting in a normalized histogram vector. The composite node representation is formed by concatenating the permission and opcode features, formulated as:

$$x_i = [p_i; o_i], \quad x_i \in \mathbb{R}^{P+O}. \tag{1}$$

To reduce redundant dimensions, zero-column filtering is applied to the feature matrix, resulting in a more compact feature space with 255 dimensions on the Drebin dataset and 249 dimensions on the CICAndMal2017 dataset.

3.3 Global Graph Encoder and Readout

In malware family classification, graph embedding is a core technique that maps high-dimensional and heterogeneous FCG into low-dimensional vectors while

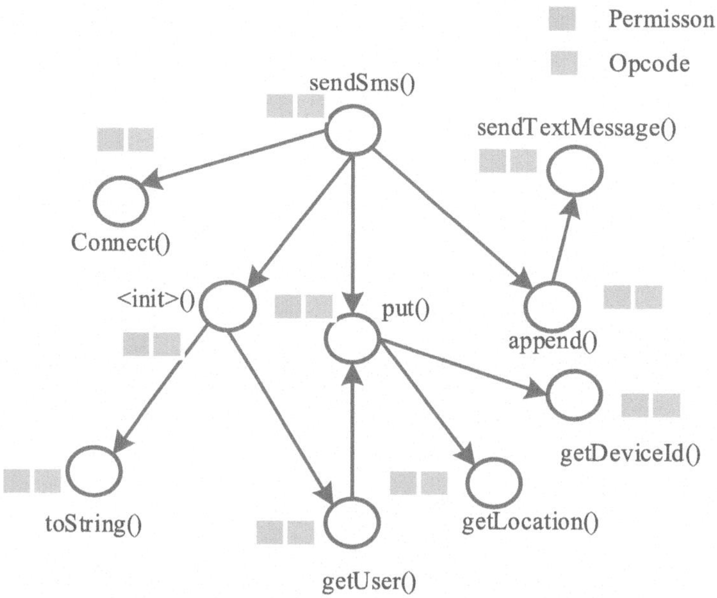

Fig. 2. Feature extraction on the function call graph (FCG).

preserving essential semantics. Traditional feature-engineering approaches (e.g., API call frequency statistics) fail to capture complex dependencies and deep behavioral patterns. In contrast, graph neural networks (GNNs) achieve automated semantic extraction through hierarchical feature propagation.

We adopt the Graph Convolutional Network (GCN) as the embedding backbone, where the key lies in the message passing mechanism: each node updates its representation by aggregating features from itself and its neighbors across layers. At the core of the GNN backbone is the message-passing mechanism, wherein each node iteratively refines its representation by integrating information from its own features and those of its adjacent neighbors across layers. The layer-wise computation that yields the updated representation $H^{(l+1)}$ from the input $H^{(l)}$ is performed via the following rule:

$$H^{(l+1)} = \sigma\Big(\hat{D}^{-\frac{1}{2}}\hat{A}\hat{D}^{-\frac{1}{2}}H^{(l)}W^{(l)}\Big), \tag{2}$$

In this formulation, $\hat{A} = A+I$ denotes the adjacency matrix after adding self-connections, $\hat{D}$ is the corresponding diagonal degree matrix where $\hat{D}ii = \sum_j \hat{A}ij$, $W^{(l)}$ constitutes the layer-specific trainable parameters, and $\sigma(\cdot)$ represents a non-linear activation function such as ReLU. For example, in the WannaCry family's encryption module, after three convolutional layers, the `encryptFiles` node captures multi-hop dependencies, encoding the full attack chain of "network detection → file encryption".

For feature aggregation, mean pooling is used as the readout function to obtain the graph-level embedding:

$$z_G = \frac{1}{|V|} \sum_{i \in V} h_i, \tag{3}$$

which preserves global statistical properties and ensures permutation invariance.

3.4 Subgraph Generation via MH-DP

The improved subgraph generator employs multi-head dynamic pooling (MH-DP) to address the limitations of single-dimensional scoring by introducing three independent scoring heads. These heads evaluate node criticality based on permission, opcode, and topology dimensions, thereby improving the feature coverage. The permission and opcode heads are defined as:

$$S^l = \mathrm{ReLU}\left(\hat{A} X^l W^l + b^l\right) \in \mathbb{R}^n, \tag{4}$$

where $l \in \{\mathrm{perm}, \mathrm{opc}\}$, and the node set $V = \{v_1, v_2, \ldots, v_n\}$ represents the set of API methods. The adjacency matrix $A \in 0, 1^{n \times n}$ is constructed to represent method call relationships, with an entry $A_{ij} = 1$ indicating that method v_i invokes method v_j. Its normalized form is derived using the calculation:

$$\tilde{A} = A + I, \quad \tilde{D}_{ii} = \sum_j \tilde{A}_{ij}, \quad \hat{A} = \tilde{D}^{-1/2} \tilde{A} \tilde{D}^{-1/2}. \tag{5}$$

The binary permission features are denoted as $X^{perm} \in \{0, 1\}^{n \times d_{perm}}$, and the opcode frequency features as $X^{opc} \in \mathbb{R}^{n \times d_{opc}}$. Nodes that receive high weighting are frequently linked to permissions categorized as high-risk, such as `ACCESS_FINE_LOCATION` for precise tracking and `RECORD_AUDIO` for ambient surveillance, which reflect the permission dependency patterns of malicious behaviors. Similarly, nodes with frequent sensitive instructions (e.g., reflective calls such as `invoke-virtual`) receive higher scores, representing dynamic loading or anti-analysis behaviors [2].

Betweenness centrality $C_b \in \mathbb{R}^n$ is adopted to measure the centrality of nodes in the control flow, defined as:

$$c_b(v) = \sum_{s \neq v \neq t} \frac{\sigma_{st}(v)}{\sigma_{st}}, \tag{6}$$

where the total shortest-path count between nodes s and t is denoted by σ_{st}, and $\sigma_{st}(v)$ gives the number of these paths that pass via node v.

$$S^{\mathrm{topo}} = \mathrm{ReLU}\left(\hat{A} C_b W^{\mathrm{topo}} + b^{\mathrm{topo}}\right) \in \mathbb{R}^n. \tag{7}$$

Nodes located on critical paths (e.g., bridging encryption and network modules) obtain higher scores, reflecting the control-flow logic of malicious behaviors.

The results of the three heads are combined through learnable dynamic weights to produce the overall node score:

$$S = \lambda_1 S^{\text{perm}} + \lambda_2 S^{\text{opc}} + \lambda_3 S^{\text{topo}} \in \mathbb{R}^n, \tag{8}$$

where $\lambda \in \mathbb{R}^3$ denotes trainable parameters, initialized as $(0.4, 0.4, 0.2)$ to balance the importance of the three heads. If, at convergence, $\lambda = [0.6, 0.3, 0.1]$, it indicates that the model relies more heavily on permission features for subgraph selection. The top-k nodes are first selected according to the overall score S:

$$V_{\text{top}} = \text{Top-}k(S). \tag{9}$$

This selection process yields the k highest-scoring nodes, though this set may not necessarily form a connected subgraph. Therefore, further processing is required to ensure that the selected subgraph is connected.

The main objective is to extract the largest connected component, as isolated high-score nodes are less meaningful. Starting from V_{top}, a connectivity detection algorithm (DFS/BFS) is applied to find the largest connected subgraph component $c_{\max}$. If the size of the resulting subgraph does not satisfy $|c_{\max}| = k$, additional nodes are selected from the remaining high-score candidates that are adjacent to the current subgraph:

$$V_{\text{candidate}} = \{v \in V \setminus c_{\max} \mid \exists u \in c_{\max}, (u, v) \in E\}. \tag{10}$$

From $V_{\text{candidate}}$, the highest-scoring node is chosen and added to $c_{\max}$:

$$V_{\text{sub}} = c_{\max} \cup \text{Top-}k\left(\{S_v \mid v \in V_{\text{candidate}}\}\right). \tag{11}$$

Finally, the subgraph node set V_{sub} and its corresponding adjacency matrix A_{sub} are used to generate the subgraph embedding h_{sub}. This embedding is derived by reusing the backbone GNN, which shares the same set of parameters as the global embedding process, ensuring efficient feature extraction.

3.5 Subgraph Readout and Aggregation

This module groups the generated subgraphs based on both semantic and structural features [16], assigning them to different clusters to enhance the discriminability of malware family classification. This module dynamically updates the cluster centers to improve clustering quality, ensuring that the optimization process adapts to evolving malicious behavior patterns. Inspired by the K-Means algorithm [18], the initial cluster center $\mu_c^{(0)}$ is obtained by averaging the embeddings of randomly selected subgraphs belonging to cluster c. Specifically, for cluster c, the initialization is given by:

$$\mu_c^{(0)} = \frac{1}{m_c} \sum_{j=1}^{m_c} h_{\text{sub}}^{(j)}, \tag{12}$$

m_c is the number of labeled samples in cluster c. If no prior cluster assignment exists, the clustering process begins by seeding the initial centers with C subgraphs that are selected randomly. The optimization process then assigns each subgraph embedding $h_{\text{sub}}^{(i)}$ to the nearest cluster according to:

$$c_i = \arg\max_{c} \cos\left(h_{\text{sub}}^{(i)}, \mu_c^{(t)}\right). \tag{13}$$

The update rule of the cluster centers is defined as:

$$\mu_c^{(t+1)} = \gamma\mu_c^{(t)} + (1-\gamma)\frac{\sum_{i\in c}\beta_{ic}h_{\text{sub}}^{(i)}}{\sum_{i\in c}\beta_{ic}}. \tag{14}$$

where γ is a momentum coefficient (set to $\gamma = 0.9$), which smooths the update process. Finally, the updated cluster centers are normalized with the L2 norm:

$$\mu_c^{(t+1)} \leftarrow \frac{\mu_c^{(t+1)}}{\|\mu_c^{(t+1)}\|_2}. \tag{15}$$

3.6 Prototype-Guided Aggregation

Prototype-Guided aggregation is based on the weighted average method of cosine similarity to combine multiple subgraph features, thereby generating enhanced representations of family prototypes. By dynamically balancing the semantic correlation between subgraphs and family prototypes, this module suppresses interference from irrelevant key nodes or noise and ultimately achieves the aggregation of family-specific features and the unified representation of cross-subgraph information.

First, the cosine similarity between each subgraph and the prototype is computed, quantifying the semantic relevance between subgraphs and the family prototype:

$$\cos_i = \frac{h_{\text{sub}}^{(i)} \cdot \mu_c}{\|h_{\text{sub}}^{(i)}\| \, \|\mu_c\|}, \quad \cos_i \in [-1, 1]. \tag{16}$$

Then, the similarity is normalized using the Softmax function:

$$\alpha_i = \frac{\exp(\cos_i)}{\sum_{j=1}^{m}\exp(\cos_j)}, \quad \alpha_i \in (0, 1). \tag{17}$$

Next, the weighted feature aggregation is performed as:

$$h_{\text{final}} = \sum_{i=1}^{m} \alpha_i \cdot h_{\text{sub}}^{(i)} \in \mathbb{R}^d. \tag{18}$$

Finally, the aggregated subgraph representation is fused with the global graph embedding:

$$h'_G = \text{MLP}([h_G \| h_{\text{final}}]) \in \mathbb{R}^d. \tag{19}$$

The final graph-level embedding h'_G is then cascaded into a fully connected layer followed by a multi-class classifier for prediction, producing the final classification output.

3.7 Loss Function

The optimization of a classification model towards learning discriminative feature representations is primarily driven by its loss function. For multi-class problems, it is important that samples are well-separated across classes while remaining compact within the same class. Center loss addresses this by minimizing the distance between features and their class centers, thereby reducing intra-class variance [19]. Therefore, a loss function $\mathcal{L}_{family}$ to achieve better family-aware representations, consisting of two parts: intra-family loss $\mathcal{L}_{intra}$ and inter-family loss $\mathcal{L}_{inter}$.

The intra-family loss is defined as:

$$\mathcal{L}_{intra} = \text{avg}_{i \in V} \left(\text{avg}_{y_G = i} \left(\cos\_sim(\mu_c, h_G^{sub}) \right) \right), \tag{20}$$

where μ_c is the cluster center of family c, and h_G^{sub} is the subgraph representation. This $\mathcal{L}_{intra}$ measures the cosine similarity between subgraph embeddings and their family centers, thus minimizing the distance between intra-family subgraph samples and their corresponding family centers.

The inter-family loss is defined as:

$$\mathcal{L}_{inter} = \text{avg}_{i \in V} \left(\text{avg}_{j \neq i, j \in V} \left(\cos\_sim(\mu_c, \mu_{c'}) \right) \right), \tag{21}$$

which measures the similarity between embeddings of different families, forcing family centers to remain distinguishable.

The combined family-aware loss is then expressed as:

$$\mathcal{L}_{family} = \log \left(\exp(\mathcal{L}_{inter} - \mathcal{L}_{intra}) \right). \tag{22}$$

Family representation h_G is obtained by FAR, and is subsequently fed into the classifier to generate predictions $\hat{y}_G$. The classification loss is the commonly used cross-entropy loss:

$$\mathcal{L}_{cel} = \sum_G y_G \log(\hat{y}_G), \tag{23}$$

where y_G is the ground-truth label of graph G.

Finally, the joint loss function combines classification loss and family-aware representation loss as:

$$\mathcal{L} = \mathcal{L}_{cel} + \lambda \cdot \mathcal{L}_{family}, \tag{24}$$

where λ is a trade-off parameter. This joint objective balances classification accuracy and family-aware discriminability, encouraging the model to simultaneously optimize for robust classification and discriminative family-level representations. As a strategy to bolster the robustness of our malware family classifier, we propose Contrastive-Enhanced FAR (CE-FAR), which introduces three levels of contrastive consistency on top of FAR:

- Global classification consistency. The cross-entropy loss $\mathcal{L}_{cel}$ aligns predictions with ground-truth labels, ensuring overall classification performance:

$$\mathcal{L}_{cel} = \sum_G y_G \log(\hat{y}_G). \tag{25}$$

- Family-level discriminative consistency. The family-level loss $\mathcal{L}_{family}$ combines intra-class compactness $\mathcal{L}_{intra}$ and inter-class separability $\mathcal{L}_{inter}$, encouraging embeddings of subgraphs from the same family to cluster closely, while different families remain well-separated:

$$\mathcal{L}_{family} = \log\left(\exp(\mathcal{L}_{inter} - \mathcal{L}_{intra})\right). \tag{26}$$

- Sample-level contrastive consistency. A supervised contrastive loss $\mathcal{L}_{proto}$ is introduced to enforce fine-grained similarity among samples within the same family while pushing apart samples from different families:

$$\mathcal{L}_{proto} = -\frac{1}{N}\sum_{i=1}^{N}\frac{1}{|P(i)|}\sum_{p\in P(i)}\log\frac{\exp(\mathrm{sim}(z_i, z_p)/T)}{\sum_{a=1}^{N}\exp(\mathrm{sim}(z_i, z_a)/T)}. \tag{27}$$

where $P(i)$ denotes the set of positive samples sharing the same family as i, and T is a temperature parameter.

Finally, the overall optimization objective of CE-FAR integrates three levels:

$$\mathcal{L}_{\text{CE-FAR}} = \mathcal{L}_{cel} + \lambda \cdot \mathcal{L}_{family} + \beta \cdot \mathcal{L}_{proto}. \tag{28}$$

4 Experiments

4.1 Datasets and Settings

We evaluate our method on two benchmark Android malware datasets: Drebin [3] and CICAndMal2017 [7]. The Drebin dataset contains 5,560 malware samples spanning 179 families. Due to extreme class imbalance with some families containing only one sample, we select the top 24 families, excluding those with fewer than 20 samples, resulting in 4,765 samples for experiments. CICAndMal2017 contains 429 malware samples from 42 families across four categories. The data preprocessing phase involved removing samples that were not successfully decompiled by Apktool, resulting in a curated collection of 424 samples for subsequent analysis. A standard 80%-10%-10% random division was applied to all datasets, constituting the training, validation, and test sets, respectively.

4.2 Results on CICAndMal2017

Since this work adopts a graph representation learning approach, we first consider graph-based methods as baselines, followed by methods that use the same datasets. For the CICAndMal2017 dataset, we conducted separate experiments on malware category classification and family classification.

Prior research in category classification has explored various feature sets. The work by Lashkari et al. [7] processed fundamental network attributes—including IP addresses, ports, and protocols—for use in machine learning systems. Taheri et al. [12] also developed specialized frameworks, with their classifier integrating dynamic API call sequences with network traffic analysis. Separately, Abuthawabeh et al. [1] investigated dialog-level network traffic as a feature source for machine learning-based categorization. For the evaluation of family classification performance, comparative analyses are conducted against the techniques introduced by Lashkari et al. and Taheri et al.

Table 1. Class classification results on CICAndMal2017

Method	Accuracy (%)	Precision	Recall
Lashkari et al. [7]	49.90	0.48	0.48
Taheri et al. [12]	83.30	0.81	0.81
Abuthawabeh et al. [1]	80.20	0.79	0.79
Jaju et al. [4]	83.72	0.83	0.83
Ours	**84.16**	**0.84**	**0.84**

As evidenced by the results in Table 1 and Table 2, our model yields state-of-the-art performance, outperforming all competing baseline methods on the CICAndMal2017 dataset. Specifically, our approach attains an accuracy of 84.16% for category classification and 75.60% for family classification.

Table 2. Family classification results on CICAndMal2017

Method	Feature(s)	Precision	Recall
Lashkari et al. [7]	Dynamic + Network Traffic	27.52	25.51
Taheri et al. [12]	Dynamic API calls	59.70	61.20
Jaju et al. [4]	Static + Image (CNN)	61.90	62.47
Ours	Static + FCG	**75.60**	**75.80**

4.3 Results on Drebin

The Drebin dataset is evaluated using several methods based on machine learning techniques as baselines for comparison.

For malware classification, CANDYMAN [9] adopts a strategy of dynamic behavior modeling via Markov chains, coupled with standard machine learning techniques. GSFDroid [8], on the other hand, focuses on graph representation learning; it constructs a function call graph (FCG) enriched with sensitive APIs through static analysis, learns from this graph using a GCN, and performs classification via an MLP. Drebin [3] employs a comprehensive static analysis approach, extracting critical information from the manifest file and transforming decompiled API and network code into feature vectors for subsequent machine learning-based classification. Jaju et al. [4] systematically evaluate different image conversion strategies (grayscale and RGB) combined with

CNN models (ResNet50, MobileNetV2, and 3C2D) on the CICAndMal2017 and Drebin datasets, analyzing their effectiveness for malware detection and family classification.

Table 3. Performance comparison on Drebin dataset.

Model	Accuracy (%)	Precision	Recall	F1-score
CANDYMAN [9]	81.8	0.80	0.81	0.80
GSFDroid [8]	91.1	0.90	0.88	0.90
Drebin [3]	93.0	0.92	0.90	0.91
Jaju et al. [4]	93.8	0.92	**0.91**	0.91
Ours	**94.8**	**0.93**	0.89	**0.92**

The results in Table 3 show that our method outperforms traditional baseline approaches on the Drebin dataset, though there is still room for improvement compared to more recent methods developed in the past two years.

4.4 Ablation Studies

The ablation experiments were conducted on the CICAndMal2017 (category and family classification) and Drebin datasets, with classification accuracy as the evaluation metric (see Fig. 3). The results clearly demonstrate the contribution of each module.

Removing MH-DP caused a significant performance decline: category classification decreased from 84.16% to 81.43%, family classification from 75.60% to 72.14%, and Drebin from 93.80% to 91.86%. This indicates that MH-DP effectively integrates complementary semantics from permissions, opcodes, and topology, and is critical for performance improvement.

The removal of FAR also led to performance degradation, particularly on CICAndMal2017, where category accuracy dropped to 82.05% and family accuracy to 73.05%. This highlights the importance of FAR in enhancing intra-class compactness and inter-class separability.

When applying FAR only, the model outperformed the two reduced variants, reaching 83.27% and 74.12% on category and family classification, respectively, and achieving the best result of 94.75% on Drebin. This suggests that FAR provides strong discriminative power in complex graph structures.

Finally, the complete CE-FAR framework achieved the best performance on CICAndMal2017 (84.16% for category and 75.60% for family), while maintaining competitive accuracy on Drebin (93.80%). Although slightly lower than FAR-only on Drebin, CE-FAR provided the most balanced and robust overall performance.

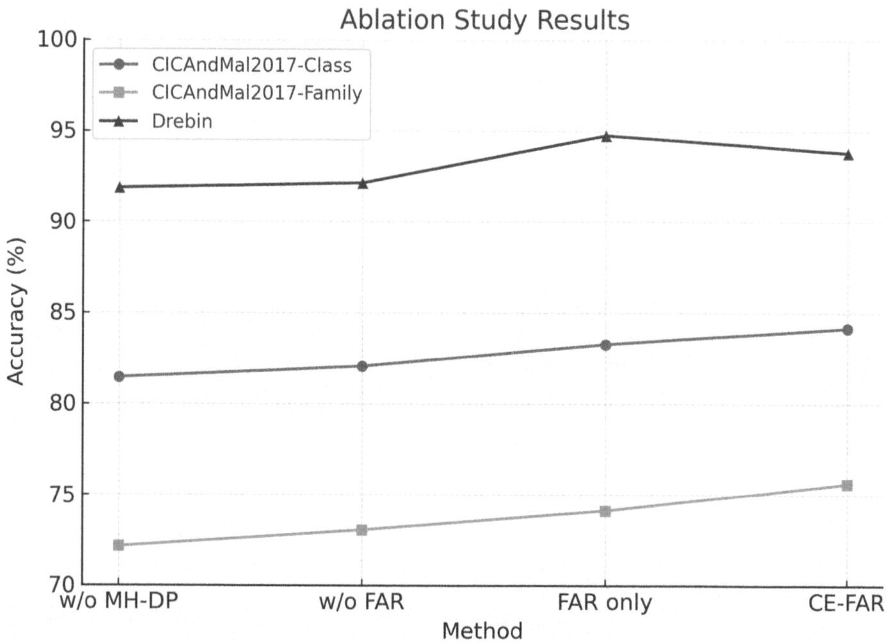

Fig. 3. Ablation study on different modules across datasets.

5 Conclusion

In summary, the experimental results demonstrate the robustness and effectiveness of the proposed CE-FAR framework across multiple datasets and tasks. The experimental results confirm that CE-FAR delivered top-ranked results for malware category and family classification on the CICAndMal2017 benchmark, with accuracies of 84.16% and 75.60%, respectively, significantly outperforming existing baselines. CE-FAR also showed superior performance compared to traditional approaches on Drebin. And although it was slightly inferior to FAR-only in certain scenarios, it still maintained overall stability and competitiveness.

Ablation studies confirmed the contribution of each module. The MH-DP module effectively improved discriminability by integrating multi-dimensional features, while the FAR module improved intra-class compactness and inter-class separability. Building on these, the incorporation of CE-FAR generally led to better feature representations and classification results.

Overall, the experiments confirm the effectiveness and generalizability of the proposed method, providing a novel and practical approach for malware family classification.

Acknowledgments. This work was Funded by Basic Research Program of Jiangsu (Grant No. BK20251747) and the Start-up Research Fund of Southeast University (Grant No. RF1028623059).

Disclosure of Interests. The authors have no competing interests to declare that are relevant to the content of this article.

References

1. Abuthawabeh, M., Mahmoud, K.W.: Enhanced android malware detection and family classification, using conversation-level network traffic features. Int. Arab J. Inf. Technol. **17**(4A), 607–614 (2020)
2. Fang, U., Li, M., Li, J., Gao, L., Jia, T., Zhang, Y.: A comprehensive survey on multi-view clustering. IEEE Trans. Knowl. Data Eng. **35**(12), 12350–12368 (2023)
3. Irolla, P., Dey, A.: The duplication issue within the Drebin dataset. J. Comput. Virol. Hacking Tech. **14**(3), 245–249 (2018)
4. JJaju, C., et al.: Analyzing image based strategies for android malware detection and classification: an empirical exploration. In: SECRYPT, pp. 863–869 (2023)
5. Jiang, B., Zhang, Z., Lin, D., Tang, J., Luo, B.: Semi-supervised learning with graph learning-convolutional networks. In: Proceedings of the IEEE/CVF Conference on Computer Vision and Pattern Recognition, pp. 11313–11320 (2019)
6. Kim, M., Kim, D., Hwang, C., Cho, S., Han, S., Park, M.: Machine-learning-based android malware family classification using built-in and custom permissions. Appl. Sci. **11**(21), 10244 (2021)
7. Lashkari, A.H., Kadir, A.F.A., Taheri, L., Ghorbani, A.A.: Toward developing a systematic approach to generate benchmark android malware datasets and classification. In: 2018 International Carnahan Conference on Security Technology (ICCST), pp. 1–7. IEEE (2018)
8. Li, Q., Hu, Q., Qi, Y., Qi, S., Liu, X., Gao, P.: Semi-supervised two-phase familial analysis of android malware with normalized graph embedding. Knowl.-Based Syst. **218**, 106802 (2021)
9. Martín, A., Rodríguez-Fernández, V., Camacho, D.: CANDYMAN: classifying android malware families by modelling dynamic traces with Markov chains. Eng. Appl. Artif. Intell. **74**, 121–133 (2018)
10. Ou, F., Xu, J.: S3Feature: a static sensitive subgraph-based feature for android malware detection. Comput. Secur. **112**, 102513 (2022)
11. Rossi, E., Chamberlain, B., Frasca, F., Eynard, D., Monti, F., Bronstein, M.: Temporal graph networks for deep learning on dynamic graphs. arXiv preprint arXiv:2006.10637 (2020)
12. Taheri, L., Kadir, A.F.A., Lashkari, A.H.: Extensible android malware detection and family classification using network-flows and API-calls. In: 2019 International Carnahan Conference on Security Technology (ICCST), pp. 1–8. IEEE (2019)
13. Velickovic, P., et al.: Graph attention networks. Stat **1050**(20), 10–48550 (2017)
14. Wang, M.Y.: Deep graph library: towards efficient and scalable deep learning on graphs. In: ICLR Workshop on Representation Learning on Graphs and Manifolds (2019)
15. Wang, Z., Zeng, K., Wang, J., Li, D.: FAGnet: family-aware-based android malware analysis using graph neural network. Knowl.-Based Syst. **289**, 111531 (2024)
16. Wu, F., Souza, A., Zhang, T., Fifty, C., Yu, T., Weinberger, K.: Simplifying graph convolutional networks. In: International Conference on Machine Learning, pp. 6861–6871. PMLR (2019)
17. Xu, Q., Zhao, D., Yang, S., Xu, L., Li, X.: Android malware detection based on behavioral-level features with graph convolutional networks. Electronics **12**(23), 4817 (2023)

18. Yi, F., Moon, I.: Extended k-means algorithm. In: 2013 5th International Conference on Intelligent Human-Machine Systems and Cybernetics, vol. 2, pp. 263–266. IEEE (2013)
19. Zhang, Z., Qi, P., Wang, W.: Dynamic malware analysis with feature engineering and feature learning. In: Proceedings of the AAAI Conference on Artificial Intelligence, vol. 34, pp. 1210–1217 (2020)
20. Zhao, L., Wang, J., Chen, Y., Wu, F., Liu, Y., et al.: FamDroid: learning-based android malware family classification using static analysis. arXiv preprint arXiv:2101.03965 (2021)

Automatic Construction of Multi-layer Knowledge Graphs with Large Language Models

Pu Li(✉), Wenzhi Si, Yunlong Wang, Songbo Zhang, and Miaomiao Jia

Software Engineering College, Zhengzhou University of Light Industry, Zhengzhou 450000, China

superlipu@163.com,

{lipu,332416020958,332416030962,332416020941,332416030959}@zzuli.edu.cn

Abstract. To jointly address ontology modeling and entity recognition in knowledge graph construction and introduce a novel multi-layer graph representation, this paper proposes a three-layer automatic construction method guided by few-shot prompts. Large language models (LLMs) perform ontology modeling, entity recognition, and relation extraction, upon which fact hypergraphs and Gaussian-based topic clustering are used to build a hierarchical knowledge graph with a basic entity layer, a fact hypergraph layer, and a topic layer. These form a three-layer "topic–basic–fact" structure that enables automatic multi-granular semantic integration and knowledge representation. Experiments on an academic social network dataset show that the proposed method achieves an ontology-modeling completeness of 91.05% and an entity recognition F1 score of 92.48, demonstrating strong graph-construction capability.The code of our proposed method is available at https://github.com/svenzhi/Auto-LLM3KG.

Keywords: Ontology modeling · Entity recognition · Automatic construction · Large language model

1 Introduction

As an important form of structured knowledge organization, knowledge graphs have been widely applied in intelligent question answering, recommender systems, and semantic search [1,2]. In particular, with the strong generalization ability of large language models (LLMs) in natural language understanding tasks, LLM-based knowledge extraction provides a new path for high-quality ontology modeling and entity recognition. It has gradually become an important approach to improving the automation of knowledge graph construction [3].

Traditional knowledge graph construction methods usually employ rule-based, statistical learning, or sequence modeling techniques for named entity recognition (NER) and relation extraction, acquiring knowledge at the triple

© The Author(s), under exclusive license to Springer Nature Singapore Pte Ltd. 2027
H. Sun et al. (Eds.): ChineseCSCW 2025, CCIS 2911, pp. 312–326, 2027.
https://doi.org/10.1007/978-981-92-0288-1_23

level from text. Although these methods achieve certain accuracy, they heavily rely on manual annotation. Their outputs are often discrete attributes and lack modeling of the overall semantic structure of entities. Moreover, most graph structures are designed in a flat form, making it difficult to represent the multi-granularity, contextual associations, and semantic abstractions required for complex knowledge organization [4].

Moreover, traditional methods still face significant limitations in structured ontology modeling and semantic abstraction. This calls for the introduction of large language models with reasoning and generative capabilities [5–8].

To address these issues, this paper proposes a three-layer automatic construction method for knowledge graphs based on large language models and prompt engineering. The method integrates ontology modeling and entity recognition into a unified stage, then builds a hierarchical knowledge graph composed of entity networks (basic layer), event hypergraphs (fact layer), and semantic clustering (topic layer). Through fact-level hypergraph construction and topic aggregation, the method enhances both organizational hierarchy and semantic expressiveness. Based on this framework, we conduct empirical validation on an academic social network dataset, and the results demonstrate strong performance in structure generation, entity completeness, and semantic coverage.
The main contributions of this paper are summarized as follows:

- We propose a novel three-layer automatic knowledge graph construction framework that unifies ontology modeling, entity recognition, and hierarchical semantic representation within an LLM-driven pipeline.
- We design a fact-level hypergraph and topic-level clustering mechanism to construct coordinated "basic–fact–topic" structures, enabling multi-granularity hierarchical semantic representation.
- We conduct extensive experiments on an academic social network dataset, demonstrating high ontology completeness (91.05%) and entity recognition F1 (92.48), verifying the effectiveness and generalization capability of the proposed approach.

2 Related Work

Most existing studies on knowledge graph construction follow a three-step pipeline of entity recognition, relation extraction, graph modeling [9–11]. As a key step, named entity recognition (NER) is usually performed with sequence models such as Conditional Random Fields (CRF) [12] or BiLSTM-CRF [13, 14] under the BIO tagging scheme, extracting basic entities such as person names, locations, and organization names from sentences. However, these methods only rely on local word sequence context, and the outputs are primarily label sequences, making it difficult to capture complete semantic structures. They also suffer from strong dependence on manually annotated data, long training time, difficulty in knowledge updating, and limited generalization and cross-domain adaptability [15].

In entity structure modeling, mainstream approaches often separate modeling from entity recognition. In this setting, the recognition stage only extracts surface fields, while ontology modeling is later defined by domain experts, lacking automated integration [16]. This "attribute separation–structure disconnection" leads to significant expressive limitations in complex applications and cannot support high-quality, reusable entity modeling.

Furthermore, most existing graph structures remain flat triples, which fail to represent complex expressions such as multi-entity co-occurrence events, semantic aggregation topics, and hierarchical contextual organization. Some studies have attempted to introduce event modeling [17], semantic nodes [18], or clustering-based summarization [19], but they still lack a unified layered semantic paradigm and have not achieved systematic integration of entities, events, and semantic abstraction in coordinated construction.

In summary, current graph construction faces three major challenges:

- How to leverage large language models to automatically generate entity nodes during recognition and avoid semantic disconnection caused by the separation of "recognition–modeling";
- How to unify entities, events, and semantic topics within graph construction;
- How to overcome the structural limitations of flat triples and achieve hierarchical, semantically extensible knowledge representation.

This work addresses these three aspects and proposes a general graph construction framework that integrates LLM-based knowledge extraction with layered knowledge representation.

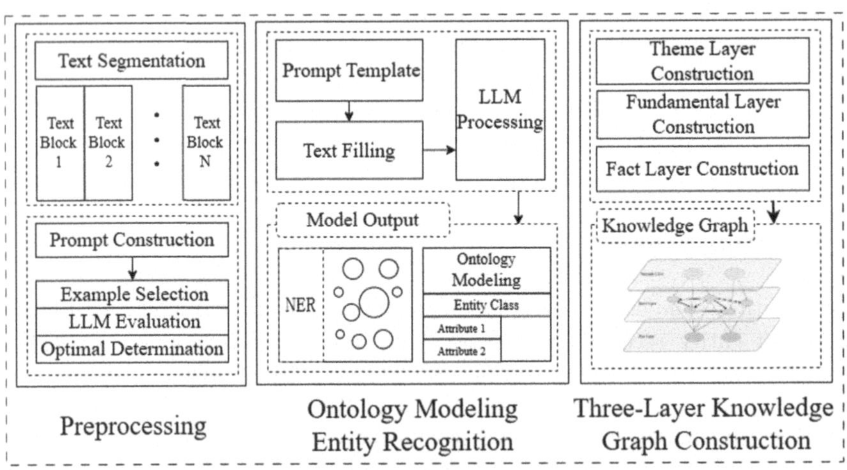

Fig. 1. LLM-based workflow for entity recognition, ontology modeling, and knowledge graph construction.

3 Three-Layer Knowledge Graph Construction Based on Large Language Models

This chapter presents the proposed automatic construction method and key technical route for knowledge graphs based on large language models. The method first leverages the semantic understanding ability of large language models and uses few-shot prompts to perform structured ontology modeling during the entity recognition stage. It directly generates entities with categories, attributes, and semantic descriptions from raw text, overcoming the limitation of traditional methods that only output discrete attribute fragments.

On this basis, the system further organizes recognized entities, events, and topics to construct a three-layer knowledge graph, including an entity network (basic layer), an event hypergraph (fact layer), and Gaussian clustering (topic layer). This design enables unified representation of multi-granularity knowledge. The overall workflow of the proposed method is shown in Fig. 1.

3.1 Ontology Modeling and Entity Recognition

Compared with traditional BIO-based named entity recognition (NER) methods that only output scattered attributes such as name, gender, and age, the proposed method not only focuses on boundary recognition but also emphasizes structured entity representation, including category, attribute, and semantic role. It effectively overcomes the limitation of conventional NER methods, which tend to produce fragmented labels without unified semantic expression during structured entity modeling.

```
-Task Objective-
Given a piece of text that may be relevant to this task, please complete the following two
items:
1. Identify all entities mentioned in the text;
2. Identify all relationships between these entities.
-Steps-
1. Identify all entities in the text. For each recognized entity, extract the following
fields:
- entity_name: the entity name, which should remain consistent with the original text;
- entity_type: the entity type, which must be one of the following list:
  {entity_types};
  - Do not add new types or modify the type names;
- entity_description: a brief description of the entity's semantic role or contextual
attributes in the text.
```

Fig. 2. Partial prompt example used in the entity recognition stage.

As illustrated in the "Preprocessing" and "Ontology Modeling and Entity Recognition" stages of Fig. 2, the proposed approach invokes a large language model with few-shot prompts to automatically identify semantic entities and their ontology structures, generating structured semantic nodes that form the content of the "basic layer" in the three-layer knowledge graph.

The prompt-based generation paradigm adopted in this stage can be seamlessly extended to subsequent stages, where the large language model continues to reason about semantic associations among entities. These structured entities are therefore not treated as isolated nodes but serve as the semantic foundation for event-level and topic-level modeling. Specifically, they provide the inputs for fact hypergraph construction and topic aggregation, enabling a smooth transition from entity-level semantics to multi-granularity hierarchical representation across the entire knowledge graph.

3.2 Three-Layer Structured Knowledge Graph Construction

Building upon the LLM-driven ontology modeling and entity recognition stage, this section focuses on constructing the complete three-layer structured knowledge graph. To achieve multi-granularity semantic representation and structured knowledge integration, the proposed method adopts a "top–middle–bottom" architecture corresponding to the topic, fact, and basic layers, respectively. The large language model continues to serve as the reasoning engine in this process, generating semantic associations and abstractions across layers through prompt-based guidance.

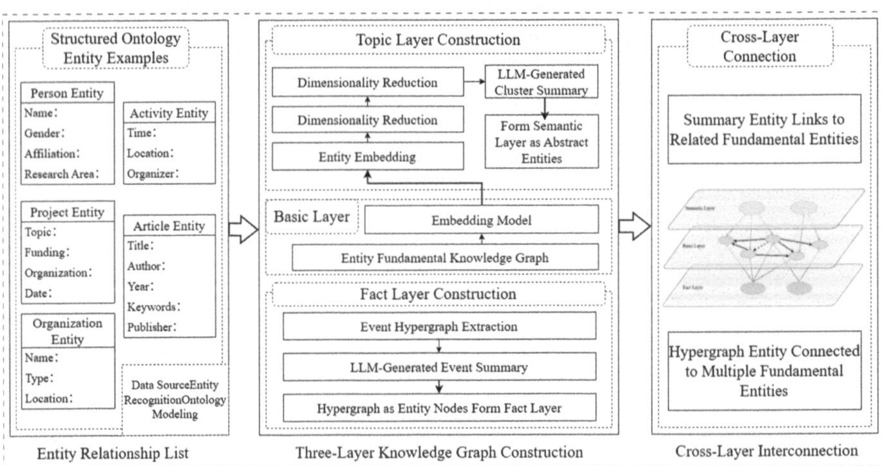

Fig. 3. Construction process of the three-layer structured knowledge graph.

As shown in Fig. 3, the construction process takes structured ontology entities produced in the previous stage as input. The system sequentially builds the basic-layer entity network, the fact-layer event hypergraph, and the topic-layer

clustering. This hierarchical process realizes entity association, event abstraction, and topic summarization, thereby forming a unified layered knowledge representation. The large language model participates throughout this pipeline to refine semantic relations, generate hyperedges, and produce interpretable topic clusters, ensuring cross-layer semantic consistency.
The overall graph structure is formally represented as:

$$G = (V, E) \tag{1}$$

where the node set is defined as

$$V = V_{\text{topic}} \cup V_{\text{basic}} \cup V_{\text{fact}} \tag{2}$$

and the edge set E represents structural connections both within and across layers. The three layers collaborate through entity co-occurrence, semantic mapping, and topic induction, establishing inter-layer relations that support multi-granularity knowledge representation and multi-level knowledge indexing from factual description to semantic abstraction.

Basic Layer: Entity Graph Construction. The basic layer serves as the middle layer of the entire graph. It is constructed based on the results of ontology modeling and entity extraction described in Sect. 3.1. The entity graph is formally defined as

$$G_{\text{basic}} = (V_{\text{basic}}, E_{\text{basic}}) \tag{3}$$

where V_{basic} denotes the set of entities extracted from text, such as "scholar name" and "research institution," and E_{basic} denotes the set of relations between entities, including semantic edges such as "published in" and "belongs to".

Fact Layer: Event Hypergraph Construction. The fact layer serves as the lower structure of the graph, modeling event knowledge in which multiple entities jointly participate. This layer adopts a hypergraph structure to represent the "many-to-many" relations between events and participating entities. The hypergraph is formally defined as

$$G_{\text{Hyper}} = (V_{\text{basic}}, H) \tag{4}$$

where $H = \{h_1, h_2, \ldots, h_n\}$ is the set of hyperedges. Each hyperedge $h_i \subseteq V_{\text{basic}}$ represents an event that connects all entities involved in it. Every event is also associated with a concise semantic description f_i generated by the LLM, forming the event fact set $F = \{f_1, f_2, \ldots, f_n\}$.

Furthermore, each event can be abstracted as an entity node $v_i \subseteq V_{\text{fact}}$, which constitutes the fact-layer entity set:

$$V_{\text{fact}} = \{v_i \mid v_i \leftrightarrow h_i \in H\} \tag{5}$$

This structure not only enhances the representation ability of complex events but also provides an intermediate bridge that establishes semantic channels between entities and topics.

Topic Layer: Semantic Topic Construction. The topic layer lies at the top of the graph and is responsible for semantic aggregation and topic abstraction of basic entities. First, entity nodes in the basic layer are vectorized, and their vectors are processed through dimensionality reduction and clustering to generate a set of semantic clusters:

$$C = \{C_1, C_2, \ldots, C_m\}, \quad C_i \subseteq V_{\text{basic}} \tag{6}$$

For each cluster C_i, the LLM generates a summarization description, forming a semantic entity S_i. This produces the summary node set:

$$V_{\text{summary}} = \{S_i \mid S_i = \text{summary}(C_i)\} \tag{7}$$

This set becomes the node set of the topic layer:

$$V_{\text{topic}} = V_{\text{summary}} \tag{8}$$

Edges are then created between semantic entities and their covered basic entities, forming the topic layer structure. This layer not only improves the interpretability of the graph but also provides structural support for cross-entity semantic extension, global reasoning, and topic retrieval.

At this point, node construction for all three layers of the graph is complete. The edge set E includes not only the intra-layer edges among basic entities E_{basic}, but also clustering-mapping edges between topic nodes and basic entities (e.g., $S_i \rightarrow C_i \subseteq V_{\text{basic}}$), as well as projection edges between fact-layer event nodes and their associated entity sets (e.g., $v_i \rightarrow h_i \subseteq V_{\text{basic}}$).

These cross-layer connections collectively form structural channels of the graph, supporting semantic propagation from local entities to global topics. Through this multi-granularity and multi-level organization, the graph achieves progressive abstraction and integration from semantic entities to events and then to topics, providing unified structural support for downstream applications such as question answering, semantic indexing, and reasoning.

4 Performance Evaluation and Empirical Study of Domain Knowledge Graph Construction

To systematically verify the feasibility and practicality of the proposed multi-layer automatic knowledge graph construction method based on large language models, this chapter conducts empirical evaluation and analysis from three perspectives. First, a Chinese scholar information dataset[1] is constructed to test

[1] https://github.com/svenzhi/ScholarInfoNER.

the accuracy, recall, and F1-score of several mainstream large language models on the entity recognition task, thereby validating their extraction ability and prompt transferability. Second, an ontology completeness evaluation metric is introduced to compare the structural modeling capability of different large language models. Third, domain-specific applications are presented to demonstrate the performance of the knowledge graph in the construction of academic social networks.

4.1 Construction and Analysis of Scholar Information Dataset

This study collects textual information from multiple academic data sources, including official university websites, Scholat.com[2], and Baidu Baike[3]. Based on the extraction results of the DeepSeek-V3 model and subsequent manual verification, we construct a high-quality Chinese entity recognition dataset tailored for the academic social network domain. The dataset covers multiple categories of academic information such as educational background, research interests, professional titles and honors, and work experience, providing strong domain representativeness and linguistic diversity.

According to statistics, the dataset contains a total of 11,207 entities (including duplicates), with 5,878 unique entities after deduplication, spanning 16 entity types. Detailed statistics are shown in Table 1.

Table 1. Statistical information of the scholar information dataset.

Item	Quantity
Total entity occurrences	11207
Unique entities	5878
Total text characters	125588
Entity types	16

The dataset is characterized by high entity density, wide category distribution, and authentic linguistic style. It can serve as an important benchmark corpus for knowledge extraction and graph modeling tasks in the Chinese academic domain, providing a solid foundation for subsequent model performance comparison and structural modeling experiments. The dataset is planned to be publicly released after formal publication to support further research and applications in this field.

[2] https://www.scholat.com.
[3] https://baike.baidu.com.

4.2 Performance Evaluation of Entity Extraction by Large Language Models

The evaluation of entity recognition adopts three standard metrics: Precision, Recall, and F1 Score, which measure the accuracy, coverage, and overall performance of field recognition, respectively.

The three evaluation metrics are defined as follows:

- **TP (True Positive):** the number of actual entities correctly recognized as entities by the model;
- **FP (False Positive):** the number of non-entities incorrectly recognized as entities by the model;
- **FN (False Negative):** the number of actual entities that the model failed to recognize.

(1) **Precision**, representing the proportion of correctly recognized entities among all entities identified by the model, is calculated as:

$$P = \frac{TP}{TP + FP} \tag{9}$$

(2) **Recall**, representing the proportion of actual entities correctly identified by the model, is calculated as:

$$R = \frac{TP}{TP + FN} \tag{10}$$

(3) **F1 Score**, the harmonic mean of precision and recall, provides a comprehensive measure of accuracy and coverage, and is calculated as:

$$F1 = \frac{2PR}{P + R} \tag{11}$$

To evaluate the performance of different large language models on the entity recognition task, four representative Chinese LLMs were selected: GLM-4-Plus, Qwen-Plus, ERNIE-4.5-Turbo, and DeepSeek-V3. These models cover different architectures and training paradigms, providing a comprehensive comparison of LLM-based entity extraction performance.

All four models completed the entity extraction task on the scholar information dataset constructed in Sect. 3.1 through API calls. A unified prompt template was applied to ensure consistent experimental settings and comparability of results. Their precision, recall, and F1 scores were recorded, as shown in Table 2.

The experimental results show that the four mainstream large language models all demonstrate strong recognition ability in the entity extraction task, with F1 scores ranging from 78.98 to 92.48. This indicates that the LLM-based entity

Table 2. Entity recognition results of different large language models.

Model	Precision	Recall	F1 Score
GLM-4-Plus	71.97	87.52	78.98
Qwen-Plus	87.70	73.59	80.03
ERNIE-4.5-Turbo	86.47	83.93	85.18
DeepSeek-V3	94.38	90.65	92.48

extraction method guided by few-shot prompts has good adaptability and practical value. Although the models show slight differences in precision and recall, their overall performance remains stable and effective for recognizing multiple types of entities in Chinese academic texts.

These results further validate the feasibility and generalizability of the proposed entity extraction method based on large language models guided by few-shot prompts, laying a solid foundation for structural modeling and multi-level graph representation.

4.3 Few-Shot Sample Size Sensitivity Experiment

To further examine the impact of sample size in prompts on entity extraction performance, four mainstream large language models—DeepSeek-V3, ERNIE-4.5-Turbo, GLM-4-Plus, and Qwen-Plus—were selected. Seven prompt configurations with different numbers of examples (1, 2, 3, 5, 8, 12, and 15) were designed to construct entity recognition experiments under few-shot settings. This setup covers a range from extremely few examples (1-shot) to the typical few-shot region (15-shot), aiming to observe trends in the number of extracted entities under enhanced prompt conditions. The experimental results are shown in Fig. 4.

Figure 4 illustrates the entity recognition scale of different models at each sample size using bar charts, providing a clear comparison of extraction capability. Overall, as the number of prompt examples increases, the number of extracted entities shows an upward trend, but fluctuations or saturation effects are observed in some models. For instance, DeepSeek-V3 reaches its maximum extraction (6179 entities) at 8 examples, then slightly decreases, suggesting that its response to prompts saturates at medium sample density. GLM-4-Plus, on the other hand, shows a sharp decline when the number of examples exceeds 12, reflecting possible contextual interference or format confusion under heavily stacked prompts.

This experiment verifies that the results of entity extraction are sensitive to the number of prompt examples. It also shows that controlling the size of few-shot prompts is important for large language models in semantic extraction tasks. In addition, the results indirectly prove that our designed prompt template is adaptable and robust. Under both small and gradually increased sample sizes, all four models keep stable extraction performance without obvious format errors

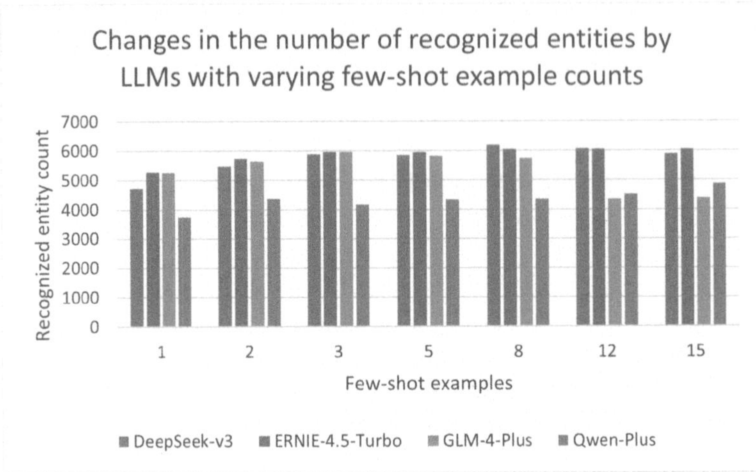

Fig. 4. The x-axis represents the number of few-shot examples provided in the prompt, while the y-axis shows the number of entities recognized by the LLM on the evaluation texts.

or semantic drift. These findings indicate that the proposed prompt template can effectively control entity boundaries, keep semantic alignment, and ensure output consistency. The experiment provides practical evidence for prompt size control and example selection, further confirming the reliability and cross-model applicability of the few-shot prompt–driven LLM-based entity extraction method in knowledge graph construction.

4.4 Ontology Modeling Completeness Evaluation

In the process of knowledge graph construction, entity recognition alone is insufficient to support high-quality semantic modeling. The structured organization of entities and the expression of semantic relations are equally important. Therefore, this study further proposes the **Modeling Completeness Rate (MCR)** as an indicator to evaluate the capability of large language models in structural modeling tasks. Specifically, MCR measures whether the model can reconstruct the true organizational structure and attribute hierarchy of entities on top of entity extraction. This indicator evaluates the coverage of structural fields in model outputs, reflecting the modeling ability of LLMs in automatic structured modeling tasks.

The metric is defined as:

$$\text{Modeling Completeness Rate} = \frac{|F_{\text{extracted}} \cap F_{\text{expected}}|}{|F_{\text{expected}}|} \quad (12)$$

where F_{expected} denotes the set of expected fields and $F_{\text{extracted}}$ denotes the set of fields actually extracted by the model.

For example, in the academic social network construction task: suppose a scholar's webpage contains six fields—name, affiliation, title, research interest, degree, and educational background—forming the expected field set F_{expected}. If the model extracts only four fields—name, affiliation, research interest, and degree—then:

$$|F_{\text{expected}}| = 6, \quad |F_{\text{extracted}}| = 4, \quad |F_{\text{extracted}} \cap F_{\text{expected}}| = 4,$$

$$\text{Modeling Completeness Rate} = \frac{4}{6} \approx 0.67$$

In this experiment, scholar data samples collected from Scholat.com were used as evaluation targets. Manually annotated structured modeling results were constructed as references. Four large language models—GLM-4-Plus, Qwen-Plus, ERNIE-4.5-Turbo, and DeepSeek-V3—were tested under a unified prompt template, and their average modeling completeness rates were calculated. The comparison results are shown in Table 3.

Table 3. Average modeling completeness rate comparison of different LLMs.

Model	Modeling Completeness Rate (%)
GLM-4-Plus	87.26
Qwen-Plus	90.06
ERNIE-4.5-Turbo	88.69
DeepSeek-V3	91.05

The experimental results show that the average modeling completeness rates of the four large language models in the structural modeling task all exceed 87%, reaching a high level overall. This indicates that under unified prompt guidance, mainstream large language models generally possess strong structural modeling capability, covering most expected fields with standardized outputs and clear semantic structures.

These findings further validate the effectiveness and stability of the proposed few-shot prompt–driven large language model approach in structured knowledge construction tasks. The differences among models are mainly reflected in the ordering or naming style of individual fields, which has only minor impact on overall modeling completeness. This demonstrates the generalizability and cross-model transferability of the proposed method.

4.5 Graph Visualization Analysis

The proposed framework integrates large language models with prompt engineering to realize the complete pipeline from data collection to entity extraction and structural modeling, requiring no manual annotation and exhibiting strong

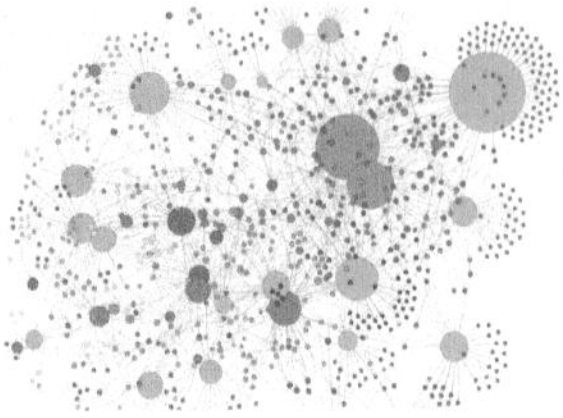

(a) Partial view of the three-layer knowledge graph.

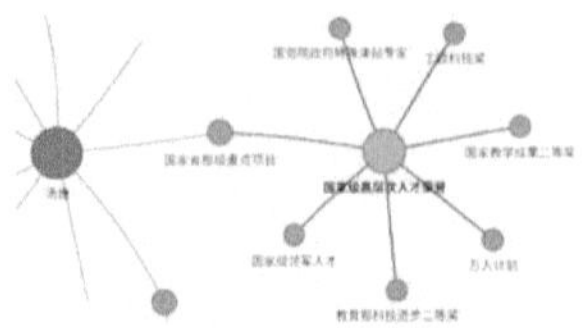

(b) Topic-layer clustering structure.

(c) Fact-layer event hypergraph structure.

Fig. 5. Visualization of the three-layer knowledge graph: (a) partial graph, (b) topic-layer clustering, and (c) fact-layer event hypergraph.

structural expressiveness. Figure 5 visualizes the resulting three-layer knowledge graph.

Hypergraph-based modeling unifies heterogeneous elements of complex events, forming cohesive structural units that enhance entity organization and event indexing. The fact layer provides a solid foundation for semantic retrieval and causal reasoning within the three-layer knowledge graph.

Compared with traditional flat graphs, the proposed "basic-fact-topic" structure enables hierarchical representations from fine-grained facts to abstract semantic topics, enhancing both the interpretability and scalability of semantic organization.

5 Conclusion and Future Work

This paper presents a three-layer automatic knowledge graph construction framework integrating large language models with prompt engineering. Covering the full pipeline from ontology modeling to graph generation, it achieves high automation, strong semantic consistency, and stable multi-level structural organization. Experiments demonstrate that the framework can generate knowledge graphs with layered semantic representations, providing reliable support for complex knowledge organization and reasoning.

In future work, the proposed "basic-fact-topic" structure will be integrated into Retrieval-Augmented Generation (RAG) frameworks as a hierarchical retrieval and context organization module. The fact layer will support fine-grained entity and relation recall, while the topic layer will guide semantic clustering and context expansion, enhancing retrieval precision and generative coherence in multi-hop question answering.

Beyond this, we will explore domain-adaptive fine-tuning for cross-domain generalization, terminology-aware entity recognition, and adaptive prompt optimization for dynamic graph updating. Integrating reasoning and evaluation modules into the construction process is another promising direction to further strengthen the framework's capability in intelligent question answering and semantic search.

References

1. Wang, M., Wang, H., Li, B., Zhao, X., Wang, X.: Survey on key technologies of new generation knowledge graph. J. Comput. Res. Dev. **59**(9), 1947–1965 (2022). https://doi.org/10.7544/issn1000-1239.20210829
2. Peng, C., Xia, F., Naseriparsa, M., Osborne, F.: Knowledge graphs: opportunities and challenges. Artif. Intell. Rev. **56**, 13071–13102 (2023). https://doi.org/10.1007/s10462-023-10465-9
3. Choi, S., Jung, Y.: Knowledge graph construction: extraction, learning, and evaluation. Appl. Sci. **15**(7), 3727 (2025). https://doi.org/10.3390/app15073727
4. Mouiche, I., Saad, S.: Entity and relation extractions for threat intelligence knowledge graphs. Comput. Secur. **148**, 104120 (2025). https://doi.org/10.1016/j.cose.2024.104120
5. Kirrane, S., Ngonga Ngomo, A.-C., Shimizu, C., Hammar, K., Hitzler, P.: Modular ontology modeling. Semant. Web **14**(3), 459–489 (2022). https://doi.org/10.3233/SW-222886
6. Kumar, P.: Large language models (LLMs): survey, technical frameworks, and future challenges. Artif. Intell. Rev. **57**(10), 260 (2024). https://doi.org/10.1007/s10462-024-10888-y
7. Wang, W., Zheng, V.W., Yu, H., et al.: A survey of zero-shot learning: settings, methods, and applications. ACM Trans. Intell. Syst. Technol. **10**(2), Article 13 (2019). https://doi.org/10.1145/3293318
8. Wang, Z., Chen, H., Xu, G., Ren, M.: A novel large-language-model-driven framework for named entity recognition. Inf. Process. Manage. **62**(3), 104054 (2025). https://doi.org/10.1016/j.ipm.2024.104054
9. Kim, H., Kim, J.E., Kim, H.: Exploring Nested named entity recognition with large language models: methods, challenges, and insights. In: Al-Onaizan, Y., Bansal, M., Chen, Y.-N. (eds.) Proceedings of the 2024 Conference on Empirical Methods in Natural Language Processing, pp. 8653–8670. Association for Computational Linguistics, Miami (2024). https://doi.org/10.18653/v1/2024.emnlp-main.492
10. Amalvy, A., Labatut, V., Dufour, R.: Learning to rank context for named entity recognition using a synthetic dataset. In: Bouamor, H., Pino, J., Bali, K. (eds.) Proceedings of the 2023 Conference on Empirical Methods in Natural Language Processing, pp. 10372–10382. Association for Computational Linguistics, Singapore (2023). https://doi.org/10.18653/v1/2023.emnlp-main.642
11. Li, Z., Zhang, Q., Zhu, F., Li, D., Zheng, C., Zhang, Y.: Knowledge graph representation learning with simplifying hierarchical feature propagation. Inf. Process. Manage. **60**(4), 103348 (2023). https://doi.org/10.1016/j.ipm.2023.103348
12. Zhang, Y., Yang, J.: Chinese NER using lattice LSTM. In: Gurevych, I., Miyao, Y. (eds.) Proceedings of the 56th Annual Meeting of the Association for Computational Linguistics (Volume 1: Long Papers), pp. 1554–1564. Association for Computational Linguistics, Melbourne (2018). https://doi.org/10.18653/v1/P18-1144
13. Li, M., et al.: Enhancing named entity recognition with a novel BERT-BiLSTM-CRF-RC joint training model for biomedical materials database. Mater. Genome Eng. Adv. **3**(1), e70001 (2025). https://doi.org/10.1002/mgea.70001
14. He, W., Xu, Y., Yu, Q.: BERT-BiLSTM-CRF Chinese resume named entity recognition combining attention mechanisms. In: Proceedings of the 4th International Conference on Artificial Intelligence and Computer Engineering (ICAICE 2023), pp. 542–547. Association for Computing Machinery, Dalian (2024). https://doi.org/10.1145/3652628.3652719

15. Abu-Salih, B.: Domain-specific knowledge graphs: a survey. J. Netw. Comput. Appl. **185**, 103076 (2021). https://doi.org/10.1016/j.jnca.2021.103076
16. Zhang, J., et al.: 2INER: instructive and in-context learning on few-shot named entity recognition. In: Bouamor, H., Pino, J., Bali, K. (eds.) Findings of the Association for Computational Linguistics: EMNLP 2023, pp. 3940–3951. Association for Computational Linguistics, Singapore (2023). https://doi.org/10.18653/v1/2023.findings-emnlp.259
17. Chen, Y., Guo, S., Liu, K., Zhao, J.: Large language models and knowledge graphs. In: Zhang, J. (ed.) Proceedings of the 22nd Chinese National Conference on Computational Linguistics (Volume 2: Frontier Forum), pp. 67–76. Chinese Information Processing Society of China, Harbin (2023). https://aclanthology.org/2023.ccl-2.6/
18. Gallardo-Delgado, A.A., Nolazco-Flores, J.A., Priego-Sánchez, Á.B., Buscaldi, D.: Large language models and knowledge graphs: a state-of-the-art exploration. SN Comput. Sci. **6**(6), 752 (2025). https://doi.org/10.1007/s42979-025-04277-7
19. Bai, X., et al.: Construction of a knowledge graph for framework material enabled by large language models and its application. NPJ Comput. Mater. **11**(1), 51 (2025). https://doi.org/10.1038/s41524-025-01540-6

Data Poisoning Attack with Diffusion Model for QoS-Aware Cloud API Recommender System

Zhen Chen[1], Taiyu Bao[2], He Liu[1], Zijia Zhang[1], Limin Shen[1], and Zeyu Tan[1(✉)]

[1] School of Information Science and Engineering, Yanshan University, Qinhuangdao 066004, China
zeyutan@stumail.ysu.edu.cn

[2] School of Cyber Science and Engineering, Wuhan University, Wuhan 430072, China

Abstract. In the era of pervasive connectivity, Cloud API serve as the primary conduits for data exchange, functional modularity and service distribution. QoS-aware cloud API recommender system (QCARS) is widely used to solve the problem of selecting high-quality cloud API with similar functions. However, the inherent openness of network environments exposes QCARS to significant security vulnerabilities, notably data poisoning, which makes the recommendations follow the will of the attacker, increasing the use risk and promotion difficulty of cloud API. This study establishes a systematic data poisoning framework for QCARS, adopting an offensive-defense perspective to standardize attack methodologies. Furthermore, it introduces a novel generative poisoning approach leveraging diffusion models. Specifically, an encoder first maps real user QoS data into a latent feature distribution. A forward diffusion process then introduces noise until the data reaches a Gaussian distribution. Finally, the model employs a reverse denoising process to iteratively sample from the noise, passing the result through a decoder to synthesize the fake user attack vector. Extensive experimental results validate the effectiveness and superiority of the proposed method. By elucidating the underlying mechanisms of poisoning attacks within QCARS, this study establishes a theoretical foundation for robust defense strategies, ultimately advancing the development of trustworthy QCARS.

Keywords: Cloud API Recommendation · Quality of Service · Data Poisoning · Diffusion Model

1 Introduction

Cloud Application Programming Interfaces (APIs) are the premier vehicle for data distribution, functional replication, and service delivery, serving as indispensable infrastructure for service-oriented development and the digital economy [1]. As enterprises increasingly embrace the API economy, they are transforming data, algorithms, and computational power using cloud APIs into public-facing services to meet the growing demand for elastic digital experiences. For

© The Author(s), under exclusive license to Springer Nature Singapore Pte Ltd. 2027
H. Sun et al. (Eds.): ChineseCSCW 2025, CCIS 2911, pp. 327–346, 2027.
https://doi.org/10.1007/978-981-92-0288-1_24

example, Baidu uses cloud APIs to provide language translation services; governments and enterprises adopt cloud APIs to awaken dormant data to leverage the multiplier effect of data elements; OpenAI brings the explosively growing intelligent chatbot into our lives via GPT cloud APIs. However, while this flourishing ecosystem offers unprecedented cloud API choice, the resulting explosion in API volume and variety [2] has created a significant discovery hurdle, potentially hindering the sustainable growth of the API economy.

To mitigate choice overload and navigate the vast repositories of cloud APIs, platforms like ProgrammableWeb, RapidAPI, and APIList have emerged as centralized hubs. While these platforms enhance search efficiency through keyword and category-based filtering, they struggle to address the high degree of functional homogeneity among cloud APIs [3]. For instance, a developer on RapidAPI may face over 100 near-identical SMS delivery cloud API services; for those lacking deep domain expertise, quickly selecting the optimal cloud APIs and services providers becomes an inefficient process of trial and error. Consequently, researchers have integrated Quality of Service (QoS) metrics, such as reliability, throughput, and response time, to differentiate cloud APIs based on non-functional performance [4]. This shift toward QoS-aware recommendation systems (QCARS) has proven instrumental in breaking the deadlock of functional equivalence, enabling more precise and personalized API selection.

While two decades of research and development have established QCARS as the standard for resolving the issue of cloud API functional homogeneity [5], their deployment in dynamic, open-network environments has introduced critical vulnerabilities. Specifically, QCARS are increasingly susceptible to data poisoning attacks, in which attackers inject malicious toxic data to manipulate recommendation logic and subvert system integrity [6]. This risk is underscored by the OWASP 2023 Top 10 API Security Threats, which identifies the expanded attack surface of open cloud APIs as a primary target for exploitation. Consequently, these persistent security anxieties represent a major bottleneck, obstructing the global adoption and trustworthiness of cloud API ecosystems.

Existing QCARSs primarily focus on improving the accuracy and diversity of recommendations [7], often overlooking data security concerns. Zheng et al. [8] pointed out that reliable QoS data is crucial for accurate cloud API QoS predictions. Manikrao et al. [9] introduced third-party agents to verify cloud API QoS registration tables to improve the credibility of QoS data. Ye et al. [10] eliminated the impact of user malicious behavior on QoS prediction performance by identifying outliers. While these agent-based verification and anomaly detection methods strengthen QoS data security, they have two key limitations. First, they fail to address data poisoning attacks that can corrupt QoS data during its collection and storage. Second, they neglect the inherent resilience of QCARSs against external malicious data interference. These gaps result in unclear mechanisms and effects of poisoning attacks on QCARSs, posing security risks for their practical deployment.

Current data poisoning methodologies for recommender systems struggle with significant structural limitations. Traditional heuristic-based attacks rely heavily on historical statistical features [11,12], which often yield low-fidelity attack vectors that lack the granularity required to target complex API composition. While recent advancements in Generative Adversarial Networks (GANs) have improved vector quality through competitive training [13–15], they remain plagued by inherent training instabilities and the risk of mode collapse. Consequently, GAN-based frameworks frequently struggle to maintain the authenticity and cross-sequence consistency of generated attack vectors, undermining their overall effectiveness in sophisticated cloud API poisoning scenarios.

To overcome these limitations, this paper establishes a comprehensive data poisoning framework for QCARS, providing both a standardized operational workflow and a formal mathematical definition of the attack surface. Central to this framework is a diffusion-based generative attack method, which masters the latent distribution of authentic user QoS data through a controlled stochastic process. By reversing a systematic noise injection procedure, the model synthesizes high-fidelity fake user profiles that are indistinguishable from real QoS data, which are then injected to subvert the QCARS's integrity. Our evaluation benchmarks this approach against both traditional and state-of-the-art poisoning methods, assessing the robustness of mainstream QCARS through a multi-dimensional lens. By elucidating these adversarial mechanisms in QCARS, this work provides the theoretical groundwork necessary to develop resilient defense strategies and foster more secure cloud API ecosystems. The primary contributions of this research are summarized as follows:

(1) We establish a generalized data poisoning framework for QCARS that formalizes the attack process. This framework allows for the generation of fake user vectors that can be precisely calibrated to specific malicious objectives and operational cost constraints.
(2) We introduce a novel poisoning approach leveraging diffusion-based stochastic modeling. By moving beyond the instability of traditional generative models, our method ensures superior training convergence while significantly enhancing the structural diversity and stealthiness of fake user profiles.
(3) We conduct a comparative analysis of our approach against state-of-the-art baselines. Our evaluation spans attack scale, intensity, and non-functional impact, while specifically benchmarking the anti-detection capabilities of diffusion-based attacks to validate their superior concealment in real-world environments.

2 Preliminaries

2.1 Data Poisoning Attack

Data poisoning involves the strategic injection of adversarial data to compromise the integrity of the original distribution. By introducing targeted bias, these manipulations distort the recommender system's logic to serve the attacker's specific objectives. As shown in Fig. 1, when a cloud API QoS dataset is poisoned, the resulting recommendation model skewness leads to the promotion of sub-optimal or malicious APIs. This degradation in recommendation quality cascades

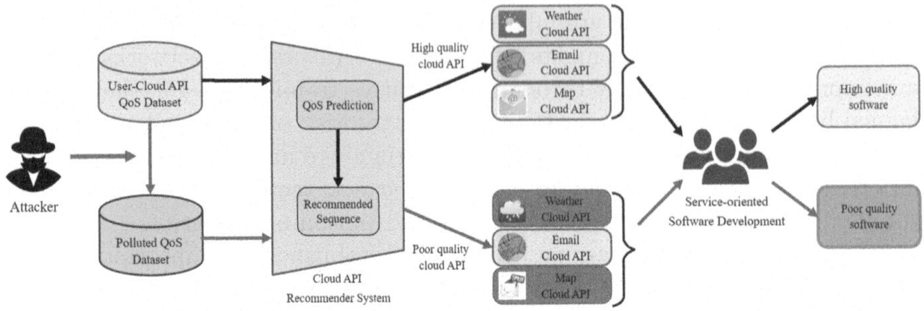

Fig. 1. Illustration of the data poisoning against QCARS.

into the software development lifecycle, resulting in lower-tier service-oriented applications that compromise both user experience and systemic security.

To evade detection, adversaries typically synthesize QoS data that closely mimics the statistical distribution of historical records before injecting it into the QCARSs. By maintaining high similarity to real QoS data, the attack achieves greater stealth while effectively manipulating recommendation outcomes. We formally define the attack process for QCARS via the injection of fake user profiles as follows:

$$Q(x_u) \oplus Q(\tilde{x}_{u'}) \Rightarrow Q(x_u, \tilde{x}_{u'}) \tag{1}$$

where $Q(x_u)$ and $Q(\tilde{x}_{u'})$ denote the QoS feature vectors of real and fake users. Specifically, x_u and $\tilde{x}_{u'}$ represent the sets of cloud API QoS values obtained by an original real user u and a generated fake user u'. The term $Q(x_u, \tilde{x}_{u'})$ designates the poisoned QoS dataset, resulting from the integration of fake profiles into the real QoS data.

2.2 Mathematical Modeling of QCARS Under Data Poisoning

In a standard operational phase, the QCARS aggregates all users' historical QoS invocation records of cloud APIs for training. Based on these historical QoS data, the QCARS generates an optimized ranking of candidate cloud APIs. This process is formalized as.

$$Q(x_u) \xrightarrow{\Gamma(v)} (a_i, a_j, \ldots, a_k) \tag{2}$$

where Γ denotes the QCARS, and v represents the target user. The tuple $(a_i, a_j, \ldots, a_k)$ constitutes the ordered recommendation sequence produced by Γ for user v in its original state, prior to any adversarial data injection.

The fundamental objective of a data poisoning attack against QCARS is to artificially increase the recommendation probability of an attacker's target API, thereby ensuring its preferential placement across the broader candidate cloud APIs. Under these adversarial conditions, the recommendation mapping is redefined as follows:

$$Q(x_i, \tilde{x}_{i'}) \xrightarrow{\Gamma(r)} (a_x, a_y, \ldots, a_k) \tag{3}$$

where $(a_x, a_y, \ldots, a_k)$ denotes the compromised recommendation sequence generated for user v post-poisoning-attack. A comparative analysis with the baseline in Eq. (2) reveals a significant systemic shift in the output of Γ. This intentional distortion successfully redirects the user toward sub-optimal cloud APIs, effectively compromising user utility and system reliability.

3 Data Poisoning Attack Framework for QCARSs

The poisoning attack framework for QCARSs mainly includes four stages, as shown in Fig. 2.

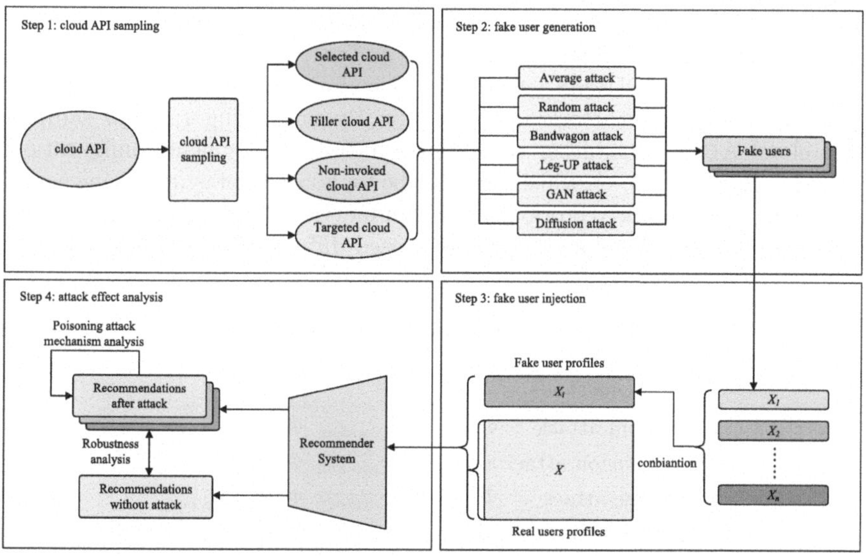

Fig. 2. QCARS poisoning attack framework.

(1) Cloud API sampling. Attackers filter a batch of cloud APIs from the cloud API repository, which can be specifically divided into selected cloud APIs, filler cloud APIs, non-invoked cloud APIs, and targeted cloud APIs. Attackers decide which cloud APIs will be invoked by fake users based on attack cost requirements and attack purposes.

(2) Fake user generation. Attackers employ generative or heuristic-based poisoning methodologies, such as average or random attacks, to synthesize fake but seemingly reasonable QoS values for the cloud APIs obtained in the cloud API sampling stage. These synthetic QoS values are then aggregated into fake user profiles, designed to bypass anomaly detection during the next injection phase.

(3) Fake user injection. The synthesized user profiles are systematically injected into the original QoS dataset to compromise the training of the QCARS.

By blending randomized combinations of adversarial vectors into the real user set, the attacker induces a targeted bias in the recommendation logic. This manipulation misleads the QCARS into prioritizing the attacker's target APIs in its final recommendation rankings.

(4) Attack effect analysis. The final phase involves a comparative performance analysis of the QCARS in its original and compromised states to quantify systemic robustness. By evaluating the destructive efficacy of various poisoning strategies, this stage demystifies the underlying mechanism of the poisoning attack in QCARS. These quantitative insights establish a theoretical foundation for developing next-generation proactive defense mechanisms and enhancing the overall resilience of QCARS.

To align with attacker's actual objectives and cost constraints, candidate cloud APIs are partitioned into four different functional subsets. Let A^S, A^F, A^ϕ, and A^T denote selected, filler, non-invoked, and target cloud APIs, respectively. The specific cloud API QoS generation logic for each subset varies depending on the underlying attack methodology. By employing random sampling across cloud APIs, an attacker can derive multiple deployment configurations, $C_i = \left({A_i}^S, {A_i}^F, {A_i}^\Phi, {A_i}^T\right)$, which serve as the foundation for synthesizing sophisticated fake user attack vectors. Table 1 summarizes the deployment strategies for five baseline attacks alongside our proposed diffusion-based approach.

Table 1. Deployment strategies of poisoning attacks

Attack methods	A^S	A^F	A^ϕ	A^T
Random attack	Φ	r_{random}	Φ	$r_{\text{max/min}}$
Bandwagon attack	r_{min}	r_{random}	Φ	r_{max}
Average attack	Φ	r_{average}	Φ	$r_{\text{max/min}}$
Leg-UP attack	$r_{\text{adversarial}}$	r_{real}	Φ	$r_{\text{max/min}}$
GAN attack	$r_{\text{adversarial}}$	r_{pareto}	Φ	$r_{\text{max/min}}$
Diffusion attack	$r_{\text{diffusion}}$	$r_{\text{diffusion}}$	Φ	$r_{\text{max/min}}$

Definition 1. Attack intensity (η). The attack intensity characterizes the quantity of target cloud APIs manipulated within a single adversarial profile. While a high value of η maximizes the attack impact on the QCARS, it simultaneously increases the risk of triggering anomaly detection mechanisms due to anomalous QoS distributions. The generation of the fake user u' under a specific intensity is formulated as:

$$f_x\left(A^S, A^F, A^T, \eta\right) = u' \tag{4}$$

where f_x denotes the generation function of the chosen attack method, u' denotes generated fake users.

Definition 2. Attack scale (μ). The attack scale defines the total volume of adversarial profiles injected into the system. As most cloud APIs operate on a pay-per-invocation model, the scale is intrinsically linked to the attacker's financial budget. The aggregation of these fake user profiles into the dataset $Q(\tilde{x}_{u'})$ is defined by the following mapping:

$$\xi\left(u'_1, u'_2, ..., u'_k, \mu\right) \Rightarrow Q\left(\tilde{x}_{u'}\right) \tag{5}$$

where $u'_1, u'_2, ..., u'_k$ denotes the set of synthesized fake users.

Following the formalization in Eq. (2), the resulting fake user attack vectors $Q(\tilde{x}_{u'})$ is surreptitiously integrated into the original training dataset, thereby subverting the recommendation logic of the QCARS.

4 Diffusion-Based Data Poisoning Attack Method

4.1 Overall Structure

As illustrated in Fig. 3, the diffusion-based data poisoning attack operates through a four-stage pipeline. First, an encoder compresses the real user's cloud API QoS interaction vector into a low-dimensional feature representation. Then, Gaussian noise is incrementally added to these features until they are transformed into pure Gaussian noise. Third, a proxy model learns to reverse this process, iteratively denoising the Gaussian noise to reconstruct synthetic, user-like features. Finally, a decoder maps these restored features into a malicious fake user attack vector.

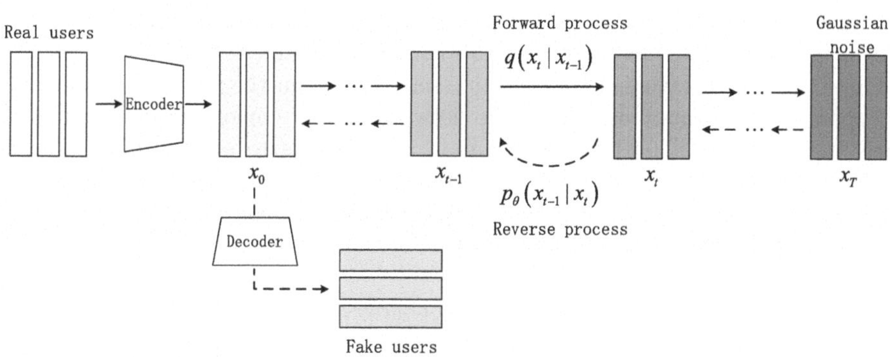

Fig. 3. Overall structure of diffusion-based data poisoning attack.

4.2 Method Design

The diffusion-based data poisoning attack utilizes a Denoising Diffusion Probabilistic Model (DDPM) to generate fake user attack vectors. By employing a Multilayer Perceptron (MLP) serving as a proxy model to reconstruct data from Gaussian noise, this method ensures stable generation and high concealment, effectively compromising the target QCARS.

Data Feature Extraction. To efficiently process the high-dimensional QoS distributions from cloud API interactions, the system employs an Autoencoder (AE) for dimensionality reduction. This architecture consists of an encoder that maps input user's QoS data to a latent space and a decoder that reconstructs the original signal. Specifically, The encoder transforms the user QoS vector x into a compressed feature representation u_{API} through a weighted linear transformation as follow:

$$u_{API} = f_{\varphi}\left(W_1 x + b_1\right) \tag{6}$$

where $f_{\varphi}(\cdot)$ is the mapping function of the encoding layer, W_1 is the weight matrix, b_1 is the bias vector. Once the backward denoising process is complete, the decoder reconstructs the fake user vector $\hat{x}$ similar to the original real user from the latent features as follow:

$$\hat{x} = g_{\phi}\left(W_2 u_{API} + b_2\right) \tag{7}$$

where $g_{\phi}(\cdot)$ is the mapping function of the decoding layer.

The above autoencoder model is trained by minimizing the reconstruction loss, which measures the squared distance between the original and generated user QoS vectors.

$$L\left(x, \hat{x}\right) = \left\| x - g_{\phi}\left(f_{\varphi}\left(x\right)\right)\right\|^2 \tag{8}$$

To optimize the autoencoder model, the objective is to iteratively update parameters to minimize the loss function $L\left(x, \hat{x}; \phi, \varphi\right)$, achieving the optimal parameter solution. When performing classification or feature extraction, using the original autoencoder may lead to identity mapping, failing to capture the unique statistical features in the training set. To prevent the model from learning a trivial identity mapping, where the network simply copies the input without learning meaningful patterns, a common approach is to set the hidden layer nodes smaller than the input layer, forcing the model to learn a compressed representation. Alternatively, one can increase the number of hidden nodes and introduce a sparsity regularization term $R(s)$, following,

$$L_{sparse}\left(x, \hat{x}; \phi, \varphi\right) = L\left(x, \hat{x}; \phi, \varphi\right) + \lambda \cdot R\left(s\right) \tag{9}$$

where $L_{sparse}\left(x, \hat{x}; \phi, \varphi\right)$ represents the loss function considering sparsity constraints, $R\left(s\right)$ is a regularization term measuring the sparsity of hidden layer activity, λ is the adjustment coefficient for regularization strength, s represents the activity value of the hidden layer.

Existing research shows that sparse representations are often more effective than non-sparse representations. The sparsity of the hidden layer can guide the model to capture the most representative features in the data while ignoring noise or unimportant information. Therefore, a sparse autoencoder is used to extract user data features.

Forward Process. After extracting the real user data features through the sparse autoencoder, the forward process systematically corrupts the QoS data feature vector x_0 by injecting incremental Gaussian noise ε over T iterations. And the time period $[0, T]$ is encoded. By introducing a proxy model such as an MLP, the simulated data at any time in the time period is polluted by noise.

Given the initial data distribution $x_0 \sim q(x_0)$, according to the transition equation $q(x_t|x_{t-1})$, different noises $\beta_1, \beta_2, ..., \beta_T$ are added over time to obtain the polluted data $x_1, x_2, ..., x_T$. At this time, when time increases and reaches moment T, the polluted data distribution will become a simple Gaussian prior distribution, i.e., $x_T \sim N(x_t; 0, \mathrm{I})$. The diffusion process is modeled as a Markov chain, where each state x_t depends solely on the previous state x_{t-1}. Therefore, the overall noise diffusion process can be represented as follows,

$$q(x_1, x_2..., x_T|x_0) = \prod_{t=1}^{T} q(x_t|x_{t-1}) \tag{10}$$

Among them, each individual step in this transition is defined by,

$$q(x_t|x_{t-1}) = N\left(x_t; \sqrt{1-\beta_t}x_{t-1}, \beta_t \mathrm{I}\right) \tag{11}$$

Since the added noise intensity during the entire noise diffusion process is a set of fixed hyperparameters, the forward process can be achieved through sampling using the reparameterization method. By defining $\alpha_t = 1 - \beta_t$ and $\bar{\alpha}_t = \prod_{i=0}^{t} \alpha_i$, we obtain the following closed-form expression,

$$q(x_t|x_0) = N(x_t; \sqrt{\alpha_t}x_0, (1-\bar{\alpha}_t)\mathrm{I}) \tag{12}$$

$$x_t = \sqrt{\bar{\alpha}_t}x_0 + \sqrt{1-\bar{\alpha}_t}\varepsilon, \varepsilon \sim N(0, \mathrm{I}) \tag{13}$$

When it is confirmed that all β_t in $\beta_1, \beta_2, ..., \beta_T$ are less than 1 and the length T of the Markov chain is sufficiently large. According to Eq. (12), it can be concluded that when $t \to T$, then $\bar{\alpha}_t \to 0$, and $q(x_t|x_0) \to N(0, \mathrm{I})$. This indicates that as more noise is added, the original information in the data gradually disappears until it eventually becomes completely random noise. The value of β generally adopts a linearly increasing method.

To facilitate the attack, each time step t is mapped to a high-dimensional timestamp embedding vector ξ_t. A proxy model (such as an MLP) is then trained to observe the data at any given moment alongside its timestamp embedding vector, the data sample will become approximately a random Gaussian noise distribution at the final moment T.

Reverse Process. The reverse process aims to reverse the forward diffusion by learning to recover the original QoS data features from Gaussian noise. Given the polluted data sample distribution at moment t and the timestamp embedding, it trains the proxy model to predict noise distribution $\varepsilon_\theta(x_t, \xi_t)$ at moment t, and use Eq. (14) to restore the data sample distribution x_{t-1} at moment $t-1$, and so on, finally restoring the original data sample distribution x_0.

$$x_{t-1} = \frac{1}{\sqrt{\alpha_t}}\left(x_t - \frac{1-\alpha_t}{\sqrt{1-\bar{\alpha}_t}}\varepsilon_\theta\left(x_t, \xi_t\right)\right) \tag{14}$$

Upon completion of the forward diffusion, the reverse denoising process is initiated to reconstruct original QoS data features from pure random noise. Theoretically, the reverse transitions $q\left(x_t|x_{t-1}\right)$ of the forward process $q\left(x_{t-1}|x_t\right)$ exists, and both maintains the same functional form. By constructing a denoising process that mirrors the noise diffusion process, the original data can be gradually recovered.

Like its forward counterpart, the denoising process is structured as a Markov chain, defined by,

$$p_\theta\left(x_0, x_1, ..., x_T\right) = p\left(x_T\right)\prod_{t=1}^{T} p_\theta\left(x_{t-1}|x_t\right) \tag{15}$$

In this chain, each step $p_\theta(x_{t-1}|x_t)$ uses a trained proxy model, parameterized by θ, to predict and remove the noise added during the forward process, gradually reconstructing the vector until the original data distribution is restored,

$$p_\theta\left(x_{t-1}|x_t\right) = N\left(x_{t-1}; \mu_\theta\left(x_t, t\right), \Sigma_\theta\left(x_t, t\right)\right) \tag{16}$$

To restore highly accurate and authentic original data, the proxy model parameters must be optimized so that the learned denoising transition $p_\theta(x_{t-1} \mid x_t)$ closely approximates the true inverse process $q(x_{t-1} \mid x_t)$ of the transition equation $q(x_t \mid x_{t-1})$ in the noise diffusion process. Since $q(x_{t-1} \mid x_t)$ is currently unknown, it cannot be directly solved. However, when x_0 is used as a conditioning variable in the diffusion process, its conditional posterior distribution $q(x_{t-1} \mid x_t, x_0)$ can be tractable and calculated as:

$$q\left(x_{t-1}|x_t, x_0\right) = N\left(x_{t-1}; \frac{\sqrt{\bar{\alpha}_{t-1}}\beta_t}{1-\bar{\alpha}_t}x_0 + \frac{\sqrt{\alpha_t}\left(1-\bar{\alpha}_{t-1}\right)}{1-\bar{\alpha}_t}x_t, \left(\frac{1-\bar{\alpha}_{t-1}}{1-\bar{\alpha}_t}\beta_t\right)\mathrm{I}\right) \tag{17}$$

Specifically, the mean $\tilde{\mu}_r(x_t, x_0)$ of the posterior distribution is given by $\frac{\sqrt{\alpha_r}\beta_r}{1-\bar{\alpha}_r}x_0 + \frac{\sqrt{\bar{\alpha}_{t-1}}(1-\alpha_r)}{1-\bar{\alpha}_r}x_t$ indicating that the mean is solely a function of x_t and x_0. The variance $\tilde{\beta}_r$ is $\frac{1-\bar{\alpha}_{t-1}}{1-\bar{\alpha}_r}\beta_r$, which depends only on the predefined noise schedule and has no learnable parameters. Thus, the denoising process simplifies to training the proxy model to estimate $p_\theta(x_0)$, which represents the likelihood of the target data distribution. By introducing Kullback-Leibler (KL) divergence based on negative log-likelihood, we can establish a variational upper bound on the negative log-likelihood. A smaller upper bound implies a smaller negative log-likelihood, leading to a larger log-likelihood, as shown in Eq. (18).

$$-\log\left(p_\theta\left(x_0\right)\right) \leq \mathrm{E}_{q\left(x_{1:T}|x_0\right)}\left[\log\left(\frac{q\left(x_{1:T}|x_0\right)}{p_\theta\left(x_{0:T}\right)}\right)\right] \tag{18}$$

This transforms into the cross-entropy upper bound $L_{VLB} \geq \mathrm{E}_{q(x_0)}\left[-\log\left(p_\theta\left(x_0\right)\right)\right]$. From this, we obtain:

$$L_{VLB} = \mathrm{E}_q \underbrace{\left[D_{KL}\left(q\left(x_T|x_0\right)||p_\theta\left(x_T\right)\right)\right.}_{L_T} + \underbrace{\sum_{t=2}^{T} D_{KL}\left(q\left(x_{t-1}|x_t,x_0\right)||p_\theta\left(x_{t-1}|x_t\right)\right)}_{L_{t-1}} - \underbrace{\left.\log\left(p_\theta\left(x_0|x_1\right)\right)\right]}_{L_0} \tag{19}$$

In the optimization objective, L_T corresponds to the initial noise distribution and has no learnable parameters, as the final diffusion scale is fixed, so it can be ignored. L_0 is similarly disregarded as a constant reconstruction term. The primary training focus is L_{t-1}, since both the posterior $q(x_{t-1} \mid x_t, x_0)$ and the transition $p_\theta(x_{t-1} \mid x_t)$ are Gaussian, their KL divergence can be simplified to the form given by Eq. (20).

$$L_{t-1} = \mathrm{E}_{x_0,\varepsilon}\left[\frac{1}{2\sigma_t^2}\left\|\tilde{\mu}_t\left(x_t,x_0\right) - \mu_\theta\left(x_t,t\right)\right\|^2\right] + C \tag{20}$$

where $\sigma_r^2 = \Sigma_\theta(x_t,t) = \tilde{\beta}_t$.

Using the parameterization method from Eq. (13) and substituting x_t into Eq. (20) allows the computation of the loss between noise terms, as shown in Eq. (21).

$$L_{t-1} \approx \mathrm{E}_{t,x_0,\varepsilon}\left[\left\|\varepsilon - \varepsilon_\theta\left(\sqrt{\bar{\alpha}_t}x_0 + \sqrt{1-\bar{\alpha}_t}\varepsilon, t\right)\right\|^2\right] \tag{21}$$

The training objective is to optimize the proxy model by simulating the noise diffusion process across all time steps. The resulting loss function is defined in Eq. (22):

$$L_{diffusion} = \mathrm{E}_{\xi_t,x_0,\varepsilon}\left[\left\|\varepsilon - \varepsilon_\theta\left(\sqrt{\bar{\alpha}_t}x_0 + \sqrt{1-\bar{\alpha}_t}\varepsilon, \xi_t\right)\right\|^2\right] \tag{22}$$

where θ denotes the set of learnable parameters within the proxy model, while ϵ is the random Gaussian noise.

Once the proxy model is trained, stepwise denoising is performed on the noise x_T sampled from a standard Gaussian distribution using Eq. (23).

$$x_{t-1} = \mu_\theta\left(x_t,t\right) + \sqrt{\beta_t}\varepsilon, \varepsilon \sim N\left(0,\mathrm{I}\right) \tag{23}$$

Finally, the denoised representation is decoded into an attack vector of fake user that mimics the real-user distribution. Since the diffusion model is trained by predicting noise, its training loss remains stable. The loss for generating poisoning samples is given in Eq. (24).

$$L = L_{sparse}\left(x,\hat{x};\phi,\theta\right) + L_{diffusion}\left(x_0,t,\xi_t;\theta\right) \tag{24}$$

5 Experiments

To evaluate the efficacy of the diffusion-based poisoning attack method and analyze its impact on the robustness of QCARSs, we conducted a series of systematic experiments on real QoS datasets. Our study is guided by the following research questions:

RQ1: To what extent does the proposed diffusion-based poisoning attack degrade the overall performance of the QCARS?

RQ2: What factors make poisoning attacks affect the performance of QCARSs?

RQ3: How do the intensity and scale of poisoning attacks influence cloud API recommendation results?

RQ4: What is the operational stability of the proposed attack method, and how resilient is it against detection algorithms?

5.1 Experimental Settings

Dataset. To evaluate the proposed diffusion-based poisoning attack method, we utilize the WS-DREAM dataset [17], which contains 1,974,675 records from 339 real users invoking 5,825 cloud API services worldwide. To simulate real-world conditions, the dataset is sparsified, reducing its density to 4%, with the remaining 96% used as the test set. Due to network fluctuations, some outliers were present in the response time data, which were removed. The statistics of the used response time dataset are summarized in Table 2.

Table 2. WS-DREAM Dataset (Response Time) Statistics

Attribute	Value (unit: s)
Num. of Users	339
Num. of cloud API	5,818
Response Time value range	(0, 20]
Avg. response time	0.9085
Num. of Interaction Records	1,873,838

Evaluation Metrics. To evaluate the prediction accuracy and attack efficacy within the QCARSs, we utilize three categories of metrics:

(1) Prediction Accuracy Metrics. Mean Absolute Error (MAE, defined in Eq. (25)) and Root Mean Square Error (RMSE, defined in Eq. (26)) quantify the deviation between the predicted cloud API QoS value ($\hat{y}_i$) and the ground truth (y_i):

$$MAE = \frac{1}{n}\sum_{i=1}^{n} |\hat{y}_i - y_i| \tag{25}$$

$$RMSE = \sqrt{\frac{1}{n}\sum_{i=1}^{n} (\hat{y}_i - y_i)^2} \tag{26}$$

where n is the total number of the tested cloud API QoS invocation records.

(2) Recommendation Performance. Hit Rate (HR@k) measures the QCARS's ability to include the target cloud API within its top-k recommendation list:

$$HR@k = \frac{1}{|A_{target}|} \sum_{a \in A_{target}} \frac{1}{|U|} \sum_{u \in U} \delta(u, a) \tag{27}$$

where $|A_{target}|$ denotes the number of the tested target APIs, $|U|$ represents the size of users, $\delta(u, a)$ is a binary indicator that equals 1 if the target API a appears in user u's top-k list, and 0 otherwise.

(3) Detection and Concealment. The F1 Score evaluates the detectability of the poisoning attack method on QCARSs by balancing Precision and Recall. A high F1 score reflects superior detection capabilities, implying lower concealment for the attack:

$$F1 = \frac{2 \times Presicion \times Recall}{Presicion + Recall} \tag{28}$$

where $Precision = \frac{TP}{TP+FP}$ and $Recall = \frac{TP}{TP+FN}$.

5.2 Data Poisoning Attack Effectiveness Analysis

To evaluate the proposed diffusion-based poisoning attack, we compared its impact against five baseline attacks (Average, Random, Bandwagon, Leg-UP, and GAN) across four categories twelve QCARSs. Specifically, 1% of fake user attack vectors were injected into the dataset. It was assumed that the density of these fake vectors matched the original dataset for optimal attack impact. Tables 3 and 4 detail the resulting shifts in MAE and RMSE, illustrating the comparative performance degradation caused by each attack method.

The experimental results in Tables 3 and 4 yield the following key conclusions:

(1) Vulnerability in Sparse Scenarios. Injecting a mere 1% ratio of fake user vectors significantly compromises most QCARSs. This underscores critical security vulnerabilities within current QCARS architectures.
(2) Superiority of Diffusion Attacks. The proposed diffusion-based attack consistently outperforms baseline methods. The diffusion attack, due to its good and stable data generation capability, can better simulate real user behavior, find weaknesses in the data distribution, and achieve effective pollution of the dataset.
(3) Reduced Robustness in Deep Learning. QCARSs based on deep learning have poorer robustness, especially when facing diffusion model-based poisoning attacks. For instance, the DeepFM algorithm experienced a 4.3% increase in MAE (rising from 0.5079 to 0.53), while the LR algorithm's MAE rose by 3.9% (from 0.6631 to 0.6895).

5.3 Explanation of Data Poisoning Attack Effects

To visualize the impact of poisoning, we compared the predictive accuracy of four representative QCARSs: arithmetic mean (AAM), collaborative filtering

Table 3. Attack effectiveness comparisons with MAE

Method	No Attack	Average	Random	Bandwagon	Leg-Up	GAN	Diffusion
GAM	.9894	.9947	.9936	.9952	.9913	.9957	**.9989**
AAM	.7149	.7208	.7214	.7230	.7198	.7224	**.7276**
UPCC	.6734	.6736	.6745	.6750	.6744	.6776	**.6798**
APCC	.8510	.8508	.8519	.8514	.8490	**.8523**	.8442
WSRec	.7290	.7288	.7297	.7293	.7263	**.7314**	.7245
Funk-SVD	.5896	.5868	.5879	.5913	.5934	.5872	**.5945**
Bias-SVD	.6018	.6026	.6076	.6076	.6112	.6047	**.6154**
SVD++	.5924	.5969	.5981	.5972	.5963	.5991	**.5992**
LR	.6631	.6689	.6742	.6785	.6823	.6834	**.6895**
FM	.7008	.7015	.7084	.7099	**.7143**	.7121	.7023
MLP	.5100	.5103	.5146	.5180	.5195	.5231	**.5238**
DeepFM	.5079	.5123	.5245	.5268	.5278	.5291	**.5300**

*Note:*For brevity, we omit the leading zero in decimal numbers (e.g., $0.xxxx$ is written as $.xxxx$) throughout this paper.

Table 4. Attack effectiveness comparisons with RMSE

Method	No Attack	Average	Random	Bandwagon	Leg-Up	GAN	Diffusion
GAM	1.9726	1.9729	1.9734	1.9736	1.9784	1.9757	**1.9802**
AAM	1.5947	1.5994	1.5996	1.6001	1.6126	1.6213	**1.6256**
UPCC	1.7267	1.7269	1.7276	1.7280	1.7233	1.7276	**1.7291**
APCC	1.9696	1.9708	1.9756	1.9787	**1.9813**	1.9733	1.9657
WSRec	1.7751	1.7762	**1.7816**	1.7801	1.7811	1.7796	1.7756
Funk-SVD	1.4843	1.4896	1.4923	1.4916	1.4934	1.4968	**1.5024**
Bias-SVD	1.3949	1.3968	1.3991	1.4008	1.4062	1.4015	**1.4085**
SVD++	1.3945	1.3965	1.3998	1.4023	1.4079	1.4120	**1.4189**
LR	1.4215	1.4269	1.4302	1.4332	1.4362	1.4298	**1.4417**
FM	1.4906	1.4924	1.4961	1.4976	**1.5024**	1.4988	1.4922
MLP	1.3635	1.3676	1.3754	1.3789	1.3765	1.3803	**1.3857**
DeepFM	1.3524	1.3598	1.3617	1.3608	1.3635	1.3669	**1.3698**

(WSRec), matrix factorization (SVD++), and deep learning (MLP). Specifically, maintaining a fixed attack scale of 10% and intensity of 20, we analyzed 120 random user-API interaction records with response times between 0 and 2 s. Predictions exceeding a 0.4 s error threshold were classified as abnormal, and vice versa.

As illustrated in Fig. 4, 5, 6 and 7, the diffusion-based attack produced a higher density of abnormal predictions and greater deviation degrees compared to traditional bandwagon, Leg-UP, and GAN-based methods. These results

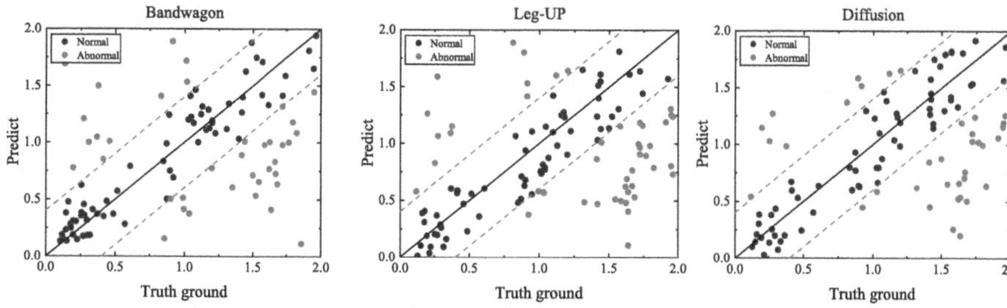

(a) Bandwagon (b) Leg-UP (c) Diffusion

Fig. 4. Prediction error of AAM under different attack methods.

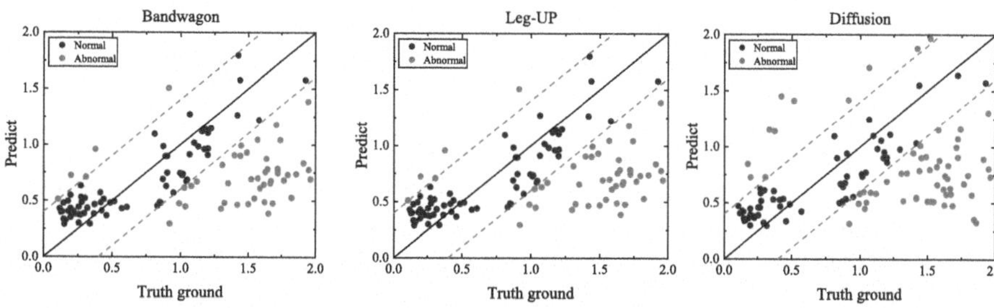

(a) Bandwagon (b) Leg-UP (c) Diffusion

Fig. 5. Prediction error of WSRec under different attack methods.

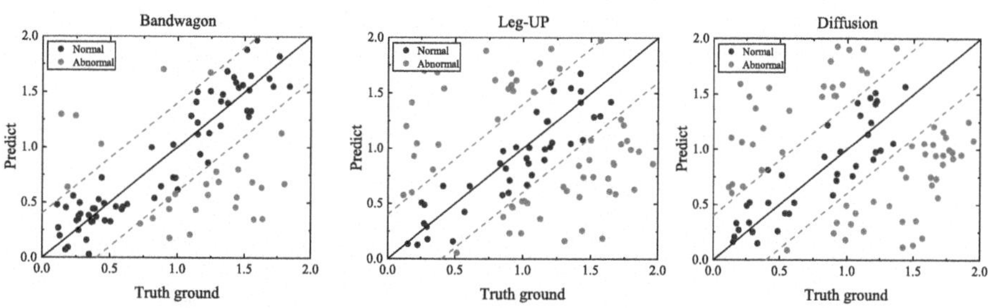

(a) Bandwagon (b) Leg-UP (c) Diffusion

Fig. 6. Prediction error of SVD++ under different attack methods.

demonstrate that diffusion-based attacks achieve superior destructive effects at a lower cost. Furthermore, the increasing error rates observed as algorithms transition from arithmetic mean to deep learning architectures indicate that modern, complex deep learning recommendation models exhibit significantly lower robustness. This vulnerability emphasizes the urgent need for enhanced data security in mainstream deep learning-based QCARSs.

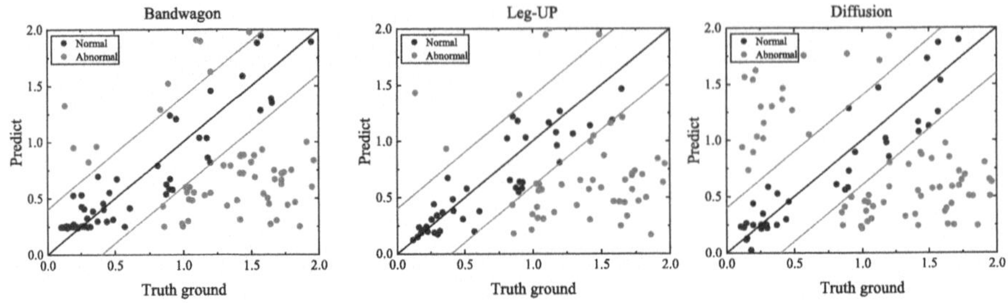

(a) Bandwagon (b) Leg-UP (c) Diffusion

Fig. 7. Prediction error of MLP under different attack methods.

5.4 Impact of Data Poisoning Attack Intensity and Scale

To evaluate the impact of the diffusion-based poisoning attack on QCARSs, we use Eq. (27) to calculate the post-attack Hit Rate (HR@k) for the target cloud API. For response time dataset, the QCARS ranks APIs in ascending order of response time (smaller is better). Since the attack aims to increase the target API's response time and reduce its recommendation likelihood, it suffices to check whether the target API appears in the reversed recommendation list.

Table 5. HR of target cloud API recommendation under parameter(a)

Method	Average	Random	Bandwagon	Leg-UP	GAN	Diffusion
UPCC	.0059	.0024	.0059	.0814	.0926	**.2614**
APCC	.0112	.0000	.0000	.0143	.0100	**.0142**
Funk-SVD	.0532	.0029	.0083	.0432	.0195	**.0560**
Bias-SVD	.0726	.0029	.0083	.0523	.0307	**.0832**
SVD++	.0838	.0236	.0177	.0258	.0820	**.1375**
LR	.0690	.0212	.0171	.0460	.0602	**.0944**
FM	.0106	.0053	.0029	.0093	.0124	**.0165**
MLP	.0361	.0448	.0454	.0840	.0950	**.1198**
DeepFM	.0094	.0053	.0088	.1920	.1770	**.1829**

The experiment sets the reverse recommendation list length to k, with attack intensities of 5 and 10 and attack scales of 0.05 and 0.1. In Tables 5, 6, 7 and 8, attack parameters are: (a) intensity 5, scale 0.05; (b) intensity 5, scale 0.1; (c) intensity 10, scale 0.05; (d) intensity 10, scale 0.1. Preliminary experiments show that without poisoning, the target cloud API never appears in the reverse recommendation list, so its hit rate without attack is omitted. For GAM and AAM recommenders, which predict response time via arithmetic mean, the results are deterministic, yielding a hit rate of 1 after poisoning; these are also omitted.

Table 6. HR of target cloud API recommendation under parameter(b)

Method	Average	Random	Bandwagon	Leg-UP	GAN	Diffusion
UPCC	.0283	.0501	.0254	.6460	.7782	**.9540**
APCC	.0153	.0000	.0000	.0424	.0460	**.0674**
Funk-SVD	.2035	.0265	.0147	.1535	.1133	**.2566**
Bias-SVD	.2395	.0260	.0171	.1432	.1180	**.2543**
SVD++	.2272	.0566	.0413	.1466	.1251	**.2319**
LR	.2118	.0307	.0289	.0426	.0531	**.2711**
FM	.1050	.0136	.0136	.0945	.0586	**.9847**
MLP	.2124	.0838	.0102	.1956	.1864	**.2991**
DeepFM	.0262	.0142	.0236	.8450	.9150	**.9917**

Table 7. HR of target cloud API recommendation under parameter(c)

Method	Average	Random	Bandwagon	Leg-UP	GAN	Diffusion
UPCC	.0080	.0059	.0029	.1313	.0799	**.2227**
APCC	.0168	.0000	.0000	.0213	.0239	**.0292**
Funk-SVD	.0271	.0029	.0029	.0196	.0218	**.0513**
Bias-SVD	.0401	.0050	.0029	.0321	.0283	**.0637**
SVD++	.0612	.0083	.0192	.0324	.0416	**.0826**
LR	.0441	.0103	.0206	.0386	.0313	**.0504**
FM	.0097	.0018	.0021	.0112	.0062	**.0142**
MLP	.0241	.0711	.0693	.0234	.0428	**.1009**
DeepFM	.0097	.0018	.0041	.0102	.0062	**.0118**

Analysis of Tables 5, 6, 7 and 8 indicates that the diffusion attack demonstrates significant advantages and attack effects among various data poisoning attack methods. By manipulating the cloud API recommendation list, the attack significantly reduces the target API's hit rate, severely degrading the user experience. Furthermore, the hit rate data shows that while increasing the attack scale markedly enhances the poisoning effect, increasing attack intensity yields diminishing returns. Excessively high intensity can even reduce attack efficacy and also increase the likelihood of fake user detection.

5.5 Data Poisoning Attack Detection

To address data poisoning attacks, recent research has focused on detecting and analyzing poisoned data at the processing level, effectively identifying and removing fake user data. To evaluate the concealment of the proposed diffusion attack, this paper employs four detection algorithms, PCA(unsupervised) [17], FAP(unsupervised) [18], SemiSAD [19](semi-

Table 8. HR of target cloud API recommendation under parameter(d)

Method	Average	Random	Bandwagon	Leg-UP	GAN	Diffusion
UPCC	.0708	.0472	.0882	.7534	.8373	**.9398**
APCC	.0360	.0000	.0000	.0623	.0690	**.0765**
Funk-SVD	.1265	.0156	.0139	.1213	.0882	**.1947**
Bias-SVD	.1327	.0204	.0156	.1430	.1027	**.1944**
SVD++	.1053	.0490	.0552	.1126	.1206	**.1481**
LR	.1558	.0407	.0263	.0765	.0628	**.2059**
FM	.0649	.0124	.0130	.0578	.0566	**.0941**
MLP	.1407	.0997	.1832	.1934	**.2292**	.2106
DeepFM	.1106	.0124	.0195	.0454	.0879	**.8994**

supervised), and DegreeSAD [20](supervised). To ensure experimental reliability, unsupervised PCA and FAP methods were evaluated using the median of five independent runs, while SemiSAD and PCA approaches employed three-fold cross-validation to maximize the utility of limited labeled data. Given the inherent class imbalance, where fake users constitute only a small fraction of the total population, standard accuracy is an inadequate metric. For instance, if 10 out of 100 users are fake, a detector labeling all users as real would achieve 90% accuracy, which is misleading. Consequently, our evaluation focuses exclusively on detection performance specifically for fake users.

Table 9. F1 of detection methods an an attack scale of 0.1

Attack Method	PCA	FAP	SemiSAD	DegreeSAD
Average Attack	.9645	.9788	.8617	.9443
Random Attack	.9550	.9732	.8858	.8948
Bandwagon Attack	.9384	.9760	.8736	.8898
Leg-UP Attack	.8552	.9665	.8230	.8572
GAN Attack	.8712	.9665	.7849	.8292
Diffusion Attack	**.8152**	**.9523**	**.7397**	**.8045**

Table 10. F1 of detection methods at an attack intensity of 0.2

Attack Method	PCA	FAP	SemiSAD	DegreeSAD
Average	.9753	.9792	.8817	.9745
Random	.9557	.9845	.9299	.9277
Bandwagon	.9870	.9898	.8979	.9164
Leg-UP	.9132	.9740	.7981	.8830
GAN	.9023	.9633	.8236	.8943
Diffusion	**.8993**	**.9633**	**.7759**	**.8560**

As shown in Tables 9 and 10, the diffusion attack has the lowest detection probability among the four methods. By modeling the forward diffusion of QoS data into Gaussian noise and its subsequent reversal, our attack method generates fake users whose QoS distributions closely resemble real users, making detection difficult. Unlike traditional poisoning methods, it avoids extreme values, which are typically used by detection systems to flag anomalies. However, increasing the proportion of injected fake users may boost short-term impact but also raises the risk of detection. Thus, attackers must balance potential benefits against exposure risks when designing poisoning attacks.

6 Conclusion

This paper explores data poisoning attacks on QCARSs and introduces a general framework for such attacks, detailing the basic poisoning attack process. Addressing the limitations of existing methods and leveraging advancements in deep learning recommender systems, we propose a diffusion model-based poisoning attack approach. This method comprises three main components: data feature extraction, forward diffusion, and backward denoising. First, the real user-invoked cloud API QoS vector is encoded to extract data feature distributions. Noise is progressively added until it transforms into pure Gaussian noise, with a proxy model trained to simulate the diffusion process. Finally, the noise is sampled and iteratively denoised to recover fake user attack vectors that replicate original QoS data features. Systematic experiments evaluating attack impact, intensity, scale, and stealth demonstrate that diffusion-based poisoning poses a significant threat to the security and reliability of QCARSs.

Acknowledgments. This work was supported by the National Natural Science Foundation of China (No. 62102348) and the Science and Technology Program of Hebei (No. 236Z0103G).

Disclosure of Interests. The authors declare no conflicts of interest.

References

1. Zhang, M., Cao, J., Sahni, Y., et al.: Eaas: a service-oriented edge computing framework towards distributed intelligence. In: Proceedings of the IEEE International Conference on Service-Oriented System Engineering, pp. 165–175 (2022)
2. Wang, L., Zhang, Y., Zhu, X.: Concept drift-aware temporal cloud service APIs recommendation for building composite cloud systems. J. Syst. Softw. **174**, 110902 (2021)
3. Qi, L., Lin, W., Zhang, X., et al.: A correlation graph based approach for personalized and compatible web apis recommendation in mobile app development. IEEE Trans. Knowl. Data Eng. **35**(6), 5444–5457 (2023)
4. Anithadevi, N., Sundarambal, M.: A design of intelligent QoS aware web service recommendation system. Cluster Comput. **22**(6), 14231–14240 (2019)

5. Eisa, M., Younas, M., Basu, K., et al.: Modelling and simulation of QoS-aware service selection in cloud computing. Simul. Model. Pract. Theory **103**, 102108 (2020)
6. Bermbach, D., Wittern, E.: Benchmarking web API quality revisited. J. Web Eng. **19**(5–6), 603–646 (2020)
7. Qi, L., Song, H., Zhang, X., et al.: Compatibility-aware web API recommendation for mashup creation via textual description mining. ACM Trans. Multimedia Comput. Commun. Appl. **17**(1), 1–19 (2021)
8. Zheng, Z., Li, X., Tang, M., et al.: Web service QoS prediction via collaborative filtering: a survey. IEEE Trans. Serv. Comput. **15**(4), 2455–2472 (2020)
9. Manikrao, U.S., Prabhakar, T.: Dynamic selection of web services with recommendation system. In: International Conference on Next Generation Web Services Practices, pp. 1–5 (2005)
10. Ye, F., Lin, Z., Chen, C., et al.: Outlier-resilient web service qos prediction. In: Proceedings of the Web Conference, pp. 3099–3110 (2021)
11. Li, B., Wang, Y., Singh, A., et al.: Data poisoning attacks on factorization-based collaborative filtering. In: Proceedings of the 30th International Conference on Neural Information Processing Systems, pp. 1893–1901 (2016)
12. Chen, L., Xu, Y., Xie, F., et al.: Data poisoning attacks on neighborhood-based recommender systems. Trans. Emerg. Telecommun. Technol. **32**(6), 1–13 (2021)
13. Wu, F., Gao, M., Yu, J., et al.: Ready for emerging threats to recommender systems? A graph convolution-based generative shilling attack. Inf. Sci. **578**, 683–701 (2021)
14. Lin, C., Chen, S., Li, H., et al.: Attacking recommender systems with augmented user profiles. In: Proceedings of International Conference on Information & Knowledge Management, pp. 855–864 (2020)
15. Lin, C., Chen, S., Zeng, M., et al.: Shilling black-box recommender systems by learning to generate fake user profiles. IEEE Trans. Neural Netw. Learn. Syst. **35**(1), 1305–1319 (2024)
16. Zheng, Z., Zhang, Y., Lyu, M.R.: Distributed QoS evaluation for real-world web services. In: Proceedings of IEEE International Conference on Web Services, 83–90 (2010)
17. Mehta, B., Nejdl, W.: Unsupervised strategies for shilling detection and robust collaborative filtering. User Model. User-Adap. Inter. **19**, 65–97 (2009)
18. Zhang, Y., Tan, Y., Zhang, M., et al.: Catch the black sheep: unified framework for shilling attack detection based on fraudulent action propagation. In: Proceedings of the 24th International Conference on Artificial Intelligence, pp. 2408–2414 (2015)
19. Li, W., Gao, M., Li, H., et al.: Shilling attack detection in recommender systems via selecting patterns analysis. IEICE Trans. Inf. Syst. **99**(10), 2600–2611 (2016)
20. Cao, J., Wu, Z., Mao, B., et al.: Shilling attack detection utilizing semi-supervised learning method for collaborative recommender system. World Wide Web **16**, 729–748 (2013)

Frequency-Enhanced and Query-Aware for Temporal Knowledge Graph Reasoning

Xian Zha, Fuyuan Zhang, Jinfan Yuan, and Jingbin Wang(✉)

Fuzhou University, Fujian 350108, China
wjb@fzu.edu.cn

Abstract. The objective of extrapolation reasoning in temporal knowledge graphs (TKGs) is to forecast absent facts utilizing past data. Most extrapolation research in TKGs concentrate on modeling global patterns of repetition in historical events, as well as local patterns of evolution in adjacent historical events, exhibiting robust efficacy in forecasting future unknown occurrences. Current models demonstrate two significant limitations in processing historical information: firstly, they focus solely on the temporal sequentiality of recent historical subgraph snapshots, ignoring the importance of temporal data relevant to the question, thereby failing to effectively capture the necessary historical context; secondly, they inadequately represent the intrinsic characteristics of historical events that display frequency and periodicity. These constraints diminish the models' expressive capacity, leading to inferior performance. This study introduces a novel model for reasoning with temporal knowledge graphs, referred to as Frequency-Enhanced and Query-Aware Temporal Knowledge Graph Reasoning (Abbreviated as **FeQua**). The model consists of three fundamental modules: (1) A global entity-aware with historical frequency information module that integrates historical frequency data to capture global historical events and pertinent historical frequency information; (2) A local two-level entity-aware and relationship evolution module that assesses the significance of query-relevant historical information at both the entity and subgraph levels; and (3) A periodic time information module that capture the cyclical characteristics of historical events through both periodic and non-periodic time encoding. Comprehensive trials on four benchmark datasets indicate that FeQua substantially surpasses current state-of-the-art models in reasoning with temporal knowledge graphs.

Keywords: Temporal knowledge graph reasoning · Query aware · Historical frequency

1 Introduction

Temporal knowledge graphs (TKGs) represents dynamic facts with timestamps through quadruples (subject, relation, object, timestamp). In contrast to classic static knowledge graphs (SKGs), temporal knowledge graphs (TKGs) are more

© The Author(s), under exclusive license to Springer Nature Singapore Pte Ltd. 2027
H. Sun et al. (Eds.): ChineseCSCW 2025, CCIS 2911, pp. 347–361, 2027.
https://doi.org/10.1007/978-981-92-0288-1_25

adept at representing the inherent dynamism of facts in the real world. As a result, they exhibit considerable potential in intelligent applications including recommendation systems [1], natural disaster forecasting [2], and traffic flow prediction [3]. Nonetheless, both KGs and TKGs are plagued by intrinsic factual incompleteness, which limits their efficacy in subsequent tasks.

RE-NET [4] employs RGCN [5] to capture graph structural information, subsequently subjecting it to sequential encoding. Using RGCN, RE-GCN [6] gathers data from nearby entities and uses gated recurrent unit(GRU) to model the relationships between past events. CyGNet [7] uses a replication generation mechanism to record how frequently global facts are repeated during historical development. TiRGN [8], on the other hand, captures recurring, cyclic, and sequential patterns in historical facts by combining historical global information with local information. HiSMatch [9] integrates background knowledge into temporal knowledge graph completion (TKGC) models via a background knowledge encoder to capture high-level associations between entities. LogCL [10] simultaneously models local and global historical information, incorporating query-aware mechanisms in both global and local graph entity encoding to achieve optimal performance. Although these studies have achieved remarkable results within the Temporal Knowledge Graph Reasoning(TKGR) discipline, two challenges still persist:

(1) Inadequate acquisition of pertinent historical information related to the inquiry. Most Temporal Knowledge Graph Reasoning (TKGR) primarily utilizes changes in entities and relationships over time to learn feature representations. They contend that, in accordance with common sense reasoning, the knowledge graph snapshot that is closer to the query time has superior predictive relevance. This assumption contains a fundamental flaw: the entities relevant to a query may exist solely in specific historical snapshots, resulting in considerable discrepancies in the influence of various snapshots on query predictions. As depicted in Fig. 1., for the query (China, collaboration, ?, t_q), Initially, concerning the significance of historical data at the entity-level, using the snapshot t_{q-1} as an illustration, the query entity : "China" has a direct correlation alone with the entity "Thailand", and its connections with "North Korea" and "United States" are indirect. Thus, for the query entity "China", the entity "Thailand" plays a more pivotal role in its query prediction compared to "North Korea" and "United States", and considerably more than other entities in the

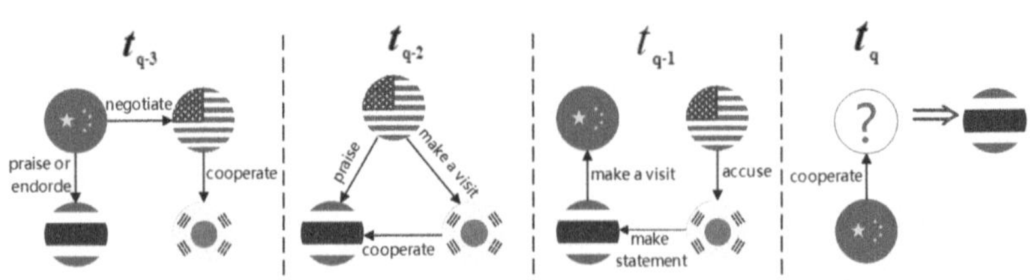

Fig. 1. An example illustrating the importance of query-awareness.

snapshot t_{q-1} that lack indirect connections with "China". Secondly, about the significance of subgraph-level historical data, the entity "China" is absent from the subgraph snapshot t_{q-2}. Thus, the snapshot t_{q-2} offers minimal, if any, value to the inquiry. Conversely, while historical facts pertaining to the entity "China" are present in the earlier snapshot t_{q-3}, they are more effective in substantiating the current query prediction than those from other sources. These behaviors expose a critical shortcoming in current methodologies: they do not discern query-relevant historical facts from entity-level and subgraph-level historical data, instead depending exclusively on temporal proximity and sequential modeling. This weakness directly compromises the model's capacity to reliably predict future facts. Consequently, designing a model that dynamically affects the acquisition of entity-level and subgraph-level historical data based on query content has become essential for improving the reasoning performance of TKGs.

(2) Fails to Effectively Capture the Frequency and Periodicity of Historical Events. Existing approaches often pay scant attention to capturing the frequency and periodicity of historical information, yet the developmental patterns of historical events frequently exhibit such characteristics. As illustrated in the two examples in Fig. 2., Barack Obama frequently imposed sanctions on Iran during his presidency, amounting to dozens of instances. Therefore, effectively considering the historical frequency of such high-frequency events is crucial for accurate prediction. Similarly, for cyclical events such as Egypt's annual January 25th revolution anniversary protests, predicting which entity the Muslim Brotherhood-led opposition will target on this day often points to the Egyptian government. Moreover, such occurrences are not isolated instances. Events demonstrating historical periodicity include the quadrennial US presidential elections, annual international summits, and United Nations-related conferences, among others. Conversely, phenomena like military conflicts, terrorist attacks, and diplomatic protests and condemnations exemplify the high frequency of historical events. Therefore, for events characterized by frequency and periodicity, effectively capturing these patterns is crucial for enhancing the accuracy of predictive models.

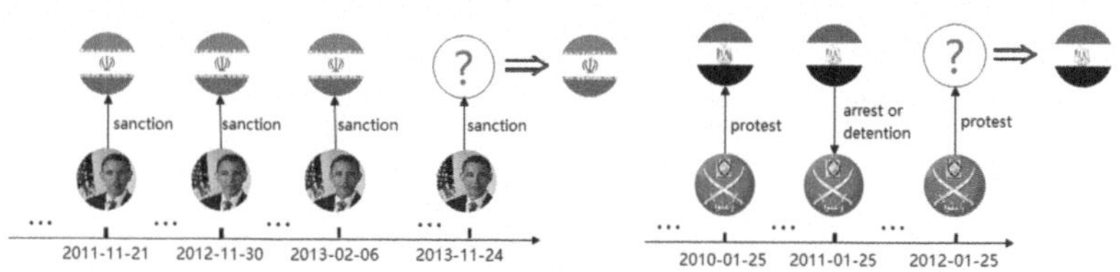

Fig. 2. Examples of periodicity and frequency of events.

In response to the previously identified problems, we suggest the FeQua model. This model utilizes a global entity-aware with historical frequency information module to identify the frequency patterns of global historical events, and the attention aware of these events on query relevance. The local two-level entity-aware and relationship evolution module acquires query-relevant entity data at both the entity and subgraph levels, effectively reflecting the sequential characteristics of recent historical events. The periodic time information module captures the periodic characteristics of historical events. The collaborative function of these modules efficiently utilizes the sequential, frequency-dependent, and periodic traits of historical events, hence improving the reliability of model prediction performance. The following succinctly describes the contributions made in this paper:

(1) For temporal knowledge graph reasoning, we provide a representation learning model, FeQua, which concurrently addresses the sequentiality, frequency, and periodicity of historical data.
(2) We design a local two-level entity-aware and relationship evolution module to efficiently capture historically significant information related to the query. The global entity-aware with historical frequency information module captures historical frequency data, along with the periodicity module, proficiently captures the frequency and periodicity of past events.
(3) Comprehensive studies on four public TKG datasets reveal that our proposed FeQua model exhibits enhanced performance relative to state-of-the-art baselines, achieving optimal results in entity prediction. Notable enhancements of 6.34%, 9.90%, 11.95%, and 9.29% are attained in the MRR and hits@1 metrics for the ICEWS18 and GDELT datasets, respectively.

2 Related Work

2.1 Temporal Knowledge Graph Interpolation Reasoning

Interpolation entails estimating unknown values by utilizing pertinent known values at the present timestamp. Interpolation-based TKGR algorithms generally fill in missing values by examining existing information within the TKG. TTransE [11] enhances the traditional TransE [12] by incorporating a shared encoding of relations and timestamps into a unified space. TA-DistMult [13] enhances the traditional DistMult [14] by interpreting features in relations and timestamps as sequences to construct temporal connections.

2.2 Temporal Knowledge Graph Extrapolation Reasoning

Extrapolation forecasts unknown values at or subsequent to a specified query time, utilizing previous data preceding that query timestamp. Extrapolation-based TKGR largely predicts future occurrences by deriving entity and connection embeddings from historical data snapshots.

RE-GCN [6] gathers data from nearby entities and uses GRU to model the relationships between past events. CyGNet [7] uses a replication generation mechanism to record how frequently global facts are repeated during historical development. TiRGN [8], on the other hand, captures recurring, cyclic, and sequential patterns in historical facts by combining historical global information with local information. HiSMatch [9] integrates background knowledge into temporal knowledge graph completion (TKGC) models via a background knowledge encoder to capture high-level associations between entities.HGLS [15] transforms TKG sequences into global graphs to explicitly connect historical entities across various temporal intervals. The hierarchical RGCN module seeks to capture long-term dependencies among items using layered graph encoding. LogCL [10] concurrently models query-aware local and global historical data, incorporating contrastive learning to improve the model's resilience to noise.

3 Problem Definition

TKG $\mathcal{G}$ can be represented as a time series composed of multiple KG snapshots, where $\mathcal{G} = \{\mathcal{G}_0, \mathcal{G}_1, \mathcal{G}_2, \cdots, \mathcal{G}_{|t|}\}$. Each KG snapshot $\mathcal{G}_t = (\mathcal{E}, \mathcal{R}, \mathcal{F}_t)$ where $\mathcal{F}_t$ represents a set of facts at timestamp t. Facts are expressed as quadruples (s, r, o, t), where subject entity $s \in \mathcal{E}$ and object entityare $o \in \mathcal{E}$ connected at timestamp $t \in \mathcal{T}$ via relation $r \in \mathcal{R}$. The TKG extrapolation task involves predicting given query $(s_q, r_q, ?, t_q)$ or $(?, r_q, o_q, t_q)$ based on a prior historical KG snapshot $\mathcal{G}_{t<t_q} = \{\mathcal{G}_0, \mathcal{G}_1, \mathcal{G}_2, \cdots, \mathcal{G}_{t_q-1}\}$. Consequently, the TKG extrapolation task can be simplified to object entity prediction.

4 Methodology

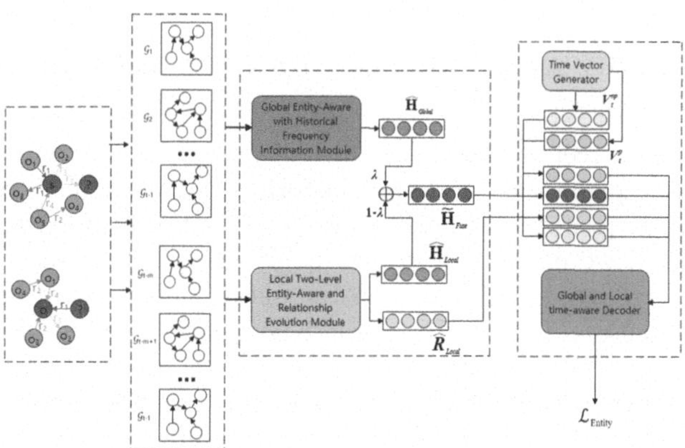

Fig. 3. The overall architecture of FeQua comprises four components: a global entity perception module with historical frequency information, a local two-level entity perception and relationship evolution module, a periodic time information module, and a multi-source information comparison loss module.

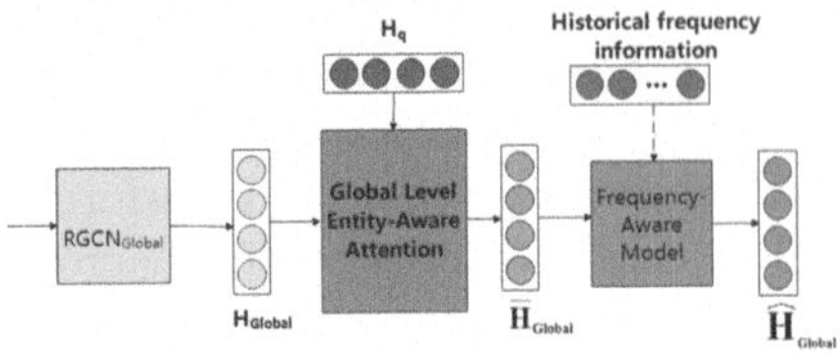

Fig. 4. Schematic diagram of the global entity perception module with historical frequency information.

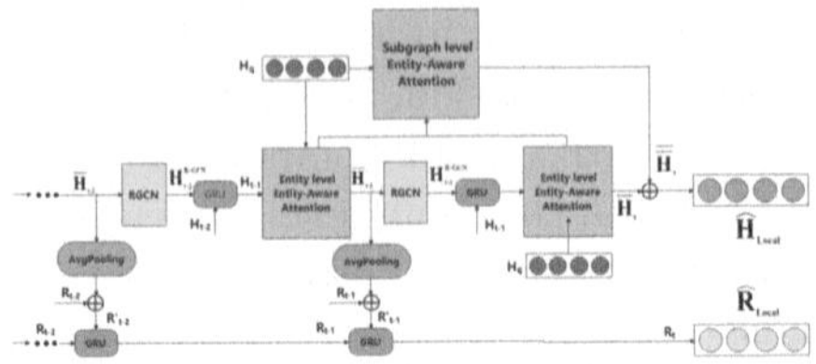

Fig. 5. Schematic diagram of the local two-level entity perception and relationship evolution module.

4.1 Architectural Overview

As shown in the Fig. 3, there are three parts to the model framework.: a global entity-aware with historical frequency information module, a local two-level entity-aware and relationship evolution module, a periodic time information module. The global entity perception module, utilizing historical frequency data, considers relevant historical information from the global that is relevant to the query. The Local two-level entity-aware and relationship evolution module utilizes a two-level entity-aware attention method at both the entity and subgraph levels to extract essential query-related information for prediction. The periodic time information module adeptly capture event periodicity utilizing periodic and aperiodic time vectors. Figure 4 and Fig. 5 respectively show the specific composition of FeQua's two core modules: the global entity-aware with historical frequency information module and the local two-level entity-aware and relationship evolution module.

4.2 Global Entity-Aware Module with Historical Frequency Information

The global entity perception module, which integrates historical frequency data, seeks to identify previously neglected historical facts within local knowledge graph snapshot sequences. For each query $(s_q, r_q, ?, t_q)$, inspired by the LogCL [10] methodology, we create a historical query subgraph by picking historical facts that are strongly associated with the query, thus capture more nuanced semantic information. In the Temporal Knowledge Graph (TKG) $\mathcal{G}_{t<t_q} = \{\mathcal{G}_0, \mathcal{G}_1, \mathcal{G}_2, \cdots, \mathcal{G}_{t_q-1}\}$, We utilize an RGCN with multi-relational modeling capabilities to encode and aggregate the structural and semantic properties of the historical subgraph, thus updating the global representations of entities pertinent to the query. We use statically initialized entity and relationship embeddings as the input features for RGCN because the global history graph lacks temporal information.

$$\mathbf{h}_{\mathbf{g}}^{\ell+1} = \mathbf{RGCN}_{\mathbf{Global}}\left(\mathbf{h}_{\mathbf{g,s}}^{\ell}, \mathbf{r}^{\ell}, \mathbf{h}_{\mathbf{g,o}}^{\ell}\right) \tag{1}$$

where $\mathbf{h}_{\mathbf{g}}^{\ell}$ denotes the output embedding of the entity at layer ℓ in the R-GCN.To keep things simple, the RGCN's final layer output is shown as $\bar{\mathbf{H}}_{\mathbf{g}}$. Besides, We use a global entity-aware attention method for global historical knowledge in order to learn pertinent historical facts.

$$\alpha = \sigma_1 \left(\mathbf{W}_1 \left(\bar{\mathbf{h}}_{\mathbf{g}} + \mathbf{h} \right) \right), \tag{2}$$

$$\hat{\mathbf{h}}_{\mathbf{g}}^{\mathbf{s_q}} = \alpha \bar{\mathbf{h}}_{\mathbf{g}}, \tag{3}$$

where α denotes the global historical information-aware attention score, $\mathbf{W}_1$ represents the learnable weight matrix, σ_1 is the softmax activation function, and $\hat{\mathbf{h}}_{\mathbf{g}}^{\mathbf{s_q}}$denotes the global representation of the entity encoded by the global entity-aware attention encoder via.

In contrast to CyGNet [7], which exclusively use one-hop target object entities pertinent to the query to enhance the learning of historical fact frequencies, we comprehensively exploit the frequency data of historical fact occurrences. By integrating frequency data into the entity representations produced by the global entity-aware attention encoder, the model can thoroughly capture event frequencies.

$$\hat{\mathbf{h}}_{\mathbf{g}}^{\mathbf{s_q}} = \mathbf{W}_2 \left(\mathbf{h}_{\mathbf{g}}^{\mathbf{Agg}} \| f_{score} \right) \tag{4}$$

where f_{score} represents the frequency score obtained by normalizing the number of historical occurrences of an event, $\mathbf{W}_2$ represents the learnable weight matrix, and $\hat{\mathbf{h}}_{\mathbf{g}}^{\mathbf{s_q}}$ signifies the final global entity representation generated by the global entity-aware module incorporating historical frequency information.

4.3 Local Two-Level Entity-Aware and Relational Evolution Module

To forecast temporal knowledge graph inquiries $q = \left(s_{t_q}, r_{t_q}, ?, t_q \right)$, it is essential to model the pertinent historical data within the knowledge graph snapshot $\mathcal{G}_{Local} = \left\{ \mathcal{G}_{t_q - m}, \mathcal{G}_{t_q - m + 1}, \cdots, \mathcal{G}_{t_q - 1} \right\}$ encompassing the latest m timestamps. We propose a local two-level entity-aware and relationship evolution module. This module architecture capture the evolutionary patterns of entities and relationships from temporal and spatial perspectives, respectively. The two-level entity-aware module subsequently selects historical data within KG snapshots pertinent to the query, depending on the representation of entity evolution. Concretely, the KG Snapshot Spatial Aggregation submodule acquires the spatial semantic framework of simultaneous facts. The KG Snapshot Time-Series Evolution submodule model temporal connections among entities and relations. The local two-level entity-aware submodule ultimately model the influence of query-relevant historical data on query prediction. The precise implementation approaches for the three submodules are as follows:

(1) KG Snapshot Spatial Aggregation Module: We utilize RGCN [5] to encode the spatial semantic structure of concurrent facts for each KG snapshot at a given timestamp. The RGCN aggregator for entity aggregation is defined as follows:

$$\mathbf{h}_{0,t}^{\ell+1} = RGCN_{Local}\left(\mathbf{h}_{s,t}^{\ell}, \mathbf{r}^{\ell}, \mathbf{h}_{o,t}^{\ell}\right) = \sigma_2\left(\frac{1}{c_o}\sum_{(s,r)\exists(s,r,o)\in F_t} \mathbf{W}_3^{\ell}\left(\mathbf{h}_{s,t}^{\ell} + \mathbf{r}^{\ell}\right) + \mathbf{W}_4^{\ell}\mathbf{h}_{o,t}^{\ell}\right) \quad (5)$$

where $\mathbf{h}_{s,t}^{\ell} \in \mathbb{R}^{|\varepsilon|\times \mathbf{d}}$ and $\mathbf{r}_t^{\ell} \in \mathbb{R}^{|\mathbf{R}|\times \mathbf{d}}$ denote the entity and relation embeddings, respectively, from the ℓth layer of RGCN within each KG snapshot at timestamp t. For simplicity, the final layer output from two RGCN layers is represented as $\bar{\mathbf{H}}_t$. C_o is a normalisation constant equal to the in-degree of object entities. $\mathbf{W}_3^{\ell}$ and $\mathbf{W}_4^{\ell}$ are parameters for aggregating object entity neighbourhood features and self-loops within the ℓth layer, respectively. $\sigma_2(\cdot)$ denotes the ReLU activation function.

(2) KG Snapshot Time Series Evolution Module: Following the acquisition of structural semantic embeddings for entities in each KG snapshot, next, we model sequence dependency of relations and entities across the latest m timestamps in the KG snapshot series. We incrementally refine entity and relation representations with GRU, the entity-oriented GRU can be articulated as follows:

$$\mathbf{H}_{t+1} = \mathbf{GRU}_{\mathbf{Ent}}\left(\mathbf{H}_t, \bar{\mathbf{H}}_t\right) \quad (6)$$

where $\bar{\mathbf{H}}_t$ denotes the entity embedding matrix after RGCN aggregation at time step t, and $\mathbf{H}_{t+1}$ represents the final entity representation updated via GRU. For relations, we follow the RE-GCN [6] model, considering both the entity and corresponding relation embeddings associated with r to obtain the relation embedding $\bar{\mathbf{R}}_t$ at time step t. Simultaneously, the relation embedding $\bar{\mathbf{R}}_t$ is updated at t via GRU. The relation-oriented GRU can be expressed as:

$$\bar{\mathbf{r}}_t = f_{ave}\left(\mathbf{H}_{r,t}\right) + \mathbf{r} \quad (7)$$

$$\mathbf{R}_{t+1} = \mathbf{GRU}_{\mathbf{Rel}}\left(\mathbf{R}_t, \bar{\mathbf{R}}_t\right) \quad (8)$$

where f_{ave} denotes the mean pooling operation, $\mathbf{H}_{r,t}$ represents the concatenated entity embeddings for relation r at timestamp t, $\bar{\mathbf{R}}_t$ is composed of all $\bar{\mathbf{r}}_t$ at time t, and $\mathbf{R}_{t+1}$ denotes the final relation representation after GRU updates.

(3) Local Two-Level Entity-Aware Module: The representations acquired for the most recent m timestamps of entities and relations through the aforementioned operations are $\left\{\mathbf{H}_{t_q-m+1}, \mathbf{H}_{t_q-m+2}, \cdots, \mathbf{H}_{t_q}\right\}$ and $\left\{\mathbf{R}_{t_q-m+1}, \cdots, \mathbf{R}_{t_q}\right\}$, respectively. We propose a local two-level entity-aware module that differentiates the significance of entities within each KG snapshot and across several KG snapshots for the query, utilizing attention methods concentrated on entities at distinct tiers. The procedural steps are as follows:

$$\mathbf{H}_{t_q}^{s_q} = \mathbf{W}_5\left[\mathbf{h}_{t_q} || f_{ave}\left(\mathbf{r}_{t_q}\right)\right] \quad (9)$$

$$\beta_i = \sigma_3\left(\mathbf{W}_6\left(\bar{\mathbf{h}}_{t_q-m+i} + \mathbf{h}_{t_q}^{s_q}\right)\right) \quad i \in [1, m-1] \quad (10)$$

$$\bar{\bar{\mathbf{H}}}_{t_q-m+i} = \beta_i \bar{\mathbf{H}}_{t_q-m+i} \quad i \in [1, m-1] \quad (11)$$

where, β_i denotes the entity-level attention weights for each entity within a KG snapshot relative to the query. σ_3 is the softmax activation function, while $\bar{\bar{\mathbf{H}}}_{\mathbf{t_q-m+i}}$ constitutes the query-aware entity matrix for the $m-i$th KG snapshot preceding the current query. For each query-aware matrix under a snapshot, we further perform subgraph-level query awareness to assign distinct weights to subgraphs across different temporal snapshots. These subgraphs are then fused to yield the final query-entity matrix.

$$\eta_i = \sigma_3\left(\mathbf{W}_7\left(\bar{\bar{\mathbf{H}}}_{\mathbf{t_q-m+i}} \cdot \mathbf{h}_{\mathbf{t_q}}^{\mathbf{s_q}}\right)\right) \quad i \in [1, m-1] \tag{12}$$

$$\hat{\mathbf{H}}_{\mathbf{t_q}} = \eta_i \bar{\bar{\mathbf{H}}}_{\mathbf{t_q-m+i}} + \bar{\bar{\mathbf{H}}}_{\mathbf{t_q-1}} \; i \in [1, m-1] \tag{13}$$

where, $\cdot$ denotes the dot product operation, η_i represents the subgraph-level attention weights for each snapshot relative to the query, and $\hat{\mathbf{H}}_{\mathbf{t_q}}$ is the final local entity representation generated at timestamp through the local two-level entity perception and relationship evolution module.

4.4 Periodic Time Information Module

Inspired by the TiRGN [8] methodology. We utilize a Periodic Time Information Module to evaluate data, thus comprehensively including both periodic and non-periodic temporal events. This module composed of two submodules: the Time Vector Generation Module and the Time Information Decoding Module.

(1) Time Vector Generation Module: Some events display cyclical repetition, like annual national celebrations or regularly scheduled international summits. The precise formulas are as follows:

$$\mathbf{v}_{\mathbf{t}}^{\mathbf{p}} = \sin\left(\omega_p \Delta t + b_p\right) \tag{14}$$

$$\mathbf{v}_{\mathbf{t}}^{\mathbf{np}} = MLP\left(\Delta t\right) \tag{15}$$

where ω_p and b_p are learnable parameter vectors, $\mathbf{v}_{\mathbf{t}}^{\mathbf{p}}$ and $\mathbf{v}_{\mathbf{t}}^{\mathbf{np}}$ represent the generated periodic and non-periodic temporal vectors respectively.

(2) Time Information Decoding Module: Following the acquisition of time vectors that are periodic and non-periodic, we utilize the Time-ConvTransE [8] for decoding purposes. To more effectively capture both event information of periodic and non-periodic, we modify the placement of time vectors within the decoder.

$$\phi\left(\mathbf{s_q}, \mathbf{r_q}, \mathbf{o}, \mathbf{t_q}\right) = \mathbf{TimeConvTransE}\left(\mathbf{v}_{\mathbf{t}}^{\mathbf{p}}, \tilde{\mathbf{h}}_{\mathbf{t_q}}^{\mathbf{s_q}}, \tilde{\mathbf{r}}_{\mathbf{t_q}}^{\mathbf{s_q}}, \mathbf{v}_{\mathbf{t}}^{\mathbf{np}}\right) \tag{16}$$

$$\tilde{\mathbf{h}}_{\mathbf{t_q}}^{\mathbf{s_q}} = \lambda \hat{\mathbf{h}}_{\mathbf{t_q}}^{\mathbf{s_q}} + (1-\lambda)\,\hat{\mathbf{h}}_{\mathbf{g}}^{\mathbf{s_q}} \tag{17}$$

$$\tilde{\mathbf{r}}_{\mathbf{t_q}}^{\mathbf{s_q}} = \lambda \hat{\mathbf{r}}_{\mathbf{t_q}}^{\mathbf{s_q}} + (1-\lambda)\,\mathbf{r} \tag{18}$$

where λ indicates hyperparameters pertinent to the amalgamation of local and global entity and relation representations, $\tilde{\mathbf{h}}_{\mathbf{t_q}}^{\mathbf{s_q}}$ and $\tilde{\mathbf{r}}_{\mathbf{t_q}}^{\mathbf{s_q}}$ represent the integrated entity and relation feature representations, respectively.

4.5 Scoring Function and Training Objective

The output of the temporal decoding module is processed through a softmax activation function to compute the final scores for candidate entities:

$$\rho^{score} = softmax\left(\phi\left(\mathbf{s_q}, \mathbf{r_{q,}}, \mathbf{o}, \mathbf{t_q}\right)\right) \tag{19}$$

This paper treats the entity prediction task as a multi-label learning problem. Consequently, the entity prediction loss is formalised as:

$$\mathcal{L}_{\mathbf{entity}} = \sum_{t=0}^{T} \sum_{(s,r,o,t)\in F_t} \sum_{o\in\mathcal{E}} \mathbf{y_t^o} log\phi\left(\mathbf{s_q}, \mathbf{r_{q,}}, \mathbf{o}, \mathbf{t_q}\right) \tag{20}$$

where $\phi\left(s_q, r_{q,}, o, t_q\right)$ represents the entity prediction probability score. $y_t^o \in \mathbb{R}^{|\mathcal{E}|}$ denotes the training label, which is 1 if the fact is true and 0 otherwise.

5 Experiments

5.1 Experimental Setup

Table 1. TKG Dataset Details

	ICEWS14	ICEWS18	ICEWS05-15	GDELT
Entities	6,869	10,094	23,033	7,691
Relations	230	256	251	240
Training	74,845	373,018	368,868	1,734,399
Validation	8,514	45,995	46,302	238,765
Test	7,371	49,545	46,159	305,241

Datasets. To evaluate the FeQua model's performance in an entity prediction task, we performed comprehensive experiments on four established datasets commonly utilized for temporal knowledge graph reasoning: ICEWS14 [16], ICEWS18 [17], ICEWS05-15 [16], and GDELT [18]. Dataset was divided into an 80% training set, a 10% validation set, and a 10% test set. Comprehensive statistical data for each dataset is provided in Table 1.

Evaluation Metrics. We utilize two commonly accepted assessment measures to evaluate model performance on temporal knowledge graph reasoning(TKGR) tasks: Mean Reciprocal Rank(MRR) and Hits@k. MRR quantifies the average reciprocal rank of genuine entities across all searches, whereas Hits@k indicates the ratio of authentic entities present among the top k anticipated outcomes. Experimental findings are presented utilizing the temporally aware filtering framework commonly utilized in recent pertinent literature, which exclusively filters quadruples that occur at the moment of the query.

Baselines. To illustrate the effectiveness of the FeQua model for TKG reasoning, we evaluated it against 13 up-to-date KG reasoning methodologies, including both SKG and TKG strategies, as well as interpolation and extrapolation techniques. Interpolation methods included TTransE [11], TA-DistMult [13]. Extrapolation methods comprise RE-NET [4], CyGNet [7], RE-GCN [6], CEN [19], TiRGN [8], HiSMatch [9], RETIA [20], CENET [21], LogCL [10], CRAFT [22], and FL-Evo [23]. CRAFT and FL-Evo stem from their own source papers, whilst the other methods are derived from LogCL.

5.2 Link Prediction

Table 2. Performance of all models on entity prediction tasks across four datasets

Model	ICEWS14				ICEWS18				ICEWS05-15				GDELT			
	MRR	H@1	H@3	H@10	MRR	H@1	H@3	H@10	MRR	H@1	H@3	H@10	MRR	H@1	H@3	H@10
TTransE (2016)	13.72	2.98	17.70	35.74	8.31	1.92	8.56	21.89	15.57	4.80	19.24	38.29	5.50	0.47	4.94	15.25
TA-DistMult (2018)	25.80	16.94	29.74	42.99	16.75	8.61	18.41	33.59	24.31	14.58	27.92	44.21	12.00	5.76	12.94	23.54
RE-NET (2020)	36.93	26.83	39.51	54.78	28.81	19.05	32.44	47.51	43.32	33.43	47.77	63.06	19.62	12.42	21.00	34.01
CyGNet (2020)	35.05	25.73	39.01	53.55	24.93	15.90	28.28	42.61	36.81	26.61	41.63	56.22	18.48	11.52	19.57	31.98
RE-GCN (2021)	40.39	30.66	44.96	59.21	30.58	21.01	34.34	48.75	48.03	37.33	53.85	68.27	19.64	12.42	20.90	33.69
CEN (2022)	42.20	32.08	47.46	61.31	31.50	21.70	35.44	50.59	46.84	36.38	52.45	67.01	20.39	12.96	21.77	34.97
TiRGN (2022)	44.04	33.83	48.95	63.84	33.66	23.19	37.99	54.22	50.04	39.25	56.13	70.71	21.67	13.63	23.27	37.60
HiSMatch (2022)	46.42	35.91	51.63	66.84	33.99	23.91	37.90	53.94	52.85	42.01	59.05	73.28	22.01	14.45	23.80	36.61
RETIA (2023)	42.76	32.28	47.77	62.75	32.43	22.23	36.48	52.94	47.26	36.64	52.90	67.76	20.12	12.76	21.45	34.49
CENET (2023)	39.02	29.62	43.23	57.49	27.85	18.15	31.63	46.98	41.95	32.17	46.93	60.43	20.23	12.69	21.70	34.92
LogCL (2024)	48.87	37.76	54.71	70.26	35.67	24.53	40.32	57.74	57.04	46.07	63.72	77.87	23.75	14.64	25.60	42.33
CRAFT (2024)	45.71	35.05	51.83	61.95	34.21	23.96	38.53	54.11	50.14	39.56	56.18	70.09	23.78	15.38	26.23	40.15
FL-Evo (2025)	48.09	35.63	55.00	71.90	35.43	24.47	39.62	57.10	52.48	40.05	58.85	76.70	24.01	16.04	25.26	39.58
FeQua	**50.86**	**40.06**	**56.68**	**72.00**	**37.93**	**26.96**	**42.70**	**59.54**	**60.00**	**49.90**	**66.43**	**79.22**	**26.88**	**17.53**	**29.22**	**45.97**
Relative Boost (%)	**4.07**	**6.09**	**3.05**	**0.14**	**6.34**	**9.90**	**5.90**	**3.12**	**5.19**	**8.31**	**4.25**	**1.73**	**11.95**	**9.29**	**15.47**	**8.60**

Table 2 present the comprehensive experimental findings for the FeQua model and the four baseline datasets. The optimal outcomes are indicated in bold, but the suboptimal results are underscored. According to the experimental findings, we note the following:

(1) The FeQua model consistently surpasses state-of-the-art techniques across all four benchmark datasets. Specifically, in comparison to the suboptimal outcome, the FeQua model demonstrates substantial enhancements in MRR across the ICEWS14, ICEWS18, ICEWS05-15, and GDELT datasets, with relative increases of 4.07%, 6.34%, 5.19%, and 11.95%, respectively.

(2) The cutting-edge model LogCL, despite accounting for query-relevant global and local historical data, inadequately captures pertinent historical factual information. Concurrently, it neglects the frequency of global historical data and fails to account for the periodicity of both global and local historical events, leading to inferior performance compared to the FeQua

model. FL-Evo improves predictive performance by identifying patterns of fact evolution and logic evolution via its respective modules. Nonetheless, it overlooks significant query-aware history data, disregarding the frequency and periodicity of historical event attributes that could enhance model predictions. CRAFT addresses the modeling of repeated historical facts but neglects the role of their occurrence frequency, resulting in lower performance compared to our model.

(3) Experimental findings demonstrate that extrapolation models surpass interpolation in performance across all datasets. Interpolation models can fill in historical gaps, they are deficient in forecasting future unknowns and modeling temporal evolution patterns. Conversely, extrapolation models exhibit enhanced performance by explicitly modeling temporal dynamics.

5.3 Ablation Study

Table 3. Ablation study results on ICEWS14 and ICEWS18 datasets.

Model	ICEWS14				ICEWS18			
	MRR	H@1	H@3	H@10	MRR	H@1	H@3	H@10
FeQua	50.86	39.98	56.68	72.00	37.69	26.60	42.49	59.38
FeQua-w/o-Local	48.23	37.32	53.91	69.62	34.83	23.60	39.38	57.22
FeQua-w/o-Global	49.38	38.03	55.39	70.89	36.78	25.55	41.50	59.05
FeQua-w/o-dlea	41.84	31.60	46.91	61.67	31.32	21.44	35.20	50.75
FeQua-w/o-fre	49.53	38.27	55.46	71.52	36.59	25.33	41.32	58.98
FeQua-w-ConvTransE	50.18	39.21	56.12	71.36	37.25	26.18	42.04	58.99

To evaluate the components influencing FeQua's prediction outcomes, we performed an ablation research on the ICEWS14 and ICEWS18 datasets, utilizing assessment measures including MRR and Hits@1/3/10. The various outcomes of FeQua are displayed in Table 3. In particular: (1) FeQua represents the comprehensive model performance; (2) FeQua-w/o-Local indicates predictions derived solely from entity representations produced by the global entity-aware encoder utilizing historical frequency data; (3) FeQua-w/o-Global signifies predictions based exclusively on entity and relation representations generated by the local two-level entity-aware encoder incorporating relation evolution; (4) FeQua-w/o-tlea refers to encoding local entity representations without the application of local two-level entity-aware processing; (5) FeQua-w/o-fre denote the encoding of global historical information entity representations without the use of historical frequency; (6) FeQua-w-ConvTransE indicates the decoding of entity and relation representations via ConvTransE instead of Time-ConvTransE.

The findings of the ablation experiment for the previously described modules are analyzed as follows: FeQua attained peak performance by integrating the advantages of all components. FeQua-w/o-Local and FeQua-w/o-Global both demonstrate a significant reduction in performance relative to the comprehensive model. This illustrates that the lack of both the local two-level entity perception and relation evolution encoder, as well as the global entity perception encoder with historical frequency data, substantially influences the model's capacity to learn feature representations for entities and relations, consequently affecting its predictive efficacy. The ablation trials of FeQua-w/o-dlea across both datasets indicate that the dlea module in the local historical information modeling component substantially improves model performance. This affirms that recent local history has substantial information detailing query-relevant behavioral patterns aligned with the sequential progression of historical events. Furthermore, for FeQua-w/o-fre, while global entity historical frequency information modeling inside global historical information modeling did not exhibit the same effectiveness as local two-level entity perception modeling, it nevertheless aided in improving model performance. The observed reduction in model performance for FeQua-w-ConvTransE, in comparison to the entire model, suggests that the periodic temporal information decoder module play a role in enhancing model performance.

Table 4. Analysis of the top three prediction results on the ICEWS14 dataset.

Query and Answer	**FeQua**	**LogCL**	**TiRGN**
Query 1: (Iran, Host a visit, ?, 2014-12-2)			
	Mohammad_Javad_Zarif (0.7619)	Majid_Takht_Ravanchi (0.4556)	Abdullah (Afghanistan) (0.1350)
Answer: Mohammad_Javad_Zarif	Aladdin_Boroujerdi (0.0736)	Mohammad_Javad_Zarif (0.1853)	Abdullah (Turkey) (0.0705)
	Majid_Takht_Ravanchi (0.0471)	Aladdin_Boroujerdi (0.1848)	Gurbanguly_Berdimuhamedow (0.0560)
Query 2: (China, Consult, ?, 2014-12-5)			
	Japan (0.5729)	Japan (0.3558)	Japan (0.1174)
Answer: Japan	South_Korea (0.2264)	South_Korea (0.1478)	South_Korea (0.1034)
	Barack_Obama (0.0551)	Mulatu_Teshome (0.1410)	South_Africa (0.1027)

5.4 Case Study

This paper verifies the effectiveness of our model in complex temporal reasoning tasks through two cases (refer to Table 4) and compares it with the LogCL and TiRGN models. For the inquiry (Iran, Host_a_visit, ?, 2014-12-2), the answer is Mohammad_Javad_Zarif. Our model accurately identified Mohammad_Javad_Zarif with the greatest confidence score, while LogCL placed him second, and TiRGN did not get a valid prediction inside the top three. The answer to the inquiry (China, Consult, ?, 2014-12-5) is Japan. Our model accurately identified the entity Japan with the utmost confidence score. While LogCL and TiRGN accurately predicted this entity, their confidence scores were markedly inferior to ours. The exceptional predictive outcomes arise chiefly from our model's three fundamental components, which not only rectify the shortcomings of LogCL and TiRGN models but also more adeptly encapsulate historically significant events pertinent to the query, as well as the intrinsic sequentiality, periodicity, and frequency of historical events. Experimental findings indicate that this method effectively addresses extrapolation reasoning difficulties in intricate temporal contexts.

6 Conclusion

This research presents FeQua, an innovative TKGR model designed for extrapolation challenges. The FeQua framework comprises three modules: a global entity perception module that includes historical frequency data, a local two-level entity perception and relationship evolution module and a periodic temporal information module. This architecture simulates intricate feature interactions and fluctuating frequency perception. Experimental findings indicate that the proposed model attains superior performance on four benchmark datasets. This confirms its efficacy in documenting historically significant events pertinent to inquiries, together with the intrinsic sequentiality, periodicity, and frequency characteristic of historical occurrences. Future endeavors will concentrate on enhancing the efficiency of obtaining historically relevant information pertinent to queries, expanding current query entity-aware to include query relationship-aware and achieve multi-dimensional awareness.

Acknowledgements. This work was supported by the Natural Science Foundation of Fujian, China (No. 2021J01619).

References

1. Guo, Q., Zhuang, F., Qin, C., et al.: A survey on knowledge graph-based recommender systems. IEEE Trans. Knowl. Data Eng. **34**(8), 3549–3568 (2020)
2. Tao, S., Cao, Q., Shen, H., Huang, J., Wu, Y., Cheng, X.: Single node injection attack against graph neural networks. In: Proceedings of the 30th ACM International Conference on Information & Knowledge Management, CIKM '21, pp. 1794–1803. ACM (2021)
3. Yang, C., Qi, G.: An urban traffic knowledge graph-driven spatial-temporal graph convolutional network for traffic flow prediction. In: Proceedings of the 11th International Joint Conference on Knowledge Graphs, pp. 110–114 (2022)
4. Jin, W., Qu, M., Jin, X., et al.: Recurrent event network: Autoregressive structure inference over temporal knowledge graphs. arXiv preprint arXiv:1904.05530 (2019)
5. Schlichtkrull, M., Kipf, T.N., Bloem, P., van den Berg, R., Titov, I., Welling, M.: Modeling Relational Data with Graph Convolutional Networks. In: Gangemi, A., Navigli, R., Vidal, M.-E., Hitzler, P., Troncy, R., Hollink, L., Tordai, A., Alam, M. (eds.) ESWC 2018. LNCS, vol. 10843, pp. 593–607. Springer, Cham (2018). https://doi.org/10.1007/978-3-319-93417-4_38
6. Li, Z., Jin, X., Li, W., et al.: Temporal knowledge graph reasoning based on evolutional representation learning. In: Proceedings of the 44th International ACM SIGIR Conference on Research and Development in Information Retrieval, pp. 408–417 (2021)

7. Zhu, C., Chen, M., Fan, C., et al.: Learning from history: Modeling temporal knowledge graphs with sequential copy-generation networks. In: Proceedings of the AAAI Conference on Artificial Intelligence, Vol. 35, pp. 4732–4740 (2021)
8. Li, Y., Sun, S., Zhao, J.: Tirgn: Time-guided recurrent graph network with local-global historical patterns for temporal knowledge graph reasoning. In: IJCAI, pp. 2152–2158 2022
9. Li, Z., Hou, Z., Guan, S., et al.: Hismatch: historical structure matching based temporal knowledge graph reasoning. arXiv preprint arXiv:2210.09708 (2022)
10. Chen, W., Wan, H., Wu, Y., et al.: Local-global history-aware contrastive learning for temporal knowledge graph reasoning. In: 2024 IEEE 40th International Conference on Data Engineering (ICDE), pp. 733–746. IEEE (2024)
11. Leblay, J., Chekol, M.W.: Deriving validity time in knowledge graph. In: Companion Proceedings of the the Web Conference, vol. 2018, pp. 1771–1776 (2018)
12. Bordes, A., Usunier, N., Garcia-Duran, A., et al.: Translating embeddings for modeling multi-relational data. Adv. Neural Inf. Process. Syst. **26** (2013)
13. García-Durán, A., Dumančić, S., Niepert, M.: Learning sequence encoders for temporal knowledge graph completion. arXiv preprint arXiv:1809.03202 (2018)
14. Yang, B., Yih, W., He, X., Gao, J., Deng, L.: Embedding entities and relations for learning and inference in knowledge bases. In: 3rd International Conference on Learning Representations, ICLR 2015, San Diego, CA, USA (2015)
15. Zhang, M., Xia, Y., Liu, Q., et al.: Learning long-and short-term representations for temporal knowledge graph reasoning. In: Proceedings of the ACM Web Conference, vol. 2023, pp. 2412–2422 (2023)
16. García-Durán, A., Dumančić, S., Niepert,M.: Learning sequence encoders for temporal knowledge graph completion. arXiv preprint arXiv:1809.03202 (2018)
17. Jin, W., Qu, M., Jin, X., et al.: Recurrent event network: Autoregressive structure inference over temporal knowledge graphs. arXiv preprint arXiv:1904.05530 (2019)
18. Leetaru, K., Schrodt, P.A.: Gdelt: Global data on events, location, and tone. 1979–2012. **2**(4), 1–49 (2013)
19. Li, Z., Guan, S., Jin, X., et al.: Complex evolutional pattern learning for temporal knowledge graph reasoning. arXiv preprint arXiv:2203.07782 (2022)
20. Liu, K., Zhao, F., Xu, G., et al.: Retia: relation-entity twin-interact aggregation for temporal knowledge graph extrapolation. In: 2023 IEEE 39th International Conference on Data Engineering (ICDE), pp. 1761–1774. IEEE (2023)
21. Xu, Y., Ou, J., Xu, H., et al.: Temporal knowledge graph reasoning with historical contrastive learning. In: Proceedings of the AAAI Conference on Artificial Intelligence, vol. 37, pp. 4765–4773 (2023)
22. Zhang, S., Wei, W., Huang, R., et al.: Modeling historical relevant and local frequency context for representation-based temporal knowledge graph forecasting. In: Findings of the Association for Computational Linguistics: EMNLP, vol. 2024, pp. 7675–7686 (2024)
23. Liu, R., Wang, X., Xie, S., et al.: Fl-evo: Jointly modeling fact and logic evolution patterns for temporal knowledge graph reasoning. Expert Syst. Appl. **286**, 128081 (2025)

Chorus: Mitigating GPU Fragmentation in LLM Serving by Unifying Prefill–Decode Disaggregation and Aggregation

Fengkai Jiang, Jinquan Zhang(✉), and Xiaoping Li

Guangdong University of Technology, Guangzhou, China
zjq8860@gdut.edu.cn, xpli@gdut.edu.cn

Abstract. Mixed workloads in Large Language Model (LLM) serving present a fundamental challenge. The resource demand ratio between the compute-intensive Prefill and memory-intensive Decode phases fluctuates dynamically. Prefill–Decode (PD) Disaggregation eliminates cross-phase interference but introduces GPU fragmentation because its rigid, whole-GPU partitioning cannot adapt to the dynamic Prefill:Decode resource demand ratio. This paper presents Chorus, a hybrid LLM serving architecture that mitigates this fragmentation. Chorus integrates a primary PD Disaggregation Subsystem with a flexible PD Aggregation Subsystem and employs a two-level adaptation mechanism. This disaggregation-first, aggregation-assisted design reconciles the isolation-elasticity trade-off, combining the benefits of both paradigms. The mechanism operates at two timescales. To address sustained demand shifts, a coarse-grained controller slowly reallocates whole GPUs, adjusting the resource partition to track long-term trends. To address transient imbalances, a fine-grained scheduler performs per-request routing. It uses a lightweight request classifier and real-time congestion signals to selectively offload requests, shaping the workload to match the disaggregation subsystem's capacity. Our evaluation shows that Chorus improves goodput by an average of 1.20x over PD Disaggregation and 1.79x over PD Aggregation systems across various cluster sizes, while meeting end-to-end (E2E) latency SLOs.

Keywords: LLM Serving · GPU Fragmentation · Hybrid Scheduling · Disaggregated Inference · Resource Management · GPU Clusters

1 Introduction

Large Language Models (LLMs) have become fundamental to a wide array of applications [1], such as conversational AI [2], code generators [3], document summarization [4], and content generation [5]. The inference process of an LLM request submitted by a user includes a Prefill phase and a Decode phase. The

© The Author(s), under exclusive license to Springer Nature Singapore Pte Ltd. 2027
H. Sun et al. (Eds.): ChineseCSCW 2025, CCIS 2911, pp. 362–376, 2027.
https://doi.org/10.1007/978-981-92-0288-1_26

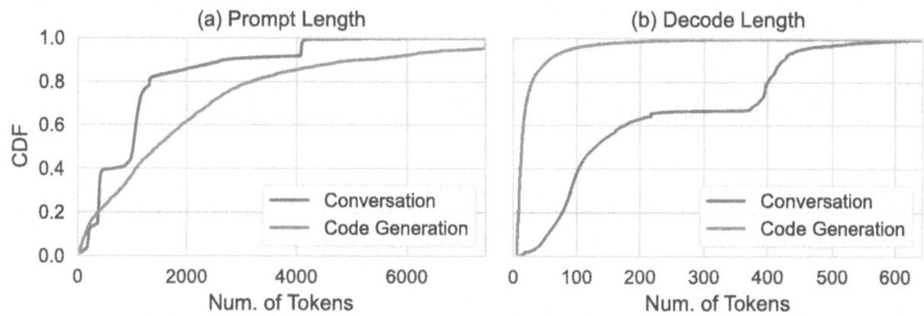

Fig. 1. Heterogeneity of production workloads, shown by the CDF of prompt and decode lengths for two distinct services. Data source: Azure LLM inference trace (via Splitwise [8]).

diversity of LLM applications leads to mixed workloads in GPU clusters, with request prompt and decode lengths (i.e., the number of tokens) varying by orders of magnitude [6,7]. This heterogeneity is evident in production data. As shown in Fig. 1, which plots the cumulative distribution function (CDF) of prompt and decode lengths from an Azure trace, different services like Conversation and Code Generation exhibit starkly different workload patterns. The interaction between the auto-regressive inference process and these varied I/O lengths creates highly diverse demands on GPU compute and memory. Consequently, a uniform resource management strategy is often inefficient for improving cluster utilization across diverse applications [16].

In this paper, we design resource management strategies for mixed LLM inference workloads. The challenges of this problem lie in:

i) **Two-Phase Nature of LLM Inference:** The compute-intensive prefill and memory-intensive decode phases have conflicting resource demands, causing performance interference when co-located on the same GPU.
ii) **Heterogeneous Resource Demands:** Request prompt and generation lengths vary by orders of magnitude, creating highly diverse resource demands across the workload.
iii) **Dynamic and Mixed LLM Inference Workloads:** The time-varying composition of heterogeneous requests causes unpredictable fluctuations in the aggregate demand for prefill and decode capacity.

These challenges expose the limitations of the two prevailing paradigms. **PD Aggregation** co-locates both phases on the same GPU, causing performance interference [8,11]. In contrast, **PD Disaggregation** uses separate GPU pools, which eliminates interference but introduces GPU fragmentation due to its rigid, whole-GPU partitioning. This rigidity creates a persistent mismatch where one pool is congested while the other remains idle [8,19].

To resolve this dilemma, we propose Chorus, a hybrid architecture guided by a "disaggregation-first, aggregation-assisted" design. Chorus uses a primary PD Disaggregation subsystem for performance isolation and a flexible PD Aggregation subsystem to absorb transient demand imbalances. A two-level mechanism adapts to workload dynamics: a fine-grained scheduler routes individual requests to mitigate transient fragmentation, while a coarse-grained controller reallocates whole GPUs to address sustained demand shifts.

Our main contributions are as follows:

i) **A Hybrid LLM Serving Architecture** that integrates PD Disaggregation and Aggregation subsystems to resolve the fundamental isolation-elasticity trade-off.
ii) **A Two-Level Adaptation Mechanism** that mitigates GPU fragmentation by combining fine-grained, per-request routing for transient imbalances with coarse-grained, whole-GPU reallocation for sustained shifts.
iii) **A Demand-Aware Routing Policy** that uses a lightweight classifier and real-time congestion signals to shape the workload, matching instantaneous demand to system capacity.
iv) **An Adaptive Chunked Prefill Controller (ACSC)** that dynamically adjusts prefill chunk size in the aggregation path to manage the throughput-latency trade-off.

2 Background and Motivation

This section reviews the two-phase inference process and analyzes the limitations of prevailing paradigms under dynamic workloads, motivating our hybrid design by quantifying the trade-off between performance interference and GPU fragmentation.

2.1 Two-Phase LLM Inference

Generative LLM inference consists of two phases with conflicting resource demands. The compute-intensive *Prefill phase* processes the input prompt in parallel to generate the first token and the Key-Value (KV) cache. Subsequently, the memory-intensive *Decode phase* auto-regressively generates the remaining tokens, a process often bottlenecked by GPU memory bandwidth due to repeated KV cache access [6,10,11]. Performance is measured by Time to First Token (TTFT) for prefill latency, Time per Output Token (TPOT) for decode speed, and End-to-End (E2E) Latency for the total request duration. The core scheduling challenge lies in managing the contention between these compute-bound prefill and memory-bound decode operations.

2.2 Dynamic Resource Demand in LLM Workloads

Mixed workloads make the Prefill:Decode (P:D) resource demand ratio time-varying along two dimensions.

First, the service mixture varies over time. Different services have distinct resource demands; for example, code generation is often prefill-heavy, while conversation is decode-heavy (Fig. 1). As the service mix changes throughout the day, so does the aggregate demand for prefill and decode capacity (Fig. 2).

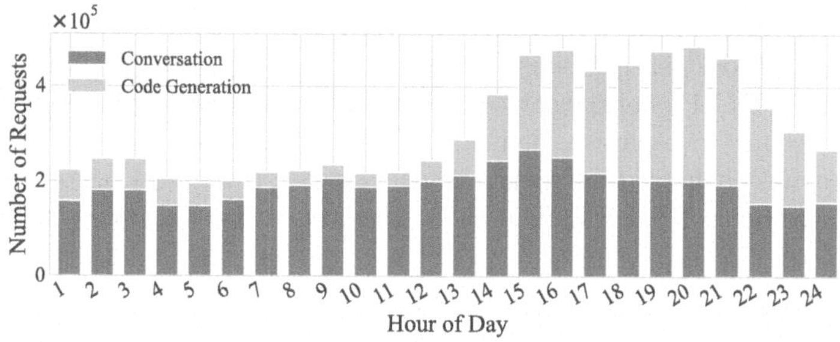

Fig. 2. Workload composition over 24 h, showing a clear diurnal pattern. Data source: Azure LLM inference trace (via DynamoLLM [9]).

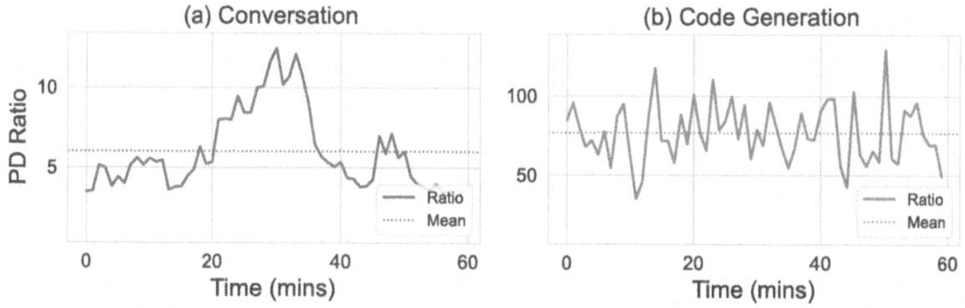

Fig. 3. Rapid fluctuation of the prefill-to-decode token ratio (N_P/N_D) over a 60-minute window. Data source: Azure LLM inference trace (via Splitwise [8]).

Second, requests within one service are heterogeneous. Prompt and decode lengths are heavy-tailed [8,20]. Session context and user behavior cause bursts. This intra-service variability perturbs the P:D ratio at short timescales. Figure 3 shows rapid fluctuations in N_P/N_D within one hour.

We model capacity needs using phase workloads $W_P = N_P/R_P$ and $W_D = N_D/R_D$, where R_P and R_D are the per-GPU processing rates. The ideal capacity ratio is $(N_P/R_P)/(N_D/R_D)$. For a fixed GPU, the hardware term (R_D/R_P) is constant, while the workload term (N_P/N_D) is volatile.

In summary, the P:D demand ratio is highly dynamic under mixed workloads. Any discrete P:D partition at whole-GPU granularity often mismatches instantaneous demand, causing queueing in one phase and idleness in the other in PD Disaggregation [8,11].

2.3 LLM Serving Paradigms

To manage the two-phase nature of inference, current systems primarily adopt one of two serving paradigms: Prefill-Decode (PD) Aggregation and PD Disaggregation.

PD Aggregation, employed by systems like vLLM [6], co-locates the prefill and decode phases on the same GPU. This model provides resource elasticity but introduces cross-phase performance interference, as compute-intensive prefill operations can block latency-sensitive decode steps.

In contrast, **PD Disaggregation**, used in systems like Splitwise [8], executes prefill and decode in separate, dedicated GPU pools. This approach eliminates interference and ensures stable performance. However, its rigid, whole-GPU partitioning introduces GPU fragmentation, a critical issue we discuss next.

2.4 The Dilemma of Prevailing Paradigms

The prevailing paradigms present a dilemma between performance stability and resource elasticity.

Observation 1 (PD Disaggregation: Performance Stability vs. GPU Fragmentation). PD Disaggregation ensures stable performance by eliminating cross-phase interference but suffers from GPU fragmentation. Its rigid partitioning creates a producer-consumer pipeline where a bottleneck in one pool (Prefill or Decode) causes the other to idle. This leads to either *Prefill Resource Fragmentation* (a Decode bottleneck) or *Decode Resource Fragmentation* (a Prefill bottleneck).

Observation 2 (PD Aggregation: Resource Elasticity vs. Cross-Phase Interference). PD Aggregation offers resource elasticity with a single GPU pool, but co-locating phases leads to performance interference. Compute-intensive prefill can create head-of-line blocking for decode steps, increasing latency variance under high load [6,7,10].

These observations reveal a fundamental trade-off. To resolve this dilemma, a hybrid design is needed to combine the isolation of disaggregation with the fine-grained elasticity required to mitigate fragmentation.

3 System Overview

Chorus is a hybrid serving architecture guided by a "disaggregation-first, aggregation-assisted" principle to mitigate GPU fragmentation. As illustrated in Fig. 4, the system consists of a Control Plane and a Data Plane. The Control Plane provides high-level coordination and implements the two-level adaptation mechanism. The Data Plane is responsible for request execution and comprises two specialized subsystems: a primary PD Disaggregation Subsystem and a flexible PD Aggregation Subsystem.

3.1 Control Plane

Chorus employs a centralized Control Plane for cluster-scale coordination. It manages per-request admission and routing, and coarse-grained GPU allocation across the Prefill, Decode, and Aggregation pools. The Control Plane is decoupled from the Data Plane and adds negligible runtime overhead. It consists of four components: the Request Classifier, the Cluster Monitor, the Global Scheduler, and the Inter-Subsystem Resource Allocator (ISRA).

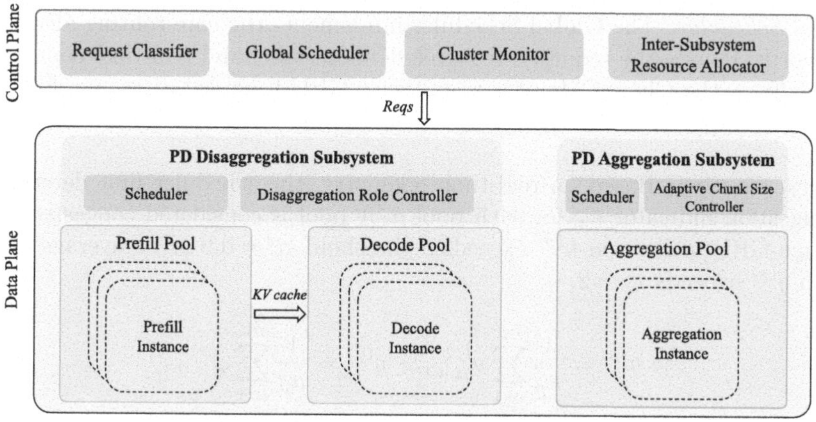

Fig. 4. Chorus system architecture.

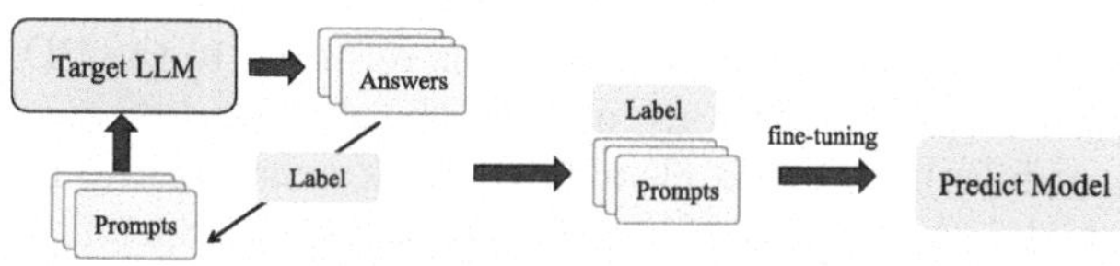

Fig. 5. Fine-tuning workflow for the lightweight decode length predictor.

Request Classifier. The Request Classifier estimates the resource profile of each incoming request. It obtains the exact prefill length, N_P, by tokenizing the prompt and predicts the decode length, $\hat{N}_D$. For the prediction, we use a lightweight RoBERTa-base model (125M parameters), fine-tuned on a dataset created by processing ShareGPT prompts with the target Llama-3-8B model [13]. The fine-tuning workflow is shown in Fig. 5. The model classifies requests into a decode-length bucket of width $B = 128$, achieving 69.4% accuracy with less than 10 ms latency.

Using the predicted bucket's midpoint as $\hat{N}_D$, we compute the resource-demand ratio $\hat{r} = (N_P/R_P)/(\hat{N}_D/R_D)$, where R_P and R_D are pre-measured peak processing rates. Based on a dynamic parameter $\alpha(t)$ from the Global Scheduler, requests are labeled *Prefill-heavy*, *Decode-heavy*, or *Balanced*.

Cluster Monitor. The Cluster Monitor samples instance-level telemetry in the Prefill (P), Decode (D), and Aggregation (A) pools. Let $p \in \{P, D, A\}$ index pools and let $i \in \{1, \ldots, n_p\}$ index instances in pool p. For instance (p, i), we measure SM utilization $u^{(p)}_{\mathrm{sm},i} \in [0, 1]$, memory utilization $u^{(p)}_{\mathrm{mem},i} \in [0, 1]$, GPU utilization $u^{(p)}_{\mathrm{gpu},i} = \max\{u^{(p)}_{\mathrm{sm},i}, u^{(p)}_{\mathrm{mem},i}\}$, and instantaneous queue depth $q^{(p)}_i \in \mathbb{N}_0$.

The monitor transmits $\{u^{(p)}_{\mathrm{gpu},i}, q^{(p)}_i\}$ to the Global Scheduler at a 100 ms interval. This high-frequency reporting provides near real-time state for responsive control. Sampling and reporting do not block the request path and impose negligible overhead.

Global Scheduler. The Global Scheduler implements the core routing algorithm of Chorus. It uses the request's resource-demand label and real-time congestion signals from the Cluster Monitor to mitigate GPU fragmentation by selectively offloading requests to the Aggregation Subsystem.

Request Routing. Based on real-time telemetry, the scheduler first determines a congestion indicator C_p for each pool p. A pool is considered congested if its average GPU utilization $\bar{u}^{(p)}$ exceeds a threshold $\tau_u = 0.9$ or its average queue depth $\bar{q}^{(p)}$ exceeds $\tau_q = 2$.

$$\bar{u}^{(p)} = \frac{1}{n_p}\sum_{i=1}^{n_p} u_{\text{gpu},i}^{(p)}, \quad \bar{q}^{(p)} = \frac{1}{n_p}\sum_{i=1}^{n_p} q_i^{(p)}. \tag{1}$$

$$C_p = (\bar{u}^{(p)} > \tau_u) \vee (\bar{q}^{(p)} > \tau_q). \tag{2}$$

The core routing logic is straightforward. By default, all requests are sent to the PD Disaggregation Subsystem. A request is rerouted to the PD Aggregation Subsystem only if two conditions are met: 1) the Aggregation pool itself is not congested ($C_A = \text{false}$), and 2) a clear bottleneck exists in the Disaggregation Subsystem that the request's profile can help alleviate. Specifically, a *Prefill-heavy* request is offloaded during a Prefill bottleneck ($C_P \wedge \neg C_D$), and a *Decode-heavy* request is offloaded during a Decode bottleneck ($C_D \wedge \neg C_P$). If both or neither of the Disaggregation pools are congested, no requests are offloaded. This logic is an O(1) operation.

Scheduler-managed $\alpha(t)$ Adaptation. The scheduler dynamically adjusts the classification bandwidth $\alpha(t)$ via a feedback loop to regulate offloading intensity. A lower $\alpha(t)$ makes more requests eligible for offloading, while a higher $\alpha(t)$ reduces it. The parameter is updated every 500 ms based on system state:

$$\alpha(t+1) = \begin{cases} \max\{1, \alpha(t) - k\}, & (C_P \oplus C_D) \wedge \neg C_A, \\ \alpha(t) + k, & \text{otherwise.} \end{cases} \tag{3}$$

With a step size $k = 0.15$, this mechanism adapts the offloading rate to congestion without overriding the main routing rules.

Inter-Subsystem Resource Allocator (ISRA). The Inter-Subsystem Resource Allocator (ISRA) manages the coarse-grained, top-level partition of GPUs between the Aggregation and Disaggregation subsystems. Operating at a slow timescale, it reallocates whole GPUs to correct sustained resource imbalances. This expensive operation is invoked infrequently to prevent oscillation. ISRA is distinct from the Disaggregation Role Controller (DRC), which manages the internal partition of the Disaggregation Subsystem.

3.2 Data Plane

The Data Plane executes inference tasks and consists of two complementary subsystems.

PD Disaggregation Subsystem. Chorus uses the PD Disaggregation Subsystem as the primary execution path to eliminate cross-phase interference and stabilize latency. After the prefill phase, the Key-Value (KV) cache is transferred from a prefill to a decode GPU. This design preserves phase isolation and enables independent scaling. The subsystem consists of a Prefill Pool, a Decode Pool, a Scheduler, and a Disaggregation Role Controller (DRC).

Prefill Pool. The Prefill Pool handles the compute-bound prefill phase. To mitigate head-of-line blocking, it uses continuous batching with chunked prefill. As the producer in the system's pipeline, its performance determines the Time to First Token (TTFT). A bottleneck here leads to high TTFT and causes *Decode Resource Fragmentation.* The pool reports its utilization and queue depth to the Cluster Monitor for global routing decisions.

Decode Pool. The Decode Pool handles the memory-bandwidth-bound decode phase, acting as the consumer in the pipeline. It uses continuous batching to maximize throughput. Its performance directly determines the Time per Output Token (TPOT). A bottleneck in this pool creates backpressure, stalling the Prefill Pool and leading to *Prefill Resource Fragmentation.* Like the Prefill Pool, it also reports its real-time telemetry to the Cluster Monitor.

Scheduler. The intra-subsystem Scheduler performs load balancing across instances in both the Prefill and Decode pools. It manages phase-specific batching and orchestrates the KV cache transfer from a Prefill instance to its designated Decode instance.

Disaggregation Role Controller (DRC). The Disaggregation Role Controller (DRC) manages the subsystem's internal resource partition (G_P vs. G_D). It operates at a slow timescale, reallocating whole GPUs to correct sustained imbalances that are not resolved by the Aggregation Subsystem's fine-grained load shaping.

PD Aggregation Subsystem. The PD Aggregation Subsystem serves as a flexible, secondary execution path designed for fine-grained workload shaping. Its primary function is to absorb transient demand imbalances by selectively executing requests offloaded from the main disaggregation path. This targeted offloading mitigates GPU fragmentation in the PD Disaggregation Subsystem, enhancing overall cluster efficiency without sacrificing performance isolation for the majority of requests. The subsystem consists of a single Aggregation Pool, a Scheduler, and an Adaptive Chunk Size Controller (ACSC).

Aggregation Pool. The Aggregation Pool executes offloaded requests end-to-end using continuous batching. This co-location model preserves data locality and provides high resource elasticity. Cross-phase interference is managed by two mechanisms: the Global Scheduler's congestion-aware routing policy, and the ACSC's adaptive prefill execution. The pool reports its telemetry to the Cluster Monitor to inform these decisions.

Scheduler. The internal Scheduler for this subsystem manages admission control and continuous batching. It works with the ACSC to apply the current pool-wide prefill chunk size at batch-construction time. In steady state, it enters a drain mode, admitting no new requests.

Adaptive Chunk Size Controller (ACSC). The ACSC mitigates head-of-line (HoL) blocking in the Aggregation Pool using adaptive chunked prefill. It sets a uniform chunk size K for the pool based on the dominant type of offloaded workload, dynamically switching its objective between maximizing prefill throughput and protecting decode latency.

Decode Protection Mode. This mode activates when the Disaggregation Subsystem's Decode Pool is congested (C_D = true), causing the Global Scheduler to offload *Decode-heavy* requests. To protect the latency of these requests, the ACSC sets a small chunk size ($K = K_{\text{small}}$). This enforces a strict time budget on prefill computations to minimize interference, as constrained by:

$$K/R_P \leq T_{dec} \implies K \leq T_{dec} \cdot R_P. \tag{4}$$

This policy ensures low TPOT variance for co-located requests at the cost of prefill efficiency.

Prefill Protection Mode. This mode activates when the Prefill Pool is congested (C_P = true), causing the Global Scheduler to offload *Prefill-heavy* requests. The ACSC's objective then shifts to maximizing prefill throughput. It sets a large chunk size ($K = K_{\text{large}}$), relaxing the time budget in Eq. (4) to improve compute efficiency for these offloaded tasks.

When the offloaded workload consists of *Balanced* requests, the controller selects $K = K_{\text{medium}}$ as a trade-off between the two objectives. The specific values for these chunk sizes are detailed in Sect. 4.

4 Implementation

We implement the Chorus prototype by extending vLLM [6] for the PD Aggregation Subsystem and SGLang [15] for the PD Disaggregation Subsystem. The prototype is deployed on a physical testbed with three NVIDIA RTX 3090 GPUs to validate its core mechanics. For larger-scale evaluations (5+ GPUs), we use the Vidur event-driven simulator [14], which is calibrated against the testbed to

Table 1. System Parameters and settings.

Parameter	Value
α_{init}	1.3
k	0.15
Congestion utilization threshold τ_u	0.9
Congestion queue-depth threshold τ_q	2
Telemetry sampling interval (Cluster Monitor)	100 ms
$\alpha(t)$ update interval (Global Scheduler)	500 ms
Prefill chunk sizes $\{K_{\text{small}}, K_{\text{medium}}, K_{\text{large}}\}$	{64, 512, 1024}
Peak steady-state per-GPU prefill rate R_P (tokens/s)	4866
Peak steady-state per-GPU decode rate R_D (tokens/s)	63

ensure high fidelity (performance metrics deviate by less than 5%). All experiments use the Meta-Llama-3-8B-Instruct model [13] and a mixed workload derived from the Conversation and Code Generation traces of the Azure LLM inference dataset [8].

System Parameters. The key system parameters used in our evaluation are listed in Table 1. These values are held fixed unless otherwise noted. The number of GPUs in the Aggregation Pool (G_A) for each cluster size is determined via offline profiling. Per-GPU processing rates (R_P, R_D) are measured using offline microbenchmarks. The Global Scheduler manages $\alpha(t)$ in-process with asynchronous updates every 500 ms, imposing negligible overhead.

5 Evaluation

This section evaluates Chorus, focusing on a performance comparison against baseline systems, an ablation study of its core components, and its sensitivity to prediction granularity. Experiments use our calibrated simulator with a mixed workload from the Azure LLM inference trace [8] and the Meta-Llama-3-8B-Instruct model [13]. Our primary metric is per-GPU goodput, defined as the throughput of requests meeting a strict E2E latency SLO, normalized by cluster size.

5.1 End-to-End Performance Comparison

This section compares the end-to-end performance of Chorus against two representative baselines for PD Aggregation and PD Disaggregation. Our primary metric is goodput, defined as the throughput of requests that meet the end-to-end (E2E) latency SLO. We measure the goodput of each system under varying per-GPU request arrival rates and across multiple cluster sizes.

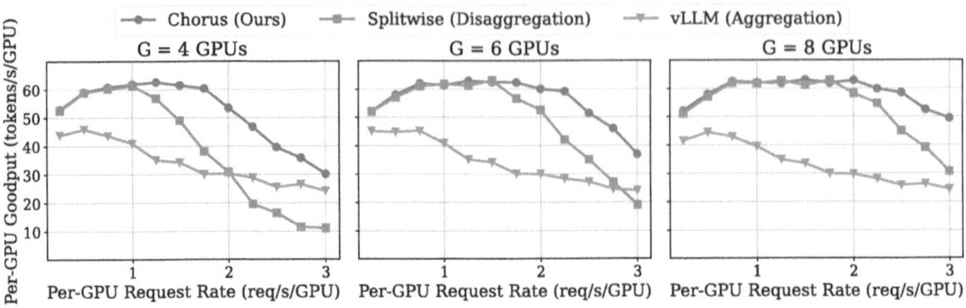

Fig. 6. Goodput on small-scale clusters ($G = 4, 6, 8$). Chorus outperforms baselines, with the largest gains on smaller clusters where GPU fragmentation is most severe.

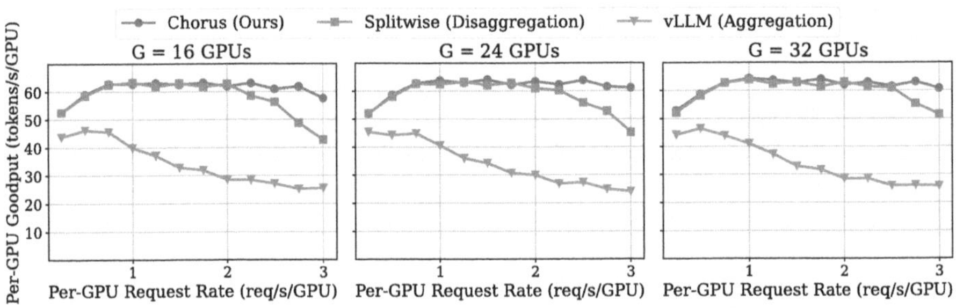

Fig. 7. Goodput on large-scale clusters ($G = 16, 24, 32$). Chorus maintains a performance advantage, though the relative gain narrows as cluster size increases.

Experimental Setup. We compare Chorus against two baselines: vLLM [6] for PD Aggregation and Splitwise [8] for PD Disaggregation. We evaluate all systems on clusters with 4, 6, 8, 16, 24, and 32 GPUs. For each configuration, we sweep the per-GPU request arrival rate up to the point where the system's goodput saturates.

Results and Analysis. Figures 6 and 7 show the results. Chorus consistently achieves the highest goodput across all tested cluster sizes and load levels. On the 8-GPU cluster, it improves goodput by up to 2.3x over vLLM and 1.6x over Splitwise at high load. The advantage is most pronounced on smaller clusters (G = 4, G = 6) due to whole-GPU fragmentation. As the cluster size increases, the relative gain narrows, but Chorus maintains a clear lead.

The PD Aggregation baseline (vLLM) suffers from cross-phase interference at high rates, causing frequent E2E SLO violations. Chorus avoids this by isolating prefill and decode, sustaining the SLO under higher loads.

The PD Disaggregation baseline (Splitwise) is limited by GPU fragmentation: rigid whole-GPU partitioning cannot track transient demand, and role switching adapts slowly and coarsely, leaving resources idle. Chorus uses fine-grained, per-request load shaping to mitigate fragmentation, improving utilization and goodput.

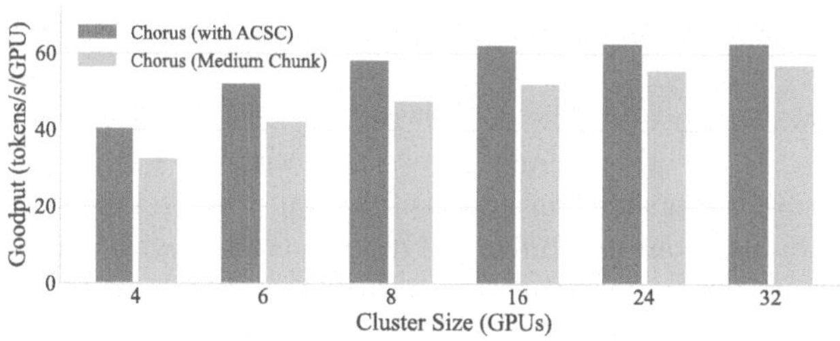

Fig. 8. Impact of the Adaptive Chunk Size Controller (ACSC). ACSC improves goodput over a fixed chunk size, especially on smaller clusters.

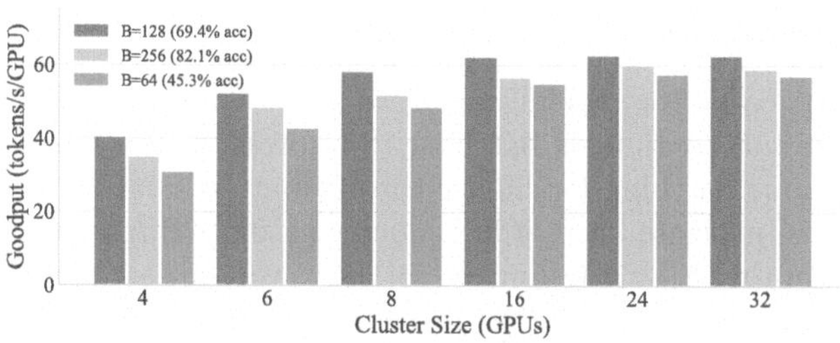

Fig. 9. Impact of prediction granularity. A bucket size of $B = 128$ provides the best goodput, balancing accuracy and precision.

5.2 Ablation Studies

We conduct two ablation studies to isolate and quantify the benefits of the core components of Chorus.

Impact of Adaptive Chunk Size Control (ACSC). This study evaluates the ACSC's effectiveness. We compare the full Chorus system against a variant with a fixed, medium prefill chunk size (K_{medium}) under a high load of 2.5 req/s/GPU.

Figure 8 shows the results. The ACSC-enabled Chorus outperforms the fixed-chunk-size variant, improving goodput by 18.5% on average. The performance gain is most significant in smaller clusters (up to 23.8% for $G = 6$), where a suboptimal, fixed chunk size creates a more severe bottleneck. The results confirm that dynamically adapting the prefill chunk size is superior to a fixed policy.

Impact of Prediction Granularity. This study assesses the sensitivity of Chorus to its decode-length predictor's granularity. The classifier's bucket size B creates a trade-off between prediction precision and accuracy.

We evaluate this trade-off by comparing system goodput under three configurations at a high load of 2.5 req/s/GPU: a fine-grained $B = 64$ (45.3% accuracy), our default $B = 128$ (69.4% accuracy), and a coarse-grained $B = 256$ (82.1% accuracy).

Figure 9 shows the results. The default setting ($B = 128$) achieves the highest goodput, striking an effective balance between prediction accuracy and granularity. The performance degradation is graceful with other settings, validating the core benefit of demand-aware routing. This robustness stems from our closed-loop control design, where real-time congestion signals can correct for misclassifications that do not lead to actual congestion.

6 Related Work

6.1 PD Aggregation

PD Aggregation co-locates Prefill and Decode on the same GPU. vLLM uses PagedAttention and continuous batching to improve utilization [6]. Orca popularizes continuous batching for higher throughput [7], and Sarathi-Serve uses chunked prefill to mitigate head-of-line blocking [10]. SOLA applies state-aware scheduling to improve SLO attainment [23]. However, cross-phase interference is an intrinsic limitation of co-location. Under mixed workloads, compute-bound prefill can delay memory-bound decode, increasing TTFT variance and TPOT at high load. Chorus differs in scope: it uses aggregation only in a small, specialized pool with an Adaptive Chunk Size Controller (ACSC). A demand-aware scheduler offloads selected requests to this pool to absorb transient imbalances, limiting interference while preserving elasticity.

6.2 PD Disaggregation

PD Disaggregation executes Prefill and Decode on different GPU pools, eliminating cross-phase interference and stabilizing TPOT. Splitwise formalizes this phase splitting for improved goodput under E2E SLOs [8]. DistServe decouples resource allocation and scheduling for the two phases [11]. Other systems enhance disaggregation with KV-cache streaming or specialized hardware-centric designs [21]. The main limitation is GPU fragmentation from coarse-grained, whole-GPU partitioning and slow adaptation via role switching, which can cause resource idleness. Chorus is disaggregation-first but addresses fragmentation by shaping incoming demand. It uses a lightweight classifier and selective offloading to an aggregation pool, avoiding role switching, reducing adaptation latency, and preserving phase isolation. System-level cluster design, such as DynamoLLM, is complementary [9].

7 Conclusion

This paper introduced Chorus, a hybrid scheduling architecture that mitigates GPU fragmentation in LLM serving. Chorus resolves the trade-off between the performance isolation of Prefill–Decode (PD) Disaggregation and the resource elasticity of PD Aggregation by integrating a primary disaggregation subsystem with a flexible aggregation subsystem.

Chorus employs a two-level adaptation mechanism. For sustained demand shifts, a coarse-grained controller reallocates GPUs at slow timescales. For transient imbalances, a fine-grained scheduler shapes the workload at a per-request level. It uses a lightweight classifier and congestion signals to selectively offload requests, aligning instantaneous demand with the system's fixed capacity. An Adaptive Chunk Size Controller further optimizes the aggregation path's responsiveness.

Our evaluation, based on a calibrated simulator, shows that Chorus substantially improves cluster-wide goodput while meeting strict latency SLOs. Compared to state-of-the-art baselines, Chorus improves goodput on average by 1.20x over a PD Disaggregation system and 1.79x over a PD Aggregation system. Our findings confirm that Chorus effectively mitigates resource fragmentation, with the most significant gains observed in small- to medium-sized clusters.

In conclusion, Chorus offers a practical and robust solution for building efficient and high-performance LLM serving systems in production environments.

References

1. Zhao, W.X., et al.: A survey of large language models. arXiv:2303.18223 (2023)
2. OpenAI: GPT-4 technical report. arXiv:2303.08774 (2024). https://doi.org/10.48550/ARXIV.2303.08774
3. Anthropic: Claude Code (2025). https://docs.anthropic.com/en/docs/claude-code/overview. Accessed Sep 2025
4. Zhang, H., Yu, P.S., Zhang, J.: A systematic survey of text summarization: from statistical methods to large language models. ACM Comput. Surv. **57**(11), 1–41 (2025)
5. Agossah, A., Krupa, F., Perreira Da Silva, M., Le Callet, P.: LLM-based interaction for content generation: a case study on the perception of employees in an IT department. In: Proceedings of the 2023 ACM International Conference on Interactive Media Experiences, pp. 237–241 (2023)
6. Kwon, W., et al.: Efficient memory management for large language model serving with PagedAttention. In: Proceedings of the 29th Symposium on Operating Systems Principles (SOSP 2023), pp. 611–626 (2023)
7. Yu, G.-I., Jeong, J.S., Kim, G.-W., Kim, S., Chun, B.-G.: Orca: a distributed serving system for Transformer-Based generative models. In: 16th USENIX Symposium on Operating Systems Design and Implementation (OSDI 2022), pp. 521–538 (2022)
8. Patel, P., et al.: Splitwise: efficient generative LLM inference using phase splitting. In: 2024 ACM/IEEE 51st Annual International Symposium on Computer Architecture (ISCA 2024), pp. 118–132. IEEE (2024)
9. Stojkovic, J., Zhang, C., Goiri, Í., Torrellas, J., Choukse, E.: DynamoLLM: designing LLM inference clusters for performance and energy efficiency. In: 2025 IEEE International Symposium on High Performance Computer Architecture (HPCA 2025), Las Vegas, NV, USA, pp. 1348–1362 (2025). https://doi.org/10.1109/HPCA61900.2025.00102

10. Agrawal, A., et al.: Taming throughput-latency tradeoff in LLM inference with sarathi-serve. In: 18th USENIX Symposium on Operating Systems Design and Implementation (OSDI 2024), pp. 117–134 (2024)
11. Zhong, Y., et al.: DistServe: disaggregating prefill and decoding for goodput-optimized large language model serving. In: 18th USENIX Symposium on Operating Systems Design and Implementation (OSDI 2024), pp. 193–210 (2024)
12. ShareGPT. https://sharegpt.com. Accessed Mar 2023
13. Meta AI: The LLaMA 3 herd of models (2024). https://ai.meta.com/research/publications/the-llama-3-herd-of-models/. Accessed Sep 2025
14. Agrawal, A., et al.: Vidur: a large-scale simulation framework for LLM inference. In: Proceedings of Machine Learning and Systems, vol. 6, pp. 351–366 (2024)
15. Zheng, L., et al.: SGLang: efficient execution of structured language model programs. Adv. Neural. Inf. Process. Syst. **37**, 62557–62583 (2024)
16. Wang, C., Zuo, P., Chen, Z., Liang, Y., Yu, Z., Yang, M.-C.: Prefill-Decode Aggregation or Disaggregation? Unifying Both for Goodput-Optimized LLM Serving. arXiv preprint arXiv:2508.01989 (2025)
17. Sun, B., et al.: Llumnix: dynamic scheduling for large language model serving. In: 18th USENIX Symposium on Operating Systems Design and Implementation (OSDI 2024), pp. 173–191 (2024)
18. Shi, X., Cai, C., Du, J., Jia, Z.: Nexus: Proactive Intra-GPU Disaggregation of Prefill and Decode in LLM Serving. arXiv preprint arXiv:2507.06608 (2025)
19. Weng, Q., et al.: Beware of fragmentation: scheduling GPU-sharing workloads with fragmentation gradient descent. In: 2023 USENIX Annual Technical Conference (USENIX ATC 23), pp. 995–1008 (2023)
20. Cheng, K., Hu, W., Wang, Z., Du, P., Li, J., Zhang, S.: Enabling efficient batch serving for LMaaS via generation length prediction. In: 2024 IEEE International Conference on Web Services (ICWS), pp. 853–864 (2024). https://doi.org/10.1109/ICWS62655.2024.00104
21. Strati, F., McAllister, S., Phanishayee, A., Tarnawski, J., Klimovic, A.: DéjàVu: KV-cache streaming for fast, fault-tolerant generative LLM serving. In: Proceedings of the 41st International Conference on Machine Learning (ICML), article 1902. JMLR.org (2024)
22. Chen, S., et al.: KVDirect: distributed Disaggregated LLM Inference. arXiv:2501.14743 (2024)
23. Hong, K., et al.: SOLA: Optimizing SLO attainment for large language model serving with state-aware scheduling. In: Eighth Conference on Machine Learning and Systems (MLSys 2024) (2024)

Deadline- and Reliability-Constrained Workflow Scheduling in GDCs

Jie Qiu, Jinquan Zhang, and Xiaoping Li(✉)

School of Computer Science and Technology, Guangdong University of Technology, Guangzhou 510006, China
2112305244@mail2.gdut.edu.cn

Abstract. In Geo-Distributed Data Centers (GDCs), electricity prices vary across regions and fluctuate over time. The workflows executed in these Data Centers (DCs) involve cross-domain data transmission and intensive computation, resulting in high electricity costs. Cloud Service Providers (CSPs) utilize Dynamic Voltage and Frequency Scaling (DVFS) technology to lower the operating frequencies of processors, thereby reducing energy consumption and electricity costs. However, this approach increases the risk of transient faults in Virtual Machines (VMs) during task execution, thereby compromising workflow execution reliability. Therefore, scheduling workflows with the constraints of deadline and reliability to minimize electricity costs is a great challenge. To address this challenge, we propose a Deadline- and Reliability-Constrained Workflow Scheduling (DRWS) algorithm, which comprises three stages: a deadline partition method based on upward rank to assign deadlines to tasks, a resource allocation method to minimize electricity costs, and a Variable Neighborhood Descent (VND)-based method to adjust the task schedule sequence. The algorithm's components and parameters are statistically calibrated using a set of randomly generated workflow instances. Finally, the proposed algorithm is compared with the state-of-the-art algorithms for similar problems. Experimental results demonstrate the effectiveness of the proposed algorithm for the considered problem.

Keywords: Deadline · Reliability · Workflow scheduling · Electricity cost

1 Introduction

Workflows consist of a large number of tasks with complex dependencies, which typically require access to geo-distributed data during execution. Therefore, GDCs, comprising DCs deployed across different regions, provide strong support for workflow execution. However, executing workflows in GDCs involves cross-domain data transmission and intensive computation, which leads to high power consumption and electricity costs. To reduce costs, CSPs employ DVFS to adjust processor operating frequencies while satisfying workflow deadline constraints. Nevertheless, lowering processor frequencies inappropriately may significantly increase the risk of transient faults in VMs during task execution,

© The Author(s), under exclusive license to Springer Nature Singapore Pte Ltd. 2027
H. Sun et al. (Eds.): ChineseCSCW 2025, CCIS 2911, pp. 377–391, 2027.
https://doi.org/10.1007/978-981-92-0288-1_27

resulting in the decline of workflow reliability and additional costs due to task retries. Consequently, providing a cost-optimal workflow scheduling schema that satisfies both deadline and reliability constraints remains a critical challenge. Furthermore, regional variations and temporal fluctuations in electricity prices introduce additional complexity to workflow scheduling.

The deadline- and reliability-constrained workflow scheduling in GDCs exhibits several notable characteristics: (1) complex workflow structure, where workflows consist of numerous heterogeneous tasks with complicated partial-order dependencies. (2) heterogeneous distributed resources, as GDCs host a wide range of computing resources with varying performance and power characteristics, and electricity prices differ across DCs and fluctuate over time due to geographical locations. (3) DVFS-induced transient fault sensitivity, since decreasing processor operating frequencies by DVFS easily incur transient faults in VMs during task execution.

This paper aims to address a workflow scheduling problem in GDCs, to minimize workflow execution cost while satisfying deadline and reliability constraints. This problem brings the following challenges: (1) workflows contain considerable tasks with sophisticated partial-order dependencies, where computational loads and data transmission volumes among tasks vary significantly, making it difficult to determine task execution sequences that meet the workflow deadline. (2) Electricity prices in GDCs differ across regions and fluctuate over time, while computing resources exhibit heterogeneity in execution speed, reliability, and power consumption, leading to variations in execution efficiency and energy consumption of the same task across different resources. Determining how to match tasks with resources to minimize the total electricity cost is a challenging problem. (3) By leveraging DVFS to lower the frequencies of processors, electricity costs can be reduced, but it simultaneously decreases workflow execution reliability. Thus, how to tune processor frequency to ensure the workflow reliability constraint remains a difficult challenge.

To address this problem, we propose a deadline- and reliability-constrained workflow scheduling algorithm in GDCs. The main contributions of this paper are summarized as follows:

(1) A mathematical model is formulated for the problem, taking into account factors such as deadline, reliability, and regional electricity price fluctuations in GDCs.
(2) A deadline- and reliability-constrained workflow scheduling algorithm is proposed, which comprises three components: deadline partition, resource allocation, and task sequence adjustment.
(3) A comprehensive set of experiments is carried out to investigate the efficiency and effectiveness of the proposed algorithm.

The remainder of this paper is organized as follows. Section 2 reviews the related work. Section 3 formally describes the problem and constructs models. Section 4 presents the proposed algorithm. Section 5 provides a comprehensive performance evaluation of the proposed algorithm. Finally, Sect. 6 concludes the paper and outlines directions for future research.

2 Related Work

2.1 Geo-Distributed Workflow Scheduling

With the advent of the big data era, workflow scheduling in GDCs has increasingly become a research hotspot. In heterogeneous resource scenarios, Topcuoglu et al. [1] proposed two classical algorithms, namely HEFT and CPOP, aimed at minimizing workflow makespan. Abrishami et al. [2] introduced a deadline partition method based on the Partial Critical Path (PCP) to minimize the execution cost of the workflow. However, these methods mainly target single data center (DC) scenarios. In GDCs, Wu et al. [3] considered original data transmission and deadline constraint, and proposed a multi-objective evolutionary algorithm to optimize makespan and leasing cost jointly. Shu et al. [4] presented a two-stage approach that integrates simulated annealing and list scheduling: the tasks of the workflow are first assigned to DCs satisfying privacy constraints, and then scheduled using a list-based heuristic algorithm according to task priorities.

2.2 Energy-Aware Workflow Scheduling

Energy optimization is a significant research field in cloud computing, with existing studies primarily focusing on DVFS, task scheduling, and renewable energy. The adoption of DVFS technology can effectively reduce energy consumption. Xia et al. [5] proposed a genetic algorithm based on a tri-chromosome encoding scheme, which incorporates task execution time encoding and employs DVFS to lower energy consumption. Similarly, Cao et al. [6] utilized DVFS to reduce energy consumption. Kumar et al. [7] integrated DVFS with a P2P load balancing algorithm, adjusting processor frequency to decrease power consumption while distributing computational load via a load balancer to avoid single-point overloads. Task scheduling is another widely used approach for energy optimization. Ding et al. [8] proposed a Q-learning-based task scheduling method to reduce energy consumption by improving CPU resource utilization. Yang et al. [9] introduced a reinforcement learning-based task scheduling algorithm that combines DVFS technology for energy efficiency. Duan et al. [10] applied a hybrid heuristic approach to enhance resource utilization and reduce energy consumption. Although higher resource utilization can lower energy consumption, it may lead to Virtual Machine (VM) overload. To avoid VM overload, Yadav et al. [11] proposed a VM migration approach based on the prediction model of CPU utilization to reduce energy consumption at overloaded VMs, while Hussain et al. [12] optimized energy consumption through dynamic VM migration. For electricity cost optimization in GDCs, Hussain et al. [13] proposed a multi-stage energy-aware workflow scheduling framework that combines VND-based DC searching, task sequence adjustment, and DVFS to minimize electricity cost. Li et al. [14] investigated the multi-workflow scheduling problem involving both generated and original data transmission, effectively reducing costs while satisfying workflow deadlines. Wang et al. [15] introduced a dynamic sub-deadline update mechanism combined with a VND-based algorithm to optimize electricity costs for multi-workflow scheduling.

2.3 Reliability-Aware Workflow Scheduling

As an important part of the QoS of cloud computing, cloud service reliability has attracted significant attention from both academia and industry. To address the issue that DVFS incurs transient faults when reducing energy consumption, Wu et al. [16] employed a checkpointing mechanism to monitor transient faults and used rollback techniques to ensure reliable task execution. Some studies adopt heuristic fault-tolerant scheduling algorithms to enhance workflow reliability. Zhang et al. [17] considered transient faults caused by DVFS and selected optimal processor frequency to balance reliability and energy consumption. Wang et al. [18] incorporated task reliability into the optimization objective and proposed a multi-objective optimization algorithm to achieve a trade-off between reliability and other optimization objectives. Furthermore, replication-based strategies also constitute another approach. Xie et al. [19] proposed an iterative two-stage replication algorithm to implement quantitative proactive replication for meeting the reliability constraint. Zhu et al. [20] developed a task allocation algorithm based on minimizing redundancy to satisfy the reliability requirements of Directed Acyclic Graph (DAG) parallel applications. Tang et al. [21] constructed a CUDA-accelerated temporal deep neural network to predict VM fault risks and triggered task backups when the predicted risk exceeded a threshold (Table 1).

Table 1. Summary of the Related Literature

Ref	Optimization Objective				Resource Characteristics			Fault-Tolerance Mechanism		Constraint		
	Electricity Cost	Energy Consumption	Makespan	Other	Geo-Distributed	Electricity Price Variability	DVFS	Replication	Checkpoint	Reliability	Deadline	Other
[1]			√									
[2]				√							√	
[4]			√		√							√
[5–8]		√					√					
[9]		√										√
[10,11]		√		√								
[12]		√										
[13–15]	√				√	√	√				√	
[16]		√					√	√	√	√		
[17,18]				√			√					√
[19–21]				√				√	√			

Compared with existing studies, the problem considered in this paper is more comprehensive. Xia et al. [5], Cao et al. [6], and Kumar et al. [7] focused exclusively on energy optimization in a single DC, without considering geo-distributed scenarios. Hussain et al. [13], Li et al. [14], and Wang et al. [15] investigated electricity cost optimization in GDCs and applied DVFS to further reduce energy consumption. However, they overlooked the increased risk of transient VM faults during task execution caused by DVFS. In contrast, this paper studies workflow scheduling in GDCs to optimize electricity cost, while explicitly accounting for the impact of DVFS on task execution reliability.

3 Problem Description

A workflow comprises multiple tasks $\{v_1, \ldots, v_n\}$, where each task v_i has a total instruction count of W_i, and the complex dependencies among tasks form a

DAG. In GDCs, each DC $D_k(k = 1, \ldots, M)$ consists of μ_k hosts $\{M_1^k, \ldots, M_{\mu_k}^k\}$, and each host M_j^k contains m_j^k heterogeneous VMs $\{V_{j,1}^k, \ldots, V_{j,m_j^k}^k\}$. For VM $V_{j,l}^k(l = 1, \ldots, m_j^k)$, the maximum instruction execution speed is denoted as $\xi_{j,l}^k$. Each VM supports Y discrete operating frequencies, sorted from low to high, denoted as $f_{j,l,y}^k(y = 1, \ldots, Y)$. The higher the operating frequency of a VM, the faster its instruction execution speed, but the greater its power $P_{j,l}^k$ due to $P_{j,l}^k \propto {f_{j,l,y}^k}^3$ [5]. Since instruction execution speed is proportional to the operating frequency, when VM $V_{j,l}^k$ operates at frequency $f_{j,l,y}^k$, its instruction execution speed can be expressed as $\xi_{j,l}^k \cdot \frac{f_{j,l,y}^k}{f_{j,l,Y}^k}$, where $f_{j,l,Y}^k$ denotes the maximum operating frequency of VM $V_{j,l}^k$. Furthermore, B_{intra} and B_{inter} denote the data transmission bandwidths within a DC and among DCs, respectively. For simplicity, the following assumptions are made:

(1) The intra-host bandwidth is considered infinite, and the corresponding data transmission time is assumed to be zero.
(2) Each VM can execute only one task at a time, and each task can be executed on only one VM.
(3) If a task fails due to a transient fault during execution, it will be re-executed until it completes successfully.
(4) The execution of each task in the workflow is mutually independent.

The electricity cost of executing the workflow is $C = \sum_{i=1}^{n} C_i$, and the electricity cost of task v_i during its execution is expressed by Eq. (1)

$$C_i = \sum_{k=1}^{M} \sum_{j=1}^{\mu_k} \sum_{l=1}^{m_j^k} \int_{T_i^B}^{T_i^F} x_{i;k,j,l} \cdot P_{j,l}^k \cdot p_k(t)\, dt. \tag{1}$$

Here, $x_{i;k,j,l}$ is a decision variable that takes 1 if task v_i is assigned to VM $V_{j,l}^k$, and 0 otherwise. $P_{j,l}^k$ denotes the power of VM $V_{j,l}^k$, and $p_k(t)$ represents the electricity price of DC D_k at time t. The finish time of task v_i, denoted as T_i^F [14], is determined by its start time T_i^B and duration T_i^D, $T_i^F = T_i^B + T_i^D$, $T_i^D = T_i^e + \max_{i' \in PR_i} \{T_{i',i}^G\} + T_i^O$. Here, T_i^e is the execution time of task v_i, $T_{i',i}^G$ represents the generated data transmission time from the predecessor task $v_{i'}$ of v_i to v_i, and T_i^O denotes the original data transmission time.

The task execution reliability follows an exponential distribution [21], defined as the probability that a task does not encounter an error during execution. The reliability of a task is calculated by $r = e^{-\lambda \cdot t}$, where λ denotes the fault arrival rate and t represents the execution time. The transient fault rate of a VM varies with its operating frequency, and a lower frequency results in a higher transient fault rate. For VM $V_{j,l}^k$ operating at frequency $f_{j,l,y}^k$, the transient fault rate [16] is given by Eq. (2)

$$\lambda_{j,l,y}^k = \lambda_{j,l,Y}^k \cdot 10^{sr_{j,l}^k \cdot \frac{f_{j,l,Y}^k - f_{j,l,y}^k}{f_{j,l,Y}^k - f_{j,l,1}^k}}, \tag{2}$$

where $\lambda^k_{j,l,Y}$ is the fault rate at the maximum frequency, and $sr^k_{j,l}$ represents the sensitivity of the fault rate to frequency scaling. Thus, when task v_i is executed on VM $V^k_{j,l}$ at frequency $f^k_{j,l,y}$, the execution reliability of the task is $r_i = e^{-\lambda^k_{j,l,y} \cdot T^e_i}$, where $T^e_i = \frac{W_i \cdot f^k_{j,l,Y}}{\xi^k_{j,l} \cdot f^k_{j,l,y}}$ denotes the task execution time. Since the execution of each task is independent, the overall reliability of the workflow $R = \prod_{i=1}^{n} r_i$ can be expressed as the product of the reliabilities of all its tasks [22].

The objective of this paper is, in GDCs, to minimize the electricity cost C of executing a workflow while considering the generated and original data transmission, electricity price variations across DCs, and task execution reliability. This is achieved under the constraints of meeting the workflow deadline d and the overall reliability constraint R^c, as formulated in Eq. (3)

$$\begin{aligned} &\mathit{Minimize} \quad C = \sum_{i=1}^{n} C_i \\ &\mathit{Subject\ to:} \quad R \geq R^c, T^F \leq d \end{aligned} \tag{3}$$

4 Proposed Algorithm

In this paper, we propose a Deadline- and Reliability-Constrained Workflow Scheduling algorithm (DRWS), which comprises three stages. The framework of DRWS is shown in Algorithm 1. First, the workflow deadline is partitioned

Algorithm 1: The Framework of DRWS Algorithm

Input: $\{v_1, \ldots, v_n\}$, d, R^c, N_{max}
Output: s^*
$\{d_1, \ldots, d_n\} \leftarrow \mathit{deadlinePartition}(d, \{v_1, \ldots, v_n\})$;
$s \leftarrow \mathit{taskSequencing}(\{v_1, \ldots, v_n\})$;
$s^* \leftarrow s$, $C^* \leftarrow \infty$, $N \leftarrow 1$;
while $N \leq N_{max}$ **do**
  $T^F, R, C \leftarrow \mathit{allocateVm}(s, \{d_1, \ldots, d_n\}, R^c)$;
  if $T^F \leq d \wedge R \geq R^c \wedge C < C^*$ **then**
    $s^* \leftarrow s$, $C^* \leftarrow C$, $N \leftarrow 1$;
  else
    $N \leftarrow N + 1$;
  $s \leftarrow \mathit{adjustSequence}(s^*, N)$;

based on the upward rank of each task, assigning a specific deadline to each task, and an initial task sequence is constructed. Second, with assigned task deadlines and the reliability requirement, tasks are allocated to appropriate VMs to minimize electricity costs, and the operating frequency of each VM for executing a given task is determined. Third, a sequence adjustment VND-based method is applied to iteratively optimize the task schedule sequence, further reducing costs.

4.1 Deadline Partition

Due to the heterogeneity of distributed resources, the instruction execution speed of the VM assigned to a task cannot be determined in advance during the pre-scheduling stage. Therefore, this paper uses the average instruction execution speed of all VMs at their highest frequency, defined as $\bar{\xi}_{fast} = \frac{\sum_{k=1}^{M}\sum_{j=1}^{\mu_k}\sum_{l=1}^{m_j^k}\xi_{j,l}^k}{\varpi}$, as the estimated execution speed of each task. Moreover, since the network bandwidth differs within and between DCs, the average generated data transmission time $\bar{T}_{i',i}^{G} = \frac{\sum_{k=1}^{M}\sum_{j=1}^{\mu_k}\sum_{l=1}^{m_j^k}\sum_{k'=1}^{M}\sum_{j'=1}^{\mu_k'}\sum_{l'=1}^{m_j^{k'}}T_{i',i}^{G}}{\varpi^2}$ and the average original data transmission time $\bar{T}_i^O = \frac{\sum_{k=1}^{M}\sum_{j=1}^{\mu_k}\sum_{l=1}^{m_j^k}T_i^O}{\varpi}$ are employed to estimate the data transmission time of each task. Based on these estimated parameters, the estimated execution time of task v_i can be expressed as $\bar{T}_i^e = \frac{W_i}{\bar{\xi}_{fast}}$, the earliest start time of the task is $T_i^{EST} = \max_{i' \in PR_i}\{T_{i'}^{EFT} + \bar{T}_{i',i}^{G}\} + \bar{T}_i^O$, the earliest finish time of task v_i is $T_i^{EFT} = T_i^{EST} + \bar{T}_i^e$, and the workflow slack time is defined as $T^{slack} = d - T_n^{EFT}$.

Within a workflow, the task with a higher upward rank has a great significant influence on the workflow finish time. The upward rank [14] is $rank_u(v_i) = \bar{T}_i^e + \bar{T}_i^O + \max_{i' \in SU_i}\{\bar{T}_{i',i}^{G} + rank_u(v_{i'})\}$. Accordingly, an upward rank-based deadline partition method is proposed, as shown in Eq. (4). Based on this method, the tasks at higher levels of the workflow—from exit to entry—are assigned more urgent deadlines, thereby reducing the risk of violating deadlines.

$$d_i = T_i^{\mathrm{EFT}} + \frac{rank_u(v_1) - rank_u(v_i) + \bar{T}_i^e + \bar{T}_i^O}{rank_u(v_1)} \times T^{slack} \tag{4}$$

4.2 Resource Allocation

The proposed resource allocation method is formally described in Algorithm 2. To ensure the reliable execution of workflow and minimize electricity cost, the schedule schema generated during the pre-scheduling phase must satisfy the workflow's reliability constraint R^c, $R \geq R^c$. To achieve this goal, the overall reliability constraint R^c be assigned to each task, such that each one only needs to satisfy its corresponding reliability requirement r_i^c during pre-scheduling. Accordingly, the pre-assigned reliability $r^{pre} = \sqrt[n]{R^c}$ [23] can be set for each task. However, directly adopting r^{pre} as the reliability constraint for each task may lead to selecting high operating frequencies, resulting in high costs. To overcome this shortcoming, the reliability constraint of a task can be dynamically adjusted during pre-scheduling [19]. Specifically, if the first $i-1$ tasks in the schedule sequence have already been scheduled, the reliability constraint r_i^c for the task v_i can be calculated by Eq. (5) based on the actual reliability r_x of the scheduled tasks and the pre-assigned reliability r^{pre} of the unscheduled tasks.

$$r_i^c = \frac{R^c}{\prod_{x=1}^{i-1} r_x \cdot \prod_{z=i+1}^{n} r^{pre}} \tag{5}$$

To optimize cost, when scheduling task v_i, its start time T_i^B is updated, the average electricity price of each DC D_k during the interval $\left[T_i^B, d_i\right]$ is determined by $\overline{p}_k = \frac{\int_{T_i^B}^{d_i} p_k(t)\,dt}{d_i - T_i^B}$, and the task v_i is assigned to the DC D_k with the lowest $\overline{p}_k$. Next, a VM is assigned to task v_i, and its operating frequency for executing

Algorithm 2: VM Allocation

Input: s, $\{d_1, \ldots, d_n\}$, R^c

Output: T^F, R, C

$C \leftarrow 0$, $r^{pre} \leftarrow \sqrt[n]{R^c}$, $T^F \leftarrow 0$, $R \leftarrow 1$;
for $i = 1$ **to** n **do**
  $T_i^B \leftarrow \max_{i' \in PR_i} \{T_{i'}^F\}$;
  $D_k \leftarrow \arg\min_{k=1,\ldots,M} \frac{\int_{T_i^B}^{d_i} p_k(t)\,dt}{d_i - T_i^B}$, $r_i^c \leftarrow \frac{R^c}{\prod_{x=1}^{i-1} r_x \cdot \prod_{z=i+1}^{n} r^{pre}}$;
  $f_i^* \leftarrow null$, $T_i^{F*} \leftarrow \infty$, $C_i^* \leftarrow \infty$;
  for $j = 1$ **to** μ_k **do**
    for $l = 1$ **to** m_j^k **do**
      $T_i^{ready} \leftarrow \max_{i' \in PR_i} \{T_{i'}^F + T_{i',i}^G\} + T_i^O$,
      $z' \leftarrow searchAvailableTimeSlot(V_{j,l}^k, v_i, T_i^{ready})$;
      if $T_i^F \le d_i \wedge r_i \ge r_i^c$ **then**
        $T_i^{avail} \leftarrow \max\{T_i^{ready}, T_{k,j,l,z'}^B\}$,
        $span \leftarrow \min\{T_{k,j,l,z'}^F, d_i\} - T_i^{avail}$, $y' \leftarrow Y$;
        for $y = Y$ **to** 1 **do**
          if $T_i^e > span \vee r_i < r_i^c$ **then**
            break;
          $y' \leftarrow y$;
        $T_i^F \leftarrow T_i^{avail} + \frac{W_i}{f_{j,l,y'}^k}$, $C_i \leftarrow calculateCost(v_i, T_i^F, f_{j,l,y'}^k)$;
        if $C_i < C_i^*$ **then**
          $f_i^* \leftarrow f_{j,l,y'}^k$, $T_i^{F*} \leftarrow T_i^F$, $C_i^* \leftarrow C_i$;
  if $f_i^* = null$ **then**
    $f_i^* \leftarrow f_{j,l,Y}^k$, $T_i^{ready} \leftarrow \max_{i' \in PR_i} \{T_{i'}^F + T_{i',i}^G\} + T_i^O$;
    $z' \leftarrow searchAvailableTimeSlot(V_{j,l}^k, v_i, T_i^{ready})$;
    $T_i^{avail} \leftarrow \max\{T_i^{ready}, T_{k,j,l,z'}^B\}$;
    $T_i^{F*} \leftarrow T_i^{avail} + \frac{W_i}{f_{j,l,Y}^k}$, $C_i^* \leftarrow calculateCost(v_i, T_i^F, f_{j,l,Y}^k)$;
  $insertTimeBlock(f_i^*, T_i^{F*})$;
  $T^F \leftarrow \max\{T^F, T_i^{F*}\}$, $R \leftarrow R \cdot r_i$, $C \leftarrow C + C_i^*$;

the task is determined. Specifically, each VM in DC D_k is traversed sequentially, with its available time slots checked in ascending order to identify a feasible slot for task v_i. The time slot search method is illustrated in Algorithm 3. Suppose an available time slot on a VM can accommodate the execution time required for task v_i at the VM's maximum frequency while satisfying both the deadline constraint d_i and the reliability constraint r_i^c. In that case, that slot is selected. Furthermore, if the task has sufficient slack time, defined as $T_i^{slack} = d_i - T_i^F$, the

VM's operating frequency can be reduced appropriately while still meeting both d_i and r_i^c, thereby further lowering cost. The cost C_i of task v_i on this VM at the chosen frequency is then calculated and recorded. This process continues across the remaining VMs, ultimately selecting the VM and frequency combination that minimizes the execution cost of task v_i. If no suitable VM is found, the task is randomly assigned to a VM at the VM's maximum frequency. Finally, insert the time block of the task v_i into the corresponding time slot.

Algorithm 3: Available Time Slot Search

Input: $V_{j,l}^k$, v_i, T_i^{ready}
Output: z'

$z' \leftarrow 1$;
for $z = 1$ **to** $h_{j,l}^k$ **do**
  $T_i^{avail} \leftarrow \max\{T_i^{ready}, T_{k,j,l,z}^B\}$, $T_i^F \leftarrow T_i^{avail} + \frac{W_i}{\xi_{j,l}^k}$;
  if $T_i^F \leq T_{k,j,l,z}^F$ **then**
    $z' \leftarrow z$;
    break;

4.3 Task Sequence Adjustment

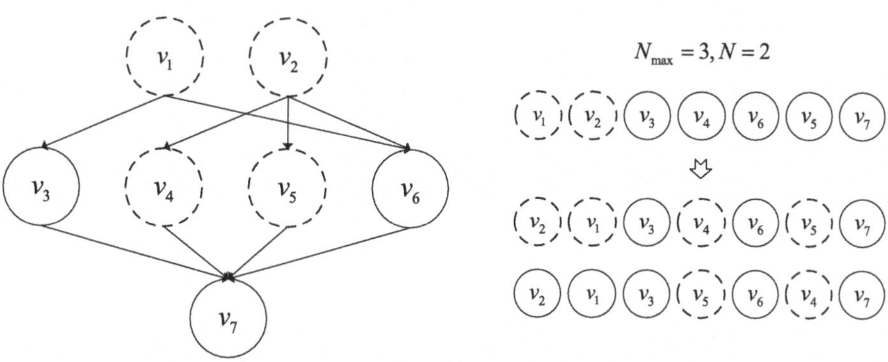

Fig. 1. Task sequence adjustment.

The task schedule sequence of the workflow has a significant impact on the electricity cost. Therefore, three initial task schedule sequence construction methods are proposed based on the upward rank, downward rank, and deadline. As the VM allocation scheme based on the initial task scheduling sequence may fall into a local optimum, a task sequence adjustment VND-based [13] is employed to explore the global optimum more effectively, which generates new schedule sequences by swapping the order of task nodes in the sequence. Since the tasks of the workflow are subject to partial order constraints, arbitrary adjustments of the task schedule sequence may violate these constraints. To preserve the partial order, tasks are divided into different levels according to $\ell_i = \max_{i' \in PR_i}\{\ell_{i'}\} + 1$, and $\ell_i = 0$ if $PR_i = \emptyset$, allowing only tasks within the same level ℓ_i to be swapped.

Moreover, balancing exploration and exploitation facilitates the search for the global optimum. Accordingly, the method initially swaps a larger number of task nodes to encourage exploration and then gradually reduces the number of swapped pairs to focus on exploitation. In this work, a total of $N_{\max}$ neighborhood structures are constructed, $N = 1, \ldots, N_{max}$. For the N-th neighborhood structure, as illustrated in Fig. 1, the $N_{\max} - N + 1$ pairs of tasks are randomly selected for swapping within the schedule sequence.

4.4 Time Complexity Analysis

In the deadline partition phase, the computation of the average generated data transmission time dominates the time complexity. Assuming that each task has an average of a predecessor tasks, the time complexity of deadline partition is $O(a \cdot n \cdot \varpi^2)$. In addition, the time complexity of constructing the initial task schedule sequence is $O(n \log n)$. The average number of VMs in a DC is $\frac{\varpi}{M}$, the number of time slots on each VM is related to the number of tasks, and the average number of tasks per VM is $\frac{n}{\varpi}$. Therefore, the time complexity of resource allocation is $O(n \cdot \frac{\varpi}{M} \cdot (\frac{n}{\varpi} + Y))$. The time complexity of task sequence adjustment depends on the number of task swap pairs, so the worst-case complexity of task sequence adjustment is $O(N_{max})$.

Finally, since a VND-based task sequence adjustment method is adopted, the number of iterations of the algorithm is uncertain due to possible neighborhood resets during the process. In the best case, the algorithm performs N_{max} iterations; if neighborhood resets occur, the number of iterations increases. Therefore, the time complexity of the proposed algorithm is

$$O(a \cdot n \cdot \varpi^2 + n \log n + N_{max} \cdot (n \cdot \frac{\varpi}{M} \cdot (\frac{n}{\varpi} + Y) + N_{max})).$$

5 Experiment

5.1 Experimental Setup

The experiments in this paper are based on the CloudSim simulation platform. Both the proposed algorithm and the baseline algorithms are implemented in Java, developed using IntelliJ IDEA 2024.1.1, and compiled with Java SE 21. All experiments are conducted on a Windows 11 machine with an Intel(R) Core(TM) i5-13500H CPU @ 2.60 GHz and 16.0 GB of RAM.

Two classic workflows, Montage and Genome, are selected. Based on the number of tasks, four scales $\{50, 100, 200, 400\}$ are considered for experiments. For

Table 2. Electricity Prices of 10 DCs During Different Periods Per Day ($\$/kWh$)

Time (UTC)	DC_1	DC_2	DC_3	DC_4	DC_5	DC_6	DC_7	DC_8	DC_9	DC_{10}
0:00	0.10	0.11	0.15	0.07	0.13	0.18	0.24	0.21	0.19	0.08
1:00	0.09	0.12	0.10	0.08	0.13	0.19	0.24	0.21	0.18	0.08
2:00	0.11	0.12	0.11	0.09	0.15	0.18	0.19	0.21	0.18	0.09
3:00	0.11	0.12	0.11	0.07	0.15	0.18	0.15	0.21	0.18	0.09
4:00	0.09	0.12	0.19	0.13	0.17	0.18	0.15	0.16	0.19	0.13
5:00	0.09	0.22	0.22	0.14	0.19	0.21	0.16	0.16	0.19	0.13
6:00	0.10	0.22	0.19	0.13	0.21	0.22	0.16	0.21	0.18	0.13
7:00	0.10	0.22	0.11	0.13	0.21	0.25	0.08	0.21	0.18	0.13
8:00	0.15	0.22	0.12	0.12	0.21	0.25	0.08	0.21	0.18	0.11
9:00	0.15	0.22	0.07	0.12	0.18	0.16	0.08	0.21	0.18	0.11
10:00	0.15	0.19	0.08	0.09	0.18	0.16	0.08	0.21	0.19	0.09
11:00	0.13	0.18	0.10	0.09	0.17	0.17	0.16	0.19	0.19	0.09

Note: Electricity prices are identical for the corresponding PM hours (12:00–23:00).

each combination of workflow type and number of tasks, five workflow instances are generated using the workflow generator, and the workflow deadline is set according to $d = T^{EFT}(1 + df)$, where T^{EFT} denotes the estimated earliest finish time of the workflow. The parameter df controls the tightness of the workflow deadline, with values $df \in \{0.2, 0.4, 0.6, 0.8\}$.

Table 3. VM Configuration

Type	VM_1	VM_2	VM_3	VM_4	VM_5
GHz/Core	2.2	2.2	2.4	2.2	2.0
MIPS/Core	1100	1100	1200	1100	1000

A total of ten DCs are configured. The electricity prices [14] of each DC during different periods are shown in Table 2. Five types of VMs [16] are configured, as shown in Table 3. Each type of VM supports five frequency levels, with the operating frequency and power at each level listed in Table 4.

In addition, the intra- and inter-data center bandwidths B_{intra} and B_{inter} are set to 10^7 and 10^6, respectively, and the sensitivity $sr^k_{j,l}$ of VM transient fault rate to frequency scaling is set to 2 [16]. Different types of VMs exhibit varying transient fault rates. First, a random variable ϕ, uniformly distributed in the interval $[1, 10)$, is defined, and then the fault rate of each VM type at its maximum frequency is determined by $\phi \cdot 10^{-5}$.

Table 4. VM Operating Frequency and Power

FV	VM_1		VM_2		VM_3		VM_4		VM_5	
	Freq (GHz)	Power (W)	Freq (GHz)	Power (W)	Freq (GHz)	Power (W)	Freq (GHz)	Power (W)	Freq (GHz)	Power (W)
1	1.4	13	1.4	15	1.6	22	1.4	11	1.2	10
2	1.6	18	1.6	21	1.8	32	1.6	15	1.4	14
3	1.8	25	1.8	30	2.0	48	1.8	18	1.6	20
4	2.0	30	2.0	54	2.2	76	2.0	22	1.8	36
5	2.2	43	2.2	95	2.4	110	2.2	32	2.0	65

5.2 Performance Evaluation

To verify the effectiveness of the proposed algorithm, the Relative Percentage Deviation (RPD) is adapted as the evaluation metric, as defined in Eq. (6), to compare the performance of different algorithms.

$$RPD(\%) = \frac{C(\pi) - C(\pi^*)}{C(\pi^*)} \times 100\% \tag{6}$$

Here, $C(\pi)$ denotes the electricity cost produced by the schedule π, while $C(\pi^*)$ represents the electricity cost obtained by the optimal schedule π^*. As shown in Eq. (6), a smaller RPD value indicates better performance.

The calibration experiments are conducted on the reliability parameter $rf \in \{0.92, 0.94, 0.96, 0.98\}$, the initial task schedule sequence construction strategy, and the neighborhood structure parameter $nf \in \{0.2, 0.4, 0.6, 0.8\}$ in the VND-based task sequence adjustment algorithm. The experiment results of all parameter and component combinations are analyzed using the Analysis of Variance (ANOVA) method, and the optimal combination is ultimately selected.

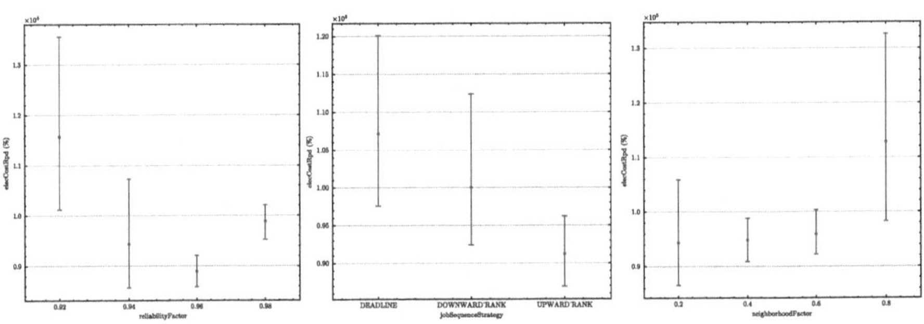

Fig. 2. The mean plots of parameters and components with 95.0% Tukey HSD confidence level intervals.

Figure 2 presents the mean plots of parameters and components with 95.0% Tukey HSD confidence level intervals. In this study, the workflow reliability constraint R^c is defined based on the reliability parameter rf and the number of tasks n, $R^c = rf^n$. The result indicates that the RPD exhibits a decrease–then–increase trend as rf increases. Specifically, as rf increases from 0.92 to 0.96, the RPD gradually decreases due to the reduction of task retries. Conversely, when $rf > 0.96$, the RPD begins to rise because of the more stringent reliability constraints. Finally, the reliability parameter rf is set to 0.96. Three task sequencing methods, based on the upward rank, downward rank, and deadline of the task, are proposed for constructing the initial task schedule sequence. The result implies that constructing the initial schedule sequence based on the upward rank is beneficial for saving costs. Thus, the upward rank-based method is chosen. In the schedule sequence adjustment method, the maximum number of neighborhood structures N_{max} is determined by the neighborhood structure parameter nf and the number of tasks n, $N_{max} = nf \times n$. The result indicates that the RPD continuously increases as nf rises. Therefore, the neighborhood structure parameter nf is set to 0.2.

In comparative experiments, the DRWS algorithm is configured with the optimal parameters and components determined in the calibration experiments. Then, the DEWS [13] and EPEE [24] algorithms are selected as benchmark algorithms to evaluate the performance of the DRWS algorithm.

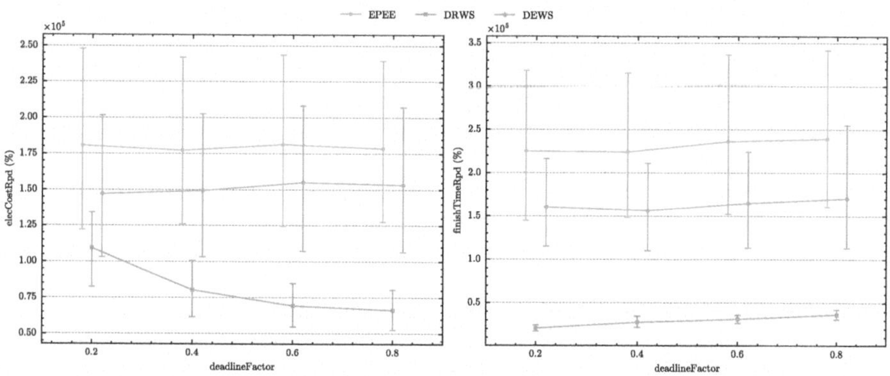

Fig. 3. The mean plots of the compared algorithms with 95.0% Tukey HSD confidence level intervals.

The mean plots of the compared algorithms with 95.0% Tukey HSD confidence level intervals are shown in Fig. 3. The results reveal significant differences among algorithms. Overall, DRWS outperforms the other, maintaining the lowest RPD of cost, which gradually decreases as the deadline is relaxed. In contrast, EPEE and DEWS incur higher RPD. Although both EPEE and DEWS use DVFS to reduce the operating frequencies of VMs to reduce cost, their aggressive frequency scaling strategies lead to more task retries and higher costs. Furthermore, DRWS also achieves the lowest finish time, with a slight increase in RPD as the deadline relaxes. The above analyses demonstrate that the proposed DRWS algorithm effectively leverages DVFS to reduce electricity costs while ensuring reliable task execution and maintaining a reasonable finish time.

6 Conclusion

In this paper, we consider the workflow scheduling problem in GDCs to minimize the electricity cost. The variability in electricity prices across different time periods and geographical locations, along with factors such as the transmission of generated and original data, workflow deadline, and VM transient faults, all pose significant challenges for cost optimization. To address these challenges, we propose a Deadline- and Reliability-Constrained Workflow Scheduling (DRWS) algorithm, which includes deadline partition, resource allocation, and task sequence adjustment. The experimental results demonstrate that the proposed DRWS algorithm consistently outperforms baseline algorithms, effectively optimizing electricity cost. As is well known, the VM fault rate is also related to aging. Therefore, future research will further investigate the comprehensive impact of VM operating frequency and aging on the workflow's execution cost.

References

1. Topcuoglu, H., Hariri, S., Wu, M.-Y.: Performance-effective and low-complexity task scheduling for heterogeneous computing. IEEE Trans. Parallel Distrib. Syst. **13**(3), 260–274 (2002)
2. Abrishami, S., Naghibzadeh, M., Epema, D.H.: Cost-driven scheduling of grid workflows using partial critical paths. IEEE Trans. Parallel Distrib. Syst. **23**(8), 1400–1414 (2012)
3. Wu, D., Wang, X., Wang, X., Huang, M., Zeng, R., Yang, K.: Multi-objective optimization-based workflow scheduling for applications with data locality and deadline constraints in geo-distributed clouds. Futur. Gener. Comput. Syst. **157**, 485–498 (2024)
4. Shu, X., Wu, Q., Zhou, M., Wen, J.: A communication-contention-aware privacy-preserving workflow scheduling method for geo-distributed datacenters. IEEE Trans. Serv. Comput. **17**(5), 1887–1898 (2024)
5. Xia, Y., Luo, X., Jin, T., Li, J., Xing, L.: A tri-chromosome-based evolutionary algorithm for energy-efficient workflow scheduling in clouds. Swarm Evol. Comput. **91**, 101751 (2024)
6. Cao, M., Li, Y., Wen, X., Zhao, Y., Zhu, J.: Energy-aware intelligent scheduling for deadline-constrained workflows in sustainable cloud computing. Egypt. Inform. J. **24**(2), 277–290 (2023)
7. Kumar, K.: P2BED-C: a novel peer to peer load balancing and energy efficient technique for data-centers over cloud. Wireless Pers. Commun. **123**(1), 311–324 (2022)
8. Ding, D., Fan, X., Zhao, Y., Kang, K., Yin, Q., Zeng, J.: Q-learning based dynamic task scheduling for energy-efficient cloud computing. Futur. Gener. Comput. Syst. **108**, 361–371 (2020)
9. Yang, W., Zhao, M., Li, J., Zhang, X.: Energy-efficient DAG scheduling with DVFS for cloud data centers. J. Supercomput. **80**(10), 14799–14823 (2024)
10. Duan, L.T., Wang, J., Wang, H.Y.: An energy-aware ant colony optimization strategy for virtual machine placement in cloud computing. Clust. Comput. **27**(10), 14269–14282 (2024)

11. Yadav, R., Zhang, W., Kaiwartya, O., Singh, P.R., Elgendy, I.A., Tian, Y.C.: Adaptive energy-aware algorithms for minimizing energy consumption and SLA violation in cloud computing. IEEE Access **6**, 55923–55936 (2018)
12. Hussain, M., Wei, L.F., Lakhan, A., Wali, S., Ali, S., Hussain, A.: Energy and performance-efficient task scheduling in heterogeneous virtualized cloud computing. Sustain. Comput. Inform. Syst. **30**, 100517 (2021)
13. Hussain, M., Wei, L.F., Rehman, A., Abbas, F., Hussain, A., Ali, M.: Deadline-constrained energy-aware workflow scheduling in geographically distributed cloud data centers. Futur. Gener. Comput. Syst. **132**, 211–222 (2022)
14. Li, X., Yu, W., Ruiz, R., Zhu, J.: Energy-aware cloud workflow applications scheduling with geo-distributed data. IEEE Trans. Serv. Comput. **15**(2), 891–903 (2022)
15. Wang, S., Duan, Y., Lei, Y., Du, P., Wang, Y.: Electricity-cost-aware multi-workflow scheduling in heterogeneous cloud. Computing **106**(6), 1749–1775 (2024)
16. Wu, T., Gu, H., Zhou, J., Wei, T., Liu, X., Chen, M.: Soft error-aware energy-efficient task scheduling for workflow applications in DVFS-enabled cloud. J. Syst. Architect. **84**, 12–27 (2018)
17. Zhang, L., Li, K., Xu, Y., Mei, J., Zhang, F., Li, K.: Maximizing reliability with energy conservation for parallel task scheduling in a heterogeneous cluster. Inf. Sci. **319**, 113–131 (2015)
18. Wang, X., Buyya, R., Su, J.: Reliability-oriented genetic algorithm for workflow applications using max-min strategy. In: 2009 9th IEEE/ACM International Symposium on Cluster Computing and the Grid, pp. 108–115. IEEE, Shanghai, China (2009). https://doi.org/10.1109/CCGRID.2009.14
19. Xie, G., et al.: Minimizing redundancy to satisfy reliability requirement for a parallel application on heterogeneous service-oriented systems. IEEE Trans. Serv. Comput. **13**(5), 871–886 (2020)
20. Zhu, J., Wang, L., Xie, G., Pei, T., Oh, S., Li, Z.: A low redundancy and high time efficiency large-scale task assignment strategy for heterogeneous service-oriented cloud computing systems. J. Supercomput. **77**(4), 3450–3483 (2021)
21. Tang, X., Liu, Y., Zeng, Z., Veeravalli, B.: Service cost effective and reliability aware job scheduling algorithm on cloud computing systems. IEEE Trans. Cloud Comput. **11**(2), 1461–1473 (2023)
22. Taghinezhad-Niar, A., Taheri, J.: Reliability, rental-cost and energy-aware multi-workflow scheduling on multi-cloud systems. IEEE Trans. Cloud Comput. **11**(3), 2681–2692 (2023)
23. Zhao, L., Ren, Y., Xiang, Y., Sakurai, K.: Fault-tolerant scheduling with dynamic number of replicas in heterogeneous systems. In: 2010 IEEE 12th International Conference on High Performance Computing and Communications (HPCC), pp. 434–441 (2010). https://doi.org/10.1109/HPCC.2010.72
24. Hussain, M., Wei, L.F., Rehman, A., Hussain, A., Ali, M., Javed, M.H.: An electricity price and energy-efficient workflow scheduling in geographically distributed cloud data centers. J. King Saud Univ. Comput. Inf. Sci. **36**(8), 102170 (2024)

MLIF: Multi-aspect Label Information Fusion for Effective ICD Coding in Long-Tail Scenarios

Yonghe Yan[1], Yujing Xin[2], Ning Liu[1(✉)], Qian Li[1], Dongbiao He[3], Teng Ma[4], Lei Liu[1], and Zhongmin Yan[1]

[1] School of Software, Shandong University, Jinan 250101, Shandong, China
202335356@mail.sdu.edu.cn , liun21cs@sdu.edu.cn
[2] Department of Oncology, Shandong Provincial Hospital Affiliated to Shandong First Medical University, Jinan 250021, Shandong, China
[3] Computer Network Information Center, Chinese Academy of Sciences, Beijing, Beijing 100190, China
[4] Alibaba Group, Hangzhou 311121, Zhejiang, China

Abstract. Automatic coding of International Classification of Diseases (ICD) assigns standardized codes to clinical texts, streamlining healthcare applications via multi-label classification. Existing methods, limited by single-faceted label representation learning and single-head label-wise attention, struggle with long-tail distributions, diverse clinical expressions, and inter-label dependencies. In this paper, we propose the Multi-aspect Label Information Fusion (MLIF) framework to address these challenges. MLIF enhances label representation learning from multiple aspects by integrating semantic information from code descriptions, contextual prototypes from clinical notes, and inter-label correlations via graph-based learning, effectively tackling long-tail distribution challenge. Multi-head code-aware self-attention and text-code cross-attention decoders further improve feature extraction and text-code alignment. Experiments on the publicly available MIMIC datasets show that our model outperforms previous models, particularly in full-code settings, while maintaining computational efficiency.

Keywords: Automatic ICD Coding · Clinical Text Processing · Multi-label Text Classification · Long-Tail Distribution

1 Introduction

The International Classification of Diseases (ICD), developed by the World Health Organization (WHO), is a global standard for classifying diseases and coding diagnostic procedures. ICD codes standardize reporting of diseases, injuries, and causes of death, as well as diagnosis and treatment worldwide. The ICD coding task maps patients' electronic health records (EHRs) to standardized ICD codes for purposes such as insurance reimbursement and resource allocation.

© The Author(s), under exclusive license to Springer Nature Singapore Pte Ltd. 2027
H. Sun et al. (Eds.): ChineseCSCW 2025, CCIS 2911, pp. 392–406, 2027.
https://doi.org/10.1007/978-981-92-0288-1_28

Manual ICD coding is time-consuming and error-prone. Therefore, researchers have explored automatic ICD coding via machine learning to reduce coder workload. Typically framed as extreme multi-label text classification task [15], it assigns multiple ICD codes per EHR document. Earlier studies employed recurrent neural networks (RNNs) [23], convolutional neural networks (CNNs) [13], or transformer-based encoders for lengthy documents representation. Label-wise attention often leverages ICD code features, such as descriptions or hierarchies, to extract code-related information [5,21].

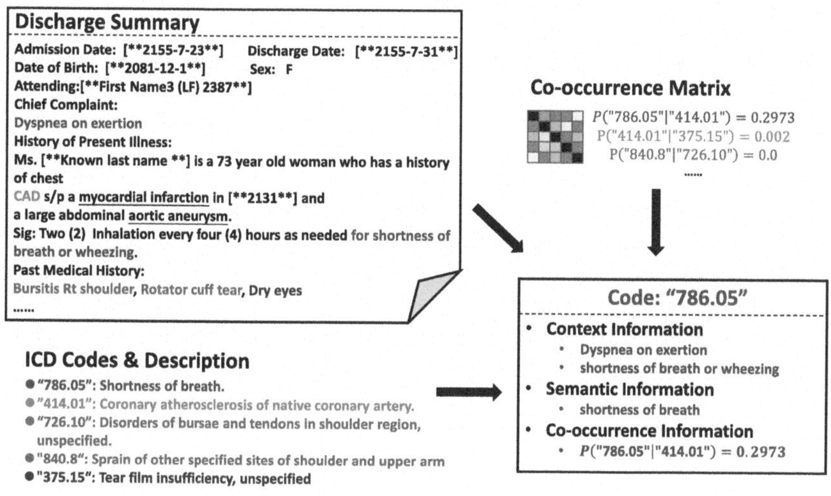

Fig. 1. Example from the MIMIC-III dataset. We marked each code and its mention in clinical documents with the same color. The code "786.05" is used as an example to show the three aspects of label information.

Despite advances, current methods face key limitations:

Limited label representation in ICD coding due to single-faceted learning and long-tail distribution challenges.

Existing approaches rely on single-faceted label representations (e.g., code descriptions or learnable embeddings), inadequately capturing ICD codes' multifaceted meanings, especially in long-tail distributions with scarce training data. In clinical practice, physicians often exhibit varied writing styles, where the way a diagnosis is described can differ. For instance, code '786.05' (standard: 'shortness of breath') may appear as 'dyspnea on exertion' in notes, as illustrated in Fig. 1. Fusing semantic, contextual, and inter-code relational information is crucial to enhance label feature learning.

Ineffective label-wise attention due to independent weight learning and single-head limitations.

label-wise attention of a single-head updates weights independently per code, hindering inter-label dependency modeling and alignment of various clinical expressions (e.g., 'shortness of breath' vs. 'dyspnea on exertion' for '786.05', Fig. 1). With limited samples, it fails to detect commonalities, resulting in suboptimal classification.

In this paper, we propose a novel **M**ulti-aspect **L**abel **I**nformation **F**usion (MLIF) framework for ICD coding (Fig. 2). To address limited label representations from single-faceted learning and long-tail challenges, MLIF fuses semantic descriptions via shared encoder, contextual prototypes from notes, and inter-label correlations three aspects, to enhance learning. To overcome ineffective single-head label-wise attention's independent weights, it employs multi-head code-aware self-attention and text-code cross-attention, similar to the Transformer decoder [22], to capture label-specific features and dependencies, enhancing clinical-code alignment. This results in a more robust and accurate ICD coding model. Our work makes several key contributions as follows:

(1) We develop a framework fusing text-label information via advanced attention, improving label-specific feature extraction and code inter-connections.
(2) A novel multi-aspect fusion module integrating semantic, contextual, and correlational views to enhance label representation learning and improve accuracy, particularly for long-tail ICD codes.
(3) Extensive experiments on the real-world MIMIC datasets showing MLIF outperforms baselines in key metrics, without external medical knowledge.

2 Related Work

Automatic ICD coding assigns ICD codes to free-text clinical records, a key task in medical NLP for decision support and reimbursement [28]. Its evolution spans traditional to deep learning methods.

Early methods employed traditional machine learning techniques. Deep learning frames coding as multi-label classification. CAML introduced CNN-attention fusion [15], extended by multi-filter residual CNNs [9], LAAT's bidirectional LSTM with label attention [23], and refinements [28]. To address sparsity and imbalance, recent works integrate external knowledge: graph neural networks for hierarchies [2], code descriptions in RAC [8], UMLS synonyms [1,28], two-stage hierarchical decoding in TwoStage [16], and contrastive pre-training with semi-structured data [11].

Pre-trained language models (PLMs) like BERT yield limited gains due to resources and overfitting [18]. Fine-tuning underperforms CNN/LSTM baselines [4]; prompt engineering improves efficacy, but costs persist [26,27]. LLMs excel in zero/few-shot generation but falter on full label spaces [3].

3 Methodology

Given a patient's EHR discharge summary $T_j = [w_1, \ldots, w_n] \in \mathcal{T}$, our goal is to assign a subset of ICD codes $\mathcal{C} = \{c_1, \ldots, c_L\}$ ($L = |\mathcal{C}|$, $n = |T_j|$). As

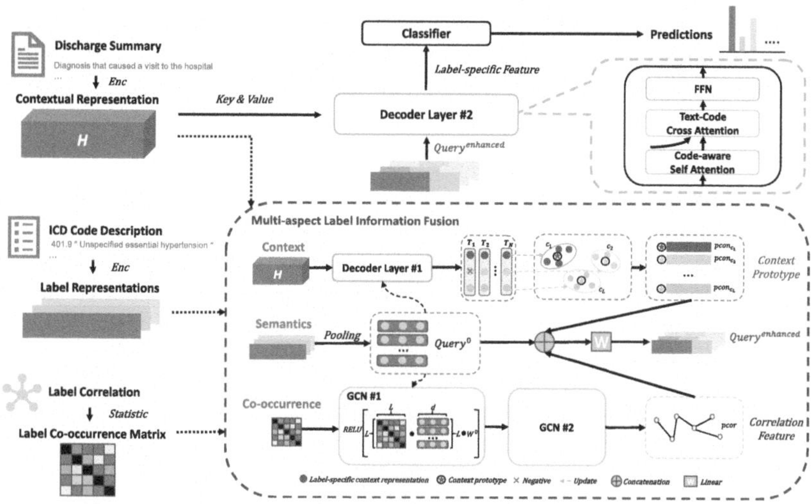

Fig. 2. The proposed **MLIF** structure.

shown in Fig. 2, the framework integrates a multi-aspect label information fusion (MLIF) module and multi-layer decoder in an encoder-decoder architecture. This uses each code as a query to capture text-label dependencies, targeting relevant sections. MLIF fuses contextual prototypes from notes, co-occurrence relationships, and semantic descriptions to enrich representations. The decoder applies code-aware self-attention and text-code cross-attention for label-specific features. The model minimizes binary cross-entropy between predictions $\hat{y}_{c_i}$ and labels $y_{c_i} \in \{0, 1\}$. Subsequent subsections detail the framework and modules.

3.1 Medical Text Encoder

Following prior work [16,23,28], we employ Bi-LSTM to encode clinical documents, effectively capturing sequential dependencies. The encoder processes input text $T_j = [w_1, \ldots, w_n]$ via pre-trained word embeddings and multi-layer Bi-LSTM:

$$[h_1, ..., h_n] = TextEncoder(w_1, ..., w_n). \tag{1}$$

This produces the text representation $H \in \mathbb{R}^{n \times d}$, where d is the Bi-LSTM output dimension.

3.2 Multi-aspect Label Information Fusion

After encoding clinical documents, we propose the Multi-aspect Label Information Fusion (MLIF) module to enhance ICD code representations by fusing semantic information from label descriptions, contextual prototypes from notes, and co-occurrence relationships. Descriptions are embedded and max-pooled via the text encoder to retain core semantics. Inspired by prototype networks [20], we aggregate note-derived contextual features into label-specific prototypes, improving rare code representations. For co-occurrences, matrix A encodes pairwise probabilities, with a two-layer GCN propagating features to capture deeper inter-code correlations. Subsequent subsections detail extraction and fusion.

Label Semantic Information Modeling: To accurately identify label-related clinical text sections, we incorporate code description features—preserving original semantics—as a label information aspect, preventing irrelevant attention during decoding. Similarly, the description corresponding to label c_i that contains s words, are embedded into code representation $q^0_{c_i} \in \mathbb{R}^d$ using the same text encoder as for clinical text, followed by max-pooling:

$$q^0_{c_i} = \text{MaxPool}(TextEncoder(w^{c_i}_1, ..., w^{c_i}_s)). \tag{2}$$

The set of description representations for all labels can be represented as $Q^0 = \{q^0_{c_1}, q^0_{c_2}, ..., q^0_{c_L}\} \in \mathbb{R}^{L\times d}$, Q^0 retains the key original semantic information. By using the same text encoder, the label feature learning process is unified with the document feature learning process, making the model easier to adapt to non-standardized clinical records.

Context Information Modeling: Inspired by prototype networks in meta-learning [20], we design label prototypes to aggregate contextual information from clinical notes, refining features especially for rare tail labels.

After obtaining the representations of clinical text H and label description representations Q^0 in the previous stage, we use the first decoder layer as a mechanism to extract contextual information, and the detailed structure will be introduced in Sect. 3.3. The first decoder takes the context representations H and label description representations Q^0 as input to obtain label-related contextual knowledge from clinical documents, serving as supplementary information beyond the label titles:

$$Q^1 = Decoder(Q^0, H, H), \tag{3}$$

Here, $Q^1 \in \mathbb{R}^{L\times d}$ is the output of the first decoder layer.

We consider that the output $Q^1 = \{q^1_{c_1}, q^1_{c_2}, ..., q^1_{c_L}\}$, obtained in Eq. (3), contains the contextual features from the clinical note related to each label. Here, $q^1_{c_i} \in \mathbb{R}^d$ indicates the result of $q^0_{c_i}$ as a query. For each label c_i, we compute the average of c_i-related contextual features $q^1_{c_i}$ of all the notes in a mini-batch as the label prototype, which will be updated throughout the training process. Although features $q^1_{c_i}$ are already associated with one label, we only consider those positive ones $\{q^1_{c_i,j}\}_{j<N_{c_i}}$ during training, where N_{c_i} is the number of the positive notes that $y_{c_i} = 1$ in a mini-batch, j denotes document index in a batch.

Then we compute the average features for label c_i in the following way within a mini-batch:

$$ave_{c_i} = \frac{1}{N_{c_i}} \sum_{j=1}^{N_{c_i}} q^1_{c_i,j} \tag{4}$$

where $ave_{c_i} \in \mathbb{R}^d$ contains contextual information about label c_i from different documents. In the next steps, we compute the label prototype and iteratively update it using the following strategy:

$$pcon_{c_i} = (1 - \alpha_{c_i}) \cdot \overline{pcon_{c_i}} + \alpha_{c_i} \cdot ave_{c_i}, \tag{5}$$

$$\alpha_{c_i} = \frac{N^{c_i}}{\overline{N^{c_i}} + N^{c_i}}. \tag{6}$$

$\overline{pcon_{c_i}} \in \mathbb{R}^d$ denotes the result of the previous batch saved offline, and will be randomly initialized at the start of training. Additionally, $\overline{N^{c_i}}$ denotes the number of all positive features of label c_i in prior batches. $\overline{N^{c_i}}$ is initially 0 and is reset to 1 after each epoch, so that subsequent training epochs contain one prototype for each label at the beginning without random initialization. For categories that do not appear in a batch, Eq. (4) is skipped, and the weight α in Eq. (5) is set to 0.

We argue that the final prototype $pcon_{c_i}$ contains context information from multiple clinical notes. The value of $pcon_{c_i}$ will be saved offline after each update for the next computation as well as the final inference stage. Therefore, the ground truth information of the labels is not needed during inference.

Label Correlation Information Modeling: In clinical practice, diseases often coexist or cause secondary conditions, leading to ICD code co-occurrences; thus, modeling label correlations enhances representations. We construct an $L \times L$ co-occurrence matrix A from training label distributions, where A_{ij} is the conditional probability of c_j given c_i. A two-layer GCN treats codes as nodes and A as edges, propagating features to capture deep inter-code correlations.

Each GCN layer processes node features $\mathrm{G}^l \in \mathbb{R}^{L \times d}$ and adjacency $\widetilde{\mathrm{A}} = A$:

$$\mathrm{G}^{l+1} = \sigma(\widetilde{\mathrm{A}} G^l \mathbf{W}^l), \tag{7}$$

where $\mathrm{G}^l \in \mathbb{R}^{L \times d}$ denotes the node features of the l-th layer, G^0 is initialized to Q^0, and $\widetilde{\mathrm{A}}$ is initialized as the co-occurrence matrix A, $\mathbf{W}^l \in \mathbb{R}^{d \times d_g}$ is the weight of each layer, $d_g = d$ in the last layer.

We take the output of the last layer as the label representations $\mathrm{G} \in \mathbb{R}^{L \times d}$, which contain co-occurrence information. The i-th row denotes the relevance features of the label c_i, denoted as $pcor_{c_i} \in \mathbb{R}^d$.

We have obtained label representations that capture three distinct aspects of information, which are treated as different facets of the same code. Thus, we aggregate them via concatenation to retain the details of each aspect. For label c_i, $pcon_{c_i}$ is a label prototype that has been fused with contextual information, while $pcor_{c_i}$ learns the knowledge of label correlation through the GCN. Then aggregate them with the original semantic features of labels to obtain the information-enhanced label features $q_{c_i} \in \mathbb{R}^d$:

$$q_{c_i} = Concat(pcon_{c_i}, q^0_{c_i}, pcor_{c_i})\mathbf{W}^E, \tag{8}$$

$\mathbf{W}^E \in \mathbb{R}^{3d \times d}$ denotes the weight of the aggregation operation. Finally, we generate augmented label representations $Q^{enhanced} = \{q_{c_1}, q_{c_2}, ..., q_{c_l}\} \in \mathbb{R}^{L \times d}$ by concatenating all the information-enhanced label features.

3.3 Label Specific Feature Extraction

In multi-label classification, the decoder extracts label-specific features from documents to assign ICD codes. Prior works [4,23] use label-wise attention for this, but single-head variants struggle to learn relevant representations amid data scarcity for rare codes.

To address this, our framework employs code-aware self-attention and text-code cross-attention for feature extraction. Multi-head attention enables focus on diverse text sections, capturing multifaceted document aspects for deeper comprehension. The decoder's attention is formulated as:

$$Attention(Q, K, V) = softmax\left(\frac{QK^T}{\sqrt{d_k}}\right)V, \tag{9}$$

$$head_j = Attention(Q\mathbf{W}_j^Q, K\mathbf{W}_j^K, V\mathbf{W}_j^V), \tag{10}$$

$$MHA(Q, K, V) = Concat(head_1, ..., head_j)\mathbf{W}^o, \tag{11}$$

where Q, K, V represent the query, key, and value of the attention input respectively, d_k denotes the dimension of the attention layer, $head_j$ refers to the result of the j-th attention head, $\mathbf{W}_j^Q$, $\mathbf{W}_j^K$, $\mathbf{W}_j^V \in \mathbb{R}^{d \times d_k}$ are the parameters of the projection layer.

1) Code-Aware Self-Attention: This component models the interrelationships among all labels. The code-aware self-attention module within the decoder captures dependencies between distinct labels and leverages information from other related labels, thereby mitigating the challenge of inadequate feature learning caused by label sparsity. Code-aware self-attention uses the attention mechanism described above and treats the embeddings of all labels as an unordered sequence without masking. It is computed according to the following formula:

$$\widetilde{Q} = MHA(Q, Q, Q). \tag{12}$$

Subsequently, the output $\widetilde{Q}$ of the self-attention layer will be used for the cross-attention.

2) Text-Code Cross-Attention: The model extracts label-specific features from documents via text-code cross-attention, where each head independently processes inputs to capture multi-dimensional document representations. This enables focus on diverse text segments, broadening attention scope and facilitating comprehensive document understanding. Passing self-attention output $\widetilde{Q}$ and text features H yields:

$$\widetilde{Q^1} = MHA(\widetilde{Q}, H, H), \tag{13}$$

$$O = FNN(\widetilde{Q}^1), \tag{14}$$

where $\widetilde{Q}$ and $\widetilde{Q}^1$ are the results of the self-attention module and the cross-attention module, respectively.

We simply express the above Eq. (12), (13) and (14) as:

$$O = Decoder(Q, H, H). \tag{15}$$

For final classification, the decoder uses enhanced representations Q^{enhanced} as queries to obtain label-specific features $S \in \mathbb{R}^{L\times d}$:

$$S = Decoder(Q^{enhanced}, H, H). \tag{16}$$

Each i-th row $s_i \in \mathbb{R}^d$ of label-specific feature matrix $S \in \mathbb{R}^{L\times d}$ is a representation of clinical text regarding the label $c_i \in \mathcal{C}$.

3.4 ICD Coding Prediction

Treating each label as a binary task, we project s_i from Eq. (16) via a linear layer to logits:

$$\hat{y}_{c_i} = \sigma(\mathbf{W}_{c_i} s_i^T + b_{c_i}), \tag{17}$$

where $\mathbf{W}_{c_i} \in \mathbb{R}^d$, and $b^{c_i} \in \mathbb{R}$ is the weight in the linear layer. We train the model using multi-label binary cross-entropy:

$$\mathcal{L} = \sum_{c_i \in C} -y_{c_i} log(\hat{y}_{c_i}) - (1 - y_{c_i}) log(1 - \hat{y}_{c_i}). \tag{18}$$

Table 1. Statistics of the datasets.

Dataset	MIMIC-II		MIMIC-III		MIMIC-IV-ICD9	
Setting	full	50	full	50	full	50
Avg. words per Doc.	1,167	1,185	1,434	1,478	1,459	1,499
Total codes	5,031	50	8,922	50	11,331	50
Training size	19,392	18,007	47,723	8,066	180,553	170,664
Validation size	1,141	1,080	1,631	1,573	7,110	6,406
Testing size	2,282	2,126	3,372	1,729	13,709	12,405

4 Experiment

4.1 Datasets

To conduct a comprehensive comparison with other models, we follow prior work and evaluate our model on the publicly available **M**edical **I**nformation **M**art for **I**ntensive **C**are (MIMIC) datasets: MIMIC-II [19], MIMIC-III [7], and MIMIC-IV [6]. Statistics are in Table 1. Primary experiments use MIMIC-III against all baselines; MIMIC-II/IV validate open-source methods. We assess under 'full' (all codes, long-tail) and 'top 50' (frequent codes) settings for generalizability and utility.

- **MIMIC-II:** [19] Following [23], 19,392 train/1,141 val/2,282 test samples. Top-50 setting filters notes with ≥1 top-50 code, removing others.
- **MIMIC-III:** [7] We use the MIMIC-III-full and MIMIC-III-top 50 datasets following the setting of previous work [15]. MIMIC-III-full includes a total of 8922 unique ICD codes.
- **MIMIC-IV:** [6] The latest release of MIMIC-IV includes two versions of ICD codes: ICD9 and ICD10. We follow the settings of MIMIC-IV-ICD [17] to create the MIMIC-IV-ICD9-top 50 dataset.

4.2 Implementation Details

Implemented in PyTorch on NVIDIA RTX 3090 (Ubuntu 18.04.6 LTS), using AdamW (lr = 0.0005, linear decay) with R-Drop [24] and early stopping on val Macro F1.

Word embeddings (dimension 100) are pre-trained on each dataset via word2vec CBOW [14]. Documents exceeding 4,000 tokens are truncated. Each decoder layer features 4 attention heads and an FFN dimension of 512; GCNs comprise 2 layers with hidden dimension 256. For the top-50 setting, we employ a single-layer Bi-LSTM (dimension 512), R-Drop factor of 12.5, batch size 16, and 20 epochs. In the full setting, we use a two-layer Bi-LSTM, R-Drop factor of 5.0, batch size 8, and 20 epochs. Dropout (0.2) follows the text encoder to mitigate overfitting. Classification thresholds are optimized on validation data. Models are evaluated over 5 random seeds (top-50) or 3 (full), reporting average test results with standard deviations.

4.3 Evaluation Metrics

Following [4,9,15], we report macro/micro F1 (macro treats codes equally for rare/common balance; micro aggregates overall). Precision@K (K = 5, 8, 15) ranks prediction probabilities.

4.4 Baseline

We compare with baselines, training from code or using reported results. Partial results for XR-LAT [10] and KBDPT [26] due to unavailable code/dataset.

- **CAML** [15]: CNN with label attention for multi-label prediction.
- **MultiResCNN** [9]: Multi-filter residual CNN.
- **HyperCore** [2]: Hyperbolic hierarchy and co-graph GCN for code relations.
- **LAAT & JointLAAT** [23]: Label-wise attention with hierarchical joint learning.
- **Fusion** [13]: Attention soft pooling aggregating local-to-global features.
- **PLM-ICD** [4]: Fine-tuned medical PLM for ICD coding.
- **LD-PLAM** [25]: Pseudo-labeling attention via document-label similarity.
- **MSMN** [28]: Multi-synonyms attention using UMLS knowledge [1].

- **KEPTLongformer** [27]: Prompt engineering with UMLS synonyms and contrastive alignment.
- **TwoStage** [16]: Hierarchical parent-to-child decoding mimicking human coders.
- **TF-GCN** [12]: Transformer with GCN for word-doc relations [25].
- **XR-LAT** [10]: Transformer with recursive training, label attention, and dynamic sampling.
- **KBDPT** [26]: Prompt learning with medical templates enhancing PLMs for multi-label diagnosis.

Table 2. Results on the MIMIC-III test set (mean ± std, in %).

Model	MIMIC-III-full					MIMIC-III-top 50			
	F1		P@K			F1		P@K	
	Macro	Micro	P@5	P@8	P@15	Macro	Micro	P@5	P@8
Single Models									
CAML	8.8	53.9	-	70.9	56.1	53.2	61.4	60.9	-
MultiResCNN	8.5	55.2	81.7	73.4	58.4	60.6	67.0	64.5	-
Fusion	8.3	55.4	81.2	73.6	58.4	61.9	67.4	64.7	-
HyperCore	9.0	55.1	-	72.2	57.9	60.9	66.3	63.2	-
LAAT	9.9	57.5	81.3	73.8	59.1	66.6	71.5	67.5	54.7
JointLAAT	10.7	57.5	80.6	73.5	59.0	66.1	71.6	67.1	54.6
TwoStage	10.5	58.4	-	74.4	-	**68.9**	71.8	66.7	-
MSMN	10.3	58.5	82.5	75.2	59.9	68.3	72.5	**68.0**	54.8
PLM-based Models									
PLM-ICD	8.4	58.0	<u>83.9</u>	<u>76.7</u>	61.1	64.8	69.6	65.0	53.0
LD-PLAM	9.9	58.3	-	75.6	-	62.9	69.9	66.0	-
TF-GCN	10.9	58.9	-	75.8	-	67.1	71.9	<u>68.2</u>	-
KEPT	10.3	58.2	-	74.9	-	<u>68.9</u>	<u>72.9</u>	67.3	-
KBDPT	-	-	-	-	-	67.7	71.9	66.5	-
XR-LAT	10.8	58.3	82.1	74.9	59.9	-	-	-	-
MLIF	**11.4** ± 0.16	**60.0** ± 0.21	**83.6** ± 0.19	**76.6** ± 0.14	**61.2** ± 0.17	**68.9** ± 0.15	**72.6** ± 0.08	**67.9** ± 0.24	**55.1** ± 0.11

4.5 Results

We compare MLIF with baselines in full (all codes, long-tail) and top-50 settings. Baselines are grouped as single or PLM-based models. Table 2 shows MIMIC-III results (**bold**: best single; <u>underline</u>: best PLM). Tables 3 and 4 cover MIMIC-II/IV.

On MIMIC-III (Table 2), MLIF outperforms baselines across most metrics, achieving top full-setting F1 scores (Macro 11.4%, Micro 60.0%; +1.1% Micro vs. TF-GCN) and balancing frequent/rare codes in long-tail scenarios. It matches PLM-ICD in P@K while surpassing in F1. In top-50, Micro F1 reaches 72.6%, equaling or exceeding prior SOTA KEPTLongformer without non-scalable prompts.

Table 3. Results on the MIMIC-II test set (mean ± std, in %).

Model	MIMIC-II-full					MIMIC-II-top 50			
	F1		P@K			F1		P@K	
	Macro	Micro	P@5	P@8	P@15	Macro	Micro	P@5	P@8
Single Models									
CAML	4.8	44.2	-	52.3	-	46.3	59.4	53.7	41.8
MultiResCNN	5.2	46.4	64.8	54.3	39.0	51.2	62.7	55.2	42.7
Fusion	4.6	45.4	63.8	53.2	38.0	54.2	64.1	56.0	43.2
LAAT	5.9	48.6	64.9	55.0	39.7	50.4	62.2	56.6	44.0
MSMN	8.3	51.0	66.8	56.5	41.0	58.9	67.9	59.0	45.2
PLM-based Models									
PLM-ICD	6.1	50.4	67.3	56.1	39.9	57.2	66.1	57.3	44.3
XR-LAT	7.3	49.9	66.7	56.1	40.2	-	-	-	-
MLIF	**8.8** ± 0.21	**51.8** ± 0.22	**68.0** ± 0.22	**57.5** ± 0.28	**41.3** ± 0.21	**59.6** ± 0.22	**68.6** ± 0.24	**59.3** ± 0.09	**45.5** ± 0.13

On MIMIC-II (Table 3), MLIF leads all metrics (full/top-50), surpassing both single and PLM-based baselines. Additionally, despite not leveraging external UMLS synonyms like MSMN, MLIF achieves competitive or superior results, suggesting that our intrinsic multi-aspect enhancements effectively mitigate data scarcity without additional resources.

On the MIMIC-IV-ICD9 dataset (Table 4), baseline performances generally improve due to the larger training instances available compared to MIMIC-II and MIMIC-III. Nonetheless, MLIF maintains its lead. The most pronounced improvements for MLIF occur in the full setting, where long-tail challenges are amplified, further affirming its efficacy in handling imbalanced distributions.

In particular, MLIF achieves the largest gains in full-code settings across datasets, with optimal Macro and Micro F1 scores. This underscores its efficacy in tacking long-tail challenges by leveraging multi-aspect fusion to enhance label representations and mitigate data scarcity for rare codes.

4.6 Ablation Experiment

To dissect MLIF component contributions, we conduct ablation studies on MIMIC-III-top 50 (Table 5), systematically removing key modules. Variants

Table 4. Results on the MIMIC-IV-ICD9 test set (mean ± std, in %).

Model	MIMIC-IV-full					MIMIC-IV-top 50			
	F1		P@K			F1		P@K	
	Macro	Micro	P@5	P@8	P@15	Macro	Micro	P@5	P@8
Single Models									
CAML	11.1	57.3	-	64.9	-	65.3	69.2	58.6	47.9
MultiResCNN	13.2	60.4	76.5	68.0	52.2	70.0	74.3	61.7	48.1
Fusion	13.2	60.3	77.4	68.6	52.3	70.4	74.7	62.1	48.3
LAAT	13.1	60.3	77.6	67.5	52.6	70.0	74.5	62.0	-
MSMN	13.9	61.6	78.0	68.9	52.8	71.9	**75.8**	62.6	48.6
PLM-based Models									
PLM-ICD	14.4	61.3	78.6	69.9	53.3	71.4	75.5	62.4	48.4
MLIF	**15.6** ± 0.20	**62.5** ± 0.21	**79.0** ± 0.10	**70.2** ± 0.13	**53.5** ± 0.09	**72.1** ± 0.08	**75.8** ± 0.07	**62.8** ± 0.11	**48.7** ± 0.05

Table 5. Results of ablation experiments on the MIMIC-III-top 50 dataset (in %).

Method	F1		P@K		Memory
	Macro	Micro	P@5	P@8	
Full Model	**68.9**	**72.6**	**67.9**	**55.1**	7.36 GB
w/o MLIF	67.5	71.4	67.1	54.4	5.18 GB
w/o Contextual	68.2	71.7	67.4	54.9	6.54 GB
w/o Correlation	68.0	72.0	67.3	54.8	5.41 GB
w/o Semantic	67.8	71.8	67.3	54.7	6.13 GB

include: **w/o MLIF**, disabling multi-aspect fusion and relying solely on the first decoder for extraction/classification; **w/o Contextual**, removing the prototype submodule (Sect. 3.2); **w/o Co-occurrence**, excluding GCN-based correlations (Sect. 3.2); and **w/o Semantic**, omitting descriptions and using learnable embeddings for guidance.

Performance drops most with **w/o MLIF**, confirming multi-aspect fusion's impact. Omitting contextual prototypes (**w/o Contextual**) or co-occurrences (**w/o Co-occurrence**) yields similar degradation, highlighting their roles in label enhancement and ICD coding. **w/o Semantic** performs worst, as absent descriptions lead to noisy, hard-to-optimize features. Overall, all modules substantially contribute.

To illustrate enhancements in prediction for ICD codes of varying frequencies via our fusion mechanism, we grouped codes by MIMIC-III-full training occurrences: 1–10, 11–50, 51–100, 101–500, and >500 (comprising 5,312, 1,825, 519, 746, and 283 codes, respectively). We evaluated MLIF, MSMN, and LAAT—trained on MIMIC-III-full—via micro F1 on test-set labels per group. As shown

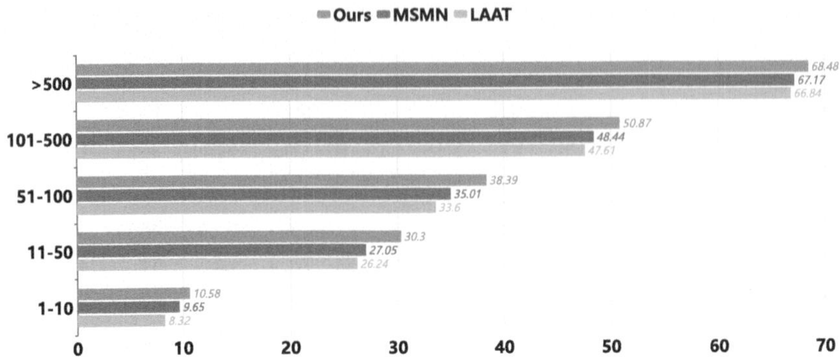

Fig. 3. Micro-F1 scores comparison under different frequencies of labels on the MIMIC-III-full dataset.

in Fig. 3, MLIF outperforms MSMN and LAAT across groups, especially for 11–500 frequencies, confirming that code-aware self-attention, text-code cross-attention, and multi-aspect fusion mitigate long-tail challenges.

Table 6. Results of different numbers of attention head on the MIMIC-III-top 50 dataset (in %).

Attention Head	F1		P@K		Memory
	Macro	Micro	P@5	P@8	
head = 1	67.3	71.6	66.9	54.5	7.22 GB
head = 2	68.5	72.0	67.2	54.6	7.30 GB
head = 4	**68.9**	**72.6**	**67.9**	**55.1**	7.36 GB
head = 8	68.3	71.8	67.2	54.7	7.66 GB

4.7 Parameter Studies

In this section, we evaluate the effect of attention head numbers on performance (Sect. 3.3; Table 6). To demonstrate our decoder's superiority over prior label-wise attention, we test 1–8 heads, distributing features across dimensions. Multi-head attention markedly exceeds single-head, especially in F1. Peak performance occurs at 4 heads, matching the 5–6 average ICD codes per MIMIC-III-top 50 document.

5 Conclusion

In this paper, we propose a novel framework integrating advanced attention decoding architectures with a multi-aspect label information fusion module to enhance representation learning for clinical texts and ICD codes. Specifically, multi-head attention decoding enables effective extraction of label-specific document features. We aggregate each label's representation prototype from clinical note contexts and fuse it with original label descriptions and co-occurrence relationships, thereby enriching label information without external dataset knowledge. Experimental results show our model outperforms baselines.

Acknowledgements. This work is partially supported by National Natural Science Foundation of China(62402294), Shandong Provincial Natural Science Foundation(ZR2022QF114)

Disclosure of Interests. The authors declare that they have no competing interests.

References

1. Bodenreider, O.: The unified medical language system (UMLS): integrating biomedical terminology. Nucleic Acids Res. **32**(suppl_1), D267–D270 (2004). https://doi.org/10.1093/nar/gkh061
2. Cao, P., Chen, Y., Liu, K., Zhao, J., Liu, S., Chong, W.: Hypercore: hyperbolic and co-graph representation for automatic ICD coding. In: Proceedings of the 58th Annual Meeting of the Association for Computational Linguistics, pp. 3105–3114 (2020). https://doi.org/10.18653/v1/2020.acl-main.282
3. Falis, M., et al.: Can GPT-3.5 generate and code discharge summaries? arXiv preprint arXiv:2401.13512 (2024). https://doi.org/10.1093/jamia/ocae132
4. Huang, C.W., Tsai, S.C., Chen, Y.N.: PLM-ICD: automatic ICD coding with pretrained language models. arXiv preprint arXiv:2207.05289 (2022). https://doi.org/10.18653/v1/2022.clinicalnlp-1.2
5. Ji, S., et al.: A unified review of deep learning for automated medical coding. ACM Comput. Surv. **56**(12), 1–41 (2024). https://doi.org/10.1145/3664615
6. Johnson, A.E., et al.: Mimic-iv, a freely accessible electronic health record dataset. Sci. Data **10**(1), 1 (2023). https://doi.org/10.1038/s41597-022-01899-x
7. Johnson, A.E., et al.: Mimic-iii, a freely accessible critical care database. Sci. Data **3**(1), 1–9 (2016). https://doi.org/10.1038/sdata.2016.35
8. Kim, B.H., Ganapathi, V.: Read, attend, and code: pushing the limits of medical codes prediction from clinical notes by machines. In: Machine Learning for Healthcare Conference, pp. 196–208. PMLR (2021)
9. Li, F., Yu, H.: ICD coding from clinical text using multi-filter residual convolutional neural network. In: Proceedings of the AAAI Conference on Artificial Intelligence, vol. 34, pp. 8180–8187 (2020). https://doi.org/10.1609/aaai.v34i05.6331
10. Liu, L., Perez-Concha, O., Nguyen, A., Bennett, V., Jorm, L.: Automated ICD coding using extreme multi-label long text transformer-based models. Artif. Intell. Med. **144**, 102662 (2023). https://doi.org/10.1016/j.artmed.2023.102662
11. Lu, C., Reddy, C., Wang, P., Ning, Y.: Towards semi-structured automatic ICD coding via tree-based contrastive learning. Adv. Neural. Inf. Process. Syst. **36**, 68300–68315 (2023)
12. Lu, P., Xue, J.: Combining transformer-based model and GCN to predict ICD codes from clinical records. Knowl.-Based Syst. **282**, 111113 (2023). https://doi.org/10.1016/j.knosys.2023.111113

13. Luo, J., Xiao, C., Glass, L., Sun, J., Ma, F.: Fusion: towards automated ICD coding via feature compression. In: Findings of the Association for Computational Linguistics: ACL-IJCNLP 2021, pp. 2096–2101 (2021). https://doi.org/10.18653/v1/2021.findings-acl.184
14. Mikolov, T., Sutskever, I., Chen, K., Corrado, G.S., Dean, J.: Distributed representations of words and phrases and their compositionality. In: Advances in Neural Information Processing Systems, vol. 26 (2013)
15. Mullenbach, J., Wiegreffe, S., Duke, J., Sun, J., Eisenstein, J.: Explainable prediction of medical codes from clinical text. arXiv preprint arXiv:1802.05695 (2018). https://doi.org/10.18653/v1/n18-1100
16. Nguyen, T.T., Schlegel, V., Kashyap, A., Winkler, S.: A two-stage decoder for efficient ICD coding. arXiv preprint arXiv:2306.00005 (2023). https://doi.org/10.18653/v1/2023.findings-acl.285
17. Nguyen, T.T., et al.: Mimic-iv-ICD: a new benchmark for extreme multilabel classification. arXiv preprint arXiv:2304.13998 (2023)
18. Pascual, D., Luck, S., Wattenhofer, R.: Towards Bert-based automatic ICD coding: limitations and opportunities. arXiv preprint arXiv:2104.06709 (2021). https://doi.org/10.18653/v1/2021.bionlp-1.6
19. Saeed, M., Lieu, C., Raber, G., Mark, R.G.: Mimic ii: a massive temporal ICU patient database to support research in intelligent patient monitoring. In: Computers in Cardiology, pp. 641–644. IEEE (2002). https://doi.org/10.1109/cic.2002.1166854
20. Snell, J., Swersky, K., Zemel, R.: Prototypical networks for few-shot learning. In: Advances in Neural Information Processing Systems, vol. 30 (2017)
21. Teng, F., Zhang, Q., Zhou, X., Hu, J., Li, T.: Few-shot ICD coding with knowledge transfer and evidence representation. Expert Syst. Appl. **238**, 121861 (2024). https://doi.org/10.1016/j.eswa.2023.121861
22. Vaswani, A.: Attention is all you need. Adv. Neural. Inf. Process. Syst. (2017). https://doi.org/10.5040/9781350101272.00000005
23. Vu, T., Nguyen, D.Q., Nguyen, A.: A label attention model for ICD coding from clinical text. arXiv preprint arXiv:2007.06351 (2020). https://doi.org/10.24963/ijcai.2020/461
24. Wu, L., et al.: R-Drop: regularized dropout for neural networks. Adv. Neural. Inf. Process. Syst. **34**, 10890–10905 (2021)
25. Wu, Y., Zeng, M., Yu, Y., Li, Y., Li, M.: A pseudo label-wise attention network for automatic ICD coding. IEEE J. Biomed. Health Inform. **26**(10), 5201–5212 (2022). https://doi.org/10.1109/jbhi.2022.3193291
26. Xie, J., et al.: Knowledge-based dynamic prompt learning for multi-label disease diagnosis. Knowl.-Based Syst. **286**, 111395 (2024). https://doi.org/10.1016/j.knosys.2024.111395
27. Yang, Z., Wang, S., Rawat, B.P.S., Mitra, A., Yu, H.: Knowledge injected prompt based fine-tuning for multi-label few-shot ICD coding. In: Proceedings of the Conference on Empirical Methods in Natural Language Processing. Conference on Empirical Methods in Natural Language Processing, vol. 2022, p. 1767. NIH Public Access (2022). https://doi.org/10.18653/v1/2022.findings-emnlp.127
28. Yuan, Z., Tan, C., Huang, S.: Code synonyms do matter: multiple synonyms matching network for automatic ICD coding. In: Proceedings of the 60th Annual Meeting of the Association for Computational Linguistics, (Volume 2: Short Papers) (2022). https://doi.org/10.18653/v1/2022.acl-short.91

Author Index

© The Editor(s) (if applicable) and The Author(s), under exclusive license
to Springer Nature Singapore Pte Ltd. 2027

H. Sun et al. (Eds.): ChineseCSCW 2025, CCIS 2911, pp. 407–408, 2027.
https://doi.org/10.1007/978-981-92-0288-1

The manufacturer's authorised representative in the EU is Springer Nature Customer Service Centre GmbH, Europaplatz 3, 69115 Heidelberg, Germany. If you have any concerns regarding our products, please contact ProductSafety@springernature.com

Printed and bound by CPI Group (UK) Ltd, Croydon, CR0 4YY
21/09/2026
02219987-0011